The
Great Thirst

OTHER BOOKS BY NORRIS HUNDLEY, JR.

Dividing the Waters:
A Century of Controversy between the United States and Mexico
(1966)

The American West:
Frontier and Region
(1969)
WITH JOHN SCHUTZ

The American Indian
(1974)

Water and the West:
The Colorado River Compact and the Politics of Water
in the American West
(1975)

The Chicano
(1975)

The Asian American:
The Historical Experience
(1976)

CONTRIBUTOR
The California Water Atlas
WILLIAM L. KAHRL, EDITOR
(1979)

California:
History of a Remarkable State
(1982)
WITH JOHN CAUGHEY

NORRIS HUNDLEY, JR.

THE GREAT THIRST

CALIFORNIANS AND WATER

A HISTORY

Revised Edition

UNIVERSITY OF CALIFORNIA PRESS

Berkeley   Los Angeles   London

University of California Press
Berkeley and Los Angeles, California

University of California Press, Ltd.
London, England

Library of Congress Cataloging-in-Publication Data
Hundley, Norris.
    The great thirst : Californians and water : a history / Norris Hundley, Jr. — Rev. ed.
      p.   cm.
    Includes bibliographical references and index.
    ISBN 978-0-520-22456-8 (pbk. : alk. paper)
    1. Water-supply—California—History.   2. California—History.   I. Title.
    HD1694.C2 H83   2001
    333.91'009794 — dc21   00-059002

Manufactured in the United States of America
15   14   13   12   11   10   09   08   07
12   11   10   9   8   7   6   5   4   3

To MY WIFE, CAROL
My parents, Norris C. and Helen M. Hundley
My daughters and their husbands, Wendy and
Craig Harris, Jacqueline and Scott Reid
And my grandchildren, Caitlyn, Sean, Mac,
and Paige—Californians all

Contents

Figures

Figures

Maps

Maps

Preface to the Revised Edition

IN THE first edition of *The Great Thirst* I noted that an attractive reason for writing the book was to tell a story that had not been told elsewhere. Compelling reasons for a revised edition are to tell the story a little better; correct errors and omissions; incorporate the findings of more recent scholarship; and, for a topic as dynamic as Californians and their water, to account for what has happened since the first edition. These considerations have resulted in the present book being significantly longer than its predecessor, with alterations and additions in every chapter, most significantly in chapters 6 and 7, which reach into the recent past and deal with major issues that were ongoing at the time of the first edition, had not yet emerged as significant, had not yet occurred, or otherwise were only briefly mentioned, if at all, at the time the manuscript went to press in 1991, the year before publication. New subjects include the victories at Mono Lake (1994) and in the Owens Valley (1997 and 1998), though in neither locale can it be said that the wars have completely ended; conflicts, attempts, and accomplishments in large-scale water marketing; the Central Valley Project Improvement Act (1992); the emergence of the CALFED Bay-Delta Program (1995); and more. Even this edition cannot pretend to have the last word on such a complex topic characterized by both fast-breaking and ponderously slow developments. Such is the fate of any attempt foolish enough to try to keep abreast of history as it is being made. An impossible task, of course, and it is further complicated because water issues are so closely intertwined with the core elements of California's (and the American West's) political, economic, legal, and cultural evolution.

Since few of the more recent events in this edition have attracted historians, I have been compelled to make numerous forays of my own into original sources and to rely on a host of individuals close to the action for interviews and documents. As with the first edition, readers should not blame others for my views or errors of fact. I do not want anyone unfairly found guilty by association.

The themes running through this account mirror those of the first edition. The most obvious is the dynamic interplay between *human values* and *what human beings do to the waterscape.* Technology, of course, plays a monumental role, for more can be done to nature with dynamite, a bulldozer, and reenforced concrete than with the Indians' digging stick. But values can place powerful restrictions on technology, whether that technology is advanced or less sophisticated. Furthermore, I want to remind readers that while science and technology are important, this book is not about those subjects. It has a different purpose. I begin by looking at California as a natural environment, before the Europeans arrived, and at how Native Americans viewed that environment as something to be manipulated, yet always within the context of maintaining their symbiotic relationship with nature. I continue with the Spanish and Mexican intruders, who, drawing on generations of experience in water-shy areas of both the Old and New Worlds, saw nature (and water especially) as a resource to be exploited, but primarily for community and, hence, national survival. Mutual rights and the common good ranked higher than individual self-interest.

That attitude toward water changed after the discovery of gold, when thousands poured into California imbued with a spirited individualism and an appetite for profit that elevated the exploitation of nature to new heights, set the stage for a system of private monopolization of land and water that has persisted into modern times, transformed political and legal institutions, and prompted California's emergence as the nation's preeminent water seeker—or, to be more precise and as emphasized in this account, California's emergence as a collection of water seekers.

Central to this story, then, is the appearance of a new kind of social imperialist whose goal was to acquire the water of others and prosper at their expense, a goal that catapulted California into a modern colossus while also producing monumental conflicts and social costs. At the same time, this is a story of extraordinary feats of fulfilling basic social needs, in which communities mobilized and focused their political energies on providing abundant clear water to multitudes of people who expressly wanted that to be done.

Another theme is how crucial government—local, regional, provincial or state, and national—has been in shaping water policy and use. During the Spanish and Mexican eras, high officials set the guidelines for local authorities. Since the U.S. takeover, the evolving complexities of the federal system have been mirrored in every major water project, with the power of Washington growing at the expense of state and local prerogatives. In the twentieth century especially, and on into the twenty-first, the impulse of Californians (and westerners generally) has been to tap the national treasury to develop water resources, with the result that the purse has inevitably come with strings attached. Thus, national involvement in California's water issues has complicated decision-making not only about harnessing water but also about reforming the system.

Still another theme is the close interrelationship between private and government interests. Under Spanish and then Mexican rule a life-sustaining hydraulic system was created that depended on the forced labor of Indians. After the U.S. conquest, private interests and governmental bureaucracies frequently aided one another in the quest for power, financial resources, and influence over policy-making. The evidence presented here does not reveal them as a powerful, highly centralized, and despotic ruling elite like that found in the irrigation society of Karl Wittfogel's classic *Oriental Despotism: A Comparative Study of Total Power* or in the works of those historians under his influence. Rather, the California record discloses a wide and often confused and crosscutting range of interest groups and bureaucrats, both public and private, who accomplish what they do as a result of shifting alliances and despite frequent disputes among themselves. Because of their multiplicity of interests, different combinations of them at different times and for different reasons worked vigorously on behalf of particular projects, but each success brought more growth, which intensified hostility and the competition for supplies always perceived as inadequate. Thus, conflict, rivalry, and localism have permeated the development process, exacerbating the human and environmental costs, with the public, until recently, cheerleading with ballots and in other ways the aqueducts, dams, and reservoirs. There is, of course, some system and order to what has been accomplished, but it is found in attitudes toward the environment, in local and regional considerations (especially California's traditional north-south rivalry), in interest-group pressures, in the give-and-take of political battle, and it is understood within the larger context of American political culture and policy-making and in the ways in which that national culture resonates in California.[1]

The previous point—the relationship between American political culture and California water policy—constitutes another theme of this study. This is not to say that individuals have not played crucial roles or that political ideologies and partisan politics always (or even primarily) explain outcomes, for this book provides considerable evidence to the contrary. Instead, it is to emphasize that, as Robert Kelley has said in his powerful *Battling the Inland Sea,* "local experience gains its full meaning for us only when we see it within the framework of national experience."[2]

When viewed from both local and national perspectives, California's water achievements have resulted ultimately from the support and encouragement of the people, who have considered themselves participants in a booming economy made possible by great hydraulic projects. These projects have included the ambitious flood control, reclamation, and irrigation programs of the late nineteenth century; the twentieth-century urban aqueducts to the Owens Valley, Mono Basin, and Hetch Hetchy; the massive federal multipurpose ventures pioneered nationally in the Boulder Canyon Project and replicated in the Central Valley Project; and California's own

State Water Project, the largest public enterprise ever undertaken by a state.

Just as the electorate has sanctioned these ventures, so too have the people of California begun to register second thoughts, especially over the last several decades. Spiraling costs, runaway urbanization, gridlocked streets and highways, environmental damage, a decline in the quality of life, heavy public expense in the exorbitant subsidies to agriculture, inefficient and wasteful water practices, the persistence of poor working conditions for those laboring in California's fields—all have contributed to mounting demands for reform.

Beginning especially in the 1960s and 1970s, this discontent produced considerable legislation in Sacramento and Washington seeking to reverse environmental despoliation; the first defeat at the polls since the 1920s of a major California water project; successful challenges to water rights long thought inviolable, such as those of Los Angeles to the Owens River and the waters of the Mono Basin; and the derailment in Congress, since the early 1970s, of nearly all major new water projects. Even so, as in the first edition, closer analysis reveals these reforms as piecemeal, fitful, and frequently more symbolic than real, especially because reforms and regulations mandated by one political administration can go largely ignored or altogether unenforced by another. The lack of *informed* and *consistent leadership* at the highest levels in Sacramento and Washington has not augured well for a state whose population continues to grow at a pace unmatched in the national experience. The unsettling results are graphically illustrated in major water-policy questions facing Californians today: accelerating urbanization of farmland and open spaces, persisting despoliation of water supplies, equity in water allocation for a mushrooming population, and continued wrangling over restoration of San Francisco Bay and the Sacramento–San Joaquin Delta. An appraisal and some suggestions in light of the historical record round out this book.

Just as with the first edition, I am indebted to many individuals for making this latest venture possible. For invaluable information, I am most grateful to Brian Thomas, Annette Hubbell, Jan Matusak, Dirk Reed, Jeffrey Kightlinger, Ed Winkler, Dennis Underwood, Dirk Marks, Steve Hirsch, Gordon Little, Keith Nobriga, Patricia Watters, and John Scott of the Metropolitan Water District of Southern California; Patrick Wright of the California Resources Agency; Steve Treanor of the California Department of Parks and Recreation; David Sandino, Mark Cowin, Jeanine Jones, Susan Tatayon, Paul Hutton, Richard Neal, and Ed Craddock of the California Department of Water Resources; Andrew Sawyer of the California Water Resources Control Board; Richard Nagel and Stephen Ott of the Los Angeles Department of Water and Power; Milton Friend of the Salton Sea Science Subcommittee; Don Cox and Linda Sánchez of the Imperial Irrigation District; Rodney Smith, economic consultant to the Imperial Irrigation District; David Nuffer of the Coalition for a Fair Water Policy; Gerald Quist of the Rincon del Diablo Municipal Water District; Steven Erie of the University of California, San Diego; Robert Campbell of the San Diego County Water Authority; S. Gale Heffler-Scott, Thomas Aiken, Julie Spezia, Donna Tegelman, Sam Cervantes, Melvin Wallace, and Debra Brower of the U.S. Bureau of Reclamation; Walter Swain of the U.S. Geological Survey; Dennis Peters of the U.S. Fish and Wildlife Service; Manuel Ybarra of the United States Section, International Boundary and Water Commission; Theodore Schade of the Great Basin Unified Air Pollution Control District; Leah Kirk of the Inyo County Water Department; Linda Vida of the University of California Water Resources Center Archives; William Ferguson of the Santa Barbara Public Works Department; Michael Johnson of the Los Angeles County Department of Public Works; Michael Stenstrom of the University of California, Los Angeles; Myron ("Mike") Fliegel of the U.S. Nuclear Regulatory Commission; Richard Blubaugh of Atlas Corporation; David Mathes of the U.S. Department of Energy; Ken Harlow and Paul Flick of *SoCal Water Resources News;* and many others. For reviewing the first edition and providing invaluable suggestions for this edition, I thank Harrison C. Dunning, Douglas Littlefield, Donald Pisani, Peter Reich, and John Scott. I owe a special debt of gratitude to Henry Vaux, Jr., and John Schutz for reviewing the entire manuscript and allowing me to benefit from their expertise. Naturally, none of the individuals supplying me with information or making suggestions for the manuscript should be associated with the views or errors found in this book. I am indebted to John Letey, director of the University of California Centers for Water and Wildland Resources, for support to obtain illustrations and maps. I am most grateful to Sergio Guillen for the maps of the CALFED Bay-Delta Program and Madge Kelley, calligrapher and cartographer extraordinaire, for her many maps that grace the book. To the University of California Press, especially to Stanley Holwitz, Laura Pasquale, Marilyn Schwartz, Suzanne Knott, and Jacqueline Volin, I deeply appreciate their making the revised edition as beautiful an example of the bookmaker's art as the first edition. I am thankful to my wife, Carol, for, as always, her good cheer, warm support, and gentle tolerance of an occasionally distracted scholar.

Norris Hundley, jr.
Malibu and Santa Barbara, California

1 The Aboriginal Water-scape: Manipulation and Near Harmony

*O*nce it was a far different place. Aboriginal California, with 275,000 to 300,000 residents by current reckoning,[1] was among the most densely populated areas in North America at the time of European contact, but the native peoples left scarcely an imprint on the waterscape or landscape. Sharp indeed is the contrast with modern California, which is largely an artificial creation. The California of the late 1990s and early 2000s supports more than thirty-four million residents, making it the most populous state in the nation, and relies for its existence on massive hydraulic works that move enormous quantities of water from areas of relative abundance, both within and outside the state, to areas of relative scarcity. Despite such impressive technological achievements, Californians are currently using more water than will be available on a long-term basis. The deficit is 1.6 million acre-feet annually, which can rise to more than 5.1 million acre-feet during drought years, with this overdraft coming from underground aquifers that are being pumped of water faster than nature can replenish it. (An acre-foot is about 326,000 gallons, the amount of water that will cover an acre to one foot in depth, or approximately what two urban families of four use in a year.)[2] Obviously, the difference between aboriginal and present California is not simply one of population size and technology but also of contrasting attitudes and values. The Indians of California held deep respect for nature, yet it was a respect that permitted them to manipulate the environment, including the most precious of nature's resources, water, without doing harm.

Living properly in aboriginal California meant, first of all, understanding and existing in harmony with the environment rather than dominating it. Nature was neither the enemy nor simply a means to an end or a commodity to be exploited for wealth or power. Rather, nature had an intrinsic value of its own. To most tribes, plants and animals shared with humankind creation and spirit in a world where all living things were interconnected and each form of life had a special function. As anthropologists Robert F. Heizer and Albert B. Elsasser have observed, "the animal's role was to supply food for men; the plant's role was to nourish both men and animals; and the human role was to gather plants and hunt animals as

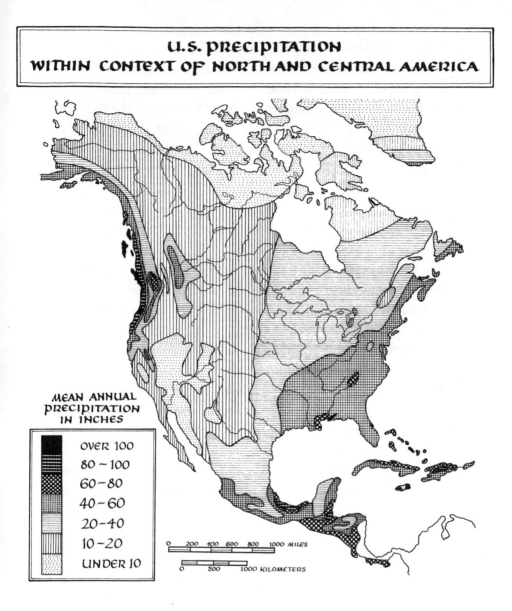

U.S. PRECIPITATION
WITHIN CONTEXT OF NORTH AND CENTRAL AMERICA

MEAN ANNUAL
PRECIPITATION
IN INCHES

OVER 100
80 ~ 100
60 ~ 80
40 ~ 60
20 ~ 40
10 ~ 20
UNDER 10

0 200 400 600 800 1000 MILES

0 500 1000 KILOMETERS

necessary for food."[3] The key words are "as necessary," for indiscriminate slaughter or wasteful gathering were abhorrent for practical and spiritual reasons. Some scholars have claimed contrary findings for other areas or times, but this worldview prevailed in California at the time of European arrival.[4] So, too, did the belief of many Indian groups that plants, animals, and even stones, springs, and trees possessed thought and feeling. Some tribes believed that human beings could transform themselves or be changed by another individual into an inanimate form or into coyotes, fish, ducks, foxes, owls, lizards, and other creatures. Death could in some tribal groups mean new life as a form of wildlife. Such ideas helped instill and reenforce a strong respect for nature that seemed to have supernatural corroboration in the regularity of the seasons, the annual salmon runs and geese migrations, and other wonders.[5]

Native Californians did not live, however, in complete harmony with nature, nor did they refrain from any significant manipulation of the environment. Like modern residents of the state, they sought to "improve" their natural world, but unlike today's developers they were sensitive to the balances in delicate ecosystems. They recognized that adverse interference with those relationships threatened their own existence as well as the natural world on which they depended and of which they were an integral part.

The tenacity with which California natives held to their values and lifestyles set them apart from most other Indian peoples of the Southwest and Mesoamerica. Their typical living patterns did not incorporate the check dams, miles of irrigation ditches, and great apartments built by the Hohokam along the Gila and Salt rivers after 300 B.C. or by the Anasazi at such places as Mesa Verde and Chaco Canyon some five hundred years before the Spaniards arrived. Nor did they live in anything like the less extensive but no less impressive or elaborate agricultural villages established several generations later and still inhabited by the Pueblo peoples of New Mexico. And they stand in stark counterpoint to the Aztecs with their *chinampas* (floating gardens) that helped make possible in the Central Valley of Mexico an urban civilization rivaling any in Eu-

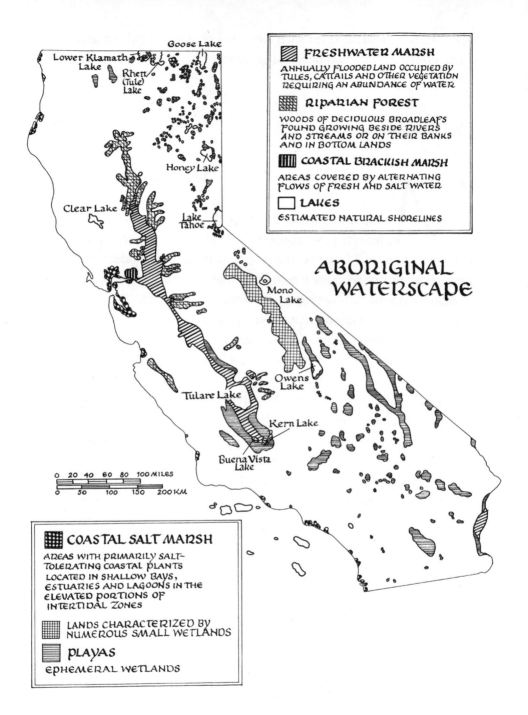

Goose Lake

Lower Klamath
Lake

Rhett
(Tule)
Lake

Honey Lake

Clear Lake

Lake
Tahoe

FRESHWATER MARSH

ANNUALLY FLOODED LAND OCCUPIED BY
TULES, CATTAILS AND OTHER VEGETATION
REQUIRING AN ABUNDANCE OF WATER

RIPARIAN FOREST

WOODS OF DECIDUOUS BROADLEAFS
FOUND GROWING BESIDE RIVERS
AND STREAMS OR ON THEIR BANKS
AND IN BOTTOM LANDS

COASTAL BRACKISH MARSH

AREAS COVERED BY ALTERNATING
FLOWS OF FRESH AND SALT WATER

LAKES

ESTIMATED NATURAL SHORELINES

ABORIGINAL
WATERSCAPE

Mono
Lake

Owens
Lake

Tulare Lake

Kern Lake

Buena Vista
Lake

0   20 40 60 80 100 MILES

0   50   100   150   200 KM

COASTAL SALT MARSH

AREAS WITH PRIMARILY SALT-
TOLERATING COASTAL PLANTS
LOCATED IN SHALLOW BAYS,
ESTUARIES AND LAGOONS IN THE
ELEVATED PORTIONS OF
INTERTIDAL ZONES

LANDS CHARACTERIZED BY
NUMEROUS SMALL WETLANDS

PLAYAS

EPHEMERAL WETLANDS

rope.[6] They had no need for such elements of material culture and hence placed no value on developing them.

The Waterscape

MOST CALIFORNIA Indians went to the water sources and settled near them rather than diverting water or storing it. Villages and population density reflected the availability of food and water, which in turn influenced lifestyles and social patterns. To understand these relationships requires recognizing that the waterscape of aboriginal California differed markedly from that of today.

In an age before massive dams and aqueducts, California's rivers flowed uninterrupted into valleys, marshes, bays, and the ocean. The great Central Valley stretches some 450 miles, is 40 to 70 miles wide, and lies between the Sierra Nevada on the east and the coastal ranges on the west. Two hundred years ago it included numerous rivers, lakes, and marshlands that were in existence more or less year-round and alternately expanded and contracted in rhythm with the seasons. They supported an abundance of fish, game, and waterfowl as well as beaver and otter. Cattails, tules, willows, and sometimes alder dominated the freshwater marshes inhabited by ducks, swans, marsh wrens, rails, and geese that darkened the sky with their enormous numbers.[7]

Preeminent in shaping all valley life were the Sacramento and San Joaquin rivers. They moved like twisting threads through the vast Central Valley trough. Draining the valley's northern third was the Sacramento, traveling some 370 meandering miles from its source in the Trinity Mountains before joining the San Joaquin in the labyrinthine waterways of the delta, whence the two rivers made their way to San Francisco Bay and the Pacific Ocean. The San Joaquin drained the larger, southern portion of the valley, but since the rains are heavier in the north its volume was only about a third that of the Sacramento. In their natural state, both rivers constantly shaped and reshaped the contours of the great valley until man-made structures dictated otherwise. Over the millennia the rivers and their tributaries during flood stage carried enormous quantities of topsoil from upland areas and deposited this rich silt across a floodplain that at the time of European contact constituted the nearly level valley floor of today.

Larger than any other comparable valley west of the Rockies, the Central Valley contained in its San Joaquin section the now vanished Tulare Lake, nearly four times the surface area of Lake Tahoe and home to an abundance of fish and vast quantities of turtles that ended up in rich soups and stews. Not far to the south were Buena Vista and Kern lakes, which now are also gone but in earlier times would often combine into a single large body of water, following an especially heavy snowmelt in the Sierra Nevada. On the San Joaquin Valley's west side and at higher elevations than the marshes, the lands were arid, receiving only slight and intermittent runoff from the Coast Range. To the east, beyond the Sierra, the floor of the Owens Valley contained swampy areas; Owens Lake held water, and, farther north, Mono Lake was full, and its islands were completely surrounded by water, providing safe habitats for millions of migratory birds. Among the migrants was the California gull, for which the area is still the largest breeding ground in the state and, except for the Great Salt Lake in Utah, in the world.[8]

In the San Joaquin, Sacramento, and coastal valleys, deciduous forests, virtually nonexistent today, grew profusely beside rivers and streams and in bottomlands. The dense and sometimes impenetrable riparian forests of willow, sycamore, oak, elder, poplar, alder, and wild grape provided shelter and food for a rich wildlife. Along the coast as well as in the inland valleys and foothills, oak savannas were more extensive and chaparral stands less evident than today, while seas of grass—tall, lush, perennial bunchgrasses now all but gone—dominated valley floors and prairies. Deer, antelope, California's own unique tule elk, rabbits, and other game animals browsed the hills and valleys in the tens of thousands. "The inland," noted a member of Francis Drake's expedition in 1579, "we found to be . . . a goodly country, and fruitfull soyle, stored with many blessings fit for the use of man: infinite was the company of very large and fat Deere, which there we sawe by thousands, as we supposed, in a heard." San Francisco Bay was then an even greater body of water than at present, ringed by large salt marshes, while the Sacramento–San Joaquin Delta teemed with fish, game, and a birdlife that numbered in the millions. "An abundance of deer, large and small, are to be met with all over the country, and geese, ducks, and cranes, on the banks of the rivers," observed Otto von Kotzebue about the delta area in 1824 during a stopover on his voyage around the world. "There was such a superfluity of game, that even those among us who had never been sportsmen before, when once they took the gun in their hands, became as eager as the rest."[9]

Wildlife was plentiful nearly everywhere, including on the vast southern California coastal plain. Because of annual rains in its bordering mountain ranges, the plain overlay a water table so near the surface that artesian springs—and even fountains—were commonplace. The ground, in effect, was filled to the brim. Similar artesian belts existed throughout California, surface expressions of the vast storehouse of groundwater that helped nurture the abundant flora and fauna on the surface. There was no Salton Sea in southeastern California, only a shallow sink sometimes containing water following a flash rain or more rarely when the Colorado River detoured into it temporarily, breaking its usual journey to the Gulf of California.[10]

The amount of precipitation that falls on California has not varied significantly between the time of European contact and the present. The annual rain- and snowfall produce approximately 200 million acre-feet. (Huge Lake Shasta, behind Shasta Dam, holds when full about 4.5 million acre-feet.) Most of this precipitation— about 65 percent—evaporates directly into the atmosphere, with nearly all the remaining 71 million acre-feet making its way into streams and, ultimately, in aboriginal times, the ocean, save for the water entering underground basins or aquifers. Over the ages, the groundwater in California's approximately 450 aquifers increased enormously, probably reaching the total estimated capacity of 1.3 billion acre-feet, or enough to cover the entire state to a depth of thirteen feet. In modern times overpumping has reduced that volume to some 850 million acre-feet, of which perhaps less than half is usable because of quality considerations and the cost of withdrawal. Of the ground and surface water presently not serving mandated environmental purposes, agriculture uses 77 percent (28 million acre-feet) and cities 23 percent (8.5 million acre-feet).[11]

The source of all this water is the Pacific Ocean. Vast clouds of moisture rise in the Gulf of Alaska or in the vicinity of the Hawaiian Islands and are driven ashore by the prevailing easterly moving wind currents (which are actually called westerlies). When the heavily laden clouds strike first the Coast Range and later the Sierra Nevada, they are driven higher into colder elevations, where their capacity to retain moisture decreases. The result is an often torrential volume of rain and snow, especially in so-called El Niño years, when a band of warm water moves east across the Pacific toward South America, altering the jet stream and worldwide weather conditions and producing for California a deluge of water. (Peruvians, who associated the phenomenon with the Christmas season, were responsible for naming it El Niño, after the Christ child.) The opposite event became popularized as La Niña: warm ocean water stretching *westward* from the mid-Pacific to South Africa, that alters the jet stream and produces in California reduced rainfall and even drought. For reasons not yet altogether understood, however, the warm-water movement back and forth, known as the Southern Oscillation, is not foolproof in its results. Fluctuations in the temperature and size of the band can produce weather variations, of course, but sometimes the effects have been even more surprising. For example, the major California floods of 1955 and 1964 did not coincide with El Niño conditions, and the moderate El Niño winter of 1976–1977 occurred during a drought. Moreover, on occasion, a dramatically larger portion of the Pacific Ocean can undergo cooling or warming and produce two, three, four, or more *decades* of severe drought or intense precipitation, hence the term Pacific Decadal Oscillation.[12]

Such erratic precipitation patterns, together with California's extraordinarily diverse landforms, help explain why the state is a land of many climates. As the clouds condense following their collision with the mountains, the higher elevations receive more moisture than the valleys, and the lowlands easterly of the Sierra—in its lee, or "rain shadow"—receive the least precipitation of all. Moreover, because the storms ordinarily originate in the North Pacific, the northern part of the state is more heavily watered than the southern. In terms of averages, precipitation varies from fifty inches annually along California's north coast to approximately eighteen inches on the southern coastal plain, and down to five inches or less in the inland desert valleys. Nearly all this precipitation arrives not in the summer growing season but between November and March.[13]

It is a mistake, however, to think of California in terms of averages and regular cycles of precipitation. The evidence, both recent and in tree rings dating from prehistoric times, reveals great variation. For example, the average annual precipitation for Los Angeles as determined over a century is about 15 inches, but that average rests on such rainfall extremes as 19 inches one year followed in consecutive years by 6 inches, 11 inches, 14 inches, 40 inches, and 11 inches.[14] Though the average varies throughout California, this pattern of extremes has remained the norm. The long-term record reveals a similar pattern of alternating cycles of severe drought and heavy precipitation. Tree-ring reconstructions not only for California but also for large portions of North America reveal evidence of what are likely extreme examples of the Pacific Decadal Oscillation phenomenon. The sixteenth century witnessed a megadrought, the most widespread, severe, and prolonged in the last 2000 years. Spreading north from Mexico, the drought, by century's end, embraced most of what is now the continental United States. Less extreme and widespread but longer droughts hit California earlier and later. A tree-ring study of stumps rooted in present-day lakes, marshes, and streams in California's Sierra Nevada indicates that the longest intervals of minimum growth (hence, a reflection of drought) were the 220 years between 892 and 1112 and the 141 years between 1209 and 1350. The lengthiest period of extreme wetness was the ninety-seven years that separated those two droughts, 1112 to 1209. The intensity of the precipitation during the wet period was so great that Mono Lake rose to a level exceeded only once in the last two thousand years.[15]

Other tree-ring studies of California for a subsequent 360-year period reveal that the third-longest interval of minimum growth was the sixty-one years from 1760 through 1820, whereas the period 1935–1944 (with an annual average precipitation in Los Angeles of nearly nineteen inches) emerges as one of maximum growth exceeded only by the almost-century-long wet spell noted above that hit more than 800 years ago. Additional lengthy periods of deficient precipitation were 1600 to 1625, 1720 to 1730, 1865 to 1885, 1928 to 1934, and 1987 to 1992. These examples represent extremes, but none of the cycles are of predictable length and they vary from place to place, with the result that some areas can be experiencing drought simultaneously with others that are literally under water. Thus, great irregularity characterizes the typical precipitation pattern throughout California. The larger point of all this, however, and a warning to modern California is that, if such extremes have occurred before, they can occur again.[16]

Waterways and Lifeways

DESPITE SUCH variation in a resource of fundamental importance, the Indians fashioned lifestyles that harmonized unusually well with their world. They had their lean, even starving, times, but they were successful enough to make California one of the most densely populated areas north of Mexico. In achieving this population, they created a

CALIFORNIA GROUNDWATER BASINS

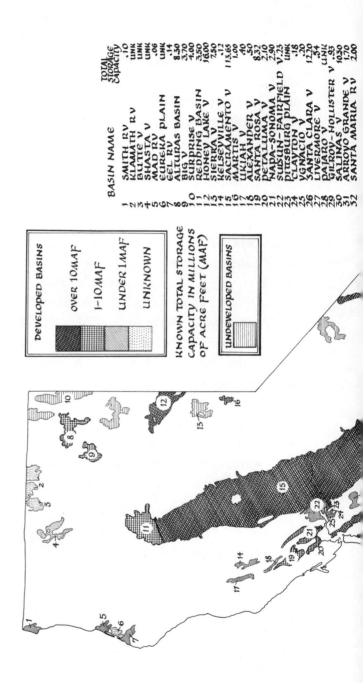

DEVELOPED BASINS

- OVER 10MAF
- 1-10MAF
- UNDER 1MAF
- UNKNOWN

KNOWN TOTAL STORAGE
CAPACITY IN MILLIONS
OF ACRE FEET (MAF)

UNDEVELOPED BASINS

	BASIN NAME	TOTAL STORAGE CAPACITY
1	SMITH RV	.10
2	KLAMATH RV	UNK
3	BUTTE V	UNK
4	SHASTA V	UNK
5	MAD RV	.06
6	EUREKA PLAIN	UNK
7	EEL RV	.14
8	ALTURAS BASIN	8.30
9	BIG V	3.70
10	SURPRISE V	4.00
11	REDDING BASIN	3.50
12	HONEY LAKE V	16.00
13	SIERRA V	7.50
14	KELSEYVILLE V	.12
15	SACRAMENTO V	115.65
16	MARTIS V	1.00
17	UKIAH V	.40
18	ALEXANDER V	.50
19	SANTA ROSA V	8.32
20	PETALUMA V	2.10
21	NAPA-SONOMA V	2.90
22	SUISUN-FAIRFIELD V	.23
23	PITTSBURG PLAIN	UNK
24	CLAYTON V	.18
25	YGNACIO V	.20
26	SANTA CLARA V	12.20
27	LIVERMORE V	.54
28	PAJARO V	UNK
29	GILROY-HOLLISTER V	.93
30	SALINAS V	UNK
31	ARROYO GRANDE V	10.30
32	SANTA MARIA RV	2.00

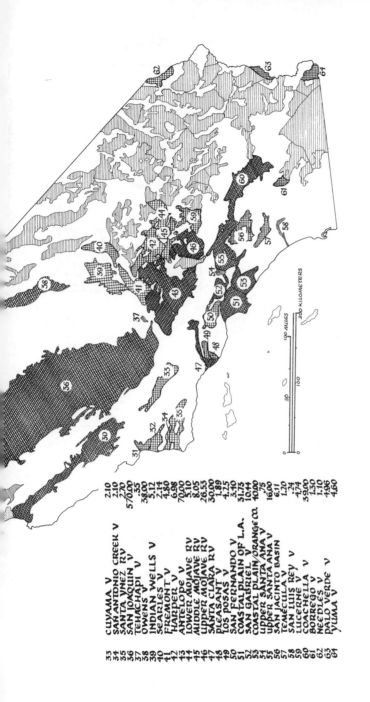

MEAN ANNUAL PRECIPITATION

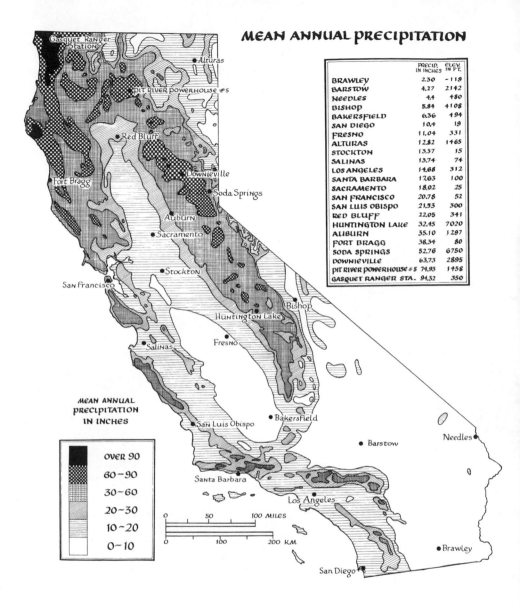

	PRECIP. IN INCHES	ELEV. IN FT.
BRAWLEY	2.30	-119
BARSTOW	4.27	2142
NEEDLES	4.4	480
BISHOP	5.84	4108
BAKERSFIELD	6.36	494
SAN DIEGO	10.4	19
FRESNO	11.04	331
ALTURAS	12.82	1465
STOCKTON	13.37	15
SALINAS	13.74	74
LOS ANGELES	14.68	312
SANTA BARBARA	17.63	100
SACRAMENTO	18.02	25
SAN FRANCISCO	20.78	52
SAN LUIS OBISPO	21.53	300
RED BLUFF	22.05	341
HUNTINGTON LAKE	32.45	7020
AUBURN	35.10	1297
FORT BRAGG	38.34	80
SODA SPRINGS	52.76	6750
DOWNIEVILLE	63.73	2895
PIT RIVER POWERHOUSE #5	74.93	1458
GASQUET RANGER STA.	94.32	350

MEAN ANNUAL PRECIPITATION IN INCHES

- OVER 90
- 60 ~ 90
- 30 ~ 60
- 20 ~ 30
- 10 ~ 20
- 0 ~ 10

0   50   100 MILES

0   100   200 KM

Map place labels: Gasquet Ranger Station, Alturas, Pit River Powerhouse #5, Red Bluff, Downieville, Fort Bragg, Soda Springs, Auburn, Sacramento, Stockton, San Francisco, Huntington Lake, Bishop, Salinas, Fresno, San Luis Obispo, Bakersfield, Santa Barbara, Barstow, Needles, Los Angeles, Brawley, San Diego variety of culture areas that echoed the potential of the different environments available to them. Anthropologists have identified six such areas: coastal, riverine, lakeshore, valley and plains, foothills, and desert. None was entirely distinct from the others but each reflected regional variations in climate, terrain, water, animals, and plants. These differences masked an even greater linguistic diversity that reflected the Indian practice of living in small isolated groups, thereby increasing the carrying capacity of the land. The native peoples belonged to six distinct language families, spoke more than a hundred dialects, and lived in numerous villages ranging in size from a few families to a population of a thousand or more. Despite such diversity, they developed social organizations and rituals to satisfy similar needs: adequate food, restoration of good health, the driving away of evil spirits, and the like. Among tribes throughout California, but especially in the dry areas, the rainmaker's ceremony occupied a place of crucial importance. The degree of that importance varied over the years, but with climatic extremes as the norm, this worthy's services eventually came into heavy demand everywhere.[17]

Water played the most significant role in village location. Unlike peoples who frequently established rivers as boundaries, California natives looked upon the entire watershed of streams, reaching back from both banks, as natural territories. Such an outlook reflected economic as well as political considerations, for it ordinarily gave a native community control of both banks of a river or stream or creek, and it provided easy access to the game and fowl that sought out such watercourses. It also meant for the community a greater variety of available resources since watersheds typically embrace several life zones where the number and kinds of plants and animals vary seasonally and according to altitude, precipitation, and climate. Control of a stream also meant access to fish, including the steelhead (a seagoing rainbow trout) that once ran the Pacific coastal streams from Alaska to Baja California—now seldom appearing as far south as Malibu Creek—and especially the highly prized king salmon that once could be found in abundance in 650

miles of uninterrupted California waterways. Fish served, therefore, as a major part of the diet for many Indians. The fresh water
of a stream or lake was also crucial in the preparation of acorns, the
principal vegetable food of most California natives. Unless the
ground acorn meal could be leached with boiling water, its tannic
acid content made it inedible. Even a less common method of removing the tannin required water: unshelled acorns were buried in
mud for as long as a year to make them palatable. Thus even those
Indians who lived along the coast and relied heavily on shellfish and
ocean catches located their villages near sources of fresh water in
order to sustain their acorn diet and to meet their personal needs.[18]

For the peoples inhabiting California's deserts, water naturally
played an even more critical role in survival. These Indians settled
near springs or an infrequent stream, often moving because of the
seasonal nature of the water supply. In their hunting-gathering activities, they depended heavily on game and mesquite berries and
especially on piñon nuts, rather than the acorn, since the otherwise
ubiquitous oak was not present in the deserts. Population density
in the desert was the lowest in California because the extreme heat,
low rainfall, and typical desert-plant cover produced fewer natural
foods than elsewhere. Among those who survived only by hunting
and collecting, village life was virtually unknown, with small bands
or even a single family being the primary unit. Water or food shortage frequently caused even these groups to splinter. Such fragmentation and isolation could profoundly affect cultural life, leading to
the development of new and distinctively different ceremonials.[19]

That California's many environments, including especially the
location and quantity of water, influenced the settlement patterns,
material culture, and lifestyles of the native peoples should not be
construed as geographic or environmental determinism. The Indians were not unthinking or passive dwellers on the land. They were
environmentally intelligent enough to survive, and usually did so
comfortably. They were also conscious manipulators of their various environments. Virtually everywhere, California natives actively practiced what could be called natural-resource manage-

ment. They did this recognizing that, above all, they were part of nature and had to manage their own lives wisely. This entailed devising social and cultural restraints calculated to ensure survival. Birth control during times of shortage provides one example. Typical, too, were rituals that prevented the overhunting or overfishing that might threaten subsistence in the future. The Yurok and Karok tribes proscribed anything that endangered the capacity of the Klamath River to attract the annual salmon runs. The Sierra Miwok and others harvested acorns carefully so as to avoid damaging the oak trees that provided their main staple. Observed an old Wintu woman in recollection: "When we . . . kill meat, we eat it all up. When we dig roots, we make little holes. . . . We don't chop down the trees. We only use dead wood."[20]

Resource management also entailed manipulating the physical environment. An especially dramatic example of such environmental alteration was the Indians' purposeful and managed use of fire, which not only aided in the production of food and material goods but also helped in reducing the threat of the horrendously destructive brush and forest wildfires so characteristic of modern-day California. The native peoples regularly burned grasslands, chaparral, coniferous trees, and freshwater marshes to flush animals and grasshoppers, provide greater access to wildlife in densely forested areas, and encourage fresh growth attractive to grazing game and important to the production of baskets and other popular items. The Miwok, Wintu, Yurok, Hupa, and perhaps other tribes grew tobacco by scattering seeds on well-watered, burned-over slopes or in the ashes of old logs to which they had earlier set fire. The Western Mono employed fire to encourage the growth of redbud shoots for making baskets, while Northwest Coast peoples obtained their basketry material by selectively firing beargrass and hazelnut. The San Diegueño, Kumeyaay, Cupeño, Pomo, and other peoples improved the productivity of edible seed plants by burning the fields containing them, just as the Choinumni Yokuts and other groups along the Klamath River fostered large berry crops by firing the older stems of bushes. Using another approach, some desert peoples appear to have regularly trimmed mesquite in order to increase pod yield, while the Cahuilla improved the livability of their desert oases by planting the seeds of desert fan palms.[21] However, the most significant form of Indian manipulation of the environment was in agriculture.

Agriculture and Cultural Patterns

OR YEARS the conventional wisdom among scholars was that the California natives did not practice agriculture: the tilling, planting, and cultivating of the soil. Some contended that native hunting and gathering practices, especially the acorn economy, were so successful that agriculture was unnecessary, whereas others emphasized the climatic obstacle posed by California's hot summers for the "usual Indian triad of corn, beans, and squash." Still others called attention to the lack of annual grasses that could be domesticated.[22] These arguments seem logical for much of California, particularly when considered along with the Indians' use of fire and other resource-management techniques, but they fail to explain the growing body of evidence that agriculture, and in particular irrigation agriculture, was being practiced long before the arrival of Europeans. At first such evidence was grudgingly labeled "incipient agriculture," "semi-cultivation," or even "irrigation without agriculture," the latter an expression coined by Julian Steward, among the most respected anthropologists of the first half of the twentieth century.[23] Recent research, however, demonstrates convincingly that some California Indians practiced agriculture on a wide scale in aboriginal times. The latest findings are strongest for two areas in California, the Owens Valley in the east and along the lower Colorado River in the southeast.

The Owens Valley is a long, narrow trough lying between the Sierra Nevada on the west and the White-Inyo Range on the east. It extends some seventy-five miles, north to south, with a width of six to ten miles. Precipitation on the valley floor averages less than six inches, but the area is well watered during much of the year by runoff from Sierra streams. There the Paiute, probably sometime around A.D. 1000, constructed an elaborate irrigation system with the largest development in the northern portion of the valley in the vicinity of the present community of Bishop. They built a dam on Bishop Creek and diverted water several miles through large earthen canals to two immense plots, one measuring about two square miles and the other approximately four-by-one to one-and-a-half miles. The plots were irrigated in alternate years in a practice similar to fallowing that promoted increased yield and lessened the chances for undesirable vegetation. The primary crops grown were native plants—yellow nut grass for protein and rich tubers and wild hyacinth for the nutritious bulblike corms. Harvesting was accomplished by turning the soil with a special wooden tool or digging stick that exposed the desired plant parts while facilitating the replanting of the soil with smaller corms and tubers.[24]

The crops were local in origin and not the melons, maize, pumpkins, and squash associated with Spanish cultivation. This in itself is evidence that agriculture developed independently in the Owens Valley and was not diffused in historic times from the missions or other colonial settlements. Nor for the same reason does it seem likely that the Paiute borrowed the practice from the agricultural tribes and pueblos in what is presently New Mexico and Arizona where the principal crops were similar to those of the Spanish settlements. To have borrowed the means (irrigation) and not the raison d'être (the crops produced) constitutes an action at variance with anthropological knowledge. Also supporting the case for independent development of agriculture among the Paiute is the fact that their words associated with the growing of crops—for example *tuvaijü*[u] (head irrigator), *tüva*[ya]*dut* (to irrigate), and *pavado* (irrigator's pole)—are Paiute and not derived from other Indian languages or Spanish.[25]

An intriguing question is why they developed agriculture. A popular theory for explaining the origins of agriculture worldwide holds that population growth is the trigger. When the natural increase in the population of an area creates a food demand incapable of being met through hunting and gathering alone, the resulting pressure prompts the development of agricultural techniques.[26] Archaeological evidence in the Owens Valley seems to support this theory, though the population pressure appears to have come from immigration and not natural increase. About A.D. 1000 the climate in the West became drier and prompted migration from less-accommodating lands of southeastern California into the Owens Valley where runoff from the Sierra, even if decreased, supported relatively abundant game and vegetation. As those resources became increasingly taxed, the Indians' settlement patterns, which had heretofore reflected only hunting-gathering characteristics, began to reveal features typical of agricultural societies. The most striking feature was a decline in nomadism and the appearance of permanent villages. Eventually the Owens Valley became home to some thirty such villages inhabited by at least two thousand people, making the region one of the most densely populated areas in the Great Basin, that vast region from the eastern borders of the Sierra Nevada to the Rockies.[27]

The adoption of agriculture would have required no great cultural leap for the Paiute. Always in close touch with their environment, the food-conscious natives of Owens Valley could not have helped but notice that the naturally occurring nutritious plants grew in more abundance in the marshlands and in areas along creeks subject to occasional overflow. It would have been but a short step to watering promising lands artificially. The natives themselves doubtless contributed to this development by their traditional dry-creek fishing practice of enlisting the help of a whole village or groups of villages to divert streams in order to gather fish from the exposed beds. The dry-creek method of fishing later became an integral part of the Indians' agricultural system, for they regularly gathered fish in this way when they dammed streams and diverted the water into their irrigation canals. The introduction of irrigation agriculture did not result in the Owens Valley Paiute becoming only farmers and occasional consumers of fish. Seldom has an agricultural society anywhere completely abandoned hunting and gathering. The Paiute continued to rely on game and especially on the piñon nut for sustenance. Agriculture's special role was to supplement the available natural foods that became increasingly inadequate, especially during the long and sometimes severe Owens Valley winters.[28]

The other California area of major agricultural development was along the lower Colorado River. There the Quechan (Yuma), Mohave, Halchidhoma, and Kamia cultivated the bottomlands between Black Canyon, near the southern tip of what is now Nevada, and the present Mexican border, while the Kamia also worked the rich soils of what is today the southern Imperial Valley. Like the Owens Valley Paiute, these peoples practiced agriculture long before the arrival of the Spanish, perhaps as early as A.D. 800 in the area where the Gila River empties into the Colorado. Agriculture there, however, does not appear to have been an independent invention, but rather diffused from tribes further east where cultivation of the soil had been going on for generations. Crops included not only some local native vegetation and a type of maize characteristic of that found in ancient Hohokam sites, but also watermelons, muskmelons, and black-eyed beans. The latter had been introduced to the New World by the Spaniards and diffused northward faster than the advance of white settlements.[29]

The river tribes had numerous plots, rather than a vast field or two like the Paiute. They relied upon the periodic floods of the Colorado River instead of building dams and canals. These overflows deposited a rich layer of silt on their plots, which they planted by punching a hole with a stick and dropping in seeds. Because the river did not always overflow and since weeds lessened the harvest, they, like the Paiute, did not abandon their hunting and gathering practices. Ordinarily, however, they could rely on agriculture for a substantial portion of their food: 50 percent for the Mohave and 30 to 50 percent for the other tribes. Their success was such that at the time of European arrival, the river tribes numbered perhaps 3,500 or 63 percent of California's desert population. As in the Owens Valley, the pressure of such numbers seems to have been the reason for the adoption of agriculture in the area, for scholars agree that reliance on natural foods alone could not have sustained anywhere near the numbers present at contact.[30]

In his fascinating study of despotism and the rise of civilization, Karl Wittfogel has argued that large-scale irrigation was possible only in a tightly ordered and hierarchical society whose members surrendered control of their labor, and much of their political and personal freedom, to a centralized authority. Wittfogel's theory does not seem to find support in the experiences of California's aboriginal irrigationists. The Owens Valley Paiute practiced irrigation on an extensive scale, requiring vast amounts of labor. The men were primarily responsible for constructing the dams and canals and the women for gathering the harvest. Their efforts, however, were communal, and freely given both in recognition of the need for a stable food supply and in anticipation that all participants would share in the harvest. Such communal efforts were not limited to irrigation but were characteristic of hunts for game, when an entire village or groups of villages joined to drive antelope or rabbits. A village or district headman supervised such efforts, but he was chosen by the people, not self-appointed and certainly not a despot. In the case of agriculture, the head irrigator was elected in the spring by a popular assembly that also approved the date for irrigation to begin. This challenge to Wittfogel joins those of others whose findings indicate that political centralization in irrigation societies varies with the circumstances. Studies of irrigation societies with vastly different social and economic structures indicate that they are as apt to be decentralized as centralized.[31]

Along the lower Colorado River, irrigation agriculture proved successful without check dams, canals, or ditches. This is not, however, to say that agriculture had no effect on the Indian societies there. The distinctive features are striking. They suggest that the river people, while certainly not subject to anything resembling despotism, could with their simpler irrigation arrangements exercise control over a wider area and command a larger following than the Paiute with their large-scale hydraulic systems. In such respects, they also differed from their nearby nonagricultural kin. The explanation seems traceable to both cultural and environmental influences. Among those lower Colorado peoples who shunned the movement toward agriculture and continued to rely strictly on a hunting and gathering economy, the basic political unit remained the patrilineal band consisting of 100 to 150 people. It operated autonomously, was governed by a leader who was ordinarily hereditary, and claimed a specific territory that it jealously guarded against other bands with which it frequently engaged in lengthy feuds. Their agricultural relatives, on the other hand, developed a deep sense of tribal—rather than band—loyalty among those speaking the same language and living within the general vicinity of one another. Leaders acquired power through individual success, rather than invoking heredity as in the band, and exercised their authority (the resolution of disputes, calling of ceremonies, redistributing gifts, selecting a course of action in critical situations) over a relatively broad region rather than over the more restricted territories of bands.[32]

Intertwined with the cultural differences were sharp contrasts in settlement patterns. The agricultural peoples ordinarily resided in individual family units spread over a considerable area. This scattering reflected the dispersed nature of the suitable farmland, which seldom existed in tracts large enough to support more than a family or two. The reason was the nature of the river. The action of the water normally produced considerable erosion and unevenness of contour, resulting in suitable plots of only an acre or two, enough for a family but clearly insufficient for a band. Also contributing to the spread-out living patterns were the frequent heavy floods that destroyed farm plots or changed the course of the river and deprived lands of water. Both eventualities necessitated habitual change of homesites.

This mobility and dispersal made it impossible for agricultural peoples to maintain the residential unity characteristic of the hunting-gathering bands and made it difficult, if not impossible, to continue political and cultural patterns that rested on such unity. Unable to identify with a particular band or headman, agricultural peoples began identifying instead with those engaged in a similar horticultural economy and who spoke the same language, lived in the same general area, and shared many of the same fears and aspirations. They selected headmen on the basis of individual achievement—their ability to persuade others of the wisdom of their choices, their generosity in distributing goods, and especially their talents for inspiring confidence through their dreams. This "dream power" became a preeminent cultural characteristic of the agricultural peoples and the means by which leaders legitimized their claims to authority. Among the nonagricultural bands dreams received no such emphasis, since heredity continued to serve as the sign of the legitimate leader. Warfare also gained great prominence among the agriculturalists. Though hunting and gathering bands engaged in protracted feuds with one another, they devoted most of their energies to subsistence. The farming peoples, on the other hand, fought more frequently, more bitterly, and on a larger scale, some even attacking tribes hundreds of miles distant. Their food resources made such ventures possible and the size of their territories assured manpower for conflicts that dwarfed those of individual bands. Warfare also helped to reenforce loyalties and maintain the tribal unity of a people scattered over a large territory.[33]

Symbiosis and Community

W ATER WAS important to the subsistence patterns and political and social customs of the agricultural peoples of the lower Colorado River and Owens Valley, but the natives did little to disturb the land. The large canals and networks of subsidiary ditches built by the Paiute are today hardly discernible even to the trained eye, a circumstance that helps explain the generations of uncertainty about the existence of agriculture in aboriginal California. To scar the land unnecessarily conflicted with their desire for symbiosis with nature and their determination to avoid any action that might lead to disaster. Such considerations probably explain the Paiute practice of annually destroying their dams once those structures had served their purpose.[34] The reliance of the Colorado River agriculturalists on the natural ebbs and flows of the river for watering their fields resulted in even fewer marks on the landscape. The contrast with modern agribusiness could not be greater.

Still another feature in counterpoint with the future was the absence among Indians of a private property right in the use of water that could be bartered or sold. Such a concept was completely alien, because water, like land, belonged to no individual but rather was interconnected with all of nature and essential for both human and animal survival. A corollary belief was a shrewd understanding of water's ultimate illusiveness. An old Wintu woman put it this way to an interviewer: "Water says this, 'Wherever you put me I'll be in my home. I am awfully smart. Lead me out of my springs, lead me from my rivers, but I came from the ocean and I shall go back into the ocean. You can dig a ditch and put me in it, but I go only so far and I am out of sight. I am awfully smart. When I am out of sight I am on my way home.'"[35]

Such wisdom notwithstanding, bands and tribes jealously defended their territories, and in doing so, they were also guarding the springs, streams, and rivers that watered those lands and attracted the game, fowl, and fish that contributed to survival. Viewed this way water belonged, if only fleetingly, to a particular community and, especially in the more arid regions, must have been the source of conflict. Yet just as later generations of Californians with a different ethic would permanently alter the landscape with their massive hydraulic structures, so too would their battles over water become monumental in scope, dwarfing any possible differences among Indian communities. The latter-day behemoths pitted vast regions and even nations against one another.

Disagreements over water were doubtless infrequent if not unknown to the vast majority of native Californians who lived in areas where precipitation was ordinarily adequate for their hunting and gathering economy. Neither they nor the minority who practiced agriculture on a regular or sporadic basis felt the need to subjugate nature. It would require the arrival of Europeans to introduce a dramatically different set of values which, in turn, would produce a different legacy.

The Aboriginal Waterscape

2 Hispanic Patterns: Community and Authority

Spain's settlement of Alta California in 1769 introduced a lifestyle and value system at sharp variance with those of the native peoples of this most distant of the empire's northern possessions. Most newcomers, especially after the first few years, were themselves of Indian and mixed-blood ancestry from New Spain (or Mexico), but the leaders of the colonization venture, as well as many of the accompanying soldiers, tended to be Old World peninsulares. It was their cultural baggage—language, religion, and customs—that predominated in the new settlements. Though sometimes modified by clashes and cultural interchanges with native peoples on earlier Hispanic frontiers, their values remained fundamentally unchanged.

Among the most persistent of the Spanish newcomers' attitudes was their conviction that nature—rivers and streams, woodlands, minerals, soils, deserts, animal and plant life in all their complexity—constituted a divine gift to be subdued and exploited in the name of God and civilization. "Man has the power," declared *Las siete partidas* (1265), the first great codification of Spanish law and the basis for the legal system introduced in the New World, "to do as he sees fit with those things that belong to him according to the laws of God and man."[1] Such a belief had centuries before helped shape Iberian institutions, none more so than those involving water. Because much of the Spanish homeland, like most of the northern periphery of New Spain, was largely a place of few rivers and sparse rainfall, customs, laws, and decrees had evolved since antiquity to reflect the fundamental importance of water and its integral role in the survival of families and local communities. Along with the emphasis on community endurance emerged an equally strong tradition stressing royal authority in matters concerning water. It was a tradition born of the long struggle to unify the Iberian Peninsula as fractious regional kings, recognizing water as a source of power and wealth, used it to manipulate allies and defeat enemies. While petty kingdoms gradually coalesced around a central monarchy, community survival and central authority persisted as the most distinctive features of Spain's attitude toward water. It carried over in promoting the overseas empire, including the settlement of California, where these customs remained dominant throughout the Spanish era (1769–1821) and the Mexican period (1821–1846).

"Apportion Water Justly and Fairly"

THERE WAS, of course, nothing new or unique about the Spanish idea of nature existing to serve humanity and its communities in virtually every imaginable way. That view has been held by many of the world's peoples, including especially those Anglo-American frontiersmen along the Atlantic Coast of North America who would transform environmental exploitation into an article of national faith before later generations would have second thoughts about such wanton destruction in the twentieth century. From time immemorial the Judeo-Christian tradition had admonished humankind to "be fruitful and multiply; abound on the earth and subdue it."[2] The Greeks and Romans had a different deity but not attitude. "All charms of life," announced Titus Lucretius Carus in the first century B.C., are found not in nature but in "ships, agriculture, city walls, laws, arms, roads." As one scholar of popular ideas about wilderness has affirmed, "the celebrations of nature, which abound in classical literature, are restricted to the cultivated, pastoral variety" and are "closely related to the fruitful or otherwise useful."[3]

For the emerging nations of Europe as for the ancients, a "fruitful" and "useful" nature meant nature controlled. Nowhere did this seem more self-evident than in water-shy areas like Spain where the compulsion to conquer both land and people had for generations dramatically altered social institutions and the countryside. Phoenicians, Greeks, Romans, Germanic invaders from the north, and the Moors from the south had contributed laws and left striking visible reminders of their ideas, especially the Romans in the massive aqueduct at Segovia and the Moors in the beautifully intricate water system of the Alhambra. Water was of such fundamental importance that its lavish display became synonymous with wealth, power, and technological sophistication. Fountains emerged as commonplace symbols of achievement. Even modest self-congratulation (and hence a modest fountain) took on special importance in a country where estates, kingdoms, towns, cities, cultivated fields, and grazing lands could not exist without an assured water supply.

The fundamental water-use unit in Spain was the local irrigation community where customs and laws had evolved over generations, drawing heavily on earlier Roman, Germanic, and Arabic experiences. Higher authorities acknowledged the importance of local considerations in water matters, a recognition of the power of tradition and the success of communities in devising principles that assured their survival. Success for them redounded to the benefit of the local kingdoms of which they were a part and, when the country finally unified under a central monarchy, to the welfare of all Spain. No noble's territory could be stronger than the communities of which it consisted, and Spain's leaders had early recognized that principle, nowhere more clearly than in arid and semiarid regions like Valencia, the "Garden of Spain." There the basic principle in allocating water was "proportionality"—people obtaining an amount in proportion to their legitimate needs and in proportion to the volume of water available. Of necessity such a determination had to be made within the context of the needs of everyone in a community, and hence the amount of water allocated to an individual was not fixed. Disputes could be appealed to higher authorities, but the community's goal was "to apportion water justly and fairly to each user and to prevent conflict."[4]

The traditional emphasis on community carried with it recognition of a water right possessed by irrigation districts, towns, and other corporate municipalities. The right was neither exclusive nor absolute, for property rights could also be private, and tradition and necessity sometimes blurred the distinction between public and private. Spain's petty kings illustrated this when they issued grants of water and land in their struggles with one another and the Moors for control of the peninsula. The private rights they created could take precedence over those of communities, though the tendency was to subordinate them when this could be done without threatening established authority. A king's preference in a newly subjugated area was to confirm the existing rights of the inhabitants as a way of winning their loyalty and reenforcing his control. "We give and concede forever to all of you united, and to each one of the inhabitants," proclaimed the conqueror of Valencia in the early thirteenth century, "all and every one of the canals, unincumbered [sic] and free, great and small, with their waters, headgates, and conduits of these same waters, as well as the spring waters, with the exception of the Royal canal."[5] The caveat about the "Royal canal" was a not subtle reminder of who was in charge.

The ouster of the Moors and the emergence of a centralized monarchy on the eve of Columbus's voyages meant that Spain's ideas about the importance and distribution of water reached America through a single powerful crown. The discoveries belonged to the royal patrimony, and the monarch followed tradition in asserting absolute authority to establish and maintain the Spanish presence.

Lessons in Survival

T HE CROWN moved quickly to secure its claims in America by replicating the familiar: a Hispanic society living primarily in cities, towns, forts, and other communities (some created in response to unique New World conditions) dependent on agriculture and cattle, sheep, goats, horses, and other animals — and all relying for survival on nearby water sources. In settling Alta California and the northern Spanish borderlands generally, Spain predominantly used three community forms: the fort, mission, and town. A form of private property, the rancho, also played a key role and sometimes took on many of the characteristics of a modest town. For some colonists on other frontiers there had been special inducements, such as precious metals or pearls or trade, but for those destined for California there were no illusions of wealth. Few, except missionaries, wanted to go to such a forlorn place where nothing even remotely valuable had been found. Mining gold or silver or separating Indians from such metals had long ago been discounted as possibilities. National security, or at least its pretext, finally sent the colonizers to California so no other nation would be tempted to occupy the region and possibly threaten the really important Spanish possessions further south.

Crucial to Spain's successful colonization of California was an acute sensitivity to water as a means of imperial expansion. To locate and control limited supplies would certainly help keep foreign interlopers out but, of far more importance as a consideration, water was absolutely essential for survival in California and throughout northern New Spain. On other borderland frontiers, particularly in New Mexico, Pimería Alta (southern Arizona and northern Sonora), and Baja California, Spaniards had learned grim lessons in desert survival. They had even delayed by decades an overland march to Alta California because of the forbidding country through which they would have to journey. When at last they were on the trail in spring 1769, the worst fears of expedition leader Gaspar de Portolá were soon realized.

"There was . . . no water" is the diary entry made by Portolá about the first evening's camp. Thereafter, entries abound in the records kept by expedition members about their concern for water—its absence, presence, quantity, quality. Sometimes they were forced to dig for it for both men and animals. Often even digging produced no results. "We had no water here except what . . . [was] carried," complained Fray Juan Crespi, "and the animals, though they had good pasture, went without drinking." Progress was torturously slow, noted Miguel Costansó, because of "the need of exploring the land one day for the next, so as to regulate the marches, according to the distance of the watering-places."[6] The deity and special saints were alternately thanked or cajoled as the circumstances seemed to require. Failure to locate water led to more fervent prayer, greater diligence on the part of scouting parties, and the taking out of some divine insurance by giving even a miserable locale a religious designation. "I named the place the Hollow of the Holy Apostles," recorded Crespi about a dry camp. The next evening, after some initial disappointments, he and his companions were more successful: "There is plenty of . . . [water] in some large pools, and although one of them is salty, the rest are . . . good. . . . I named the place Holy Cross of the Pools of the Bay of Todos Santos."[7]

Expedition leaders were under strict orders to identify sites for permanent settlements, including missions where the natives could be brought to the white man's God and trained to produce the food and clothing needed to sustain the imperial foothold. Because of the shortage of priests and the scattering of the Indians throughout the countryside in scores of small villages (the Spaniards called them *rancherías*), imperial policy dictated bringing the Indians to the missions rather than pursuing the hopeless goal of establishing a mission in each village. This necessarily required knowledge of the whereabouts of large numbers of potential converts, but just as important, it demanded information about timber for building and firewood, lands suitable for cultivation, and especially springs, streams, and rivers. To Spain, survival of the empire in California would depend upon what had enabled it to survive in other watershort areas: establishment of an irrigated agricultural base relying on Indian labor. When the Indians had become sufficiently "civilized," the missions were to be secularized—that is, transformed into corporate *pueblos* (villages or towns), with the inhabitants receiving title to individual land grants and the surplus holdings going to other settlers deemed worthy. It was a process designed to produce, at least in theory, a large population of loyal and productive Spaniards in a precariously held corner of the empire.

The colonists had hardly entered Alta California when they found in San Diego an attractive site for the first mission and *presidio* (fort) as well as rendezvous point for other expedition parties coming by land and sea. There was a splendid, protected harbor, "a large river," "good arable land," impressive stands of "willows, cottonwoods, and alders," and "many large villages of heathen." Though natural harbors were scarce, the presence of the other features determined the location of most settlements, especially the missions that became the most numerous expressions of Spanish presence. Typical was Mission San Antonio de Padua which rose in a "large [interior] valley full of oaks" with "many heathen in the vicinity" and "near a river which was running with a good deal of water" that could "irrigate the . . . extensive land." Francisco Palóu's glowing description of another locale—"good streams of water," "fertile land," "heathen" in "neighboring villages," "cottonwoods, willows, and other trees, thickets of blackberries, and innumerable wild grape vines"—prompted the founding of San Gabriel, eventually among the most productive of all the missions. San Luis Obispo emerged in a place "having two small arroyos of water, with plenty of land which could be irrigated with a little labor" supplied by nearby Indians noted for their "docility" and "affection."[8] With such attention to site and Indian settlement patterns, the Franciscans eventually established a chain of twenty-one missions over a period of fifty-four years.

Spain's heavy reliance on missions followed well-established precedent, but such a policy was exceedingly difficult to implement in the first years. California Indians belonged to many culturally distinct societies with no labor systems of their own on which the Spaniards could superimpose their institutions as they had done with the peoples of central Mexico. As the missionaries struggled to recruit and train the dispersed populations, the presidio with its soldiers and government officials emerged for a time as the predominant institution, though even its existence remained precarious. Eventually there were four of them hugging the coast—at San Diego (1769), Monterey (1770), San Francisco (1776), and Santa Bárbara (1782).

Though preeminently military fortifications, presidios were expected to generate their own food and clothing and eventually to achieve the formal status of a civil pueblo. Progress was disappointingly slow. In 1773 Viceroy Antonio María Bucareli y Ursúa, driven by a "desire that population may be more speedily assured," admonished the commandant in charge of the first two presidios at San Diego and Monterey to exercise his authority "with respect to distributing lands" and to include among the grantees those Indians most dedicated "to agriculture and raising cattle."[9] Such orders notwithstanding, presidio residents proved hardly able to perform their military tasks, much less feed and clothe themselves.

The failure of the military garrisons prompted imperial authorities to order the establishment of pueblos and to charge their residents with provisioning themselves as well as the inhabitants of the presidios. In time, three pueblos were established: at San José (1777), Los Angeles (1781), and Branciforte (1797). The instructions for the founding of all of them made expressly clear the importance of sound water planning. "For the foundation of the pueblo of la Reina de los Angeles," stipulated Governor Felipe de Neve in August 1781, "all the lands should be ascertained which can have the benefit of irrigation" and "the pueblo is to be located . . . so that the whole or the greater part of the lands for cultivation . . . should be opened." Neve set out in detail the layout of the streets, main buildings, and plaza, his orders being tempered by the practical reminder that the site "be slightly elevated . . . guarding against the risks of sudden overflows" from the nearby Los Angeles River, then known as the Río Porciúncula. San José had been founded four years earlier with similar concern for agricultural development. It was located along the Guadalupe River where the soil was rich and where poplar, laurel, and willow trees grew in abundance. When Governor Diego de Borica ordered his soldiers to select the site for the province's last pueblo, at Branciforte (near present-day Santa Cruz), he instructed them to find a location with "abundant land and water . . . as are found [at] . . . San José and N Sra de los Angeles."[10]

Misjudgments

S PAIN'S CLOSE attention to water supply and physical planning did not automatically guarantee success. Erratic precipitation patterns, then as now, suggested an abundance of stream flow in some areas that longer experience proved were more akin to deserts than oases. Part of the explanation for the inability of presidio residents to meet their food needs was the lack of sufficient water for irrigation. The military's understandable concern about defensive considerations in selecting a site sometimes clouded early appraisals of water supply and led to miscalculations.

Missions as well as presidios occasionally suffered because of faulty judgments about water availability. A half dozen of them had to relocate at least once because of floods or drought. Such was the fate of the first permanent European settlement in Alta California at San Diego. There the fathers established the mission near a broad fertile valley which they sowed with wheat that heavy rains and floods then destroyed. A lesson seemed learned, for the next crop was planted at a higher elevation, but it too was lost when reduced rainfall lowered the level of the river to a point where the irrigation system became ineffectual. The colonists eventually overcame the problem, but only after relocating the mission, which became the supply depot for the nearby presidio, at a site six miles upstream where different topography and better engineering saw San Diego eventually emerge as the fifth most productive mission in the province. Also among those missions relocated because of an inadequate water supply was Junípero Serra's own headquarters at San Carlos Borromeo. Originally founded in 1770 at Monterey, a year later it was shifted about four miles south to Carmel where, Francisco Palóu noted, "water flows the whole year through" and "it would be easy to retain enough . . . to irrigate as much as might be wished of the plain that is in sight." [11]

Relocation was not confined to missions. The pueblo at San José had to be moved to another site shortly after its founding when heavy rains, poor drainage, and a broken dam turned the original locale into a quagmire. Continuing problems with marshy soil would require a second move. As with San Diego, residents learned that too much water could be as serious a problem as too little. [12]

Prayer rather than relocation became a more frequent response to capricious weather cycles. According to one account, a harried and distraught missionary at San Antonio de Padua drafted an Indian shaman into God's service when he learned the man was a

Remains of the water-powered gristmill, reservoir, and filter system at Mission Santa Bárbara. (Courtesy of Santa Barbara Historical Society)

rainmaker. The priest locked up the shaman with the warning that he would remain incarcerated until he ended the drought. The Indian told the priest to put the congregation in the church and to bring him a barrel of water. He then performed a special ritual which, according to the account, was followed by rain.[13]

The pueblo of Branciforte was not so fortunate. Despite its location on the San Lorenzo River and Francisco Palóu's prediction twenty years before its founding that the site was "fit not only for a town, but for a city, without wanting any of the things necessary," the community never achieved success.[14] There were many problems. Settlers lacked "experience and energy," many of them were infected with syphilis, there was inadequate government support, and there was a constant boundary dispute with the nearby ("scarcely a stone's throw" away) Santa Cruz Mission. The fundamental difficulty involved land and water. Although Branciforte had an abundance of superior grazing land, the prime irrigable tracts lay on the mission side of the river and beyond reach of the settlers. As a result, the pueblo, according to an official, was "not capable of sustaining the residents in its district."[15] From its founding in 1797, Branciforte reached an unimpressive population high of 101 in 1803 before beginning a slow descent into oblivion.

Royal Authority and Community Rights

WHETHER SUCCESSFUL or plagued by trouble, California's earliest settlements and the waters for sustaining them came under Spain's highly complex legal system. When the decrees and statutes governing communities in the New World had grown to the thousands, as they had by the late eighteenth century when Portolá set out on his expedition of colonization, the possibilities for confusion and controversy had become monumental. As early as 1681 Spain had been compelled to compile and codify the enormous number of laws pertaining to the New World in the *Recopilación de leyes de los reynos de las Indias,* but thereafter the decrees and legislation so multiplied that another edition—the *Novísima recopilación*—was necessary in 1805. Despite the volume of laws, there was remarkable clarity on fundamental issues, and key among them was the Spanish crown's position as the preeminent owner of the lands and waters of the New World.

The monarch as sovereign of Castile (it was Isabella as queen of Castile who had underwritten Columbus's voyage to America) held title in fee simple to all New World land, minerals, and water claimed by Spain. From this premise derived the chain of title to all property. The crown, or as was common practice at the time of Portolá's expedition, its designees, could grant outright ownership or merely a temporary right of use. Until the monarch made such an allocation, all residents of the New World shared the royal patrimony in common. "We have ordered that the pastures, woods, and waters be common in the Indies," proclaimed the monarch in 1541 in a decree reaffirming an even earlier pronouncement, ". . . and the foregoing shall be enforced where no title or grant of ours orders differently." [16]

To the missions of California, the grants of land and water, though gargantuan in size, were always strictly temporary and usufructuary. Title remained in the crown with the missionaries serving as trustees for the Indians. Responsibilities of trusteeship included not only Christianizing the natives and training them as agriculturalists and herdsmen but also providing them, as the viceroy instructed California's military commander in 1773, with "sufficient . . . water to drink and for irrigation of the fields" they farmed in common as well as for any individual plots they cultivated on their own. This must be done with an eye to the future, admonished the viceroy. "As the mission settlements are hereafter to become cities, care must be taken in their foundation," including building "the houses . . . in line, with wide streets and good market squares." To make the missions more attractive to Indians, the viceroy empowered the commander to designate the future pueblo's common lands and, as with the presidios, to issue individual land grants "to such Indians as may most dedicate themselves to agriculture and the raising of cattle." [17] In this way, the viceroy underscored the mission's importance in the colonization scheme even though his hope for future Indian pueblos would go unfulfilled when the missions were finally secularized in the 1830s.

Civil pueblos and presidios had title from the outset to four-square-league sites (a league was approximately 2.6 miles), and within this area of roughly twenty-seven square miles their residents, military as well as civilian, received house lots and lands for pasturing livestock and growing crops. These allocations became permanent if the residents met certain prescribed requirements for developing them. [18] Although the residents could obtain title to their individual land grants, they could not obtain title to water. Under Spanish law, water in a municipality did not belong to separate in-

Flume in rock wall built to carry water from the reservoir to the garden at Mission Santa Bárbara. (Courtesy of Santa Barbara Mission Library Archive)

dividuals, but rather passed from the monarch to the entire community as a corporate body.

Since all of Spain's major settlements in California and the borderlands were destined at least theoretically to become corporate municipalities, an understanding of community water rights can be found in a document known as the Plan of Pitic. Approved by royal officials about 1783 and thus contemporaneous with the settlement of California, the Plan was drafted as the founding charter of Pitic (now Hermosillo), Mexico, but it immediately gained acceptance as the controlling instrument for pueblos established throughout the *Provincias Internas,* virtually the entire borderlands of present-day northern Mexico and the southwestern United States.[19]

Fundamental to the Plan of Pitic was the principle, derived from Iberian tradition, that a town's waters should be shared by all residents. "Pastures, woods, waters, hunting, fishing, stone quarries, fruit trees, and other privileges shall be for the common benefit of the Spaniards and Indians residing therein," declared a key passage of the Plan, echoing a royal decree issued in 1533. Governor Pedro Fages's instructions to his agent in Los Angeles reaffirmed the same principle: "Care must be taken to make it clear that the citizens understand . . . what is held in common, such as the . . . water."[20]

That admonition possessed little real meaning when water was abundant, but when it was in short supply, as was often the case, Spanish legalisms took on great significance. Since the water was "for the common benefit," no one had a superior right that could be exercised to the detriment of others. As in the irrigation communities of Spain, this meant that no person or family had a right to a specific volume of water. The quantity varied according to individual and community needs and according to the available supply. The goal, as the Plan of Pitic stipulated, was to allocate water with "equity and justice," and the authority responsible for assuring such fairness was the local *ayuntamiento* or town council whose members were elected by the residents.[21]

Such delegation of power—technically from crown to local government and ordinarily through viceroy, governor, and commander of the nearest presidio—reflected wisdom drawn from generations of Iberian experience. As formally expressed by the Plan of Pitic, it meant that local governments knew best "the community and public which they represent" and the kinds of actions that would be "most useful and necessary." Among the powers accorded the ayuntamiento, none was more important than its authority to appoint (or call for the election of) a special administrator or *zanjero* to oversee the irrigation system. To those individuals went the loftiest of responsibilities: "the care of distributing" to residents "the benefit of the waters in proportion to the need of their respective crops." If an owner, through "carelessness or indolence," failed to take the allotted share, then a laborer would be hired to make the diversion for the ne'er-do-well, who would then be billed for the service. Similarly, if a zanjero failed to allocate water fairly, he could expect to be dealt with summarily, as occurred in Los Angeles in 1836 (under the regime of the Republic of Mexico) when the ayuntamiento "decided to reprimand" the errant official and authorize an election for his successor as soon as "the neighborhood could be gathered."[22]

Not all the land allocated to a pueblo or its residents carried an irrigation right, but water for grazing if not for cultivation was anticipated for most of the four square leagues. A pueblo's holdings were ordinarily divided into several categories: *solares* (lots for houses); *suertes* (farmlands); *propios* (public lands worked in common or rented to generate municipal income); *ejidos* (common lands available for pasturing a few animals); *dehesas* (larger common pasturelands lying beyond the ejidos); *montes* (common woods); and *baldías* (vacant common farmlands). Irrigation rights usually accompanied only the propios and some of the suertes. In California a suerte measured 200 *varas* by 200 varas (a vara is approximately thirty-three inches; thus a suerte equaled about 6.9 Anglo-American acres), and at the beginning of colonization, each family received four suertes (or just under 28 acres) on the outskirts of a pueblo with water available for two.[23]

A town's authority over water extended to all uses, not just to those for irrigation. When the Los Angeles ayuntamiento in 1839, during the Mexican era, granted a resident permission to build a mill, it did so with the clear understanding that he "not interfere with the flow of the water . . . into the river" so it would be available downstream for use by others. Approval of a similar request five years later required the grantee to "build his own ditch and outlet, so as not to damage the road and main ditch." As might be expected, the ayuntamiento outlawed the wasting of water and levied especially severe fines on those who allowed their irrigation ditches to overflow and damage roads, alleys, or other property. If a break should suddenly occur in the *zanja madre* or main irrigation ditch supplying the community, the "person nearest . . . [the] breakage must immediately repair" it.[24] Such action served to affirm that water, from the earliest days of settlement in the towns of both Spanish and Mexican California, remained what Iberian custom and law had long before determined—a community resource and responsibility.

Community Obligations

THE COMMON right of town residents to an equitable share of water carried with it the responsibility of each inhabitant to help build and maintain the zanja madre (also frequently referred to as the *acequia madre,* which still exists in modern Santa Fe, New Mexico, under that name) and the related canal system as well as any necessary *saca de agua* (or dam). Because of the unreliability of supply ships from Mexico and the necessity of getting crops in as soon as possible, construction of the water system began even before the erection of churches, houses, and public buildings. Hastily assembled huts had to suffice, often for several seasons, as priority went to replicating the water delivery network that had assured survival on earlier frontiers.

The experience of the settlers at Los Angeles was typical. Although the forty-four original colonists of el pueblo de la Reina de los Angeles on the Porciúncula had finished their main irrigation ditch less than two months after founding the community on September 4, 1781, the shelters they provided for themselves and for their animals remained incomplete and makeshift at best for years. The situation improved only as they, and especially the Indians they induced to work for them, completed the principal branch ditches (eventually eight of them) to the zanja madre and developed a steady rhythm of irrigation agriculture. San José, established four years earlier in 1777, had a similar experience, and even twenty years later, the residents there, like those in Los Angeles, were living in rude tule huts "since," complained an official, "they are not able to attend to . . . construction without abandoning the sowings with which they earn their living." Those responsible for establishing Branciforte in 1797 sought to learn from this experience by insisting that adobe houses be built early and at royal expense. That wish became victim to an impoverished treasury as the colonists found themselves living in temporary shelters as they labored on a dam, a system of ditches, and a well.[25]

Authority for enforcing community compliance in constructing and maintaining water systems rested with the ayuntamientos or other elected officers at self-governing pueblos, with local officials appointed by the governor at those presidios and communities lacking civil government, and with the priests at the missions. The time required of pueblo and presidio residents to build, clean, and repair the system was in proportion to the size of the holdings for which they received water.[26] Failure to perform prescribed labor drew stiff fines. As individuals and communities prospered, inhabitants frequently satisfied their responsibilities by hiring substitutes or persuading the town council to do so with rental revenue from the propios or municipal farmlands. A common practice was to order vagrants and jailed criminals (usually Indians) to work off their sentences by laboring on public works.

A community's responsibility for a water system extended to the quality as well as the quantity of the supply. Water channeled through the zanja madre had to satisfy many purposes before being abandoned—watering animals, irrigating crops, and satisfying a variety of domestic household needs. Such multiple uses held potential for great harm since the water for animals, laundry, and sewage and garbage removal was also needed for drinking. Detailed ordinances imposed by the central government as well as local authorities sought to prevent pollution, especially of the water destined for human consumption. The task then, as today, seemed never-ending, with the difference being no threat from industrially generated toxic wastes.

Illustrative was the *lavandería* (or laundry tank), the most common water-use device not developed exclusively for agriculture. About three feet wide, two feet deep, twelve or more feet long, and usually lined with tiles, it possessed a two-foot mortar apron running along each side to accommodate the washers and to permit the effluent to return to the tank. Water ran continuously through the lavandería, often entering through the mouth of a stone gargoyle and then exiting through clay conduits that eventually discharged into the fields. The system kept the wash water out of the domestic supply while the lye soaps of the day did not harm the crops.[27]

The lavandería system reflected not only concern for public health but also the belief that water should be used many times before allowing it to escape or return to the stream from which it had been taken. A typical pattern would find water diverted by a dam or lifted by a *noria* (or waterwheel) into the zanja madre of a mission, presidio, or pueblo. From there it might be channeled to a gristmill and then to a reservoir settling basin from which it would pass through a filter on its way to a public fountain, next to a lavandería, and from there perhaps to a pottery or tannery. Drainage would then be filtered before being diverted onto the fields.

Such an elaborate system invited opportunities for abuse by the careless, who were constantly being admonished, fined, and slapped with new ordinances. In Los Angeles (where documents of the Mexican period have survived in significant numbers) the town council was constantly battling to maintain the potability of the community's drinking water by going after those putting trash in the zanja madre, bathing or washing their clothes in it, laying drain pipes into it, or building cesspools too near it.[28] The right to share water in common meant nothing if the supply was polluted.

Lavandería *at Mission Santa Bárbara. (Courtesy of Santa Barbara Mission Library Archive)*

Community Rights and Private Rights

J UST AS Hispanic practice assured an equitable water supply to the residents *within* a community, so, too, did it guarantee water to other communities along a common watercourse. "The residents and natives," stipulated the Plan of Pitic, echoing earlier ordinances and decrees, "shall equally enjoy the benefits of the . . . water . . . that may lie outside the lands assigned to the new settlement, in common with the residents and natives of the adjoining and neighboring pueblos."[29] The only water to which a community, or anyone for that matter, could claim an exclusive right was that originating on the property itself. Hence, water taken from springs and wells belonged solely to the owner of the land—whether it be the community or an individual—where the springs and wells were located. This was a hallowed legal principle traceable to medieval Spain and to a faulty understanding of the interrelationship between water above ground and below. Even that right did not permit an owner maliciously to use water so as to deny it to others or to withhold it from a town lacking an adequate supply. A town that acquired such groundwater from a landowner, however, had to compensate the owner, a requirement not unlike that embodied in today's principle of eminent domain.[30]

Thus, with the exception of groundwater, no community or individual could assert a paramount or exclusive right to a river or a stream or to precipitation regardless of where it fell. This principle extended even to very old villages. When Spain colonized the upper Rio Grande Valley of New Mexico in the sixteenth century, it encountered native pueblo agricultural communities dating back many centuries. Their priority of right became an important but not the only consideration of imperial authorities in allocating waters and settling disputes during times of shortage.[31] If priority had become the sole criterion, Spain could not have maintained a presence in those areas where the pueblos required (or whose future growth would require) all available water.

In making grants of land and water in coastal California, the Spanish did not have to contend with precontact Indian agricultural villages as in New Mexico, but the steady growth in the number of missions, presidios, and pueblos nonetheless increased the potential for conflict over water. Officials recognized the threat. The dispersed location of the missions reflected in part a deliberate attempt to minimize disputes and assure success. Presidios and pueblos, however, tended to be near missions where they could secure a priest for special ceremonies, solicit labor from the attached Indian community for onerous tasks, obtain supplies in times of shortage, and offer defensive aid when needed. Though pueblos and presidios were few in number, this proximity to missions was a source of constant concern to religious, military, and civil authorities.

Ranchos posed a special concern. Ultimately numbering more than 800, but amounting to only a couple dozen or so prior to secularization of the missions in the 1830s, ranchos represented grants of private property and consisted of vast amounts of land. The earliest grants were especially large, with the three given by Governor Pedro Fages in 1784 embracing some 36,000 acres, 74,000 acres, and 300,000 acres, respectively. A few later ranchos were as tiny as 20 acres, but most embraced thousands of acres, with a grant of 15,000 to 20,000 acres considered small.[32] Ordinarily, private grants in the Hispanic legal system carried a right to use water only for domestic purposes and for livestock, but not for irrigation or to operate mills unless the grants specifically permitted such activities. When they did authorize irrigation, less than 10 percent of the property usually received the designation *de riego* (irrigable land) or *labor* (cropland for which irrigation was implied). Water rights could subsequently be obtained (or increased or reduced) as a result of petition, purchase, or judicial decree. An owner with no irrigation right, who nonetheless turned water onto his lands, could have his uses later affirmed if no one complained for a long period of time, ordinarily ten years under Spanish and Mexican law.[33]

Most rancho holdings in California were near the missions, where many of the early grantees served as guards, or near the presidios and pueblos, where most rancheros maintained a residence. Provincial authorities moved cautiously on requests for rancho land. When Governor Pedro Fages initiated the rancho system in 1784, he knew that he was not doing so in a vacuum and attached provisos to his allocations. He awarded Rancho San Rafael to José María Verdugo on condition that Verdugo "not prejudice the . . . Mission [San Gabriel], nor the inhabitants of the Reina de los Angeles, and . . . [that] some one [be] in charge [of the rancho], without being exposed to the Gentile Indians, nor in any manner injuring them." Similarly, when he allocated the lands of the future Rancho Los Nietos in the same year to Manuel Pérez Nieto, he did so "provided no harm is done to the Mission San Gabriel nor to the Pagan Indians of its environs in any manner whatsoever." After Verdugo took possession of his property and amassed hundreds of head of livestock, he admitted to the governor that he had also built a dam for "the irrigation of a moderate portion of land," but he assured him of his compliance with the terms of the grant: "I neither prejudice the natives . . . nor the residents of the [pueblo] . . . [nor] the Indians of all the Country round about and therefore I turn my eyes to your Honor."[34] The dam posed no problem, for the governor confirmed the grant, but pledges like Verdugo's did not prevent disputes and certainly did not stave off abuse of the Indians, which came in many forms, not least from the missionization process itself. Legally, however, the natives, both Christian and *gentil* (unbaptized), possessed rights to lands and waters, ephemeral as those rights ultimately became.

As Governor Fages's stipulation suggested, the rights of rancheros (and by implication other individuals) were ordinarily inferior to those of communities—presidios, pueblos, missions, Indian villages. From the beginning of Spanish colonization in the New World and on into the Mexican era (1821–1846), the law distinguished between private rights and those of communities, and emphasized the preference of the latter over individuals, especially during the critical initial years of settlement.[35] What was usual, however, was not invariable. The water rights of communities could— and did—vary according to circumstances. Governor Fages's insistence that Verdugo and other rancheros "not prejudice" the missions or pueblos or Indians "in any manner" did not mean recognizing in those settlements a prior and absolute right to a common water source. In a dispute between an individual and a community or in a dispute involving different kinds of communities, the principles of "equity and justice," as enunciated in the Plan of Pitic and other regulations, became the fundamental test of fairness. In some provisions of the Plan of Pitic, private rights were singled out for protection against community abuse. For example, in the establishment of new towns, the Plan cautioned that "there shall not result injury to any *private individuals*." This concern about an earlier settler reflected official policy, but, as already noted, it was not to be construed so literally as to make Spanish colonization impossible. Once a town was established, the Plan of Pitic forbade the residents from abusing the rights of individuals living elsewhere. It authorized water judges to prevent a town resident from taking "a greater quantity than . . . his share" when this caused "injury to the owners situated on the land beyond."[36]

California rancheros had good reason to appreciate such flexibility in the legal system. They were private landholders, but many of their ranchos became communities in fact if not in law—home to numerous immediate family members, relatives, *vaqueros* (or cowboys), and other laborers, all responsible to the ranchero as family head and *patrón*. Devoted primarily to cattle raising and to the hide and tallow trade, these rancho communities also frequently planted extensive fields with fruit orchards, vineyards, corn, beans, onions, potatoes, hemp, and other crops. Springs, artesian wells, and nearby streams and rivers irrigated the tracts and watered the cattle and other domestic animals. Ranchos, like towns, presidios, and missions, often developed their own zanja madre with its maze of appurtenant laterals and catch basins. Significantly, two of the first three ranchos created in California in 1784 had the word *zanja* (ditch or canal) in their original names as explicit recognition of water's importance and the range of projected activities.[37]

When Rights Collide: Bien Procumunal

BUT THE real test of rights for allocating water and land emerged in the clash of interests and not in legal codes and adherence to ritualistic formulas. Not surprisingly those clashes tended to occur in areas where the two institutions most responsible for agricultural development—pueblos and missions—were close to one another. Records for California are sparse, but those that survive underscore the Hispanic system's flexibility and emphasis on sharing water.

Later generations sometimes interpreted differently the Hispanic system, occasionally with far-reaching results. Beginning in the late nineteenth century and on into the twentieth some southwestern communities asserted a so-called pueblo water right. Tracing it to the rights protected by the Treaty of Guadalupe Hidalgo (the peace treaty ending the Mexican-American War in 1848 and awarding the present Southwest to the United States), they claimed the pueblo water right entitled them to a prior and paramount right to nearby rivers. Los Angeles has been the most aggressive and successful city in advancing such a claim and has persuaded the California courts to award it exclusive rights to the Los Angeles River and the runoff of the entire 500-square-mile watershed, a victory that helped assure Los Angeles's emergence as the preeminent city of California and the West. Only San Diego, California, and one other city—Las Vegas, New Mexico—have formally won judicial recognition of a pueblo right, but the courts based those decisions on Los Angeles's earlier victory and refused to consider contrary Spanish and Mexican documents and laws.[38] Neither the principles of Spanish and Mexican law nor the water disputes engaged in by Los Angeles during the Spanish and Mexican periods seem to support the pueblo water rights theory.

On at least three occasions, the pueblo of Los Angeles battled over water with Mission San Fernando, founded sixteen years after the town and the major upstream community also dependent on the Los Angeles River. Father Vicente de Santa María had selected the site in the northern part of the broad valley that eventually bore the mission's name not only because of the numerous Indians but also "because it has much water, much humid land, and . . . pastures . . . very suitable for cattle." Some three decades earlier, a member of the Portolá expedition had also commented favorably on the "very pleasant and spacious valley" and its "friendly and docile" inhabitants, while later a squatter from Los Angeles had demonstrated the area's potential by establishing a rancho and hiring local Indians to tend his "field of corn, beans, and melons" and work as "cattlemen, irrigators, bird-catchers, foremen, [and] horsemen."[39]

When the missionaries formally established San Fernando in 1797, they selected the rancho site (about ten miles north of the

Los Angeles River) for their main buildings, evicted the squatter, and recruited nearby natives to develop an agricultural and grazing enterprise that eventually spread over and beyond the nearly 200-square-mile valley. As early as 1810 some 963 neophytes (baptized Indians) were herding 11,500 head of cattle, horses, goats, and other livestock and harvesting 9,700 bushels of wheat, corn, beans, and additional crops, not including the produce of vineyards and orchards for which reports were not required.[40]

The year 1810 witnessed a challenge from Los Angeles, which objected to a mission dam at Cahuenga on the southern edge of the valley because it was "cutting the flow of the river" to the pueblo. The commander at Santa Bárbara, as the local authority in the area, conducted an investigation, compiled a nineteen-page report, and then forwarded it to the governor for final action. Unfortunately for future historians (and lawyers as well), the report was lost in the San Francisco earthquake and fire of 1906, leaving only two summaries—one, a single-page digest prepared by a late-nineteenth-century scribe in the employ of historian Hubert Howe Bancroft; and the other, a slightly longer (and somewhat differently worded) summary produced in the 1870s by attorneys employed by Los Angeles to advance the city's pueblo water claims.[41]

The Los Angeles version contains statements not found in the other draft that seem to lend support to the city's cause: the Santa Bárbara commander is described as issuing a "demand that the dam should be removed" and the missionaries are represented as agreeing to "yield all right" to the dam and implicitly to any water impounded by it. The attorneys later challenging Los Angeles in the 1890s objected to the summary and many of the city's other documents—but they did so on the ground that those materials were irrelevant, not inaccurate. Accuracy was immaterial to them, and they apparently did not independently examine the original file. Among their contentions was that Los Angeles had years earlier forfeited its claim to a pueblo water right, if any existed, by failing to assert such a claim in the 1850s before the U.S. Land Commission, which had the responsibility for determining rights under the Treaty of Guadalupe Hidalgo.[42] The loss of the original file makes impossible any attempt to verify the Los Angeles version, but confidence in it is undermined by the city's translation errors in other documents that were offered in evidence and by the city's frequent habit of omitting key passages from its quotations of Spanish and Mexican law, especially those emphasizing when water should be shared in common.[43]

Though the city's summary is suspect, it does concur in certain essentials with the shorter digest prepared by Bancroft's assistant. Taken together, the two documents agree on the following about the 1810 incident: the waters diverted by the mission at Cahuenga came from the Los Angeles River; pueblo residents became concerned because of the diminished flow and complained to the Santa Bárbara commander; the padres expressed a desire to irrigate only a small portion of land and would cease farming that area if their actions should cause "the least damage" to the residents of Los Angeles; and the Santa Bárbara commander forwarded to the governor the documents that he had collected.

Nothing is known of the governor's action, but it seems unlikely that he recognized in Los Angeles a prior and paramount right to the river's water—the heart of what later became known as the pueblo water rights doctrine. In neither summary did the townspeople, commander, or missionaries assert or acknowledge such a claim. If the original nineteen-page file had contained clear language to that effect, the Los Angeles attorneys in the late nineteenth century would surely have pounced on it. Nor did the missionaries' willingness to stop diversions at Cahuenga if they harmed the pueblo imply a prior right of the pueblo. When the dispute is viewed within the context of other information not heretofore considered by courts and legal scholars, it seems to reflect the traditional Hispanic desire to arrive at a settlement that would be equitable for all participants in the dispute.

The padres wanted to irrigate a small field at Cahuenga, but they did not think it important enough to justify causing "the least damage" to Los Angeles. Their reasons (and those of the other partici-

53

pants in the incident), while not expressed in the surviving fragmentary record, seem to emerge clearly in what was common knowledge of the day. The mission had access to water sources other than the river itself and the tributaries flowing directly into it. Springs, marshes, and streams could be found in a variety of locales on Mission San Fernando's vast holdings, and two years earlier, in 1808, a masonry dam had been built north of the mission's main buildings (and nearly twelve miles north of the river) to capture runoff there.[44] While the mission possessed a variety of water sources, Los Angeles could count on only a single supply of any importance: the adjacent river. Later years would reveal that the mission's water sources were interconnected with the river through vast underground reservoirs or aquifers below the surface of the San Fernando Valley that were fed by local precipitation and floodwaters from the surrounding mountains. Pressure forced some of this groundwater to the surface along the valley's southern edge where it emerged in the channel of the Los Angeles River. Lacking such knowledge of the river's origin, observers would have noted only that Los Angeles possessed a sole dependable water supply while the mission had multiple sources, including springs and marshes that drew upon underground water which, according to Spanish law, belonged entirely to the possessor of the overlying land—in this case, the crown, which had granted the mission usufructuary rights to the land and water.

Weather patterns of the time also must have helped shape attitudes just as they affected the available water supply, including the flow of the Los Angeles River. When compared to other waterways of North America, the Los Angeles River seems puny with its annual average surface flow of about 40,000 acre-feet, a minute fraction of the Rio Grande's 9.4 million acre-feet and the Colorado River's 14 million acre-feet, two rivers that in turn are dwarfed by the Columbia and Mississippi Rivers, which have flows in excess of 100 million acre-feet. Yet even the Los Angeles River's 40,000 acre-feet could not be counted on, for the volume fluctuated dramatically in response to unpredictable cycles of drought and surplus.

Measurements taken in modern times over a twenty-nine-year period revealed a low of 1,660 acre-feet and a high of about 165,000 acre-feet.[45]

Ordinarily, diversions upriver at Cahuenga would have posed no problem for the small pueblo (with a population at this time of 365, including nearby rancheros and their families), but the 1809–1810 water year was far from normal. It was the driest period in a drought that, with only brief interruptions, had begun twenty-eight years earlier.[46] During the early drought years, the abundant groundwater in the valley would have prevented a significant decline in the river's flow, but as the dry period lengthened and intensified, the effect on supply would become readily apparent. The sharp decline in rainfall would also have depleted the water available to the mission and enhanced the value of irrigation at Cahuenga, but the mission's various water sources seem to have held up reasonably well during the extended drought. In 1806, the Indians at San Fernando had brought in the largest harvest in the mission's history, some 12,900 bushels of wheat and other crops. Although the harvest fell to less than 2,000 bushels in 1807 and 1809, it exceeded 6,000 bushels in the intervening year of 1808 and reached 9,700 bushels in 1810, the second best year since the mission's founding and the year when Los Angeles lodged its protest. The increased harvest of 1810 at least partially reflected the return of heavy rains in the latter part of that year, but when Los Angeles complained in March, southern California was still locked in severe drought. San Fernando by this time, however, could count on help from other missions if supplies ran short. As early as the 1790s the fathers had devised a system for sharing surpluses from the more prosperous missions with those that were less fortunate—a system that was soon working so well that, despite the dry years, there were surplus commodities for trade to residents outside the missions and to foreigners.[47]

Los Angeles and the other pueblos had been less fortunate during these early years, even in periods of normal rainfall. Far from fulfilling their purpose of supplying the presidios, they frequently failed to meet their own needs and went into debt to the missions or relied on them for handouts to feed and clothe themselves. As late as 1820 Father Joaquín Pascual Nuez of Mission San Gabriel noted that "the families of the Pueblo of Los Angeles did not come to mass because they were nearly naked and we were the sorry observers of their want, and even the older girls went without shirts for lack of them and no way of obtaining any."[48] Under the circumstances, the desire in 1810 of townspeople and the military commander to stop diversions at Cahuenga that were "cutting the flow of the river" and the missionaries' willingness to cease irrigation at Cahuenga if it harmed the pueblo seem responsible reactions to a crisis and in harmony with the Hispanic concern for "equity and justice."

Sensitivity to Los Angeles's continuing precarious situation occurred a half dozen years later when the padres at San Fernando petitioned the governor to demarcate officially the mission's southern boundary. When first established, mission territories were hazily defined, ordinarily stretching from one mission to another with the line separating them lying somewhere in between. This sufficed until other land grants became numerous enough to cause misunderstanding, and in 1817 the padres at San Fernando asked for a clear determination of their holdings, one that would specifically include the Cahuenga area. Precipitation had increased (the years from 1810 to 1821 witnessed unusually heavy rainfall in southern California), but Los Angeles was still struggling economically and the governor was concerned about the effect of the missionaries' request on the community. He agreed to the padres' petition after ascertaining from Los Angeles officials that "it would not cause any injury to the Pueblo." He then awarded both land and water to the mission, expressly acknowledging his "obligation of favoring . . . San Fernando, for the necessity it represented to provide for [the] Neophites [sic], in consequence of the great dryness that they experienced, to enable them to gain . . . subsistence."[49] In making the grant, the governor was not giving the mission a prior right to the river's flow any more than the actions of 1810 had given a prior right to the pueblo. He was merely recognizing that the mission, like the pueblo, had legitimate claims to water and that the extent of those claims depended on considerations of equity.

A similar affirmation occurred in 1836 during a second confrontation between Los Angeles and San Fernando. By that time, the mission had been secularized and its lands made available for distribution by the government. In the interim, the governor had appointed an administrator, as he had for missions elsewhere, to oversee the former mission holdings. The San Fernando official had promptly set about "damming the river water at Cahuenga," an action that alarmed Los Angeles residents, who two years before had experienced unusually heavy rainfall and floods preceded by a decade of drought. These experiences caused them to view the dam as a double threat: it might deprive them of water during a drought and it might give way during a prolonged storm, releasing floodwaters that would destroy the town's reservoir and perhaps cause other damage. The ayuntamiento sent a committee to investigate, and its findings calmed fears. The dam, reported the town attorney, had so far caused no harm, and the "man in charge of San Fernando had promised him that in case . . . [the] dam would break and do some damage to the city reservoir . . . he would repair . . . [it] at his own expense, and that if the river should run short of water . . . he would break [the] . . . dam and let all the water run out."[50] This seemed to more than satisfy Los Angeles residents who neither demanded the dam's destruction nor asserted exclusive claims to the river.

Eight years later in 1844 San Fernando precipitated a third confrontation with the pueblo when, according to the Los Angeles *alcade* (mayor), it "put a dam in the river and took out more water than was necessary." The alcalde and the priest at San Fernando resolved this dispute as readily as the earlier ones. The priest "came to my house," recalled the alcalde, "and we drank some wine together, and we arranged the matter and he removed the dam." This recollection came from the alcalde thirty-three years later while testifying on behalf of Los Angeles's pueblo right theory. At the time of the incident, he remembered, the "general impression was that the town . . . had a special grant of the waters of . . . [the] river, but," he pointedly noted, "I have never seen any written instrument of it."[51] Nor did he give any indication that he had invoked that "general impression" about an alleged "special grant" in persuading the priest to remove the dam. Rather, what happened in 1844 resembles what had occurred in 1810 and 1836: equity demanded that the dam be removed; the priest, after drinking "some wine" with the alcalde, recognized the need to take appropriate action; and the dam came down.

Significantly, there is no evidence that the city invoked an exclusive claim to the river between 1840 and 1846, primarily a dry period, when the Mexican governor carved from the former mission lands six ranchos whose owners followed typical patterns of cattle raising and irrigation agriculture that relied upon springs, wells, and often direct access to the Los Angeles River. One of the grants, Rancho Cahuenga, included the area earlier disputed by Los Angeles, while it and three of the remaining ranchos—Providencia, El Encino, and Ex-Mission de San Fernando—occupied sites embracing both banks of the Los Angeles River.[52]

In northern California a long-running dispute in the late eighteenth century between the pueblo of San José and Mission Santa Clara over lands and the water of the Guadalupe River also led to compromise and sharing of resources. The padres had never looked warmly on the pueblo because of its proximity—less than a league—to the mission, and their chagrin led to official protest following floods that forced relocation of the mission (though it remained approximately the same distance from the pueblo) and further clouded already uncertain boundaries. The controversy continued for more than two decades with the priests complaining to governors and viceroys that pueblo residents were illegally taking land and water needed by the Indians. The dispute also became a vehicle for challenging the legitimacy of the town itself, for the missionaries combed through the regulations governing New World settlement for those that seemed to support their cause. "The laws state distinctly," complained Junípero Serra in 1782 to his superiors in Mexico City, "that all of that territory, and the water rights too, are the property of the Indians living in this mission." The towns-people replied in kind. Although not challenging the legitimacy of the mission, they complained bitterly about Indians trespassing on their lands and illegally growing crops and cutting wood.[53]

Charges, countercharges, untimely deaths of key officials, and transfer of San José to a new location delayed resolution of the dispute until 1798. The governor, following a careful investigation ordered by the viceroy, then cut through the rhetoric of the opponents by affirming the need of both town and mission for water and land and by imposing a solution. Henceforth, the Guadalupe River became the boundary and common source of water for pueblo and mission, with the additional caveat that townspeople could gather wood in the coastal ranges on the mission side of the river.[54]

The Hispanic practice of investigating water disputes—albeit sometimes in an overly prolonged fashion—and arriving at a practical judgment that sought to accommodate the interests of all parties was typical of the borderlands generally. In Texas in the mid-eighteenth century a civil pueblo, the *villa* of San Fernando de Béxar, battled with five missions over the waters of the San Antonio River and San Pedro Creek. On two occasions, the viceroy was forced to intervene when neither side budged from its demand for all the water. The missionaries insisted there was "hardly enough water to supply . . . their lands," and since they had arrived first, they believed the government should relocate the pueblo elsewhere. The settlers countered that their survival required all the available water. On each occasion, the viceroy instructed the adversaries to share the supply. "I do hereby order the governor of the Province of Texas to make the distribution of the waters . . . in such a way that all may enjoy its benefits," he declared in 1733, reaffirming a similar decree issued a year and a half earlier. And "it shall be done with the clear understanding that in case there is an insufficient supply for continuous utilization, it shall be used by turns . . . so that . . . everyone may enjoy its benefits." A study of water use in Hispanic New Mexico found a similar emphasis on sharing and no evidence that a pueblo "had a right to enlarge its claim to water without consideration of the legitimate needs of other users, individuals, or communities."[55]

In analyzing Hispanic water disputes in locales other than California, historian Michael Meyer adduces seven criteria employed in adjudicating conflicts: legal rights; legal title; prior use; need; injury to a third party; purpose of the water use; and equity and the common good. The last was predominant and in a fundamental sense embraced and tempered the others. This was a deeply embedded social outlook, as legal scholar David Langum has observed, "a philosophical focus . . . on the reconciliation of conflict and the accommodation of conflicting interests, serving the greater interest in the community and its harmony."[56] Thus, the California experience with water reflected the general Hispanic commitment to *bien procumunal*—the common good—a concept that defied precise definition, encouraged flexibility, and was incompatible with monopoly.

The Darker Side

THE CONCEPT of "common good" was also invariably ethnocentric when transformed into action, a lesson learned early by the native peoples of the New World. Their land and water rights were often reduced to little more than a cipher, while their labor was commandeered on behalf of God, country, and other men's profits. Shielded somewhat from this process were those Indian communities, like the Indian pueblos of New Mexico, with long-established agricultural traditions that the Spaniards went out of their way to safeguard but not to the extent of giving them a prior and paramount right to water. They, like all communities, were obligated to share supplies, though they frequently complained that their share was too small.[57] In California, where there were no such preexisting Indian agricultural settlements in the areas occupied by the Spaniards, the opportunities for abuse were great.

Hispanic Patterns

Playing a powerful role in the exploitative process was the Hispanic system of water control and management. From the beginning at California's missions and almost that early at the presidios, pueblos, and ranchos, Indians erected the hydraulic works on which the new colony depended for survival. They hauled the rock for dams, dredged the canals, and performed the never-ending drudgery of keeping ditches open and free of weeds, silt, and other debris. Thus, the water system became a mighty vehicle and reason for mobilizing and controlling the labor of native peoples. The missionaries' call for souls was doubtless sincere, but so too was their desire for a vast workforce that would gain experience for constructing the missions and other buildings by first transporting water to parched fields and then bringing in crops to sustain the laborers and residents elsewhere in the colony. Indians eventually tilled perhaps 10,000 acres at the missions in addition to laboring at their other tasks as builders, herdsmen, and artisans.[58]

Legally, Spain viewed the Indians as free people, not as slaves, but their labor had long been recognized as essential to the empire's survival, the more so in exposed frontier outposts where non-Indians were both few in number and anxious to find others to perform the more onerous but necessary tasks of settlement-building. Hence, in California, as elsewhere in Spanish America, freedom for native people did not mean the liberty to live as they had earlier, but rather carried with it the obligation to labor on behalf of the well-being of society. In practice, this blurred the distinction between freedom and slavery.

Even more desirous than the missionaries for command of Indian labor were the residents of the presidios and pueblos and the owners of the ranchos. These *gente de razón* (or people of reason, as the non-Indians called themselves) wanted native Californians to perform the same tasks demanded of them at the missions—with this major difference: the Indian labor at the missions, while forced, was essentially communal and, according to Sherburne Cook, "in theory always, and in practice usually . . . devoted to the welfare and improvement of the Indian himself."[59] Indian labor in the towns and on the ranchos primarily promoted the welfare and interests of non-Indians, although during the early years, marketplace forces frequently shielded the natives from abuse while also encouraging many of them to avoid the missions.

Indians quickly learned that conversion meant confinement to the closely watched neophyte village on the mission's grounds with permission to leave coming only grudgingly and often not at all. The priests' attitudes reflected their concern about the sinful occasions presented by the civil and military towns and their need of Indian labor for a higher calling—and a more elaborate irrigation system, among other responsibilities—at the mission. Reluctance to grant Indians permission to leave stiffened as mission populations fell, especially beginning in the 1820s, in response to increased deaths from disease and to runaways disenchanted with mission life and prospects. Townspeople from the outset reacted to the missionaries' desire for a captive population by encouraging Indians to avoid baptism and to work for them rather than the priests. As inducements they ordinarily paid the Indians with what they sought: blankets, sombreros, a portion of the crops they harvested, or other goods that seemed especially practical or attractive or both. "The Indian is errand boy, cowboy and manual laborer for them—in fact, general factotum," observed one not-so-impressed missionary.[60]

As early as 1787 the governor enhanced the attractiveness of towns by establishing a code of conduct for dealing with Indians, which provided for the punishment of residents who mistreated them—and to punish them in the presence of their victims.[61] As a result, relatively harmonious ethnic relations prevailed at first in the presidios and pueblos as irrigation systems were built, crops planted and harvested, and buildings erected—all at minimal expense and effort on the part of the gente de razón. The few rancheros of these early years benefited as well and for similar reasons.

The situation changed in the 1830s when secularization was decreed by the Mexican government and when Indians either abandoned or were defrauded of mission lands intended for them. Many now crowded into the towns. Some refugees from the mission villages flatly refused to work, not wishing to exchange the regimen of the padres for that of others, while most of the remainder discovered that their numbers exceeded the capacity of local economies to absorb them. Numerous Indians found refuge in liquor and gambling, which often gave way to violence, nearly always directed at one another. Local town councils at first viewed these disturbances with dismay until more cunning civic leaders argued that inebriated Indians presented an opportunity, not a problem.

In Los Angeles, the increased incidence of drunkenness coincided with the need for major repairs to the main irrigation ditch. The town council in 1836 authorized the arrest of drunken Indians and required them to work off their sentences on the water system. In time, new ordinances in Los Angeles and elsewhere increased the involuntary workforce by broadening the category of offenses— vagrancy, begging, loitering, and the catch-all "leading an immoral or profligate course of life." Similarly, the tasks to which Indians could be assigned multiplied until the system served private as well as public labor needs, amounted to slavery in all but name, and persisted well into the American period.

On the ranchos, which increased sharply in number following secularization and employed thousands of Indians, debt peonage frequently accomplished what the townspeople achieved by ordinance. Indians could take up work voluntarily on a ranch, but the law prevented them from leaving unless they had documentation attesting that they were not in debt to their former employer. Seldom was such an Indian able to avoid debt and achieve freedom of movement.[62]

The Indians of California found little comfort in the Hispanic society they labored to maintain. Lofty ideals about the common good accompanied by incarceration, forced labor, disease and death, and a hydraulic system as an instrument of coercion took on a relevancy best understood by the victims. Still, while no society can boast about its policy toward indigenous peoples, Spain and Mexico did develop a remarkably equitable arrangement for allocating scarce water resources, at least among non-Indian inhabitants. Higher authorities set the guidelines with the preeminent emphasis on community needs and responsibilities, though not to the exclusion of individual rights. Water was a resource to be shared—shared in common among the residents of a settlement, shared among the various kinds of communities (missions, presidios, pueblos, Indian villages) along a common water source, and shared between communities and such private landholders as rancheros, although community rights generally took precedence over those of individuals.

Viewed from the vantage point of the twenty-first century, Hispanic principles contrast sharply with the individualism and monopolistic impulses of those who flocked to California following the American conquest in 1846. Admittedly, Spain and Mexico's imprint on the waterscape differed significantly from that of aboriginal Californians, but it paled in comparison with what was to come.

3 The American Takeover: Laissez-Faire, Localism, and Monopoly

The conquest of California by the United States in 1846 and the discovery of gold two years later ushered in a sequence of events that profoundly altered the vast new American acquisition. The Indian population of some 150,000, about half the precontact level, continued its precipitous decline to less than 20,000 by century's end as the newcomers' diseases, weapons, and destruction of native food supplies took their toll. Mexican Californians and their social and economic institutions also reeled and sometimes gave way before the waves of new residents from around the globe and especially from the eastern United States. The population boomed from some 10,000 non-Indians in 1846, to 100,000 three years later, to nearly 1.5 million by 1900.[1] The growth in numbers accompanied an even more rapid transfer of privately owned land from native *Californios*—the name usually applied to the non-Indian peoples of California—to in-flooding Americans as towns and cities proliferated and massive commercial and agricultural development brought revolutionary changes to the land- and waterscape. The transformation of the environment reflected not only a mushrooming population and American technology but also the values of a society mesmerized by a myth of superabundance. It was a myth traceable to those earliest frontiers along the East Coast and reenforced as settlement pushed into vast expanses containing apparently unlimited quantities of fertile land, timber, wildlife, and other natural gifts seemingly ordained for Americans by creation and capitalism alike.

In their ideas about nature generally, the newcomers and their Spanish and Mexican predecessors differed more in emphasis than in principle. Both looked on the environment as a source of wealth rather than as an end in itself—as a means of political, social, and economic gain rather than as something worth preserving for intrinsic values of its own. Both also came from societies with legal traditions that sanctioned diverting water from streams when economic necessity or survival so dictated. For Californios and for Americans in the eastern United States this included diverting water for such critical activities as meeting household needs, watering animals, and operating mills, while for Californios irrigation was, of course, a time-honored practice and one the invaders would readily, if not always smoothly, adopt.[2]

Yet there were also sharp differences between the two peoples. Although Hispanic tradition and the long experience with aridity had produced a society stressing the preeminence of community rights and recognizing in government sweeping authority in allocating resources, the newcomers came from a tradition that valued individual rights and minimal government interference. As historian Robert Kelley has observed, they were the embodiment of a mid-nineteenth-century American political culture that left them "confident, impatient, entrepreneurial, defiant of life's limitations, and determined actively to possess and develop the enormous . . . expanse that had now opened before them."[3] Though their political culture set them apart from California's preconquest residents, it did not constitute a monolithic set of beliefs and practices. Rather, it served both to unite and divide Americans. An understanding of that culture nationally makes it easier to comprehend why Californians manipulated their waterscape as they did following the American takeover.

American Political Culture

A S AN individualistic, freedom-loving people, Americans from the outset of their republic shared a fundamental distrust of government reflected in their Constitution, which separated authority among the several branches on the principle that liberty is best preserved when governmental powers war with one another.[4] Agreed on that essential, Americans also from the beginning differed on how far the distrust of government should go. Those coalescing around Thomas Jefferson and then Andrew Jackson, and who by the second quarter of the nineteenth century labeled themselves Democrats, believed that at the national level the least government was the best government and that authority should be overwhelmingly concentrated locally. They vigorously opposed a strong activist central authority that used the public funds of all to benefit a few through such means as internal improvements (canals, roads, river and harbor projects), tariffs, monopolies, and land grants. At best this was a misuse of the people's money; at worst it invited corruption. Those sharing these views included by mid-century many who distrusted an activist government for special reasons of their own—southern Democrats fearful of attempts to contain and root out slavery, and ethnic minorities, especially Irish Catholics of the northern cities, concerned that a powerful government might proscribe their fondness for whiskey, their religion, and their parochial schools. Localism and laissez-faire were the Democrats' political shibboleths.

In contrast to this strong antiactivist government position emerged another faction sympathetic to the ideas of Alexander Hamilton and whose members by the time of the California gold rush made their political home in the Whig party. Their heartland was the Northeast, especially Yankee New England where their Puritan legacy left them convinced that they were as much God's religious agents as political vehicles for creating a morally and economically strong America. On economic issues, in particular, they attracted kindred spirits elsewhere, including many in the upper and lower South. Henry Clay of Kentucky summarized their national program in the pre–Civil War years in his "American System." Its premise was that a government safely checked by the Constitution and by regular elections could promote a strong national economy through internal improvements, a tariff keeping out foreign goods and allowing domestic factories to develop, and in general intervening with large-scale and centrally designed plans encouraging development of the country. Such goals, in the Whig view, required an educated leadership, a belief reinforced by the traditional New England emphasis on learning but at variance with the Democratic notion that anyone was capable of running the nation.

Though the Whig party collapsed during the intense North-South debate over slavery, its philosophy reemerged in 1854 in the Republican party, essentially a Whig party without southerners and more Yankee in sentiment because of the realignment. The Civil War crisis and the splitting of the Democratic party along North-South lines propelled into power the Republicans, who quickly implemented their nationalist agenda: internal improvements, tariffs, a national banking system, and uniform currency. With the war's end, rancor over Radical Reconstruction, political corruption, immigration policy, and other issues brought a resurgence of Democratic strength and, except for brief periods of strong Republican ascendancy, a return to policies emphasizing nonactivist government, localism, and laissez-faire.

The Whig/Republican and Democratic political cultures with their contrasting views of the role of government arrived in California with the hordes following the discovery of gold in 1848. Since most newcomers were Democrats (southerners and ethnic minorities, especially Irish Catholics, from northern working-class neighborhoods), their views prevailed throughout much of the latter half of the nineteenth century. Thus, in California as in the nation's capital, distaste for activist government, preference for local decision-making (reenforced and sometimes sparked by local experiences), and emphasis on individual enterprise became the norm except for those less frequent occasions of effective Republican control.[5] When the newcomers' enthusiasm for wealth and laissez-faire encountered California's environmental realities—gold, aridity, great fertile valleys—the consequences were profound for the state, the West, and the nation.

"First in Time, First in Right"

AMERICANS CROWDING into California following the gold discovery found water essential for the pans, sluices, rockers, long toms, and most other devices used to work the promising gravels. On earlier mining frontiers in Georgia and Alabama, the availability of water had not been a problem, but in California the relatively fewer rivers and

Early mining methods, including such water-dependent devices as pan, rocker or cradle, long tom, sluice, and flume. (Courtesy of California History Room, California State Library, Sacramento)

smaller amount of precipitation posed a serious obstacle. It was compounded by the ore-bearing soil often being at some distance, frequently many miles, from a stream or river. Common sense called for diverting water—and divert it the miners did, from as far away as was necessary and practical through wooden sluices, iron pipes, ditches, and whatever else worked.[6]

Common sense also demanded putting some kind of control on the diversions. In a water-shy country with a rapidly growing population, even the most single-minded gold seekers recognized that uncontrolled diversions would eventually mean insufficient water and economic disaster for all. Since no guidance came in the crucial years of the 1850s from the usually Democrat-controlled federal government, which had jurisdiction over the public land where virtually all the gold discoveries occurred, the newcomers drew on the familiar when it proved practical and improvised when it did not. As for the familiar, there was a hallowed frontier tradition emphasizing the superior claims of the first persons to settle an area. It was a principle that western settlers had early reenforced by banding together in extralegal associations or claims clubs and frightening away latecomers intent on outbidding them when public lands were finally put up for auction. This emphasis on the rights of first arrivals found special appeal among the midwesterners rushing to California, for they came from a region where the government's mineral policy in the local lead mines was in complete disarray. Still, Washington itself had recently recognized the principle of priority in the Preemption Act of 1841, which promised the first settler on public land the right to buy a homestead for the minimum price as soon as the government had surveyed the area and put it on the market.[7] In actuality, Washington had neither the desire (it faced a surfeit of distractions in the pre–Civil War years) nor the manpower to survey and sell the land in the California mother lode. Moreover, the hordes pouring into the diggings did not want to buy a homestead. They wanted gold—to find it, take it, and move on to another promising site.

Necessity, tempered by the traditional emphasis on the superior claims of the first arrivals and by the Democratic majority's instinctive Jeffersonian wish to resolve issues locally, produced a solution straightforward in its simplicity: the right to a gold claim went to the first person working it. And the government, out of similar considerations of necessity, tradition, and political culture, left the miners alone. "This is public land," the American military governor in California told them, "and the gold is the property of the United States; all of you here are trespassers, but as the Government is benefited by your getting out the gold, I do not intend to interfere."[8] That the governor did not have the troops to eject them, even if he had wanted to, made his forbearance ring rather hollow.

It was only natural that the miners established the same principle of priority—"first in time, first in right"—in determining rights to the water, which was absolutely necessary to work a claim. The premium lay in being the first to use water with the assurance that latecomers could not deprive one of that right. The only requirement for maintaining one's preeminent position was continued diligence in using the water to work the claim. Implicit in such a system (and subsequently made explicit in law) was the principle that no one

Flumes could carry enormous volumes of water over great distances, as this flume and the one opposite still do in northern California. (Courtesy of Pacific Gas and Electric Company)

acquired property in running water itself—the *corpus* of the water—but only a right to divert and use the flow. Cessation of beneficial use meant an end of the right, thus allowing someone else to use the water. As hammered out initially in myriad gold camps and rigorously enforced by local miners' courts, these principles be-

came known as the arid region doctrine or the doctrine of prior appropriation.[9]

The new doctrine received state approval for the mother lode country in 1851 when the legislature ratified the "customs, usages, or regulations established and in force at the bar, or diggings" and congressional endorsement followed in 1866 for public lands generally.[10] Congress's action was especially noteworthy for two reasons. First, it represented Washington's abandonment of its so-far unexercised authority over water distribution on public lands. In removing itself, Congress officially recognized what had already taken place—the applicability of "local customs, laws, and the decisions of courts"—thus effectively acknowledging in the states the power to regulate water rights (an authority they still largely possess, but which the federal government reclaimed in certain particulars in the twentieth century). Second, Congress's endorsement of prior appropriation not only governed "the use of water for mining" but also its use for "agricultural, manufacturing, or other purposes." With this step Congress, like the miners and military governor earlier, was recognizing reality, for by then the new doctrine was being applied to virtually every conceivable use and had moved well beyond its origins in California. (Riparian water rights, to be discussed later, had also gained legal recognition as a result of the state legislature's adoption in 1850 of the common law, thereby setting the stage for enormous complications.) Eventually all western states endorsed the appropriation doctrine in some form, and nine states—Colorado, Nevada, Idaho, Utah, Wyoming, New Mexico, Arizona, Montana, and Alaska—chose it as their sole water law.[11]

The appropriation doctrine resembled Hispanic water law in its emphasis on *use* as the decisive consideration for developing a region; but unlike Hispanic practice, it grounded water rights on personal initiative, not on an imperial decree or administrative order. It established priority of use, not considerations of equity or justice, as the determinant of who got water and how much. Under the new system, many people could divert water from a river where there had been an earlier appropriator, but in times of shortage (and they were frequent), the latecomers would lose all the water they were using before the first-comer would be affected. There was no sovereign authority as in Spanish and Mexican California to arrange for pro rata sharing of the reduced flow or a weighing of individual needs against the total supply. In addition, this new right came to be seen as a personal property right that could be accumulated on a stream (or many streams), just as a person might accumulate other forms of property, which could be sold piecemeal or all at once without selling the land.[12] The right, as noted earlier, continued only so long as a person exercised "due diligence" in diverting the water and using it beneficially (the "use it or lose it" principle), but in a dry country, few allowed themselves to fall afoul of this requirement.

Thus the new law, as it emerged in nineteenth-century California, ratified the survival instincts of a profit-driven people in an arid land. It endorsed swift commandeering of water resources and rapid economic development, and it gave no advantages to communities over individuals, though towns and cities could condemn rights that individuals had acquired. Not surprisingly in a region where water was recognized at once as a necessity and a readily acquirable source of power and wealth, this situation encouraged individual and corporate tendencies to monopolize as much of it as possible. This tendency surfaced early in the mining districts and led not only to friction among miners but also to monumental environmental despoliation.

Hydraulicking and Environmental Destruction

EVEN AS novel legal principles emerged in the mother lode country, miners began exhausting the more easily worked placer deposits and devising new technologies and capitalization methods to get at the less accessible pay dirt. Some greatly lengthened the miles of ditches and flumes to bring water to their sluice boxes, while others diverted entire streams to expose rich gravels in the riverbeds, and still others invested in networks of tunnels and costly stamp mills to work quartz deposits. The expense of these enterprises required cooperation among miners and, as costs and profits spiraled, resulted in companies underwritten by urban investors in San Francisco and increasingly in the East and Europe.

Some firms profited so well in supplying water to the new en-

Hydraulic mining at North Bloomfield in Nevada County. (Courtesy of California History Room, California State Library, Sacramento)

terprises that they avoided mining altogether and devoted their energies to acquiring water rights and selling the precious commodity. This angered many individual gold seekers who objected to paying for something so vital to their survival. They insisted that water and mining were inextricably bound and that the appropriation doctrine sanctioned the use of water only by those directly involved in mining and not by outside interlopers wishing to market water.[13] When the state supreme court disagreed with them in 1855 and upheld the retailing of water, the impact was immediate. Businesses selling only water as well as those commandeering water for their mining operations multiplied apace. Corporate control of mining lands and nearby streams soon became standard practice.

Among the most profitable of the new entrepreneurial ventures was hydraulic mining, a California invention that subsequently spread, some would say like a plague, to other parts of the nation and world. As early as the mid-1850s the miners, with their canvas hoses, began washing away thick layers of soil and rock to expose gold in long-buried prehistoric (Tertiary) streambeds. Two elements, technology and capital, propelled hydraulic mining to national prominence, with the promise of the one attracting the other. In 1853 when a miner from Connecticut named Edward Matteson attached a nozzle to a hose and revealed how water pressure could be used to produce wealth, he piqued the interest of investors who invaded the diggings with their "hydraulic giants," iron behemoths that resembled cannons, weighed nearly a ton, and could wash away hillsides, meadows, stands of timber, and even mountains in their entirety. "The effect of this continuous stream of water coming with such force must be seen to be appreciated," noted a horrified observer, for "wherever it struck it tore away earth, gravel and boulders. . . . It is impossible to conceive of anything more desolate, more utterly forbidding, than a region which has been subjected to this hydraulic mining treatment." [14]

As the destruction was extraordinary, so too was the reward, which by the mid-1880s amounted to a return of about three to one—$300 million in gold on investments totaling $100 million in equipment and property. Such profits encouraged around-the-clock operations with illumination for night work at first supplied by torches, then in the 1860s by oil-burning locomotive headlights, and eventually by electric lights after the North Bloomfield mine pioneered the practice in 1879. One massive system at Cherokee in Butte County stopped only once in twelve years, and then for the funeral of President James Garfield. The resulting demand for water drove the hydraulickers to redouble their efforts to acquire nearby streams. Through purchase, filing on abandoned claims, extralegal force, and court battles with competitors, they built hydraulic empires of dams, reservoirs, flumes, ditches, pipes, and hoses. All this in turn required knowledge of advanced engineering principles, now introduced for the first time on a large scale in the West and later used to build other great public and private projects. The Cherokee operation at its height had four reservoirs supplying water through a hundred miles of ditches, flumes, and pipes to sixteen "hydraulic giants" that daily spewed out 40 million gallons of water, three times the volume used in San Francisco at the time. In 1880 as hydraulicking neared its peak, the industry in California had about 20,000 employees, more than 7 million cubic feet of water in reservoirs, and 6,000 miles of ditches, excluding countless minor lines. In addition, great tracts of forest had been clear-cut to supply the timber for the huge operations, thereby speeding erosion and increasing the debris washed into streams.[15]

The environmental havoc wreaked by such a gigantic enterprise spread far beyond the mining country. Rivers of mud flowed downstream, killing fish, polluting water for people and animals, and filling in and then obliterating river channels, thus greatly exaggerating the natural tendency toward annual flooding on the central flatlands of the Sacramento Valley. Marysville, Sacramento, and other towns rushed levees into place only to see them overtopped or swept away. Thousands of acres of farmland—orchards, field crops, houses, and barns—were buried under mining detritus, while inland shipping from Sacramento to San Francisco Bay slowed appreciably and sometimes ceased altogether. The unfettered private enterprise that in the 1840s and 1850s promoted rapid mining of gold by individuals had by the 1880s produced corporate giants increasingly excoriated by the public and especially by farmers, whose growing economic and political importance began challenging and then surpassing that of the mining interests.[16]

Still, the power of corporate mining and the inability of the laissez-faire-oriented legislature to implement a broad drainage plan to protect farmers (and, it was hoped, allow hydraulicking to continue as well) frustrated reform efforts for years. The fact that the hydraulickers were discharging into streams that carried the debris down into the navigable rivers of the flatlands made the issue a federal matter under the U.S. Supreme Court ruling of *Gibbons* v. *Ogden* (1824). Also, under ancient common law, it was illegal to use one's property in any way that would damage property belonging to someone else.

Finally, in 1884 the Ninth U.S. Circuit Court of Appeal in San Francisco issued an injunction shutting down the entire hydraulic mining industry on the grounds that its operations inevitably damaged the property of others and practically destroyed the navigability of the Sacramento and Feather rivers. This remarkable action in *Woodruff* v. *North Bloomfield,* one of the earliest federal environmental decisions (if not the first such decision), held that dumping debris into rivers violated both common and statutory law and jeopardized commerce.[17] A chastened hydraulic industry sought to continue but under regulations so strict that survival became impossible. For nearly three decades, however, community and environmental concerns had run a distant second to individual and especially corporate desires to seize water and blast away at the landscape in a frenzied quest for riches.

The Politics of Flood Control

THOUGH HYDRAULICKING increased alarm over flooding in the Sacramento Valley, flooding there long antedated the heyday of the gold rush era and remained a serious problem generations after mining had fallen on hard times. Early attempts to grapple with the problem illustrate how water overabundance has frequently been as serious as shortage. They also reveal how public policy-making in California resonated with decisions made in Washington that reflected the Jeffersonian emphasis on laissez-faire and localism.[18]

Northern California's Sacramento Valley is an enormously fertile area about forty miles wide that stretches some 150 miles from present-day Red Bluff in the flatlands below the Trinity Mountains to the delta behind San Francisco Bay. As former miners turned to cultivating the rich soils, they discovered the awesome power of the Sacramento River, which regularly transformed the valley into a vast inland sea a hundred miles long that usually persisted well into summer, with much of the valley remaining swampland year round. Under such conditions, agriculture was precarious where not impossible, the growing season short, and property damage often extensive.

Responsibility for dealing with the problem rested with the state, which owned the valley's half-million acres of swamp and overflow land (as well as some 1.5 million acres of similar land elsewhere in California). Such lands had been granted to all the states by the Arkansas Act of 1850 on condition that the state reclaim the land for agriculture. Congress, dominated by Democrats for whom centralized planning was anathema, had no interest in embarking on a federal flood-control scheme, and would not for more than a half century. California might have initiated a comprehensive project of its own, but when it finally got around to addressing the issue in 1855, its Democrat-controlled legislature was no more willing than Congress had been to trust centralized authority. It delegated major responsibility for flood control to the counties, which had the important task of determining which lands were actually swamp and overflow properties. The legislature also sought to prevent the reclaimed lands from falling into the hands of wealthy speculators by limiting sales to a maximum of 320 acres at a dollar an acre (increased to a 640-acre maximum three years later) and making a local official responsible for enforcing the law. As for the actual accomplishment of flood control, the legislators put their faith in laissez-faire. Farmers looking out for their individual self-interest, the lawmakers believed, could be trusted to build levees around their plots to ward off floodwaters and dry out swamplands.[19]

Whigs and then Republicans, convinced of the need for a centralized plan, criticized these efforts as piecemeal and lacking adequate coordination. They also rapped the Democrats for failing to heed the warnings of local officials who insisted that numerous small plots could not be effectively drained or protected. They argued that large holdings of the size that men of wealth could purchase and afford to protect with substantial levees and drains should be the preferred course of action. Their position soon seemed vindicated when the small, helter-skelter protective works proved not only incapable of deflecting floods but actually increased damage

Sacramento under flood, 1850. (Courtesy of California History Room, California State Library, Sacramento)

by contributing to higher water levels before they, in turn, were overtopped and destroyed.

An opportunity for a radically different approach came with the outbreak of the Civil War and a split of the Democrats into pro-southern and pro-northern factions. California Republicans, together with those Democrats at least temporarily inclined because of the wartime emergency to accept the idea of an activist government promoting the general welfare, secured passage of a Reclamation and Swampland Act in 1861.[20] It called for a valley-wide plan designed and directed from Sacramento. Specifically, it created a Board of Swampland Commissioners, a public body and the first independent state agency—that is, a body with governing powers which was not part of the executive branch—in California history. The commissioners were elected by the legislature and vested with authority to design a flood-control program reflecting the topography of the valley, not individual landholdings. Since the topography varied, the design and location of the levees and drains would also vary in harmony with geographic reality.

To implement the plan locally (that is, to levy taxes and build the actual works) the 1861 statute authorized the state board to create

Sacramento inundated in 1862. (Courtesy of California History Room, California State Library, Sacramento)

a new type of legal entity, the *swampland district* (later known as reclamation district), an institution that Californians later modified for a host of other purposes ranging from irrigation to sewage disposal and fire protection. These swampland districts could be established on petition of at least a third of the landholders in an area "susceptible to one mode or system of reclamation." Though the districts had to build the protective works according to guidelines established and enforced by state-appointed engineers, the districts as local entities made the state programs less objectionable to those uncomfortable with centralized authority.

Bold as the 1861 act was, it failed. Overconfidence played a major role, since engineers lacked the detailed technical studies of flood flows and the equipment required for what hindsight would prove to be a gargantuan task. A few years later, by the time the state board recognized the need for more information and more formidably designed (and hence more expensive) works, floodwaters had destroyed the new levee systems, which were low and weak by comparison with the giant modern structures in the valley, thoroughly embarrassing the advocates of valley-wide planning. Undermining them further were bitter debates in the state legislature over Radical Reconstruction policies then being enacted by Congress to create racial justice in the postwar South. These angry arguments destroyed the political coalition that had made possible the board's creation. Outraged over attempts to guarantee civil rights to blacks, "Short Hair" Republicans (former Democrats) joined with Democrats long sympathetic to the South in attacks on the concept of activist government. A by-product in 1866 was elimination of the Board of Swampland Commissioners and delegation of its authority to county boards of supervisors. Two years later, with the legislature firmly in Democratic control and a Democrat as governor, the reversal became complete with passage of the Green Act.[21]

The Green Act of 1868 epitomized the Democratic commitment to localism and laissez-faire. It permitted a group of purchasers (or even a single buyer) who had acquired as little as half of a given tract of land to create a swampland district and build any kind of levee and drainage system around it. This mirrored not only disenchantment with state-directed policy but also distrust of engineers as lacking the practical common sense of farmers committed to protecting their own holdings. The law also recognized the earlier warnings of local officials that large holdings could be more effectively protected than smaller ones by removing all restrictions on the amount of swamp and overflow land a person could purchase. Removal of acreage restrictions harmonized with the Democratic emphasis on laissez-faire but it also opened the possibility of land being monopolized by speculators. The legislature's response to the dilemma was to set the price of land at a dollar an acre in the hope that this would keep farms within the reach of those of modest means. For those who drained swamplands, the law offered to do the most, promising to return their purchase price as soon as they could show that they had cultivated their property for three years. Not long after, even that requirement was replaced by weaker conditions that generally went unenforced.[22]

For the next half century the Green Act represented state flood-control policy in California. It persisted even after evidence mounted that it promoted monopoly, rather than small irrigated farms, and failed to prevent massive flood damage. Within three years, virtually all of the more than 2 million acres of state swampland had been snatched up, much of it in private holdings of enormous size. A legislative investigation in 1871 produced a list of thirty individuals possessing a total of some 430,000 acres of swampland, or an average of approximately 16,300 acres apiece. Others, embarrassed about such disclosures, purchased land through dummy entrymen, with a former state surveyor general suspected of acquiring 300,000 acres in this way. The legislature, though incapable of registering embarrassment, acknowledged that the situation had gotten out of hand when in 1874 it restored the 640-acre maximum that a person could purchase. By then, however, all the swampland was gone, including vast tracts of dry land that state agents misrepresented as swamps and secured for themselves or transferred to others for a bribe. Not a few large landholders were known locally as "admiral" or "commodore" on the basis of rumors that they had secured their swamp and overflow land by testifying they had been over it in a boat—a boat placed in a horse-drawn wagon.[23]

The Green Act failed to curb flood damage largely because it resulted in a return to the earlier practice of atomized protective systems, with only the largest (and most expensive) levees of the wealthy affording some semblance of security. Even that was achieved by deflecting floodwaters across less well guarded nearby properties belonging to someone else, and ultimately proved a temporary palliative, since the largest protective works also gave way during periods of massive runoff. Republican attempts, most notably in 1880, to reintroduce valley-wide planning at the state level failed when engineering knowledge again proved inadequate to the task and served only to intensify the Democrats' opposition to what they considered excessive and unwise authority in Sacramento.[24] Thus, laissez-faire, localism, and monopoly became standard practice in flood-control planning just as they had in the allocation of water for mining.

Riparian Rights

W HILE MANY Californians battled floods to make a living and those in the water-scarce gold country armed themselves with the appropriation doctrine to seek their fortunes, others adopted different means to achieve wealth. Some invoked a water law at sharp odds with the principles devised by the miners. Their allegiance was to riparian rights, long the prevailing system in England and the eastern United States where rainfall in abundance and rivers flowing year-round were the norm. Riparianism shared with the doctrine of prior appropriation the principle that no one could acquire a property right to the corpus of the water itself, only to its use, but otherwise the two systems were striking in their differences. Unlike the appropriation doctrine, riparianism emphasized location and mere legal possession (that is, owning a piece of land through which a stream flowed), not priority of appropriation or even actual use of the water, as the prime considerations in establishing a water right. It guaranteed owners of land bordering a stream the full natural flow, less only what was needed upstream to satisfy domestic needs, including the watering of livestock, but did not authorize withdrawals for irrigated agriculture. Riparian owners' rights were equal in that all could use the water so long as they did not impair the rights of other riparians. Thus, unlike the situation under the appropriation doctrine, they could not—and this included even the first person on a stream—divert as much water as they wanted or wherever they wished. Also unlike the appropriation doctrine, use did not create the right and nonuse did not terminate it. In later years this would be called the "rocking chair" principle: landowners could simply sit and look at their water, and no one could deprive them of their right and use the water elsewhere. Location alone determined the right, which simply resided in the ownership of land bordering the stream.[25]

Though the two doctrines differed sharply, both gained legal recognition early in California: appropriation in the gold country and riparianism when the first legislature in 1850 adopted the common law of England as the basic system of law to be followed by the state's courts—later modified, of course, by statutory law (laws enacted by the legislature) and case law (decisions made by the courts, which were based, where appropriate, on the state and federal constitutions).[26] That action automatically fastened riparianism on the state because it was part of English common law. Adoption of the common law was the usual practice of new states, and in California it was done with little thought to the principles being developed in the goldfields.

For nearly three decades the state dealt with the problem of two contradictory legal systems by reaffirming the legitimacy of both and seeking to soften their differences. The legislature's approval of riparianism in 1850 was followed a year later by its endorsement of mining customs (and hence appropriation in the diggings) and then by its inclusion of both doctrines in the 1872 civil code. Similarly, the state supreme court balanced its approval of prior appropriation in *Irwin v. Phillips* in 1855 with its finding for riparianism in *Crandall v. Woods* two years later.[27] This willingness to accommodate the apparently incompatible was due in the early years of statehood to the tendency of nearly all water users in a particular area to invoke one or the other of these systems. In other words, a patchwork of legal ideas existed. Initially this meant that the vast majority of newcomers—who were miners in the mother lode country—opted for the appropriation doctrine.[28] Even those who owned land adjacent to a stream preferred appropriation except in those better-watered areas where riparianism became the norm for virtually everyone. As with so much else in these early years, localism and laissez-faire prevailed.

At the outset, however, there was one aspect of riparian law that held the potential for major conflict. This was the prohibition against diverting water except for domestic needs. Experience showed that some irrigation was frequently necessary if agriculture was to be possible in even the better-watered areas. Here the courts revealed flexibility, not only responding to local necessity but also taking a cue from eastern states, which had begun modifying their riparian law tradition in favor of some appropriation practices—for example, diverting water for a milldam or to float barges through a canal. As early as 1865 the California supreme court agreed to permit limited irrigation in areas where the riparian doctrine applied. So long as the use was reasonable and confined to land adjacent to a stream, the court had no qualms about broadening the riparian doctrine in this way.[29] Such relative harmony began breaking down, however, as settlers in ever-increasing numbers began moving out onto the floors of the vast interior and coastal valleys where water was less abundant than in the foothills, frontage along streams was in shorter supply, irrigation was not the primary interest of everyone, and monopoly of land and water was the goal of many.

Monopoly and a Clash of Rights

SETTING THE stage for conflict were speculators, ranchers, farmers, and would-be farmers. There had not always been intense interest among the newcomers in the valleys, especially the great Central Valley. The earliest emigrants to California had looked with dismay at the broad expanse before them from their trails on the downward slope of the Sierra Nevada. Most arrived in summer when the Central Valley was dry, the temperature was soaring, and haze obscured their view. One migrant, after making his way to the valley floor and losing sight of the mountains in the haze, exclaimed in befuddled amazement, "My God! We're out of sight of land."[30]

Such disappointment did not last. Among the first to see the potential of California's many valleys were the speculators. They came looking for investment opportunities for the profits wrested from mining or other commercial ventures that boomed following the gold rush. They eyed the more than 13 million acres (out of California's 100 million) locked up—but not securely, as the U.S. Land Commission and federal courts would demonstrate—in Spanish and Mexican rancho grants. They were also attracted to the even vaster public lands, where a special beneficiary was the Central (later Southern) Pacific Railroad with a bequest from Congress that exceeded 3.5 million acres in California alone by the early 1880s. The sale of those lands was to pay for constructing the railroad. Additionally, nearly 8.5 million acres of state land that California had received from the federal government were to be sold either as swamplands or for the benefit of schools and colleges.[31]

Shrewd speculators with ready cash bought, bribed, and forged their way into estates, dwarfing those of most European bluebloods. William S. Chapman and Isaac Friedlander used dummy entrymen to evade the restrictions of state and federal law, acquire rancho, school, and swamplands for a pittance, and amass holdings in excess of a million acres each in the Central Valley. They were unique but not alone. As early as 1873, some 122 others had acquired estates averaging 72,000 acres. There were also many small farmers trying to eke out an existence on a handful of acres, but even the inclusion of their holdings meant that in 1870 an average farm was still a large 482 acres. By century's end, 62 percent of the state's 28 million acres of farmland was in holdings of a thousand acres or more.[32] This pattern of big landholding has persisted into modern times as a distinctive characteristic of California agriculture.

Some purchasers acquired property for the purpose of selling it as soon as population pressures and the availability of transportation networks drove up prices, but this was not the usual pattern. Most took advantage of local markets and the extension of the railroads out into and through the Central Valley to reap returns by working their lands, with cattle ranching and wheat growing attracting most attention. Earlier the Mexican rancheros had benefited mightly from the gold rush demand for beef, but by the mid-1850s disaster was overtaking them in the form of a glutted market, horrendously expensive litigation costs incurred in defending their land titles, mounting debts from purchasing luxuries they could no longer afford, and severe drought followed by floods that killed thousands of cattle. The land rapidly changed hands, ordinarily in large unsubdivided holdings. It went to lawyers in lieu of fees, on the auction block to the highest bidder in order to satisfy overdue taxes, and to speculators for cash payments that the Californios applied with increasingly diminished effectiveness to their debts that skyrocketed as a result of immense rates of interest. The displaced rancheros and the numerous vaqueros and artisans who depended on them for their livelihoods drifted into the lowest-paid unskilled jobs in the countryside as well as in the newer cities emerging in the coastal areas.[33]

The change in ownership did not necessarily mean a change in land use. Anticipating an increased demand for beef as the state population continued to expand rapidly, many of the new American landowners kept the former ranchos stocked with cattle. Other investors in the Central Valley and elsewhere carved ranches out of the public domain and supplemented them with purchases of small private tracts. Wherever the new owners appeared, they made water a top priority, acquiring as much frontage along streams and rivers as possible. For most ranchers, riparianism became the doctrine of choice since it assured them a continuous flow of water for their livestock and periodic flooding of bottomlands for the growing of alfalfa and hay.

Because of the vagaries of weather and market, wheat growing attracted much greater attention than ranching. It soared after the late 1860s in response to suitable environmental conditions, the availability of seasonal labor (mostly Mexicans, Mexican Americans, Indians, Chinese, and other ethnic minorities), an expanding rail and ship transportation network, and an almost insatiable foreign market served through shipments to Liverpool, England. California produced an especially fine variety of hard wheat much prized in world markets. The Central Valley in particular came under the sway of wheat barons whose wide and level estates easily accommodated massive gangplows and great steam combines that only their great wealth could afford.[34]

Especially enhancing the attractiveness of wheat were the bountiful harvests obtainable without irrigation. This success was due to dry farming, a practice requiring rainfall no greater than that ordinarily available at the time in the Central Valley. Deep plowing after rains brought runoff into the subsoil where it was prevented from evaporating by means of a shallow dust blanket created by a special machine that pulverized the surface. This reservoir of moisture enabled the growing of vast quantities of grain that propelled California from eighth in wheat production in 1869 to second (behind only Minnesota) by 1889. The success of the wheat barons, while dramatic, was nonetheless always precarious. Rainfall, though usually sufficient for dry farming, was not always so. Droughts and crop failures did occur—and with sufficient frequency and severity to make growers uneasy. In 1863–1864, 1870–1871, and 1876–1877 drought hit so hard that even scrupulously practiced dry farming could not prevent total crop loss for many, especially in the southern San Joaquin Valley.[35]

So long as most large owners remained committed to wheat and dry farming, they showed no preference for a particular water doctrine. This began changing in response to the droughts and also to the example of small farmers who lived around the periphery of the big estates and along streams in the Sierra Nevada foothills. They demonstrated the attractiveness of irrigation during periods of slight rainfall, a point even more forcefully underscored by the long tradition of successful irrigation on former Spanish and Mexican holdings in southern California and elsewhere. During the American period irrigation expanded on many of those lands. By 1867 some 10,000 acres in Los Angeles County alone were being watered, with the state's largest vineyards standing beside the Los Angeles, San Gabriel, and Santa Ana rivers. Enhancing the attractiveness of irrigation were improvements in the 1870s in the refrigerated railroad car. This meant that high-return specialty crops produced through irrigation—vegetables, grapes, apricots, cherries, oranges, and lemons—could be shipped safely to rapidly growing eastern cities, thus generating profits for farmers on even small holdings of between ten and fifty acres.[36] The irrigationists' success became not only an object lesson to larger landholders in how to survive during periods of drought, but also in how to maximize returns. If profits could be safely made on small irrigated plots, then big profits could surely be made on big acreage, which could either be subdivided and sold at "appropriate" prices or retained and farmed as an estate.

Entrepreneurs responded with a variety of schemes. In the late 1860s and 1870s some, aided as Donald Pisani has shown by a growing public belief that the irrigated family farm would produce "a more homogeneous, virtuous, middle-class society," rushed into the real-estate market with water and land ventures such as the Fresno Canal and Irrigation Company, the Farmers' Irrigation Company of Merced, the San Joaquin and Kings River Canal and Irrigation Company, and other similar enterprises. Many who subdivided and sold some of their holdings realized significant profits by providing dams, ditches, planted crops, and a water right. Land magnate William S. Chapman helped pioneer such merchandising at his Central California Colony near Fresno where in 1875 he offered twenty-acre homesteads for $1,000. Four years earlier, an equivalent amount of land along Los Banos Creek could be obtained for only $100 and prepared for irrigation for an additional $250. Few promoters had the imagination, capital, and cunning of Chapman, who sold every lot in his colony within three years and still remained among the state's largest landowners.[37]

Chapman, however, had numerous near imitators, and their successes as well as the hoped-for earnings of the small farmers who purchased their tracts and the landless looking for the means to secure places of their own produced a clear-cut attitude toward water. These irrigationists and would-be irrigationists constituted an army as committed to the appropriation doctrine as the miners had been. It was a commitment that intensified as the irrigation frontier in California advanced from only 60,000 acres in 1870, to nearly

300,000 ten years later, and to a million acres by 1890.[38] The enemy increasingly became identified as the large ranchers who owned lands adjacent to a river and invoked the riparian doctrine to keep their cattle well watered and to prevent nonriparian owners upstream from making diversions to their properties at some distance from the rivers.

Yet big landowners could frequently be found on both sides of the issue. They tended to be the holders of great estates with investments in both irrigation and cattle and hence as flexible in their attitude toward the law as they were in their ways of turning a profit. They easily alternated their allegiance between the two water laws depending on which economic interest was being pursued on their vast and often separated holdings.

For small farmers and the thousands of landless who hoped someday to get a stake of their own, appropriation seemed the *only* reasonable law for a democratic country. To them, appropriation was the "people's" law while riparianism served the interests of only a few wealthy landowners. By the 1870s they no longer found consolation in the willingness of the California courts to tolerate some irrigation under the riparian doctrine. To the small or would-be farmer this tolerance was fundamentally flawed, since it applied only to the owner of land along the bank of a river. There simply was not enough such riverbank land to accommodate all those who sought it, especially in a state where a family, if given a chance, could make a decent living on only a handful of irrigated acres. Moreover, the banks of most streams were already owned by a small number of nabobs, most of whom seemed uninterested or only peripherally interested in irrigation. "The consequences of depriving all, or all but riparian owners, from irrigating are simply frightful to contemplate," declared a state irrigation convention in 1885. "Which is better?" asked the delegates:

> That a few men, the limited few who own the [river] bank, should have the exclusive use of the stream to water their stock, all irrigation be stopped, all the progress of the past be

blotted out, and ruin and destruction be brought to all the prosperous and happy homes of which now irrigation is the cause, the life and the only hope; or that the stream be used so as to irrigate the greatest amount of land which it is capable of irrigating so as to stimulate production to its widest limits, so as to build up homes of plenty and happy firesides, and rich and prosperous communities and peoples . . . ?

The answer seemed self-evident: "We submit to your good judgment that the . . . common law of England, as expounded by the Courts, [is] . . . repugnant to and inconsistent with the climate, topography and physical condition of the State and the necessities of the people."[39]

Such anger reflected a groundswell of popular opposition to riparianism that in the 1870s and 1880s spilled over into legislative halls, election campaigns, and an epic conflict in the courts. The success of agriculture, it was widely believed, lay in vanquishing the riverbank monopolists through water law reform. Major legal change did occur, but the results hardly merited the label *reform*.

Lux *v.* Haggin *and the California Doctrine*

THE POPULAR notion that the conflict between appropriation and riparianism was a battle between the "people" and monopolists received a severe jolt when the two systems finally clashed head-on in a monumental legal battle between 1879 and 1886 that ended in the *Lux* v. *Haggin* decision. That state supreme court ruling saddled California with a new system of water law (one later imitated by eight other western states), but it failed to alter the pattern of land and water rights concentrated in relatively few hands. This hardly seems surprising, since the principal antagonists in the struggle were among the state's wealthiest land (and water) barons. Theirs was a battle between giants, but who else except the extremely well-to-do could have afforded a fight that lasted so long, involved two appeals to the state supreme court, and produced an opinion running 200 pages, still among the longest on record anywhere?

A man with the unlikely name of James Ben Ali Haggin initiated the struggle. Taking his middle name from a Turkish physician grandfather, Haggin hailed from a prominent Kentucky family and practiced law before going in 1850 to California where he opened an office in Sacramento. He soon realized that the big money was being made in commerce in San Francisco, and there he went to make several fortunes, first as moneylender and then as investor in Wells, Fargo & Company, in the Anaconda Copper Company, in the mining ventures of George Hearst, in railroads and utility companies, and finally as the owner of a vast empire of 1.4 million acres in Arizona, New Mexico, and California, with most of his California holdings concentrated in the Central Valley.[40]

Haggin's agent in his business ventures was William B. Carr, a Bay Area politician described by the San Francisco *Argonaut* as belonging to "a ring of mercenary bandits who steal to get office and who get office to steal."[41] What Carr lacked in scruples, he more than made up for in shrewdness. He knew that Central Valley land without water was virtually worthless, so in 1873 he and Haggin set about trying to secure a monopoly on water rights for their holdings along the lower Kern River in the San Joaquin Valley. First, they established cordial relations with the local farmers who owned the few canals of any consequence at the time. They told the farmers that bigger irrigation works would produce bigger profits, and they described a painless way to raise the necessary investment capital: issue stock. This the farmers did, and then Haggin graciously agreed to purchase the stock in large quantities—large enough to gain control of the farmers' companies *and* their land and create his own Kern County Land and Water Company. He eventually acquired more than 400,000 acres in the valley, much of it through the buying of former rancho property and the use of dummy entrymen who filed on federal and state lands.[42]

At first, Haggin's canal investments were perceived as support for the small irrigators as was his willingness to hire local people to excavate additional canals and laterals to his own property and theirs. He testified often and spiritedly about his desire to pepper the countryside with modest homesteads irrigated by "industrious farmers." "My object has not been, nor do I wish to monopolize large bodies of land," he proclaimed, "but I desire to make valuable and available that which I have, by extending irrigating ditches over my lands, and when these lands are subject to irrigation, to divide them up and sell them out in small tracts with the water rights necessary for irrigation." [43]

Nonetheless, while Haggin eagerly acquired land and developed it, he postponed selling it. The reason lay in the integral role these properties played in his larger economic empire. On the million acres that he owned in Arizona and New Mexico he raised livestock dependent on the alfalfa and other grains harvested on his California holdings. To sell his alfalfa fields to a host of small farmers growing high-yield specialty crops for eastern markets would disrupt the flow of profits from his interdependent investments.

Yet Haggin was a charmer. Despite his foot-dragging about parting with his land, he successfully masked his livestock-agriculture interests, convinced the public of the sincerity of his intentions to subdivide and sell his holdings, and emerged in the late 1870s as the champion of the small farmer and the appropriation doctrine. He was helped immeasurably in his deceit by his choice of enemies. They were two similarly acquisitive monopolists who in 1879 invoked the unpopular riparian doctrine against him.

When Henry Miller and Charles Lux mounted their attack on Haggin, they did so as economic equals. They owned more than a million acres in Oregon, Nevada, and California with some 120,000 acres of that in Kern County. Unlike Haggin, they had come from modest backgrounds, yet in ambition and cunning they were every bit his equal. Miller, a German immigrant, had arrived during the gold rush all but penniless—with only "six dollars and a walking stick" to his name. [44] He sensed right away that his future lay in business, not in the diggings, and he opened a butcher shop, practicing the only trade he knew. To meet the growing demand for beef, he used his profits to buy cattle and then land for pasturing his increasing herds, a move that led to his partnership with Charles Lux, another butcher-turned-entrepreneur and an equally hard-driving Alsatian immigrant with as shrewd a business sense as his own. When drought devastated the state's livestock herds in the 1860s, the partners took advantage of the cattlemen's plight and bought entire ranchos and parts of others at bargain prices and then increased the herds on their new holdings. Like Haggin, they also used dummy entrymen to acquire massive additional tracts of state and federal land, always making sure their property had access to water. Through acquisition of riverbank properties, they effectively gained control of grazing over even vaster acreage. One of the most promising of their acquisitions now became the scene of an epic battle with Haggin. It was a large estate, most of it swampland, at the lower end of the Kern River and a short distance west of Bakersfield.[45]

Miller and Lux viewed suspiciously Haggin's digging of canals upstream of their Kern County holdings. Their concern turned to alarm after 1877 when drought combined with increased upstream diversions to virtually dry up the river and eliminate water reaching their livestock at river's end. Within two years thousands of their cattle had died. They appealed to Haggin and other upriver appropriators to release enough of the flow so they could maintain their ranching operation. Specifically, they asked for a fourth of the river's flow and offered to forgo all their riparian rights to the remainder. Haggin was in no mood to deal. He was buoyed by the growing public outrage at the riparian doctrine and confident that the courts would side with his—and the people's—preference for prior appropriation.

Miller and Lux reacted angrily to Haggin's rebuff, with Miller, the dominant member of the partnership, especially outraged. Described by a business acquaintance as "selfish, grasping, indomitable, thrifty, with a wondrous brain that schemed and twisted and generally routed his opponent," Miller decided to teach Haggin a lesson. In May 1879 he and his partner took him to court. The public sensed immediately the larger issues at stake and anxiously awaited the outcome. Especially attentive were the small and would-be irrigationists who, according to the Bakersfield *Kern County Californian,* firmly believed that "on the issue of this suit hangs, in great measure, the fate of all of us." Haggin's "success," they announced, will be "that of the entire community, and its sympathies are most warmly with . . . [him] in the present emergency"—a message echoed in newspapers throughout the state.[46]

Two years later the lower court ruled for Haggin, for prior appropriation, and for the "people"—but the win was temporary. Miller and Lux appealed to the state supreme court, and on two occasions (the last in 1886), the court found for them in the landmark decision of *Lux* v. *Haggin.*[47] In doing so, however, the court also found a way to obfuscate the issues and deliver something less than a clear-cut victory for riparianism. It held that the riparian doctrine was law in California, citing as evidence the first legislature's adoption of the common law in 1850, but it also ruled that under certain conditions the appropriation doctrine would prevail. The result was the creation of a legal hybrid, known subsequently as the "California doctrine" after its place of origin, that eventually spread to eight other states—Washington, Oregon, Nebraska, Oklahoma, Texas, Kansas, and North and South Dakota—where, as in California, climatic and other conditions fostered the development of competing water-law systems.[48]

The *Lux* v. *Haggin* decision was complex but its essential points were these: (1) riparian rights inhered in all private lands, including public lands when they passed into private ownership; and (2) an appropriator could possess a right superior to a riparian if the appropriator had begun using water from a stream *before* a riparian had acquired his property. Put simply, both systems were legitimate and timing determined which prevailed in a conflict.

To a public adamantly opposed to riparianism, approval of that doctrine under any circumstances was anathema. In this instance the disappointment was especially galling because the caveat about timing provided no consolation. The reason was simple enough. By now, virtually all the riverbank land in farmable areas had passed into private ownership—and it had done so without being subject to any substantial earlier appropriations. In other words, riparians held a distinct legal advantage. They tended to be the ranchers who had acquired their holdings from Spanish and Mexican grantees (whose water rights antedated the American conquest and were protected by the Treaty of Guadalupe Hidalgo) or had pieced their properties together with public-land purchases. Thus, small and would-be farmers found nothing to praise in the decision and much to criticize. In a stronger position were the appropriators with big estates. They often found they had protected, or could protect, themselves through the purchase of large amounts of riverbank land in the vicinity of their holdings. Even if they did not avoid a lawsuit—or, as in the case of Haggin, chose not to avoid one— their property and other financial resources gave them a distinct advantage not possessed by the small irrigationists. Haggin himself demonstrated the force of such an advantage in the wake of the *Lux* v. *Haggin* decision.

Haggin had lost his battle with Miller and Lux, but the loss turned out to be more symbolic than real. Legally he lost because he had diverted water *after* the riparians Miller and Lux had obtained their land. The water they won, however, came in a rush in the spring, was more than they needed, and could not be controlled or stored since all practical dam sites were upstream and belonged to Haggin. "There is more water than we can use, and it does not come at the right time of the year," confessed Henry Miller following the court decision. "It comes in a great flood early in the spring, and in the hot months of summer the river is dry." So, like the good businessman he was, Miller offered Haggin a deal. "You builds me a reservoir, and I gives you two-thirds of the water." And thus it was done, underscoring that among wealthy combatants there were no real losers.[49]

The land barons emerged from the courtroom virtually unscathed and in possession of water and estates, but lesser Californians found the *Lux* v. *Haggin* decision an enormous headache and bitter disappointment. Besides anger over continued recognition of riparian-ism, there was dismay about the complex, contradictory, and jerry-built legal system that the court had saddled on the state. It soon proved a field day for lawyers, who filed suits with such abandon that no single issue appeared more often on state court dockets than water disputes. Even the nabobs soon tired of these antics, with Henry Miller later complaining as an old man that he had spent $25 million on legal fees, much of that maintaining his hold on water rights.[50] The less fortunate, even if the law seemed in their favor, could seldom afford to wage court battles, though enough people still found the means to keep judges busy and water attor-neys wealthy.

The Irrigation District and the Persistence of Monopoly

THE PUBLIC'S initial disappointment with *Lux* v. *Haggin* fo-cused overwhelmingly on the court's continued recogni-tion of riparianism, a doctrine (thanks to Haggin's won-drous ability to obfuscate his intentions) seen as destructive of California's potential for small irrigated farms. A flurry of bills were introduced in the legislature to limit or abolish riparian rights, but within only months the public began to see that the appropriation doctrine was not a panacea either and that the real enemy was monopoly, whether by riparians or appropriators. Snoopy newspaper reporters examined county records and found that a relatively small number of people had filed appropriation claims on nearly all California's rivers and often for several times more water than was available. Thus, abolishing riparian rights would merely surrender the field to another set of monopolists and their attorneys. "Private ownership and control of the waters of the state," declared the *Stockton Daily Independent,* "is far more to be dreaded than the objectionable law of riparian rights."[51]

Once alerted to what they perceived as the real evil, small and would-be farmers rallied around the ideas of C. C. Wright, a lawyer from the Central Valley town of Modesto who advocated a popular solution: provide the public with power to take water and land, by means of condemnation, from the huge estates and to create community-controlled *irrigation districts.* His proposal won his immediate election to the legislature where in 1887 he secured unanimous approval of the Wright Act.

The new law represented an effort to foster community values, promote small family farms, and curb the monopolistic excesses produced by the rampant individualism of California's pioneer capitalists. It also reflected the prevailing Jeffersonian emphasis on localism and laissez-faire, and this ultimately contributed mightily to its undoing. The act authorized the residents of an area to form local districts, elect a board of directors, issue bonds and raise revenue, purchase (including the authority to invoke condemnation if required) land and water rights, and distribute water. Except in a few closely circumscribed particulars, the state had no control over these functions. As Wright himself put it, the legislature had now "created a special government for the one purpose of developing and administering the irrigation water for the benefit of the people."[52] It was a "special government" modeled on the swampland district, but as that district had been radically localized in the Green Act.

The small and would-be farmers who championed the Wright Act believed that the local and democratically controlled district represented the most effective weapon against speculators and large landholders. All local residents (whether landowners or not) who were eligible to vote in state elections could cast ballots on district issues. In addition, all were taxed on the value of their property (town lots and buildings as well as rural land), not on whether they received irrigation water. The tax burden, it was thought, would force those holding land for speculative purposes or for the growing of wheat to sell at reasonable prices in small tracts to irrigationists. The new law also reflected the belief that an entire community had a stake in an irrigation enterprise, and everyone—farmers as well as those providing them goods and services—would share in any agricultural success. Also clearly evident was the element of coercion. Once a district had been created with a two-thirds vote of the electorate, even the most reluctant property owner had to go along.

In some ways, the irrigation district was reminiscent of Hispanic institutions. Unlike the situation under either riparian or appropriation law, the water right resided in the district, not with individuals or private corporations. In times of shortage, all users would share equally in the reduced flow, thus serving to reinforce what was essentially a community enterprise. Also as in pre-American California, irrigation districts derived their authority from above—in this case, the legislature—but there was a significant difference: Sacramento had neither Spain's generations of experience gained from living in water-scarce environments nor that country's centralized administration for dealing with aridity. This lack of experience and an overall plan proved a decisive flaw. There were those, including the state engineer and the California Grange, an organization of mostly small farmers opposed to monopoly and strongly in favor of irrigation, who were of a different mind. They argued vigorously for more comprehensive solutions directed from Sacramento, but the popular passion for localism and laissez-faire prompted the legislature not only to roundly reject such ideas but also to abolish the office of state engineer.[53]

At first many Californians viewed the Wright Act as the hoped-for panacea. It prompted creation of numerous irrigation districts and increases in irrigated acreage in the late 1880s and 1890s. Waves of landless and small landholders rushed to take advantage of the new law. As early as 1889 California led the nation in irrigated agriculture with nearly 14,000 farmers irrigating a million acres, most of them between Stockton and Bakersfield. Many of these farmers had earlier secured land around the Central Valley's periphery, where there were flowing watercourses emerging from the high country, while others had obtained acreage from some of the large landowners, including the railroad. Still others had found ways to circumvent the monopolistic grasp of the large landholders. In the 1890s with the appearance of the modern pump, some turned to groundwater, which was subject to no legal restraint and still remains largely unfettered. And there were those who simply gambled, clandestinely diverting water from a stream in the hope that earlier riparians or appropriators would either not notice or ignore them.

As early as 1857 in *Crandall* v. *Woods,* the state supreme court had allowed many to turn the gamble into a firm right through a device known as "adverse prescription." If irrigators could maintain their unauthorized diversions for at least five years without legal challenge, the right to the water was theirs. It was a loophole that provided many latecomers with legitimate access to water, but attempts to take advantage of the law in this way frequently led to extensive litigation that the poor could ill afford to pursue. Nonetheless, through such means and the Wright Act's encouragement, the irrigated lands increased in the decade after 1889 by some 50 percent to nearly 1.5 million acres at century's end. Much of this was devoted to specialized farming—nuts, vineyards, vegetables, fruit orchards—where small plots yielded impressive returns. Indeed, some 64 percent of the value of all California crops derived from such commodities. At the same time, farm sizes decreased, especially in those areas where irrigation had expanded most rapidly. In Fresno County, for example, the average farm in 1900 was half the size it had been twenty years earlier and in Los Angeles County, 40 percent smaller.[54]

The gains were more illusory than real. The Wright Act proved a limited success at best. The state's irrigated area expanded, but not as greatly as expected—1.5 million irrigated acres out of a total of 28 million acres of farmland was hardly an impressive figure—and much of that occurred on the large estates. While the size of the average farm declined, the drop was not dramatic: from 426 to 397 acres between 1880 and 1900. Moreover, most of the agricultural land (62 percent of it) remained in large ownerships exceeding a thousand acres. Wheat, while gradually giving way to the specialty crops encouraged by the railroad and refrigerator car, still dominated in many places. Especially disconcerting was the high rate of failure of the irrigation districts, with most surviving only a few years. In the Sacramento Valley, for example, only one of the seven districts created there enjoyed even partial success.[55]

Irrigation districts faced formidable barriers. Opposition from the large landowners, particularly in the form of court challenges, proved costly and time consuming. Heavy reliance on the courts necessarily followed from the Wright Act's decision to localize authority rather than to establish a statewide administrative agency that could issue rulings without necessitating the use of lawyers and expensive lawsuits. Also contributing to the high rate of failure was extraordinarily expensive court-ordered compensation for condemned land and water rights, severe drought in 1889, depression in 1893, ignorance about irrigation farming techniques, and fraudulent schemes of speculators seeking to profit from land sales in areas where the water supply could not support irrigation. Such obstacles made it extremely difficult to sell the bonds needed to cover the cost of the irrigation works, a task made impossible when the interest rate that districts could pay—and the Wright Act restricted the rate to 5 percent—was below what investors could obtain elsewhere. There were no limits on the size of a bond issue, however, and when buyers were available, a district's indebtedness often soared beyond reason, encouraging fraud and waste.[56]

Despite such setbacks, the district idea began spreading to other states where it enjoyed remarkable success because of changes made on the basis of the California experience. Thus, it joined such other California inventions adopted elsewhere as the appropriation doctrine, the California doctrine, and hydraulicking. By the 1890s in California, however, the irrigation district concept, which had been introduced with such enthusiasm only a few years earlier, was largely a failure—until it was revived and reformed in the early twentieth century.

Localism and the Search for Alternatives

N OT ALL those who established small irrigated homesteads and communities had been swept up in the irrigation district movement. Decades earlier, the Mormons had suggested a different approach when they
sought to replicate in California a settlement pattern pioneered in
the Great Basin of Utah. It was a pattern reflecting a broad, centrally directed plan. At San Bernardino in 1851 Brigham Young established the first of what was to be a corridor of communities linking Salt Lake City with the Pacific. The venture proved short lived,
however. Troubles in Utah prompted Young to recall the residents
in 1857, but before departing they established a successful agricultural village modeled after the church-administered and commu-
nally worked settlements in the Salt Lake Valley.[57]

Subsequent efforts mirrored the popular passion for free enterprise and localism, with the most successful of these experiments
being an innovation known as the *mutual water company*. It prospered primarily in southern California, where the land barons and
speculators had gotten off to a slower start than in the north with
its gold-rush catalyst. The slower growth permitted smaller venture
capitalists to secure land and water at reasonable expense, at least
in the beginning. German immigrants pioneered the mutual water
company idea at Anaheim, which a group of San Francisco investors
first established in 1857 on former rancho land at a site about forty
miles southeast of Los Angeles and along the Santa Ana River. The
enterprise was soon taken over by the settlers themselves, whose
goal was a planned agricultural community—vineyards and wines
were their first interest—on about 1,200 acres. They subdivided
the land into twenty-acre farm tracts and half-acre town lots, setting aside additional acreage for schools, shops, and public buildings. Like the later irrigation districts formed under the Wright Act,
their venture was community owned and directed, but unlike the

irrigation districts, it was a private business association, not a governmental, tax-raising political unit created by a special statute with rigid specifications. Thus, it was under the complete control—the mutual control—of the water users themselves.[58] Put another way, the irrigation district was similar to a municipal corporation, like a small town with limited functions and run by its citizens, while the mutual water company was a private corporation run by its owners.

Most crucial to economic survival was the community water company, in this case, the Anaheim Water Company, created by the settlers to hold all water rights and to build needed check dams and canals. Since this was a business venture, residents owned and controlled it through possession of stock, at first one share apiece for the original fifty owners, which entitled each settler to water for farmland and a town lot. This share carried with it the responsibility to maintain the system and also a vote on company policies, chief of which was that the company could not make a profit and water had to be sold at cost. Unlike the members of the irrigation districts, only those who actually used the water (that is, owned the company) could vote, though in time as some colonists obtained more land and used more water, they secured more votes. Such increases also included the obligation to pay a greater share of costs for the upkeep of the system.

The mutual water company, with its emphasis on local ownership and payment based on benefits received, proved an impressive success at Anaheim. Within four years the original fifty settlers had increased to 300 and the venture continued to grow at a remarkable rate, encouraged by the arrival at Los Angeles of the Southern Pacific in 1876 and the Santa Fe in 1885, and inspiring imitators throughout southern California at Riverside, Etiwanda, Ontario, and elsewhere.

As at Anaheim, private investors frequently established the settlements that later evolved into communities organized along the lines of mutual water companies. Ordinarily these developers were

George Chaffey's colony at Ontario, looking northward along Euclid Avenue toward the San Gabriel Mountains. (Courtesy of Security Pacific Historical Photograph Collection, Los Angeles Public Library)

small operators in comparison with the land barons of the Central Valley, and their practice was to relinquish control (although sometimes doing so only under pressure) to the settlers. This was the experience at Riverside, founded in 1870 and made nationally famous following the first planting of the navel orange three years later. Not until the mid-1880s, however, did the water-users wrest control of the water company from its profit-driven owners by buying them out and introducing an era of prosperity that became the envy of the state and an attraction to thousands of newcomers from the East.[59]

The preeminent promoter of the mutual water company idea was George Chaffey, a Canadian engineer who arrived in 1880 and within two years had left his mark first at Etiwanda; then at his "Model Colony" of Ontario (named for his home province), which he laid out in 1882; and later at Whittier. At Etiwanda he and his brother purchased 1,500 acres that they subdivided into ten-acre tracts, established rights to a nearby stream, pioneered the use of concrete pipes to prevent water loss, took advantage of the new technology of hydroelectricity generated with moving water to provide lighting, and went to great pains to raise sufficient capital to assure a well-planned and successful community. Also critical to Chaffey's success was the principle of one share in the company (and one vote in determining its policies) for each acre held. Two years later at Ontario, he achieved even greater popular success. He began by purchasing all conflicting water claims along nearby San Antonio Creek, thus assuring his community a firm water supply. He then designed an elaborate network of canals, established a college, banned saloons, provided a public transportation system, and laid out broad streets (most notably 200-foot-wide Euclid Avenue) planted with shade trees. Within ten years Ontario boasted 2,500 settlers on prosperous farms of ten to twenty acres. That Chaffey was not an ordinary speculator became abundantly clear when he voluntarily sold his water rights and water companies to the residents of his communities at reasonable prices and inspired other settlers to adopt mutual water company principles at Pomona, Pasadena, Redlands, and elsewhere. His successes attracted worldwide attention and in 1885 brought him an invitation to replicate his ventures in Australia.[60]

The Rainmakers

MUTUAL WATER companies proved more successful than the Wright Act's irrigation districts, but neither broke the near monopolistic control of water enjoyed by California's land barons. Community irrigation advances remained piecemeal at best, and outside of southern California, even those limited undertakings stagnated. Frustration became rampant, and it intensified during the last decade of the century when severe drought proved especially crippling to the less fortunate. Willing to grasp at almost any scheme promising relief, many gave way to an irrational return to ancient superstitions:

they invested their hopes and sometimes their money in the promises of "rainmakers."

Fresh from exploits on the Great Plains where drought had hit with a vengeance ten years earlier than in California, the rainmakers arrived in the 1890s with their secret chemicals and machines to redeem the state. Boasting a formula that "there is not enough money to buy," the Inter State Artificial Rain Company descended on Pixley in the San Joaquin Valley in 1892, secured a contract from a local group, and put its "rain persuader" to work. Early results were nil, but before the agreement expired, rain began falling not only on Pixley but also throughout much of California and as far east as Nevada, Utah, and Arizona. The U.S. Weather Bureau office in San Francisco proclaimed the experiment a "fizzle," while a farmer south of Pixley grumbled that the rain played havoc with his chores.[61]

Inter State had its defenders, but few had a good word for Clayton Jewell, a Kansan who arrived near Los Angeles in the dry summer of 1899. At first residents enthusiastically greeted him and his machine that emitted "a certain perfume which hurt the throat." After he spent sixty hours bombarding the heavens with the foul gas, everyone had had enough. Jewell called it quits, returned his advance payment, exited quietly and quickly, and apparently left the rainmaking business altogether.[62]

California's—and the nation's—most famous rainmaker was Charles Hatfield, who arrived in southern California with his parents during the real estate boom of the 1880s and within a decade had launched a career that would reach well into the twentieth century. His fame eventually brought him contracts from as far away as Guatemala and the Yukon, but most of his activities centered in the San Diego and Los Angeles areas. Hatfield attributed his success to a mixture of nearly two dozen secret chemicals that he "aged" for several days and then poured into pans and placed atop towers where they would evaporate and, so he claimed, bring rain. The odor produced by the chemicals, according to one spectator, resembled "a limburger cheese factory . . . broken loose," while another witness drolly speculated that the stink was the secret of Hatfield's success: "These gases smell so bad that it rains in self-defense."[63]

Hatfield's successes and failures remained local news until 1905 when he burst on the national scene following an exhibition at Los Angeles. He had earlier got the city's attention by producing (or so many believed) a third of an inch of rain at nearby Altadena with his "chemical affinity highball." When the local weather forecaster derided his claims, he told Los Angeles officials he would provide the city with eighteen inches of rain during the current season for a thousand dollars. Since that amount of precipitation had fallen only seven times in the preceding twenty-seven years and not at all in the last twelve, his offer attracted newspaper headlines and then greater publicity when the weather forecaster denounced him as a charlatan and imposter.[64] The rains came as Hatfield promised, and when he offered to toss in a couple more inches for good measure, the city folk demurred, one of them turning to poetry to explain why.

> It has drizzled and sprinkled and rained and poured
> The lightnings have flashed and the thunders have
>   roared. . . .
> You've earned your money, you've done your work well.
> Of your rain-making history surely will tell,
> So now, if you really love us all well
> Mr. Hatfield—do—let—up.[65]

Hatfield's success won him a spot on the lead float in Pasadena's Rose Parade and spread his fame across the nation and even to London where he was billed as the "World's Greatest 'Rain-Maker.'" Requests for his services as speaker and bringer of precipitation poured in as the now self-proclaimed "Professor" Charles Hatfield talked about "watering the desert of Sahara," dissipating London's fogs, and "drenching Kansas." Not all, or even most, of his future experiments produced rain, but there were enough triumphs to keep him busy, the most famous occurring in San Diego.

Charles Hatfield mixing a "chemical affinity highball." (Courtesy of Security Pacific Historical Photograph Collection, Los Angeles Public Library)

Hatfield's rainmaking tower at Morena Reservoir. (Courtesy of Department of Special Collections, Charles E. Young Research Library, UCLA)

In December 1915 Hatfield promised officials of drought-stricken San Diego what seemed to be a miracle: "I will fill Morena Reservoir to overflowing between now and next December 20, 1916, for the sum of $10,000, in default of which I ask no compensation."[66] With nothing to lose, the city grabbed the offer, and within a month record rains not only filled the reservoir but also washed out rail lines, bridges, crops, streets, and houses with loss of lives and damage claims of $3.5 million. Announced one exasperated farmer: "Let's pay Hatfield $100,000 to quit." Others vowed to lynch him. Once the reservoir filled to overflowing, Hatfield took down his equipment and demanded his fee. San Diego at first balked—the deluge was "an act of God" and not Hatfield's doing, claimed the city attorney—and then agreed to pay on condition that the rainmaker assume responsibility for all the damage claims. Hatfield refused, took the issue to court, and saw it languish there for more than two decades before being dismissed. The lack of a written contract with the city proved the undoing of his suit as did the distraction of much new business generated elsewhere by the publicity that he gained because of the incident.

Despite the notoriety of Hatfield and those like him, rainmaking proved at best a temporary palliative. Precipitation patterns could not be demonstrated to have changed because of such activities, and the U.S. Weather Bureau remained a harsh critic, arguing that the rains followed usual patterns that had nothing to do with chemicals spewed into the air. Later generations of scientists would dispute some of these contentions, but there is no evidence that the rainmakers of this era used chemical combinations similar to those employed today. Moreover, the erratic nature of California precipitation produced many more failures than successes, making it early apparent that rainmaking held no prospect for increasing the available water supply. Well before the turn of the century, Californians began looking for other ways to meet their water needs and to circumvent the monopolists of land and water. Frustrated by the many failures and only piecemeal gains, many increasingly pressured government to play a more active role.

The Progressive Impulse:
From Laissez-Faire to Centralized Planning

ASHINGTON HAD not ignored the problem of aridity in the West, but neither had it moved decisively or successfully to eliminate the abuse of federal land laws or to adjust them to the requirements of a water-shy environment. After all, the country was still in the era when most Americans assumed, and desired, that the states and local government would provide essentially all the governing in domestic matters that was needed. In 1878 John Wesley Powell—of what a year later would be designated the U.S. Geological Survey—had helped open a slowly dawning era in which people began to make Washington ever more a center of national studies and, eventually, guidance and governance. After a close investigation of the West and its natural resources, first commissioned by Congress in 1867, Powell argued eloquently for a completely new approach to western land and water in his monumental *Report on the Lands of the Arid Region of the United States.* Yet Congress, captivated by the instinctive Democratic emphasis on localism and laissez-faire, reacted coldly to his plan for reform directed by a single powerful federal agency. Westerners at that time shared such distrust and were also openly hostile to his essentially bleak message: "There is not sufficient water to irrigate all the land which could be irrigated." [67]

When Congress did act, it stumbled. The Desert Land Act (1877) had offered 640 acres for a modest price to anyone who would irrigate a portion of the land, but the measure, because of the use of dummies and other frauds by speculators, land companies, and cattlemen, encouraged monopolistic holdings, not irrigation. Similarly, the Carey Act (1894), which promised a million acres to any western state that would reclaim them with irrigation, had proved a disappointment because of flaws in design and the depressed conditions following the panic of 1893. [68] Such feeble and fragmentary efforts, together with the concentration of western land and water in relatively few hands, brought heightened demands for reform and for more effective government involvement.

Of monumental importance in helping to shape attitudes was the panic of 1893, until that time the severest depression in the history of the United States. Great fortunes were lost, businesses were destroyed, and tens of thousands were thrown out of work. In the West, suffering was especially severe for those already hard hit by the droughts of the 1880s and 1890s. When Democratic President Grover Cleveland adhered to his party's traditional laissez-faire policy and did nothing to ameliorate the situation, he reaped a whirlwind of criticism. It became so widespread and deep among the public that it helped propel a transformation in the balance of power in Washington and in many northern and western states, including California, that lasted for most of the next four decades. Large numbers of working-class voters joined with merchants, businessmen, and professionals of America's rapidly growing urban middle class to support the Republican party with its emphasis on activist government—this time government increasingly in the hands of those committed to a thorough overhaul of political and social institutions at all levels. The reform impulse emerged most dramatically in the Progressive Era, and though it waned thereafter, Republicans remained in control of the White House (except for the years when Woodrow Wilson brought his own brand of Democratic Progressivism to the presidency) until the Great Depression.[69]

At the heart of the reform ideology was the fervently held belief that government action should be guided by morally correct and intellectually informed decisions. This followed naturally from the old Whig (and then Republican) sense of morality and faith in education as a prerequisite to responsible exercise of authority, but it took on a new urgency in the complex world of turn-of-the-century America. A highly technical society facing baffling urban and industrial problems and dwindling natural resources concentrated increasingly in the hands of a few, argued the Progressives, required highly trained technicians—"experts": engineers, statisticians, lawyers, economists, geologists, agronomists, and the like—to design realistic solutions to social ills. Such an attitude rested on a great faith in formal learning, as opposed to the traditional Democratic belief that anyone could manage the nation, and on the elitist concept that experts should be allowed to go about their work free from the caprice of popular interference.

In the everyday world of practical politics, the Progressives' ideas took the form of scores of specialized agencies and commissions insulated from legislative bodies as well as the public. To the reformers, the prime goal of these commissions, especially those responsible for developing and managing natural resources, became the promotion of economic democracy by giving the people greater opportunities and a larger share of the nation's resources through the elimination of waste, inefficiency, and stealing. Expressed as a policy for positive action, the battle cry became "conservation"—conservation for future use of timberland, water supplies, and other scarce resources vital for the nation's sustained economic and political health. To achieve conservation with speed and efficiency was a goal that lent itself easily to the traditional Whig/Republican emphasis on centralized planning by government. Thus, the Progressive conservationists, as J. Leonard Bates has noted, sought "economic justice and democracy." And they hoped to achieve those goals, as Samuel P. Hays has succinctly observed, through "the transformation of a decentralized, nontechnical, loosely organized society, where waste and inefficiency ran rampant, into a highly organized, technical, and centrally planned and directed social organization which could meet a complex world with efficiency and purpose."[70]

Toward the Reclamation Act

SPEARHEADING THE drive for federal help in dealing with the West's water and land problems was a cadre of easterners and westerners whose professed goal, in numerous speeches and writings, was the moral regeneration of the nation. This goal would be accomplished by the creation of western irrigation communities peopled by the unfortunate: merchants and professionals bankrupted by depression or possessing skills no longer in demand in the new industrial order; workers displaced by the machine age; and farmers destroyed by drought. Relocated into communities of small homesteads, these family farmers, through cooperative efforts in distributing water and marketing crops, would, according to the reformers, achieve dignity and serve as a counterpoise in American society to the rampant individualism that in states like California had led to monopolistic land and water holdings and thousands of landless agricultural laborers.

Federal support and guidance were seen by these moral and social reformers as essential to the fulfillment of their hopes. First off, the communities had to have water, and the only promise of significant new supplies lay in trapping floodwaters now lost because the dams required were too expensive, even for the wealthy. The affordable (that is, small) private dams had all been built. Only the federal government possessed the means to construct the much larger new facilities and the authority to deal effectively with complex issues of water rights on those rivers that crossed state and international lines.

Preeminent in preparing the public for acceptance of this reform agenda calling for large-scale development was a crucial figure in the 1890s, William E. Smythe, a tall, sober, driven man whose commitment to agrarian and communitarian values formed the intellectual and emotional core of what became virtually a religious movement. "I had taken the cross of a new crusade," he later recalled. "It was not merely a matter of ditches and acres, but a philosophy, a religion, and a programme of practical statesmanship . . . that had fallen to my hand and [I] knew that I must cut loose from all other interests and endeavor to rouse the Nation to a realizing sense of its duty and opportunity."[71] A newspaperman and founder in 1891 of the journal *Irrigation Age,* he at first believed, in a fashion typical of the political thinking of the era, that the states should play the major role in reclamation, but soon changed his mind as he pondered the obstacles and weighed the practical advice of such experts as Hiram M. Chittenden, the distinguished engineer in the U.S. Army Corps of Engineers. In an 1897 report to Congress, Chittenden argued that only "through the agency of the General Government" would it be "possible to secure the best development." Smythe's conversion, like that of so many others in the dawning Progressive Era, to federal involvement and to faith in the technical knowledge of experts like Chittenden was complete. "Here was a clear suggestion of a workable plan," Smythe announced. "When Uncle Sam puts his hand to a task, we know it will be done. Not even the hysteria of hard times can frighten him away from the work. When he waves his hand toward the desert and says, 'Let there be water!' we know that the stream will obey his command."[72]

Smythe discovered a kindred spirit in the charismatic California lawyer and publicist George H. Maxwell, who railed at the failures of the Wright Act in his native state and abandoned a lucrative law practice to become a "militant evangelist" in Smythe's crusade. In 1899 he created the National Irrigation Association and lobbied successfully for support throughout the country and among leaders in both political parties. Joining him early in the campaign were highly placed engineers in the U.S. Geological Survey as well as Nevada Congressman Francis Newlands, who linked with eastern conservationist Gifford Pinchot to help win Theodore Roosevelt's endorsement. All shared the popular Progressive notions then sweeping the country that urged governments, both state and national, to use science and technology to advance American life. Pressure for action nationally, like that on state government, also came on the heels of the extreme western droughts of the 1880s and 1890s that in turn coincided with the severe depression of the 1890s. To the committed believers, harsh and shattering events demanded bold action. When Theodore Roosevelt took office following William McKinley's assassination in 1901, reclamation received such a high priority from this enthusiastic conservationist that in less than ten months Congress passed the landmark Reclamation Act of 1902.[73]

The legislation clearly reflected the desire of the irrigation crusaders for a national plan centrally administered and financed to promote small, irrigated homesteads. It authorized the Secretary of the Interior to conduct field surveys, build storage works, divert water, and withdraw from entry public land for irrigation. As a concession to the states' traditional control over water distribution, the act required the Secretary to proceed in conformity with state water laws, but it expressly limited the amount of land that a property holder could irrigate. Those filing for public land within a project could obtain homesteads ranging from 40 to 160 acres, while nearby private landowners could also secure project water, though only for 160 acres. On Congress's intent to help small farmers obtain and cultivate their own property, the law was unequivocal: "No right to the use of water for land in private ownership shall be sold for a tract exceeding 160 acres to any one landowner, and no such sale shall be made to any landowner unless he be an actual bona fide resident on such land, or . . . residing in the neighborhood."[74] The water made available with federal funds was not for absentee speculators, corporations, or other big landowners. "This bill is drawn exclusively for the protection of the settler and actual homebuilder," declared Congressman Eben Martin of South Dakota, "and every possible safeguard is made against speculative ownership and the concentration of the lands or water privileges into large holdings."[75]

Those goals prompted the inclusion of provisions stipulating that lands within a federal irrigation project would be free and that settlers would pay only for the works built to bring water directly to their fields—and those payments could be spread over time (at first ten years, but later extended when that proved impractical). As noted, adjacent lands in private ownership before a project was built could also obtain water, but only for 160 acres. Excess lands remained dry or could be sold, although not at a price inflated because of the federal project. Such protections not only assured the support of western reformers but also attracted votes needed for passage from other regions. "These lands are being opened to settlement for all the people, whether they now reside in the East, South, or West," stated Representative Oscar Underwood of Alabama. "If this policy is not undertaken now, this great Western desert will ultimately be acquired by individuals and great corporations . . . and it will be impossible to ever convert it into homestead lands for our own people or to build up the population of this Western country."[76]

To carry out the policy, the Interior Secretary created a new agency, the Reclamation Service, and charged it with constructing the first works with proceeds from western land sales; later works would be built with funds paid by settlers for construction on the earlier reclaimed lands. Within a few years the Reclamation Service discovered a major new source of revenue in the hydroelectricity generated at its dams, and in 1906 it secured congressional approval to apply those funds to irrigation costs. In later years Congress authorized even more sources of revenue, such as receipts from federal power licenses and mineral and oil leases. Thus apparently well funded and protected against speculators and great corporate and individual wealth, the Reclamation Service sent engineers throughout the West to fulfill the dream of those in California and elsewhere for a homestead of their own.

California's landless and small farmers with precarious or inadequate water rights greeted the new law as they did the other changes of the Progressive Era: with an optimism borne of a half century of frustration. Statehood had begun with a similar—indeed, more robust—sense of optimism that had both encouraged and been tempered by rapid economic development, environmental exploitation, and monopolization of land and water resources. Those developments had reflected and been encouraged by a political culture emphasizing laissez-faire and the local concentration of power and decision making. The burden of change fell heaviest on the Indians, of course, and then on the displaced Californios, the landless of all ethnic groups, and the small and would-be farmers, while leaving the wealthy land and water barons virtually unscathed except for their legal bills. Innovations such as the swampland district, the irrigation district, and the mutual water company represented at best partial advances because they required information and technologies not yet available, or sought to use local means to resolve a problem requiring centralized planning and funding. Other developments, such as prior appropriation, the hybrid California legal doctrine of water rights, and hydraulicking, benefited few at the expense of many.

With the economic cataclysms of the 1890s and the emergence of Progressivism, American political culture shifted from an emphasis on the laissez-faire principles of the Democrats to the activist government leanings of the Republicans, who captured Sacramento (and most other western and northern capitals) as well as Washington, D.C. The effect was immediate, with perhaps nothing in water-resource policy more graphically illustrating the change than the Reclamation Act, a spirited venture in centralized planning on behalf of the less fortunate and an attempt to bring about greater equity in landholding and water-use patterns. Only the future would reveal the ultimate fate of this dramatic attempt at reform.

In the meantime, still another voice began calling for public help in resolving water problems. Not surprisingly in a state that from its beginnings had been among the most urban in the country, this voice came from burgeoning metropolitan areas, which sought water for drinking, bathing, sewage, fire fighting, and industry rather than growing crops. Their demands, like those that had precipitated unrest over land and water rights in the countryside, would profoundly alter California's political and economic fabric as well as its waterscape.

4 Urban Imperialism: A Tale of Two Cities

Cities dominate modern California just as they do much of the nation and the world. In California, community living in villages, towns, and eventually vast metropolitan areas has

almost always been the norm. Indian settlements and Hispanic presidios, pueblos, missions, and rancho complexes characterized the
human landscape of pre-American California. For several decades
following the gold rush, California's population took a rural tilt,
but by the turn of the century most residents called urban areas
home, something the rest of the nation would not do until the
1920s.[1] This meant that Californians grappled early with the problems of city living. Among the most formidable issues by century's
end, especially for the fastest-growing areas, was the demand for
ever greater supplies of water.

By the 1890s, San Francisco and Los Angeles were in the vanguard
of western cities that were searching for additional water sources.
San Francisco had burst forth almost overnight as the West's greatest metropolis in the wake of the gold rush, mushrooming from a
hamlet of some 300 in 1846 to a bustling urban area of 56,000 in
1860 to over 340,000 by the turn of the century, when it became
the nation's eighth-largest city. Mining, freighting, the railroads, as
well as banking, manufacturing, shipping, and a magnificent harbor,
combined to make San Francisco "The City" to most Californians.
In the early 1900s Los Angeles began to challenge its northern rival
for preeminence as mild climate, fertile soils, the availability of a
vast coastal plain that invited urban expansion, good transportation
networks, and abundant oil discoveries worked their magic on the
southland. From about 1,600 residents at the time of statehood
(1850), Los Angeles jumped to 100,000 by century's end, and then
during the second decade of the twentieth century bypassed San
Francisco to become the state's most populous city.[2]

The rapid development of both areas accompanied and encouraged a vigorous boosterism in which local leaders, particularly
those in Los Angeles, viewed growth as an end in itself and water
as the chief means of sustaining it. The result was a new kind of imperialism—an urban water imperialism led by public, not private,
entities which aimed at controlling local and then ever more distant
water sources, and relying for strength on a carefully orchestrated
use of government power and the public treasury. Both cities re-

flected the Progressive Era emphasis on activist government, attracted national admiration as well as scorn, inspired urban areas elsewhere to imitate their example, and prepared the way for the massive federal and state hydraulic works of the later twentieth century.

Los Angeles: From Hispanic Village to American City

L OS ANGELES outdid San Francisco in both imagination and aggressiveness in pioneering the new imperialism even though it got off to a much slower start following the American conquest. For some two decades, it remained primarily as it had begun: an agricultural village of irrigation ditches, vineyards, orchards, and assorted field crops. Ultimate authority over the water system, it must be emphasized, was public. Inheriting unusual powers, for an American local government, from its Spanish and Mexican predecessors, the town council established by the state legislature in 1850 succeeded "to all the rights, claims, and powers of the Pueblo" and thereby continued directly to control the community's water system. In traditional Hispanic fashion it appointed a *zanjero* to issue permits, regulate water distribution, and collect special water taxes and fees. With the help of deputies, the zanjero maintained an Indian labor force (nearly all the Indians, as before the conquest, were working off fines) to keep open and expand the network of canals that by the 1870s served about 4,500 acres. "Extending irrigation is of the most vital importance to the future of . . . Los Angeles, and which requires the earnest attention of this body," proclaimed the council in 1873, echoing what had long before become conventional wisdom among residents.[3]

In little more than a decade, however, commerce had supplanted agriculture as the most crucial activity within the city's boundaries, though water remained the acknowledged means for sustaining the new prosperity as it had the old. Rapid population growth lay behind the change. From a community of only 4,300 in 1860, Los Angeles's inhabitants nearly tripled by 1880 and then increased to more than 50,000 ten years later in the wake of railroad competition for transcontinental passengers. A real estate boom turned passengers into settlers who made their living in shops, mercantile establishments, small manufacturing firms, transportation, and a variety of other service and commercial enterprises.[4]

The transformation in the economy received official notice. "The necessity of irrigation within the city limits," announced the mayor in 1887, "does not now exist to any great extent as most of the vineyards or orchards have been subdivided and made into residence sites for our rapidly increasing population."[5] Thus began that process, the replacement of farmland by homes and businesses, which continues into the twenty-first century to be the core process, widely deplored, of California life. This shift in land-use patterns had been preceded nearly two decades earlier by the abandonment of public canals (except for agriculture) and the inauguration of private enterprise as the agency to supply water for domestic needs. It was a decision reflecting the pro–private enterprise values of the newcomers and their desire, in harmony with the traditional Jeffersonian distrust of activist government, to avoid expanding the powers of the town council to deal with new and pressing needs.

The growing population demanded a more efficient and sanitary network of covered pipes rather than the open ditches where the menace from pollution was ever present. Not even the availability of allegedly good-quality water sold door-to-door in jugs and buckets and later from horse-drawn water carts quieted fears or lessened residents' desires for a new and safer domestic system, one that could also offer fire protection in a town where adobe structures were giving way to wood-frame buildings. Threats from disease and a smallpox epidemic in 1863 forcefully underscored the need for action. "The dread disease worked its ravages especially among the Mexicans and Indians, as many as a dozen of them dying in a single day," recalled Harris Newmark about the smallpox

A Los Angeles wheel for lifting water from the river. (Courtesy of Security Pacific Historical Photograph Collection, Los Angeles Public Library)

outbreak, "and these sufferers and their associates being under no quarantine, and even bathing *ad libitum* in the *zanjas,* the pest spread alarmingly." Even before the epidemic, the city had turned to private enterprise for a solution. While retaining direct control over the agricultural ditches for which the zanja system seemed adequate, the common council for the first time in 1857 granted a franchise to William G. Dryden "to supply the city with water."[6]

Change did not assure improvement. The council ended up contracting for short periods with several different firms, whose massive wheels to lift water from the river fell victim to floods and whose wooden pipes leaked more water than they carried, creating

The water wheel on the zanja madre *of Los Angeles. (Courtesy of Security Pacific Historical Photograph Collection, Los Angeles Public Library)*

mud holes in the streets and so embarrassing one of the early contractors that he committed suicide in the town council chambers. The council, mightily embarrassed itself and anxious to be rid of the problem, redoubled efforts to identify a stable firm, and in 1868 it believed it had done so with the Los Angeles City Water Company. The council awarded the company a thirty-year lease in exchange for an annual fee of $1,500 (lowered to $400 two years later) and promises of iron pipes, fire hydrants, reservoirs, and free water for all public buildings.[7]

Even prior to the change from agricultural village to commercial city, local leaders had concluded, in a decision carrying within it the heart of the Los Angeles story for the next century and a half, that their community required not only a more secure water supply but also a larger one if it were to become more than a humdrum place on a map. They realized that the town was not developing in a vacuum, for as it grew so did the surrounding countryside—and often at a faster rate. In 1860 and 1870 Los Angeles County had more than twice as many residents as the city; in 1880, more than triple the number; and in 1890, still twice as many. The county was considerably larger in size, of course, but large numbers of new-comers settled in areas like the San Fernando Valley that were also dependent upon the Los Angeles River for watering orchards, live-stock, and field crops. As in Spanish and Mexican times, the presence of these upstream settlers after the American takeover aroused concern because they diverted water that city officials believed Los Angeles needed for its future growth and because, as well, their ac-tions threatened an immediate source of municipal revenue. For years Los Angeles had used its diversion system to sell water not needed within the city limits to nearby customers. It was an ideal arrangement that allowed the city to profit during times of water surplus while also assuring a standby supply to meet droughts and the demands of future growth. By the early 1870s, community leaders, openly fearful that upstream diversions threatened this arrangement, launched the first of several bold plans that would transform Los Angeles into the nation's most famous water seeker and the state's (and West's) preeminent metropolis.

Legerdemain and the Pueblo Water Right

In 1874 the city began a campaign to control the Los Angeles River by declaring war on upstream water users. It did so by turn-

Original reservoir of hewn planks atop a brick foundation. Los Angeles plaza, c. 1860. (Courtesy of Los Angeles Department of Water and Power)

ing to the courts, which nationally were beginning to bestir themselves and take a more active, interventionist role in public economic affairs by unlimbering and putting to use that ancient and powerful judicial weapon, the injunction.[8] Essentially it was an order from the king, or "court," to someone to cease and desist from doing something not illegal by statutory law but harmful to someone else and, therefore, illegal under the case law (that is, court-made law) embodied in the venerable law of equity. By reaching for this weapon, Los Angeles was helping to initiate that historic swing, in water law matters, away from the democratic process as found in elected legislatures and to the courts, which to the present day remain peculiarly the source of much of the most important governing law in water management.

Los Angeles singled out for a test case Leon Baldwin, owner of extensive irrigated acreage formerly part of Rancho Los Feliz, located just northwest of the city. In seeking an injunction to shut down Baldwin's operations and those of several smaller irrigators in the area, Los Angeles faced a formidable obstacle. Though state water law lacked clarity and invited attorneys to use their imagination, the two major doctrines evolving in California case (not statutory) law—prior appropriation and riparianism—seemed to challenge rather than support the city's strategy. As noted in chapter two, Los Angeles had begun diverting water before the rancho owners, rather latecomers on the scene (most in the 1840s), initiated irrigation, but current case law permitted latecomers to take water from a river if no one else objected and even recognized that they could establish a firm right under the principle of adverse prescription if the objections were too long (more than five years) in coming.[9] Hispanic law had also acknowledged that long use (more than ten years) could result in the establishment of a right where none existed before. Since the lands owned by Baldwin had been irrigated without objection long before he had purchased them in 1871 and even before the rancho's creation during the Mexican era in 1843, the law as conventionally understood by the courts seemed to favor him—and, ominously for the city, others like him with property long irrigated from the river.

A skillful city attorney devised an argument that at least theoretically met the challenge. John Godfrey possessed not only imagination but also an almost legendary reputation for persuasiveness. That talent he demonstrated most dramatically one day in rowdy El Monte where he went to visit the wife of a close friend who had recently been murdered. After leaving the widow, he encountered

*Main Street in Los Angeles, looking south from Temple Street, 1885.
(Courtesy of Los Angeles City Archives)*

a crowd about to lynch the killer. "Charity for the widow and or-
phans," he shouted, "should be considered before justice for the
killer." With that, he passed his large hat among the crowd, which
slowly dispersed.[10] In the sedate job of a city attorney, his goal was
acquiring for his community all the water in the adjacent river. He
knew that the Treaty of Guadalupe Hidalgo obligated the United
States to recognize Mexican property rights in the territories acquired from Mexico, and one of those rights, he decided, was a special pueblo water right. "Pueblo de Los Angeles," Godfrey announced to the local district court in July 1874, "was, from its first
settlement, the owner of . . . all of the water flowing in . . . [the]
river."[11]

   This was an extraordinarily audacious claim, for it flew in the
face of a basic principle of the appropriation doctrine, riparianism,
and all Western systems of water law dating back to antiquity: no
one owned water flowing in a natural stream or river. "The right is
not in the *corpus* of the water," declared the California supreme

court in its first decision dealing with a water controversy in 1853, but "to its reasonable use." Put simply, the right existed in *using* water: "It is laid down by our law writers, that the right of property in water is *usufructuary*."[12] The forty-four residents of Los Angeles in 1781 could not have conceivably been using all the river's water at the time of "first settlement," and Godfrey made no attempt to prove that they had done so then or thereafter. Instead, he contended that Spanish and, later, Mexican law had given the town title to the river, and he introduced scores of documents as well as testimony from longtime residents as purported proof. About the same time, he urged Los Angeles to advance its cause by seeking statutory help in the legislature, which responded immediately in 1874 with a law approving amendments to the city charter, one of which vested in Los Angeles the "exclusive right to all of the water flowing in the River of Los Angeles."[13] The statute delighted city fathers and marked the first of numerous later occasions when the state would support Los Angeles's quest for water.

Still, the new law meant nothing if the courts chose to ignore or overrule it, and that was precisely the goal of Baldwin, his fellow defendants, and their attorneys. They vigorously denied the existence of such a pueblo right and emphasized their rights as riparians and as claimants under the law of adverse prescription. They pointed out that Los Angeles had never interfered with irrigation on their property until now and had even specifically approved diversions there as far back as 1816. Pueblo officials had done so under the mistaken impression that the site lay within the town's boundaries and was under its jurisdiction. Later the town council had not rescinded that approval or protested the diversions when a rancho was created there in 1843 or when the U.S. government in 1858 had issued a patent to the rancho owners indicating that no part of the property lay within the town's boundaries. The defendants concluded their rejoinder to Godfrey by going on the offensive and taking a sharp slap at Los Angeles for its "inadequate and antediluvian water works." If the city made "proper expenditures and improvements," they scolded, it could "irrigate all of the lands within the city limits and four times as much below the city limits." However, this was secondary to the defendants' major contention: They, as riparians, prescriptive users, and successors in title to the former rancho lands, were entitled to "a fair proportion of water"—the amount they were "now so using."[14]

To attorney Godfrey's deep disappointment, the court ruled against him. Neither the lower court (on two occasions) nor, in 1879, the state supreme court was moved by the claims or evidence he presented. The supreme court all but dismissed him out of hand in an opinion that did not fill a page: "The claim set up by the city in this action—that the city is the owner of the *corpus* of the water in the Los Angeles River—finds no support in the evidence." Rebuffed in court, Los Angeles finally got what it wanted from Baldwin, but only after five years and a payment in hard cash. In 1884 it purchased his diversion site and interests for $50,000 in gold—a handsome price for the time, though one that did nothing to advance the city's pueblo right claim.[15]

Despite the inauspicious beginning, Los Angeles officials pressed forward aggressively, only this time they took direct action rather than relying on the courts when they singled out another group of landowners on former Rancho Los Feliz property. In May 1879, just four months after the loss to Baldwin, the city destroyed diversion works on the property and, in a move that clearly revealed its preoccupation with future growth and present revenue, immediately offered to reopen the canals if the owners would pay for the water "upon the same terms" as the city "sold water to other parties."[16] Outraged, the landowners refused the blackmail offer and sought a court order to regain control of their diversion facilities.

The local court sided with them, yet it did so in a peculiar opinion that left them uneasy and vulnerable. The court agreed that they, like Baldwin earlier, were "riparian owners . . . entitled to a reasonable use of waters"—the amount they had been using when Los Angeles intervened—and that they had "always been in exclusive . . . control of their ditches," a ruling that seemed to imply that they had never been subject to the city's jurisdiction. On the other hand, the court also appeared to give credence to the city's pueblo right claim when it stated that Los Angeles, earlier as a pueblo and later as an American city, had "at all times exercised control of and claimed the exclusive right to use the [river's] waters," and that this authority had been "duly recognized . . . by the owners of the land." [17] Godfrey was pleased with this finding but dismayed with the court's decision to award water to the landowners. The court seemed to have accepted his fundamental contention but not its logical conclusion. If the city had an "exclusive right," Godfrey reasoned, then it should be able to deny others use of the river's waters. He appealed the decision.

When the upstream landowners appeared before the state supreme court, they acknowledged that they, too, found the lower court's reasoning confusing. "We confess that there may be some difficulty in interpreting the findings so as to make them consistent." Nonetheless, they struggled resolutely to do so, drawing special attention to parts of the earlier opinion that seemed to favor them and undercut any alleged pueblo right. In particular, they emphasized the lower court's statement that the diversion canals had "always" been in the "exclusive control" of the landowners and their predecessors, thus challenging the notion that Los Angeles's rights extended over the entire river. The city's authority over water, they contended, had never reached beyond the town's boundaries, and although Los Angeles's attorneys introduced numerous Spanish and Mexican documents, they produced no law or decree from those governments indicating otherwise. Rather, in citing documentary evidence of their own, they sought to undermine any reasonable belief in a pueblo right. As added support, they stressed the precedent set by the *Baldwin* court's rejection of the right's existence. [18]

The supreme court was less concerned with precedent and evidence than with the lack of "harmony" in the lower court's decision. In 1881 in *Feliz v. Los Angeles,* it satisfied its own sense of symmetry by overruling the lower court and allowing Los Angeles to shut down the upstream diversion facilities. In doing so, the justices skirted the pueblo right issue and avoided reversing the *Baldwin* decision. That is, they behaved in the classic fashion clung to by Anglo-American courts: They defined the issue before them as narrowly as possible, thus focusing on what absolutely had to be decided and not ranging beyond it into irrelevancies. By this means, the courts kept the basic principle of *stare decisis* (respect for precedent, or "the [prior] decision stands") and therefore their moral authority alive, as it would not be if they regularly made large shifts in direction. The court in this case grounded its decision on the city's contention that "all the owners of land on the stream, from its source," had "recognized" the town's "right to all the waters of the river" and had "dug their ditches" with the "permission and consent of the municipal authorities." In short, acknowledgment of the city's right, not any Spanish or Mexican law, was the decisive issue in the court's reasoning. "We have not examined the rights of the defendant as they existed under Spanish and Mexican laws, applicable to pueblos, for the findings in this case render such examination unnecessary." [19]

This reluctance disappointed city officials, and they became further disgruntled when the court, in almost an afterthought at the end of its opinion, violated its own disclaimer about not defining the city's rights by specifying a right Los Angeles did *not* have. "We do not intend to be understood as holding, nor do we hold, that the city has the right at any time to dispose of the water for use upon lands situated without the [city] limits, to the injury of . . . other owners of land bordering on the river." [20] In short, Los Angeles could not sell water to customers outside the city if this deprived downstream riparians of a needed supply. With this caveat, the court struck directly at what had become a steady source of municipal revenue and also clearly limited Los Angeles's grand claim to an unrestricted right to "all the waters" of the river.

Because of the court's refusal to define clearly the pueblo right, there was always the possibility that the claim might be effectively negated in a future ruling. City officials decided not to press their luck and backed off until the late 1880s and early 1890s when spiraling population growth, renewed dreams of metropolitan grandeur, and occasional years of below-average precipitation prompted renewed court action.

The city's initial response to water-short years was to push additional levees and dams into place to trap as much of the river's flow as possible, and to put in underground catchment galleries where the river's waters tended to pond, above and below ground, at its "narrows" upstream. At the narrows was the subterranean rock formation, or sill, which held back the waters of the aquifer underlying the San Fernando Valley, in effect the underground reservoir that for so long had released its waters downstream, in and below the river's bed, to supply Los Angeles.

The construction efforts and increased rainfall often created a surplus, prompting officials to follow their earlier policy of selling it to customers outside the city limits. When this resulted in cutting off the supply to people downstream from the city in the 1890s, it constituted a direct challenge to the *Feliz* decision. Officials now, however, had reason to believe the courts might side with them and also substantially reenforce their pueblo claim. The cause for their optimism was the famous decision in *Lux* v. *Haggin,* handed down in 1886 by the state supreme court. Although *Lux* dealt primarily with the conflict between the riparian and appropriation doctrines, it had also touched on the pueblo water right, noting that the legislature had recognized such a right in Los Angeles and suggesting that it might be almost unlimited in scope: "It appears . . . [a] riparian proprietor could not . . . interfere with the common use or destiny which a pueblo on the stream should . . . [give] to the waters."[21] These remarks, while incidental to the case and thus not legally binding, nonetheless buoyed the spirits of Los Angeles officials as they began selling surplus water, knowing full well their action would not go unchallenged.

The challenge came in the early 1890s, and after wending its way through the legal system produced in 1895 perhaps the most important decision in the history of Los Angeles. In *Vernon Irrigation Co.* v. *Los Angeles,* the state supreme court addressed squarely for the first time the pueblo right question. There was indeed such a right, concluded the court, and it guaranteed Los Angeles "all the waters of the river"—a prior and paramount right to as much water as would ever be needed. City officials were ecstatic, though their enthusiasm was tempered with one disappointment. While the lower court in the case had upheld the city's renewed attempt to sell surplus water to outsiders, the supreme court ruled otherwise: Los Angeles's "right could be asserted only to the amount needed to supply the wants of the inhabitants."[22] That qualification was disconcerting but the city took consolation in knowing that, while others could use surplus water, when the city needed it, the city could have it. More importantly, the attention given the pueblo right by the court established the city's claim as strongly as could reasonably be expected.

In arriving at its decision, the court had examined numerous documents relating to Spanish and Mexican history and law. Virtually all of this material, however, had been supplied only by Los Angeles. The opposing attorneys presented almost no documentary evidence challenging the city's interpretation of the pueblo claim because they considered such material irrelevant. They argued that the case should be decided on riparian and appropriation principles, insisting that if Los Angeles had ever held such a pueblo right, the city had forfeited it by not asserting it before the U.S. Land Commission, which in the 1850s had the responsibility for determining rights claimed under the Treaty of Guadalupe Hidalgo. "All the evidence offered [by Los Angeles] to prove what is the law of Spain and Mexico, or of California, is, if it is correct, useless, and if it is not correct, it is worse than useless," declared Vernon's attorneys. "These are the same documents that were introduced in the case of the City of Los Angeles vs. Baldwin, and which the Court dismissed with the simple statement that the proposition that the City of Los Angeles owned the waters of the Los Angeles river [sic] finds no support in the evidence."[23]

The attorneys adopted this strategy in part because their client, unlike the opponents of Los Angeles in the *Baldwin* and *Feliz* cases, did not claim rights dating to the pre-American period. The practical result of their strategy, however, was to give an edge to Los Angeles, for once the court decided to focus on the pueblo right question, much of the evidence readily available to it in the arguments and briefs presented by both sides supported Los Angeles's position. The court could have consulted the voluminous *Baldwin* and *Feliz* records cited by Vernon's attorneys, but to do so would have reflected a sincere desire to understand Hispanic water law and practice. As legal scholar Peter Reich has argued, the judges had no such desire. Like Californians generally at the time, they were caught up in a popular culture that romanticized the state's Spanish past—its everyday life, architecture, relations with Indians, institutions, and much more—seeing it not as it was but rather as it ought to be.[24] The judges in *Vernon* were less interested in Spanish legal reality than in what the Los Angeles city council, the state legislature, and now they affirmed *should* exist: a pueblo water right allowing Los Angeles to become a great city.

Spanish and Mexican law did, of course, emphasize the preference of community over individual rights, but that preference was neither rigid nor absolute. More importantly, Hispanic law did not vest exclusive rights to a stream in a single community, not even in the first pueblo established in an area. In effect, the *Vernon* decision transformed the Hispanic preference for community rights into a rigid formula favoring a specific community: Los Angeles. In so doing, it issued an ominous warning to all others along the river—not only to private property owners but also to the new towns that had emerged during the last decade. During the years immediately following *Vernon,* the courts affirmed that the right extended to the vast reservoir (with a storage capacity in excess of 900,000 acre-feet) which lay beneath the San Fernando Valley and fed the Los Angeles River.[25] There would be future challenges to the city, but the *Vernon* decision constituted the bedrock for Los Angeles's claim to all the water of a five-hundred-square-mile area.

The city celebrated the 1895 victory by annexing in the same year Highland Park, a 904-acre tract on the northeast. When doubts

LOS ANGELES CITY ANNEXATIONS 1851~1920

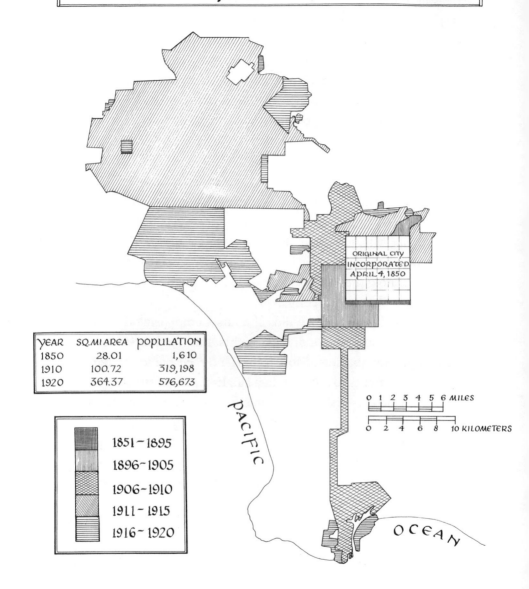

ORIGINAL CITY
INCORPORATED
APRIL 4, 1850

YEAR	SQ.MI AREA	POPULATION
1850	28.01	1,610
1910	100.72	319,198
1920	364.37	576,673

PACIFIC

OCEAN

0 1 2 3 4 5 6 MILES

0 2 4 6 8 10 KILOMETERS

1851~1895
1896~1905
1906~1910
1911~1915
1916~1920

surfaced that the restriction of water use to the city limits might mean the old pueblo boundaries of four square leagues, Los Angeles persuaded the state supreme court to quash those fears in 1899 by winning from it, in the case of *Los Angeles v. Pomeroy,* a ruling that the pueblo right applied to areas annexed by the city. Expanding the city's boundaries was at once seen as a way of justifying—indeed requiring—more water to build an even more magnificent metropolis. As one official noted, "If you don't get the water, you won't need it."[26] The roots of empire had been established.

Girding for Expansion: Municipal Control

Visions of greatness meant nothing unless the water rights were accompanied by actual control of the supply itself. The city had bargained away its authority over the now all-important domestic supply in 1868 in the thirty-year lease to the Los Angeles City Water Company. It was a move regretted almost as soon as it had been taken. Even that decision had been hotly contested and approved by the city council on a split vote of four to two. Critics appeared immediately, and as the lease neared its expiration date, they included virtually the entire community. By then the principal objections were to excessively high rates and poor service. While the firm had profited handsomely ($10 in profits for every $15 collected annually from each household, according to one survey), fire hydrants often malfunctioned and water pressure was either nonexistent or so low, complained an exasperated resident, that "the supply is grossly inadequate for ordinary domestic uses."[27]

More alarming was the discovery that the company had begun threatening the city's pueblo claim. A portion of the water supplied by the company came from springs located on its property and not connected to the Los Angeles River system. To increase the supply from the springs the company secretly drilled a tunnel tapping into the river and then created a new corporation and transferred the springs to it.[28] With this move, the company thought it had found a way to assure itself a future water supply regardless of what happened to the lease. When the maneuver became public, the city's decision to let the lease expire in 1898 became a foregone conclusion.

So, too, was Los Angeles's determination never again to repeat its experience with leasing. In 1903 residents approved an amendment to the city charter specifying that "no . . . water rights now or hereafter owned . . . shall be conveyed, leased, or otherwise disposed of, without the assent of two-thirds of the qualified electors"—a barrier set high enough to virtually assure municipal control in perpetuity.[29] It was a commitment made all the stronger because it reflected firsthand personal dissatisfaction with private service rather than being solely the product of reform advocated by Populists, Socialists, Progressives, and others urging municipal ownership of public utilities in these years. The city's action also mirrored strong distaste for permitting something as fundamentally important as a water system to be buffeted by partisan politics.

Here the electorate shared the emerging Progressive movement's emphasis on commission government—turning complex issues like water and transportation over to commissions of right-minded citizens capable of gathering necessary information, drawing on the advice of scientific experts, and reaching appropriate decisions free from popular caprice. The same charter revision making it all but impossible to lease or sell the city's water rights also established a five-member Board of Water Commissioners appointed by the mayor with the approval of the city council. Their terms were for four years, but once in office they never had to stand for election, and their control over policy, over the naming of the superintendent responsible for operating the system, and over funds generated by water rates became formidable, though by no means absolute. They had to seek council approval for rates and for permission to put bond issues before the people, who had the final word on major projects. They could also be forced to resign—and were, especially in the 1930s as a result of disagreements over public power policies and charges of corruption—or to fire subordinates when public pressure became sufficiently intense. Still, they also achieved in the new charter a significant measure of isolation from the public in whose name they thereafter claimed to act.[30]

Thus, by shortly after the turn of the century, Los Angeles had established strong municipal control over its water system and rights to all the water of the Los Angeles River Basin. This victory at home soon seemed as pyrrhic as it had been initially impressive. Fully confident about Los Angeles becoming the West's greatest metropolis, city leaders had already begun welcoming with open arms nearby towns and communities eager for annexation since it brought them access to the area's largest dependable water supply. Some adjacent areas had joined their futures to Los Angeles's even before the legal and municipal ownership issues had been fully resolved. As early as 1900 the city's original four square leagues (some twenty-seven square miles) had nearly doubled (to forty-three square miles), while the population, as a result of the annexations and the arrival of newcomers, also doubled during the preceding decade to 100,000. When the population nearly doubled again during the next four years at the same time that groundwater in local aquifers was on the decline, the superintendent of the new municipal water system startled the public by announcing that the Los Angeles River, despite its vast capacity, could not long support the city at its current growth rate. "The time has come," he proclaimed in 1904, "when we shall have to supplement its flow from some other source."[31] It was a declaration with monumental consequences, opening a chapter in Los Angeles history still charged with controversy.

The Owens Valley Caper

The superintendent of the water system making the announcement was William Mulholland. His central role in Los Angeles water development is as clear as his beginnings were inauspicious. After a brief visit as a merchant seaman in 1874, he arrived to stay in 1877 at the age of twenty-two, a penniless Irish immigrant. Taking a job as a common laborer, he tended ditches for the Los Angeles

William Mulholland. (Courtesy of Los Angeles Department of Water and Power)

City Water Company then battling the city over its lease arrangement. A sober, single-minded man with an enormous capacity for hard work, he soon caught the attention of company officials— though in a rather peculiar way. As the firm's president was making an inspection one day, he noticed the young man's vigorous efforts with a shovel. Stopping his carriage, he asked Mulholland his name and what he was doing. "It's none of your damned business!"

came the shouted reply with no glance upward at the questioner, who went quietly on his way. When Mulholland learned a short time later to whom he had spoken, he fully expected to be fired and went to pick up his pay and quit before the president returned to the office. He arrived too late. The president was already there, but instead of firing him he promoted Mulholland to foreman as a reward for dedication to his job.[32]

Mulholland's capacity for work was matched by a quick mind, an extraordinary memory, and an eagerness to learn all he could about the company and its technical operations. Within eight years he was superintendent, a position to which he was reappointed in 1902 when the water-distribution facilities were purchased by the city following the expiration of the company's lease. It is testimony to Mulholland's brilliance and dedication that the city would hire him when the company that he served was held in such low esteem. In the public mind he was separated from the company's owners, who were viewed as more interested in profits than in fulfilling their obligations and in allowing Mulholland to do the best of which he was capable. This was a perception that gained wide support during the negotiations between the city and water company over the price to be paid for the company's facilities. To the chagrin of his employers, Mulholland frequently told the city to offer less for certain sections of the system that he knew to be overpriced. There was also a more practical reason why the city secured his services. He had committed to memory not only the company's entire distribution system of pipes, gate valves, hydrants, pumps, and ditches, but also the details of its complex operation. Little existed on paper, for Mulholland was a notoriously poor record keeper and seldom at his desk. The city almost had to hire him in order to understand and maintain the system it had acquired.[33]

Once in control, Mulholland, with the support of the Board of Water Commissioners, issued a flurry of orders that soon made Los Angeles's water department the envy of the state. He began by cutting water rates and then installing meters throughout the city, thereby encouraging customers to avoid wasting water while at the same time generating additional revenue for rebuilding the out-moded system for a growing population. He was so successful that he even produced a profit: some $1.5 million for the city in four years. Such achievements (and others followed) earned him wide public respect and allowed him to create a virtual fiefdom within city government. They also brought financial rewards. Mulholland eventually became the highest-paid public official not only in the city but also in the state—perhaps the surest measure of water's importance to Los Angeles.[34] Not surprisingly, he won an immediate sympathetic hearing when he proclaimed the need to obtain additional water for Los Angeles.

At the time of Mulholland's announcement in 1904, he had already decided on the probable new source of water: the Owens River, some 235 miles to the north on the eastern side of the Sierra Nevada. He kept that information to himself, the Board of Water Commissioners, and only a few other city officials from whom he secured permission to launch a secret investigation. He wanted to do nothing that would precipitate a stampede of speculators into the valley causing land values to skyrocket. The idea of an Owens Valley aqueduct was not original with him but came from Fred Eaton, a former Los Angeles mayor and before that an engineer, first with the Los Angeles City Water Company and then with the city. Since the 1890s Eaton had advocated a gravity canal from the Owens Valley, an idea that Mulholland had initially considered unrealistic. "We have enough water here in the [Los Angeles] river to supply the city for the next fifty years," he told Eaton in 1893. "You are wrong," Eaton replied. "You have not lived in this country as long as I have. I was born here and have seen dry years, years that you know nothing about. Wait and see."[35]

As early as 1901 the Los Angeles growth rate had convinced Mulholland that the city would need more water if it were to become the metropolis envisaged by local boosters. At that time he had settled on no specific source, studying at least five alternatives, before finally targeting the Owens River for a more careful investigation and then persuading the Board of Water Commissioners, the

Fred Eaton. (Courtesy of Security Pacific Historical Photograph Collection, Los Angeles Public Library)

mayor, and other city leaders to endorse his decision. Water from Owens Valley, he believed, could support a population of two million, some ten times the present number of Los Angeles residents, and also allow the city's "boundaries . . . [to] be greatly extended."[36]

Mulholland's choice of the Owens Valley derived largely from the booster mentality that he shared with other city leaders, but

Eaton's enthusiasm rested primarily on hopes of personal enrichment. While Mulholland was still trying to decide where to go for additional water, Eaton began quietly securing options on land, with its associated water rights, in the Owens Valley with the intention of persuading the city to build an aqueduct in exchange for half the water. He intended to distribute his half of the supply to people outside the city limits. That scheme failed when he could not attract sufficient capital to secure all the necessary water rights, when the city objected to a joint venture, and when the U.S. Reclamation Service announced its strong disapproval. The Reclamation Service, which had launched an investigation for an Owens Valley project of its own and had withdrawn all public lands in the area (that is, removed the possibility of their being transferred into private hands), vowed to fight any undertaking not publicly owned and controlled. Reclamation officials, however, because of budgetary constraints, incomplete studies, and sympathy for Los Angeles's water need, had not fully committed themselves to a federal project and left open the possibility of withdrawing in favor of the city. They left no doubt, however, as to their position about public ownership at a confidential meeting with Mulholland and Eaton in November 1904. "The Reclamation Service . . . could not aid the City of Los Angeles unless the project was exclusively a municipal one."[37] When city officials promised that it would be solely a Los Angeles undertaking, the Reclamation Service shared its preliminary studies with Mulholland.

Eaton now changed his tactics, offering to transfer to Los Angeles at cost the land and water rights he had secured and tendering his services as the city's agent in obtaining the remaining rights needed to acquire the valley's water for the aqueduct. When Mulholland's own investigations confirmed Owens Valley as the ideal water source, Eaton's offer won ready acceptance by Mulholland and city leaders. To them, the arrangement seemed a bargain, for it removed Eaton as a middleman, transferred his rights to the city at no markup in price, and secured the services of a person with first-hand knowledge of the valley. What Eaton did not tell Mulholland

Source of the Owens River at Big Springs. (Courtesy of Los Angeles Department of Water and Power)

and the others was that he had another plan for making money—and his arrangement with the city would be ideal for promoting that scheme. It would also terribly exacerbate Los Angeles's relationship with the Owens Valley.

Thus far, utmost secrecy had been maintained about the city's deal with Eaton and the decision to secure water rights in the

Owens Valley. Not a secret, however, was the investigation being conducted by the Reclamation Service into the feasibility of an irrigation project in the valley. That question had serious implications for the city's plans. In the summer of 1903 residents of the valley had warmly welcomed the arrival of Joseph B. Lippincott, the Reclamation Service supervising engineer for the southwestern United States. What they did not know was that Lippincott was a man with sharply divided loyalties. Besides being on the government payroll, he had a prosperous private consulting practice, and his biggest client was the city of Los Angeles; what's more, Fred Eaton was one of his closest friends. With hardly a nod to the obvious conflict of interest, Lippincott, as soon as he learned of the city's plans, decided that the valley's water should go to Los Angeles rather than to a Reclamation Service project. Although later claiming not to have known about Eaton's special arrangement with the city, he quietly gave his friend access in March 1905 to public land office records that enabled him to obtain options to purchase for Los Angeles (though his being agent for Los Angeles was not yet publicly known) the additional land and water rights needed to supply an aqueduct. Lippincott, for his part, while not telling his superiors all that he was doing on behalf of Los Angeles, revealed enough about his financial ties, sympathies, and actions to alarm them. As historian Abraham Hoffman notes, they warned him that he "courted conflict-of-interest charges and rendered the Reclamation Service vulnerable to scandal." Their failure to take stronger action, however, revealed their own equivocal attitude about a federal project in the valley.[38]

Not all Eaton's purchases were made as a public-spirited resident of Los Angeles. He had a plan for recouping that hoped-for personal enrichment that had disappeared with the collapse of his original scheme. He secured an option on a ranch containing the major portion of the only feasible reservoir site in the valley. He knew the land's value, and he did not intend to sell it at cost. Indeed, he did not intend to sell it at all. Instead, he offered the city a "perpetual right and easement" to build a small dam on the reservoir site and

Los Angeles Board of Water Commissioners, 1905. Left to right: John J. Fay, Jr., John M. Elliott, Moses H. Sherman, William Mead, and Fred L. Baker. (Courtesy of Security Pacific Historical Photograph Collection, Los Angeles Public Library)

half the ranch on which it lay for $450,000, an amount approximately double the property's value. He did not want to sell the land, because if Los Angeles did not build a reservoir—and at the time the city had no plans to do so—or delayed years before building one, he planned to use the area for raising cattle. If the city would not accept his offer, then he would offer the land to others, an offer which if taken (and Eaton indicated that he had a group of eager buyers) would jeopardize plans for a project wholly municipally owned and controlled.

When Mulholland learned of Eaton's offer—in reality, a demand—he was outraged, "dealing with him at swords' points and arms' lengths" over the matter. After two days of wrangling in June 1905, Mulholland capitulated. Although Los Angeles had no present desire for a reservoir, Mulholland could not rule out the necessity of one in the future. Moreover, with Los Angeles in possession of the reservoir rights, the city would control all important valley links in the proposed aqueduct and also satisfy the Reclamation Service demand for a publicly owned project. City possession of the reservoir site would, in addition, essentially quash any lingering possibility of a Reclamation Service project in the valley. To develop such a project would require the federal government to condemn Los Angeles's rights through eminent domain, a move that city leaders believed would be a political impossibility. Thus, in the view of Mulholland and the Board of Water Commissioners, Los Angeles had no choice but to accept Eaton's terms. "There was a fear," water commissioner John M. Elliott later explained, "that if other parties obtained the rights of the . . . reservoir they might, in the future, interfere with the City's water supply, and . . . for that reason alone, if for no other, it was wise for us to take every precaution to protect the City in the future." [39]

The city acted hastily on Eaton's offer because the secrecy that it had so zealously maintained was beginning to break down, primarily as a result of suspicions aroused in the Owens Valley by Eaton's purchases and by the frequent appearance together there of Eaton and Lippincott. The prying questions of valley residents began coming at a time when some key land and water rights remained to be secured by the city. While Eaton and Lippincott fended off challenges about possible wrongdoing, Mulholland himself raced to the Owens Valley and obtained options on all the remaining land needed to supply the aqueduct. On July 29, 1905, came his announcement to the Board of Water Commissioners: "The last spike has been driven" and "the deal by which Los Angeles city becomes the owner . . . of the purest snow water has been nailed." Later the same day the *Los Angeles Times* broke the secrecy

that had shrouded the affair with the headline: "TITANIC PROJ-
ECT TO GIVE CITY A RIVER."

An Aqueduct for the Future

Despite the hoopla, two major hurdles to an Owens Valley aqueduct still remained. First, the federal government had to give its approval. Los Angeles's purchase of the reservoir site had effectively
derailed any realistic hope for a Reclamation Service project in the
valley, but the city could not go forward without Washington's permission to build the aqueduct across federal lands lying between
Los Angeles and the Owens River. The other obstacle was money.
Mulholland had to raise funds—nearly $25 million, an enormous
amount at the time—to pay off the land options secretly acquired
by the city and to construct the aqueduct. Since money, especially
to secure firm title to the land and water rights, represented the
most pressing need, it received first attention. A more cautious person might have asked the voters for the funds in installments in order to build the aqueduct in sections and not frighten the public
with a large initial request. (This was a tactic later used with regret
by San Francisco to build its own water project.) Mulholland, however, boldly insisted on obtaining the entire amount before beginning construction and won the overwhelming support of the Board
of Water Commissioners and the city council. Then in two elections, the first in 1905 (for $1.5 million for the necessary rights) and
the second in 1907 (for $23 million for construction), the Los An-
geles electorate cast overwhelming ballots (fourteen to one and ten
to one, respectively) authorizing a total of $24.5 million in bonds to
underwrite the project.[40]

The lopsided votes reflected the public's commitment to growth
and the widespread belief that the entire community would benefit
from the project. The chamber of commerce, the Municipal League,
the Merchants and Manufacturers Association, and all leading civic
and commercial organizations threw their support behind the bond

The Los Angeles River near the narrows and looking north from Elysian Park, 1909. (Courtesy of Los Angeles City Archives)

issues. A special investigative committee of prominent business-men reported on the eve of the 1905 election that the project would give the city "as much and as good water as it will at any time require." Grumblings from private power interests about the electricity to be generated along the aqueduct and sold by the city and reports about profits to be made by unscrupulous investors in San Fernando Valley real estate were swept aside by predictions that "every acre of dry land in Los Angeles county will be provided with sufficient water." Moreover, announced the *Los Angeles Herald,* "lawns . . . could be kept perennially as green as emerald and greater Los Angeles could go on swimmingly in its metropolitan progress." To which the *Examiner* added there would be water enough to supply "a city of 2,000,000 population" and to accommodate the "annexation" of "nearby towns, thereby greatly reducing the cost" of the project.[41]

Despite such enthusiasm, Mulholland could not resist the temptation to engage in an occasional scare tactic to assure a victory that did not seem to need it. Scholars disagree on whether Los Angeles had been in a severe drought since the mid-1890s, but it seems unlikely that the city was on the verge of the "water famine" that Mulholland and other water department officials stated would occur without new water. Rainfall had averaged 11.5 inches since 1895 (about 3.5 inches below the long-term average) and 12.6 inches during the five years prior to the election. The public, nonetheless, was not regaled with rainfall data. Instead, Mulholland talked of the current "emergency" and wistfully declared: "If we could only make the people see the precarious condition in which Los Angeles stands! If we could only pound it into them!" Pound it into them he did, emphasizing that worsening of the situation could lead to immediate devastation. "If Los Angeles runs out of water for one week," he announced shortly before the election, "the city within a year will not have a population of 100,000 people." For a city with double that number of people at the time, such a statement hardly encouraged confidence in a future that did not include Owens River water. The *Los Angeles Examiner* was not much more encouraging. Based on calculations of its own, it editorialized that even if the present supply remained stable, the city would be able to accommodate fewer than 300,000 people, and at the present growth rate it would reach the maximum number in less than five years. "This indicates the need to move quickly," warned the *Examiner*.[42]

If all this were not enough, the summer heat conveniently supplied the coup de grace. The first bond election was scheduled for early September, ordinarily the hottest time of the year in Los Angeles—and 1905 was no exception. Thermometers frequently approached and exceeded 100 degrees in the weeks just prior to the balloting. The unsurprising result was increased water use and a decline in reservoir capacity that Mulholland did not allow to pass unnoticed. "This illustrates better than anything else could," he announced a week before the election, "the absolute necessity for securing a source of water supply elsewhere. We must have it." Yet Mulholland did not blame the current situation entirely on the weather since he and his staff believed that much water was "being wasted by too liberal sprinkling and irrigating of flower beds and lawns." "It will be necessary . . . to install many new meters and thus cut the waste of the city's water"—a step he soon took." [43]

Despite sharply increased rainfall during the next two years, the public's enthusiasm persisted into the 1907 bond election when, again, all the leading civic and commercial groups registered their vigorous endorsement and joined to create an Owens River Campaign Committee to direct their efforts. There were rallies, slide shows, and teas, while churches designated an "Aqueduct Day" and brochures were distributed by the thousands. Despite extraordinarily low precipitation three years later in 1910 (less than five inches), the local supplies were capable of supporting more than the 300,000 people that the *Examiner* claimed. Los Angeles's population in fact reached 500,000 before the aqueduct was completed, but in part due to Mulholland's metering and other improvements to the water system, as well as to stepped-up efforts invoking the pueblo water right and shutting down groundwater pumping and diversions outside the city limits, the city still had enough water for its needs. One point emerges clearly in all this: Los Angeles did not need the aqueduct to rescue it from immediate disaster but, rather, to allow it to grow. As William Kahrl has aptly noted: "The city needed the aqueduct, but it was a need founded in prospect." [44]

An added benefit was the hydroelectricity that the city could generate along the route of the aqueduct for homes, businesses, and trolleys. The community's appetite for electrical energy had increased enormously since it was first introduced in 1882 to light the outdoor downtown area, three years later to power streetcars, then in 1890 to light homes, and shortly thereafter to drive numerous other machines. Private power, angry at the city's intention to go into the electricity business, opposed the aqueduct, but public enthusiasm for the overall project, voter disenchantment with private enterprise's earlier record in managing the city's water supply, and divisions within the ranks of private power (the Pacific Electric and Power Company endorsed the aqueduct because owner Henry Huntington figured his future profits lay more in getting water to his real estate landholdings than in producing electricity) over-whelmed the opposition in the 1905 and 1907 bond elections. In 1910 residents voted almost eight to one for bonds to build munic-ipally owned generating facilities (Huntington opposed this move since he believed its defeat would help his power company while posing no threat to the aqueduct) and a year later the public gave an even stronger endorsement (nine to one) to a city-owned electrical distribution system. This did not mean that municipalization came easily, for private power was strong enough to defeat bond issues aimed at expanding the city's distribution system in 1913, 1923, and 1929. Still, advocates of municipal ownership persisted, and by 1936 Los Angeles had absorbed the distribution networks of all pri-vate firms and was operating the largest urban electrical system in the nation.[45]

As soon as Los Angeles's leaders had obtained the public's en-dorsement of the first bond issue for the aqueduct and considered the second a certainty, they began lobbying in Washington for the necessary right-of-way from the federal government, over whose lands the water would be transported. Emphasizing that Owens River water would benefit far more people if it were taken to Los Angeles than left in the valley, they gained a major ally in President Theodore Roosevelt. "It is a hundred or thousandfold more im-portant to the State and more valuable to the people as a whole," affirmed Roosevelt, "if [this water is] used by the city than if used by the people of the Owens Valley." Despite last-ditch efforts by valley residents to kill the bill or amend it in a way that would pro-vide them with a reclamation project, the President's support proved decisive. In June 1906 Congress granted the right-of-way.[46]

Construction of the aqueduct began in 1908, and five years later, on November 5, 1913, the first Owens River water poured into the San Fernando Valley. Mulholland had completed the project on time and within budget—a remarkable accomplishment for any era. Present for the ceremonies celebrating the event were bands playing bright airs, a soprano whose high notes bounced off the nearby hills, and 30,000 cheering onlookers who wildly applauded

Releasing Owens River water into the San Fernando Valley on November 5, 1913. (Courtesy of Los Angeles Department of Water and Power)

as the valves were turned and water cascaded down the spillway. "There it is," Mulholland proudly proclaimed in a laconic utterance since immortalized in countless quotations. "Take it!"[47]

The San Fernando Valley: Insider Information for Private Gain

Among those anxious to take it were nearby communities, ranchers, and farmers, many of them deprived of water by Los Angeles's aggressive assertion of its pueblo right to all the water in the Los Angeles River, and others made fearful by the gradual depletion of their local wells and streams as newcomers expanded agricultural and town-building activities throughout the southern

The crowd celebrating at the Owensmouth Cascades, near Sylmar, on November 5, 1913. (Courtesy of Los Angeles Department of Water and Power)

coastal plain. Since the new water supply greatly exceeded the city's current needs, many officials urged selling the surplus in order to reap the greatest profits possible until Los Angeles needed the water. Mulholland disagreed, arguing that it would be a "base deception" to sell water that would likely have to be reclaimed by the city after "innocent purchasers" had "probably made millions of dollars worth of improvements dependent on the water."[48] In-

*Jawbone Siphon construction site, north of Mojave, on the Los Angeles
Aqueduct. (Courtesy of Los Angeles Department of Water and Power)*

stead, he urged making the surplus available only to areas that could
be annexed and assured a steady water supply.

Mulholland's views prevailed, sparking renewed demands for
urban expansion and even creation of a special Annexation Commission to set the terms for acquiring new city territory and sharing
surplus water. "Annexation and consolidation," proudly announced
the new commission, "will give Los Angeles standing as the me-

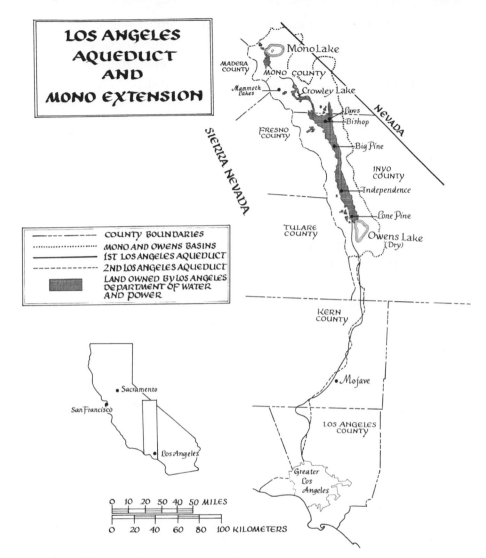

LOS ANGELES
AQUEDUCT
AND
MONO EXTENSION

COUNTY BOUNDARIES
MONO AND OWENS BASINS
1ST LOS ANGELES AQUEDUCT
2ND LOS ANGELES AQUEDUCT
LAND OWNED BY LOS ANGELES
DEPARTMENT OF WATER
AND POWER

Mono Lake
MADERA COUNTY
MONO COUNTY
Mammoth Lakes
Crowley Lake
NEVADA
FRESNO COUNTY
Laws
Bishop
Big Pine
INYO COUNTY
Independence
Lone Pine
TULARE COUNTY
Owens Lake (Dry)
KERN COUNTY
SIERRA NEVADA

Sacramento
San Francisco
Los Angeles

Mojave
LOS ANGELES COUNTY
Greater Los Angeles

0   10   20   30   40   50 MILES
0   20   40   60   80   100 KILOMETERS

tropolis of the Pacific Coast. . . . Wherever the aqueduct water is placed—be it north, south, east or west—there will the greatest development of the future be found, and that development should be a part of, and help constitute the Greater Los Angeles that is to be."[49] By the end of 1915 the city had nearly tripled in size, expanding from 108 square miles to 285 square miles, with the largest single acquisition being the San Fernando Valley.

The rapidly expanding boundaries, economic development, and profits generated by the arrival of Owens River water created many personal fortunes, some so large that they aroused suspicions of corruption. Eaton had profited, of course, from his purchases on behalf of the city, but no individuals seem to have made more money than investors in a San Fernando Valley land syndicate that purchased 16,000 acres for $35 an acre (there would later be a second syndicate and more purchases) and then sold them for millions once water arrived in the valley. Critics of the city at the time and since charged that the aqueduct was the result of a conspiracy—that the whole Owens Valley project had been originally conceived by members of the San Fernando Valley land syndicate who, in order to make valuable their dry and nearly worthless property, bribed key city officials to bring in Owens River water and then to annex the valley to the city so that their lands would have permanent access to that water and be worth a fortune.

The most recent and thorough inquiries into this question by Abraham Hoffman and William Kahrl agree that there is no evidence to support such a theory. A reexamination conducted in the preparation of this book supports that conclusion. Eaton, not the members of the land syndicate, conceived and promoted the aqueduct idea that Mulholland subsequently adopted and persuaded city leaders to put on the ballot. Neither Eaton nor Mulholland owned or had options on acreage in the San Fernando Valley when the decision was made to build the aqueduct. Mulholland eventually invested in some valley real estate, but not as a member of any syndicate, and he did so after news of the aqueduct had become public knowledge and after voters had approved both aqueduct bond issues.[50] Still, there is evidence, much of it circumstantial, that the land syndicate took advantage of privileged information to make a fortune on San Fernando Valley real estate.

The syndicate was the San Fernando Mission Land Company, and its members included railway and real estate entrepreneur Henry Huntington, Union Pacific president E. H. Harriman, *Los Angeles Times* owner Harrison Gray Otis, and *Los Angeles Express* owner Edwin T. Earl, among others. Through their company these men secured an option to purchase San Fernando Valley land on November 28, 1904, less than two months after Mulholland had returned from his initial reconnaissance to the Owens Valley and told the Board of Water Commissioners that he was "favorably impressed" and only a week after the city had obtained copies of the Reclamation Service's engineering reports, thus revealing that agency's sympathy for Los Angeles. The syndicate finally purchased the land on March 23, 1905, the same day that news reached the Board of Water Commissioners of Fred Eaton's having secured an option on the bulk of the reservoir site lands in the Owens Valley. The obtaining of that option seriously compromised any lingering Reclamation Service plans for a project of its own in the Owens Valley and all but assured the city's acquisition of Owens River water which, as noted earlier, was a volume of water so great that it exceeded Los Angeles's foreseeable needs and left a surplus for nearby areas like the San Fernando Valley.[51]

To see these closely timed events as coincidences begs credulity, the more so in the face of evidence that a short time later the syndicate gained a new partner, Moses Sherman, who was also a member of the Board of Water Commissioners. The conclusion seems inescapable that Sherman used privileged information gained by his membership on the water board to enrich himself and his soon-to-be partners. He was already well known to the syndicate members, and since the turn of the century he had been a close friend and business associate of Harry Chandler, son-in-law of original syndicate member Harrison Gray Otis of the *Times*. Neither Sherman nor the other syndicate members originated the idea of the aqueduct but they profited handsomely from it, eventually securing most of the valley before reselling it. It was an age before the use of insider information for private gain was illegal but not before it was considered questionable—if not reprehensible—behavior. Not everyone with access to the same privileged information obtained by Sherman acted on it. "In that San Fernando Valley I neither bought then nor own now a dollar's worth of land there," later explained John M. Elliott, a member of the water commission. "I wanted to keep myself free from suspicion of having acted from any foreknowledge because of my official position."[52] Sherman apparently had no such scruples, and neither did the two syndicate members who owned newspapers. Otis's *Times* and Edwin Earl's *Express* vigorously lobbied the public not only for passage of the aqueduct bonds but also for annexation of the San Fernando Valley by Los Angeles.

Rival newspapers—William Randolph Hearst's *Los Angeles Examiner* and Samuel Clover's *Los Angeles News*—uncovered evidence of the syndicate's activities during the campaigns for the bond elections, but the information failed to dampen the public's enthusiasm for either the aqueduct or annexation. When the charges became an issue in the mayoralty election of 1911 and expanded to include the conspiracy theory involving collusion between the syndicate and Mulholland as well as other Los Angeles officials, the city created an Aqueduct Investigation Board. In August 1912 the board issued a report that pleased no one. "No direct evidence of graft has been developed," but "the Aqueduct affords opportunities for graft, and if this Board had had the necessary time to develop all facts along lines suggested by individuals, a knowledge of human nature indicates that men would have been found who had succumbed to temptation."[53] The result was that those who believed that everyone involved had been exonerated and those who insisted that the aqueduct was the product of a syndicate-city conspiracy continued to press their views. Over the years, the conspiracy thesis proved especially attractive to writers and found support in such popular accounts as W. A. Chalfant's *The Story of Inyo* (1922; revised edition, 1933), Morrow Mayo's *Los Angeles* (1933), and Carey McWilliams's *Southern California Country* (1946) as well as in the motion picture *Chinatown* (1974).

Los Angeles's Water Colonies

Owens Valley residents found conspiracy a readily believable explanation for their plight. They reacted bitterly to Los Angeles's plans, the way the city had moved secretly through the valley, and the probability of having lost forever a reclamation project of their own. They appealed for public sympathy and waged a vigorous campaign but succeeded only in furthering Los Angeles's imperialistic ventures in the valley.

As soon as the city's plans became known in 1905, valley residents, led by the Inyo County Board of Supervisors; local businessmen; and talented nature writer and novelist Mary Austin and her husband, Stafford, a federal land office employee, singled out J. B. Lippincott for special criticism. They denounced his collusion with Eaton and Los Angeles and urged Washington to resurrect its program for a Reclamation Service project in the valley. They failed to shake the President's conviction that the water would better serve the public good in Los Angeles than in the Owens Valley, but no one in the Reclamation Service found it easy to defend Lippincott, and some highly placed officials, including Assistant Chief Engineer Arthur Powell Davis, found it impossible. "I am convinced," stated Davis in August 1905, "that Lippincott is so blind to the public interest and so biased by private and selfish considerations that it will be impossible to secure loyal service from him."[54] When a special investigation ordered by the Secretary of the Interior agreed that Lippincott's actions were "indefensible" and that "for the good of the Reclamation Service, he should be separated from it," the Secretary prepared to fire him but then backed off out of fear that the dismissal would publicly embarrass the Service at a time when it was trying to get its newly created program under way in the West. Lippincott was allowed to remain so long as he abandoned his private consulting practice. He promised to do so, but never did, resigning in 1906 to take a higher-paying job with Los Angeles as assistant chief engineer for construction of the aqueduct.[55] He would not be the last well-placed federal employee to end up on the city's payroll.

Believing themselves abandoned by the President, betrayed by the Reclamation Service, and misled by Los Angeles, Owens Valley residents remained deeply embittered. For about a dozen years, their anger was assuaged by the city's practice of taking water at the lower end of the valley after the settlers' needs had been met and by the prosperity brought to the area by aqueduct construc-

A dynamited portion of the Los Angeles Aqueduct, 1927. (Courtesy of Security Pacific Historical Photograph Collection, Los Angeles Public Library)

tion, a railroad connection that opened local goods to outside markets, and World War I demands for increased agricultural production. In the 1920s old hatreds resurfaced as Los Angeles's diversions occurred higher and higher up the valley in response to the city's booming population growth (a hundred thousand newcomers arriving annually) and to drought. The problem was that the increased diversions came at a time of drought in the Owens Valley as well as the city—the worst on record for the valley.

In 1923, to silence opposition and to solidify its control over the valley, Los Angeles, at Mulholland's urging, began purchasing most of the remaining land and water rights not held by the city (because they were not vital to keeping valley water flowing to Los Angeles) or by the federal government. Those who sold at good prices had few complaints. But those denied top dollar or who, like the businessmen in the valley's towns, saw their livelihoods and property values nosedive as the farmers and ranchers departed after selling their land (and water rights) to Los Angeles became outraged and then violent. They dynamited the aqueduct on numerous occasions and attracted the attention of reporters who aroused national sympathy for the valley's plight and touched off a debate in Los Angeles over the wisdom of the city's policy. Embarrassed by the publicity and anxious to safeguard its water supply, the city responded in the only way it knew how—with more purchases. It decided to buy off the remaining opposition by securing *all* the private property in the Owens Valley. By 1933 it had acquired a vast possession—virtually all the farms, ranches, and towns of Inyo County.[56]

Among those hit hardest by the decline in economic activity were the valley's oldest residents, some 800 Paiute. Although their land and water rights were under federal protection, this meant nothing since the lands they possessed were worthless for agriculture and the little income they earned came from off-reservation jobs that disappeared as the white residents packed and left. After several false starts, the city finally acknowledged an obligation to the Indians, and with approval of the federal government negotiated a settlement in 1939 providing the Paiute with better lands and assured water rights.[57]

In the meantime, Los Angeles's victory in quieting Owens Valley opposition resulted in an unanticipated costly by-product. Ownership of extensive valley acreage brought with it a heavy property tax burden. The city eventually began selling many of the town properties (less, of course, any water rights) to merchants catering to the rising recreational business in the area. Tourists, most of them, ironically, from Los Angeles, flocked to the valley and surrounding countryside in search of hunting, fishing, skiing, and backpacking and to enjoy the beauty of Mount Whitney and see the stands of bristlecone pine, the world's oldest living trees. Still, Los Angeles—in particular, the Department of Water and Power (in 1925 the municipal water and electrical departments were combined under a single board of commissioners)—remained owner of the bulk of valley land and water rights not under federal control. (The federal government forbade development on virtually all its lands so as to keep the water flowing to Los Angeles.)

The city's Owens Valley colony soon increased dramatically when Los Angeles moved its water acquisitions northward into adjacent Mono County. In 1930 the city electorate, told that a water famine was imminent, approved a nearly $40 million bond issue, much of it going for an extension of the Owens River aqueduct system into the Mono drainage basin. Construction began four years later and was completed by 1940.[58]

As with the water from Owens Valley, there was no legal need for haste in using the entire new supply—in fact, the just-finished aqueduct was not large enough to move all of it—because the state Water Rights Board interpreted leniently the "due diligence" requirement for Los Angeles to divert and use water. Until the board decided otherwise, the city would have an almost perpetual standby supply for the future. Also like the earlier Owens Valley venture, this one received decisive help from highly placed Reclamation Service officials. They were Arthur Powell Davis, who had moved up the ranks to become head of the service from 1914 to 1923, and Frank E. Weymouth, chief engineer in the early 1920s, who advanced the project by supporting policies preventing settlers from taking up federal land in the area. Unlike Lippincott before them, they were not caught up in a conflict of interest, but Weymouth's efforts were later rewarded with a lucrative position in the city's Department of Water and Power.[59]

With vast stretches of the Owens and Mono basins under its control, Los Angeles became almost a caricature of its earlier self—a megalopolis connected by a ribbon of steel and concrete to "water colonies" hundreds of miles away. Earlier victories at home in acquiring the Los Angeles River had prepared the way for—indeed, demanded—victories elsewhere to sustain the growth and prosperity that city leaders and the electorate took for granted. It was a metropolis sustained by a network of rivers, aqueducts, and single-minded public employees, chief of whom was William Mulholland. By the time Mulholland had secured his greatest engineering achievements, however, he had become one of their most tragic victims.

The Tragedy and Legacy of the Expert: William Mulholland

In 1928 William Mulholland dropped out of sight, a ruined man forced to resign in disgrace. The immediate cause of his downfall was the collapse of a dam with the loss of hundreds of lives and millions of dollars in property damage. It was a disaster resulting directly from his success in acquiring new land and water rights in the Owens Valley in the 1920s.

Mulholland's purchases had led to the departure of farmers whose irrigation practices had regulated the flows entering the aqueduct. Thereafter regulation had to be provided by new reservoirs such as St. Francis Dam, a facility forty miles north of Los Angeles in San Francisquito Canyon. The dam rested on unstable geological formations detected years earlier in 1911 by Mulholland while making plans to bring the aqueduct through a tunnel and into the canyon at a point high above the canyon floor. The purpose was to take advantage of the drop to generate hydroelectricity, but the fractured schist on the west canyon wall led to precautionary measures to protect the aqueduct. "As the face of the canyon opposite the lower [aqueduct] power line is exceedingly rough," Mulholland reported to his superiors, "and the dip and strike of the slate such as to threaten slips, . . . this portion of the line was . . . placed well back under the mountain." Constructing St. Francis Dam later, Mulholland failed to take adequate precautions, a failure exacerbated by his refusal to allow outside, independent experts to examine the site and his plans, a norm of the day among responsible dam builders. On the night of March 12, 1928, the dam failed, sending a wall of water into the Santa Clara Valley that took at least 450 lives, while destroying towns, farms, and rural communities, before emptying into the ocean near Ventura some fifty-five miles downriver. The devastation led to numerous investigations, with most agreeing with the coroner's jury: "The construction and operation of a great dam should

Ruins of St. Francis Dam, looking upstream. (Courtesy of California Commission to Investigate the Causes Leading to the Failure of St. Francis Dam)

never be left to the sole judgment of one man, no matter how eminent."[60]

Mulholland implied that saboteurs were at fault but eventually accepted full responsibility for the disaster. It left him a broken man, and no one doubted his sincerity when he told the coroner's jury: "I envy . . . the ones who are dead."[61] With the dam collapse coming on the heels of the negative publicity generated by his latest purchases in the Owens Valley, he and other city officials recognized he had to go. Neither his earlier successes nor his insulation from the electorate was enough to protect him. The Board of Water Commissioners even considered firing him while the investigation was still under way, but finally allowed him to take a leave of absence until the reports were completed. He was then permitted to resign in November 1928 after which he lived quietly until his death seven years later.

More than any other person, Mulholland shaped Los Angeles's water policy and laid the foundation for the modern city, but he did it within the context of the Progressive movement and with the full and enthusiastic support of the electorate. This vast program was no creature of an autocratic government sitting on high, though it was proposed and argued through by a small group. It was, rather, firmly based in the wishes of the people, who for many years into the future would greet such proposals with acclamation, regarding those who conceived and brought them to reality as great public benefactors. They supplied *water,* that precious substance that all cherished, for it meant survival, growth, and prosperity in an arid land.

Mulholland seemed to epitomize the Progressive expert, self-taught though he was, and much admired for his ability to meet the complex challenges of modern urban America. In reality he was also impatient, obsessed with achieving his goals, and ignorant about much that was taught in the new schools of professional engineering. The gaps in his knowledge and his incautiousness produced great loss of life in the collapse of St. Francis Dam. Additionally, his limited technical knowledge about cement and geology cost the city millions of dollars when it later had to reconstruct portions of the Owens aqueduct, deal with the aftermath of the dam failure, and absorb losses associated with the abandonment of another dam after construction was well under way.[62] Still, the professional engineers of the day, though not blind to his failures, recognized him as a man of unusual achievement and one of their own. *Engineering-News Record* on his death acknowleged "the unfortunate failure of the St. Francis dam," but emphasized Mulholland's "brilliant career as an engineer," and *Western Construction News* described him as an "outstanding water supply engineer" while also noting the same "disaster" and observing that he was a "doer" whose "accent was heavy on the urge to overcome obstacles" rather than to study "a problem in all its phases, patiently eliminating errors and inaccurate deductions." Withal, however, he represented a type of engineer that the profession "has, and needs."[63]

As a builder Mulholland was also as much a creature of the city's booster mentality as any other resident. There had been earlier steps of monumental importance that prepared the way for his accomplishments: the city's establishment of a pueblo water right that gave it mastery over the Los Angeles River Basin, and the city's reassertion, at strong popular urging and in harmony with Progressive principles, of municipal control of water resources. Mulholland built upon these gains by creating an efficient, modern municipal water system and then, through secrecy and winking at the moral lapses of others if not of himself, by leading the campaign to take the water of the Owens Valley and establishing a precedent that inspired imitators throughout the state and the West.

As early as 1920 the Owens aqueduct, with the aid of harbor facilities at San Pedro, had helped Los Angeles surpass San Francisco in population to become the premier port city on the West Coast. Additionally, the development of local groundwater supplies throughout the southern coastal plain and the promise of new water helped Los Angeles County as early as 1910 to become the national leader in agriculture. With the infusion of water into the San Fernando Valley and arrival of additional supplies from the Mono Basin and elsewhere, it maintained that distinction until the 1950s, when farms and orchards rapidly gave way to homes and streets. Driving this development, and constituting Mulholland's preeminent legacy, was his policy of bringing in water in advance of need. It was a policy designed with a great city in mind and for a distant future. As late as 1980 and with a population of 3 million, Los Angeles could meet 80 percent of its water needs with imported supplies from the Owens Valley and Mono Basin.[64]

When Mulholland resigned in 1928 the city's oil, motion picture, real estate, and tourist industries were booming; the Department of Water and Power had become the most powerful municipal agency in the United States; and Los Angeles was preparing to embark on a new phase of water seeking that would reach across the American Southwest. Such remarkable achievement had not come without great human, psychic, and economic costs: the St. Francis Dam collapse, the bitterness associated with the Owens River aqueduct, the virtual elimination of ranching and agriculture in the Owens Valley, and the widespread distrust of Los Angeles that led the state legislature in 1931 to enact a county-of-origin law (a statute authorizing a county to retain within its borders water originating there and required to meet future needs).[65]

Los Angeles did not stand alone in exciting fear, envy, and mixed feelings about the price exacted by growth. San Francisco had slipped behind its southern rival, but it was nonetheless among the nation's largest cities and second only to Los Angeles in the West. Moreover, like Los Angeles, its modern prosperity rested heavily on aggressive municipal leadership emphasizing a special water imperialism of its own.

San Francisco: Instant City with an Instant Water Problem

SAN FRANCISCO'S location in coastal northern California, alongside a magnificent bay into which empty the state's largest rivers, hardly suggests a water-shy site, but the water that surrounds the city on three sides is salty and the climate is semiarid. Precipitation averages only twenty inches, and fog, not rainfall, is the area's most distinctive characteristic during the summer growing season. Although founders of the presidio and mission in 1776 encountered poor sandy soils and scanty local fresh water supplies, strategic considerations dictated a settlement at the entrance of the bay. The unimpressive springs, wells, and streams— no source was anywhere near as large as the river from which Los Angeles took its name—met the slow-growing community's needs until the gold rush led overnight to a booming metropolis.

As in Los Angeles, but sooner because of the influx of newcomers, the Hispanic system of municipally controlled open ditches and a few water peddlers gave way in San Francisco to profit-minded entrepreneurs going door-to-door with their wagons jammed with water barrels for eager customers. By the early 1850s water was being shipped by barge from Marin County while other firms competed with one another and the city to increase the yield from local sources with dams, flumes, and reservoirs. Giving a special urgency to these efforts were the six fires that destroyed the city between 1850 and 1852. Responding to the widespread fear of continued holocausts, a group of investors successfully lobbied the state legislature in 1858 for a franchise to provide water in exchange for allowing the city to draw upon the supply to extinguish fires. The newly created Spring Valley Water Works began delivering water four years later while at the same time consolidating the earlier competing firms under its control and purchasing nearly all the water sources and watershed surrounding the city.[66]

This reliance on private enterprise, like Los Angeles's experiment with leasing its water system to a private company, caused trouble from the outset—and for the same reasons: inadequate supply, poor service, and exorbitant rates. "The whole subject of an increased water supply," complained an exasperated mayor, "ought to be . . . with the view of making it a public enterprise to be owned by the city, so that the people may have an unrestricted use of water without price, other than the tax required to build the works and keep them in order."[67]

The growing demand for municipal control took a major step

forward in 1874 when San Franciscans obtained approval from the state legislature to create through purchase or condemnation a public system of their own. City leaders decided to circumvent Spring Valley Water Works by purchasing a large fresh-water source in Alameda County's Calaveras Valley, only to have Spring Valley undercut them by buying it before they could complete the transaction. The city next sought to purchase the Spring Valley system, but that gambit constantly foundered because of sharp differences over what constituted a fair price. Finally, in 1900, after twenty-six failing years in this effort, and as Progressive ideas gained momentum locally and nationally, San Franciscans obtained the state legislature's approval of a new city charter that mandated municipal ownership of utilities.[68] The earlier desire for a city-owned water system was now replaced by a legal requirement for such a system.

The challenge was to implement the mandate. All knew that taking over Spring Valley would be expensive whether the company's assets were obtained through a negotiated sale or by condemnation and purchase. Many had come to doubt the wisdom of either course, believing that the company's combined water sources would not long meet the city's growing needs. Attention turned to distant sources free from private control. They were considered and rejected until the mayor, city engineer, and Board of Public Works finally settled on the Tuolumne River. The Tuolumne drained a large portion of the Sierra Nevada, including Hetch Hetchy Valley, a canyon 170 miles east of San Francisco. About three and a half miles long, a quarter to three-quarters of a mile wide, and with perpendicular granite walls rising 2,500 feet, the valley seemed an ideal reservoir for capturing enough superior-quality Sierra runoff to meet the city's needs for the foreseeable future. Damming it would also allow for other dividends: the generation of hydroelectricity to supply the Bay Area's growing demand for power, thereby producing revenue to help underwrite the cost of the project.

Like Los Angeles's decision to tap the Owens River, San Francisco's deliberations were kept secret, and—as the city later candidly acknowledged—for essentially the same reasons: "To prevent

Hetch Hetchy Valley as it was. (Courtesy of City and County of San Francisco)

certain privileges and rights that may be of vital importance from falling into the hands of speculators, private individuals or private corporations adverse to the interests of this city."[69] San Francisco had already learned a harsh lesson when Spring Valley had purchased the Calaveras Valley water rights just as the city thought it had wrapped up that deal. Thus in 1901, San Francisco Mayor James Phelan quietly filed for rights to the water of the Tuolumne River. His agent in doing so was the same Joseph B. Lippincott who would shortly help his friend Fred Eaton and Los Angeles secretly acquire rights to the water of the Owens River.

James D. Phelan. (Courtesy of City and County of San Francisco)

Hetch Hetchy Predicaments: The Federal Government and Boss Ruef

For San Francisco, as for Los Angeles, there was a complication involving the federal government. Hetch Hetchy was located on federal land in the northern part of Yosemite National Park. This had its attractive side in the absence of private property owners who could complicate and make more expensive the city's plans. Federal control of the area, however, meant that building a dam in the valley and securing a right-of-way for an aqueduct would require Washington's approval—in this case, that of the Secretary of the Interior. The city anticipated no problems. In 1902 Phelan, again acting quietly and as a private citizen, applied for the necessary approvals. Once that was done, city officials, confident of quick federal authorization, announced publicly their intentions in July as Phelan made plans to transfer his claims to San Francisco.[70]

The city's optimism was short-lived. The Secretary of the Interior denied Phelan's request as well as another filed immediately by the city on the grounds that a Hetch Hetchy reservoir would detract from the area's "wonderful natural conditions and marvelous scenic interest." The Secretary's rejection also clearly indicated that Spring Valley Water Works had not been idle since the city announced its plans. San Francisco did not have to go to the Sierra Nevada for water, concluded the Secretary, because Spring Valley "has the ability to increase the supply to adequately meet the needs of the city almost indefinitely."[71]

Hetch Hetchy advocates disagreed, but they were in no position to launch a counterattack because, for reasons unrelated to the water issue, they fell from power almost as soon as Phelan had filed his application with the Interior Department. Conflict between the business community and organized labor had in 1902 brought city government under the control of the Union Labor Party whose political boss, Abraham Ruef, and his puppet mayor, Eugene Schmitz, were more interested in making money than in promoting a municipal water system relying on Hetch Hetchy. Hope for Hetch Hetchy remained barely alive in the Board of Public Works, and Ruef, in exchange for the promise of a handsome bribe, tried to quash it entirely within a few years. A private firm, Bay Cities Water Company, which held rights along tributaries of the American and Cosumnes rivers, offered Ruef a million dollars to persuade Mayor Schmitz and the board of supervisors to purchase its assets and to abandon Hetch Hetchy. Ruef jumped at the opportunity. With promises of payoffs of his own to board members, he obtained a resolution from the supervisors in February 1906 agreeing to "refrain from expending further money, energy or time" on Hetch Hetchy and to investigate other possibilities.[72] In April, as he began lining up votes favorable to Bay Cities, his scheme unexpectedly received a major boost from the San Francisco earthquake and especially the fire that followed. The conflagration raged out of control for three days and destroyed most of the city. Ruef and his fellow conspirators claimed that the problem was lack of water—actually there was plenty of water in Spring Valley's reservoirs; the problem was damaged water lines—and used the disaster to emphasize the need for acquiring Bay Cities.

The ploy worked—for a while. Then rumors of a corrupt bargain began circulating, which former Mayor Phelan encouraged by publicly criticizing the city administration. In September Fremont Older of the *San Francisco Bulletin* entered the fray with a ringing editorial: "Only by one means—BRIBERY—can it be brought about that the Hetch Hetchy project shall be abandoned by the city."[73] Others joined in the attack, from which neither the Bay Cities scheme nor Ruef recovered. Evidence of widespread and flagrant corruption resulted in the Union Labor Party being turned out of office in 1907 and in Ruef's indictment, conviction, and imprisonment.

The notoriety and change in administration breathed life once more into the Hetch Hetchy plan. In 1907 a new San Francisco city engineer probed the attitudes of Washington officials and encountered a Secretary of the Interior, James R. Garfield, less inclined than his predecessor to permanently lock away resources for aesthetic reasons and more committed to municipal ownership of public utilities. Garfield had also become convinced that the earthquake and fire demonstrated San Francisco's need for a new water supply. In May 1908 he granted the city's request for a right-of-way permit. "Domestic use, . . . especially for a municipal water supply," he explained, "is the highest use to which water and available storage basins . . . can be put."[74] San Francisco leaders cheered the news.

Secretary Garfield's action elated San Francisco officials but it touched off a firestorm of opposition that raged for five years, attracted national attention, and threatened to scuttle the project until Congress intervened in 1913. The opponents of a Hetch Hetchy dam came primarily from three sources. Spring Valley Water Works, with good reason, viewed the project as a threat to its monopoly and profits. Equally alarmed were farmers near the San Joaquin Valley communities of Modesto and Turlock who claimed prior rights to the waters of the Tuolumne. These local and regional protests attracted little attention outside California, and San Francisco officials felt they could neutralize them with relative ease. Not so the opposition coming from another group with a national following, wilderness advocates, who had claims of being more committed than San Francisco to serving the public's needs.

These most vocal of protestors urged that Hetch Hetchy be preserved for enjoyment by all Americans rather than transformed into a reservoir for use by a minority. The conflict here was essentially a split within the conservation movement itself—between those who emphasized conserving resources through careful management for later use and those dedicated to preserving forever in their natural state unique and beautiful wild places. Both sides agreed on the need to stop wasteful abuse of the nation's dwindling natural resources and both counted among their number scientists and others who, as historian Michael Smith has noted, believed that "in certain instances . . . a natural feature or region should warrant preservation in its natural state."[75] However, in an arid land where scarce water supplies and magnificent natural wonders were often in the same locale or otherwise closely interrelated, clashes became inevitable. The first confrontation of national significance occurred over Hetch Hetchy.

Spiritual leader of the opposition and vigorous beyond his seventy years was John Muir, already viewed as a legend by many of his contemporaries. A Scot by birth and naturalist by training, he had

John Muir in his beloved Yosemite Valley, with Royal Arches and Washington Column to the left. (Courtesy of William E. Colby Memorial Library, Sierra Club)

arrived in California at age thirty in 1868 and immediately fallen in love with the grandeur and beauty of the Sierra Nevada. As often as possible he journeyed to the high country, publicized it in numerous writings, argued for its preservation, and in 1890 helped bring about the creation of Yosemite National Park. Two years later he joined a group of San Francisco residents in establishing the Sierra

Club, dedicated to enlisting "the support and co-operation of the people and the government in preserving the forests and other natural features of the Sierra Nevada." To Muir, Hetch Hetchy was one of the most precious of those "natural features." Indeed, though he found its canyon walls "less sublime in height than those of Yosemite," he believed that "its groves, gardens, and broad, spacious meadows are more beautiful and picturesque."[76]

San Francisco's plans for Hetch Hetchy dismayed and bitterly angered Muir. "Dam Hetch Hetchy!" he roared. "As well dam for water-tanks the people's cathedrals and churches, for no holier temple has ever been consecrated by the heart of man." Aesthetically beautiful wild places were for Muir divinely inspired creations, "God's best gifts," where "the hand of God" and "Nature's love" could be experienced firsthand as "recreation grounds for soul and body." Since wilderness—including "every crystal, every flower"—was a "window opening into heaven, a mirror reflecting the Creator," those who threatened it were serving "the Prince of the powers of Darkness" and the "Almighty Dollar." The issue, quite simply, was one of good against evil. Preservation became in Muir's mind identified with his "God of the Mountains," while utilitarian principles served "Satan," "Mammon," and "raging commercialism."[77]

Following Interior Secretary Garfield's issuance of the permit to San Francisco in 1908, Muir enlisted the support of like-minded people and organizations across the country. He appealed to the growing number of Americans questioning the national fascination with material growth and emphasis on economic profit over spiritual vitality and aesthetic appreciation. "The National habit is to waste the beauty of nature and save the dollars of business," lamented Lyman Abbott, editor of the *Outlook* in a biting attack on the Hetch Hetchy plan. "If this country were in danger of habitually ignoring utilitarian practice for the sake of running after sentimental dreams and aesthetic visions we should advise it to cut down the California big trees to shelter its citizens from the weather, and to dam the Tuolumne River in order to instruct its citizens in the use of the bathtub. But the danger is all the other way." Offering a similar critique of "this wanton sacrifice of the public interest" and the materialistic values that he associated with the project was Robert Underwood Johnson of *Century*. "One of the retarding influences of American civilization [is] . . . that 'Good is only good to eat.' . . . The citizens of San Francisco . . . will do well to exhaust every other possibility of meeting their needs before giving their consent to the ruin of one of their imperial State's greatest natural treasures." *Suburban Life, The Nation,* the *New York Times,* the *Boston Transcript,* and other periodicals and newspapers echoed the refrain, while women's clubs, outdoor groups, teachers, and professional organizations denounced the project to the President and Congress.[78]

San Francisco was as uncompromising as Muir and his allies. "Short-haired women and long-haired men" belonging to "so-called nature loving societies" is how the city engineer described the preservationists, while the *San Francisco Chronicle* castigated them as "mushy esthetes." The city's advocates also sought to capture the moral high ground by accusing Muir of furthering private greed. Defeat of the Hetch Hetchy project, they warned, would only strengthen Spring Valley Water Works's "control [of] the present water supply." At best Muir and his followers were "mistaken zealots who are witlessly being used as catspaws by these grasping interests." Moreover, their narrowmindedness had blinded them to the recreational values of the lake that would be created by the dam. The public, observed city officials, would certainly benefit more from boating, fishing, and swimming than staring at a canyon now accessible to few. Besides, a Hetch Hetchy lake would be doubly precious: it would be a thing of beauty, "as beautiful as the other lakes which add charm to the landscapes of the Sierras," while at the same time affording "a supply pure in quality and sufficient in size to meet the present and all future demands of the city."[79]

Muir and his supporters found it difficult to challenge San Francisco's claims about the need for additional water or to persuade a public not as committed to preservation as later generations would become that a man-made lake was a lesser order of beauty. They also suffered from the unfair association with Spring Valley and from the disadvantage of having to persuade the Interior Department to reverse an earlier decision favorable to San Francisco. Perhaps their greatest obstacle was the public perception of their being out of step with the Progressive Era's emphasis on the need to conserve resources for efficient and sustained use rather than setting them aside permanently. These difficulties, especially the latter, surfaced within the Sierra Club itself, eventually producing a bitter schism when some members threw their support to the Hetch Hetchy project and forced Muir to participate in creating a counter group, the Society for the Preservation of the National Parks, to lead the fight against the dam. Such internal bickering as well as preservationist battles on other fronts—to establish a Kings Canyon park, obtain more land for Yosemite, create a national park service— translated into a chronic shortage of money, an overworked staff, and exhaustion for Muir and others in the forefront of the fight.[80]

San Francisco, in contrast, drew upon the city's extensive bureaucratic and financial resources, including $45 million in bonds approved by voters in January 1910 for construction of the first phase of the project. City residents were willing to take the gamble, so confident were they of Muir's defeat. In addition, major contributions of time and money came to the city's cause from wealthy supporters like William Kent and Rudolph Spreckels. To combat such mounting strength, the preservationists turned increasingly to arguments based on practical rather than aesthetic considerations and calculated to allow San Francisco to obtain more water while at the same time keeping Hetch Hetchy in its natural state.

Toward a Utilitarian Triumph

The preservationists discovered that their most appealing argument was their claim that alternative water sources were available to San Francisco. It was a contention first effectively made by two Reclamation Service engineers less than a month after the San Francisco bond vote in 1910, and it prompted a new Secretary of the Interior, Richard Ballinger, to warn San Francisco that he would rescind his predecessor's permit unless the city demonstrated that no alternative sites existed. To keep the city on the defensive and, it was hoped, doom the project, the preservationists hired an engineer of their own whose findings reenforced the Reclamation Service report.[81]

As San Francisco's city engineer, Marsden Manson, prepared his counterattack, he discovered to his delight that the data on which both the Reclamation Service and preservationists relied came from the same source—a consulting engineer in the pay of the Spring Valley company. Armed with this damning information, he privately intimated to Interior Secretary Ballinger that he could publicly embarrass him and the Reclamation Service. Ballinger immediately got the not-so-subtle message, and to head off unwanted revelations, he turned the question of alternative water sources over to an allegedly impartial Advisory Board of Army Engineers. As a measure of his concern about possibly damaging revelations, however, he established the inquiry in a way that virtually assured an outcome favorable to San Francisco.

Ballinger charged the advisory board with appraising San Francisco's contention that the Tuolumne River was the only source capable of meeting the city's needs, but he provided the board with neither funds nor staff for an independent investigation. The result was that the board had little more to work with than the data supplied by San Francisco. And what the city provided was a classic example of obfuscation through excess. There was a massive amount of statistical data accompanied by profuse illustrations, but cost estimates that would allow comparisons with alternative sources were incomplete or missing altogether. The advisory board hardly seemed to care. Without the means to conduct its own study, the safe course seemed to be in not challenging the permit already issued to the city. "Sufficient data are lacking as well as time and funds for making adequate investigations," acknowledged the board in its report of February 1913 to the Interior Secretary, but "sooner or later" Hetch Hetchy will have to be dammed, and it might as well be sooner.[82]

San Francisco was delighted, but the flaws in the appraisal process could not be kept a secret and the preservationists responded with outrage. Ballinger had left office before the report was issued, and his successor, also due to leave Washington in a few weeks with the retiring William Howard Taft administration, was anxious to rid the Interior Department of responsibility in the matter. Less than a week after the advisory board released its findings, he announced that approval of Hetch Hetchy would now require a mandate from Congress. The Secretary's position reflected not only the political sensitivity of the issue but also Taft's uncertainty about the legality of the executive branch granting rights-of-way through federal land. When President Woodrow Wilson took office a few weeks later, he did not reverse the ruling, probably because of the embarrassment it might create since his new Interior Secretary was Franklin Lane, a former San Francisco city attorney and strong supporter of the Hetch Hetchy project.[83] Besides, a congressional act authorizing the project would eliminate the multiple problems that had been created by the constantly shifting positions of individual Secretaries in the past.

Franklin Lane's strategy was to let Congress become the focal point of debate while he marshaled the administration's forces in support of the Hetch Hetchy dam. Congressman John E. Raker of California—political ally of former San Francisco Mayor James Phelan, who would shortly be elected to the U.S. Senate—introduced the necessary legislation in April 1913, thereby revitalizing the national debate over the project. All the old arguments were marched out, with each side claiming to represent the public's interests, only this time the preservationists focused their energies on what seemed to them the most vulnerable part of San Francisco's argument—the question of alternative water sources. They identified other water sources, emphasizing especially the Mokelumne River, another Sierra-fed stream that they felt could meet San Francisco's water and power needs and avoid despoiling Hetch Hetchy. There was merit to their contention, proven later with hindsight when the East Bay cities built an aqueduct to the Mokelumne. Even at the time, San Francisco had a report from a young assistant engineer in the water department pointing out the potential of the Mokelumne, but the city's chief engineer, Marsden Manson, had denigrated that report and in 1912 had locked it away.[84]

Hearing rumors of the suppressed report but denied access to it and incapable of financing their own investigation, the preservationists could buttress their position with no hard data and began losing ground with members of Congress growing weary of the debate. Muir and his allies were also feeling the effects of their battles on other fronts and their inability to counter successfully the argument that a recreational reservoir could benefit more people than a secluded valley. Just when the situation seemed darkest, a man emerged from the shadows claiming he could prove that San Francisco water leaders had deliberately lied in claiming that the Hetch Hetchy project was superior to developing the Mokelumne.

The hoped-for savior was Eugene Sullivan, whose possession of water and power rights on the Mokelumne River should have made even the unwary think twice before joining forces with him. Regrets were not long in coming. Because of the sensational nature of Sullivan's allegations, the House of Representatives accorded him a full day during hearings on the Raker Bill. Sullivan rambled at length about his wish to do "good to my brother man," but when pressed for proof of his charges, he admitted he had none and began retreating from his earlier position.[85] Sullivan's disastrous showing embarrassed the preservationists and provided San Franciscans with wonderful additional publicity that they played with consummate skill.

The outcome now became a certainty, particularly since the Raker Bill contained provisions recognizing the prior rights of the Turlock and Modesto irrigation districts, limiting use of the Tuolumne's water to domestic and other municipal needs, and prohibiting San Francisco from disposing of project water or electricity

Hetch Hetchy Reservoir and O'Shaughnessy Dam. (Courtesy of California Department of Water Resources)

to private firms for resale. First the House and then the Senate decisively approved the measure and sent it to President Woodrow Wilson, who signed it into law in December 1913. "I have signed this bill," observed Wilson in a statement epitomizing the utilitarian triumph, "because it seemed to serve the pressing public needs of the region . . . and yet did not impair the usefulness or materially detract from the beauty of the public domain."[86]

Urban Imperialism

Hetch Hetchy shortly after construction of the dam. (Courtesy of Philip Hyde)

The Ironies of Victory

To John Muir, "Satan & Co." had emerged the victor, though he hoped that some good would "come out of this dark damn-dam-damnation."[87] A year later he was dead, with his hope unfulfilled and before he could realize the irony in Wilson's statement. Perhaps it was just as well, for he would have lived only to see a Hetch Hetchy reservoir seldom visited by anyone, largely because it is not a lovely or hospitable sight. In the summer when the reservoir is most accessible, the sun's heat radiating off the water's surface and the granite walls makes the area most uncomfortable, while the canyon sides are scarred by the telltale bathtub rings created by the fluctuating water level. In the drier seasons, the surface often falls low enough to expose the tree stumps and other debris of a once magnificent wilderness sacrificed to urban growth. So much for the

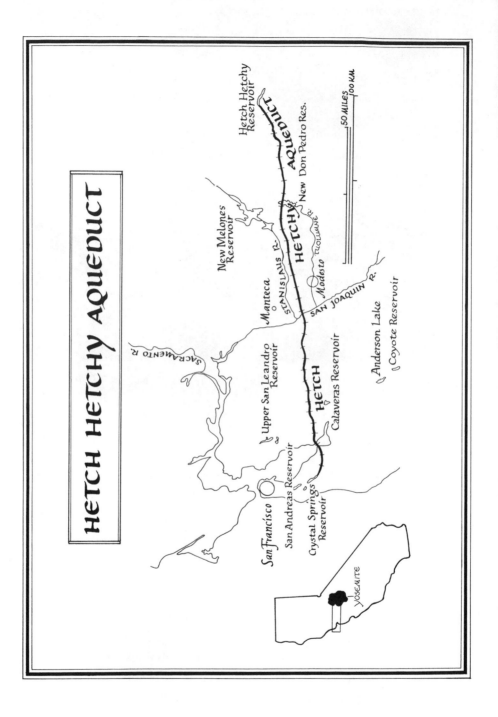

HETCH HETCHY AQUEDUCT

argument that the reservoir would benefit more recreationists than would a secluded valley.

There were other twists. The aqueduct completed in 1929 from the Mokelumne River to the East Bay demonstrated the capacity of that source to support a dense metropolitan area, but if San Francisco had tapped the Mokelumne, the East Bay cities would have undoubtedly turned to another river to meet their needs. It seems safe to say that the Tuolumne and Hetch Hetchy Valley would have been high on their list of choices.

A far more telling irony involved a major reason San Francisco had launched its Hetch Hetchy campaign in the first place—to establish a municipal water and power system. In many ways, the city's triumph in securing the Raker Act complicated that goal because of the law's stipulation that San Francisco could not sell or give away project water or hydroelectricity to a private firm. Since Spring Valley Water Works owned the city's water distribution system and because duplicating its local reservoirs would be impossible, the practical effect of the Raker Act was to mandate San Francisco's purchase of Spring Valley. The sale took years to consummate and occurred only after much haggling over price and after voters had repeatedly rejected bond issues to buy the company—in 1910 (before passage of the Raker Act) and again in 1915, 1921, and 1927—on the grounds that the proposed cost was exorbitant. Not until 1928 did the electorate provide the necessary two-thirds approval for $41 million in bonds to make the sale. Even then, the onset of the Great Depression delayed the actual transaction until 1930 because of the city's difficulty in locating buyers for its bonds.[88]

The mandate for a public power system took considerably longer to satisfy and even then required sleight of hand to accomplish. The city began generating hydroelectricity along its Hetch Hetchy system as early as May 1918 to aid in construction and also to help meet the power demands created by World War I. However, just as with the water, the city had no electricity distribution facilities of its own and was relying upon private companies. Because of the

Michael M. O'Shaughnessy. (Courtesy of City and County of San Francisco)

wartime emergency, the Federal Power Administration temporarily waived the Raker Act requirement and authorized sales to a private power company which in turn resold the energy to the public. That firm was soon absorbed by Pacific Gas and Electric, a giant consortium of private utility firms that strongly opposed the city developing its own system and thereby cutting into PG&E's profits.[89]

As it turned out, San Francisco had no desire to do so. Since the arrangement saved the city the expense of building its own distribution facilities at a time when it was financially strapped by payments on the bonds for the Hetch Hetchy project, it continued selling its power to PG&E for resale after the wartime emergency had passed. Federal authorities remained quiet until complaints about PG&E's profits began arriving, many from people never resigned to the damming of Hetch Hetchy. Under a contract approved by the

O'Shaughnessy and some of his crew. (Courtesy of City and County of San Francisco)

San Francisco County Board of Supervisors in 1925, PG&E supplied the city with power for street lighting and municipal streetcars and then purchased the remaining Hetch Hetchy power for $2.4 million annually, which it promptly turned around and sold to city residents for $9 million.[90]

Put on notice by the federal government, San Francisco officials tried to bring the city into conformity with the law, but the residents refused to budge. Eight times between 1927 and 1941, they rejected as too expensive bond issues that would have established a municipal distribution system or purchased the facilities of PG&E. Two attempts to amend the Raker Act also failed. Then, with the outbreak of World War II, the federal government once more ceased pressing for compliance with the law. The war's end in 1945 brought continued federal collusion with the city in its policy of noncompliance, this time by resort to a clever ruse: Washington proclaimed San Francisco the official retailer of Hetch Hetchy power. In practice, nothing really changed. Technically, the city distributed the

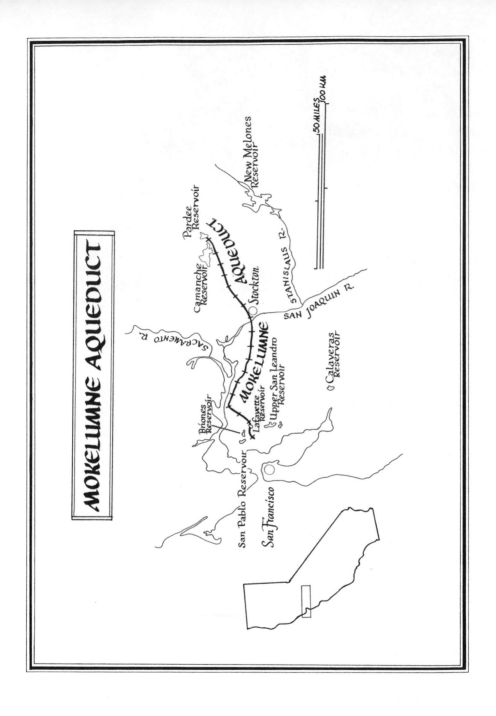

power, but it did so in name only by paying PG&E a handsome consideration for use of the company's distribution system.[91] So much for the concept of a municipal power system.

Water finally reached San Francisco from Hetch Hetchy in 1934 at an eventual cost of $100 million when all the bills for the 155-mile aqueduct were totaled. This was some $23 million more than the original estimate, largely because city officials opted for the time-consuming (and more costly because of inflation) practice of asking the electorate to approve bonds at different stages of construction rather than all at once at the outset as Los Angeles had done. City Engineer Michael M. O'Shaughnessy was primarily responsible for this policy—"Give me the ten million now and I'll be back in a couple of years for twenty-three million more to finish the job"—and the public soon groused that his initials, M. M., stood for "More Money." Delays and additional expense also resulted from the tedious struggle to bore a twenty-five-mile-long tunnel through the Coast Range, the longest in the world at the time. Deliveries arrived none too soon, for the city's growth had already exceeded local supplies and three years earlier had required diversions from the East Bay to meet shortages. (Encountering fewer obstacles, the East Bay had completed its aqueduct to the Mokelumne in only six years from site selection to delivery of water in 1929.)[92]

The water and electrical power of the Hetch Hetchy project far exceeded the demands of San Francisco, which sold the surplus to nearby communities. Such sales to municipalities and other public agencies were not prohibited by the Raker Act and had been anticipated before the project's approval when San Francisco invited Bay Area cities to participate in the undertaking. East Bay communities responded favorably at first but then decided to go their own way out of fear of being politically swallowed by San Francisco. Others were less afraid. The place of the East Bay dropouts as customers was eventually taken by cities south of San Francisco and along the southern bay in Alameda and Santa Clara counties. Continued rapid growth throughout the area, especially following World War II, brought increased demand, and San Francisco voters, delighted at the prospect of having their neighbors share the cost of maintaining and expanding the project, approved $115 million in bonds in 1961 to increase the aqueduct's capacity. By the late 1970s San Francisco was importing nearly six times as much water as it did with the original Hetch Hetchy project. By then as well it was selling more than half its water to outsiders and bringing in nearly $33 million annually in combined water and power sales to maintain the system.[93]

Such a gargantuan enterprise made it little wonder that city officials rejected out of hand the suggestion made in 1987 by Ronald Reagan's Secretary of the Interior that Hetch Hetchy be returned to its natural state. The suggestion was politically motivated and made to deflect criticism of the administration's poor record on environmental protection. Still, many engineers and environmentalists believed that the valley could be restored and that alternative water and power sources could be found. Virtually no San Francisco official, however, was willing to undertake such a venture. "I'll do all in my power to fight it," proclaimed San Francisco Mayor Dianne Feinstein. "It's dumb, dumb, dumb."[94] Not everyone agreed, but there are presently no plans to turn off the Hetch Hetchy tap.

A Comparison of Two Cities

MUCH SEEMS similar about the San Francisco and Los Angeles searches for water. They were ambitious young cities convinced that progress and growth were synonymous; that abundant water was an essential ingredient for metropolitan greatness; that municipal control of water and power would be the most efficient and least costly vehicle for expansion (though San Francisco nodded on this one in its arrangement with PG&E); that less-populated and -developed areas were obligated to surrender their resources and independence to the needs of the new urban empires. Both Los Angeles and San Francisco hid their motives when targeting their more distant water sources, relied on federal cooperation (and connivance), took advantage of conflicts of interest, sought water not only for their future needs but also for a vaster area and population, and relied on public funding to fight their adversaries and build their water and hydroelectric empires. Their arrogance aroused widespread concern about their tactics and prompted unanticipated results. San Francisco pushed the public toward a greater appreciation of wilderness, while both San Francisco and especially Los Angeles generated the fear that led to the county-of-origin legislation.

Equally important, and frequently overlooked in this present age when segments of the public automatically equate cities with environmental destruction, both Los Angeles and San Francisco reflected Progressive values nationally that were ascendant when the two cities launched their projects. They provided the people what they obviously wanted: clean, fresh, abundant, and inexpensive water. This demand was of a piece with the public's insistence on pure food and drugs; on playgrounds, schools, and good universities; on cheaper and better transportation; electric power through municipal departments; regulated access to natural resources so as to conserve them; and the host of other achievements associated with Progressive Era reforms. That Progressivism had its darker side, especially in its racism and treatment of ethnic minorities outside the favored Anglo-Saxon pale, should not obscure its nobler accomplishments.

Nor should the ascendance of Progressive ideas be allowed to mask the conflicting interests battling among themselves in both cities. Opponents of municipal electric power were preeminent in San Francisco, but even in Los Angeles they were strong enough to defeat three bond issues to expand the city's distribution system, thus making municipalization a costly and piecemeal process not complete until the mid-1930s. Additionally, conflicts over water

Trees and houses climbing a San Francisco hillside above the bay.
(Courtesy of Redwood Empire Association)

rights in both cities; connivance for special gain by the likes of Fred
Eaton, Boss Ruef, Moses Sherman, and the San Fernando Valley land
syndicate; and much more make it clear that neither Los Angeles
nor San Francisco operated as monoliths. Similarly, in the San Francisco and Los Angeles searches for water, the peculations of some
individuals and the unfortunate fixation on growth for its own sake

by city officials and the public alike should not conceal the success of both cities in providing the public with a clean and inexpensive resource crucial to human survival.

There were also significant differences in the experiences of the two cities. Los Angeles, on the one hand, used its pueblo water theory to establish supremacy over local supplies and then built on that victory at home to advance more ambitious schemes. San Francisco, on the other hand, acquired control of local supplies only after first securing leverage through its monumental Hetch Hetchy venture. It never occurred to early San Franciscans to advance a pueblo rights argument, something one might have expected them to be more inclined than Los Angeles to do in view of the far fewer local water sources. That they did not do so seems in itself a telling commentary on the legitimacy of that notion. By the time Los Angeles had invoked the idea, Spring Valley Water Works had already gained effective control of San Francisco's local water supply and distribution system, which the company refused to surrender until it obtained a handsome price in 1930.

Los Angeles's reliance on the pueblo right helped produce still another major difference between the cities. That right restricted the sale of Los Angeles River water to customers within the city limits, and to circumvent it, Los Angeles (even before the arrival of Owens Valley water, which was free of the restriction) began spreading its boundaries to embrace communities anxious to share in the expanding metropolis's water legacy. It was an arrangement mutually agreeable to the new suburbs and to the boosters of a greater Los Angeles. San Francisco faced no pueblo right restriction. Free to sell to other municipalities and surrounded by communities either opposed to absorption or capable of meeting their water needs in other ways, San Francisco marketed water and hydroelectricity to customers well beyond its borders. For the northern city, unlike for Los Angeles, tribute in the form of revenue, rather than acquisition of territory, became the distinctive feature of empire. Of course, another distinctive feature shared by both was the command of massive volumes of water from distant sources.

Los Angeles and San Francisco began planning their major forays

Hollywood from Olive Hill (later Barnsdall Park), 1895. (Courtesy of California Historical Society/Ticor Title Insurance Collection, Department of Special Collections, University of Southern California)

to the Owens Valley and Hetch Hetchy at about the same time, but Los Angeles completed its aqueduct before San Francisco even had congressional authorization to begin. Another half-dozen years passed before electrical power became available in the northern city on even a temporary basis, and twenty-one years before water flowed through the Hetch Hetchy aqueduct. To a considerable extent, these delays reflected the far greater complexity of the situation that San Francisco faced, including more and better organized opponents: the Spring Valley Water Works, anxious to hold onto its monopoly and profits; the corrupt Union Labor Party in a city noted for the influence of organized labor; and preservationists who successfully aroused nationwide concern about a dam in a national park. In addition, San Francisco expended much time and energy futilely trying to negotiate a right-of-way with the Interior Department while Los Angeles went directly to Congress and demanded the necessary approval. San Francisco also encountered

The same location in 1926. (Courtesy of California Historical Society/Ticor Title Insurance Collection, Department of Special Collections, University of Southern California)

unanticipated difficulties in construction and resistance from voters who, unlike those of Los Angeles, took years to approve purchase of Spring Valley's facilities and repeatedly rejected attempts to establish a municipal power system.

The delays also reflected how much less San Francisco was a child of the Progressive Era than was Los Angeles. Just as the initial stimulus for Progressivism in the state came from southern California, so too did the enthusiasm for Progressive political forms come earlier and with greater effect from the southland.[95] Precisely because Los Angeles so early created a powerful commission led by the passionately driven William Mulholland, the city was able to move decisively ahead. That commission, insulated from direct popular control in classic Progressive fashion and under the influence of the tough, single-minded Mulholland, allowed for the emergence of the Los Angeles Department of Water and Power, the most powerful such municipal agency in the nation. Such an amalgam of polit-

University of California, Berkeley campus, in 1900. North Hall, Mechanical Arts Building with Annex, Bacon Art and Library Building, and South Hall, all viewed from the road north of Harmon Gymnasium. (Courtesy of The Bancroft Library, University of California, Archives Picture Collection UARC pic 3:73d)

ical culture, a powerful institutional base, and a dominating personality played a crucial role in allowing the southland city to hold sway over its region, bypass San Francisco as the state's population and industrial center, and eventually emerge as the preeminent city of the West and one of the leading metropolises of the world.

For both cities, however, and for their urban imitators as well, the volumes of new water transformed landscapes and encouraged lifestyles in sharp counterpoint to California's essentially desert environment. In San Francisco the voracious appetite of Golden Gate Park for water—at one point the bill reached $400,000—long antedated and became a compelling reason for the Hetch Hetchy aqueduct. Trees, flowering shrubs, and lawns marched in lockstep with the subdivisions that moved relentlessly across nearly treeless expanses and sometimes barren fields and eventually up hillsides, as reinforced concrete, steel, and glass permitted developers to offer newcomers homes with views. Soon flatlanders and also many

Aerial view of Berkeley campus, about 1966. (Courtesy of The Bancroft Library, University of California, Archives Picture Collection UARC pic 3:267)

in aeries were boasting swimming pools, some with eye-catching waterfalls and fountains, especially in southern California, destined to become the swimming pool capital of the world. Urban areas north and south saw imported, water-gulping grasses and trees (elm, maple, coral, birch, sweet gum, and others) replace the native oaks and plants as real-estate agents scurried to deliver on the idyllic new Eden promised migrants from the East and Midwest.[96]

The newcomers, in turn, happily acquiesced in the mythmaking, filling their gardens with camellias, ferns, azaleas, marigolds, birds of paradise, and other exotics made available by a mushrooming nursery industry, while also turning out in the tens of thousands as curbside cheerleaders for such annual events as the Rose Parade. Architects (mostly newcomers themselves) encouraged the trend, with the Greene brothers (Charles and Henry) in the south and

Bernard Maybeck in the north filling once treeless neighborhoods with sculpted wooden bungalows. Others opted for the stark, obviously nonarboreal Mediterranean and Mission Revival styles, though they quickly sited them among stands of eucalyptus, conifers, and palms while relying on the bougainvillea's bright red, purple, and orange flowers and green leaves to soften the glare of stucco. Next came the modernists, Rudolph Schindler, Richard Neutra, Cliff May, and their imitators, whose emphasis on "bringing the outdoors inside" made gardens and greenery as indispensable to architecture as blueprints. "Landscape was so important to Neutra," observes architectural historian Thomas Hines, "that when photographers came to take pictures of a new house, Neutra would hold up branches to ensure that the house was seen through a bower of foliage."[97] The resulting "urban forests" that spilled across the city landscapes of California offered dramatic testimony to the magic wrought by the state's modern-day water wizards.

Los Angeles and San Francisco demonstrated what could be accomplished locally with well-organized and no-nonsense drives for water. Those early achievements found admirers, and nowhere was the enthusiasm greater than among federal and state planners who sought to emulate their urban counterparts on an even grander scale.

5 Hydraulic Society Triumphant: The Great Projects

The spectacular success of Los Angeles and San Francisco excited admiration and much envy among federal and state engineers whose own water schemes by the 1920s had produced meager results if not outright failure. The Reclamation Service (Bureau of Reclamation after 1923) had set out following its creation in 1902 with high hopes of making the desert bloom, fostering homesteads, and re-forming society. During the next two decades, morale plummeted, disappointment suffused the agency, and congressmen openly called for its reorganization or elimination. In California, state water planners escaped the opprobrium heaped on Washington's efforts, but that was largely because the public expected less of them, though they chafed at their inability to get their own projects off the drawing board.

Within four decades there was a complete turnabout as the California Department of Water Resources and the U.S. Reclamation Bureau boasted power and influence almost unimaginable to earlier generations. By the 1960s the state had embarked on the largest and most expensive water project ever devised, while the Reclamation Bureau had achieved international fame for its massive dams and hydroelectric plants in California and elsewhere in the West. This transformation accompanied California's emergence as the nation's number one agricultural state (first achieved in cash income in 1929 and then maintained consistently after 1949), as a world leader in urban and industrial development, and as the most populous state in the union after 1963.

At the heart of these changes in California and Washington was an aggressive policy of seeking water on an even grander scale than before. Its proponents included private citizens, businesses, and government on all levels—local, regional, state, federal—sometimes working at cross-purposes but cooperating often enough to transform first southern and then central California into powerful engines for marshaling and transporting water with profound repercussions not only for the entire state but the American Southwest and Mexico as well. The transformation found graphic expression in three massive hydraulic ventures—the Boulder Canyon, Central Valley, and State Water projects—whose evolution mirrored and reenforced shifting patterns in the political culture of the state and the nation.

The Boulder Canyon Project

....

THE TERM *Boulder Canyon Project* masks a multidimensional undertaking that had a deep impact on the state, the West, the entire country, and northwestern Mexico. Its origin can be traced to the turn of the century and to the merging of two forceful ideas. The first belonged to Arthur Powell Davis, nephew of John Wesley Powell, the prominent nineteenth-century geologist who had unsuccessfully urged the federal government to reform land and water laws and who had gained wide public fame as the one-armed explorer who in 1869 had led the first expedition down the Colorado River and through the Grand Canyon.[1] Arthur Davis had grown to manhood inspired by his uncle's exploits and the West's rugged beauty. He followed Powell into the U.S. Geological Survey and later was among the first to sign on with the newly created U.S. Reclamation Service. His attention immediately focused on the Colorado River, the site of his uncle's greatest feats and now, he believed, the means for achievements of his own.

Arthur Davis brought more to his job than ambition. Like other Progressive Republicans, he had deep faith in the role of experts (he himself held a degree in civil engineering), worshipped efficiency, and viewed the federal government as a major instrument for social and political reform. He also shared the irrigation crusaders' belief in the nobility of the small farmer, abhorrence of monopoly, conviction that restoration of the nation's moral fiber lay in reclaiming desert wastes so that more farmers could be put on the soil, and a commitment (albeit a flexible one, as events would reveal) to local control. Though he romanticized the small farmer, Davis was convinced that the West's water supply problems were so enormous and complex that their solution required central planning and federal funding on an unprecedented scale. Intelligent planning, he believed, had to take into account the hydrology of entire river basins. He set for himself an extraordinary goal: harnessing the 1,400-mile-long Colorado River, the sole dependable water supply for a vast area of 248,000 square miles (roughly the size of Texas) that embraced parts of seven American states and two in Mexico.[2]

"I . . . considered problems in all the Western States," Davis later explained, "but there [was] . . . none which . . . excited my interest and imagination and ambition so much as the development of the Colorado River basin." Such an undertaking, he recognized, could not be achieved with the small local projects anticipated in the Reclamation Act and being designed by his fellow engineers. Instead, he concluded as early as 1902, it required "large storage reservoirs" with the keystone structure being a massive dam on the lower river "built as high as appears practicable."[3] Davis was ahead of his time, however, for his ambitions were not shared by his more cautious colleagues in the Reclamation Service. Still, he took heart in the agency's early engineering triumphs, most notably the Salt River Project in southern Arizona where the Reclamation Service designed its first multipurpose undertaking—for flood control, storage for irrigation, and generation of hydroelectricity—and built Roosevelt Dam, completed in 1911, which at 280 feet from bedrock remains the world's highest rock masonry dam. That success and the building of other impressive masonry or concrete storage facilities at such western sites as Shoshone (Wyoming 1910), Arrowrock (Idaho 1915), and Elephant Butte (New Mexico 1916) demonstrated the Reclamation Service's engineering competence at a time when dam failures were common, and prepared it for the more grandiose tasks envisioned by Davis.[4] His opportunity finally came when campaigners for a different scheme of Colorado River development inadvertently gave him a chance to resurrect his plans.

The Imperial Valley Impulse

Those advocates were settlers in a scrubby southeastern pocket of California whose foremost desire was for a canal, not a dam. Location largely explained their attitude. Their homes were in the Imperial Valley, an arid but large and immensely fertile area of 600,000 acres just across the Colorado River from Arizona and immediately north of the Mexican border. The settlers' existence depended on water that entered the valley, where summer temperatures could approach 120 degrees, by way of an overflow channel from the Colorado River, the Alamo Canal, that dipped below the border into Mexico before turning northward and entering the United States. To free themselves from dependence on that waterway and the host of problems that it had created with Mexico, the settlers wanted a canal completely within the United States—an All-American Canal, they called it.

In 1901 when water had first reached the valley through the Alamo, there had been jubilation. Responsible for the engineering was George Chaffey, the developer famed for his accomplishments at Etiwanda and Ontario and now returned from his Australian ventures and looking for new opportunities. His reputation and his genius in renaming the area (formerly known as the Colorado Desert) immediately attracted settlers—2,000 within eight months and continued steady increases thereafter.[5]

Disaster struck in 1905. During the previous year the private company delivering the water, without consulting Chaffey who had by then severed his connection with the firm, opened a new intake on the Colorado River. This one, unlike Chaffey's original cut, was below the border in Mexico because the U.S. federal government had threatened to use its control over the river—based on the stream's alleged navigability—to shut down the firm's operations and enable the new Reclamation Service to take over Imperial Valley development. The company had also felt pressured into making the cut because its diversion facilities north of the border had become clogged with silt, causing settlers to complain bitterly about lack of water. The new intake restored water flow and freed the company from the possibility of a Reclamation Service takeover, but faulty maintenance left the opening vulnerable to floods. In the spring of 1905 a surge of high water tore out the flimsy diversion works and soon the entire Colorado River was pouring through a break a mile wide and sweeping back northwestward into the valley, destroying buildings, drowning crops, and transforming the nearby Salton Sink into the Salton Sea. It took two years and millions of dollars to return the river to its old course, reestablish a secure intake in Mexico, and restore a regulated flow through the Alamo Canal.[6]

The flood was not the only price paid by the Imperial Valley for its new intake below the border. In exchange for allowing the diversion, Mexico demanded up to half the water taken from the river. At first the concession posed no problem but this changed as population and agriculture expanded on both sides of the border, frequently requiring diversion of the entire stream during periods of low flow and, after Mexico had taken its share, necessitating the rationing of water in the more intensely developed Imperial Valley. Fear about economic survival turned to anger when Mexico refused to share in maintenence costs of the canal and charged duties on equipment taken below the border to shore up the levee system. The appearance of refuse, dead horses, and even human bodies in the canal, which carried water for domestic uses as well as agriculture, intensified concern. Especially galling was the news that the bulk of the land being developed in Mexico—some 840,000 acres—belonged to a Los Angeles syndicate whose most notable member was Harry Chandler, son-in-law of Harrison Gray Otis and soon to become publisher of the *Los Angeles Times,* who was even then anticipating great profits from the Owens Valley project as a member of the San Fernando Valley land syndicate. Imperial Valley residents feared that Chandler and his partners would find a way to keep all the Colorado River water for themselves. "These Mexican . . . lands," they protested, "menace us like a great sponge, which threatens to absorb more and more water, until such time as they will take all of the natural flow of the river."[7]

The valley's concerns coalesced into a vigorous demand for an All-American Canal. Because the cost of such an aqueduct exceeded the settlers' resources, they turned to Congress for help, rallying behind the Imperial Irrigation District, a public agency created in 1911 to take over the local water system and to lead the fight. In 1919 they finally found a sympathetic member of the House who introduced a bill authorizing construction of the canal.

The proposed legislation immediately caught the eye of Arthur Powell Davis, now director and chief engineer of the Reclamation Service, who saw it as a perfect opportunity to raise anew his dream of harnessing the Colorado River. By this time the agency's early engineering successes at Salt River and elsewhere were well known. The canal made sense, concluded Davis, but only if it were part of a larger design. To build such an aqueduct without also constructing dams to control "the flood menace" would doom the canal to a short life. Moreover, only with storage to catch the heavy flows of flood times could substantially more water be made available for the Imperial Valley and the entire Southwest. "The Imperial Valley problem . . . ," Davis told all who would listen, "is inseparably linked with the problem of water storage in the Colorado Basin as a whole."[8]

Davis argued with more than the conviction of a longtime advocate of Colorado River development. He was also a man under fire and anxiously looking for a major triumph to redeem his reputation and that of the Reclamation Service. The agency's engineering successes had not automatically produced reclamation successes. Congress had passed the Reclamation Act nearly two decades earlier amid high expectations but those hopes had turned to disillusionment. Few of the Reclamation Service's projects were paying their way, most farmers were abandoning the ventures, and only a paltry 7 percent of the West's irrigated acreage could be attributed to the government. The fault lay not entirely with the Reclamation Service, since political interference in site selections, general agricultural depression following the end of World War I, intense economic and legal struggles among westerners over water, and eastern opposition to competition from western agriculture hampered progress. Other reasons for the dismal showing—selection of settlers who lacked irrigation skills and faulty cost estimates—seemed to most critics, however, a reflection of poor planning by the Service.[9]

How better to counteract such impressions than with a massive project whose success would overshadow previous failures? Like others in earlier times, Davis sought vindication not in defending past actions but in future achievement. And his vision of achievement broadened to the most gargantuan multipurpose project yet contemplated, one that dwarfed the pioneer effort on the Salt River in its ambitious plans for flood control, irrigation expansion, generation of hydroelectricity, and—as a special concession to that group of potential allies from the Imperial Valley—an All-American Canal.

Not everyone greeted the idea of a multipurpose project with enthusiasm. Among those decidedly unsympathetic was the U.S. Army Corps of Engineers, long an antagonist and rival of the Reclamation Service for large construction projects in the West and still unhappy over Congress's passage of the Reclamation Act in 1902. The Corps, a century older than the Reclamation Service, had both military and civil engineering functions. Military responsibilities included constructing forts and supply lines and maintaining engineering instructional programs, while civil functions dealt with navigation improvement and flood control. It was in the civil realm that friction developed with the Reclamation Service, for the Corps viewed dams and hydroelectric generation as impediments to navigation. And flood control, it believed, could be best achieved through massive levee systems alone (that is, no dams), a strategy at odds with the Reclamation Service's desire for reservoirs that could hold water for agricultural and many other purposes. Eventually, as dam building became almost a national fad, the Corps softened its opposition to reservoirs and even began building dams and launching multipurpose projects (sometimes in uneasy cooperation with Reclamation's engineers).[10] For the present and into the future, however, the Corps was more nemesis than friend of the Reclamation Service, a relationship worsened by competition between the two agencies for congressional appropriations.

More outspoken in their opposition to Davis's grand plan were lobbyists from the Imperial Valley. Davis considered their support essential, but at first they resisted tying their canal scheme to his more complex, expensive, and, inevitably, controversial undertaking. Nonetheless, they found it difficult to counter his logic about the relationship between flood control and security for a canal—and the Imperial Valley. Without dams on the river, the valley would always remain vulnerable to a repetition of the 1905 disaster, a reality that residents could not push from their minds. "Each year . . . when the river rose with the snow-melt in June," recalled William Warne, who as a youngster lived on a valley farm and would later rise to prominence in federal and California water agencies, "there was anxiety that it would break into the valley again." Nor could valley residents ignore the support for Davis's ideas coming increasingly from elsewhere in California as booster organizations, chambers of commerce, and city governments discerned benefits for themselves in a major Colorado River project. Valley residents bowed to what seemed inevitable. In April 1922, following extensive engineering field studies under the direction of Davis, two Republicans fully in accord with their party's commitment to centralized planning—Congressman Phil Swing, whose constituency included the Imperial Valley, and Senator Hiram Johnson of California, the former Progressive governor—introduced the Boulder Canyon, or Swing-Johnson, Bill. It called for a large dam on the lower river "at or near Boulder Canyon," a hydroelectric plant to generate sufficient revenue to repay the cost of the dam, and an All-American Canal.[11]

It had taken two decades for Davis's ambition to merge with the Imperial Valley's wishes and create a powerful political engine for water development. But the struggle for the project had only begun, and Davis would not be around to oversee or take credit for its completion. Unable to fend off the Reclamation Service's critics, he was ousted from his job a year later, but his successor, Californian Elwood Mead, was equally committed to the undertaking and more adept at addressing the problems that had brought down Davis. Mead's tenure as head of the newly renamed Bureau of Reclamation (1924–1936) witnessed the bureau's emergence as the world's preeminent builder of massive water projects.[12]

The Colorado River Compact

News of the Boulder Canyon Bill elated Californians but sent shock waves elsewhere throughout the American Southwest, especially alarming the residents of the other six states in the Colorado River Basin—Wyoming, Utah, Colorado, New Mexico, Arizona, and Nevada. They greeted Congress's action with the same foreboding with which Owens Valley settlers had received news of Los Angeles's plans to acquire and take away their water. Deep regional fears of and dislike for California, current then and still alive and well in the West, were stirred. To many westerners California was not only a lurid and morally corrupt society—with its Hollywood flappers and strange ethnic mixture of Asians and midwesterners and Italians, of Catholics, Jews, and Protestants—it was also a behemoth, the largest and fastest-growing state in the basin, and one supremely arrogant. It contributed less water to the river (almost nothing) than any other state and yet had introduced legislation authorizing projects that essentially benefited only California—the All-American Canal and a large dam regulating the flow so that California could take even more water.

"The bill," complained an Arizona leader, "appears to view the whole situation from a California standpoint." The other basin states wanted to expand their agriculture and attract more people and industry. They, too, wanted their own versions of California boom and economic opportunity, and they demanded big projects of their own, pointing out that in some areas they faced an impending water crisis that required immediate attention. "The most serious problem that confronts us at this time," announced a Denver official, "is the future water supply. Unless a construction program is formulated . . . that will bring to Denver and the agricultural communities surrounding it more water . . . any great future growth in Denver's population must be made at the expense of the agricultural communities surrounding it."[13]

The opposition to California and the Boulder Canyon Bill hardened to the point of intransigence only two months after the legislation was introduced when the U.S. Supreme Court handed down a long-awaited decision on water disputes between states. In _Wyoming v. Colorado_ (1922), the court held that the doctrine of prior appropriation applied to states recognizing that doctrine and shar-

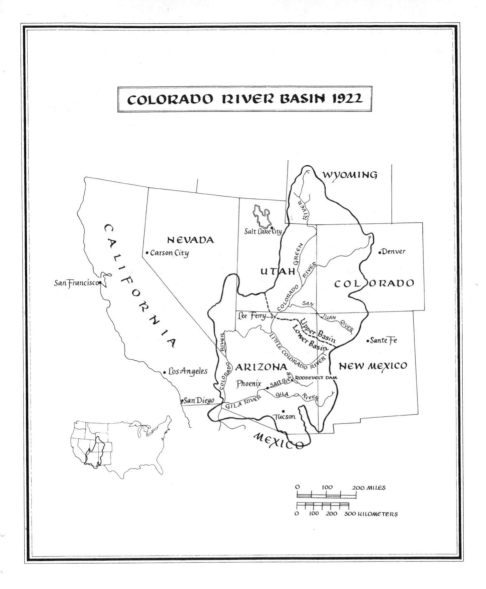

COLORADO RIVER BASIN 1922

ing a common water source.[14] A principle that had earlier applied to residents *within* a state now applied to the states themselves: first in time, first in right. Since all the Colorado Basin states recognized the appropriation doctrine, the message of the Boulder Canyon Bill was clear. Passage of the measure would enable California to gain the lion's share of the river's waters before anyone else, and thus by the doctrine of prior appropriation severely limit growth elsewhere, especially in the upper Colorado Basin where isolation, longer winters, and shorter growing seasons meant slower development.

Vigorous resistance to the bill led to a prolonged six-year battle that resulted in enactment of legislation only when California agreed to some major concessions that still limit the state's actions. The first was the Colorado River Compact, the earliest interstate compact (or treaty) involving more than two or three states to be negotiated under the Constitution's compact clause (Article I, Section 10), and one that sparked numerous similar agreements on other rivers, though none would involve as many states or deal with as large an area or as complex a set of problems. The Colorado pact was negotiated in November 1922, dividing the river's waters between the upper and lower sections of the basin. This agreement foresaw the delivery of 7.5 million acre-feet to the upper basin states (Wyoming, Colorado, Utah, New Mexico) and a similar amount to the lower basin (California, Arizona, Nevada). In addition to this basic allocation, the lower basin could increase its share by an additional million acre-feet (presumed by the negotiators to come from lower-basin tributaries).[15]

The compact effectively suspended the law of prior appropriation between the two basins, thus setting aside a large portion of the river's flow for the upper states until they were ready to use it. In exacting the concession from California, the upper states had a powerful weapon in their control of key congressional reclamation committees where they threatened to keep the Boulder Canyon Bill bottled up unless they got what they wanted. Their control was good for only so much leverage, however. It did not give them sufficient advantage to force projects of their own into the Boulder Canyon Bill, since they lacked engineering studies—studies that would take many years to complete—identifying specific projects. Californians, however, had their engineering reports, thanks to earlier work by Arthur Powell Davis, as well as Davis's congressional testimony that a high dam in the Boulder Canyon area should precede construction anywhere else on the river. Also tempering the upper basin's influence was the flood threat on the lower river. There was widespread fear that a destructive flood could occur at any time, and if one did, Congress would likely rush through the Boulder Canyon legislation with little heed to upper-basin objections. Thus, both sides found reasons to compromise their differences and agree to the Colorado River Compact.

New Players and New Battles

California's acceptance of the compact led to a second concession. The catalyst lay in Arizona's as-yet unsatisfied needs and desires. The newly elected governor of Arizona and many state leaders almost immediately denounced the compact and repudiated their representative who had signed it. The fundamental problem was that while the compact suspended the law of prior appropriation between the basins, it did nothing about modifying the law as it applied to the states *within* each basin. Of the three lower-basin states, this obviously did not bother California, which had nothing to fear from its slower-growing neighbors. It could get legal claim to the water before they could advance a reasonable need for it. Nor did it alarm Nevada, since at that time those portions of its territory that could benefit from the Colorado River were quite small and the water needed for them was readily conceded by Arizona and California. Arizonans, however, viewed California as suspiciously as did the upper basin. The one person who did not was the Arizona representative at the compact negotiations, W. S. Norviel, who believed that California's "ultimate development" was "definitely well-known" and presented no obstacle to Arizona's future growth.[16] To his chagrin, he soon discovered that neither his fellow Arizonans nor Californians, for that matter, shared his optimism.

Norviel returned home from the compact negotiations to find that the new governor, a Democrat, believed that the political issue of a lifetime had been dropped into his lap. George W. P. Hunt accused Norviel and his fellow Republicans of allowing their fascination with central planning and interstate schemes to overlook local needs. He denounced them for failing to assess adequately Arizona's future water requirements and urged the state legislature to take no action on the compact until it had secured "accurate and adequate information."[17] When studies confirmed potential water and hydroelectric power uses not anticipated in either Arizona or California, he mounted a campaign against the compact and the Boulder Canyon Bill, now amended to include the Colorado River pact among its provisions.

In early 1924 Governor Hunt's opposition became shrill and uncompromising when he learned of a new and powerful competitor for the Colorado River. William Mulholland showed up in Washington, D.C., and boldly announced to Congress: "I am here in the interest of a domestic water supply for the city of Los Angeles."[18] The city had earlier expressed support for the Boulder Canyon Bill in order to obtain some of the electricity to be generated at the high dam on the river, but now Mulholland announced the city's intention to get water as well. Indeed, he soon made it clear that he was lobbying not only for Los Angeles but also for communities scattered across the vast southern California coastal plain.

The drought of the early 1920s that, as noted earlier, had sparked Los Angeles's renewed aggressive purchases of land and water rights in the Owens Valley had also prompted interest in the Colorado River. Mulholland realized that tapping the Colorado would require an extraordinarily expensive aqueduct and pumping system to lift the water over the high ridges separating the river from the coastal plain. He decided to persuade nearby communities to help pay the costs, and to assure their receptiveness to the idea he warned of an impending "disastrous water shortage." His predicted arrival for the disaster varied from eight to ten to twelve years by the late 1920s (the earlier drought had ended in 1926), but few noted the discrepancies, and in 1928 numerous communities joined to create the Metropolitan Water District of Southern California (MWD). Creation of the new agency appreciably slowed Los Angeles's geographic expansion, since access to a reliable water supply seldom now required annexation. Earlier planning, noted a city water employee, "assumed that all the area in Los Angeles County, with the exception of that north of the mountains, would eventually be in the city of Los Angeles."[19] Future planning envisaged a city smaller in size but still requiring enormous volumes of water to meet the expectations of those who believed Los Angeles had an almost unlimited potential for population and industrial growth. Nor did the existence of the new agency mean for decades to come any diminution in the city's influence over southland water policy.

Not surprisingly, Los Angeles emerged as the preeminent, though not absolute, power in the MWD, largely through possession of the largest bloc of votes on the board of directors. The initial bill to create the agency stipulated that a member community's votes, as well as its share of imported water and project costs, would be determined by assessed property valuation. For Los Angeles, this would have meant possession of nearly 80 percent of the votes, water, and costs. Other potential members of MWD did not balk at the size of Los Angeles's financial burden or water share (it was widely believed that there would be enough water for everyone into the foreseeable future) but, fearful of being swallowed by the city, they refused their approval until the enabling legislation capped Los Angeles's votes at 50 percent. That number meant that the city still had a formidable position, since a member community's votes had to be cast as a bloc, thereby requiring Los Angeles to acquire the support of only one other member to pass most measures. Moreover, its command of half the votes allowed it to block actions that it opposed. For those measures requiring a two-thirds vote, the city's barrier to success was higher, occasionally requiring compromise or abandonment of a proposal. Los Angeles, however, still held veto power over measures that it opposed. The city's votes, water share, and portion of the costs would decline as new members joined MWD, but for twenty-five years Los Angeles controlled half the votes.[20]

Despite the city's imposing presence within MWD, it consciously avoided the role of tyrant, sometimes out of a desire to foster unity on issues of greater importance to it and at other times to

LOS ANGELES CITY ANNEXATIONS 1920-1990

PACIFIC

OCEAN

YEAR	SQ.MI.AREA	POPULATION
1930	441.74	1,238,048
1940	450.80	1,504,277
1990	468.80	3,485,398

0 1 2 3 4 5 6 MILES

0 2 4 6 8 10 KILOMETERS

1850~1920
1921~1930
1931~1940
1941~1990

disarm threats. In 1948, for example, when Los Angeles, because of uncertainty over the quantity of water in the Colorado River, opposed the admission of new MWD members, an angry local community had a bill introduced in the state legislature requiring MWD directors to vote as individuals rather than as a bloc. The threat was enough for Los Angeles to drop its proposed ban, and in return, the bill to alter voting practice was quietly shelved. Also checking the city's authority and that of MWD were communities like Beverly Hills, Santa Monica, Burbank, Glendale, and others that had independent groundwater supplies and remained aloof from the agency. Los Angeles's desire, especially during the early years, to persuade these and enough other communities to join MWD in order to assure its success and to spread costs kept the city from trying to eliminate assessments based on property value and to substitute a flat water rate. That action, frequently demanded by city residents, would have reduced Los Angeles's financial burden but at the risk of frightening away current and potential MWD members whose costs would have to be increased to cover what Los Angeles was no longer contributing. Such considerations tempered Los Angeles's authority, encouraging cooperation, compromise, and unanimous votes of the board on most issues, while still leaving the city the single most powerful influence on MWD (and hence on the coastal plain, for which MWD supplied water).[21]

MWD also obtained what Mulholland and other city leaders had provided for the Los Angeles Department of Water and Power commissioners: insulation of the board of directors from politics and popular control. In a continued application of Progressive Era concepts of strong administration by expert-guided independent commissions (southern California, it will be remembered, had been the home base of Progressivism in the state), all members were appointed by the chief executive officer of the community that they represented; none ever had to stand for election.[22]

Thus armed with an efficient and powerful new vehicle for acquiring water, Los Angeles reaffirmed its alliance with the Imperial Valley and Bureau of Reclamation, redoubled its efforts on behalf of the Boulder Canyon Bill, and propelled Arizona's Governor Hunt into frenzied attacks on the bill and compact. This new situation convinced many southwestern leaders that California had to be checked with something more than just the compact. Those in the forefront of such thinking were, as before, in the upper-basin states.

Compromises and Enactment

The emergence of Los Angeles as a major player in Colorado River politics and Arizona's intransigent opposition to the compact sent shudders throughout the upper basin. According to the terms of the compact, that agreement would not take effect until all seven basin states and Congress had ratified it. Arizona's strong opposition made ratification impossible while at the same time intensifying upper-state fears that a devastating flood on the lower river might stampede Congress into passing river-control legislation. With a regulated river and no compact, California could take as much water as it wanted. To guard against such a calamity, the upper basin urged Congress to take two steps: (1) permit the pact to become operative with the approval of only six states; and (2) require California to limit itself to a specific portion of the lower basin's allocation. The first action would assure protection of the upper states against California (six state legislatures, including that of California, had already ratified the compact), while the second would protect them against Arizona.

The upper basin's reasoning was straightforward: so long as Arizona refused to approve the compact, that state was not bound by the document's terms. Hence, if California should establish rights to all (or nearly all) the water allocated to the lower basin by the compact, then Arizona, not subject to the compact's restrictions, could obtain the water it needed by simply establishing prior rights to the water of the slower-developing upper basin. The solution to this problem, concluded the upper states, lay with California. That state had to be restricted so that enough lower-basin water remained for Arizona to develop without threatening the upper basin's supply. As a leader from Colorado observed: "The States of the upper basin much prefer a 7-State compact, but they desire a compact of some kind, and with a provision under which . . . California . . . steps into the position of guarantor, so that the upper basin [states] would be reasonably assured . . . they then could go ahead safely in developing their irrigation enterprises and taking water for domestic use."[23]

Congress, after prolonged and heated debate, finally in 1928 gave the upper states what they wanted. It amended the Boulder Canyon Bill to authorize a six-state compact and to limit California to 4.4 million acre-feet plus no more than half of any surplus water unallocated by the compact. Arizona applauded the idea of a limitation, but felt the actual limitation imposed was inadequate and persisted in its objections to the bill and to the compact. Congress made one last effort to promote peace by adding another amendment to the bill giving its prior approval to a special proposed lower-basin pact that would apportion: 4.4 million acre-feet and half the surplus to California; 2.8 million acre-feet, half the surplus, and all the water in the Gila River to Arizona (the Gila was a Colorado River tributary almost entirely within Arizona, which that state did not want to share with anyone); and 0.3 million acre-feet to Nevada. This suggested settlement would one day take on new meaning in the hands of the U.S. Supreme Court, but at the time neither Arizona nor California found merit in it. Nonetheless, there were enough other inducements in the bill as amended for it to win the support of California and all the other basin states except Arizona: provisions for a six-state compact; the California limitation of 4.4 million acre-feet plus half the surplus; a high dam on the lower river; and the All-American Canal.

The bill contained one other major element that provoked sharp debate and threatened to undo the bipartisan coalition emerging in favor of the legislation. This was a provision stipulating that the dam's construction be paid for primarily from sales of hydroelectricity. While advocates of public power wanted the federal government to build the generating plant and sell the power as a measure of breaking the near monopoly (and undercutting the high prices) of private power, others denounced such a possibility as socialistic or worse. They insisted that private industry alone be accorded that opportunity. Phil Swing, the bill's chief architect in Congress, finally forged a compromise by persuading combatants to leave the decision on who would install and operate the power plant to the Secretary of the Interior.[24]

At last Congress approved the bill in December 1928, the Senate by an overwhelming six-to-one margin (54 to 11) and the House by a substantial majority of 167 to 122. In both chambers, Democrats joined with Republicans in almost equal numbers to back a measure that, in promising jobs, water for cities and more farms, elimination of potentially devastating floods, and checks on California's water ambitions, seemed altogether warranted. Two months later, on March 4, 1929, the California legislature agreed to the limitation imposed by Congress and not long after President Herbert Hoover declared the Boulder Canyon Act in effect.[25]

Californians had finally gotten their much-sought legislation, albeit with some important restrictions attached. When it came to water, they had clearly emerged as a powerful force both feared and courted in the West and even in Washington, where the Reclamation Bureau was ecstatic about the giant hydraulic works that it was charged with building and managing. The Secretary of the Interior added to those responsibilities in 1930 by authorizing the federal government to build the hydroelectrical generating facilities and, in a move to placate the advocates of both public and private power, to lease those facilities to a private firm (Southern California Edison) and a public entity (the city of Los Angeles). The two lessees would then generate electricity that they would sell to other private firms and public agencies (including themselves) for resale.[26] The process was complicated, but it essentially put both public agencies and private firms into the electricity business on the lower Colorado River.

The Boulder Canyon Project Act, by authorizing the nation's first great multipurpose project, marked the Reclamation Bureau's emergence as the mightiest federal agency in the American West. In addition, it was a sign, hardly noticed in the enthusiasm, of the Bureau's increasing inattention to its original mandate to promote small family farms.

The Imperial Valley and the Betrayal of Reclamation Law

Evidence of something different in the Bureau's values was reflected in its relationship (through the Interior Department of which it was a part) with the Imperial Valley following passage of the Boulder Canyon legislation. The new law resulted in Hoover Dam (built in nearby and better-suited Black Canyon, rather than Boulder Canyon, and the world's largest at its completion in 1935), which regulated the river and permitted construction of the All-American Canal that began delivering water to the Imperial Valley in 1942. That water, provided at subsidized rates (no interest was levied on the federal funds expended for constructing the delivery system), stabilized the valley's irrigable area at about 440,000 acres and brought a measure of security and prosperity unknown before. It also helped fasten a landed elite onto the area.

Even as the Boulder Canyon legislation made its lengthy and troubled journey through Congress, the Imperial Valley was undergoing major change with the bulk of the irrigated acreage passing from small dirt farmers to a select group—absentee landlords with holdings averaging between 300 and 700 acres and some as large as 3,000 acres. A combination of good water years and none of the disastrous floods as predicted helped produce millions of dollars in farm revenue. Those profits and the promise of a regulated river and the All-American Canal had attracted great sums of investment capital from Los Angeles, San Francisco, and elsewhere. The financiers and speculators snapped up small plots, transforming them into large-scale factory farms under managers who naturally sought to secure maximum returns on their investments. Most of the few farmers who did not sell out to handsome outside offers used their agricultural profits and expanded bank credit to enlarge their own

Hoover Dam in Black Canyon of the Colorado River was completed in 1935. (Courtesy of U.S. Bureau of Reclamation)

holdings, hire managers, and retire to the cooler temperatures and comforts of the coastal cities. That left the valley populated by a handful of owners and operators at the top of the social pyramid and a large underclass of laborers, most of Mexican origin, who toiled for agribusiness by keeping the irrigation ditches open and bringing in the bountiful crops.[27]

The Boulder Canyon Act had, however, provided the Reclamation Bureau with the means of breaking up the Imperial Valley's corporate estates. The act's benefits (Hoover Dam regulated the river, and the All-American Canal freed the valley from dependence on Mexico) theoretically subjected the area to the acreage limitation and residency requirements of reclamation law. Owners, in other

Hoover Dam at night. (Courtesy of U.S. Bureau of Reclamation)

words, were not supposed to receive water for more than 160 acres and had to reside on the land or in the immediate vicinity. In 1930 Northcutt Ely, executive assistant to Secretary of the Interior Ray Lyman Wilbur, stated that he could "see nothing to do but enforce" the law. That announcement immediately made Ely the object of a vigorous lobbying campaign in which valley landowners argued for exemption, principally on the grounds that the area had been substantially developed before passage of the Boulder Canyon legislation. Ely, without benefit of a formal solicitor's ruling, now reversed himself and prepared a letter that Secretary Wilbur signed exempt-

The All-American Canal on its way through the California desert with water for the Imperial and Coachella valleys. (Courtesy of U.S. Bureau of Reclamation)

ing the valley. That Ely's generosity did not go unrewarded became apparent shortly thereafter when he left office with the retiring Herbert Hoover administration and became the Imperial Irrigation District's Washington attorney. His role and Wilbur's letter subsequently became the subject of debate and litigation, but their action had a profound impact by allowing concentrated landholding to continue in the valley. Three decades later the average farm was about 500 acres (some 200 acres more than the average farm holding nationwide by then) with some holdings ranging from 5,000 to 9,000 acres. By then as well, the Imperial Valley was on its way to acquiring one of the highest poverty rates in the nation, with nearly 90 percent of the farm personnel there (most of Mexican birth or parentage) classified as "lower class" in a study of social stratification in agricultural areas of the United States.[28] So much for the dream of irrigated small farms and social reform in the Imperial Valley.

Parker Dam and Lake Havasu on the Colorado River. (Courtesy of Metropolitan Water District of Southern California)

New Water and Accelerated Urbanization

The most profound impact of the Boulder Canyon legislation was on cities, rather than on farmers either large or small, and especially on southern California's cities. Completion of Hoover Dam in 1935 was followed a year later by a hydroelectric power plant that began sending all the power generated to southern California. Eventually Arizona and Nevada contracted for limited amounts of power, but for years the only market was in California. Even before the dam and power plant were constructed, the Metropolitan Water District of Southern California had taken steps to assure itself an aqueduct.

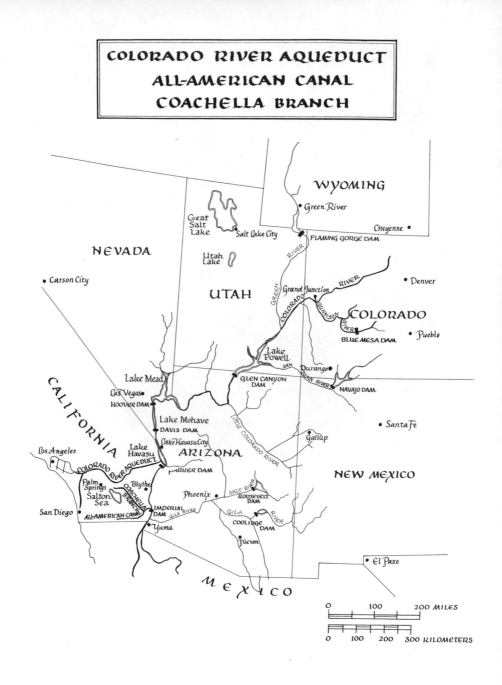

COLORADO RIVER AQUEDUCT
ALL-AMERICAN CANAL
COACHELLA BRANCH

WYOMING

• Green River

• Cheyenne

Great Salt Lake

• Salt Lake City

FLAMING GORGE DAM

NEVADA

Utah Lake

• Carson City

UTAH

Grand Junction

• Denver

COLORADO

Lake Powell

BLUE MESA DAM

• Pueblo

Lake Mead

GLEN CANYON DAM

Durango •

NAVAJO DAM

Las Vegas

HOOVER DAM

CALIFORNIA

Lake Mohave

DAVIS DAM

• Santa Fe

Los Angeles

Lake Havasu

Lake Havasu City

Gallup

COLORADO RIVER AQUEDUCT

ARIZONA

NEW MEXICO

PARKER DAM

Palm Springs

Blythe

COACHELLA BRANCH

Salton Sea

Phoenix •

SALT RIVER

ROOSEVELT DAM

San Diego

ALL-AMERICAN CANAL

IMPERIAL DAM

GILA RIVER

GILA

COOLIDGE DAM

• El Paso

• Yuma

Tucson

MEXICO

0	100	200 MILES

0	100	200	300 KILOMETERS

The Coachella Branch of the All-American Canal delivers water to more than 50,000 acres in the Coachella Valley. (Courtesy of U.S. Bureau of Reclamation)

In 1931 the district's voters by a margin of five-to-one approved a $220 million bond issue to finance the project, and two years later work began on a diversion dam near Parker.[29]

That proved too much for Arizona, still bitter over the Boulder Canyon Act and railing against California in the press and the courts. A new state governor, as uncompromising a foe of California as George Hunt had been, called in the militia to prevent any attempt to anchor the dam to the Arizona side of the river. Only half in jest, the *Los Angeles Times* sent a "war correspondent" to observe the "impending movement of . . . troops into this theater of war to pro-

Contrast of desert and cropland in the Imperial Valley. (Courtesy of U.S. Bureau of Reclamation)

tect the State of Arizona from invasion by all or part of the State of California." An army of five soldiers coordinated movements with an "Arizona Navy" of two ferryboats as the governor announced to the world: "We may get licked in the affair, but we will go down fighting." At this point the Secretary of the Interior ordered construction halted and moved the conflict into the U.S. Supreme Court, which sided with Arizona on the grounds that the Boulder Canyon Act had not specifically authorized a dam at Parker. When Congress speedily remedied that omission in 1935, Arizona was forced to stand aside and construction resumed.[30]

In June 1941 the first water reached the coastal plain through MWD's 242-mile-long aqueduct. Mulholland's "disastrous water shortage" had failed to materialize in the intervening years (and he had long since ceased to be a force, having resigned in late 1928 and died seven years later). His fears that Los Angeles and its neighboring communities might lack adequate supplies seemed unwarranted. The new water, like that earlier from the Owens Valley, exceeded current needs and helped underwrite a future of massive growth. But that, of course, had always been the dream of Mulholland and the voters who regularly endorsed his projects—a water supply capable of supporting the sustained growth of a great metropolis through the most severe of future droughts. At least as early as 1940 planners in the Los Angeles Department of Water and Power concluded that the Mono extension essentially freed the city from reliance on the Colorado. Not until the 1960s would the member communities of the MWD begin using all the Colorado River water brought through the massive system and even then Los Angeles took little of the supply. As late as the mid-1980s the city had never taken more than 10 percent of the share to which it was entitled.[31] Thereafter, however, as will be discussed later, a new combination of circumstances emerged to cast doubt on Mulholland's dream of a water-secure Los Angeles.

The availability of Colorado River water beginning in the 1940s nonetheless had a profound psychological effect on city leaders and planners. It obliterated any sense of restraint about Los Angeles's capacity to absorb ever more people and industries. For surrounding communities, the abundant new supply, including the vast quantity of water unneeded by Los Angeles and available to them, encouraged growth otherwise not possible. The impact could be seen throughout the southern California coastal plain where the water and electricity arrived just in time to meet—and encourage—the demands of the Second World War and postwar boom.

Los Angeles's population almost doubled to nearly 3 million between 1940 and 1970, while that of the four coastal counties of Los Angeles, Ventura, Orange, and San Diego increased two and a half times to more than 10 million during the same period. The growth in numbers accompanied an equally impressive expansion in man-

Beverly (later Sunset) Boulevard at Sepulveda Canyon (upper left), Los Angeles, 1933. (Courtesy of UCLA Department of Geography Air Photo Archives)

ufacturing (aircraft production, shipbuilding, housing construction), service industries (banking, gasoline stations, grocery stores, restaurants, and, especially after World War II, tourism), and research and development centers (Rand Corporation in Santa Monica, the Jet Propulsion Laboratory in Pasadena)—all further stimulated by an infusion of federal dollars, some $35 billion for California alone during the war years, 10 percent of the national total and nearly 60 percent of all federal expenditures in the West. In addition, by the late 1980s the people of urban southern California, through water and power charges, had contributed approximately 76 percent of the $351 million cost, including interest, of constructing and operating Hoover Dam, with the Metropolitan Water District of Southern California alone providing $96.4 million. Made heady by the phenomenal transformation, the Metropolitan Water District

*The same location in 1969, with Sepulveda Canyon almost filled by
Interstate Highway 405. The earlier nearly barren hillsides to the right
are covered with houses surrounded by trees and other foliage. (Courtesy
of UCLA Department of Geography Air Photo Archives)*

as early as 1952 officially proclaimed there was no limit to what it
could accomplish. In the so-called Laguna Declaration it promised
all the water required "to meet expanding and increasing needs in
the years ahead."[32]

The larger significance of California's Colorado River interlude
was not lost on even casual observers. A state that contributed
hardly a drop to the river had, with the help of the federal government, gained control of an enormous volume of water. Moreover,
unlike Los Angeles's Owens Valley venture (especially as reflected
in the roles of Joseph B. Lippincott and Fred Eaton), there was nothing sinister or conspiratorial about the process, for it had been fought
out in the light of courtrooms, legislative halls, and public elections.
It had resulted in restrictions on California as well as victories,

The intersection of San Vincente and Fairfax in Los Angeles, 1922.
(Courtesy of UCLA Department of Geography Air Photo Archives)

though on balance the victories were striking and helped assure California both preeminence in economic hegemony over the American West and a formidable position in the national and world economy. So, too, did another massive hydraulic venture in the Central Valley.

The Central Valley Project

ALIFORNIANS FROM the days of the gold rush had dreamed of transforming the Central Valley into an agricultural paradise. The hydraulic miners had challenged that vision with their environmentally destructive hoses that washed away entire mountainsides, but even before their more abusive practices were outlawed, geologists and other

The same intersection in 1966. (Courtesy of UCLA Department of Geography Air Photo Archives)

experts had concluded that sustained productivity in the valley would require major manipulation of the state's waterscape. To them this judgment seemed reaffirmed by the lessons learned by 1900 from the collapse of the cattle and wheat dry-farming ventures, as well as from the generally poor showing of most mutual water companies and irrigation districts.

The Central Valley appeared to be a geographical paradox. A phenomenally rich and broad alluvial plain, some 450 miles long and 40 to 70 miles wide, it was watered by streams draining the Sierra Nevada on the east and the coastal ranges on the west. As speculators, developers, farmers, and would-be farmers saw it, however, nature had short-changed the area. Precipitation was light and came mostly after the growing season had ended.

Also troubling was the runoff from rivers which ordinarily arrived in great floods and in uneven quantities in the valley's northern and southern portions. The northern section, the Sacramento

Whitsett Pumping Plant, two miles above Parker Dam on Lake Havasu and the starting point of the Metropolitan Water District's Colorado River Aqueduct. (Courtesy of U.S. Bureau of Reclamation)

Valley, contained a third of the land while generating two-thirds of the water. At flood stage the swollen Sacramento River and its tributaries wreaked great havoc at Marysville, Sacramento, and other downstream communities, farms, and ranches. In the southern portion, the San Joaquin Valley held most of the land and contributed a smaller volume of water, but that runoff could still cause severe property damage in the flood season. During the rest of the year, there was enough water to irrigate only a limited amount of land along both the San Joaquin and Sacramento rivers before the two streams met and then meandered through the delta area before emptying into San Francisco Bay. In unusually dry years, the delta could be adversely affected, since saltwater from the bay moved upstream against the diminished current, crippling farming and threatening the new industrial and municipal ventures along the lower delta.

Progressive Era Promise and Disappointment

The flood threat in the Central Valley as well as other obstacles throughout California to the creation of irrigated family farms and to meeting growing municipal needs seemed at first less formidable as a result of the reforms initiated following the election in 1910 of Progressive Republican Governor Hiram Johnson. Under Johnson's leadership, the legislature in 1911 ordered the gathering of data on a wide range of resources, including "water, the use of water, [and] water power, . . . for the purpose of . . . reforming the laws of this state." Three years later, in a referendum election, the public approved a new code asserting state sovereignty over water, giving municipal water uses priority over agriculture and mining, and establishing a state water commission and charging it with eliminating litigation over water rights. As a first step in reducing the court battles, the commission required all appropriators to secure a state permit for a specific quantity of water.[33] Earlier, individuals could do as little as post a claim on a river for any volume that struck their fancy, file a copy with a local recorder, and then try to resolve disputes with other claimants in court if not with weapons.

Johnson and his Progressive followers also sought to promote irrigation and curb monopolists by breathing new life into the irrigation district concept. In characteristic fashion, they significantly increased state supervision by making it virtually impossible for districts to be created or to issue bonds without state certification as to their economic soundness and promise of success.[34]

Still another dramatic example of the Progressive emphasis on centralized planning and conservation was renewed efforts at flood control along the Sacramento River. Major engineering structures

The Metropolitan Water District's Colorado River Aqueduct travels 242 miles from Lake Havasu to its terminal point at Lake Mathews near Riverside. (Courtesy of Metropolitan Water District of Southern California)

began appearing in the late 1890s, but the most significant developments occurred after 1911 when the legislature created a state Reclamation Board and vested it with authority over all protective works in the valley. The Board then joined with the U.S. Army Corps of Engineers to implement a valley-wide plan—the Sacramento Flood Control Project—that laid out a carefully designed network of levees and bypasses to prevent floodwaters from moving across the valley floor and creating havoc. Agricultural development boomed as the new levee system was pushed into place, but experts still sought the security that only a comprehensive plan calling for large dams and massive reservoirs could provide.[35]

Even those fortunate enough to obtain reasonably well-protected land and an assured water supply faced formidable obstacles. Such lands commanded premium prices that steadily increased as their availability declined and demand went up in response to population growth. Costs of production also climbed as a reflection of equipment purchases and land preparation—leveling, ditching, planting. For those who settled in areas, especially in the San Joaquin Valley, where the only water in significant volume was underground, an added expense was the gasoline- or electricity-powered pump that became available by the late nineteenth century. This innovation proved a boon to agriculture, but its long-term blessings were mixed. From less than a million irrigated acres in 1900, such lands in the Central Valley expanded to about three times that area during the next four decades, though the advances produced unwanted side effects.[36] The cost of pumping increased as the water table fell and farms faced the possibility of exhausting the underground aquifers. In some areas, the higher costs forced the abandonment of fields, while in others the declining water table had led by the 1920s to the death of native flora and great numbers of ancient oak trees. The U.S. Reclamation Service hardly made a difference when it first entered the valley. As Donald Pisani has shown, its projects were few, small-scale, and hampered by inadequate resources, opposition from large landowners fearful of the 160-acre limitation, and confrontations with the Army Corps of

Engineers whose primary interest was maintaining the navigability of the Sacramento River, not providing for irrigation.[37]

By the 1920s the dismal record of the Reclamation Service in the Central Valley and in California and the West generally had produced tens of thousands of bitterly disappointed farmers and would-be farmers. The Reclamation Act, viewed by many as the most promising Progressive-Era reform for combatting monopoly and promoting the family farm, had failed on both counts. Nor had the Progressive reforms on the state level fared much better. Hiram Johnson's water commission, touted as the means for eliminating litigation over water rights, had been unable to do so because of court challenges, inadequate funding, and insufficient power to enforce its decisions. More promising at first were the improvements to the irrigation district and the changes that followed. Greater state control over district organization and financing, together with increased demands for specialty crops (intensified by booming agricultural prices during World War I), improvements to the refrigerator car, and revenues from district hydroelectricity sales that reduced farming costs, led to rapid growth in new districts and irrigated acreage. The number of districts statewide increased from a handful in 1913 to nearly ninety by the late 1920s, while the land watered by these agencies mushroomed more than eightfold to 1.6 million acres by 1930, increasing the state's total irrigated area to 4.5 million acres, the highest in the nation. "It seemed to me," noted Frank Adams, head of the California Division of Irrigation, "everyone wanted to form an irrigation district then."[38] The number of farms also increased (from about 73,000 in 1900 to more than 150,000 by 1935), while the average farm size dropped appreciably from just under 400 to slightly more than 200 acres during the same period.

Yet such figures, impressive as they were, did not mean significant advances for the family farm or setbacks for monopoly. While the number of farms increased, the percentage of land in larger holdings not only remained high but rose dramatically. In 1920, for example, 60 percent of the land was in farms of a thousand acres or more, and within fifteen years, the percentage had increased to 70.[39]

Hydraulic Society Triumphant

Not only was more land being held by fewer owners, those owners were increasingly dictating water policy at the local level. This followed the revitalization of a practice first introduced in the late-nineteenth-century swampland district: property-weighted voting. When deciding important issues, those district members with more land had more votes. In 1921 this principle reemerged in a new kind of organization, *the water storage district,* a novel response to those large landowners desiring to construct and control local reservoirs. Unlike the one-man, one-vote requirement of the irrigation district, the water storage district allocated votes on the basis of the value of an owner's holdings—in this instance, one vote for each $100 of assessed valuation. Within a year the Kern County Land Company and two other conglomerates had petitioned to create such districts in the San Joaquin Valley. The Kern County company, as an example, unsurprisingly brought off an election creating a 250,000-acre district in which it held almost half the votes.[40]

Most large landowners were not interested, however, in spending their own money for reservoirs of any appreciable size so long as there remained the possibility that the state and federal governments would do it for them. The power of that belief resulted in only nine water storage districts being created in the next half century. The concept of property-weighted voting, however, was another matter altogether. It readily appealed to the increasing numbers of big growers, resulting in the creation of a host of new water districts serving a variety of purposes. Many of them were established by special acts of the legislature, and all of them incorporated some form of property-weighted voting for important measures. At the same time, agriculture continued to concentrate in ever fewer hands. The number of farms over a thousand acres increased their combined property from 17.6 million acres in 1920 to nearly 25 million acres in 1945. That trend as well as the number of special districts accelerated even more dramatically in the decades that followed.[41] Thus did the family farm and local democracy fade from the California countryside.

The agricultural depression following World War I, the cycle of floods and droughts, the mounting costs of operation, and the declining water table took their toll, especially on the smaller farmers, who with increasing frequency lost their lands and fell into tenantry or migrated to the rapidly growing cities with their myriad job opportunities. The larger farms and great landowners who had subdivided few, if any, of their holdings found it easier to survive—and profit—by taking advantage of economies of scale and the availability of an inexpensive, mobile labor force to harvest their crops. They relied primarily on the Chinese in the late nineteenth century and then, after federal legislation forbade their immigration, the Japanese until the Gentlemen's Agreement of 1907–1908 and the Immigration Act of 1924 barred their entry. In the 1920s they turned to Asian Indians, Filipinos, Mexicans, and Mexican Americans, with the latter two groups supplying 70 to 80 percent of the agricultural workforce by 1930.[42]

Farming advanced in California during the early decades of the twentieth century, but there was always a tenuous quality about it, especially for those in the Central Valley and including even the large landowners. The big growers, as well as those with less acreage and those who only dreamed of securing a farm, sought the security of a comprehensive water program—a program that captured floodwaters otherwise going to waste at sea (later generations would question this concept of "waste") and that only government could afford to undertake. Some at first worried that help from government, whether based in Sacramento or Washington, would restrict their freedom of action, but they worried less about this in the face of the mounting seriousness of the problems they confronted.

Toward a State Plan

The search for a comprehensive water plan for the Central Valley went back at least to 1856 when the California surveyor general called for a "system of reclamation . . . for the whole State where required."[43] Thereafter, others echoed that theme and both the state and federal governments launched investigations, with the massive studies of state engineer William Hammond Hall graphically detailing the problems. No one advanced a substantive proposal until 1919 when increased population and heightened difficulties in the valley and delta prompted Robert B. Marshall to publicize a dramatic plan. A highly respected former member of the U.S. Geological Survey, he had spent years surveying the topography of California. He drew on that knowledge to design a bold project that promised something for every major part of the state. His "Marshall Plan" called for a large dam on the upper Sacramento River and two aqueducts for varying distances on either side of the Central Valley to reclaim vast sections of the Sacramento and especially San Joaquin valleys from their current waterless or low-water conditions, to provide water to San Francisco Bay cities, to improve the navigability of the Sacramento River, and to prevent saltwater intrusion into the delta. For southern California, the project would divert the Kern River to Los Angeles and the south coast by way of a tunnel through the Tehachapi Mountains. Some 12 million acres would be reclaimed in the Central Valley as well as in neighboring Santa Clara, Livermore, and Concord valleys, while Los Angeles would receive four times the volume of water then arriving through the Owens aqueduct. Revenue for the vast scheme would come from the sale of water and electricity generated at state power plants erected along the system.[44]

Despite its promise of something for nearly everyone, Marshall's plan failed to gain approval either in the legislature (where in 1921 it passed the senate but failed in the assembly) or in three modified versions that went on the ballot as initiatives and were rejected by voters in 1922, 1924, and 1926. Nor did Marshall, who harbored ambitions for a state senate seat, help matters by flip-flopping on his own plan, opposing the 1922 initiative, favoring an identical initiative two years later, and then returning to the opposition in 1926. To a great extent, Marshall's plan became a victim of its huge price tag (estimated by Marshall himself to be as much as $800 million) and of nationwide agricultural surpluses in the 1920s that made any increase in farmland seem senseless. The depressed crop prices also aroused opposition among the more successful irrigation districts, which feared a decline in their land values if more acreage became available. The most intransigent critics were private power firms angry over the provision for state power plants which they denounced as "sovietization." While strong support for the idea came from Progressive Republicans (including significant financial contributions from such Progressive stalwarts as Rudolph Spreckels, William Kent, and John R. Haynes), the influence of Progressives waned on some issues in the mid-1920s and then after 1930 as they came to constitute a minority among the increasingly more conservative Republicans who dominated the legislature. Even with the aid of moderate Republican governor William Stephens, they found it exceedingly difficult to counter the vigorous opposition from Pacific Gas and Electric and Southern California Edison as well as those criticizing Marshall's plan on other grounds.[45]

Also joining the naysayers were professional engineering groups, which believed that Marshall had failed to collect adequate data on storage sites. Another concern was the north's fear that it might someday need the water sent south. Los Angeles's pummeling of the Owens Valley and retaliatory dynamite attacks on the aqueduct during the 1920s had raised a specter that no northerner wanted repeated on a statewide scale. To many, the most serious drawback was riparian law. The holders of riparian rights along Central Valley streams, it was feared, could delay, if not prevent altogether, the large-scale water transfer envisaged in the plan.

During the next decade, several developments combined to overcome the major obstacles to a comprehensive water plan. The most troublesome involved riparian law. California courts, it will be recalled, had broadened the doctrine to permit riparians (those who owned property adjacent to a river) to engage in irrigation so long as they recognized that all riparians on the same stream possessed a similar right. As a practical matter, this meant that riparians had reciprocal rights and an obligation to use water reasonably with respect to one another. The problem was that riparians insisted they had no obligation to be reasonable—that is, avoid wasteful practices—in their dealings with appropriators on the same stream.

(Appropriators, it will be remembered, ordinarily lived some distance from the rivers whose waters they used under the law of appropriation.) In 1926 the state supreme court in *Herminghaus* v. *Southern California Edison* agreed with them. Riparians, announced the court, could not be deprived of their rights to a river's flow, including floodwater, even if they used the water wastefully. The decision effectively prevented appropriators from building dams on rivers claimed by riparians and trapping the floodwaters absolutely necessary for new development at some distance from the streams, or for recharging distant and declining underground aquifers.[46]

The ruling shocked the public into howls of protest which culminated in 1928 with a popularly voted initiative amending the state constitution and prohibiting any "waste or unreasonable use" of water. The "rocking chair" theory of riparian rights was gone; riparian owners could no longer just sit by an adjoining water course and, even though not using it, claim a right to its undiminished flow. To survive a challenge from an appropriator, a riparian had to put water to *"reasonable beneficial use."* Debate would continue on the meaning of "reasonable" and "beneficial," but the amendment removed a significant hurdle to statewide water planning and established a principle that legal experts agree remains "the central theme of modern California water rights law."[47]

Anticipating approval of the amendment, the legislature during the previous year authorized the state to establish water rights in its own name—to the floodwaters that it intended to trap—and absolved the state of the requirement to diligently use the water in order to maintain its rights. In this way, the state could acquire and hold on to rights until its projects were constructed. As for northern California's fear of a repetition of the Owens Valley incident on a statewide scale and its wish for assurance that it could someday get back water sent south, the legislature responded in 1931 with the county-of-origin law, a statute applying only to appropriations for the state project and stipulating that counties could retain water rising within their boundaries if needed at any time in the future.[48] Not everyone—north or south—felt comfortable with the law, and

many questioned its constitutionality, but it helped win the support of some who otherwise would have resisted a statewide plan.

Two remaining major obstacles to a comprehensive program for
the Central Valley were engineering data and cost. These difficulties were partly overcome in 1931 when State Engineer Edward
Hyatt unveiled a plan that, while still impressive, was considerably
scaled back in comparison to Marshall's proposal. The Hyatt price
tag was estimated at $500 to $600 million ($200 to $300 million less
than Marshall's) and the engineering requirements were fewer and
better detailed. During the decade following the legislature's rejection of Marshall's plan in 1921, both the state and federal governments had collected and analyzed great quantities of data on state
water resources and needs. The proposal that Hyatt released in
1931, christened the "State Water Plan" (not to be confused with the
State Water Project launched nearly three decades later), required
Californians to shoulder the bulk of the cost, but there would also
be contributions from Washington for those aspects which involved
federal responsibility: flood control and navigation improvement.[49]

Stripped to its essentials, the Hyatt proposal, like Marshall's,
called for: (1) a major reservoir on the Sacramento River (at the
present-day site of Shasta Dam) to store floodwaters; (2) regulated
releases to improve navigability along the lower Sacramento and to
prevent saltwater intrusion in the delta, while also providing additional fresh water for the growing cities, industries, and farms along
the southern delta; (3) an interconnected canal and reservoir system
for taking the Sacramento River water, which had been stored behind Shasta Dam and slowly released, out of the delta and down
into the much drier San Joaquin Valley; and (4) an aqueduct from
the Colorado River to the southern California coastal plain. The entire undertaking, as in the Marshall Plan, was to be paid for by water and power sales.

Almost immediately, however, the proposal was modified in one
important particular. Since southern Californians had already taken
steps to secure Colorado River water on their own and feared that
involvement with the state would unnecessarily delay and compli-

cate their plans, they asked not to be included in any future undertaking. With the absence of southern California, Hyatt's so-called State Water Plan automatically became essentially a Central Valley project, transferring water from the northern Sacramento Valley to the San Joaquin Valley.

American Political Culture and the Central Valley Project

The release of Hyatt's plan coincided with the most severe economic catastrophe in American history, the Great Depression of the 1930s. That crisis had profound consequences for American political culture generally as well as water policy and projects both nationally and throughout the West. Measured by the number of people thrown out of work, businesses destroyed, banks made insolvent, farms and homes lost through foreclosure, tenants evicted from the land, city dwellers thrown onto the streets, and overall social misery, the depression of the 1930s was unprecedented, far surpassing the panic of the 1890s, until then the greatest financial debacle experienced by the country. On that earlier occasion, Democratic President Grover Cleveland's failure to respond with effective countermeasures to the crisis or to address boldly other social problems long building in the rapidly urbanizing and industrializing nation had led to strong popular rejection of him and his party. The repudiation was so overwhelming that it shifted the country's political balance of power over to the Republicans until the 1930s, as voters rallied around that party's traditional commitment to strong and active government, centralized planning, and Progressive Era reforms. The party secured such a tight lock on the White House that it surrendered only to Democrat Woodrow Wilson (also a reformer and believer in an activist central government) during the next four decades.[50]

The eruption of the Great Depression found a Republican as President, Herbert Hoover, who was soon reaping the same public scorn for inaction earlier heaped on Democrat Cleveland. Hoover actually did much more to combat the economic emergency facing him than Cleveland had done years before, but in the public's view he failed to do nearly enough. Voters summarily rejected him, as they had Cleveland, and in the election of 1932 placed their confidence in Franklin D. Roosevelt's promise of a New Deal for all Americans. Though a Democrat, Roosevelt, like the Progressive Republicans of an earlier era, pledged to bring the full authority of the national government to fighting the depression. Once in office, he orchestrated the passage of a panoply of laws and the creation of a multitude of agencies aimed at providing relief, recovery, and reform. The staggering volume of activity made earlier Republican efforts seem minuscule by comparison and prompted widespread public perception that Democrats had replaced Republicans as champions of centralized planning and a strong, activist government. There was much truth in the popular perception, for profound readjustments had been taking place in American political culture that were producing reverberations throughout the nation.

To a great extent, the readjustments reflected changes in emphasis rather than a complete repudiation of earlier values. Whig/Republican ideology had always been sensitive to the needs of business, viewing the creation of a national environment favorable to investment and industrial development as a major responsibility of the central government. Thus, Republicans of the early twentieth century, like their nineteenth-century predecessors, advocated protective tariffs and internal improvements like highways, canals, and water projects as legitimate activities of government. During the Progressive Era, though their record on suffrage and their policies toward ethnic minorities were badly flawed, they also had an especially sensitive social conscience. It emerged forcefully in reforms like those providing for workers' compensation, publicly owned hydroelectric plants to assure fair rates and serve as a check on the so-called power trust, and pure food legislation, just as their moral values had earlier found expression in demands that blacks be freed and given civil rights.

During the 1920s, however, as business flourished and as the nation's cities filled with hundreds of thousands of immigrants from southern and eastern Europe, Republicans increasingly came to believe that the promotion of business and restriction of immigration (Whigs/Republicans had always frowned on the cultural baggage of newcomers) were the only really important functions of an activist government, with business far and away the more important of the two. In practice, such thinking led to the elimination or nonenforcement of numerous regulations hampering business in its search for profits; repudiation of the earlier Progressive support for public power (as had already begun in the struggles for the Boulder Canyon and Central Valley projects); and opposition to government at the national level assuming responsibility for social problems like unemployment and welfare. Relief for the unemployed and destitute, according to Republicans, even in times of severe economic dislocation, should be provided through voluntary efforts, charitable organizations, state and local governments, and by the affected individuals themselves who, it was believed, often merely had to work harder to retain and advance in their jobs. Thus, when it came to programs on behalf of the general public, Republicans, on the eve of the Great Depression, had begun taking over and espousing the old Democratic principle of laissez-faire—a principle that restricted Herbert Hoover's ability to move effectively against the economic catastrophe that greeted him.[51]

The Democrats, meanwhile, had been moving toward the earlier Whig/Republican preference for a strong, activist government, but in the spirit of their traditional mood of distrust of powerful business interests. Cautiously at first in the industrialized states (New York, Illinois) from about 1910 on, and at the national level during the administration of Woodrow Wilson (1913–1921), and then dramatically in response to the upheaval of the 1930s depression, they abandoned their traditional laissez-faire stance and transformed the federal government into a vigorous engine for large-scale, centralized planning and reform. They found a powerful constituency in the general American public hard hit by the depression, and especially among the Jews, Italians, Russians, Poles, Greeks, Czechs, Slovaks, and other new immigrants suffering from mass unemployment and who had also been alienated by the Republicans' anti-immigration legislation of the 1920s. Following FDR's election in 1932, the Democrats solidified their support among voters with a barrage of laws regulating business; providing workers with jobs, the right to bargain collectively, and minimum wages; and assuring relief and Social Security benefits to the unemployed, sick, and elderly.[52]

The cataclysm of the Great Depression did not cause the Democrats or Republicans to abandon altogether their traditional goals, but, rather, to make a shift in tactics.[53] Democrats remained firmly wedded to the Jeffersonian/Jacksonian ideals of individual freedom and protection of civil liberties, but they now saw the safeguarding of those freedoms in a strong, activist central government that could assure citizens a decent standard of living. Similarly, Republicans continued to stress the old Whig emphasis on government support for national economic development (through tariffs, highways, water projects, and the like) and friendliness toward business. Thus they now identified such support with greater laissez-faire and less government activity of any sort, especially when it came to the regulation of business, the promotion of public hydroelectric power ventures that competed with private business, and the support of social welfare programs.

Still, whenever broad political shifts occur, there are those whose values and tactics cause them to harmonize uneasily, and frequently not at all, with the new majorities in their political parties. Some Democrats looked suspiciously on novel federal programs that they believed restricted individual freedom, undermined traditional labor relationships, and encouraged minority bloc voting and class warfare. They often hid behind the banner of states' rights and sided with Republican opponents of some New Deal programs. Similarly, many Republicans refused to abandon their Progressive ideals, which they now believed flowered in the New Deal policies of FDR.

This possibility for party labels to mask a range of political beliefs became especially pronounced in California where a system known as "cross-filing" (enacted in 1913 during the Progressive Hiram Johnson administration) allowed a candidate to become the nominee of more than one political party for the same office. Candidates who won the primaries of both major political parties could count on almost certain victory in the general elections. Such a system downplayed the importance of party labels while enhancing the value of name recognition, a consideration that worked to the advantage of incumbents. Though Democrats established a three-to-two voter registration edge over Republicans during the depression, Republicans, the longtime incumbents in most elective positions, proved more adept at manipulating the cross-filing system and maintaining their control of the nominating process of both parties. They were aided immeasurably by a state press that was overwhelmingly Republican and by unofficial party associations (especially the California Republican Assembly, founded in 1934) that united local groups behind specific candidates.

With the exception of one four-year period (1939–1943), Republicans continued to control the governorship, as they had since the 1890s, and did so for three decades after the depression's onset. A Democratic landslide in 1958 finally led to the elimination of cross-filing the following year. Throughout the same period, Republicans outnumbered Democrats in the state senate and fell behind in the assembly only for six years (1937–1943). Such success tended to produce Republican officeholders who (while generally to the right of their Progressive predecessors) carefully avoided emphasizing their Republicanism before a largely Democratic electorate, who tended to be pragmatic rather than political ideologues, and whose positions on resource development and other issues frequently made party loyalty a matter of secondary importance.[54]

The realignment within American political culture during the depression formed the new context in which water projects and policy generally were worked out during the next half century. It was a culture in which the two major parties could, despite their different positions, unite on the need for massive water projects and sometimes reach a compromise on such issues as public power, acreage limitation, and ultimate ownership of the projects. Within California, it was also a culture shaped by the peculiarities of cross-filing (so long as that system remained in place) and by sharp regional differences over water policy that frequently cut across party lines and pitted the more humid north against the arid south. Signs of these changes had already emerged before the depression, but with that economic catastrophe and during the decades that followed, the new alignment of values and strategies moved forcefully to the forefront, nowhere more graphically than in the struggle over the Central Valley Project.

From State to Federal Project

In 1933, two years after State Engineer Edward Hyatt had released his Central Valley plan and with California and the nation in the depths of the depression, the state legislature endorsed the Central Valley Project (and $170 million in bonds for construction of initial units). Though the margin of victory in the senate was narrow (two votes more than the majority needed), the assembly overwhelmingly approved the measure by a tally greater than five to one.[55] The affirmation reflected the project's relatively low estimated cost; compelling engineering studies; a severe drought that had gripped California since 1929 and would continue until 1935; the need for hydroelectricity for the state's farms, cities, and manufacturers; the promise of fresh water to combat saltwater intrusion and to meet the urban, industrial, and agricultural needs in the delta area; and the assurance of jobs that the project would create for the unemployed (20 percent of the state's population was on relief), a consideration that caused the earlier concern about a glutted agricultural market to pale by comparison.[56]

Nonetheless, approval had not come easily. Though voters nationally were evicting Republicans from office in wholesale numbers, the party in California, primarily through cross-filing and avoidance of extremes, would maintain control of the governor's mansion and both houses of the legislature for most of the 1930s,

1940s, and 1950s. In 1933, the Republicans overwhelmingly out-numbered the Democrats in the legislature—nine to one in the sen-ate and more than two to one in the assembly. With few exceptions the Republican majority, and some Democrats as well, resisted at-tempts (coming primarily from a handful of Progressive Republi-cans) to incorporate meaningful public power provisions into the Central Valley Project (CVP) Bill. Many objected to public power in principle, while others favored it, but not at the risk of getting the water project bogged down in a controversy with private power. Both groups did an about-face only when confronted with disturb-ing news from Washington. Depressed economic conditions made it abundantly clear to all that only the federal government could af-ford to purchase the construction bonds or otherwise provide fund-ing for the CVP. When New Deal administrators learned that the California legislature planned to enact a bill without adequate pro-vision for public power, their message was clear: no public power, no federal help. The result, in the words of one state senator, was "a complete capitulation to . . . public ownership."[57]

For the legislators, including the Republican majority, the shift came quickly because of their conviction that the project was far too important for California agriculture and business recovery gen-erally to sacrifice on behalf of any single interest. Besides, so far as public power was concerned, the Republican Herbert Hoover ad-ministration had earlier (in 1930) made an important concession by allowing public agencies as well as private firms to sell electricity generated at Hoover Dam. In July 1933 Republican state legislators joined with Democrats to approve a CVP bill containing strong pub-lic power provisions by a vote of twenty-three to fifteen in the sen-ate and fifty-eight to eleven in the assembly. Though a majority in both parties supported the legislation, a sizable portion of Republi-cans in the senate (about 40 percent of those voting) and a smaller number in the assembly (16 percent) registered dissent. The Dem-ocrats, as well, had some naysayers, but only one in the senate (out of a total of four who voted) and just three in the assembly (of the twenty who voted), though their percentage of negative votes in the assembly (15 percent) was similar to that of the Republicans (16 percent). Analyzed by region, the tally revealed that the strongest support came, not surprisingly, from Central Valley delegates in both houses of the legislature. A similarly strong endorsement came in the assembly from northern representatives (above the Tehachapis) as well as those from the south, but in the senate the two regions only barely approved the project.[58] Thus, the measure had bipartisan and north-south support, but among Republicans and in both regions there were a significant number of dissenters. Still, a Central Valley Project Bill had finally been passed, and the legislature sent the measure to the governor who promptly signed it into law.

The struggle renewed almost at once, this time statewide. Warned that private power planned to strike back with a referendum campaign, Republican Governor James Rolph sought to deflect the threat by announcing publicly his strong support for the Central Valley Project: "If any special interests try to block this measure or delay it in any way, I am prepared to fight them to the last ditch of my executive authority."[59] He said nothing about the public power provisions in the new legislation, a reflection of his hope that, by not mentioning the matter, private power might back off.

Rolph's strategy failed. Under the vigorous leadership of PG&E, opponents collected 85,000 signatures in less than two months and forced a referendum election. Southern Californians (excluded from the project as they had requested) also joined the opposition on the grounds that they objected to being taxed to help the north. Moreover, no projects for the south meant no jobs for residents there. Southern California's large orange-growing establishment, fearful that additional water would accelerate citrus production in the valley, slammed the proposal because of the competition it threatened to encourage. Rolph and Republican advocates of the CVP continued to emphasize the state's need for the project, with most saying little or nothing about power. Yet those supporters in the Democratic party (as well as the Progressive Republicans committed to public power) underscored the law's hydroelectricity provisions in addition to its other benefits, a stance taken as well by the Grange, the League of Municipalities, and organized labor. Proponents also stressed that the CVP was a "rescue project," designed not to bring new lands into production but to save acreage already developed and threatened with destruction by drought and the depletion of groundwater supplies.[60]

In December 1933 voters sustained the Central Valley Project, but the margin of victory was slim (33,600 votes out of more than 900,000 cast), owing to Los Angeles County's two-to-one opposition. In the north, nearly 70 percent of the voters in the counties surrounding San Francisco Bay supported the project, while all but one of the twenty-seven Central Valley counties approved it. Not surprisingly, the San Joaquin Valley registered overwhelming enthusiasm, delivering a five-to-one endorsement. Madera, Kings, Kern, and Tulare counties each returned a favorable vote greater than fifteen to one, and in Tulare County, where the declining water table had become especially hazardous, it reached thirty-three to one.[61]

The victory at the polls did not guarantee the Central Valley Project. Power and water revenues were supposed to pay for it, but first the bonds had to be sold to build the dams, canals, and power plants. Because of the worsening economy, California leaders did not even try to market the bonds but, as they had already anticipated doing, hurried instead to Washington for help. They had all along expected federal aid for flood control and navigation improvement, and had hoped that Washington would purchase the bonds or even provide interest-free loans or an outright grant for much of the construction. Now they asked the federal government to shoulder the entire burden.

President Franklin D. Roosevelt, open to almost any proposal that would create jobs and soften the depression's harshness, proved sympathetic. In 1935 he released emergency relief funds so that construction could begin, stipulating that the allocation was made "in accordance with the reclamation laws." Two years later, after a brief scrap with the Army Corps of Engineers, which sought

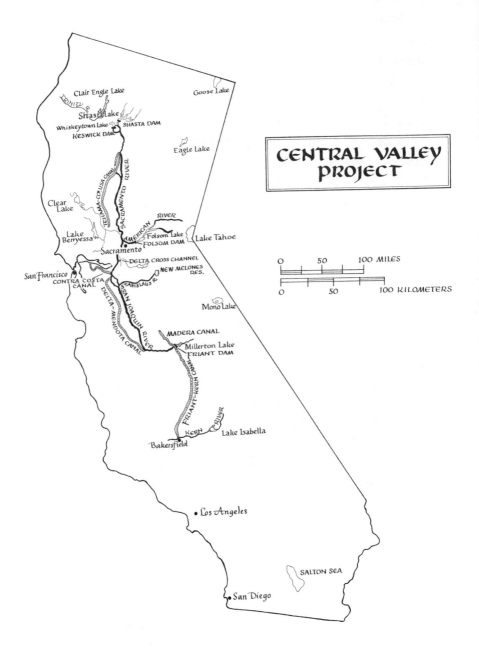

Clair Engle Lake

Goose Lake

TRINITY

Shasta Lake

Whiskeytown Lake — SHASTA DAM

KESWICK DAM

Eagle Lake

Clear Lake

American River

Folsom Lake

Lake Tahoe

FOLSOM DAM

Sacramento

Lake Berryessa

DELTA CROSS CHANNEL

San Francisco

NEW MELONES RES.

CONTRA COSTA CANAL

STANISLAUS R.

DELTA-MENDOTA CANAL

SAN JOAQUIN RIVER

Mono Lake

MADERA CANAL

Millerton Lake

FRIANT DAM

FRIANT-KERN CANAL

KERN RIVER

Lake Isabella

Bakersfield

Los Angeles

SALTON SEA

San Diego

TEHAMA-COLUSA CANAL

SACRAMENTO RIVER

CENTRAL VALLEY PROJECT

0   50   100 MILES

0   50   100 KILOMETERS

the Central Valley undertaking for itself, he secured formal congressional approval for the Reclamation Bureau to take over the project.[62] Thus what had started as a state undertaking now became a federal project, delighting the Reclamation Bureau, which was still heady from its gains in the Boulder Canyon Act. The change was to have profound consequences not only for the Central Valley but also far beyond California's borders.

A Project at Last

The federal takeover assured realization of the Central Valley Project, but its completion came slowly, piecemeal, and often with bitter clashes over policy that linger into the present. In its essentials, the project by the early 1950s consisted of several major dams to control floods, prevent saltwater intrusion into the delta, improve navigation on the lower Sacramento River, and provide irrigation water: Shasta and Keswick dams on the Sacramento and Folsom Dam on the American River, all of which would capture floodwaters and release them when needed into the Sacramento Valley's streams for irrigation; and New Melones Dam on the Stanislaus River and Friant Dam on the San Joaquin. (Folsom and New Melones were later additions to the original CVP, built by the Army Corps of Engineers in 1955 and 1978, respectively, and operated by the Reclamation Bureau.) In addition, it included four principal canal systems moving water in several directions for different purposes: the Tehama-Colusa Canal bringing water down into a section of the northern Sacramento Valley, on the west side; the Delta Cross Channel and Contra Costa Canal to impede saltwater intrusion into the delta and provide water for the farms, cities, and industries of the delta area; the Delta Cross Channel and Delta-Mendota Canal for moving water into and through the San Joaquin Valley; and the Friant-Kern and Madera canals serving irrigation needs in the San Joaquin Valley with runoff collected at Friant Dam from the Sierra Nevada. When completed, the Central Valley Project consisted of 20 dams and reservoirs and 500 miles of canals for man-

Shasta Dam and Lake Shasta on the Sacramento River near Redding, California, are the major northern components of the Central Valley Project. (Courtesy of U.S. Bureau of Reclamation)

aging 9 million acre-feet of water supporting 2.5 million city dwellers, 3 million acres of farmland, and a vast array of fish and other wildlife. In addition, it generated 5.6 billion kilowatt hours of electricity annually at eleven power plants for some 2 million people, receiving $34 million in power sales to help pay for the project.[63]

Work on the Central Valley Project began in 1937 with the first power available for sale in 1944. Delivery of water to the San Joaquin Valley took even longer, not arriving until 1951 through the Delta-Mendota Canal, some fourteen years after the Reclamation Bureau had begun construction and had expended nearly a half billion federal dollars, more than two and a half times the $170 million authorized by the state in 1933 and a gigantic infusion of federal money into the state economy. In part, the delays and high costs were due

Delta Cross Channel near Walnut Grove, California. Water is diverted from the Sacramento River through the Delta Cross Channel into Snodgrass Slough. It then flows through natural channels to the Tracy Pumping Plant where it is lifted into the Delta-Mendota Canal and sent south. (Courtesy of U.S. Bureau of Reclamation)

to shortages of material and personnel following America's entry into World War II. Time-consuming and expensive struggles invoking eminent domain to secure rights-of-way and water rights also hindered progress as did inflation and changes to the state plan mandated by discoveries in the field.[64] The delays were also due to bitter differences over two far-reaching policy issues: public versus private power and the 160-acre limitation provision. Both raised the question as to who should benefit from the cheap power and water that would be made available at taxpayers' expense.

Friant Dam, a key link in the Central Valley Project, is northeast of Fresno, impounds the San Joaquin River (creating here Millerton Lake), and makes possible diversions into Friant-Kern Canal (at right) for delivery as far south as the Bakersfield area. (Courtesy of U.S. Bureau of Reclamation)

Roosevelt's decision in 1935 to make his emergency allocation to the CVP subject to reclamation statutes and Congress's subsequent action putting the Reclamation Bureau in charge of the project automatically subjected the undertaking to reclamation law. That law mandated that project water could be used on only 160 acres. All irrigated acreage in excess of the limit, according to a 1926 amendment to the Reclamation Act, had to be sold within ten years at a price that reflected the value of the land prior to the arrival of project water. These conditions mirrored the purposes of the original 1902 legislation: to reclaim arid land, promote the family farm, and prevent speculators and large landowners from profiting at government expense. Landholders benefited from the government in two principal ways: they were not charged interest on the funds advanced by Washington to build the water delivery systems, and their operating costs were reduced by the revenue obtained from the sale of hydroelectricity generated at government plants.

The problem in the Central Valley was that all the land within the

Friant-Kern Canal about two miles below Friant Dam. (Courtesy of U.S. Bureau of Reclamation)

project area had passed into private hands long before the Reclamation Bureau's arrival. Moreover, the bulk of it was in holdings far greater than 160 acres and much belonged to absentee owners. This is not to say that most farmers held excess lands. About a dozen years before project water arrived, a government study revealed that 89 percent of the owners in three representative San Joaquin Valley counties held 160 acres or less. Most of the irrigable land (66 percent of it), however, was in holdings that exceeded the limit. And the bulk of that excessive land was in only a few hands: fewer than 6 percent of the owners held 53 percent of the excessive lands.[65]

Another provision of reclamation law that came in for sharp debate concerned hydroelectricity. The law (a 1906 amendment to the original legislation) stipulated that power generated at Reclamation Bureau plants be used to construct and maintain the projects, with surplus electricity being leased at the lowest possible cost and "preference" given to "municipal purposes."[66] Private power companies had all along vigorously opposed government distribution of power as "socialistic and un-American." When the California legislature had originally approved the CVP as a state project in 1933, it had authorized only public power production with sales preference to public agencies, a decision reaffirmed by voters in the referendum election on the issue later that year. Private power firms refused to admit defeat, however, and now that the CVP was a federal undertaking, they waged a protracted struggle to undermine the public power provisions of reclamation law.

The Battle over Acreage Limitation

For nearly a decade following Washington's decision to put the Reclamation Bureau in charge of the Central Valley Project, federal officials soft-pedaled the controversial aspects of reclamation law. As with the Boulder Canyon Project, the Reclamation Bureau did not want to jeopardize an opportunity to get beyond past failures and become identified with enterprises of national and international distinction. This problem did not exist everywhere. On the lands irrigated with water from Grand Coulee Dam in the state of Washington, the Bureau could enforce restrictions on landholding without arousing vested interests and jeopardizing an enormous project. Grand Coulee, when completed in 1942, was a mile long, three times larger than Hoover Dam, and would serve the largest irrigation development ever underwritten by the federal government. Moreover, Congress had passed special legislation on that project in 1937 limiting holdings to small parcels of 40 acres and then six years later allowed the size to increase, but only to a maximum of 160 acres and only if the Secretary of the Interior agreed that the additional land was necessary to maintain a viable farm.[67]

The sharp contrast with the many estate-size farms in California stemmed primarily from the lack of irrigation in the Grand Coulee area prior to the project's completion and from the absence of groundwater as an alternative source and a way of skirting federal acreage limitation. Furthermore, in California during the depression years, unlike at the as-yet uncompleted Grand Coulee, Reclamation Bureau officials were reluctant to do anything that might jeopardize the economic recovery of the vast farmland already developed. Then, too, there was always the chance that the rival Army Corps of Engineers, not subject to reclamation law and already engaged in flood-control efforts in the Central Valley, might mount a takeover bid. In 1943, however, Washington's policy of ignoring reclamation law in the Central Valley abruptly ended, unnerving California's growers and sending them hurrying for ways to protect themselves.

Precipitating the turnaround was a decision reached by Secretary of the Interior Harold Ickes, who for several years had contemplated taking such action. He shared Roosevelt's concern about the depression's downtrodden and found special cause for alarm in the contrast between the miserable plight of migratory farmworkers and the success of agribusiness so vividly described in 1939 in John Steinbeck's *Grapes of Wrath* and Carey McWilliams's *Factories in the Field*. So long as the field-workers had been primarily ethnic minorities, they had largely escaped the attention of even the most ardent New Deal reformers. That neglect, together with pressure coming especially from western and southern growers to exempt farm labor from New Deal reforms, had deprived field hands of the improved wages and working conditions and the right to organize given to industrial workers in federal and state legislation. The cheap labor costs made possible by the employment of these unfortunates had constituted a special subsidy provided growers by an America unaware of or uninterested in this agricultural underclass. By the 1930s nearly two-thirds of California's farmers were relying on hired workers, but most employed only a handful of people to work several days. Those primarily benefiting from serflike workers were a minority: 10 percent of the farmers, who by 1935 were producing more than half the crops with 75 percent of the harvest workforce.[68]

By the 1930s, however, the farm workforce had undergone a major transformation, with the majority for the first time consisting of whites, many with their families, who had flooded into California from the Dust Bowl area. These were people with whom the majority of white Americans found it easier to identify, especially when their sufferings were graphically described by Steinbeck, McWilliams, and other critics. While Steinbeck aroused national public sympathy for them with his best-selling novel, McWilliams documented the brutal tactics of grower organizations like the Associated Farmers and set forth a bold solution to the problem: transform the large agricultural estates into farms collectively owned by the people working them. Ickes and Roosevelt seemed unwilling to go that far, but they did believe reform was mandatory. Reclamation projects should "give first chance to the 'Grapes of Wrath' families of the nation," asserted the President. To which Ickes added: "It is the age-old battle over who is to cash in on the unearned increment in land values created by a public investment."[69]

Anticipating the uproar that a policy reversal would create in the Central Valley, the Reclamation Bureau dragged its heels on reform and further angered Ickes by supporting congressional measures exempting two projects from the 160-acre limitation: the Colorado–Big Thompson Project in Colorado in 1939 and the Truckee Project in Nevada a year later. Preoccupied with other matters, Ickes did not learn of the exemptions and the approval given them by his subordinates until Congress had acted (though Congress stipulated that the exemptions were not precedents for other projects). To circumvent the Bureau's conservative bureaucracy, Ickes, his resolve strengthened by the cheap power of the Tennessee Valley Authority and the prospect of more public power from the huge Bonneville Dam nearing completion on the Columbia River, created a Water and Power Division in his office. When even that proved unsatisfactory, he named a new commissioner of reclamation sympathetic to his views. Then, in October 1943, Ickes, his new commissioner, and President Roosevelt publicly announced their intention to enforce reclamation law. That law's "provisions against water and land monopoly and against speculation in improved lands," declared Ickes, "not only protect the farmers today, but will protect all of the returning soldiers as well as all of the farmers who move into the . . . other great land openings of the future."[70]

Growers reacted instantly and bitterly. The California Farm Bureau Federation, the Irrigation Districts Association of California, and other agribusiness interests pressed for investigations to determine the feasibility of the state's purchasing the Central Valley Project (CVP), and thus evicting the federal government. The anger proved no respecter of party lines. In early 1944, a Tulare farmer serving as a Democrat in the House of Representatives introduced a rider to an appropriations bill exempting the Central Valley Project from the acreage limitation. The Interior Department, he announced, had to be stopped from "trying to socialize agriculture and force Communism upon the people of the San Joaquin Valley." Besides, he cautioned, the department's policy could put land into the wrong hands: "Remember the Japanese and the trouble we had with them."[71] The rider passed in the House but ran into stiff opposition in the Senate where Robert M. La Follette, Jr., of Wisconsin, a Progressive champion of the New Deal who had earlier held public hearings into corporate agriculture's violations of farmworkers' rights, rallied enough support to kill the measure.

In the same year, proponents of acreage limitation gained another victory by including the restriction in legislation authorizing the Army Corps of Engineers to build dams on rivers flowing into the eastern Central Valley. Growers had lobbied hard for construction by the Corps because the acreage limitation did not apply to that agency's projects. The Corps had enough support in Congress to get the assignment, but neither it nor the growers could derail a stipulation in the law making the projects—which eventually included Pine Flat Dam on the Kings River, Folsom on the American, and New Melones on the Stanislaus—subject to reclamation law. Subsequent legislation mandated that the irrigation waters of the completed projects be under the specific control of the Reclamation Bureau. As for maneuvers for state ownership of CVP, Ickes dashed them—at least for the time being—by quoting a purchase price of $357 million.[72]

In the meantime, the resolve of acreage-limitation advocates stiffened in 1944 when they reviewed the findings of Walter Goldschmidt, a young anthropologist from the University of California in the employ of the Bureau of Agricultural Economics. Goldschmidt had studied social patterns in two sharply different Central Valley towns. Dinuba, surrounded by farms averaging about sixty acres, had residents with more evenly distributed incomes, a higher standard of living, a richer community life, more schools and parks, access to more local businesses, and fewer farm laborers than Arvin, situated among farms averaging some 500 acres in size. Dinuba had not only smaller farms but more of them—nearly five and a half times more. All of which led Goldschmidt to conclude that the "differences in the communities may properly be assigned confidently and overwhelmingly to the scale-of-farming factor."[73]

"Technical Compliance": A Bipartisan Legacy

The growers' defeats in Congress and studies like Goldschmidt's signaled a high point in the government's efforts to enforce acreage limitation that now began a turnaround. Even earlier, the related issue of working conditions of farm laborers had ceased to be a matter of public concern. World War II had siphoned white field hands into the military and urban defense industries, leaving agricultural work, as before, to politically weak ethnic minorities (mainly of Mexican descent by this time) who remained underpaid, outside of politics, and unable to organize, now primarily because of the government's "bracero program." That program, which was initiated in 1942 and would last more than two decades, brought in workers from Mexico whose wages were set sufficiently low to undermine attempts of domestic laborers to improve their own incomes and conditions. As earlier, a minority of large farmers employed the vast majority of farmworkers and thus reaped the largest benefit, in increased profits, from this subsidy. A measure of the new climate of opinion was the Bureau of Agricultural Economics's decision to withhold publication of Goldschmidt's study. When after two years it finally appeared in print in 1946, it did so as an obscure U.S. Senate committee publication. The findings, however, were too explosive to remain overlooked, especially by an agribusiness that had anticipated Goldschmidt's results and had begun attacking him as an unpatriotic and "silly professor" while he was still gathering data in the field.[74]

Of more immediate importance in undercutting efforts at acreage limitation was Roosevelt's death in 1945 and the resignation of Ickes and his commissioner of reclamation not long after in 1946. There followed a reversal of policy in practice, if not in theory. The new commissioner, Michael Straus, although sporting "a set of formidable eyebrows that ought to have intimidated any valley grower," had different priorities than his predecessor as well as sympathetic superiors who left him alone. Straus was less interested in reform than in continuing the Bureau of Reclamation's growth into becoming one of the biggest and busiest bureaucracies in the nation. He succeeded, and in large part because of the climate of support provided by the new Harry S. Truman administration. It shared the widespread fear in America at large of an inevitable post–Second World War depression like that of the 1930s. Thus, the Truman administration believed that economic expansion was, in the words of one of the President's key advisors, "the very essence of our development as a nation."[75]

Indeed, so important did economic growth become in the thinking of the Truman administration that it submerged the earlier New Deal emphasis on enforcing reclamation law and redistributing the excess lands into family holdings. Instead, as Clayton Koppes has noted, administration officials had become convinced that "the wartime partnership between government and business had proved capitalism capable of an almost unlimited expansion that would obviate the need for redistributive policies."[76] Veterans who might take up farming for the first time or return to that life were seen as having innumerable and more attractive job opportunities in the nation's booming industries and cities. This change of circumstances, concluded the members of an Interior Department seminar as early as 1945, called for recognizing the role of "farms operated as business enterprises" as well as small-scale family units.[77] In other words, the traditional dream of government-fostered small farming, to aid social health, was dying. There was strong resistance to revising reclamation law, but nonetheless a willingness to consider compromises and overwhelming enthusiasm for the Reclamation Bureau expanding its activities to keep pace with the demands of the metropolitan areas for food and the irrigation needs of the farms supplying them. Under Truman, what was good for the Bureau of Reclamation was seen as good for the nation. Congress became more generous to the Bureau than at any time before or since, awarding it sums never contemplated earlier, including a record appropriation for a single year of $359 million in 1950.

Such success rested on a Bureau policy of trying to accommodate all major interest groups. Reclamation Commissioner Straus worked ceaselessly to curry Congress's favor and to disarm potential critics inside and outside of Washington. During his first year in office he ran into continued stiff opposition over the Bureau's still official policy of enforcing the acreage limitation requirement. Especially outspoken was California's Democratic Senator Sheridan Downey, a former left-winger (he had been Upton Sinclair's running mate for lieutenant governor of California in the End Poverty in California, or EPIC, campaign of 1934) who, at least on the question of acreage limitation, had moved to the right with all the fervor of the converted. In 1947 he introduced a bill to exempt from the restriction not only the Central Valley Project but also, in an obvious bid for wider support, two projects outside California as well.

Downey claimed he acted out of a desire to help both large and small farmers, but his tangled explanations found support only from agribusiness and its allies. The National Grange (representing mostly small farmers), organized labor, the Disabled American Veterans, National Catholic Rural Life Conference, and numerous other groups found him unconvincing if not incomprehensible. In still another move in 1947 to influence public opinion, Downey published *They Would Rule the Valley,* the "they" being allegedly misguided Reclamation Bureau officials who were determined to "bring ruin to thousands of our California farmers and return to the desert hundreds of thousands of now rich and productive acres."[78]

Straus wanted to appease, not confront, Downey and others like him, the more so because they had persuaded California officials to explore once more the possibility of buying the Central Valley Project from the federal government and thus eliminating the 160-acre limit. Taking a major project from the Bureau at a time when Straus wanted to preside over unprecedented expansion, not shrinkage, was anathema to the new commissioner. The happy solution to the threat—for him at least—was "technical compliance."

Straus believed that he could not openly abandon the excess land law, because to do so would deprive the Bureau of needed votes of easterners in Congress who generally looked unfavorably on federal support for western reclamation projects. So long as reclamation could be viewed as "a settlement and homesteading program"— and the 160-acre limitation was essential to such a view—their support could be counted on. Straus's policy, as revealed during the debate on Downey's bill to suspend the acreage limitation requirement, was to defend the law while at the same time telling growers how to get around it through "technical compliance." Such compliance took several forms. If a corporate farm was owned by stockholders, each could obtain water for 160 acres. Another possibility would be for a grower to deed land to his relatives and children. An owner could also deed land to employees and then lease it back. Perhaps the most imaginative device was the "accelerated payment" in which wealthy landowners could avoid disposing of excess lands by paying off all construction charges for their irrigation systems in a lump sum before the ten years had passed, at which point reclamation law mandated that they must sell their excess land. The theory was that once the federal government had been paid back, it could not force owners to dispose of excess lands—a theory that ignored the continuing enormous subsidies in the form of cheap taxpayer-provided water going to those landowners.[79] Such loopholes did not seem unreasonable to agribusiness leaders, since earlier the Reclamation Service had successfully done something just as imaginative. In 1916 it had construed the law to allow a husband and wife water for 320 acres.

Straus's willingness to go along with technical compliance had the desired effect: Downey's bill died in committee and the Reclamation Bureau secured enough support in Congress to expand its operations to a grand scale, which by the late 1960s included supplying water to 8.5 million acres of western farmland, generating over 33 billion kilowatt-hours of electricity, and providing 2 million acre-feet of water to municipalities. In addition, the Bureau achieved on paper virtually perfect compliance by Central Valley Project lands with the acreage limitation restriction. Without legally changing the law, the Bureau, as Clayton Koppes has observed, had administratively changed it "to reinforce the most skewed land-tenure pattern in the nation."[80]

The Bureau's action had implications for the entire West, since the technical compliance strategies devised for California were adopted by many water districts elsewhere. Persistence of large landholdings in the valley also received added strength from the Bureau's nonenforcement there (as in the Imperial Valley) of the reclamation law's residency requirement as well as the prohibition against selling land at a price inflated because of the availability of federal water. Failure to enforce the latter provision not only enabled sellers to reap great profits but also made it increasingly difficult for all but the wealthy to purchase farmland.[81]

The policies introduced by Straus continued into the Republican administration of Dwight Eisenhower, though with this difference: Republicans (at first, anyway) chafed at the duplicity, denounced the restrictions as threats to the free enterprise system, and complained generally about the size and cost of government. In a stance reflective of their post–Progressive Era/New Deal emphasis on laissez-faire, they criticized reclamation law's restraints as futile, discriminatory, and federal interference in matters better left to state and local governments and private business. Washington's participation in water-resource development was necessary, acknowledged Eisenhower in his first message to Congress in 1953, but that participation had to be more cost-effective and within the framework of "a partnership of the States and local communities, private citizens, and the Federal Government."[82]

As the new administration tried to determine the practical meaning of "partnership," to define the precise roles of the various players, and to identify where costs could be cut, it slowed construction on some projects and stopped work altogether on others. The result was a graphic illustration of how the Republicans' pre–New Deal emphasis on an efficient overall program had given way to localism, for each reclamation project was now subjected to an individual, time-consuming analysis. The delays and reduced expenditures soon produced enormous resentment in the West that spilled over into the congressional elections of 1954. Western Democratic victories helped that party regain control of Congress, lost two years earlier in Eisenhower's landslide capture of the White House.[83] Stung, the administration immediately saw the wisdom of forming a "partnership" with Congress that brought water-resource development nearly back to the level of the Straus years.

Similarly, the restrictions in reclamation law became the target of attacks calculated to produce political gains rather than actual changes in a law that, essentially ignored, was not otherwise worth the bother. Criticisms reflected the Cold War hysteria and McCarthyism of the 1950s. When California Democratic Congresswoman Helen Gahagan Douglas announced support of acreage limitation, Republicans cited her position as evidence of communist leanings. The Interior Department, like other agencies in the new administration, began the wholesale firing of "rabid New Dealers," "security risks," and those capable of being "intimidated or blackmailed by communists."[84] Some seven thousand Interior personnel, including Straus, left its employment during a two-year period, but the old Straus policy of technical compliance remained firmly in place. The Eisenhower administration, with technical compliance alive and well, had no reason to fight for changing a law that went unenforced, while Congress, under Democratic control after 1954, believed it had nothing to gain and much to risk politically by changing a policy introduced during the Democratic Truman administration.

The Truman-Eisenhower consensus on resource policy persisted long into the future, perhaps nowhere more clearly than in the person of Floyd Dominy. Eisenhower's last commissioner of reclamation, Dominy remained in office through the Democratic John Kennedy and Lyndon Johnson administrations. Indeed, though the political balance of power would shift in the coming decades and reclamation law would undergo change, the policy of technical, rather than actual, compliance with the law would persist to the present.

Public versus Private Power

The dispute over hydroelectricity generated by the Central Valley Project was nearly as intense as the battle over acreage limitation. The private firm of Pacific Gas and Electric, with a virtual monopoly over power distribution in northern and central California, adopted a strategy similar to the one it followed in the conflict over Hetch Hetchy power and waged an aggressive campaign to prevent the Reclamation Bureau from competing with it. At first PG&E concentrated on securing the right to distribute all the power generated in public facilities, even that destined for the Bureau's own water-pumping plants. This was a struggle that the utility waged in both Sacramento and Washington, D.C. In California it drew upon strong Republican and grower support in the late 1930s and early 1940s to defeat bills that would have enabled public agencies to build local government-owned facilities to receive power from a federal distribution network. In Washington, PG&E lobbied with uneven success against appropriations allowing the Reclamation Bureau to construct its distribution system, but the private utility received a major boost with the outbreak of World War II, which deprived the Bureau of materials and priorities for transmission lines. To meet the wartime demand for electricity, PG&E obtained short-term arrangements to deliver power (at a profit) to its own customers and to public agencies.[85]

In this struggle, PG&E found a powerful ally in big agriculture. Though the company and the growers had battled one another over initial approval of the Central Valley Project, with PG&E opposed because of the public power provisions, the growers now joined the utility in fighting the government's attempt to market power. The reason, paradoxically, lay in the Reclamation Bureau's low-cost power policy. On the one hand, the Bureau's intention to sell the electricity cheaply would result in little revenue for reducing the cost of—and hence the farmers' payments for—their government-constructed irrigation systems. PG&E, on the other hand, would charge higher rates, thereby producing not only profits for the company but also more revenue for reducing the costs of the farmers' systems. The possibility of higher rates did not bother the large farmers, since their lands were mostly in the San Joaquin Valley, where there were currently no plans to transmit project power. Most power sales were planned for the farms, cities, and industries of the Sacramento Valley and along the delta. Thus, the fight over hydroelectricity was not only a struggle between public and private power, but also among valley residents, with the large growers of the south speaking primarily through the California Farm Bureau Federation, and the small landowners rallying around the Grange, an organization especially strong in the north. Boasting a membership of 25,000 "dirt farmers," the Grange declared itself at war with monopoly in general and the "huge octopus-like power companies in particular."[86]

The battle raged throughout the 1940s. Republican Governor Earl Warren (1943–1953)—a man years earlier inspired by California's great Progressive Republican governor, Hiram Johnson, who had preached using government to achieve social justice—angered the conservative members of his party by siding with the advocates of public power. Warren, perhaps the most popular governor in California history, epitomized those Republicans who, in a state where Democratic voters outnumbered Republicans by three to two, benefited from the state's cross-filing system by downplaying their party affiliation, taking advantage of name recognition (he had earlier been state attorney general), and emphasizing programs of broad public appeal—in the case of Warren, programs emphasizing expanded governmental services like those sought by New Deal Democrats. Warren was unusually successful at getting what he wanted, but in the public power struggle his intervention did little more than help to prolong the fight until 1948 when a severe power shortage forced a congressional review of the issue and a compromise settlement.[87]

The settlement benefited PG&E and agribusiness more than the Bureau and the public. Equally telling, it was an agreement in harmony with the "technical compliance" mentality that had suffused the Truman administration and the Democrat-controlled Congress. The settlement took the form of the so-called wheeling agreement of 1951. In this arrangement, the Bureau obtained power lines to operate its pumping stations and then transmitted the excess power to PG&E. The utility then "wheeled," or delivered, electricity at Bureau-approved rates to those public agencies that had contracted with the government for power—but with the important proviso that the existing number of public agencies, which at the time was small, could not be increased. The remaining power, amounting to more than 80 percent of the electricity then being supplied by the Bureau, was sold by PG&E to its own customers.[88] These customers paid considerably more for electricity than what the public power advocates had expected them to pay if the government had provided it.

Privately, Reclamation Bureau officials expressed disappointment, hoping that the agreement would prove temporary (it would have to be renewed in 1961) and that the Bureau would eventually be able to provide direct service. Publicly, however, Commissioner Michael Straus hinted at no reservations: "the wheeling contracts are . . . accepted by both sides. It is accepted by us."[89] Just as Straus's desire to accommodate, rather than confront, opposition had led him to adopt his "technical compliance" policy for acreage limitation, so, too, did it encourage his blessing of this arrangement. The Grange voiced regret at the cap placed on the number of public agencies that could receive "wheeled" power, but agribusiness found nothing to criticize. Two years later, the Republican Eisenhower administration, after encouraging and then ignoring PG&E's efforts to gain control of even the transmission lines to the Bureau's own pumping stations, left the arrangement in place, renewing it in 1959, three years earlier than necessary. In 1967 the Democratic Lyndon Johnson administration, in further evidence of bipartisan agreement on the issue, renewed it once more, this time to the year 2005.[90]

PG&E had succeeded in limiting sales to public agencies and profiting handsomely. Since most of the purchasers of power lived in the state's urbanizing areas, California's city dwellers subsidized (and continue to subsidize) PG&E while also heavily subsidizing rural agribusiness with the revenues that reduce the costs (and hence the farmers' payments) for the government-constructed irrigation systems. Two decades following the 1951 wheeling agreement, the comptroller general of the United States estimated that electricity users were contributing approximately 20 percent of the $1.5 billion in subsidies going to Central Valley Project farm operators.[91]

By nearly all measures, California agribusiness and its allies seemed by the late 1940s and early 1950s to have transformed the Central Valley Project into a vehicle of great corporate aggrandizement. The subsidies obtained from power customers and taxpayers as well as the technical compliance loopholes in reclamation law represented impressive achievements. However, the large growers were, first of all, shrewd businessmen who recognized that their success depended on much that was ephemeral. The concept of technical compliance rested simply on administrative manipulation of the law, not on an actual change in legislation. What had been manipulated once could be manipulated again—and perhaps not in their favor. State purchase of the Central Valley Project, as a way out of their dilemma, was again dismissed in 1954 as too costly in view of the Reclamation Bureau's latest price tag—twice the value of all the physical structures.[92] Even if the price had been right, a sale would have been politically difficult given the Bureau's commitment to expanding, not dismantling, its empire. Many agribusiness leaders had already concluded that their best interests lay in broadening their base of support—in persuading the people of California to underwrite a water plan that would benefit the entire state while also serving corporate agriculture in the Central Valley. They therefore emerged as the strongest force in a movement that eventually culminated in California's most gigantic of hydraulic undertakings: the State Water Project.

The State Water Project

A STATE PROJECT encompassing the Central Valley promised two immediate benefits to the large growers. First, those taking water from a state enterprise would not be subject to federal reclamation law. Second, a state project, by serving as an alternative to federal water for many valley farmers, would cause the Reclamation Bureau to think twice before invoking reclamation law against those now benefiting from the technical compliance loopholes. Yet a successful campaign for a state venture required an argument with broad appeal to voters throughout California. This seemed ready-made in the state's explosive growth during World War II and the immediate postwar period when industrial capacity mushroomed and population increased at a phenomenal rate. Some 3,600,000 newcomers arrived in the 1940s and an even greater flood entered in the 1950s, averaging a half million new Californians each year.

The shock troops in the new struggle for water were San Joaquin Valley landowners, especially those in Kings and Kern counties along the southwestern side and at the southern end. Besides wishing to escape the dreaded acreage restriction, they sought water for an area as vast as it was dry. Among the largest property owners was the Kern County Land Company, a direct descendant of the giant corporation created by James Ben Ali Haggin of *Lux* v. *Haggin* fame and still controlled by his heirs and those of a partner, Lloyd Tevis. Neither he nor they had delivered on his promise to subdivide the land into small homesteads. Of the more than 400,000 acres owned by the company in California, most was in Kern County, and the greater portion of that, nearly 224,000 acres, was along the valley's west side and could not be developed without a major infusion of new water, since it was outside the CVP area and because wells there yielded only brackish supplies incapable of growing crops. This area, which stood to benefit directly from state water, contained some of the largest corporate landholdings in the United States: Standard Oil with 89,810 acres (94 percent of them irrigable); Kern County Land Company, 223,534 (99 percent irrigable); Buena Vista Associates, 25,254 (100 percent); Belridge Oil, 24,627 (100 percent); Tidewater Oil, 23,009 (99 percent); General Petroleum, 16,619 (99 percent); Shell Oil, 15,353 (99 percent); Occidental Land and Development Company, 14,462 (98 percent); E. M. and E. C. Still, 13,039 (98 percent); Richfield Oil, 12,395 (98 percent); Southern Pacific Company, 11,605 (100 percent); Southern Pacific Land Company, 15,060 (100 percent); Allison Honer Company, 10,240 (100 percent); and Tejon Ranch (whose principal stockholder was the Times Mirror Company, publisher of the *Los Angeles Times*), 38,689 acres (96 percent irrigable).[93]

Vigorous support for the state project, as for the Central Valley Project earlier, also came from those who relied upon groundwater to irrigate many thousands of acres. By the late 1940s in the San Joaquin Valley, just prior to CVP water being introduced into the area, there were some 35,000 wells mining 6 million acre-feet of groundwater annually, 60 percent of all the water pumped in the state. The arrival of the CVP supply in 1951, described by proponents of the project in the 1930s as being intended to "rescue" acreage already developed and threatened by water shortage, and not to bring new lands into production, did nothing to lessen reliance on pumping. Rather, the mining of groundwater and agricultural expansion accelerated throughout the valley. In a typical 1,300-square-mile area on the central-west side, the volume of pumped water increased from a million acre-feet to 1.2 million acre-feet in two years in the early 1950s, a rate acknowledged by both state and federal experts as "far in excess of replenishment."[94] In large areas, the very surface of the land subsided as much as thirty feet as water was pumped out, producing "squeezed," compacted aquifers that could never again be refilled with water, whether from rainfall or direct injection.

Some continued to mine groundwater rather than take any risk with acreage limitation by using Central Valley Project supplies. Others pumped because their lands could not be reached by laterals from the CVP. Still others took water from the Central Valley Project but used that supply to develop new lands while continuing to pump groundwater for the older acreage. In nearly all instances, the results were the same: falling water tables (from an average of fifty-five feet below the surface in the early 1930s to three or four times deeper by the 1940s and 1950s), increased pumping costs, pollution of aquifers by agricultural runoff, and land subsidence.[95] The operative principle seemed to be: make profits while you can, and when you cannot, persuade government to intervene. As for the ecological damage, the less said (little was really said) the better. Even those lands for which surface water, primarily from the Kern River, was available had declined in productivity because of the higher concentration of salts in the water resulting from heavy irrigation upstream.

A State Plan

Nothing can be accomplished without a plan, and in 1945 the state legislature, responding to concerns about groundwater, acreage limitation, population growth, and rapid urbanization, took a major step toward creation of a state project by approving a State Water

Resources Act. It vested in the state the authority for coordinating water development and created a new agency, the Water Resources Board, to inventory all water supplies and "to formulate plans for . . . solutions for the water problems of each portion of the State." In 1951 the board reported that 40 percent of the runoff in California's rivers emptied into the ocean along the northern coast—"wasted" was the clear implication—while the "greater demands" were in central and southern California. "The greatest challenge" facing the state, announced the board, was "redistribution of the water supply from areas of surplus to areas of deficiency." Planners projected (fairly accurately as it turned out) a population in excess of 21 million Californians by 1980. (The population at the time was about half that number or 11 million).[96]

Those pushing for a state project could hardly have asked for a greater incentive, but they got one when the Reclamation Bureau released in the same year a plan to develop the water resources of a great portion of the West through a series of interbasin transfers. The Bureau wanted to divert much of Oregon's Klamath River into central and southern California and, in exchange, to send some California water elsewhere: a portion of the American River to Nevada, and Owens Valley water to the Mojave Desert. Water planners in metropolitan southern California reacted with a resounding "no" to surrendering any of their water—especially Owens River water—and they joined with San Joaquin Valley farmers in hooting down the proposal and drawing attention to a statewide plan offered in May 1951 by State Engineer Arthur Edmonston. It called for the world's tallest dam near Oroville on the Feather River, a tributary of the Sacramento and the state's heaviest-flowing wild (still un-dammed) stream, to control floods and collect runoff for delivery along a 750-mile route, first to the delta and San Francisco Bay area (to help prevent saltwater intrusion and to dilute pollutants), then to the San Joaquin Valley (through an aqueduct along the desolate west side), and finally across the Tehachapis to the cities and industries of southern California. Known at first as the Feather River Project after the principal water source, it was later officially renamed the California Water Project when state officials began casting about for a grander designation.[97]

The legislature advanced Edmonston's plan with three major actions. First, it authorized the project and appropriated funds for necessary detailed studies late in 1951. Second, in 1956, following the greatest flood on record in northern and central California, which inundated 100,000 square miles, took sixty-four lives, and caused over $200 million in property damage, much of which could have been prevented by a dam on the Feather River at Oroville, it created a superagency considered essential to carrying out such a massive undertaking. The new Department of Water Resources brought under a single leadership the fifty-two formerly independent state agencies responsible for some aspect of water planning and development. Third, in 1959 it approved the Water Resources Development Bond Act, also known as the Burns-Porter Act, authorizing $1.75 billion in bonds plus enough revenue from the state's offshore oil deposits to pay for a first phase (storage facilities and aqueduct system) estimated to cost $2.5 billion. A second phase also received authorization, though the specific projects were purposely left vague so as to give water officials the widest possible latitude: the bill referred to those "additional facilities" deemed "necessary and desirable" to supply future needs, including those of the delta.[98]

This was a broad mandate—so broad that the second phase held promise of never ending as long as a single drop of California water remained unused. Such an open-ended authorization also meant an uncertain final price tag since future projects and funding would have to be pursued on the installment plan, reminiscent of San Francisco's Hetch Hetchy project. At the time, however, the estimated $2.5 billion for the first phase seemed a staggering enough amount. And the $1.75 billion in bonds was a record sum for a water project, nearly as much as the entire California budget, and the largest bond issue ever considered by any state. Indeed, its enormity led the legislature to make it subject to voter approval at an election scheduled for November 1960.

The election served to highlight sharp differences that had emerged as the project moved through the legislature. Not surprisingly, the greatest enthusiasm for the plan came from those representing the San Joaquin Valley where the landowners had become even more ardent in their support after 1958 when they failed to get the U.S. Supreme Court in *Ivanhoe* v. *McCracken* to do what Congress had refused to do: give an outright exemption to Central Valley Project lands for the 160-acre limitation.[99] The strongest opposition came from northerners adamantly against sending their water south. Measures that would control floods, promote northern development, and prevent saltwater intrusion into the delta were permissible—indeed, strenuously sought by some—but surrendering water to agribusiness and southern California aroused bitter opposition. The opponents were not limited to the north, however, for they also included many southern Californians who objected to the project because of the shadow cast by the 1931 "county of origin" legislation. They had no desire to obligate the south to pay for a gigantic water system that the north might someday shut down.

Playing the decisive role in securing compromises that got the bond issue through the legislature and before the electorate was Governor Edmund G. "Pat" Brown, who had made statewide water planning a top priority of his new administration. In his approach to the issue, Democrat Brown differed sharply from his Republican predecessor, Goodwin Knight. Prior to becoming governor, Knight, who had been lieutenant governor under the popular Earl Warren, was a favorite of the Republican right wing, sharing its post–New Deal preference for limited government and laissez-faire. When Knight became governor following Warren's resignation to become chief justice of the United States, he moved toward the center of the political spectrum in a bid to capture the followers of Warren.[100] Though many questioned the sincerity of his conversion, he became an advocate of increased workers' compensation, mental health programs, old-age pensions, and unemployment insurance as well as an opponent of such antiunion proposals as right-to-work legislation.

When it came to a comprehensive state water plan, however, Knight's old doubts about enlarged governmental powers resurfaced. While he acknowledged a need for the state project, he failed to work actively for it and became an advocate of the 1956 bill creating the Department of Water Resources only following the disastrous flood of the previous year and a state assembly report condemning the "gross duplication, conflicting areas of authority and overlapping on all levels and in all areas of state activity concerning water."[101] Once the 1956 measure had been enacted, Knight reverted largely to inaction, taking few initiatives, insisting that a state project would have to await a constitutional amendment protecting the interests of both north and south (a goal that even his advisors concluded was impossible to achieve), and effectively abdicating responsibility to the legislature where regional and partisan differences stymied all attempts to rally around a bill for a state water project.[102]

In 1959 Pat Brown brought to state government generally and water planning in particular a strong, activist attitude: "We want new blood, new ideas, and new ways of dealing with old problems."[103] In most instances, he brought merely the activist principles of the Democratic party nationally, though during the early part of his administration, he concentrated most of his energy on the water issue. He was thoroughly convinced that the development of new water resources was crucial to the state's future growth and prosperity—and to his own place in history: "I was *absolutely determined* that I was going to pass this California Water Project," he declared. "I wanted this to be a monument to *me*."[104]

That Brown sought a monument in a massive hydraulic undertaking comes as no surprise in a state where such projects had long been viewed as possessing both symbolic and real significance. But his willingness to risk political failure at the very outset of his administration by tackling a controversial issue of statewide importance on which his fellow Democrats were divided reflected not only his conviction that the undertaking was "good for the state" but also supreme confidence in his political skills. "When you run for public office you have somewhat of a missionary complex," he later recalled. "You think you're the . . . only person that can do this job and that's the way I felt about the California Water Project."[105]

Brown had good reason for such self-assurance, for he came into office with overwhelming popular support, having crushed by a million-vote winning margin his Republican opponent, William Knowland (who had angered the public with heavy-handed tactics preventing Knight from running for reelection as governor). Brown was the state's first Democratic governor in nearly two decades, and he carried enough fellow party members along on his coattails to produce its first Democratic legislature in the twentieth century.[106] As it turned out, he needed all the support he could muster for the state water plan.

Pat Brown personally told the legislature of his commitment to a state project and participated actively in drafting the necessary legislation. Working closely with leaders in the senate and assembly through Ralph Brody, his special advisor on water matters (Brody went on to become chief counsel for the Westlands Water District, a recipient of federal water through the CVP and a dogged opponent of acreage limitation), Brown won over needed legislators by avoiding all talk about a constitutional amendment and providing two major concessions. To northerners he offered a special companion measure—the Davis-Grunsky Act—authorizing $130 million of the bond sales for local projects, most, if not all, assumed to be in the north. Some of these, like "Pauline's Puddles" (the name given to five tiny man-made lakes that Assemblywoman Pauline Davis of Plumas County exacted as the price for her vote), were spelled out in detail. Southern Californians posed a special problem. At one point the Metropolitan Water District advocated a cheaper, stripped down, go-it-alone plan to build an aqueduct to the Eel River on the north coast, but when that gambit reaped a whirlwind of criticism from state officials and also from those who saw the Eel plan as an attempt to repeat the Owens Valley grab statewide, MWD abandoned it. To placate southern Californians worried that the north might someday invoke the county-of-origin legislation and prevent water going south, Brown secured an amendment stipulating that the water contracts could not be abrogated while the bonds remained outstanding. (Subsequently the contracts were scheduled to terminate in 2035 or when the bonds were paid off, now projected to be about 2029.)[107]

The size of the bond issue was pegged at $1.75 billion, the largest such issue ever contemplated by any state. The original plan had been to build a project capable of meeting the state's projected needs to the year 2020, but the estimated cost of $4 billion was considered beyond the possibility of public approval. Brown and his advisors finally settled on a project costing an estimated $2.25 to $2.5 billion ("We hadn't priced it out to any exactitude," he later admitted) and capable of meeting projected needs as of 1990. Because even that price tag was considered too high, Brown decided to ask the public for $1.75 billion and then seek the balance from tideland oil revenues, which would later be repaid with interest by water and power users after the bonds had been retired. "The $1.75 billion, plus tideland oil revenues . . . ," he concluded, "would complete the canal throughout the state."[108] Water requirements beyond 1990 might be met by the desalination of seawater, but if that proved economically infeasible, then they could be met through the construction of new facilities financed, it was hoped, by leftover bonds. The idea here was that the tideland revenues might be large enough to permit the state to save enough bonds to build the newer projects. No one knew whether there would be adequate tidelands revenue or leftover bonds or even the precise kinds of future projects that might be needed, but, as noted earlier, Brown and his advisors nonetheless added language to the bill authorizing a vague second phase of the state project: "Such additional facilities . . . as the [D]epartment [of Water Resources] shall determine to be necessary and desirable to meet local needs . . . and to augment the supplies of water in the Sacramento–San Joaquin Delta."[109]

This second phase later became the subject of a bitter statewide battle in its own right but, for the present, allusion to it in the bond measure helped Brown win over those concerned about the more distant future.

To maintain his legislative coalition, Brown also refused to make certain concessions. Despite pressure from the Grange, some labor organizations, the California Water and Power Users Association, and other consumer groups, he resisted two demands in particular: that public agencies be given preference as customers for power generated by the project and that an acreage limitation be placed on users of project water. Such restrictions, in light of the sharp north-south rivalry that Brown was trying to paper over, would doubtless kill the undertaking. To deflect as much criticism as possible, however, Brown announced his agreement with the purpose of the demands (to prevent "unjust enrichment"), insisted there were better means to achieve that purpose (he did not say what they were and later confessed that he "was never convinced that the small farmer could succeed or would be good for the economy of the state"), and then used his influence to have the issues referred for study to a legislative committee (from which neither they nor any other recommendations emerged).[110]

Brown's adroit maneuvers won legislative approval for the bond measure, known as the Burns-Porter Act, though enactment required Republican support. Democrats substantially outnumbered Republicans in the legislature (they constituted nearly 60 percent of the assembly and 70 percent of the senate), but preliminary balloting on amendments and other measures revealed that defections (almost entirely northerners) left the party short of the majority needed to guarantee passage of the bill. With the aid of Republicans and intense lobbying by Brown, the vote for the measure became a comfortable twenty-five to twelve in the senate and fifty to thirty in the assembly. A majority in both parties supported the legislation in the senate, though a considerably greater portion of Democrats voted no (about 38 percent) than Republicans (18 percent). Not surprisingly, nearly all the senate dissenters of both parties were northern Californians, with no negative votes being cast by southern Californians and only two coming from the San Joaquin Valley. In the assembly, the percentage of Democratic opponents was less than half that in the senate, and those naysayers, with one exception, were northerners. The representatives from the San Joaquin Valley—all Democrats—voted seven to one for the bill. Assembly Republicans registered two-to-one opposition to the measure, with northerners nearly unanimous in their hostility. Still, there were enough proponents among both assembly Republicans (33 percent of them) and Democrats (83 percent) to easily pass the bill, which Brown happily signed into law on July 10, 1959.[111]

Thus both regional and partisan considerations explain the outcome, but Brown later expressed his personal belief that he would have been unable to prevent certain defeat if he had not just been elected by a landslide. Even then, he confessed, he had "begged, pleaded, urged, and cajoled" to get his way. "I don't think any other Governor would have got that bill through at that time. I don't think I would have got it through if I didn't have the muscle of a million votes."[112]

Brown's cajoling and concessions (those he made and those he refused to make) persuaded the legislature to put the bond measure on the ballot, but they did little to quiet the more intransigent opponents in and out of government. Northern critics remained especially outspoken, some arguing that the promised local projects would be inadequate, if not unwanted, and insisting that it made more sense for people to go to the water than vice versa (that is, southern Californians should move to the north if they wanted water). Others feared that the county-of-origin guarantee would mean little once those in the south had been using northern water for the fifty or more years covered by the contracts.

There were also objections on financial grounds, with claims that cost estimates had failed to take adequately into account the future effects of inflation. These same critics contended that the estimates of future population growth were exaggerated and, thus, so too was the projected market for water. "If the voters go ahead," cautioned the *San Francisco Chronicle,* "they are taking a desperate plunge into the unknown" and authorizing a "blank check to irresponsibility." In an attempt to silence such objections, the state retained two independent consulting firms to assess the financial and engineering aspects of the project. Their reports affirmed that the funding would be adequate—barely so—as long as inflation did not reduce current purchasing power. The *Los Angeles Times* greeted this news with a headline proclaiming that the project "GETS SOUND RATING IN TWO REPORTS," while on the same day the *San Francisco Chronicle* headlined: "STATE WATER PLAN CALLED IMPOSSIBLE."[113] So much for unbiased reporting.

Organized labor split on the project, with steelworkers, Teamsters, and operating engineers favoring it as a source of new jobs, while the California Labor Federation (the voice for all AFL-CIO affiliates in the state) registered strong opposition because the enterprise would allow corporate agriculture to enrich itself unjustly by evading the acreage restriction. Sharing this latter view was the California Grange. Announced Grangemaster J. D. Quinn: "The thought of subsidizing several millions of acres of land on the western side of the Central Valley to large corporate interests is shameful."[114] Equally unconscionable to many labor and liberal groups was any aid that might strengthen agribusiness's traditional policy of fighting farmworkers' attempts to organize. Nonetheless, a majority of the chapters of the League of Women Voters favored the project.

Though southern California was to receive a major portion of the diverted water, many there continued to oppose the project even after Brown secured protection for their contracts. Chief among them was the Metropolitan Water District, representing most users, which still worried publicly about the county-of-origin guarantee. Protection of the contracts for a specified period only served as a reminder that the south could become vulnerable as soon as the bonds were retired. Still, this was not a concern that privately mattered much to the MWD's board of directors. It was a part of their arsenal of arguments against the project but they, like most northern political leaders, had confidence in the soundness of the engineering studies indicating enormous surpluses in northern rivers. More troubling to board members was California's ongoing battle with Arizona over the Colorado River. That struggle was once again in the U.S. Supreme Court, and some MWD members feared that construction of the state project would weaken California's position in the litigation.[115] Of far greater importance was the matter of cost. No one on MWD's board doubted that the project was affordable, but they disagreed sharply about how the costs should be distributed. Though that dispute remained out of the public eye and confined to the boardroom, it shaped MWD's public stance on the bond issue.

At the heart of MWD policy was the peculiar situation of Los Angeles. The city's growth rate was only a third to half that of neighboring communities represented on the board of directors. This had led to the anomaly in which Los Angeles was using very little Colorado River water and yet continuing to pay for the larger volume for which it had contracted. Put another way, Los Angeles was using less than 9 percent of the Colorado supply being delivered by MWD while paying taxes on 62 percent of the district's operations.[116] In effect, most of the Colorado water to which the city was entitled and for which it was paying supported the growth of other southern California communities that now wanted even more water to sustain their record expansion. Los Angeles did not object to their desire to bring more water south. Indeed, city leaders shared that wish, the more so after the attempt to tap the Eel had failed and now that Arizona had launched a major challenge in the Supreme Court. Also driving them as always was their vision of an even greater city and the enormous volume of water needed to achieve and sustain it. That goal, as it had been for earlier generations, remained elusive, since the presence of scores of cities throughout the region (smaller but no less ambitious versions of Los Angeles) meant there could never be quite enough water to provide complete peace of mind or make possible a metropolis that could not somehow be grander with just a little more water. There was also the belief that growth was inevitable or, at least, should be. "You couldn't kick people out or build a fence to keep them out, and you had to have industry to support the people when they came in here," declared Preston Hotchkis, a Los Angeles native and water leader. "So I just knew we had to have more water, and the only place we could get it . . . was the California Water Project."[117]

There was the matter of financial reality, however. Los Angeles officials had reached the point where they vehemently refused to pay any more than they absolutely had to surrender to get the water they sought. What brought the issue to a head was the proposed financing of the two branch aqueducts designed to distribute water below the Tehachapis. The West Branch, coming down through Castaic just above Los Angeles, would tie into a feeder network from which MWD could serve all its customers. MWD board members, including those representing the city of Los Angeles, agreed with state officials that the agency should pay for this aqueduct. However, sharp debate erupted over the East Branch Aqueduct, which would run southeasterly through the Antelope Valley and then cross the San Bernardino Mountains in distant San Bernardino County. Because the potential customers that it would serve could not afford to build it on their own, state officials insisted that MWD would have to contribute a substantial amount—approximately $80 million—to the cost. Sharing this view were some MWD board members, especially those in San Bernardino, Riverside, and San Diego counties, who felt their needs could be more effectively served by the East rather than the West Branch. Most Los Angeles board members refused to go along, insisting that the East Branch was unnecessary and a financial burden that the city should not be asked to share. Its construction would also deprive MWD of monopoly control over the distribution of state water in southern California. The Los Angeles opponents used their control of the largest single bloc of board votes to lead the district in opposition to the bond proposal.[118]

As the election approached and as Brown barnstormed the state telling everyone within earshot that "it's better to have problems with water than problems without water," Los Angeles found it increasingly difficult to hold the MWD members together. Many grew fearful that the board's refusal to endorse the State Water Project would mean its defeat. Individual MWD members began breaking ranks, endorsing the project and revealing publicly their differences with Los Angeles. Then just four days before the election, a majority of Los Angeles's representatives on the MWD board, finding themselves virtually isolated and making enemies of longtime friends, reversed themselves. Since the city's representatives, under MWD rules, had to cast their votes as a bloc, the board now officially endorsed the state plan and signed a contract for project water that included a provision obligating it to help pay for the East Branch Aqueduct. The victory was not clear-cut, however. Joseph Jensen, chairman of the board and one of the dissenting Los Angeles representatives, persuaded the city council to withhold its endorsement of the project. This was partially but not entirely offset by the mayor's announcement that he strongly supported the undertaking.[119] With the situation now sufficiently muddled, all that remained was the ballot.

On November 8, 1960, voters approved the bonds with a winning margin of only about 174,000 ballots out of 5.8 million cast, or three-tenths of 1 percent. With the exception of Yuba and Butte counties, the north rejected the proposal, but the Yuba "yes" vote was lukewarm (294 ballots made the difference) and Butte County's stronger endorsement (two to one in favor) is explained by its being the locale of the high dam on the Feather River. Southern California delivered the slight but decisive winning edge because of the overwhelming support of voters there. Orange County residents endorsed the bonds by a two-to-one margin, while Riverside and San Bernardino counties approved them by a three-to-one vote and San Diego County four to one. Los Angeles County delivered the largest single bloc of "yes" votes—some 1.3 million—but it also registered the largest number of naysayers—slightly more than a million—a sign of confusion created by the MWD infighting and the hard-fought nature of the campaign. Despite the close vote, state Director of Water Resources William Warne saw the the outcome as reaffirming a bedrock principle: "California . . . must always in

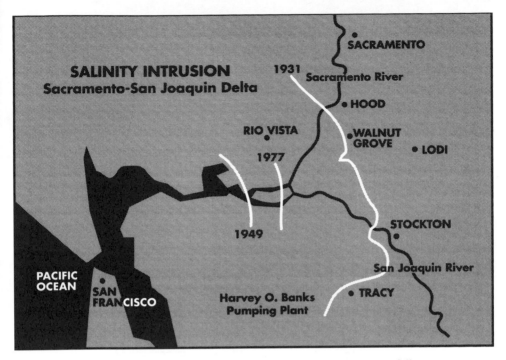

Saltwater intrusion into the Sacramento–San Joaquin Delta in 1949, following completion of Shasta and Friant dams; in 1931, a severe drought year prior to the completion of the Central Valley and the State Water projects, whose freshwater releases help repel salinity; and in 1977, the state's driest year on record. (Courtesy of the Water Education Foundation)

the future be willing, as no one else is willing, to . . . sustain . . . growth and development." [120]

New Water, Growth, and Inequities

Construction soon began on the State Water Project and proceeded steadily, with water reaching Alameda County in 1962, the San Joaquin Valley six years later, and then crossing the Tehachapis in 1971. By year's end the West Branch Aqueduct was completed to Castaic Lake (a holding facility for project water) and by 1973, with the filling of Lake Perris in Riverside County (also a holding facility), the first phase of the state project had been completed. Water poured into southern California at a rate that would have topped

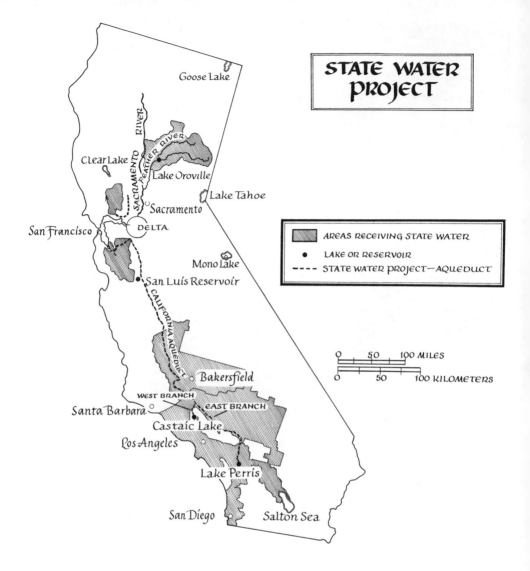

STATE WATER PROJECT

Goose Lake

SACRAMENTO RIVER

FEATHER RIVER

Clear Lake

Lake Oroville

Lake Tahoe

Sacramento

San Francisco

DELTA

Mono Lake

San Luis Reservoir

CALIFORNIA AQUEDUCT

Bakersfield

WEST BRANCH

Santa Barbara

EAST BRANCH

Castaic Lake

Los Angeles

Lake Perris

San Diego

Salton Sea

☐ AREAS RECEIVING STATE WATER
● LAKE OR RESERVOIR
---- STATE WATER PROJECT—AQUEDUCT

0   50   100 MILES
0   50   100 KILOMETERS

Governor Edmund G. (Pat) Brown initiating service on his "monument to me"—the State Water Project—on July 10, 1962. (Courtesy of The Bancroft Library, University of California, Berkeley)

the Rose Bowl in Pasadena every hour and a half. Even earlier (by 1963) contracts had been secured for nearly all of the minimum volume of water that the project was expected to yield: 4 million acre-feet. Eventually thirty agencies contracted for a total of 4.2 million acre-feet. The largest volume (2.5 million acre-feet) was contracted for by southern California with the next-largest allocation (1.35 million acre-feet) scheduled for the San Joaquin Valley and nearly all of that for Kern County, while the smallest volume (about

Oroville Dam on the Feather River, completed in 1967 and a key element in the State Water Project. Below the waters of Lake Oroville are such early mining settlements as Bidwell's Bar. (Courtesy of California Department of Water Resources)

0.4 million acre-feet) was destined for the central coast and the north.[121]

Predictions of economic disaster by some early opponents failed to materialize. Helping considerably was an unexpected windfall in tideland oil and gas revenues. Although the interest rate on the bonds had to be increased with voter approval in order to sell them in an inflated market and to repay loans from the state general fund needed to cover initial overdrafts, the project was paying for itself by the 1970s. Relatively little revenue (13 percent) came from power consumers since nearly all the electricity generated, plus more than twice as much more, was needed to pump the water south. After 1983, however, the generation of electricity was integrated into the project, which succeeded not only in supplying all its power needs at cost but also in generating revenue from sales of surplus energy. Contributing to this happy situation was the tax-exempt status of the project and the federal government's payment for flood control aspects, though the amount was very small (only 1 percent) and even less than what the state paid from the general fund for fisheries, wildlife preservation, and recreation (3 percent).[122]

Ultimately, the burden of paying for the bulk of the project (80 percent) fell on the water users, with the corporate farmers of Kern County receiving their water at bargain rates. They accomplished this in four ways. First, in 1961 they persuaded the county's residents to create the Kern County Water Agency on a basis whereby every taxpayer agreed to help fund the imported water. As a practical matter, this meant that the residents of Bakersfield, the county's largest city, absorbed most of the costs on the theory that what was good for agribusiness was good for urban dwellers. Second, the growers then obtained a water rate that reduced their costs (and the costs of other users as well) by the amount of revenue generated by power sales at Oroville Dam. At first, the contract eliminated this subsidy for large landowners by calling for a two-dollar premium per acre-foot on water used to irrigate holdings in excess of 160 acres (or 320 acres for a married couple). This was Pat Brown's attempt to deliver on his promise of "no unjust enrichment," but he acknowledged that "it wasn't very substantial" and was merely "a bone" thrown to those who had earlier sought an acreage-limitation provision in the bond legislation.[123] When Ronald Reagan captured the governorship, he eliminated this modest surcharge, thus restoring the subsidy to the growers.

Third, the Kern County landowners secured another subsidy as a result of the price charged for the size of the water-moving system. Ordinarily those costs are based on the capacity of the aqueduct. Under such an arrangement, the farmers would be charged more than urban areas for the stretch shared by both because agriculture's peak summer demands exceeded those of cities and thus required construction of a system larger than that needed by urban dwellers. The farmers rejected such an arrangement, however, insisting that costs be allocated on the basis of the volume of water

California Aqueduct, the principal north-south artery in the State Water Project. (Courtesy of California Department of Water Resources)

going to users. This approach decidedly favored the farmers since their total water entitlement was only about half that of southern California. Ultimately, the two sides compromised, agreeing to a cost midway between volume and capacity, which still represented a significant subsidy for agribusiness. Nonetheless, the compromise recognized, as state Water Resources Director Harvey Banks noted, that "under the formulation of the project, [agriculture] had to take the first cut in the event of shortage." To Banks, who supported the agreement, this created a situation in which "equity" favored a cost break for the farmers. MWD objected at first, but finally went along because without a contract with the farmers there would be no project.[124]

The fourth development reducing even further the costs of large landowners was a special rate for surplus water that they negotiated with the state and the Metropolitan Water District. Until southern Californians were ready to use their water, the farmers agreed to purchase it at about $13 an acre-foot, the cost of transporting the water, instead of the approximately $43 that it would otherwise cost if they paid their share of the capital expense of the project. State officials and the farmers justified the lower price on the grounds that this supply was temporary and would not be applied directly to irrigation but, rather, used to replenish overdrafted groundwater basins.[125]

The theory behind the special rate for surplus water may have had a ring of plausibility to it but the reality was another matter. The state water brought south (like the federal CVP water earlier) was used primarily to develop new farmlands while groundwater pumping continued unabated. The result was an overdraft on aquifers in the southern San Joaquin Valley (Kern County) that increased by 7 million acre-feet (for a cumulative overdraft of 17 million acre-feet) by the late 1970s. Thus corporate farmers in Kern County got an even better deal than they had anticipated (though they did so by further depleting and degrading the valley's underground supplies), and all without the dreaded acreage restriction. They also got it at the expense of metropolitan southern Californians who were legally obligated to pay for the water for which they had contracted but did not now need. That payment amounted to a subsidy to agriculture that by the mid-1980s was $25 million a year.[126]

Just why the Metropolitan Water District agreed to the special rate for water (at first it objected) is not altogether clear. William Warne, director of the Department of Water Resources at the time, suspected that MWD had extracted from the farmers a promise to support the agency on "some political issue." He could not imagine, however, "what issue was serious enough to cause Met to shift on this issue," and the available recollections of those state and MWD officials in a position to know are silent on the subject.[127] Politics may have played a role but a more likely explanation is simply that MWD preferred to get some reduction on its bill for water that it

Wind Gap Pumping Plant on the California Aqueduct in southern Kern County. (Courtesy of California Department of Water Resources)

California Aqueduct, East Branch, Antelope Valley. (Courtesy of California Department of Water Resources)

could not use rather than get no reduction at all. The special price was doubtless the best deal that it could negotiate with the growers. As Governor Brown later observed about the surplus water: "What are you going to do with it? If they didn't buy the surplus water it would flow to the sea. So we had to get rid of it at bargain rates." These particular bargain rates ended in 1988 when southern California's water requirements eliminated the surplus.[128]

Another strong incentive for developing new farmland in the 1960s came from the federal tax code. It allowed investors to deduct as business expenses their development costs, thus prompting them to rush new fields into production as soon as water became available. In Kern County, they concentrated at first on such specialty crops as almonds and citrus which grew especially well along the valley's west side. Then, when the Internal Revenue Service, under heavy criticism for providing tax subsidies to the wealthy, ended the tax break for citrus and almond orchards in 1969 and 1970, investors poured their money into grapes, olives, and pistachios. The result was glutted markets and nosediving prices that devastated many of the state's small growers. Corporate agriculture, however, had no trouble surviving and even benefiting as a result of its economies of scale, access to additional capital, and freedom from acreage limitation. The public failed to benefit from the glutted market because the special contracts negotiated by the large growers with the processing companies produced no decrease in retail prices.[129]

Inexpensive state water for farmers only further encouraged unwise uses already long practiced by those relying on heavily subsidized and hence cheap federal water ($3.50 to $8 an acre-foot). Farmers continued to reap profits from low-value, water-intensive forage crops such as alfalfa (primarily for the dairy industry), which by the late 1970s accounted for more than 60 percent of all the water used on state farms (and agriculture in general was then using 85 percent of all the water consumed in California). These practices, in turn, contributed to product surpluses, adversely affecting competing farmers in rain-supplied parts of the United States. When federal quotas on cotton were removed in 1982, for example, California farmers, encouraged by the abundance of cheap water, rushed vast fields into cotton production, thereby bringing depressed conditions to many small farmers in the southern states and their local economies. That a higher, and hence less heavily subsidized, price for water would not contribute to such economic dislocations but, rather, encourage greater efficiency was confirmed by economic studies indicating that as water prices rose, low-value and water-intensive crops were taken out of production.[130]

As earlier, another form of subsidy to growers was the underpaid agricultural workforce, whose wages and working conditions remained stagnated as a result of the wartime bracero program with Mexico, which was extended until the end of 1963 as a result of the Korean War and the pressure of growers and allied interests. Even when embarrassing disclosures of mistreatment and exploitation, together with the outrage generated by the struggle over civil rights, ended the program, special federal loopholes (some later incorporated into the Immigration Reform and Control Act of 1986) and increases in the number of undocumented workers migrating from Mexico provided growers with enough field labor to prevent widespread and meaningful attempts to unionize workers and improve conditions. Also aiding the growers was the state's failure to effectively enforce a 1975 law (the California Agricultural Labor Relations Act) assuring workers secret and fair elections to determine union representation, and destructive rifts over policy among labor organizers themselves, including those associated with César Chávez's United Farm Workers of America. Despite much publicity and some gains, the United Farm Workers (UFW) had ground to a virtual standstill by the end of the 1980s with membership down from a high of 100,000 to, according to union sources, 20,000, or, according to other estimates, less than 12,000. Though at one time the union had contracts with nearly all California grape growers, it possessed not a single such contract in 1989. That situation improved slightly during the following decade (although Chávez's death in 1993 removed a powerful force), nonetheless by the end of the 1990s UFW membership, by its own account, stood at only 27,000 nationwide (compared to a farm workforce of some 230,000 in California alone) as the union struggled unsuccessfully to recover its earlier vitality.[131]

The advocates of California's great hydraulic projects cared little about agricultural working conditions and less about studies pointing out the nature, extent, and inequities of subsidized water for farmers. They preferred instead to emphasize what they and their predecessors had traditionally stressed: the state's enormous population and economic growth. From about 16 million people in 1960 the state increased to nearly 18 million three years later (making California the most populous state in the union), and to some 30 million by 1990, with most of the increase occurring in the south. Even before the aqueduct of the State Water Project moved into southern California, subdividers, real-estate agents, contractors, bankers, and industrialists had gone into action, transforming ever vaster tracts of countryside into city. By the time the aqueduct crossed the Tehachapis in 1972, pushed by four mighty pumps, each capable of powering a battleship, water in the southland was too expensive, even for temporary use, for all but the most highly specialized crops. The great profits came from responding to public demand and planting houses and shopping centers on what had been the oak-studded hills and flatlands of the western San Fernando Valley, Conejo, Thousand Oaks, and Orange and San Diego counties. Eventually, the combination of jobs (even if reachable only by sitting for hours in an automobile), desire for cheap housing, and availability of water that made all the rest possible pushed the megalopolis into areas once considered wastelands—Antelope Valley and the Mojave Desert—as well as the far inland sections of the coastal counties and adjacent Riverside and San Bernardino counties.

Such growth prompted planners to dream even grander schemes designed, as one former employee of the Department of Water Resources noted even before the state aqueduct was completed, to transform California into "a system of water channels . . . knit . . . so intricate as to make every rivulet give account of itself."[132] That goal had been brought dramatically close by the gargantuan Boulder Canyon, Central Valley, and State Water projects—projects that private interests and governmental bureaucracies (federal, state, regional, local) had struggled to shape for reasons of their own and projects desired by the public, as reflected in ballot returns and votes of elected representatives. Even those opposed to the undertakings ordinarily objected because of the manner in which the benefits would be distributed, not because of philosophical opposition to the way in which water was to be harnessed and used.

Yet, as state water planners designed bold new projects, their world began to change rapidly. Competitors challenged Californians for water they thought was securely in their control, and critics sought to undermine the traditionally popular desire to put nature in a straitjacket.

6 Hydraulic Society on the Defensive

The years immediately fol-

lowing inauguration of the

State Water Project brought

unprecedented challenges

to California's numerous

hydraulic planners. Court

decrees eliminated major water supplies and threatened others, while the public, reflecting national concern over environmental abuse and increasing skepticism about the old, unquestioned belief in growth for its own sake, rejected new projects and forced urban, state, and federal strategists to emphasize better management of available sources—the increasingly central theme and thrust of water policy in California from the mid-1960s onward. Those who traditionally looked upon cheap and abundant water as a birthright reacted with alarm but not resignation as they grappled with environmental militants and devised strategies to slow, if not undermine altogether, threats to the old order.

Arizona v. California

THE FIRST major setback to California's water seekers came only three years after voters had approved the bonds launching the State Water Project. In 1963 the U.S. Supreme Court issued a monumental decision affecting the Colorado River, the source of more than half the water used in southern California. Instigator of the suit was Arizona, which, as noted earlier, had been battling with California over the Colorado since the days of the Boulder Canyon legislation. That fight had grown more intense as Arizona boomed during the war and postwar years, attracting people, industry, and capital (both federal and private), with much of the new money financing urban and agricultural expansion in the state's heartland, embracing Phoenix and Tucson. Since the rivers of central Arizona were now fully developed, irrigators had turned increasingly to groundwater supplies, which they pumped with such intensity that by the late 1940s and early 1950s they were encountering problems even more severe than those of California's Central Valley—rapidly falling water tables with exhaustion of some aquifers, abandonment of once productive fields, and land subsidence.[1]

Arizonans in 1947 turned to Congress for help, asking for equity and a major project like that accorded California in the Boulder Canyon Act. They quickly coalesced around a so-called Central Arizona Project that would bring Colorado River water through a 241-mile-long aqueduct to replace shrinking groundwater supplies and breathe new life into the urban and rural economies. In the early 1950s Congress repeatedly refused on the grounds that Arizona's unresolved dispute with California left it unclear whether Arizona had rights to enough water to make the project feasible.[2]

Bitterly disappointed and unwilling to continue futile negotiations with California, Arizonans in 1952 asked the U.S. Supreme Court to impose a settlement favorable to them. If the Central Arizona Project were to become a reality, such a settlement would have to award Arizona about a million acre-feet (enough for nearly 8 million people) that California was then using. Raising the stakes further was a treaty that the United States had negotiated with Mexico in 1944 guaranteeing that country 1.5 million acre-feet from the Colorado River. The treaty water was to come from surplus unallocated by the Colorado River Compact with any shortfall being supplied by the upper and lower basins. Among the California interests, in light of the treaty, most vulnerable to a Supreme Court decision favorable to Arizona would be the Metropolitan Water District of Southern California whose water contracts had a lower priority than the agricultural lands of the Imperial, Coachella, and Palo Verde valleys and the Yuma Project (California Division)—all of which drew from the Colorado River.[3]

With stakes so high it is little wonder that the trial in *Arizona* v. *California* became one of the longest, most expensive, and most hotly contested in U.S. Supreme Court history. After eleven years of testimony by some 340 witnesses and arguments by nearly fifty lawyers (California alone had sixty people working full-time on the case behind the scenes), the court in 1963 delivered an opinion that took virtually everyone by surprise. It did not endorse the legal position of either state, but the practical result of its action was a tremendous victory for Arizona. The court grounded its decision on the Boulder Canyon Act of 1928. Congress in that legislation had given its prior approval to a lower-basin compact that it hoped Arizona and California would find acceptable. Congress's actions, according to those who introduced the amendment adding the proposed pact to the legislation, was "not [to] be construed hereafter . . . as being the expression of the will or the demand . . . of the Congress," but, rather, a timesaving and conciliatory gesture on the part of that body. It would save California and Arizona from having to come back to Congress later since no compact between states could take effect without congressional approval. California and Arizona rejected the suggested pact, but thirty-five years later the Supreme Court in *Arizona* v. *California* startled everyone by holding that Congress had indeed expressed its "will" and "demand" in 1928. It was a decision, as close subsequent analysis has revealed, based on a faulty reading of the historical record, and it took aback not only the adversaries but also constitutional lawyers who knew of no precedent for such a congressional allocation of water between states. This bothered the court not at all. It held that Congress in the Boulder Canyon legislation had created "its own comprehensive scheme for . . . apportionment," giving Arizona all the water in its tributaries—differences over the tributaries had been at the heart of the dispute between Arizona and California—plus 2.8 million acre-feet from the main stream of the Colorado. Since this allocation was considered large enough to make practical a Central Arizona Project, Congress authorized it five years later, in 1968.[4]

Now it was California's turn to be bitterly disappointed as water planners pondered the impact of the decision on the state. Under the ruling, California received 4.4 million acre-feet plus half of any surplus. This was the same formula to which the state had limited itself back in the late 1920s in order to get congressional approval of the Boulder Canyon legislation, but with this difference: state leaders had then believed there would be a substantial surplus and they had also hoped they would be victors in their struggle with Arizona. On the basis of these expectations, they had contracted with the Secretary of the Interior for a total of 5,362,000 acre-feet

of Colorado River water and built expensive aqueducts with sufficient capacity to carry that volume—which they were using by the
1960s. They had gambled and lost. Later, and more accurate, stream-
flow studies indicated that there was considerably less water in the
river than earlier believed. Those studies, when adjusted to reflect
the obligation to Mexico and the court's award to Arizona, indicated little likelihood of any surplus. Thus, as Arizona began taking
its share of water and as the upper states and Mexico used increasingly more of what was already legally theirs, Californians would
be forced to cut back their uses by 962,000 acre-feet. Of that amount,
about 70 percent (662,000 acre-feet) would have to be surrendered
by MWD.

This realization frightened MWD board members in 1964 into
increasing their contracts with the California Department of Water
Resources for state water by half a million acre-feet with the balance
of the shortfall to be offset by Los Angeles importing more water
from the Owens Valley and Mono Basin. Other southern California
agencies sought to protect themselves by increasing their demands
for state water by an amount nearly similar to MWD's. These increases resulted in an equivalent volume of water not being available to the San Joaquin Valley, thus shrinking the valley's share
from the 2.25 million acre-feet envisaged in the 1950s to 1.35 million acre-feet.[5] The impact on agriculture would not be felt immediately since farmers could still use the water (and at heavily discounted rates) until it was needed by the southland, and that would
occur gradually. Nonetheless, Department of Water Resources officials, by reallocating water rights in the wake of the *Arizona* v. *California* decision, made it clear that in a contest between cities and
farmers for state water, *cities held the advantage.*

That reality prompted corporate farmers to begin agitating for
the building of water-development projects anticipated for subsequent phases of the State Water Project. They formed alliances with
southern California municipalities worried that many of their contracts for state water would go unfulfilled as northern California
grew, eventually causing residents there to invoke the county-of-

origin protection and keep more of the supply at home. As plans were readied for a new water-development offensive calling for large projects that would further transform California's waterscape, forceful new opponents to such strategies were also making themselves heard.

The Environmental Movement

ALIFORNIA'S SETBACK in its designs upon the Colorado River coincided with an era of great social and political upheaval. The civil rights struggles of the 1950s, 1960s, and early 1970s and the unpopular Vietnam War caused Americans to reexamine the discrepancies between the ideals of their Declaration of Independence and Bill of Rights and the realities of Jim Crowism, segregated housing and schools, and racial discrimination in all its nuances. Others had long denounced such inequities, but now as the nation awakened more fully to the social injustices being fought through sit-ins, freedom rides, and voter-registration drives and as the carnage of a war that seemed unwinnable touched increasingly more families, Americans demanded change, sometimes taking to the streets in the hundreds of thousands to emphasize their resolve.

The challenge to authority swept across the full spectrum of American life and included the questioning of long-held values about the environment, nature, and wildlife. Such challenges were nothing new. John Muir had waged a holy war in a futile attempt to preserve Hetch Hetchy, and Aldo Leopold not too many years thereafter had insisted that "ethics . . . be extended to land"; that the morality of an action be determined by whether "it tends to preserve the integrity, stability, and beauty of the biotic community."[6] There were others of similar mind, but all were somewhat out of sync with popular opinion until the years following World War II.

Concern for the environment intensified during the postwar era as unprecedented national prosperity and modern conveniences not only freed most Americans from worrying about obtaining basic necessities but also provided them with leisure time to address larger social and environmental issues. As Samuel P. Hays has observed, "The search for environmental quality was an integral part of [the postwar] . . . rising standard of living."[7] For many their search began, as such quests often do, at home as people sought to improve their immediate surroundings by purchasing a house in a more pleasant suburban or countryside setting. Attention then turned to preserving vacation areas and increasingly to other environmental issues beyond the control of single individuals but of concern to all: the impact of modern industrial society on unique natural wonders, on wildlife, and on such fundamentally important elements for life as clean air and water. No single person or issue was responsible for the modern environmental movement and studies indicate significant differences among the states, but Rachel Carson's *Silent Spring,* published in 1962, helped set off a popular outpouring of concern. Her book focused somewhat narrowly on the danger of pesticides, especially DDT, to wildlife, but it had wide appeal and, together with the blowout of the oil platform in the Santa Barbara Channel in 1969 and Earth Day the following year, galvanized popular attitudes that had been evolving throughout the 1960s and earlier.[8]

Quick to capitalize on the new concern were many political leaders, especially those in the Democratic party already predisposed by the wrenching experiences of the Great Depression and the Second World War to favor a strong, activist government working for social welfare. As the party most attractive to blacks and other newly self-conscious ethnic minorities, its commitment to reform had recently taken on renewed vitality as had its instinctive distrust of powerful corporate and industrial interests because of their potential for economic repression and now environmental destruction. Democrats did not monopolize the environmental movement, and their commitment varied regionally (being especially strong on the Pacific Coast and in New England and the upper Midwest). Still, their presence was preeminent, remaining vigorous through the 1970s and 1980s (analyses of congressional voting patterns reveal their support for environmental reform as being nearly twice that of Republicans), checking, if not eliminating, the attempts of the Republican Ronald Reagan administration (1981–1989) to use Reagan's executive authority to reverse earlier advances.[9] This pattern persisted into the 1990s. These national struggles reverberated within California, though there, as in earlier contests, debates over water issues were more reflective of regional considerations and the individual self-interests of the state's myriad water seekers and managers than they were of political ideologies.

Congress first responded with a host of environmental laws during the years roughly bracketing the Democratic administrations of John Kennedy and Lyndon Johnson (1961–1969) and extending into the early presidential years of Richard Nixon (1969–1974): Clean Air acts in 1963, 1967, 1970, and 1990 (California pointed the way in 1960 with the first statute requiring smog-control devices in automobiles); Clean Water acts in 1960, 1965, 1966, 1972, 1977, and 1979; the National Environmental Policy Act in 1969, which required federal agencies to prepare an environmental impact statement on any action likely to have a major effect on the environment; the creation of the federal Environmental Protection Agency in 1970; the Wilderness Act of 1964, which initially set aside 9 million acres as permanent wildlands; Endangered Species acts in 1966, 1969, and 1973; the National Wild and Scenic Rivers Act in 1968; the National Trails Act of 1968; and many other examples of reform through statute and ultimately through the courts whenever legislation alone seemed inadequate. California echoed the national concern with its own Clean Water Act in 1969 (the Porter-Cologne Water Quality Control Act); Endangered Species Act (1970 and 1984); San Francisco Bay Conservation and Development Commission (1969); Environmental Quality Act (1970), which mandated state and local agencies to prepare an environmental impact report when their activities might affect the environment; Wild and Scenic Rivers Act (1972); Coastal Act (1976); and similar measures that tended to elicit greater support in the north than in the south, and to find it equally strong among members of both political parties.[10]

Against this background California's water seekers played out their attempts to follow traditional policies. They had fair warning of the public's tougher attitude toward water projects, with a particularly telling incident occurring in the 1950s when the Reclamation Bureau sought congressional approval to build a dam on the Green River at Echo Park near the Colorado-Utah border. Originally endorsed by the Democratic Harry S. Truman administration and then blessed by Republican President Dwight Eisenhower, the project seemed a shoo-in because of such bipartisan support, but the idea also attracted critics, and in 1950 the Sierra Club, Izaak Walton League, Wilderness Society, and others joined forces to block the Bureau and its prodevelopment supporters. Since the resulting reservoir would flood the unique and beautiful canyons of Dinosaur National Monument, it precipitated the biggest fight over wilderness preservation since Hetch Hetchy and was waged with particular ferocity for six years. Like that earlier struggle, it became a civil war in which both sides labeled themselves "conservationists," one group arguing for conservation for use through dams and hydroelectric power and the other campaigning for conservation through preservation of unique wilderness areas. This time the preservationists prevailed, successfully eliminating Echo Park from the bill (enacted in April 1956), though their acquiescence in the same legislation to a dam on the Colorado River at Glen Canyon in northern Arizona was a concession they later came to regret.[11]

Another dramatic preservationist victory occurred in the 1960s when the Reclamation Bureau again sought congressional approval for a major project, this one to build two dams as part of the Central Arizona Project (CAP). A major purpose of the dams was to generate the hydroelectricity needed to pump water to the Phoenix and Tucson areas. Since one of the dams would be located in Marble Canyon, just east of the main gorge of Grand Canyon, and the other in Bridge Canyon, immediately west of Grand Canyon, environmentalists once more reacted with a great outcry and vowed to kill the legislation. After a lengthy battle that again captured national attention, the dams were dropped in favor of a coal-fired hydroelectric plant. Even California got something out of this struggle. Having lost to Arizona in the Supreme Court, it now sought to turn that defeat into victory by using its greater influence in the House of Representatives to derail the Central Arizona Project, a decision that made it an unwitting ally (temporarily) of the preservationists. In exchange for dropping its opposition, California wrung a major concession in the bill from Arizona: that state agreed never to deprive California of 4.4 million acre-feet even if it meant shutting down the Central Arizona Project. With such compromises all around, the CAP Bill passed Congress in 1968. Even then, appropriations for actual construction came slowly and in dribs and drabs because of lingering concern about the environment and doubts about the accuracy of river-flow estimates. More than two decades passed before the Central Arizona Project reached completion in 1993 and only in 1997 did the state begin taking its full apportionment of 2.8 million acre-feet.[12]

The preservationist victories were not unqualified triumphs. The dam at Glen Canyon inundated one of North America's most remarkable natural wonders, but this only caused the Sierra Club to issue a public mea culpa—most movingly in Eliot Porter's beautiful *The Place No One Knew* (1963)—and to redouble its resolve against developers. An added embarrassment, and also a spur to greater vigilance on the part of preservationists, was the pollution subsequently generated by the coal-fired plant that still fouls the air over Grand Canyon, Bryce, Zion, and Cedar Breaks. These mixed results notwithstanding, water developers everywhere recognized the public's growing uneasiness with business as usual.

That message was driven home again to Californians a few years later when the U.S. Army Corps of Engineers released plans to construct a dam at Dos Rios on the Middle Fork of the winding and unpredictable Eel River. The opposition, intensified by Indian activists because the dam would flood the Round Valley Reservation, attracted such widespread support that then-Governor Ronald Reagan, with a mixed record on the environment but not yet the notoriously insensitive figure he would become as President, helped kill the proposal in 1971. A year later, the desire to further protect the Eel as well as other untamed rivers along the north coast resulted in a state Wild and Scenic Rivers Act. Modeled on the federal legislation of four years earlier, it prohibited diversions (except for meeting modest local needs) on sections of five rivers, including portions or all of their tributaries: the Smith (the state's only major undammed river), American, Klamath, Trinity, and Eel (with the latter's protected status targeted for reconsideration in 1984). Though not as stringent as the federal law that also protected watersheds (particularly through close management of logging in national forests), it nonetheless removed from development rivers earlier earmarked for the State Water Project. In 1972 the National Water Commission also disappointed developers by urging less emphasis on large projects like those traditionally advocated by the Bureau of Reclamation and more attention to efficient management of available water supplies.[13]

The Peripheral Canal Fight: Round One

THE EVENT that more than any other rudely awakened California's water establishment to its vulnerability was the battle over the so-called Peripheral Canal. At stake was a great deal more than a canal—indeed, the name masked a far more grandiose enterprise that became a symbol of the clashing ideologies that had emerged over traditional state water policy. The issue's importance derived in part from its being the first crystallization of the long-anticipated second phase of the State Water Project, a phase that the earlier enabling legislation had broadly defined as virtually anything that lawmakers wanted to add to the state project to help meet local needs or augment the supply reaching the delta. Many water leaders insisted that the inauguration of this phase did not require a vote of the people or the legislature, since it had already received approval in the general election of 1960.[14] Yet, if there was not enough money (leftover bonds and tidelands oil revenue) to construct the project, as seemed increasingly likely, legislative action would be required to secure the needed funding. The possibility of obtaining the legislature's help improved significantly after 1964 when the U.S. Supreme Court ordered that representation in the state senate be based on population rather than area. This gave the more populous and water-shy south, already in control of the assembly, a commanding edge in the legislature. No one, however, likes a bully, especially one contemplating an engineering package more expensive than the original bond issue for the State Water Project. The challenge for the south was to get the north's water with the north's cooperation and with revenue from all of California.

The ostensible major purpose of the Peripheral Canal was to combat the old problem of saltwater intrusion into the delta behind San Francisco Bay. Despite earlier ameliorative measures, the situation had only worsened as delta communities and farms increased their own consumption of fresh water and as growth accelerated around the bay. Growth also further reduced the runoff that had earlier gone to the delta from the Tuolumne, Mokelumne, and other Sierra streams, which now went in increased volume by aqueduct directly to growing cities and industries. Further compounding the problem were the enormous diversions for the Central Valley and State Water projects from the Sacramento and San Joaquin river systems. Occasionally the damage extended beyond the delta when, during periods of low flow and drought, ocean water advanced far enough inland to be sucked into the state and federal aqueducts going south. Also affected adversely was the wildlife of the delta and adjoining Suisun Marsh, regions that were breeding grounds and migratory way stations for fish and waterfowl. Many fish, including striped bass and king salmon, became confused by the reverse movement of ocean water. Millions of eggs and fry ended up in the pumps sucking water southward. There was also serious disruption of salmon breeding grounds.[15]

State and federal planners had long recognized the need for bold action to save the delta, but they counted themselves political realists and designed a plan calculated, they hoped, to protect the delta while also providing more northern water for the San Joaquin Valley and southern California. In 1965, the Interagency Delta Committee released a plan for a 43-mile-long, 400-foot-wide, 30-foot-deep unlined ditch in the shape of a broad eastward-swinging curve—hence, the name Peripheral Canal—that would begin at a site on the Sacramento River fifteen miles below the state capital and then move south, skirting and bypassing the eastern edge of the delta, to the state and federal pumping plants near Tracy.[16]

Such a canal appealed to those in the south because it would assure that the water entering the San Joaquin Valley would be of the same quality as that diverted upstream on the Sacramento. To protect the delta, gates would be located along the canal's length for releasing enough fresh water to prevent saltwater intrusion. According to planning estimates in 1966, the canal, together with appurtenant reservoirs and other facilities, would make available 7.8 million acre-feet annually for the State Water Project and Central Valley Project, salvage 2.25 million acre-feet that "would otherwise have to be released from storage and wasted to the ocean for water quality control at the federal and state export pumps," and provide 1.3 million acre-feet to meet the needs of the delta. The total capital costs were estimated at $179 million with the state's share pegged at $55 million and the federal government's at $124 million.[17]

Despite the steep price tag, many believed that a plan promising so much and having the endorsement of the California Department of Water Resources, Bureau of Reclamation, and Army Corps of Engineers was destined for success. Southern California water leaders, reeling from their loss to Arizona in the Supreme Court, greeted it enthusiastically as did agribusiness in the San Joaquin Valley. There farmers had a vested interest in maintaining a water supply in excess of urban southern California's needs and hence available to them at cut-rate prices. "The ability of our farmers to pay for water and finance . . . local distribution works is being stretched to the limit," complained the Kern County Water Agency in 1969. "Any

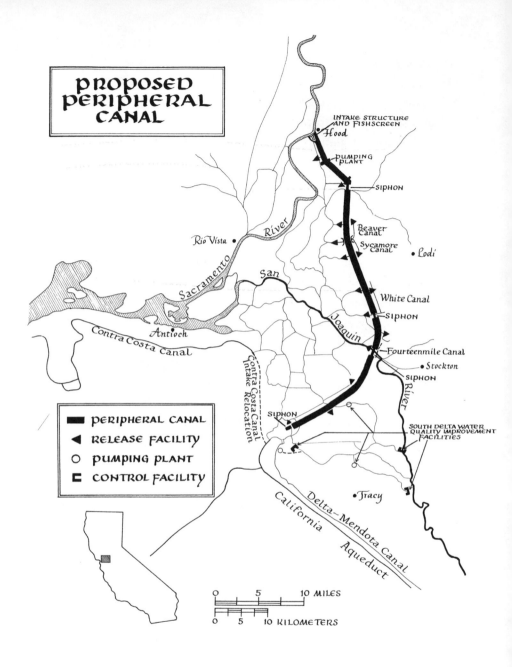

PROPOSED
PERIPHERAL
CANAL

INTAKE STRUCTURE
AND FISHSCREEN
Hood

PUMPING
PLANT

SIPHON

Beaver
Canal

Sycamore
Canal

Lodi

White Canal

SIPHON

Fourteenmile Canal

Stockton

SIPHON

SOUTH DELTA WATER
QUALITY IMPROVEMENT
FACILITIES

SIPHON

Tracy

Rio Vista

Sacramento   River

San

Joaquin

River

Antioch

Contra Costa Canal

Contra Costa Canal
Intake Relocation

Delta–Mendota Canal

California   Aqueduct

PERIPHERAL CANAL
RELEASE FACILITY
PUMPING PLANT
CONTROL FACILITY

0   5   10 MILES

0   5   10 KILOMETERS

modification in the . . . proposed Federal and State plans for a joint Peripheral Canal Project . . . could be disastrous to Kern County." [18]

Also in support of the canal were many valley farmers who had found it cheaper to continue pumping groundwater than to take state water, thus continuing the old cycle of draining aquifers faster than they could be replenished and ignoring the future consequences of their actions, as they had always done in the past, on the assumption that there would be plenty of imported surface water available when they needed it. Agribusiness as well as the south's cities found additional reason for a Peripheral Canal enterprise in state reports pointing to deficiencies in the first phase of the State Water Project. Contracts had been issued for 4.2 million acre-feet, but recent studies indicated that little more than half that amount was then being delivered or likely to be delivered in the future. The reasons: increasing water needs in the north, and losses due to evaporation along the aqueducts and at the reservoirs already in place. Also attracted to the Peripheral Canal proposal were many delta interests as well as the state Department of Fish and Game, which took heart in the predictions of environmental renewal and improved health of fish, birds, and other wildlife. [19]

The canal also immediately attracted critics. As the public became more familiar with the plan, old regional charges of a southern water grab emerged, only this time they were accompanied by sharp attacks on agribusiness as well as alarmed cries from the new army of environmentalists. The battle raged with varying intensity for seventeen years before the issue was decided.

As before, northern Californians were at the forefront of the opposition, attacking the canal as merely the south's latest gambit to steal their water. Each successful earlier venture had led only to another, and unless the cycle were broken, they argued, it would not end until every northern stream had been channeled to southern California. The fact that the State Water Project would not generate enough water to fulfill all the contracts, they contended, reflected exaggerated projections, not imminent disaster. "We consider it to be self-fulfilling prophecy," declared two highly critical University of California researchers, "for the state to promise more than it can deliver and then to use those promises to justify further supply expansion."[20] The reality, they charged, is that the farmers generally and Californians in particular have plenty of water and are wasting much of it through inefficient irrigation practices on farms and lack of water conservation policies for both rural and urban areas.

When even state studies confirmed that more than a million acre-feet were lost in the Imperial and Central valleys through evaporation and seepage from unlined canals (and the Peripheral Canal would be unlined), the critics redoubled their demands for reform, emphasizing the availability of important new—and so far largely ignored—technologies. Sprinkler irrigation was nearly 20 percent more efficient than the use of open ditches and drip irrigation could be greater than 50 percent more efficient, yet the vast majority of California's irrigated farms (80 percent) relied on ditches.[21] Not every area possessed conditions that permitted the use of such techniques, but those that did should adopt them, insisted critics.

Farmers remained largely unmoved. Why should they adopt such expensive methods, they asked themselves (and sometimes the public), when it was far cheaper to pour their subsidized (at public expense) water onto their fields and to rely on new sources of supply (also developed at public expense)? Their position, though hardly popular with the opponents of the Peripheral Canal plan, was altogether reasonable. It simply reflected the public's traditional willingness to subsidize water supply but not water conservation.

Many canal opponents recognized the inherent weakness in demanding conservation without also reforming the water system. They launched a vigorous attack on the subsidies that they believed were at the heart of the modern water problem. In speeches, brochures, pamphlets, and articles in *Cry California,* the *California Journal, New West* magazine, the *Public Affairs Reports* of the University of California's Institute of Governmental Studies, and elsewhere, they hammered away at their theme: the state and federal governments should reform their policies and require water users to pay their fair share of a project's cost. Only then, they contended, could society hope to reverse a system requiring "the overdevelopment of rivers and streams and the overconsumption of water by agriculture at a very high public cost."[22]

Especially notorious, in the view of critics, were the federal government's subsidies to agribusiness resulting from abuse of reclamation law. To opponents of the Peripheral Canal, nothing so epitomized that abuse as the Westlands Water District, the site of the Reclamation Bureau's latest project in California. Westlands then consisted of 545,000 acres of incredibly rich land in a seventy-mile-long strip that roughly paralleled today's Interstate 5 in the San Joaquin Valley. In the early 1960s when the Reclamation Bureau began constructing a multimillion-dollar distribution system for the area as the newest unit in the still expanding Central Valley Project, nearly all the land was held in vast tracts by individuals or major corporations. In 1968 when water arrived, corporations and individuals, mostly absentee, still held the bulk of the land—11 percent of the owners possessed 84 percent of the land, with an average holding consisting of 1,650 acres. During the ten-year grace period that followed when owners could obtain subsidized water for all their acreage, the average benefit was $950 an acre or $1.6 million for each of those owners among the select 11 percent. Even the remaining owners, whose holdings averaged forty acres, came away with benefits of about $40,000 each because of the subsidy. The end of the grace period did not mean an end to the subsidy, however, since the Reclamation Bureau's technical-compliance loopholes effectively nullified the requirement to sell off holdings in excess of 160 acres. Moreover, those who elected to sell some or all of their acreage found the Bureau willing to approve selling prices inflated because of the federal project. This violation of reclamation law, according to a University of California researcher, resulted in a windfall of some $400 an acre to those Westlands owners disposing of land during the decade following the arrival of water.[23]

"What has occurred," discovered George Baker, an investigative reporter for the McClatchy newspapers, "is a class shuffle game in which land is sold or resold or leased to former associates, syndicates, foreign corporations or Caribbean-based tax havens."[24] What also helped make it possible was the state's willingness (through the State Water Project) to join with the Reclamation Bureau in building San Luis Dam, which regulated the water delivered to the Bureau's distribution system at Westlands. The local guiding spirit behind this entire web of support was Ralph Brody, formerly a Reclamation Bureau attorney and then special counsel to Governor Pat Brown during the struggle to win approval of the State Water Project in 1960. He was now the manager and chief counsel of the Westlands Water District.[25]

Feeling more directly threatened by the Peripheral Canal and hence more emotional and dogged in their opposition were delta residents, especially those in Contra Costa County whose cities and farms received the brunt of the damage from saltwater intrusion. The few who at first thought the canal would be their salvation soon joined the vast majority who saw it as an unmitigated threat. The canal would be furnished with gates to permit the release of fresh water into the delta, but nowhere in the plan were the delta's water rights spelled out. Moreover, there was no clear understanding or agreement on just how much water the delta required during the different seasons of the year to prevent damage and maintain a healthy environment for wildlife. "We don't want to give the Metropolitan Water District the plumbing to suck us dry in a drought year," announced a representative of the Central Delta Water Agency.[26] As early as 1969 delta water agencies joined to pass a resolution denouncing the canal and then fought it in both Congress and the state legislature.

Vigorously aiding those efforts were environmentalists in California and across the nation who were alarmed not only by the threat to the delta but also to the entire state. To support the Peripheral Canal, they believed, was to promote further ecological destruction in the San Francisco Bay area, the ocean, the Central Valley, and the already overgrown and polluted megalopolis of southern California. There was also fear that the volume of water to be sent south was so great that it would require removing the north-coast rivers from their wild and scenic status under state law. The Sierra Club, Friends of the Earth, the Planning and Conservation League, Friends of the River, and similar organizations joined with other opponents to stall, if not derail, the canal project by success-fully invoking state legislation (the 1970 California Environmental Quality Act) requiring an environmental impact report, that pow-erful new weapon in the environmentalists' crusade. The prelimi-nary draft of that report, released in 1974, was generally favorable to the project, but it acknowledged adverse effects, including in-creased salinity in the delta and particularly for Suisun Marsh, the nation's largest contiguous marsh and a major wintering ground on the Pacific Flyway.[27] The news caused the opposition to become even more intransigent.

Heightening the alarm of the opponents and exacerbating their anger was the refusal of San Joaquin Valley and southern California interests as well as the Reclamation Bureau to acknowledge any re-sponsibility for maintaining water quality standards in the delta. According to them, the state and federal governments were respon-sible only for the quality of the water entering the aqueducts of the Central Valley Project and the State Water Project—that is, at the southern border of the delta. The California Water Resources Con-trol Board contended otherwise, and in 1971 ordered the Reclama-tion Bureau and the state Department of Water Resources to increase releases from their dams according to a complex set of criteria. The Interior Department promptly announced that the state had no le-gal authority over federal projects. San Joaquin Valley farmers and then Washington sought to block implementation of the board's order by filing lawsuits that never fully resolved the issue through-out the long battle over the Peripheral Canal.[28]

Despite the lengthy and acrimonious struggle, California's gov-ernors remained supporters of the canal, perhaps not least because of the preponderance of voters in the south. Former Democratic Governor Pat Brown saw it as the natural outgrowth of his State Water Project, and Republican Governor Ronald Reagan, whose power base was in the southland, considered it essential to continued economic prosperity. It was he who in 1971 announced that the state would build the project on its own when the federal government began registering doubts about sharing costs and otherwise foot-dragging in response to concerns of the Environmental Protection Agency, the U.S. Geological Survey, and others. Though remaining firmly convinced that the canal should be built, Reagan relaxed his pressure for it when his Department of Water Resources director concluded that it could be "put on the deferred list" until the mid-1970s.[29] The issue then carried over into the Democratic administration of Edmund G. "Jerry" Brown, Jr.

When Brown took office in 1975 with his emphasis on "small is beautiful," "era of limits," and conservation of resources, he buoyed the spirits of canal opponents. He seemed nothing like—indeed, appeared to be under an extraordinary compulsion not to be like— his father. He reaffirmed this impression with his appointment as head of the state Resources Agency a Sierra Club member, Claire Dedrick, who publicly announced that the canal "ought to be killed, dead." Brown then ordered a reappraisal of the proposal and a study of alternatives.[30]

After nearly two years of hearings (which revealed no changes in the battle lines) and data gathering and assessment, state water officials reaffirmed their basic commitment to the canal. Playing no small role in influencing their judgment was the drought that hit California shortly after Brown took office and led to rationing, especially in parts of the hard-hit north, before it ended two years later, with the final year (1977) being the driest on record. Southern California was spared the worst of the dry spell because of abundant runoff in the Colorado River Basin that allowed it to voluntarily shut down for a time the state aqueduct, thereby increasing the supply available to the north. The south warned, however, that such generosity could not be expected during a future drought in the Colorado basin or when Arizona began taking its full entitlement to the river. The message was clear: the south remained thoroughly committed to the Peripheral Canal.

So, too, did the state Department of Water Resources. The

drought had brought the delta to the edge of disaster and helped precipitate the court battles between the state and Reclamation Bureau over water quality responsibilities. As the legal conflicts raged, with the Bureau insisting that the burden for maintaining quality rested solely on the state, California water officials concluded that the canal was absolutely mandatory for protecting the delta and meeting the water needs of the south. "We felt there was a need for more water [and an] . . . environmentally oriented package," observed Water Resources Director Ronald Robie.[31]

Governor Brown in 1977, beginning a shift to a more conservative stance and without waiting for a formal recommendation from his staff, abandoned his neutral position and publicly announced his support for the canal. As in many earlier water battles, regional considerations and the pressures exerted by individual interest groups became more compelling than party ideology in influencing decision making. The pressure from southern California, agribusiness, and the drought proved persuasive. He recognized the need, however, to respond to northern concerns by establishing water quality standards for the delta and by making the decision to go ahead on the project subject to federal acceptance of those standards, as well as Washington's equal participation in the costs for the facilities to maintain them. "I want you to sit down and hammer out legislation to carry out this project," he told key legislators.[32]

In 1977 and 1978 Brown made no headway. At first the legislature's bills did not meet his requirements and later, when they did, northerners denounced the environmental protections as too weak and southerners insisted they were too strong. Another obstacle was the Interior Department's continued insistence that it was not— and would not allow itself to be—legally bound by state water quality standards. The Interior Department became even more intransigent in July 1978 when the U.S. Supreme Court in *California v. U.S.* held that the state could attach conditions to federal water-rights permits but only so long as the state's directives did not clearly conflict with congressional legislation. The two sides promptly returned to court, disputing whether the state's authority conflicted with congressional intent. In the meantime, until the question was settled the Interior Department expressed a willingness to abide by state requirements except in years of severe drought like 1976 and 1977, a gesture that served only to further inflame environmentalists since the delta was most at risk during droughts.[33]

Brown tried again in 1979. To the north, he promised amendments to the state constitution making California alone responsible for guaranteeing water quality in the delta and also protecting the north-coast rivers by stipulating that storage projects on the state's wild rivers would require a two-thirds, rather than simply a majority, vote of the legislature. To the south, he offered not only the canal and supporting facilities but also the promise that the constitutional guarantees would be worded so as not to take effect until the canal had legislative approval. In addition, he bowed to farmers' demands that the bill contain nothing that would open the door to management of groundwater.

No one was completely happy with the proposal and many openly opposed it, but after debating no fewer than fourteen different bills, a majority of lawmakers in the south-dominated legislature agreed to go along. In late January 1980 the senate, by a twenty-four-to-twelve margin, passed the Peripheral Canal Bill. Significantly, with only one exception, every state senator from southern California and the San Joaquin Valley supported the measure, and the sole dissenter represented an area in which the valley constituted but a small portion of a district reaching across the Sierra Nevada into eastern California. Similarly, every senator from the north except one rejected the canal. Support for the legislation came from a majority in both parties (71 percent of the Democrats and 60 percent of the Republicans) but regional considerations clearly dominated in the voting outcome. A little more than five months later, in early July, the assembly went along with an endorsement of fifty to twenty-eight. There, too, while the measure received bipartisan support (60 percent of the Democrats and 71 percent of the Republicans), regional considerations were preeminent, with the north rejecting and the south approving the canal with almost the same near unanimity they had demonstrated in the senate.[34]

In the meantime, the legislature, a few weeks earlier in June, had voted to put the proposed constitutional amendment protecting the delta and north-coast rivers on the ballot. San Joaquin Valley representatives objected to the move, but delegates from southern California, sensing a need to compromise and knowing that valley agriculture would face cutbacks during shortages before their urbanized areas would be denied water, joined overwhelmingly with the north to send the measure to the voters. When it appeared on the ballot in November 1980 as Proposition 8, the electorate approved it by a close but decisive margin (54 to 46 percent) in which the north, understandably, registered strong support. San Francisco endorsed it three to one, but Los Angeles County voters, unlike their representatives in the legislature, dragged their heels, giving it a winning edge of only 121,000 ballots out of nearly 2 million cast.[35] The battle might have seemed over, but it now entered a new stage.

The Peripheral Canal Fight: Round Two

GOVERNOR BROWN betrayed uneasiness about the legislation that he had helped generate when he waited eleven days before announcing his intention to sign it. During this period not even the members of his staff knew his plans. He flew to Los Angeles and scheduled a television address for the evening of July 18, 1980. That morning, recalled state Water Resources Director Ronald Robie, who still knew nothing of Brown's decision, the governor "went into a little room and hand-wrote his statement, consulting with me regularly, and by three o'clock it was almost done. It was to sign it."[36]

For a long while into his television address Brown kept his decision to himself. He began with an uncharacteristic invocation of his father's memory for obviously political reasons. "Twenty years

Prelude to a renewed battle. Governor Jerry Brown signing the Peripheral Canal Bill into law on July 18, 1980. (Courtesy of California Department of Water Resources)

ago . . . my father . . . presented to the people a water project that was one of the most ambitious in the world. . . . Deserts were turned green and crops were shipped all over the world, helping to maintain California as the number one agricultural state." Having made this gesture to agribusiness and established that "there is nothing unusual in transferring water from one part of the State to another,"

Brown then spent the remainder of his talk trying to depict the new legislation as if it were every environmentalist's most fervent wish—it "imposes strict and unprecedented environmental safeguards," "restricts the power of the State to move water," and marks the "end of an era . . . of growth without strict conservation." Only toward the end of his speech did he announce: "I'm going to sign."[37]

Brown's plan was to disarm criticism from the environmentalists whom he viewed as the real threat to the Peripheral Canal package. He was only half right in his appraisal of the potential opposition, and it was a miscalculation that he compounded during the months that followed when he appealed to President Jimmy Carter's Secretary of the Interior, Cecil Andrus, to put the north-coast rivers under the protection of the federal Wild and Scenic Rivers Act. Such action would effectively place the rivers (including the Eel whose status as a protected river under state law had been scheduled for reconsideration in 1984) off limits to dam builders. At bottom, this constituted an intensification of the Proposition 8 guarantees, which provided that protection would cease as soon as the developers could muster a two-thirds vote of the legislature. The Interior Secretary agreed with the request, setting aside 1,235 miles of northern rivers just hours before leaving office in January 1981. A coalition of water agencies and farm and business groups then appealed to the courts to reverse the Secretary's action on the grounds that he had failed to provide adequate time for public comment. The U.S. Supreme Court years later upheld the Secretary's decision, but for the present Brown only succeeded in antagonizing agribusiness and the south by seeking to give more protection to the north's rivers and in reminding environmentalists that, even with the passage of Proposition 8, the north-coast rivers would remain vulnerable without federal protection.[38]

Brown's overtures to the environmentalists fell on deaf ears. They immediately joined with delta residents and an overwhelming majority of northerners to launch a campaign for a referendum to repeal the canal legislation. Their determination intensified when the legislature, responding to southern and agribusiness pressure, killed a measure that would have required recipients of state water to adopt groundwater management and water conservation programs. In little time, the coalition of anticanal groups had collected 850,000 signatures, more than double the number necessary, on petitions calling for the public referendum. It was scheduled for the statewide election in June 1982.[39]

The campaign preceding the election was among the most hard-fought and costly (more than $6 million was spent) in California history. It was also filled with surprises. The contest had no sooner gotten under way than the California Farm Bureau Federation, traditionally a strongly Republican and prodevelopment organization representing fifty-four county agricultural groups and a claimed 10,000 individuals, reversed itself and came out against the canal at its annual meeting in December 1980. The reason: not because it opposed the project (it had long sought the canal) but because it objected to Proposition 8's protection—albeit qualified protection—of the north-coast rivers and the delta. Although approved by the voters, Proposition 8 would not take effect unless the canal gained approval, thus both the canal legislation and Proposition 8 were subject to the referendum election scheduled for June 1982.[40]

"We do not feel we should bankrupt our future," declared the Farm Bureau president, "by locking up the north coast rivers as the price for securing the Peripheral Canal." Brown's action, complained the Bureau, was tantamount to saying: "Okay, boys, you can have your canal, but you can't have any more water to put through it" than currently comes down the Sacramento River. The Farm Bureau saw its opposition as encouragement to the legislature to come up with something better. So, too, did the J. G. Boswell Company and Salyer Land Company, among the largest corporate farms in the state and the heaviest contributors to the campaign against the project. They favored a less costly channel through the delta and one free of environmental regulations. The *Sacramento Bee* described the Farm Bureau and its allies as "throwing out . . . [their] Peripheral Canal baby with the bathwater of Proposition 8." Other farmers shared that view, especially corporate agricultural and oil interests in the southern San Joaquin Valley, including Shell Oil, Getty Oil, and the Tejon Ranch Company which contributed substantial sums to the procanal campaign.[41]

Environmentalists and northern California opponents of the canal welcomed the turnabout by the Farm Bureau as warmly as they disagreed with the bureau's reasons. Some of them even joined with Boswell and Salyer in a coalition called Californians for a Fair Water Policy to fight the project, though they also promised to battle the Boswell-Salyer channel if it were ever put forward. They were convinced that both Proposition 8 and the legislature's canal act were flawed. Proposition 8 would establish constitutional guarantees for water quality standards for the delta and for river protection, but these could be changed by another initiative or a two-thirds vote of the legislature. With southern Californians already in the majority in the legislature and "expected to increase" their control there, opponents feared that the south would "move to repeal this amendment." "Federal protection is much more difficult to overturn," they noted, but the "water lobby . . . went to court to try to keep the federal government from extending that . . . protection" and the outcome of the litigation remained in doubt.[42]

As for the Peripheral Canal project, opponents faulted it for the same reasons they had done so all along: the south did not really need the water and was subsidizing agribusiness, which continued to contribute market-glutting surpluses (and those surpluses included not only such commodities as forage crops and cotton but also sometimes even specialty crops like olives and almonds); the project contained no requirement for effective water conservation and groundwater management programs; it was too expensive; and, most importantly, the delta ecology—indeed, the ecology of the state—was too fragile to risk with such a complex and gargantuan undertaking. Despite the protections written into the canal legislation, the opponents remained haunted by the possibility of "mismanagement" of the intricate system of gates and releases on which the success of the whole enterprise rested. And suffusing the opposition and influencing even those unable or unwilling to grasp the more complex issues was widespread cynicism and distrust: "Legal promises can be broken by the legislators who make them." Former state Senator Peter Behr of Marin County in the north graphically captured the popular attitude toward the south: "You can't contain a thirsty beast in a paper cage."[43]

Much was also made of the cost of the project, a sensitive issue at a time when the economy had momentarily slowed and when taxpayers were still upset at the burdens that had led to sweeping property-tax relief a few years earlier. The state's estimates had risen steadily as the passage of time and addition of new facilities pushed costs ever upward—from an initial $179 million in 1966, to $210 million by 1973, to nearly $2.5 billion on the eve of the election, with the last figure expected to exceed $5 billion by the year 2035 after being adjusted for inflation. When state Water Resources Director Ronald Robie sought to hedge on his department's latest calculations by acknowledging that "cost estimates are difficult to come up with" and he "won't even guess" at expenses after the year 2000, opponents did it for him, predicting costs as great as $23 billion and insisting that southern Californians would pay the lion's share while most of the water would be used for decades in the San Joaquin Valley (especially Kern County) at subsidized prices. Whatever the ultimate price tag, the state admitted that California water users would pay for the bulk of the project (about 96 percent, including repayment of bonds and tidelands oil revenue) with the balance for flood control, recreation, and fish and wildlife enhancement coming from federal and state taxpayers. This was quite a change from the estimate of a decade and a half earlier when the federal government alone was expected to cover nearly 70 percent of what was to have been a smaller and much less expensive undertaking.[44]

The intensity of the attack further alarmed the already skittish Governor Brown. Planning a run for the U.S. Senate, he began backing away from the controversy, claiming that he was overworked and his energies were needed to combat crime. "Hey, I'm working 12 hours a day. I can barely keep up. I have so much to do as gov-

'I love it . . . I love it not . . . I love it . . . I love it not . . . I love it . . .'

Governor Jerry Brown ponders the Peripheral Canal (Editorial cartoon by Ken Alexander in the San Francisco Examiner, *March 29, 1981. Reprinted with permission of the* San Francisco Examiner. © *1981 San Francisco Examiner)*

ernor."[45] Lieutenant Governor Mike Curb, a southern California Republican intent on taking over Brown's job as soon as it became available, also sensed that the canal was in trouble. He dropped his earlier support and came out against the project, now claiming that it was too expensive (and also picking up major campaign aid from Boswell and Salyer for his gubernatorial race).

Brown's vacillation throughout most of the campaign and Curb's flip-flop on an issue of vital concern to his region's water establishment did neither man any good and probably contributed to the defeat both suffered in their bids for new offices. Nonetheless, the two politicians had correctly gauged the discontent over the canal. On June 8, 1982, the electorate approved the referendum repealing the

Peripheral Canal legislation (and rejecting the Proposition 8 protections) by a decisive margin of more than three to two—63 to 37 percent.[46]

With the exception of the San Joaquin Valley, the vote generally reflected traditional regional differences, though southern California's enthusiasm was weak in comparison to earlier water project elections. (Southern California is defined here as generally the area below the Tehachapis and embracing eight counties: Los Angeles, San Bernardino, Ventura, Santa Barbara, Riverside, Orange, San Diego, and Imperial.) One southern county (Santa Barbara) actually rejected the canal, and voter turnout in those counties supporting it was low. Northern voters, on the other hand, went to the polls in great numbers and an overwhelming 90 percent registered opposition. Breaking with tradition were San Joaquin Valley residents who joined with the California Farm Bureau Federation in rejecting the canal. Of the eight counties located wholly or partially (though significantly) in the valley, only one (Kern) favored the project (reflecting the strength there of the procanal corporate agriculture and oil interests), but it did so by less than 17,000 votes out of more than 84,000 cast. A measure of the regional differences in intensity was Los Angeles County's less than two-to-one vote for the canal, Marin County's thirty-two-to-one and San Francisco's nearly twenty-to-one rejection of it, and the San Joaquin Valley's three-to-one opposition. Pollsters later claimed that the single biggest consideration in voters' thinking was cost (58 percent of those questioned so testified), though other factors also played a major role in the outcome. Forty percent believed the project would harm the environment and 28 percent singled out the delta and bay as being especially threatened.[47]

The result represented a milestone in California water history: the first rejection of a major project since the 1920s. Though defeated, the Peripheral Canal concept was not dead. The north remained (and remains) convinced that the delta requires greater protection, while agribusiness and southern California political leaders of both parties continued to angle for new supplies of water. In 1984 Governor George Deukmejian, a southern Californian, sought passage of a cheaper and shorter "through-delta" bill, but the legislature refused to go along with the Republican chief executive. When a return of drought conditions became particularly severe in 1990, the Metropolitan Water District of Southern California, already uneasy because of the increased demands of the southland's expanding population, began lobbying in Sacramento for a resurrection of the canal idea. At the same time, a prominent Democratic member of the Los Angeles County Board of Supervisors proposed revival of an old plan to import water into the state from the Columbia River Basin in the Pacific Northwest. "You've got to be kidding," responded government officials in Oregon and Washington, who proclaimed their unequivocal opposition. A hydrologist in the state Department of Water Resources pronounced the plan feasible but "frightfully expensive" and subject to virtually insurmountable environmental and political barriers. Not intimidated by such talk, Alaska Governor Walter Hickel a short time later dusted off another old plan, this one to pipe 2 billion to 3 billion gallons of water to southern California and other arid areas from his state—for a hefty price, of course. This proposal, like so many others being trooped out, was pronounced "technologically feasible" but suspect for a host of practical reasons.[48]

Serious cracks also appeared among southland water leaders in the mid-1980s. Some San Diego County officials disavowed the Metropolitan Water District's "single-solution" insistence on new projects. "Create some kind of incentive to use less water" was the message that San Diego's representative on the MWD board gave to the agency. MWD's management publicly scoffed at the suggestion but began negotiating with Imperial Valley farmers for rights to water lost there to seepage. What remained clear was the north's resistance to any new state plumbing for the south. That resistance received strong encouragement from the U.S. Supreme Court in 1985 when it upheld the Secretary of the Interior's action four years earlier placing the north-coast rivers under the protection of the federal Wild and Scenic Rivers Act. It would thereafter require an act of Congress to remove them from the national system.[49]

The defeat of the Peripheral Canal represented the most serious setback for the state's water establishment following the *Arizona* v. *California* loss, but the idea would forcefully emerge again in the 1990s. In the meantime, water leaders faced additional challenges. Among the most significant were those involving the oldest and most experienced water hustler of them all, Los Angeles. From the 1970s into the 1990s the city had to defend itself from determined challenges to three sources of water that it considered uniquely and safely its own: the Los Angeles River, the Owens River, and Mono Basin.

The Pueblo Water Right Challenged

D ESPITE LOS ANGELES'S long-touted pueblo water right (upheld back in 1895 by the state supreme court), several nearby communities in the San Fernando Valley escaped the city's metropolitan grasp, maintained their independence, and continued pumping groundwater. During the boom years following World War II they increased the rate of extraction until 1955 when Los Angeles, asserting its prior and paramount pueblo right to all the waters of the Los Angeles River, decided to teach the upstarts a lesson and filed suit against them in county superior court. City attorneys expected a quick decision, but the court, in a surprise move, found merit in the defendants' claims and decided to reopen the question of the origin and meaning of the pueblo water right.

Thirteen *years* later, following an analysis of hundreds of historical documents and close questioning of expert witnesses, the trial court dropped a bombshell. "The so-called 'pueblo water right,'" it concluded, "had no support in Spanish or Mexican law and . . . its statement in some of the [earlier] cases was based solely upon erroneous translations, incomplete and inaccurate citations, and unsupported conclusions drawn therefrom."[50] The judge awarded the parties rights to the water each had been using, a decision that reduced by nearly a third the water under the San Fernando Valley claimed by Los Angeles.

Los Angeles promptly appealed to the state supreme court, which in 1975, in *Los Angeles* v. *San Fernando,* overruled the lower court and upheld the city's pueblo claim. It did so, however, even though noting that the "data on Spanish-Mexican law and history" demonstrated neither "conclusively . . . the existence of the pueblo right" nor "its non-existence." Nonetheless, the court concluded that it should abide by the principle of *stare decisis*—the tendency of courts to let stand prior decisions, especially older ones whose undoing would have far-reaching effects. On the basis of that principle and its reading of the evidence, the court concluded there was "a reasonable basis for a judicial determination that the right did and still does exist."[51]

The lower court had also considered and then dismissed invoking stare decisis on several grounds, but especially because it believed that the evidence on which the earlier decisions rested was unpersuasive: "In none of the cases . . . has there been a single reference to a Spanish or Mexican law that used the words 'pueblo water right' or any equivalent phrase or parallel to that legal theory."[52] The supreme court entertained no such scruples, all of which led a couple of perplexed legal scholars to pronounce the court's reasoning "manufactured" and a product of "its zeal to save face over its prior decisions." Whatever the explanation, Los Angeles had once more—but after a good scare—reaffirmed its hold on the river bearing its name and forced its challengers, who were denied San Fernando Valley groundwater, to contract for higher-priced supplies (nearly three times more expensive) from the Metropolitan Water District.[53]

Mono Lake and the Public Trust Doctrine

WHILE STILL locked in conflict over the pueblo water right, Los Angeles encountered an even more formidable threat to another of its sacred watering holes: the Mono drainage basin, an area just north of the Owens Valley and east of the Sierra Nevada that it had begun tapping for water in 1941 when it extended northward its Owens Valley water-gathering system. Almost immediately affected was Mono Lake, an awesome 500,000-year-old roughly circular saline body of water about thirteen miles across at its widest point and eight miles at its narrowest. "This solemn, silent, sailless sea—this lonely tenant of the loneliest spot on earth," as Mark Twain described it in *Roughing It,* was all that remained of a once vast inland sea of 300,000 square miles.[54]

Possessing no outlet, Mono Lake had acquired a level of salinity in which only a single type of brine shrimp and one kind of brine fly could survive, but they were adequate enough to support on the lake's small islands the nation's second largest breeding ground for California gulls. The lake is also located along a major flyway and serves as a stop-off for such migratory birds as grebes and phalaropes on their way south from the Arctic. While the gulls and grebes feast on the shrimp, the smaller phalaropes refuel on the flies. Since there are no fish, the birds, numbering at least a million annually, have no competitors for the local food supply. That supply and the wildlife, however, depend for their existence on the lake. Ominously, the lake began declining at the rate of about a foot a year after Los Angeles completed its Mono extension on the eve of World War II and began taking water from the streams feeding the area. In 1970 the city's impact on the lake increased significantly when Los Angeles completed a second aqueduct through the Owens Valley and into the Mono Basin. The rate of decline increased to a foot and a half annually as some 90,000 acre-feet a year or 17 percent of the city's total annual supply came from the area.[55]

Mono Lake: "Lonely tenant of the loneliest spot on earth."—Mark Twain.
(Courtesy of Water Education Foundation)

Ironically, Los Angeles did not then need the additional water. The supply coming earlier from Mono Basin as well the Owens Valley, together with the city's entitlements to deliveries from the Colorado River and through the state project (which tapped the Feather River), assured Los Angeles more water than it was expected to require. The problem was that the water from these latter two sources was more expensive than that from Mono or the Owens Valley. Moreover, the less water that Los Angeles took from the Colorado and from the state project meant more for other southern California communities and for San Joaquin Valley farmers. Keeping them happy provided Los Angeles with allies on other issues of importance to the city. That consideration had begun weighing heavily in Los Angeles's thinking during the 1950s when these "allies" and state planners became upset over the city's refusal to exercise fully its Owens Valley and Mono rights, thereby freeing up water for others. Reacting to the dismay, the state Water

Rights Board in 1959 reversed its earlier flexible interpretation of the "due diligence" requirement of the appropriation doctrine and threatened to cancel Los Angeles's unexercised rights.[56] The city might have challenged such an action, for it was no longer dependent solely on the board for a broad reading of the law. The state legislature in 1943 and 1945 had enacted statutes encouraging leniency toward cities (their "rights . . . should be protected to the fullest extent necessary for existing and future uses") and giving them a higher priority ("water for the municipality . . . shall be considered first in right, irrespective of whether it is first in time").[57] State pressure and the need for allies proved more compelling than a fight, however, and the city hurriedly constructed the second aqueduct, since the first one did not have the capacity to move enough water.

Completion of the aqueduct accelerated the decline in the water level of Mono Lake, increased the concentration of salts in the remaining water, and caused scientists to predict the death of the brine shrimp and flies and the disappearance of the birds. Within forty years of Los Angeles's first diversions, the two aqueducts had caused the lake surface to fall by forty-five feet, the volume of water to decrease by half, and the salinity nearly to double (to two-and-a-half times that of the ocean). Though the lake level had fluctuated over the previous thousands of years in response to changing climatic conditions, scientific studies indicated that the present reduced surface was solely the result of Los Angeles's actions. In the late 1970s the receding water level exposed a land bridge to Negit Island, allowing coyotes access to rookeries where they cut a deadly swath through the gull population. The birds then migrated to smaller islets where they bred successfully until the declining surface in 1981 and again during the 1987–1992 drought connected the two larger islets to the mainland, permitting intrusion by coyotes and once more forcing departure of the gulls.[58]

An eerie measure of the lake's destruction was the growing band of white salt crust that emerged behind the receding water line and filled the air with choking alkaline dust during windstorms. Punc-

California gulls feeding on brine shrimp near a tufa grove on Mono Lake.
(© Liane Enkelis)

tuating parts of the lake surface and perimeter were stark white monoliths or tufa created by the interaction of alkaline lake water and fresh water from springs. These unique towers were formed under water and exposed by the declining lake level. They were often toppled when undercut by waves striking at their bases, and frequently damaged by vandals when completely exposed.

The deterioration of the lake and the local ecosystem first aroused a group of young biologists and students at several university campuses, including Stanford and the University of California, Davis. They obtained a National Science Foundation grant to study the area, and when their findings confirmed their fears, they created the Mono Lake Committee in 1978 and alerted environmental organizations throughout the state and nation. The state responded by creating a task force "to develop and recommend a plan of action to preserve and protect the natural resources in Mono Basin."[59] The members included federal, state, and county delegates as well as a representative from the Los Angeles Department of Water and Power. All except the Department of Water and Power member recommended in 1979 that the city reduce its water diversions from the Mono Basin by 85 percent so that the lake level would rise. They felt that this goal could be achieved if the city conserved as much water as it had during the drought of 1976–1977, made greater use of wastewater, and obtained any additional supplies that it needed from the Metropolitan Water District. Though having only minority representation on the task force, the city had enough influence in the legislature to quash an attempt to implement the recommendations.

Los Angeles's influence was especially formidable because it rested on a powerful array of interlocking interest groups that went far beyond the city. In resisting the task force, Los Angeles received the strong support of MWD which, already gun-shy because of the *Arizona* v. *California* decision, had no desire to see the city increase its share of the agency's water. Offering even more encouragement to Los Angeles in its diversions from Mono Basin were San Joaquin Valley farmers who knew that any water increases for Los Angeles provided by MWD would come at their expense. The surplus water available to them through the State Water Project would disappear as soon as MWD needed it. Thus, the advocates of Mono Lake had not taken on Los Angeles alone, formidable though the city might be. Indirectly and directly, they had entered into conflict with other powerful water interests. And those interests believed the law was squarely on their side. When the state recognized Los Angeles's rights to Mono Basin water in 1940, it acknowledged that the environment would be harmed but believed it could do nothing about it.

Faced with such formidable economic, political, and legal obstacles, the environmentalists devised a novel counterattack. In 1979 the National Audubon Society, Friends of the Earth, Mono Lake Committee, and other allies filed suit against Los Angeles, claiming that the city's diversions violated the doctrine of "public trust." This was a principle developed decades earlier to protect navigation in streams also subject to water rights. Now for the first time it was invoked to protect an area of ecological and scenic value.[60] Just as the state possesses a responsibility or "public trust" to maintain navigable waterways, argued the environmentalists, so too does it have an obligation to prevent Los Angeles from diminishing the public's use and benefit of Mono Lake. Los Angeles vigorously disagreed, falling back on the legitimacy of its rights under the appropriation doctrine and insisting that the public trust concept made no sense in an arid environment where water diversions were necessary for survival. Note well, the city's attorneys also admonished, that an adverse decision for Los Angeles would also be an adverse decision for San Francisco, San Diego, and other urban areas relying on water imported from elsewhere.

The local superior court agreed with Los Angeles, but the state supreme court rejected that view in 1983 with a decision every bit as ominous as Los Angeles feared. No water, ruled the court in *National Audubon Society* v. *Superior Court of Alpine County,* can be taken from a stream, lake, or other natural source without a careful assessment of the harm that might be done. The state can allow the use of water by cities and others, but in doing so it does not surrender all interest in the water; rather, it retains an interest in trust for the public.[61]

The decision did not come as a complete surprise, for the environmental legislation of the 1960s and 1970s had allowed for government-ordered appraisals of the impact of development on ecosystems. However, as noted legal scholar Harrison C. Dunning observed, "Until now the mandate was not so clearly stated and was therefore easier to evade."[62] Put another way, no longer could a water developer get away with merely arguing that a use was reasonable and beneficial. Now the courts or appropriate state agency had the responsibility of assessing the effect on the environment and could order a decrease in diversions or might allow them to continue if they were found to be a "practical necessity." The question was one of balancing the city's need for water against the public's need for the lake and its ecosystem—in other words, according to Dunning, "the public right to use water in place." In this instance, the court backed away from rendering a final judgment and contented itself with recognizing the applicability of the public trust doctrine, the need for a "reconsideration of the allocation of the waters of the Mono Basin," and the "concurrent jurisdiction" of the courts and state government in determining the "allocation."[63]

Even this was too much for Los Angeles, which denounced the state supreme court's decision as "radical" and appealed to the U.S. Supreme Court, claiming that the ruling violated city property rights protected by the Fourteenth Amendment. Supporting the appeal were MWD and the Association of California Water Agencies as well as the states of Wyoming and Idaho, which feared the decision could affect the entire West. The high court refused to hear the appeal, thus clearing the way for the joint court-state action called for in the decision: the reappraisal and modification of Los Angeles's diversions from Mono Lake.[64]

That action was interminably slow in coming, largely because of unsympathetic state officials—newly elected governor George Deukmejian and his appointee to head the Resources Agency were advocates of Los Angeles—who favored sending the issue back to the superior court that had sided with the city. Despite the delay, a series of wet years softened anxieties by eliminating the land bridges at Mono Lake (thereby allowing the gull population to recover) and by diluting the salt concentration, but all viewed the respite as temporary. This was confirmed in the late 1980s by three disturbing reports, one prepared by the National Research Council, the executive agency within the National Academy of Sciences; another by the Community and Research Institute of the University of California, Santa Barbara; and the third by the U.S. Forest Service. (The Forest Service had been made responsible for managing the Mono region when Congress created the Mono Basin National Forest Scenic Area in 1984.) All three agencies agreed that if Los Angeles continued its current diversions, the lake's ecosystem would soon die.[65]

By 1986 Mono Lake's water level, though slightly higher than a few years earlier, was still dangerously low and declining. It stood at about 6,380 feet above sea level, some thirty-seven feet lower than when diversions began. A more graphic observation was that the lake by then contained approximately half the water it held when Los Angeles arrived. An additional ten-foot drop would lead to reduction of the brine fly population that supported nearly 200,000 phalaropes; another ten-foot drop would reduce the brine shrimp that supported the 50,000 gulls and grebes; with still another ten-foot drop virtually all the islands would be connected to the mainland and gulls would no longer nest at the lake. The National Research Council's report, issued in 1987, predicted that the lake would continue to decline until it stabilized at 6,330 feet as an essentially dead sea. The UC Santa Barbara study, released a year later, was noteworthy because it detailed the year—2012—when the lake's ecosystem was likely to "cease to function" and also the annual volume of water—nearly 38,000 acre-feet—that the city would have to forgo to keep the lake from declining further. This volume represented slightly more than 40 percent of Los Angeles's average historical diversions. Seven months later, the U.S. Forest Service announced that the city would have to reduce its diversions even more, up to 75 percent, in order to protect the lake's ecosystem. Despite its responsibility for managing the area, the Forest Service had no authority to force Los Angeles to cut back its uses since the legislation creating the Mono Lake scenic area specifically safeguarded existing water rights.[66]

City officials did not dispute the reports but instead emphasized the costs to Los Angeles of cutting back on Mono water. Merely to stabilize the lake at its present level, they complained, would require surrendering water equivalent to 10 percent of Los Angeles's total supply. In addition, there would be $10 million in lost revenue from the sale of electricity generated by the water traveling through the aqueduct. Environmentalists responded by asking the courts to intervene and by insisting that considerable water could be saved if Los Angeles became more serious about conservation. Taking the lead were the Audubon Society and California Trout, Inc., the latter a nonprofit organization dedicated to promoting "wild" trout populations. In 1989, in the landmark decision of *California Trout* v. *State Water Resources Control Board,* they persuaded a California appellate court that the city had to reduce its diversions to prevent the destruction of fisheries. Fate played a role in that decision, since the fisheries had developed below city diversion dams following heavier than usual Sierra snowfalls in the mid-1980s. The melt had coursed over spillways and into streams that not only fed Mono Lake but also restored trout habitats destroyed earlier by Los Angeles's diversions. Because state law now forbade destroying a fishery to supply an aqueduct, the court sided with the environmentalists and directed the state Water Resources Control Board to determine the extent of the city's cutback. About the same time, the Audubon Society and Mono Lake Committee obtained a preliminary injunction from an El Dorado County superior court judge halting all diversions until the lake surface increased to 6,337 feet above sea level. That was the height considered by the Mono Lake Committee's experts to be minimally necessary to preserve the ecosystem. The lake's surface was then two feet below that minimum, having fallen five feet in the previous three years. The environmentalists had sought a complete halt until the entire matter could be settled by trial but under the circumstances were pleased to get any respite they could.[67]

These actions brought Los Angeles a great deal of unfavorable publicity, much of it national (in *Harper's, National Geographic, Time, Smithsonian, Audubon, Sports Illustrated*) and some of it local. "Los Angeles should realize by now that it never will win," editorialized the *Los Angeles Times*. Feeling the pressure and upset with its public image as villain, the city in late 1989 agreed to seek a negotiated settlement with its chief nemesis, the Mono Lake Committee. The committee had grown into an enormously powerful lobby, boasting 18,000 members, an annual budget of $700,000, and donated legal services from a large San Francisco firm. Weighing heavily in the thinking of city leaders was action by the state legislature which, at the prodding of both sides, in September 1989 had established a

$65 million Environmental Water Fund to help the city develop alternative water supplies—but with the stipulation that no funds would be made available unless the city and the committee jointly applied for them. The Mono Lake Committee's incentive for supporting the legislation and entering negotiations was fear that time was not on its side. "Litigation is our strongest suit," observed a committee leader, "but although Los Angeles is on the losing side of the lawsuits, Mono Lake is on the losing end in terms of time."[68]

The talks soon soured when Los Angeles, citing drought conditions in the early 1990s, tried to get the El Dorado County superior court to lift its injunction against diversions. In April 1991 the court announced its refusal to budge until the lake had stabilized at the 6,337-foot level. This order was to remain in effect until the state Water Resources Control Board completed its study and issued an order of its own, which the El Dorado court could then accept or reject.[69]

A major breakthrough came in October 1993 when Governor Peter "Pete" Wilson, who had succeeded Deukmejian two years earlier, placed himself squarely alongside the environmentalists. Drawing on recent studies by the state Department of Fish and Game, he demanded that Mono Lake be raised to 6,390 feet. Wilson, like Deukmejian, was a Republican and outspoken opponent of federal acreage-limitation, but, unlike his predecessor, he had long been a champion of Mono Lake, supporting the move to make it a national monument when he was in the U.S. Senate and persuading the reluctant Deukmejian to sign the state law creating the water fund to encourage Los Angeles to develop alternative supplies. Such high-level support for the lake notwithstanding, the Los Angeles Department of Water and Power (DWP), to no one's surprise, balked, a spokesman protesting that "for the next 35 years, Los Angeles would get little or no water from the basin." The resistance soon folded, however, when the city's newly elected Republican mayor, Richard Riordan, an advocate of efficiency and critic of unnecessary conflict, and his fresh appointee as head of DWP called for a settlement.[70]

Within two months, in December 1993, the city and the Mono

Lake Committee had hammered out an agreement that permanently reduced by about a third Los Angeles's diversions from the Mono Basin and called for expenditures from the state water fund to bring in a replacement supply. That supply was to come primarily from wastewater reclamation in the San Fernando Valley. The agreement then went for review (and an environmental impact report) to the state Water Resources Control Board, which approved it, but not before increasing slightly the lake level to 6,392 feet (in order to eliminate the dust problem) and requiring Los Angeles to "expeditiously" develop and execute plans for restoring fish and waterfowl habitats in the streams feeding the lake. Once the city had accomplished those tasks, it could increase its exports from the basin to an annual average of 30,800 acre-feet, a far cry from the 100,000 acre-feet that sparked resistance. DWP attorneys reacted angrily to the new burdens, but with the mayor and other city officials clamoring for a settlement the outburst was short-lived. Helping to quash it was the Mono Lake Committee's tenacious yet savvy executive director, Martha Davis, who offered to assist in the city's search for funds to do the restoration work. By day's end on September 26, 1994, the two sides again had a deal—sixteen *years* after the Mono Lake Committee had initiated the struggle in 1978.[71]

The achievement, as environmental activist and historian John Hart has observed, was monumental: "At Mono Lake in 1994, for the first time ever in California, water was removed from the grasp of an anointed appropriative user and assigned, not to some rival diverter, but to an environmental purpose: the restoration of the lake and its feeder streams." Nonetheless, as David Carle, longtime ranger at the Mono Lake Tufa State Reserve, has cautioned, the courts had not mandated that "Mono Lake must *absolutely* be protected, but rather that *balancing* must occur between 'beneficial domestic uses' of diverted water and the lake's public trust values. Public trust values are, in great part, a subjective product of changeable attitudes and beliefs"—as the long struggle with Los Angeles dramatically demonstrated.[72] Still, the emergence of the public trust doctrine was of towering importance as a means of preserving and restoring the environment. In determined hands, it put Los Angeles on the defensive and eventually, through the decisiveness of a new mayor, allied the city with efforts on behalf of nature. Perhaps it might do the same in restraining other water hustlers throughout the state and nation.

Owens Valley War: Renewed and Cooled But Not Over

IN RECENT years Los Angeles has been as fully engaged in battling the residents of Owens Valley as it has the defenders of Mono Lake. For a while relations between the valley and city noticeably improved. The aqueduct bombings and inflamed tensions of the 1920s gave way to grudging acquiescence as those valley residents who remained in the wake of Los Angeles's land and water-rights buying spree profited from vacationers (most from Los Angeles) pouring in and through the area to ski, backpack, hike, hunt, and fish in the clean mountain air and uncrowded wilderness areas. Some valley dwellers and conservationists were even conceding that the city's rapacious water policy had redounded to the great benefit of the environment and wildlife. The area had been kept in an open, undeveloped condition, rather than being transformed, as was the Imperial Valley, into a region of intense irrigated farming. "We recognize that Los Angeles is probably the savior of the valley," stated a Sierra Club spokesman. "Our goal is to preserve the valley as it is now."[73]

That goal was abruptly challenged in the years after 1970 when Los Angeles completed the second aqueduct to the area, which led not only to the conflict over Mono Lake but also to renewed hostilities with the Owens Valley. In the valley, the aqueduct was followed by the city's initiation of a massive groundwater pumping program that destroyed natural vegetation, dried up springs and artesian wells, accelerated erosion, and transformed much of the valley into a barren desert swept by dust storms.

Valley leaders, working through Inyo County government,

sought vainly to negotiate a compromise. When talks collapsed in 1972, they turned to the courts and filed for an injunction under the state's Environmental Quality Act of 1970 to stop the new pumping program and require the city to prepare an environmental impact report (EIR). The Third District Court of Appeal in Sacramento agreed to the need for the report and for twenty-five years into the future remained the arbiter over what constituted an acceptable EIR. The court's actions, however, reduced rather than stopped the pumping. Los Angeles retaliated by cutting off all water to valley recreational activities as well as to the modest amount of local agriculture and cattle ranching it had permitted. The county superior court then forced the city to restore service in what became a tit-for-tat exchange that lasted for more than a decade as the courts at all levels tried to outdo one another in readjusting the rate of pumping and as Los Angeles called upon its creative writing skills in preparing self-serving environmental impact reports during a period when environmental law itself was rapidly evolving. The comic opera aspect of the struggle had its darker side as old bitterness resurfaced with the blowing up of a section of the aqueduct in 1976, the shooting of an arrow attached to a stick of dynamite into William Mulholland Memorial Fountain in Los Angeles, and destruction of a city-owned gate that prevented water from reaching a popular valley lake.[74]

As the struggle wore on, Los Angeles became increasingly convinced that it should cut its losses and seek a negotiated settlement. Despite its battery of attorneys, engineers, and publicists, the city, as in its Mono Lake battle, found it impossible to counteract adverse publicity that it was once again raping the Owens Valley. A more practical reason for changing strategy was the city's failure in 1977 and 1981 to win court approval of its environmental impact report—a report that the state court of appeal described as "impermissibly truncated" and based on unrealistic "synthetic" data that "makes a sham of the EIR process and invalidates the EIR."[75] With no acceptable report, the city could pump only a portion of the water it sought and even that amount, warned the court, could be further reduced or eliminated altogether.

Owens Valley residents also welcomed negotiations. They never intended to prevent water going to Los Angeles. To them, the diversions were a fait accompli, and common sense indicated that no court would take water from a city of more than 3 million and return it to a county of 18,000. They were adamantly opposed, however, to Los Angeles draining away so much water, especially through pumping, that the valley suffered intolerable environmental damage. They also recognized that the struggle threatened to break them financially. Their small population base could ill afford the astronomical legal fees generated by the prolonged court fights. When they tried to raise additional funds by taxing at a higher rate the valley land owned by the city's Department of Water and Power, the city took them to court, thereby further increasing their legal costs. Added to these burdens was Inyo County's inability to regulate the city's pumping operations on its own. In 1980 county residents passed such an ordinance, but three years later the superior court rejected it on the grounds that only the state could regulate water. "Disappointing but not unexpected" was the comment of Inyo County's attorney, while Los Angeles, though pleased, adopted a conciliatory attitude. "I'm hopeful that we can now make a serious effort at working out a settlement with the county," announced the Department of Water and Power administrator in charge of the aqueduct.[76]

Both sides then entered into talks that began in 1984 with agreement to a "cooling-off" period of as long as five years during which neither party would resort to lawsuits. The first task was to arrive at a mutually acceptable short-term pumping program so that careful studies, conducted by the U.S. Geological Survey, could be completed and form the basis for a permanent agreement. The talks got off to a good start with the creation of an Inyo County–Los Angeles standing committee given responsibility for determining how much water could be pumped each year and what portion of that would be allowed to go to the city. In the eventuality that committee members failed to agree on a specific amount for a given year, they devised a formula establishing a rather wide range of diversions available to Los Angeles—106,000 acre-feet to as much as

210,000 acre-feet—but a range that neither side wanted to live with for more than a short period. The city welcomed the arrangement since the courts had limited it to 108,000 acre-feet, and Inyo County accepted the plan because Los Angeles and the county had to adopt conservation measures whenever the formula was invoked. Los Angeles also agreed to try to reverse environmental damage already done, to cut the rates charged to valley water users, and to reimburse Inyo County for its share of the cost for the geological studies. As a further gesture of goodwill, the city indicated that if it were forced to cut back on diversions from Mono Basin, it would not seek to make up those losses with increased demands on the Owens Valley.[77]

The talks between the city and valley went so well that in 1986 the standing committee agreed to release some water back into the Owens River for the first time since 1913. As a sign of peace, an official from the city and another from the valley planned to turn the valve together, but when it came time to do so, each pulled in the opposite direction. After a brief fluster of embarrassment, they agreed on the correct maneuver, but observers wondered if this were a harbinger of things to come.[78]

Just as the five-year truce period neared its end, the two sides, drawing in part on studies prepared by the U.S. Geological Survey, agreed on a long-term formula for guiding future groundwater pumping. Their first accord, released in March 1989, was hooted down by valley residents as providing inadequate safeguards, just as winds kicked up enormous gray clouds of fine alkaline dust off the exposed bed of dry Owens Lake that impaired visibility and created a health hazard. Five months later a tightened-up version placing regulation of pumping in a technical group appointed by city and Inyo officials received the endorsement of the Inyo County Board of Supervisors and the Los Angeles City Council, but strong resentment among many valley residents continued. Lack of a limit on pumping and distrust of the regulatory mechanism remained sore points as criticism of the Board of Supervisors mounted and plans were made to file new lawsuits. "They haven't seen anything yet," proclaimed an angry Lone Pine attorney. The anger spilled over into the defeat of one county supervisor's bid for reelection, the forcing of another into a runoff election scheduled for November 1990, and an attempt to recall the remaining three supervisors at the same election, the first recall effort in Inyo County history.[79]

Meanwhile, fear of seeing the agreement scuttled and worsening drought conditions that exacerbated the environmental damage caused by Los Angeles's pumping in the valley prompted the city in April 1990 to temporarily suspend taking groundwater from the area. That decision received reenforcement five months later when Los Angeles released its latest environmental impact report (prepared jointly with Inyo County). The report finally acknowledged the serious environmental damage caused by the pumping following completion of the second aqueduct and recommended mitigation measures. The decision to suspend pumping and the more evenhanded environmental impact report lessened tensions in the valley and led to failure of the recall effort. Voters, however, decisively rejected the supervisor forced into the runoff who had angered residents by expressing fewer doubts about the agreement with Los Angeles. (Contributing to his defeat was the belief of many people that he had been in office too long—twenty-five years.)[80]

Both sides acknowledged that the disclosures in the environmental impact report mandated changes in the 1989 agreement if any sort of meaningful accord were to be achieved. Following public hearings and tough negotiations, a settlement was announced in 1991. The agreement, through a closely monitored management program, sought "to avoid . . . significant adverse effects in the Owens Valley" and required Los Angeles to take specific steps to improve the situation: "rewatering" fifty-three miles (later increased to sixty miles) of the "dry channel" of the lower Owens River, establishing "off-stream ponds and wetlands," and undertaking other "environmentally oriented projects." The city obligated itself to pay Inyo County some $2 million annually to enforce the agreement, to "conduct water and environmentally related activities," and "to offset Inyo County's reduced tax base due to the ownership of lands by Los Angeles."[81] The city also had to transfer permanently to Owens Valley towns the water systems (at a price of $1 each) owned by the Department of Water and Power.

Though the agreement could allow Los Angeles to pump more groundwater than it could take under court order, the amount would still be a far cry from what the city had sought with no restrictions on its actions. The obligations and the fact that environmental considerations, not Los Angeles's needs, controlled pumping made city council members less than enthusiastic. Also "not completely satisfied" were Inyo County supervisors and residents, especially those upset by what they considered an overly vague and inadequate EIR on the agreement. Angering them as well was the harm caused by the original aqueduct in drying up the formerly 110-square-mile Owens Lake, thereby creating conditions that produced the lung-choking alkaline dust clouds carried by winds as far as San Bernardino and Bakersfield. Others unhappy were the Paiute who felt they should have been parties to the agreement so that more attention could have been paid to their lands and water rights. Still, the Inyo County Board of Supervisors and the Los Angeles City Council felt satisfied enough in October 1991 to give their unanimous approval to the agreement.[82]

That action only sparked another round of fighting. Los Angeles and Inyo had no sooner submitted their agreement and accompanying environmental impact report to the Third District Court of Appeal for approval and an official end to the conflict than opponents objected to the EIR as flawed. These were no ordinary adversaries, for they included not only valley residents (organized as the Owens Valley Committee) but also, among others, the Sierra Club, the California Department of Fish and Game, the state Lands Commission, and the Indian Water Commission, the last representing the Paiute. Eventually all but the Indians—who reported reaching "a settlement" with Los Angeles and dropped out of the case only later to dispute that settlement—filed briefs as *amici curiae* (friends of the court). These amici had no quarrel with the goals of the Los Angeles–Inyo agreement—we "applaud these efforts to solve this historic battle cooperatively"—but they sharply criticized the means. In particular, they charged that the EIR failed to describe accurately the impact of Los Angeles's "water management practices" on the valley's environment *prior* to completion of the second aqueduct in 1970. "Instead of analyzing the cumulative impacts of eighty years of water exports, the City chooses to discuss mitigation of only a small portion of these impacts by limiting its analysis . . . to those that occurred between 1970 and 1990." That omission, declared the state Lands Commission and Department of Fish and Game echoing the other amici, had been compounded by another failure: "Details of the mitigation of [even] these identified impacts is incomplete, vague, and misleading."[83]

Now began years of additional study and negotiation over Los Angeles's groundwater pumping, which eventually ended happily in March 1997 with an agreement that essentially gave the critics what they had demanded: restoration of the pumping-decimated lower Owens River to what it had been before Los Angeles began diverting water in 1913. The goal now was the creation of "a healthy, functioning . . . riverine-riparian ecosystem" incorporating "multiple resource values" and "based upon holistic management principles . . . of promoting biodiversity and sustainable uses." The terms required numerous studies and specific enhancement plans for fish, wildlife, and plants, including threatened and endangered species, with the cost of these activities and their implementation to be met by Los Angeles. The amount of water that the city would have to surrender would not be known until later, but some estimates placed it at more than 10 percent of Los Angeles's eastern Sierra supply. The winners in this long struggle were the Owens Valley ecosystem, wildlife, fish, and the well-paid attorneys for both sides. In May 1997, the Third District Court of Appeal formally declared this particular fight at an end.[84]

But this victory did not mean the war was over. The latest agreement, while promising ecosystem restoration and a "continuous flow . . . in the river" dealt only with the lower river and not with its delta or another issue of increasing bitterness: the Owens Lake

Owens Lake dust storm descending on the community of Inyokern, 1979. (Courtesy of Great Basin Unified Air Pollution Control District)

dust clouds. Winds blowing sometimes in excess of forty miles per hour across the exposed bed polluted the air annually with 4 million tons of salt crystals laced with arsenic and toxic metals that clogged lungs, aggravated heart conditions, triggered asthma attacks, and brought on coughing and infections. "When we see the white cloud . . . ," declared a local physician, "the E[mergency] R[oom] and doctors' offices fill up with people." The particulate count was the highest in the nation, sometimes reaching a density twenty-five times greater than allowed by federal health standards. "It gets so bad you can barely see the house across the street," complained a resident. "It's not that you can't breathe, it's more like you don't want to breathe."[85]

Taking the lead in seeking to end the hazard was the Great Basin Unified Air Pollution Control District, the air agency for the Owens Valley. In late 1996, following thirteen years of study, the district invoked the federal Clean Air Act of 1990 and released a plan requiring Los Angeles to remedy the intolerable situation. The plan, offered as a preliminary proposal for public comment while the mandated environmental impact report was being prepared, called for Los Angeles to surrender 51,000 acre-feet (13 percent) of its Owens Valley supply for a combined water, vegetation, and gravel mitigation project covering selected portions of the lake bed totaling thirty-five square miles. Estimated to cost $70 million up front and then $25 million annually thereafter for maintenance, the plan would require a 9 percent ($1.78 a month) average rate hike for city water customers.[86]

True to form, the Los Angeles Department of Water and Power resisted the valley's proposal, denouncing it as ill-conceived, unworkable, and exorbitant. In a traditional scare appeal for allies elsewhere, DWP officials claimed that any cut in the city's Owens Valley supply would mean taking more water from the north (and, hence, the already threatened delta) and from the Colorado River, thereby decreasing the supply available to other communities, especially those belonging to the Metropolitan Water District of Southern California (MWD), which was already skittish because of cutbacks during the drought year of 1991. The tactic had the desired result. "You cannot add 50,000 acre-feet to the demand without having an impact somewhere," stated an alarmed MWD official. "You trade one environmental issue for another."[87]

Owens Valley residents held their ground. Buoying their hopes was the federal Clean Air Act's requirement that states had to produce plans for cleaning up foul air by 1997 and implement them by 2001. Failure to do so would result in the U.S. Environmental Protection Agency imposing a solution and possibly economic sanctions as well. While optimistic, residents were all too familiar with Los Angeles's dogged ability to delay and obfuscate issues to believe that a resolution would come easily. That became abundantly clear after May 1997 when the valley's air-pollution district released its final plan (and accompanying environmental impact report) for restoring the region's air quality. The water requirement and restoration strategy remained essentially as in the preliminary plan, but the cost estimate had increased by $21 million to $91 million (the estimate for annual maintenance remained the same). Los

Angeles roared its displeasure, repeating earlier objections but now adding new ones: the cost would actually be three times greater than the valley's already increased estimate and monthly rates for city water customers would likely be more than double ($4) the earlier calculation. DWP officials vowed to bring legal action.[88]

The threat of a lawsuit was not unexpected, but for valley residents it raised the specter of again falling victim to protracted and financially draining battles with the city. Nonetheless, the air-pollution board refused to change course. On July 5, 1997, in a six-to-one vote, it formally adopted the mitigation plan and ordered Los Angeles to implement it. "We have to do it," insisted a board member. "If we have to have a lawsuit, I'd rather have one for doing the right thing." Under prodding from Los Angeles mayor Richard Riordan, DWP backed off from court action and offered to negotiate, but during the months that followed nothing changed. The city produced an unacceptably stripped-down proposal to control the dust and then appealed to the California Air Resources Board (which possessed veto power over local air-pollution efforts) to reject the valley's plan.[89]

By mid-1998, as the state Air Resources Board wrestled over what action to take, pressure mounted for DWP to cease its delaying tactics and eliminate the pollution in the Owens Valley. Looming in the immediate future was the federal government's deadline for a mitigation plan (extended to August 1999 in order to accommodate the latest talks). So far as valley air-pollution officials were concerned, the deadline could not come too soon, for they were convinced that the EPA would find persuasive their own thorough analysis and carefully crafted plan. "We would be just as happy to have the feds come in," announced Theodore Schade, head of the air district's Owens Lake effort.[90]

Also outspokenly fed up with the city was the *Los Angeles Times,* which from the outset had lambasted DWP officials for having "dug in their heels . . . to fight to the last drop of water" and for their "blustery defiance and threats of rate increases and legal challenges." Such "sorry behavior does not distinguish the DWP," protested the

Times. The agency has to accept "responsibility for the mess it created" and "get back to work on the . . . problem." "It's time to settle this case, time to stop the torrent of legal words and documents, time to let the water flow."[91]

Though DWP seldom revealed cracks in its ranks, a profound change was taking place in its uppermost leadership, making it more receptive to complaints like those voiced by the *Times.* Most striking was the appointment of S. David Freeman to the top post of general manager in September 1997. Admired for his achievements in the public power industry, most notably for helping to turn around the beleaguered Tennessee Valley Authority, he had been tapped by Mayor Riordan to guide DWP through a monumental challenge laid down a year earlier by the state legislature: the deregulation of electricity producers and the highly competitive period expected to follow. Ever since 1939, when Los Angeles purchased the last private utilities serving the city, DWP had led a protected existence as monopoly provider of electricity to an extraordinarily large group of captive customers—the city's residents, businesses, and government agencies.[92] This market security had encouraged bureaucratic overgrowth, inefficiency, and inattention to cash flow that had led to an enormous debt burden. Riordan wanted his new appointee to overhaul DWP and make it competitive in the approaching open market.

No sooner had Freeman accepted his post than he faced an unexpected crisis of enormous proportions. Investigative reporters for the *Times* revealed that DWP was $7.5 billion in debt, with close to $5 billion of that not on the agency's balance sheet and hidden from the public. DWP officials had tried to conceal startlingly shortsighted overinvestments in inefficient, especially coal-fired, generating plants. These blunders, concluded Freeman and his advisors, meant that deregulation posed not a challenge but a life-or-death struggle for the agency. Freeman embarked on a massive cost-cutting program calling for immediate reduction of the workforce by 2,000 employees (the largest in city history), early retirements, a wide range of other budgetary slashes, and the elimination of layers of bureaucracy—all calculated, as he put it, to "transform [DWP] from a monopoly into a highly effective competitor . . . provid[ing] low rates . . . as well as protecting the environment and encouraging economic development in the city."[93]

When Freeman found time to focus on such other serious issues as the Owens Valley imbroglio, he moved with equal decisiveness. He reviewed the relevant documents and announced that what he found in them "made me cringe": DWP officials emphasizing costs rather than the health of valley residents. He personally took command of the city's negotiations, announcing that "everybody in this country is entitled to healthful air quality." That said, he was still constrained by the agency's financial crisis and asked Owens Valley leaders for a more flexible timetable that would allow for the possibility of achieving the desired air quality by treating a smaller portion of the lake bed—22.5 square miles rather than 35 square miles. Valley air-pollution officials readily agreed, in part because Freeman's request came with a willingness to be open-ended with the city's mitigation efforts: work would continue until the air in all the communities around the lake met federal standards no matter how many square miles had to be treated. The schedule, as approved on July 15, 1998, called for the treatment of 10 square miles of the lake bed by the end of 2001, another 3.5 square miles in the following year, and an additional 3 square miles in 2003. Thereafter, 2 square miles a year would be added until federal air requirements were satisfied. The expectation was that success could be achieved by 2006 at a cost of $120 million and use of 40,000 acre-feet of the city's Owens Valley supply. A review would be conducted in 2003 to determine if the pace had to be increased to meet the 2006 deadline.[94]

Leaders on both sides were elated. "It's a victory," proclaimed the air-pollution district's Theodore Schade. In hearty agreement was Ruth Galanter, Los Angeles city council member and chair of the council's DWP oversight committee. "We represent people who have long-standing resentment toward [one another]," noted Galanter, "and both sides said to hell with that and decided to work together to solve a legitimate problem." No one, however, was more pleased than DWP's S. David Freeman, whom all credited with the breakthrough. "We are now pledged, if the [Los Angeles] City Council approves this, to stay with the job until the job gets done," he promised. Unanimous approval for the agreement came within two weeks from both the city and valley air authority. All that remained was fulfillment of Freeman's promise.[95]

But nothing is simple when it comes to Owens Valley matters. Two years later, while Freeman's commitment to eliminate the dust storms and DWP's earlier promise to restore the lower Owens River seemed to be on track, the city sent a shock wave through the valley by reopening the groundwater pumping issue supposedly resolved years earlier. In late July 2000 a DWP spokesman announced the agency's intention of increasing its pumping of fresh groundwater from 63,000 acre-feet annually to some 93,000 acre-feet. "Our people believe we can increase pumping without causing damage to the environment," declared the spokesman. He then followed that with a statement suggesting that Los Angeles had learned nothing over the last century, much less the last decade: "We have a mission, and that's to provide reliable low-cost water to L.A. and do it responsibly." In response, the U.S. Geological Survey held that groundwater pumping should not exceed 75,000 acre-feet a year from *all* sources in the valley. An increase, warned a USGS hydrologist who had carefully studied the valley, would devastate native plants. "There's no free lunch," he observed. "The whole valley is interconnected." Residents throughout the area feared not only the loss of remaining plants and trees but also, for those who had them, their life-sustaining wells. "If our wells go, we go" was the common refrain of alarm. Freeman's attempt to calm rising tensions—"We continue to work with Inyo County to develop a mutually acceptable pumping proposal"—held the promise, but not necessarily the reality, of peace.[96]

If this latest contretemps can be resolved and newer ones not emerge—no small assumption in light of the preceding ninety-five years of on-again, off-again fighting—the two sides will have achieved a series of settlements as monumental as the peace agreement over Mono Lake. For decades, the plight of the Owens Valley had illustrated more graphically than any similar issue in the nation that environmental legislation did not assure environmental protection. *Perhaps* still another agreement between the valley and Los Angeles will demonstrate that protection can be achieved when there is a combination of dogged determination, imaginative use of the law, and enlightened leadership.

The Fight for the Right to Instream Use

P ARALLELING THE Mono and Owens Valley battles was another closely related environmental struggle over the legality of invoking an appropriative or riparian right on behalf of so-called *instream uses*—water for native plants, wetlands, animals, and fish as well as for aesthetic and recreational purposes. Preservationists—especially at first those concerned with sustaining or restoring fish populations—sought to exercise such rights through state agencies that had a mandate to protect wildlife and the environment, or directly by purchasing the rights of others for instream purposes (necessary since virtually no unappropriated supplies remained). They believed funding for such purchases (and the costs were apt to be heavy) could be raised from the thousands of people flocking into the Sierra Club, Wilderness Society, and similar organizations as well as from those demanding more and better outdoor recreational opportunities.

These expectations hit a formidable roadblock in 1979 when a state court of appeal ruled in two separate cases (one brought by the Department of Fish and Game and the other by California Trout) that water could not be appropriated for instream flows. The decision, which sustained the state Water Resources Control Board's earlier refusal to acknowledge such a right, held that an instream appropriation did not constitute "use" as defined by law: exercising physical control over water.[97] The ruling reenforced the exploitative tradition of *using* water, but it also prompted environmentalists to redouble their efforts, most importantly by successfully invoking, as noted earlier, the public trust doctrine on behalf of Mono Lake in the 1983 *National Audubon Society* v. *Superior Court of Alpine County.* That decision upheld the public's right to use water in place but, emphasized the court, such a right could not be exercised willy-nilly; it had to be balanced against the rights and needs of conventional water users. This caveat mandated careful studies and appreciably slowed by years getting sufficient water to save Mono Lake. In the interim, some water, but nowhere near the amount needed for the lake, resulted from California Trout's subsequent imaginative discovery of a new way to keep water in a stream. Citing a state Fish and Game requirement that dam owners had to release enough water to maintain downstream fisheries, California Trout, as explained earlier, convinced the California court of appeal in 1989 to reduce Los Angeles's diversions from Mono Basin.[98]

Then, two years later, came a major and clear-cut victory for the right of instream use. In 1991, at the urging of a now more environmentally sensitive state Water Resources Control Board, the legislature effectively quashed the 1979 court rulings against appropriations for instream uses. "Any person entitled to the use of water," stated the new statute, "whether based upon an appropriative, riparian, or other right" could, with the approval of the state Water Resources Control Board, use the water for "preserving or enhancing wetlands habitat, fish and wildlife resources, or recreation." A major breakthrough had been achieved, though by this time those battling on behalf of Mono Lake and Owens Valley were sufficiently locked into other legal strategies that they chose not to exercise the new option. Had it been available earlier, their struggle for victory might have ended much sooner. By early 1999, the Water Resources Control Board had approved only two requests for instream uses, and they were for fairly small purposes on Butte Creek, a tributary of the Sacramento River, and at Petaluma, but they set a precedent for much larger proposals then pending and still larger ones anticipated. "The instream right has tremendous potential," stated a Water Resources Control Board attorney in 1999, "primarily because there is lots of money for such uses in recent state and federal legislation."[99]

An Increasingly Vulnerable Southland

THE RIGHT of instream use and Los Angeles's surrender of water for Mono Basin and the Owens Valley reflected a powerful sea change already well under way and having profound implications for Los Angeles and for southern California in general. The court-ordered decreases in the city's Owens Valley pumping operations beginning in the 1970s and in its supply from the Mono Basin dating from the late 1980s had resulted in Los Angeles increasing its dependence on the Metropolitan Water District (and thus on water from northern California and the Colorado River). City-mandated conservation measures to make up for the water no longer arriving were, as usual, not yet the option selected. Instead, Los Angeles, relying on MWD for less than 10 percent of its water until the mid-1980s, looked to the agency for 65 percent in drought years like that of 1991 and 34 percent in years of average precipitation. That situation, in turn, put an additional burden on MWD, already overstretched because of ballooning population growth in its service area (up more than 4 million since 1980 to 16 million by the late 1990s).[100] Ringing mightily hollow because of all this was MWD's 1952 promise in its Laguna Declaration to supply all the water needed by its member agencies.

MWD now had the awesome responsibility of serving more than three hundred cities and unincorporated areas at a time when Los Angeles's influence over the agency was much less than in earlier years. The city had more votes on the MWD board than any other agency, but the number of member agencies had grown from the original thirteen to twenty-seven, whose total assessed valua-

tion (and, hence, voting power) far exceeded that of Los Angeles. The block of votes controlled by Los Angeles had fallen dramatically (from 50 percent in 1928 to about 21 percent by the late 1990s), while some fast-growing agencies were rapidly approaching par with the city (the San Diego County Water Authority and the Municipal Water District of Orange County possessed 16 percent and 13 percent of the board's votes, respectively). Despite Los Angeles's fewer ballots, the city and other board members recognized the need to cooperate in adopting conservation measures, especially in periods of drought. During the 1987–1992 drought, with MWD expecting to fall short of its customers' demands, the board joined with city officials throughout southern California in calling for residents to cut back voluntarily on water use. When volunteer efforts proved inadequate, the board in April 1991 cut its water deliveries by 31 percent overall (to be achieved by reductions that ranged from 20 percent for residential and industrial customers to 50 percent for agriculture) and ordered rate increases to make up for the anticipated lost revenue in water sales. These actions, in turn, forced nearly all member agencies to adopt a host of mandatory rationing measures.[101]

Public criticism, the courts, legislation, and drought radically altered Los Angeles's relationship with the Owens Valley and Mono Basin. The city learned that *rights* to water did not automatically guarantee water. Agribusiness, MWD, the state government, and Californians generally—all inevitable participants in these struggles—learned (or were constantly being reminded by the courts of) the same lesson. Traditional claims to supplies for agriculture, industry, and "progress" now had to be balanced against competing needs of birds, fish, animals, land, and the water source itself. Humankind did not live for exploitation alone. Thus, the capturing of great volumes of water to meet the needs anticipated by one generation could fail dramatically to meet the needs considered crucial by a future generation. The challenges to Los Angeles, the setback to the state in *Arizona* v. *California,* and the defeat of the Peripheral Canal were reminders that in an arid land not even the most successful water seekers are invulnerable. Nor was the environment, as the continuing and worsening despoliation of San Francisco Bay, the delta, and much more was making (and would continue to make) abundantly clear.

7 Water Policy at a Crossroads

The setbacks to California's water seekers during the last three decades did not break their spirit or prevent some telling victories in behalf of the old cause. Similarly, the resistance of state as well as national voters to massive new projects because of soaring costs and intense opposition by environmentalists has not ushered in an era of reform as many hoped and some even predicted. There has been reform, but it has been piecemeal, pale in comparison to continued abuse of the waterscape, frequently occurring only after a serious environmental loss, and lacking in leadership at the highest levels. Though Democrats have remained more willing than Republicans to champion reform, their commitment has frequently dissolved under multiple pressures: the persistence of powerful regional forces, the factionalism among the state's myriad water interests that has intensified as environmentalists have become an increasingly major player in water policy decisions, the emergence of a promising (though in need of appropriate constraints) market in water, the durability of the traditional notion that water exists to be *used,* and the enormous complexity of the state water system.

Tradition versus Reform: The Fate of the Stanislaus River

NOTHING BETTER illustrates the relationship between dramatic alteration of the waterscape and piecemeal reform than the struggle to preserve an awesomely beautiful and rugged stretch of the Stanislaus River, a stream that rises high in the Sierra Nevada north of Yosemite before eventually joining the San Joaquin River west of Modesto. Small dams built on upper branches in the early twentieth century gained little attention even though they flooded scenic areas. The inundated locales were neither comparable to Hetch Hetchy nor had a John Muir to champion them. Nor did the public exhibit concern when New Melones Dam was approved in 1944 as part of the Central Valley Project and reauthorized as a larger undertaking eighteen years later—to be built by the Army Corps of Engineers and managed by the Bureau of Reclamation. This was still an era when dam building was equated with the creation of jobs and conservation. The little opposition that existed was local and directed not against damming the river or its tributaries but at the acreage-limitation provision and especially at plans to export the water rather than to use it in the immediate vicinity of the watershed.[1]

By the 1970s when construction finally got under way at New Melones, the plans for the dam called for the nation's fourth highest structure that would flood twenty-six miles of the Stanislaus, an amazingly beautiful stretch that included one of the country's most boated (some ranked it second in that use) white-water rapids. The area also boasted a wide-ranging difficulty factor that, depending on the time of year, could challenge the most experienced river runner and also accommodate the greenest novice. The dam would not only destroy the rapids but also flood archaeological and historical sites, Indian petroglyphs, wilderness areas, and the West Coast's deepest limestone canyon. This was more than enough to arouse canoeists, scientists, preservationists, and a host of kindred environmentalists. State and federal agencies had taken steps to mitigate the project's effect on wildlife, fisheries, and water quality, but those now alarmed were not interested in mitigation but in preserving a unique natural area.[2]

Even before water could back up behind New Melones, opponents had transformed the struggle into a national fight. In 1972 they held up construction for a year and bought valuable time to organize their efforts by claiming in federal court that the environmental impact statement for the dam was inadequate. The court disagreed, but in the meantime, they gathered a hundred thousand signatures on a petition asking Republican President Richard Nixon to halt construction and consider alternatives. When he remained unmoved and Republican Governor Ronald Reagan's Director of Water Resources challenged the whole notion of river preservation ("Wild rivers—who needs 'em?"), the opponents created Friends of the River and, aided by the Sierra Club, the Environmental Defense Fund, Friends of the Earth, and countless volunteers, campaigned

New Melones Dam and Reservoir. (Courtesy of California Department of Water Resources)

for an initiative on the 1974 state ballot—Proposition 17—to quash the proposed dam.[3]

The initiative proponents ran head-on into formidable resistance from water leaders at all levels of government as well as agribusiness, Pacific Gas and Electric, the California Chamber of Commerce, and the contractors working on New Melones, all of whom insisted that they were the Stanislaus's true friends and that only a no vote on the initiative, in the words of the campaign to stop the dam, would "Save the River." The Stanislaus, they protested, was not really a wild river because of the small dams built upstream decades earlier. "Stop the 'Wild River' Hoax!" became a major theme in their attack.

Spearheading the opposition and serving as its most effective voice was Californians Against Proposition 17, an organization masterminded by a veteran public relations firm that outspent Friends of the River nearly two to one ($419,000 to $238,000), pouring the money into newspaper and especially television ads. The single biggest contribution ($175,000) came from the contractors building the dam, but donations of $5,000 or more also came from manufacturers of heavy farming equipment, Goodyear Tire and Rubber, Texaco, and PG&E, among others. Friends of the River received no single contribution over $5,000, avoided costly television and newspaper ads entirely, and relied on brochures, mailings, and door-to-door canvassing by an army of unpaid volunteers. They also won the endorsement of Democrat Jerry Brown who, making his initial bid for the governor's office on the same ballot, visited the dam site not long before the election, took a paddleboat trip on which he nearly got tossed overboard, and announced not long after: "I support Proposition 17. The $270 million allocated for building the dam could be used to fight pollution and to create more jobs . . . than would be created due to construction of the dam."[4]

Brown squeaked to victory but the initiative, at least in part reflecting the power of money and television, lost, though only barely so (53 percent to 47 percent). A subsequent poll revealed that most voters had become confused by the conflicting campaign ads—especially the extent to which the Stanislaus was really a "wild river." Focus on that point overlooked the fact that hardly a river remained anywhere without some development along its course and that at issue in the election was whether Stanislaus Canyon would remain undeveloped. Not surprisingly, strongest opposition came from the San Joaquin Valley, with southern California and the Central Valley (except for Shasta and Yolo counties) also casting negative votes but generally by narrow margins. Major support was restricted to the Bay Area.[5]

Defeated at the polls, the opponents now pinned their hopes on the courts. A year earlier the California Water Resources Control Board, at the urging of environmentalists, had refused the Reclamation Bureau's application for a permit to fill the reservoir because the Bureau had not documented the need for additional irrigation water. Without that evidence, explained the Water Resources Control Board, it could not determine whether the irrigation need "will outweigh any damage that will result to fish, wildlife and recreation in the watershed above New Melones Dam."[6] The board's action— which also pointedly acknowledged Stanislaus Canyon as a "unique asset to state and nation"—outraged Bureau officials. They had never before been required to produce such documentation. Now a dam was being built that they might not be able to fill.

The Reclamation Bureau immediately appealed to the federal district court and then the court of appeal, which found against the Water Resources Control Board; but the board promptly countered with an appeal of its own to the U.S. Supreme Court, where in 1978, in *California* v. *U.S.*, it won—at least theoretically. In a decision, as noted earlier, with implications for state attempts to set water quality standards for the delta, the court concluded that the Reclamation Bureau had to "follow state law in all respects not directly inconsistent with" congressional intent. When the Supreme Court remanded to the district court the question of whether the state's action met the legal test, it set the stage for years of additional decisions and appeals.[7] In the meantime, construction on the dam continued, and with it, the threat that a sudden rush of floodwaters could be captured at New Melones and backed into Stanislaus Canyon, inundating the area.

The opponents now shifted their attention to Congress, which had the authority to halt construction or reduce the dam to a size that did not endanger the canyon. Lobbying proved as time consuming as court battles, allowing completion of the dam and giving advocates a new argument: it would be economically wasteful not to fill the finished structure to capacity. Old arguments also received new emphasis, especially the advocates' claim that the struggle was essentially one of "recreation versus food," a reference to the fact that so many leading opponents were white-water canoeists and rafters. In the meantime, the dam's builder, the Army Corps of

Engineers, not embroiled in the lawsuits hampering the Reclamation Bureau, allowed water to begin backing up behind the dam.

In a dramatic gesture, one of the river rafters, Mark Dubois, in May 1979 chained himself to bedrock near the rising water level, announcing: "The life of the 9-million-year-old Stanislaus Canyon is far more significant than my short tenure on this planet." Governor Brown, who had avoided the issue since the defeat of Proposition 17 and his narrow election, sensed a political opportunity too good to pass up. "I urge you to instruct the U.S. Army Corps of Engineers," he wired Democratic President Jimmy Carter, "to halt the filling of the New Melones Dam. . . . The beauty of the Stanislaus Canyon and the life of Mark Dubois deserve your personal intervention."[8]

The Corps recognized it was in a no-win situation and spilled water from the dam, but not before television, newspapers, and magazines again brought the struggle to a nationwide audience. Opponents then persuaded Congress to consider legislation adding the Stanislaus to the federal wild and scenic river system. They also tried to stall the complete filling of the reservoir by arguing that, if only partially full, it could still provide most of the anticipated benefits while sparing upper Stanislaus Canyon. President Carter, who strongly sympathized with the proenvironmentalist members of his party in Congress, was no friend of western dam-building projects, especially those promising heavy subsidies to a small number of beneficiaries. He promised to sign any bill preserving the river. Following that announcement, the *Los Angeles Times* reversed its earlier support of New Melones and called for congressional intervention. "We think a case can be made that the rapids of the Stanislaus belong under the protection of the Wild and Scenic Rivers Act, and we hope Congress will agree."[9]

In September 1980 the bill's opponents, emphasizing the earlier defeat of Proposition 17 and economic benefits in the form of irrigation water and hydroelectricity, prevented the bill from clearing the crucial House Interior Committee—but only by two votes. The Republicans lined up solidly against the Stanislaus, while the Dem-

Stanislaus River rapids below Grapevine Gulch, now flooded by New Melones Dam. (Courtesy of Tim Palmer)

ocrats split. The election of Republican Ronald Reagan as president two months later, together with the indifferent support of Governor Jerry Brown and the lack of an open commitment on the part of California's Democratic Senator Alan Cranston, undermined the efforts of environmentalists to regroup. When the wet years of 1982 and 1983 sent more water than usual down the river, Stanislaus Canyon was lost. Seeing now no practical reason to withhold the permits sought by the Reclamation Bureau, the Water Resources Control Board issued them in March 1983.[10]

New and Old Challenges to Dams and Levees

THOUGH THE environmentalists failed to defeat New Melones Dam, the long struggle encouraged their efforts in the contemporaneous fight against the Peripheral Canal and steeled them in their determination to prevent similar losses elsewhere. Since preservationists nationally had joined in the campaign, the Stanislaus emerged as a new rallying cry and source of inspiration across the United States. "People began to talk more about the joy, the wonder, and the spirituality brought by rivers," noted Tim Palmer, a member and chronicler of movements to save the Stanislaus and other endangered rivers. "The Stanislaus brought out feelings of reverence for the natural world, where rivers are a source of life and a center for attention. The river was a sacred and holy place."[11] Such sentiments reflected a newer emphasis among preservationists. Before the 1970s, the stress had been on preserving land and biotic communities, but now rivers had clearly joined that group of wonders deserving protection. The earlier battles over Hetch Hetchy, Echo Park, and Grand Canyon had been less over the rivers than over the canyons that would be flooded. Now the public had been dramatically told—and many had come to fervently believe—that rivers could be as sacred as the wilderness areas through which they flowed.

"Why save a river?" asked Palmer. "Because it is the unspoiled Eden, right here, available to all. Why save a river? Because it is a river."[12]

The struggle over the Stanislaus did not create this attitude, for it had surfaced years before, most vividly in the passage of the federal Wild and Scenic Rivers Act of 1968, prohibiting dams and other projects adversely affecting the designated rivers, and in a similar state law four years later.[13] Nevertheless, selection of rivers for both systems languished until the loss of the Stanislaus aroused the public as nothing before had done. That lesson fueled resistance to development of California's north-coast rivers and streams elsewhere in the nation. Looked at this way, the Stanislaus fight was not so much about the loss of a river as an early chapter in a story about preserving the few partially wild rivers left and demolishing dams on other streams to restore their freedom.

By the end of the 1990s California had named eleven rivers to its wild and scenic system (Klamath, Scott, Salmon, Trinity, Smith, Eel, Van Duzen, American, West Walker, East Fork Carson, South Fork Yuba) and prohibited dam construction on a twelfth (the McCloud). The McCloud, while protected from dams, was kept out of the system for fear that a tougher federal wild river designation might follow, thus restricting logging in the area—an acknowledgment of that industry's influence. Equally telling about the nature of the protection afforded to all these streams was that the legislation applied only piecemeal—for example, to ten miles of the East Fork Carson, thirty-eight miles of the West Walker, and fifty-three miles of the McCloud and its tributaries. Following a similar pattern was the federal wild and scenic rivers program, which by the mid-1990s included portions of most rivers in the state system plus sections of the Middle Fork Feather, Tuolumne, Merced, Kings, North Fork Kern, South Fork Kern, Sisquoc, Big Sur, and Sespe Creek. A significant difference between the federal and state legislation is that the Federal Energy Regulatory Commission can override the state system and issue a license to construct a dam. This loophole and the protection of rivers in snatches testify to the past, and continuing, power of the development ethic within the United States.[14]

The recent construction of the Metropolitan Water District of Southern California's massive Diamond Valley Lake (boasting a capacity of 800,000 acre-feet) demonstrates that dam building is still alive—but with a difference. Diamond and Domenigoni valleys were dammed to create the enormous reservoir, yet no river was sacrificed in the process. Moreover, this offstream facility is encircled by 9,000 acres set aside by MWD as a wildlife preserve. When it comes to dam building today, the focus is primarily on studies to raise the height and increase the capacity of dams at multiple sites: San Vicente Reservoir in San Diego County; Kaweah and Success lakes in the southern Sierra; Millerton Lake behind Friant Dam, northeast of Fresno; Los Vaqueros Reservoir in Contra Costa County; Lake Shasta, California's largest artificial body of water, near Redding; and elsewhere. Raising Shasta Dam, which is two-thirds of a mile long, another 6 feet to a height of nearly 1,100 feet would cost $122 million and produce an additional 300,000 acre-feet. A Reclamation Bureau study has also considered raising the dam 100 feet and the maximum possible of 200 feet, with the former move nearly doubling Lake Shasta's volume from 4.5 million acre-feet to 8.5 million acre-feet at a cost of nearly $4 billion, about 30 percent of it going to relocate railroad tracks, an interstate highway, and resort facilities and to construct new bridges and tunnels. At 200 feet, Shasta's crest would lengthen to nearly a mile, reservoir capacity more than triple to 14 million acre-feet, and the cost increase to $5.8 billion, with 31 percent of that going for relocation and reconstruction. Prompting these studies have been estimates of future population growth, recent droughts, heavy flooding like that in January 1997, and the lack of remaining dam sites.[15]

Such testimony to an ongoing faith in dams and reservoirs has been accompanied by an increasing willingness to acknowledge that these structures can become obsolete and should give way to a higher purpose. An important recent example is Chatsworth Reservoir, located just north of downtown Los Angeles in the western San Fernando Valley. Created in 1919 with the construction of two earth-filled dams, the reservoir supplied irrigation water for agriculture and then, as the area urbanized, served the domestic needs of the new residents. Not long after the transition, it became apparent that water good enough for agriculture did not always satisfy the quality standards required for people. In 1969, the Los Angeles Department of Water and Power (DWP) drained the reservoir and began a massive effort to enlarge and upgrade it. That overhaul came to an abrupt halt three years later when the powerful 6.6 Sylmar earthquake rattled the area, destroying freeway bridges, a large hospital only a month old, and taking sixty-four lives. Subsequent studies revealed the Chatsworth Dams to be seismically unsafe and financially impractical to replace.[16]

Abandoned as a reservoir, the 1,300-acre site became a drain on city resources, requiring $250,000 a year to maintain, principally against trespassers and illegal dumping. When an appraisal placed a value of $50 million on the property, DWP jumped at the opportunity to cut its losses and make money by announcing that the land would be sold at public auction. The news provoked a roar of protest from citizens angry at the prospect of losing precious open space in a city with too little of it, and from environmentalists who wanted the area set aside as a nature and historic preserve. The latter possibility gained momentum as word spread that the reservoir had become a major stopover point on the Pacific Flyway for osprey, prairie falcons, red-winged blackbirds, Canada geese, red-tailed hawks, kingfishers, and a host of other species; home to a rich assortment of animal wildlife, including foxes, deer, and coyotes; studded with a six-acre lagoon, a valley oak savanna, and indigenous grasses and shrubs; a locale of historic Native American sites; and a popular field-trip destination (with DWP approval) for schoolchildren. In 1999 protesters persuaded DWP to set aside 1,300 acres as a preserve. Such a natural refuge would have been impossible if dams and reservoirs had not kept at bay for nearly a century the shopping malls, gasoline stations, car washes, housing tracts, and asphalt that now surround this sanctuary.[17]

The destruction of dams is not a recent phenomenon. In 1970 Sweesey Dam on the Mad River in northwestern California was knocked down so that Chinook salmon could once more spawn upstream. Across the country hundreds of dams were and continue to be destroyed, but most are small and no longer serving the purpose for which they were built. Even those still useful can come down if alternative means are available, as is increasingly possible. A case in point were four small irrigation dams on Butte Creek in northern California that were demolished in 1998 in favor of other technologies for regulating and moving water to farmland. Their elimination brought new life to Butte Creek, which, even with dams, had boasted the state's largest run of spring salmon. That run, however, had been infinitesimal compared to the hundreds of thousands of migrating fish in the pre-dam era that may now return to the creek. Encouraged by this action, Friends of the River stepped up efforts to revive salmon and steelhead stocks and to restore rivers by targeting more than two dozen dams scattered throughout the state for demolition. Most were small, but they also included the 280-foot-high Englebright Dam on the Yuba River, 198-foot Matilija Dam on a tributary of the Ventura River, 173-foot-high Iron Gate Dam on the Klamath, and "the mother of all dam removal proposals in California," O'Shaughnessy Dam blocking Hetch Hetchy Valley.[18]

Opening greater possibilities to dam removal is the policy currently being followed by federal energy regulators. There are 146 hydroelectric dams in California (250 nationwide) whose licenses are due to expire in the first decade of the twenty-first century. Where renewals were once routine, regulators now hold public hearings on whether the adverse environmental impact of these dams outweighs their usefulness. A negative decision for the 162-year-old, 917-foot-long Edwards Dam on the Kennebec River in Maine led to its demolition in 1999, the first dam ordered destroyed by the U.S. government on behalf of conservation. What the future holds for California is not altogether clear, but the dam busters elsewhere are ambitious. In the Northwest they are inquiring into the feasibility of demolishing four dams—at a cost of $500 million to $800 million—on the Snake River, the chief tributary of the mighty Columbia River. Built primarily for the generation of hydroelectricity, the dams provide only 4 to 7 percent of the region's power needs while driving toward extinction once-renowned salmon runs despite the expenditure of $3 billion to bring them back. Removal of the structures would dwarf all other dam-removal projects in the nation and has generated surprise and opposition. "It's amazing. It's like the pope talking about [allowing] abortion," declared an official with the National Marine Fisheries Service. Nonetheless, it is the U.S. Army Corps of Engineers, the agency that built the dams, that in a turnaround initiated the study that could lead to demolition of the structures.[19]

Regardless of the outcome on the Snake River, the irony is irresistible: in an age when a dam-building agency can no longer find funds to put up dams, it can now seek survival in accepting available resources to pull them down. The about-face has been accompanied by changes in philosophy as reflected in Interior Secretary Bruce Babbitt's remarks at the ceremony celebrating destruction of the dams on Butte Creek. "Dams are not like the pyramids of Egypt that stand for eternity. They are instruments that should be judged by the health of the rivers to which they belong." Such words were in sharp contrast to those of one of Babbitt's predecessors, Secretary of the Interior Harold Ickes, at the dedication of Hoover Dam in 1935. "Pridefully, man acclaims his conquest of nature."[20]

Dams at Risk

The certainty is that even the largest, most massive dams are as doomed as the small ones currently being knocked down. Many were flawed from the outset and led to premature collapse and tragic loss of life, as occurred in 1928 with William Mulholland's St. Francis Dam, in 1963 with the Baldwin Hills Dam near Culver City, in 1976 with Idaho's Teton, and others. But no dam can guarantee absolute safety. Minimum standards require protection from a hundred-year flood for metropolitan areas and a ten-year flood for farming regions. These expressions refer to past flood frequencies, meaning that a hundred-year flood is estimated to occur once a hundred years (or has a 1 percent chance of occurring in any year) and a ten-year flood is estimated to occur once in ten years (or has a 10 percent chance of occurring in any year).[21]

The reality is that planners have only a vague idea about the frequency and intensity of floods. What was considered a hundred-year flood on the American River near Sacramento in 1940 ranks today as only a twenty-year flood. Folsom Dam, completed on the American River in 1955 to withstand a 250-year storm, was reassessed following the floods of 1986 and 1997 and declared good enough for just a sixty-year event. The purchase of additional space for flood runoff in Lake Folsom then led the U.S. Army Corps of Engineers to conclude that Folsom Dam and the levees along the American River were capable of handling a seventy-seven-year storm. A year later in 1999, however, the National Research Council announced that existing facilities could contain a hundred-year flood. Such examples underscore the inescapably deceptive quality to all flood forecasts and appraisals, the more so since those making them have based their computations on data reaching back in time only a relatively short period. Figures on stream flow have been gathered on just a few rivers in the West for more than fifty years, and on none for more than a century and a half, beginning approximately with the American conquest of northern Mexico in 1846. Since western rivers have been flowing for an immense period of time, this offers a pathetically inadequate statistical base for projections—especially in a region in which wild fluctuations in rainfall are the norm.[22]

Thus, even the great Central Valley, with dams on the headwaters of virtually all major streams that enter it, is not absolutely secure. Flood protection for the more heavily watered Sacramento Valley was planned around the flood of 1907, until recent years the largest on record with runoff of 600,000 second-feet (a discharge of one second-foot produces nearly two acre-feet a day). Then, in February 1986, a massive storm produced nearly *double* that volume. The dams held but there was still property damage in excess of $150 million; 50,000 people were driven from their homes, and

Sacramento Valley flooding, February 1986. (Courtesy of California Department of Water Resources)

twelve people died. Eleven years later, in January 1997, an even more powerful storm again wreaked havoc on the Sacramento Valley and this time on the San Joaquin Valley as well, resulting in the state's largest flood disaster on record with at least nine deaths, more than 120,000 people forced to flee their homes, nearly 300 square miles under water, and $2 billion in property damage. The devastation prompted state planners to reexamine earlier hydrology studies and to conclude with as much mumbo jumbo as science that the 1986 and 1997 floods were "about sixty-year events." That conclusion was an admission that the future could produce even

Feather River in flood at Marysville, January 3, 1997. (Courtesy of California Department of Water Resources)

more massive inundations, a point already tellingly made by Robert Kelley, distinguished historian of flood-control efforts in central California: "The Sacramento Valley, after all, is millions of years old, storms have been coming up from far out in the Pacific for many millennia, and Americans are only into their second century—but a tiny slice of time—of observing floods in that venue."[23]

Scientists are currently investigating the history of floods in ancient layers of rock. Among the findings of a study of a 5,000-year record of big floods in the American Southwest is that such events do not occur in hundred- or ten-year or in any other such cycle but instead in clusters that coincide with wet, cool, El Niño–like events. This research is only in its infancy and the lack of adequate data recently caused a Fresno flood official to throw up his hands and announce: "We don't know if we're in a wet cycle or a dry cycle." Europeans with their longer history have learned what Americans are only beginning to realize. The Netherlands, for example, has

Flooding in the San Joaquin Valley, January 1997. (Courtesy of California Department of Water Resources)

planned for a 1,250-year flood along the Rhine River, while nations bordering the North Sea coast have prepared for a 10,000-year event.[24]

Complicating any planning is the fact that most dams in California and throughout the West are not always built only—or even primarily—for flood control but for other reasons: irrigation, the generation of electricity, water storage for cities. Sometimes these other purposes are given priority, as in 1997 when a dam near Modesto was nearly full of water destined for summer agricultural use. The operators misjudged the intensity of an incoming storm and only at the eleventh hour made large emergency releases that inundated property and homes downstream.[25]

Other major problems are the aging of dams and the failure to maintain them properly. In January 1997 torrential rainfall along the San Joaquin River nearly turned Friant Dam into Friant Falls when water came within four inches of going over the top and

Friant Dam on the San Joaquin River on January 4, 1997, when flooding upriver nearly turned the dam into Friant Falls. (Photo by Mark Volkoff. Courtesy of U.S. Bureau of Reclamation)

flooding the outskirts of Fresno, the nation's sixth-fastest-growing city. Contributing to the near disaster was the failure of the emergency spillway gates to open. Only heroic, last-minute adjustments opened the gates enough to prevent calamity. Two years earlier, a spillway gate at Folsom Dam that had not been properly maintained for fifteen years broke and released nearly half of Folsom Lake, a loss calculated at $2.4 million for the water alone.[26]

Such incidents have not been unique to California but are symptomatic of a national problem. "Our system of reservoirs in the United States can be compared to a person in their middle ages," recently stated an expert on dams at the University of Nebraska. "As we age, we face more problems." This became patently clear (though the public was kept largely in the dark) at Glen Canyon Dam in 1983 when Colorado River floodwaters gouged enormous holes in the concrete, nearly undermining the structure and releasing Lake Powell, the second largest reservoir in the nation. If the dam had collapsed, the raging torrent might have toppled Hoover Dam downstream, creating a flood, according to a University of Arizona hydrologist, unlike any other on the Colorado "since the Ice Age. . . . It would be a disaster beyond what nature is capable of."[27]

The Impermanence of Dams: Earthquakes, Silt, Neglect, and Flawed Planning

Another ever-present threat to flood-control works and dams in California comes from earthquakes. A moderate temblor in 1971 nearly caused the collapse of the Lower San Fernando Valley Dam and damaged the Upper San Fernando Valley Dam, placing in jeopardy 80,000 people below those structures. Four years later an earthquake near Oroville Dam seemed to have been triggered by the weight of the water in the reservoir and seepage into the underlying strata. Some experts subsequently concluded that later seismic activity at Oroville, and even the earlier earthquake, actually resulted from the sudden drawdown on the reservoir in summer and fall rather than the winter and spring filling. According to this theory, the rapid emptying of dams can increase fault instability.[28]

Concern about a potential disaster at the proposed $2.5 billion, 700-foot-high dam at Auburn on the North Fork of the American River above Sacramento and adjacent to the city of Auburn led to interruption of construction following a 5.7 magnitude quake in 1975 that rattled the area. A major reason for a dam at Auburn is to eliminate flood threats that downstream Folsom Dam, according to studies conducted after its construction, could not contain. Following the quake, the Reclamation Bureau reported that failure of a dam at the Auburn site, which lies above a seismic fault (though not the one that ruptured in 1975), would send a 100-foot-high wall of water downstream, washing out Folsom Dam, destroying Sacramento and three military air bases, flooding hundreds of thousands of acres of farmland, and imperiling the lives of 750,000 people. Despite the fears of many, Auburn still has its advocates who, in 1992 and again in 1996, sought to win congressional approval for a somewhat downsized (508-foot, $1 billion) and renamed structure (Detention Dam). They failed both times, and by the late 1990s the struggle had shifted to finding ways to reconfigure and otherwise strengthen Folsom Dam in order to counter the flood danger on the American River. In the meantime, the flood threat there remains, just as it does in the Bay Area where water from Hetch Hetchy aqueduct continues to pour into Crystal Springs Lakes located on the San Andreas fault above San Francisco.[29]

Earthquakes aside, virtually all the dams in California (there are some 1,400 of them[30]) will eventually silt up and cease to function. The state's (and the West's) watersheds do not consist of solid rock but of crumbling sandstone and quartz, as well as loose soil, and the mountains are steep, often covered with only sparse growth, and actively eroding. Speeding up the process is human activity—recreational vehicles, road building, cross-country bicycles, motorcycles, and even hiking. Exacerbating the problem yet further are fire-suppression policies (now being questioned and sometimes modified) that allow forests and brush areas to grow unnaturally dense. When lightning or arsonists ignite such places, massive firestorms devour all vegetation in their path, setting the stage for the next thunderstorm to send enormous "debris flows" of mud and boulders into creeks, rivers, farmland, homes, and reservoirs.

No one is seriously studying the approaching crisis of debris-filled reservoirs. "When I was commissioner . . . and raised the issue," stated Daniel Beard, Reclamation Bureau head from 1993 to 1995, "the answers I got back were nonanswers. There wasn't anybody in the organization I felt was on top of the issue." At present, the life of old dams cannot be appreciably prolonged and the promise of new ones is not encouraging in today's climate of resistance; moreover, nearly all the best sites have been taken. Inevitably, the reservoirs, including those at Lake Mead, Hetch Hetchy, and on the Stanislaus, will become vast bodies of mud crossed by rivers tumbling over dams transformed into waterfalls. This future is not thousands of years away but only a few hundred and much less for smaller dams. Illustrative is the principal mountain reservoir for the city of Santa Barbara. Completed in 1920, it is already half filled with silt, as is the reservoir at Cresta Dam on the Feather River, completed three decades later in 1950.[31]

No single agency has appraised the integrity of the nation's network of dams, and Stanford University's National Performance of Dams Program (created in 1994) has produced little of value because of underfunding and lack of cooperation from the Reclamation Bureau, Army Corps of Engineers, and state dam-safety officials. In 1997 the *Sacramento Bee* launched an investigative team (Tom Knudson and Nancy Vogel) whose careful reports reaffirmed the worst fears of many. Among the findings: maintenance needs have escalated as dams have aged while funding for repairs has remained constant or declined; only 10 percent of downstream populations at risk have warning or evacuation plans; dam safety (as earlier at Friant and Folsom) is sometimes given a lower priority than delivery of electricity and water. "The dangers are growing— and the need for change has never been more urgent," warned the investigators.[32]

The *Sacramento Bee*'s revelations also disclosed the reality of chaotic flood management in which the responsible local, state, and federal agencies follow different guidelines. Development-driven local authorities frequently support building on floodplains, assuming that such requirements as elevated foundations will keep homes and businesses dry and revenue from permits and taxes rolling in. Federal agencies tend to look with horror at such construction but then turn around and offer national insurance that encourages building—and rebuilding—in flood-prone areas. The National Flood Insurance Program was created in 1966 on the recommendations of two federal task forces whose rationale was straightforward: flood-control expenditures had been unable to prevent losses ($7 billion spent between 1936 and 1966 had not averted annual increases in losses) and some settlement on floodplains was inevitable, making it preferable for those residents to have flood insurance rather than to expect the federal government to indemnify them for losses. The legislation provided for the purchase of repeatedly damaged property but the initiative had to come from owners, thus doing little to prevent repetitive losses. California is the pacesetter in build-and-rebuild behavior with $3.4 billion in flood damage between 1990 and 1997 (almost 10 percent of the nation's total). At the same time, 6,000 people a month are moving into the Central Valley, the state's largest floodplain and among the biggest in the nation.[33]

That kind of population pressure, together with developers' dreams of windfall profits, led to a bewildering proposal in January 1997. As San Joaquin River floodwaters were receding, Fresno developers filed plans to build several hundred condominiums and houses and two golf courses in the river's bottomlands. When questioned about the wisdom of the project, one of the investors, while standing at the proposed site where only days earlier he had rescued ten horses trapped in four feet of surging river water, replied: "I don't need anyone's protection."[34]

There is no groundswell for reforming the nation's dam and flood policies, but scattered calls for change have emerged, especially in selected attempts to accept rivers for what they are and to work with them. These efforts take the form of allowing floods to move out onto portions of a floodplain and fallow farmland, spreading sediment over a larger area, a practice widely adopted in Europe and beginning to emerge in California and elsewhere in the United States. Others have focused on the dangers posed by the aging flood-control infrastructure and are demanding more funding for maintenance, while some local governments are resisting attempts to push development onto floodplains. Still others in many parts of the nation are urging abandonment of the hundred-year flood standard in favor of a more realistic measure reflecting historical flood patterns found in ancient geological strata, tree rings, and elsewhere.[35]

Scattered voices are also calling for reform of the National Flood

Insurance Program. In the meantime, the Federal Emergency Management Agency (FEMA) requires communities to prohibit new development on hundred-year floodplains and demands those already there to purchase federally subsidized flood insurance. The insurance is also available to anyone else who feels the need for it. Many critics are calling for decreasing coverage for recurring losses, since 30 percent of flood insurance claimants have filed more than once. Other reformers, however, want the insurance made mandatory for residents of any flood-prone area, regardless of the projected frequency of the threat, on the theory that they will think twice about settling there, and if they do, they will, as noted earlier, be covered for losses and not ask for handouts from FEMA. Many want the government out of the disaster insurance business altogether.[36]

Such disparate and sometimes conflicting voices weaken the efforts at change. Nonetheless, there is an emerging belief that the most effective way to control floods is to prevent unreasonable and abusive use of the land in the first place. According to environmentalist Luna Leopold of the University of California, Berkeley: "When you rely on structural works . . . rather than saying, 'We will control land use,' then you are bound to fail. We're attacking the problem of floods when we should be attacking the problem of land use."[37] As a goal for future planning, this admonition seems to make much good sense. As a principle for undoing or mitigating all past questionable decisions that have permitted millions of people to live, work, and farm in areas that today's planners might proscribe, it suggests a complex course of action demanding commitment, technical and scientific knowledge, and common sense. Public agencies are not noted for possessing such characteristics.

Los Angeles: A Vexing Lesson
in Dams, Levees, Floods, and Public Policy

A case in point has been the handling of Los Angeles's namesake river. Many more entities than the city have been involved, for the river's reach and capacity to flood hundreds of square miles have also brought into play Los Angeles County, the U.S. Army Corps of Engineers, the Federal Emergency Management Agency, and scores of local communities, among many other interested parties. Despite the river's natural tendency to occasionally leap its banks and wreak great havoc, most notably for the twentieth century in 1914 and 1938, people settled in large numbers on its floodplain, in part induced by the false sense of security created by the water-control projects constructed following the major disasters. The 1914 devastation resulted in formation of the Los Angeles County Flood Control District a year later and a rash of projects in the 1920s, including, in 1929, Pacoima Dam, which at 372 feet in height was then the tallest concrete-arch dam in the United States. The flood of 1938, the most destructive on record in Los Angeles County with 81 deaths and property damage of $47.3 million (throughout all of southern California there were 87 deaths and $78.6 million in damage) brought in the U.S. Army Corps of Engineers, which unleashed a torrent of concrete encasing the river. Except for a few tiny portions that somehow survived as reminders of what Gaspar de Portolá witnessed in 1769, the Los Angeles River became fifty-one miles of storm drains, dams, and reservoirs stretching from north of the San Fernando Valley to the ocean at Long Beach. Thereafter, settlement accelerated along the supposedly harnessed river's eighty-two-square-mile lower floodplain until, by the 1990s, some 500,000 people and 123,000 homes and businesses valued at more than $17 billion were scattered among fourteen cities and communities located there.[38]

By then as well, alarmed water leaders were predicting disaster unless massive new flood-control measures were taken. As early as 1980, local public works engineers and the Army Corps of Engineers found evidence that the system was failing: sticks, twigs, and other debris left atop the concrete channels and levees by receding water following heavy rains. The Corps confirmed that the concrete and steel enveloping the lower river and its tributaries no longer met minimum standards and would be breached in the event of a hundred-year flood with $2.3 billion in damage. The reasons:

The destruction of the Southern Pacific Railroad bridge over the Los Angeles River during the flood of 1938. (Courtesy of Los Angeles County Flood Control District)

earlier designs were based on too short a storm record and planners following the 1938 flood had misjudged the rate of future urbanization on the river's headwaters in the San Fernando Valley. They had counted on the valley's farmlands and citrus groves to absorb torrential rains and runoff from the Santa Monica Mountains, but as the citrus groves and agriculture gave way to subdivisions, businesses, asphalt, and concrete, the runoff had no place to go except to increasingly overburdened creeks and storm drains feeding the river.[39]

Moving deliberately—and slowly in view of the threat—the Corps and Los Angeles County finally released in 1992 a $364 million plan to elevate channel walls four to eight feet along twenty-one miles of the river's lower reaches, modify twenty-seven bridges to accommodate the higher walls, and reenforce the land side of vulnerable embankments. That proposal aroused environmentalists who rallied behind the Friends of the Los Angeles River and urged a design providing not only for storm protection but also for a more natural river consisting of wildlife habitats and portions of reclaimed floodplain transformed into riverside parkland where people could stroll, sit, jog, or bike. Though a novel idea for Los Angeles, other cities, including Chicago, San Antonio, Cleveland, and Memphis, had shown that rivers could be reborn and incorporated into the life of a city.[40]

Such a river was not then meant for Los Angeles. The Army Corps of Engineers, after taking more than a decade to produce its plan, now strenuously objected that restoration would entail delays, increase exposure of residents to flood danger, and prolong the period during which residents with federally insured mortgages would have to purchase costly flood insurance (a requirement at first postponed, then enforced, and, finally, gradually eliminated altogether as revetment-building went forward with a complete phase-out targeted for spring 2001, if not earlier). When city leaders in the affected area sided with the Corps, so, too, did the Los Angeles County Board of Supervisors. Concrete, thus, begat more concrete. Though protests from environmentalists continued, construction began in 1995 with the federal government eventually being responsible for 75 percent of the cost.[41]

A modest environmental advance came in 1999 when the California legislature created the San Gabriel and Lower Los Angeles Rivers and Mountains Conservancy. Given a grand charge—"to provide open-space, low-impact recreational and educational uses, water conservation, watershed improvement, [and] wildlife and habitat restoration and protection"—the agency had to operate under severe restraints: an inadequate budget of $700,000; denial of authority to exercise the power of eminent domain in acquiring property; and a prohibition against doing anything that could be construed as "infringing" on flood-control operations.[42]

Far more impressive advances came in 2000, first in March when voters overwhelmingly approved Propositions 12 and 13 earmark-

The Los Angeles River, prior to channelization, just above Los Feliz Boulevard in 1936. (Courtesy of Los Angeles County Flood Control District)

ing $4 billion for environmental enhancements and then in June when Governor Gray Davis approved legislation setting aside a portion of that money plus state funds for a total of $88 million to "green" the Los Angeles River under the leadership of the California Department of Parks and Recreation with the cooperation of the state Resources Agency and the Santa Monica Mountains Conservancy, among other participants. Plans called for a "Los Angeles River Parkway" consisting of five staggered parks (Compton-Slauson, Arroyo Seco, Elysian Valley, Taylor Yards, and Tujunga) connected by walking and biking paths along the upper rivershed as well as by naturally vegetated flood-control basins and spreading grounds. The Friends of the Los Angeles River were jubilant. "It's such a blessing, and it's incredibly exciting," declared the executive

The same location after riprap paving had begun. (Courtesy of Los Angeles County Flood Control District)

director. "The things we've been talking about for years are finally reaching a level of acceptance." Well, almost acceptance, for the concrete walls lining the river will remain—at least for the time being. "The changes . . . will lead to the next step," observed an optimistic local leader, "when people will ask, 'Why do we have all that ugly cement in there, and isn't there something that can be done to beautify that?'"[43]

Vulnerable Levees and the Delta

While levees are critical to thousands of floodplain residents in Los Angeles, they are also crucial to Californians elsewhere, nowhere more so than in the Sacramento–San Joaquin Delta through which passes the drinking water for two-thirds of the state's population and the irrigation water for over 7 million acres. The delta consists of approximately a thousand square miles of floodplain

Rubio Wash, which enters the Los Angeles River by way of the Rio Hondo, in its natural condition. (Courtesy of Los Angeles County Flood Control District)

crisscrossed by two rivers and scores of meandering sloughs. The rich soil of the fifty-two islands and immediately adjacent mainland supports highly productive farms. The area also boasts major transportation networks, towns, and the homes and businesses of 300,000 people, most of whom live along the perimeter. Yet because this region's peaty soil, now bared to the sun and wind by farming (the delta was formerly a vast region of swampy islands), is drying out, the area is sinking at an annual rate of two to five inches, faster than any other place on earth. Islands that were at sea level a century ago are now as much as twenty to thirty feet below sea level and protected by old and increasingly precarious levees.[44]

The only barrier between disaster and delta communities and farms is the 1,100 miles of dirt-and-aggregate levees, usually built of local fill dredged from nearby waterways, that have been frequently breached during past floods on the San Joaquin and especially the Sacramento rivers. Levees, like dams, are vulnerable to

Rubio Wash as channelized and transformed into a storm drain, the fate of most urban washes, creeks, and streams. (Courtesy of Los Angeles County Flood Control District)

earthquakes in which the shaking introduces water into the structure, resulting in liquefaction, abrupt loss of sheer strength, and collapse. Breaks in the protective system have also resulted from a combination of high tides and wind coming from the west. Before 1950 most failures were caused by waters overtopping the levees; since 1950, two-thirds of the failures have resulted from structural erosion when water, usually moving at high velocity, saturates and erodes the levee's interior (in a process called *piping*), then exits at the base on the land side, causing the levee to collapse. As the levees have aged, the breaks have understandably come more often and resulted in greater damage, with more than 150 occurring in the twentieth century, most of them in the northern delta. This pattern does not take into account the effect of possible global warming, the so-called greenhouse effect that predicts an accelerated sea-level rise as a result of greater concentrations of carbon dioxide and

The channelized Los Angeles River after a storm, 1965. (Courtesy of California Department of Water Resources)

trace gases in the troposphere because of human actions. The experts disagree about the probability of such a phenomenon, although the Environmental Protection Agency believes the threat is real and has recommended planning for a four-foot sea rise in the next fifty years and an eight-foot increase in the next century. Most vulnerable are those levees built and maintained by landowners and reclamation districts. While all the levees constructed by the Corps of Engineers meet federal standards (35 percent of the total), half of the other levees do not (about 33 percent of the total). Estimates to overhaul the entire system run into the billions of dollars.[45]

The threat is not just to delta farms and communities but also to the agriculture and cities of the San Joaquin Valley and southern California. The delta is at the heart of the state's water transport sys-

An aerial view of the delta near Antioch, California, showing some of the many islands created by the crisscrossed waterways at the confluence of the Sacramento and San Joaquin rivers. (Courtesy of U.S. Bureau of Reclamation)

tem, for an average 60 percent of the water passing through the area is diverted elsewhere (less in drought years and more in times of heavy precipitation), mostly southward into the aqueducts of the Central Valley and State Water projects. The area also plays a major role in commerce, serving the Sacramento and Stockton Deep Water channels through which more than 3 million tons of goods are shipped annually.[46]

In 1976 the California legislature placed responsibility for maintaining the delta's levee system on the state Department of Water

Resources and authorized a paltry $2,000 annually to carry out the task. In the 1980s, as the need for a greater effort became apparent, the legislature increased funding to $2 million and then $6 million a year, a sum to which the federal government, in recognition of its responsibility to maintain the navigability of the shipping channels, added $400 million. So long as there is no global warming or, if it does occur (and there is increasing evidence it is under way), it takes place slowly enough so that its effect can be overcome, the Department of Water Resources believes that it has adequate means to maintain the levees. Many others remain unconvinced, especially those not only alarmed about floods, earthquakes, and aging dams but also fearful that global warming is a probability rather than possibility (a National Research Council panel concluded in January 2000 that the Earth's "warming trend . . . is undoubtedly real"), and that planning for it cannot wait for concrete evidence of sea-level rise. "If we wait to see the train coming, it will be too late to get off the tracks," warned Robert Buddemier, associate division leader for environmental projects with the Lawrence Livermore National Laboratory.[47]

Environmental Crisis: Bay, Delta, and CALFED

BY THE mid-1980s, the delta's vulnerability because of the inadequate levee system had combined with multiple other problems to create a monumental hazard and statewide embarrassment. Pollution and a decreasing water supply because of upstream diversions were fouling not only the delta but also San Francisco Bay and the entire estuary. Tests during the '80s and into the '90s revealed high levels of selenium, bromide salts, Diazinon (a popular residential pesticide), and other wastes (especially organic carbon) introduced by local industrial discharge, drainage runoff, and saltwater intrusion from the ocean. On a single day enough mercury for 31,000 thermometers washes down the Sacramento River into the bay and delta. About half the mercury originates in abandoned mines where it was used to extract gold from ore during the nineteenth century, while the other half comes from automobile exhaust and discarded household items. Though scientists disagree about the mercury levels that pose a health risk, few doubt that the toxic soup of chemicals pouring into the bay and delta constitute a threat to public health and the complete ecosystem—wetlands, fisheries, and wildlife, including more than 30 endangered species and 800,000 water birds annually.[48]

Wetlands are at the heart of the survival of much else, for they not only serve as habitat for fish, fowl, and a rich abundance of animal wildlife but also enhance water quality by absorbing and filtering pollutants, reduce the destructiveness of floods by slowing their flow, increase water supply by recharging aquifers, prevent seawater intrusion by acting as a freshwater barrier, and control erosion by preventing soil and silt from moving downstream toward the ocean. The bay and delta, especially Suisun Marsh, contain the state's largest expanse of wetlands and yet they constitute only a fraction of the approximately 5 million acres that originally existed in California. Some 454,000 acres remain in the state, reflecting a loss of more than 90 percent, the greatest decline of wetlands in the nation. Most were lost to agriculture and much of what remained fell to urbanization, both processes encouraged by federal, state, and local policies reaching back into the nineteenth century and extending well into the twentieth century that reflected the popular desire to drain such "useless" areas and make them "productive." The federal Clean Water Act of 1972 (and as reaffirmed by Congress in 1977) theoretically protected wetlands and required mitigation for any loss, but their disappearance continued, primarily because of lax enforcement of the law. (Today, the remaining wetlands are concentrated in five areas: San Francisco Bay, Suisun Marsh, the Central Valley, Humboldt Bay, and Klamath Basin.) Also frustrating attempts to address the myriad other threats to the health of the bay and delta was the confusion created by the

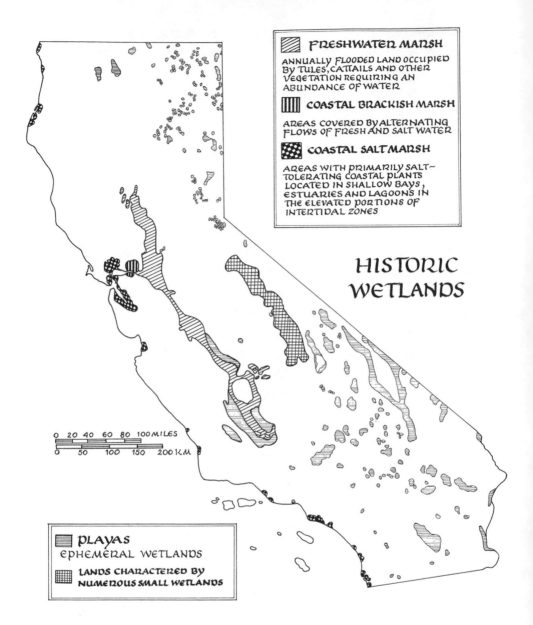

FRESHWATER MARSH

ANNUALLY FLOODED LAND OCCUPIED BY TULES, CATTAILS AND OTHER VEGETATION REQUIRING AN ABUNDANCE OF WATER

COASTAL BRACKISH MARSH

AREAS COVERED BY ALTERNATING FLOWS OF FRESH AND SALT WATER

COASTAL SALT MARSH

AREAS WITH PRIMARILY SALT-TOLERATING COASTAL PLANTS LOCATED IN SHALLOW BAYS, ESTUARIES AND LAGOONS IN THE ELEVATED PORTIONS OF INTERTIDAL ZONES

HISTORIC WETLANDS

0 20 40 60 80 100 MILES
0 50 100 150 200 KM

PLAYAS
EPHEMERAL WETLANDS

LANDS CHARACTERED BY NUMEROUS SMALL WETLANDS

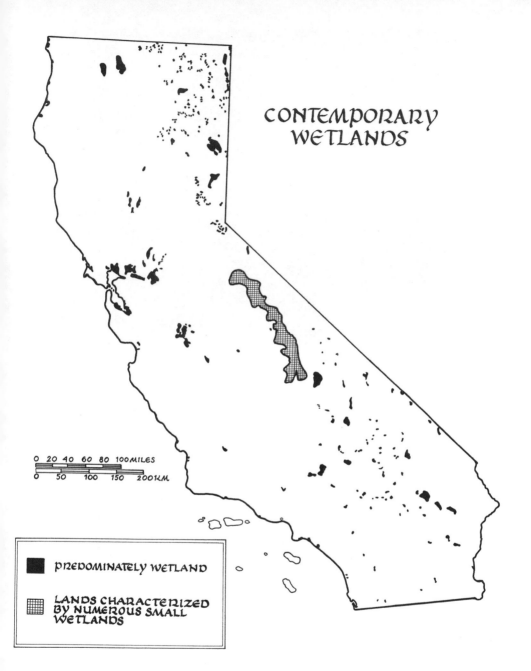

CONTEMPORARY
WETLANDS

0 20 40 60 80 100MILES
0   50   100   150   200KM

PREDOMINATELY WETLAND

LANDS CHARACTERIZED
BY NUMEROUS SMALL
WETLANDS

Suisun Marsh, San Francisco Bay. (Courtesy of California Department of Water Resources)

Interior Department's long-standing refusal to acknowledge that it was legally bound by state water standards and, in particular, the inept performance of a weak and ineffective state Water Resources Control Board.[49]

The Water Resources Control Board had been created in 1967 and given two primary responsibilities: assuring that water diverted from California's rivers and streams was put to beneficial use, and preventing water pollution. As for the latter duty, the panel of five members (appointed to four-year terms by the governor) was charged with guaranteeing "the highest water quality reasonable . . . for use and enjoyment by the people of the state." By the mid-1980s it was clear that the board had failed miserably in this responsibility. The state auditor general complained that the regional boards (nine had been created in the original legislation to assist the main board and handle enforcement) were operating with many out-of-date pollution-measurement standards and ne-

Coastal wetlands, San Mateo County. (Courtesy of California Department of Water Resources)

glecting to effectively curb violators. The legislative analyst added that the legislature was getting little information about pollution-control efforts and that the state board paid little attention to what the regional boards were doing.[50]

The problems were not all of the state board's doing. Governors Jerry Brown and George Deukmejian had cut budgets (with resulting decreases in staff) just when the legislature, responding to public complaints, passed statutes increasing the board's workload. At the same time, the board's authority was diluted as a result of bureaucratic infighting that saw some of its power shifted to other agencies. The Department of Health Services emerged with primary responsibility for controlling toxic discharges (and with many of the board's most experienced personnel), while the Department of Food and Agriculture became the paramount agency controlling pesticide use. The underfunding, staff cuts, and splintering of authority severely undercut enforcement as did strong opposition from agricultural and industrial interests, which managed to prevent the reappointment of at least one board member who was particularly outspoken in defense of the environment. Underscoring the board's impotence was its ineffectual plan (adopted as Decision 1485 in 1978) to protect the fisheries, wildlife, and ecosystem of San Francisco Bay and the delta.[51]

Alarmed by the board's erosion of power and the Interior Department's refusal to acknowledge an obligation to abide by state water standards, a group of environmentalists and northern California officials turned to the courts. In 1986 they persuaded the California Court of Appeal, in *United States* v. *State Water Resources Control Board,* to let stand a four-year-old court ruling giving the state authority to place restrictions on federal and state projects. The court of appeal not only upheld the state's control over federal projects but also, in its so-called Racanelli decision (named for the judge who issued the opinion), emphasized the broad sweep of state authority over water quality and quantity and ordered the board to take more aggressive action by invoking the public trust doctrine. The decision possessed enormous potential for effecting change. The court's insistence that the board play a more active role in protecting the environment had the practical effect of vesting the board with authority to rethink rights to the entire supply sent south through both the State Water Project and the Central Valley Project.[52]

Apparently admonished, the Water Resources Control Board began hearings less than a year later aimed at developing a plan to carry out the court's mandate. When the board released its draft report two years later in November 1988 it aroused criticism from all sides. San Joaquin Valley farmers and southern California water agencies blasted it for calling for reductions in water exports south to their 1985 levels. According to the board's calculations, this would limit exports to 5.5 million acre-feet (considerably less than the 6 to 7 million acre-feet sought by many) and permit an additional 1.5 million acre-feet for protecting the delta. For the Metropolitan Water District of Southern California, it would mean being restricted to 700,000 acre-feet of the 2 million acre-feet of the State Water Project deliveries for which it had contracted. The report concluded that southern California could continue to grow at its current rate— 400,000 new residents annually—by adopting more stringent conservation measures. "Fundamentally flawed," replied farmers about the recommendations, while southern California water managers claimed the plan would "effectively institutionalize drought" and was "a dagger plunged into the heart of the Southland." Both groups complained that the problems involving pollutants in San Francisco Bay were caused by the communities surrounding it rather than by a shortage of fresh water.[53]

Though at first pleasantly surprised at the magnitude of the proposed reductions, northern officials, fishermen's lobbies, and environmentalists were soon denouncing the recommendations as inadequate, especially for their failure to guarantee a specific volume of water for flushing San Francisco Bay of pollutants. The *Los Angeles Times,* trying desperately in the years following the Peripheral Canal defeat to appear less parochial, sympathized with the need to do more for the bay and delta but, under intense pressure from southern California water officials, reverted to form. While at first it editorialized that the board's "goals . . . are sound," that "there is far too much waste," and that "the bay and delta are natural treasures that must be protected," it was soon denouncing the recommendations as "flawed," unpersuasive in their call for an "increase of water for fish life in the . . . Delta," and designed to punish "unfairly" southern Californians, who criticized the plan "with justification."[54]

Not only the *Times* buckled under pressure. Less than three months following the report's release, the chair of the Water Resources Control Board announced that he was dropping from the report any mention of a limit on water exports south. "That thorny question," he offered, would be dealt with "later." Few observers doubted there was a connection between this announcement and the fact that the chair, under heavy fire from agribusiness interests and southern California water leaders, was publicly fishing for a reappointment to the board. He subsequently got his renewal, but when the board announced its final plan in 1991, the U.S. Environmental Protection Agency, responsible for approving it under federal law, promptly rejected it for depriving the bay and delta of too much water. That action and the State Water Resources Control Board's obvious lack of resolve brought an outpouring of federal activity to fill the void and by default propel the U.S. government into spearheading the effort for water quality standards for the bay and delta.[55]

The lead came from Congress with passage in 1992 of the Central Valley Project Improvement Act, not incidently cosponsored by an exasperated Congressman from the Bay Area, George Miller. Though focused primarily on the Central Valley, the legislation had major implications for the Sacramento–San Joaquin estuary by setting aside 800,000 acre-feet of Central Valley Project water for environmental and wildlife purposes, creating a $50 million annual fund to finance fish and wildlife restoration, and prohibiting new water contracts (except for fish and wildlife) until all environmental actions stipulated in the act had been completed. At the same time, under the authority of the Endangered Species Act (1973), federal agencies moved forward with a flurry of activity on several fronts. By invoking a nearly twenty-year-old law to correct a wrong that antedated the legislation, the agencies underscored a perennial and sad political reality: enactment of a law did not automatically produce the desired result; only a willingness to *implement* the law held that *possibility*.[56]

In 1993 alone, the National Marine Fisheries Service announced regulations that were more restrictive than those proposed by the state Water Resources Control Board; the U.S. Fish and Wildlife Service declared the delta smelt a threatened species and called for tighter requirements on the operations of the State Water and Central Valley projects; and the Environmental Protection Agency released proposed standards for the bay and delta to replace those of the Water Resources Control Board that it had earlier rejected.[57] Such energy not only aroused resentment among upstaged state agencies (some of them as disappointed as federal officials with the Water Resources Control Board's ineffectiveness) but also threatened to create regulatory gridlock and stall progress. Wiser heads now called for what often had been missing from the California water experience: state-federal cooperation.

The first significant step toward that collaboration came in June 1994 when state and federal delegations met to bring order to bureaucratic morass and design a meaningful restoration plan. Representing California was the Water Policy Council, created expressly so the state's multiple water agencies could finally speak with something approximating a single voice. A similar body formed to represent a host of U.S. agencies was the Federal Ecosystem Directorate. The two groups, consisting of fifteen agencies, came together in May 1995 as CALFED, aptly described by a California Department of Water Resources official working on behalf of CALFED as a "collection of federal and state agencies with their own responsibilities and authorities trying to work together to improve efficiency." Their first task: to devise a long-term plan for saving and restoring the estuary.[58]

The targeted issues were water quality and supply, fish and wildlife, endangered species, levee protection, and the relevant actions mandated by the Central Valley Project Improvement Act. CALFED placed management responsibilities in an executive director and federal-state team assisted by technical experts from both sides. Public input came from a thirty-one-member Bay-Delta Advisory Committee consisting of representatives of California's urban, agricultural, environmental, business, fishing, and other interests with a stake in the estuary's future. Such careful organizational planning reflected a desire not to repeat the last—and disastrous—attempt to deal with bay-delta problems: the ill-fated and nastily divisive Peripheral Canal proposal of 1982. The dogged attention to planning produced an auspicious beginning. Within six months CALFED cut through the thicket created by years of bureaucratic and interest-group infighting to announce interim water-quality standards (known as the Bay-Delta Accord) that would govern until a long-term solution was in place. The price tag to implement the interim accord—about $400 million—was to be shared by the state and federal governments.[59]

The crucial test began in 1996 when CALFED, after nearly two years of study and analysis, released three restoration plans for public scrutiny, and when voters endorsed a $995 million water bond with two-thirds of the money earmarked as a down payment for rescuing the delta. One of them (called Alternative 3) resembled the earlier Peripheral Canal proposal in a particularly striking way. It called for taking water out of the Sacramento River (but only about half as much as was sought with the Peripheral Canal) and conveying it in a forty-four-mile earthen ditch around the central delta, where fish spawn and salmon migrate, to the pumps sending it south. That proposal emerged simply because CALFED's studies, like those earlier for the Peripheral Canal, indicated that such a conveyance would bring better-quality Sacramento River water directly to the aqueducts going south and hence would mean significantly better drinking water for southern Californians. (The harmful bromide salts alone in drinking water supplies from the delta were in concentrations greater than was found in the drinking supplies of 90 percent of the nation.) Though cleverly disguised as the Open Channel Isolated Facility, the colorless name did nothing to hide from the public its similarity to the 1982 proposal.[60]

Neither of the other two plans proposed to divert water around the central delta. One of them (Alternative 1) called for the status quo, allowing water to reach the pumps through the existing system of channels, while the other (Alternative 2) would substantially increase the flow to the pumps by modifying the current

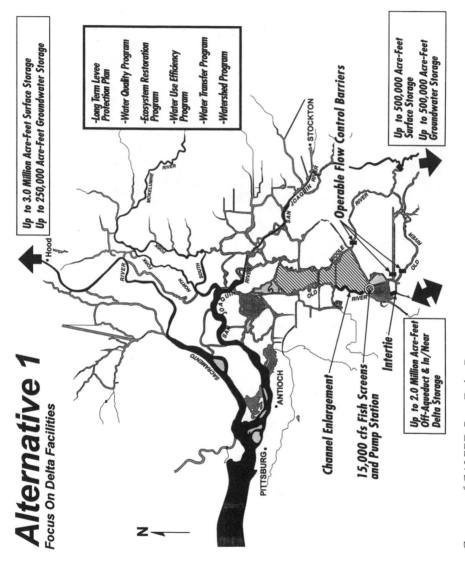

Alternative 1
Focus On Delta Facilities

N

Up to 3.0 Million Acre-Feet Surface Storage
Up to 250,000 Acre-Feet Groundwater Storage

-Long Term Levee
 Protection Plan
-Water Quality Program
-Ecosystem Restoration
 Program
-Water Use Efficiency
 Program
-Water Transfer Program
-Watershed Program

Up to 500,000 Acre-Feet
Surface Storage
Up to 500,000 Acre-Feet
Groundwater Storage

Operable Flow Control Barriers

Channel Enlargement

15,000 cfs Fish Screens
and Pump Station

Intertie

Up to 2.0 Million Acre-Feet
Off-Aqueduct & In/Near
Delta Storage

• Hood

MOKELUMNE RIVER

NORTH FORK
SOUTH FORK
RIVER

SAN JOAQUIN

SACRAMENTO

PITTSBURG •

• ANTIOCH

SAN JOAQUIN RIVER

STOCKTON •

MIDDLE RIVER

OLD

OLD RIVER

Courtesy of CALFED Bay-Delta Program

Alternative 2
Focus On Delta Facilities

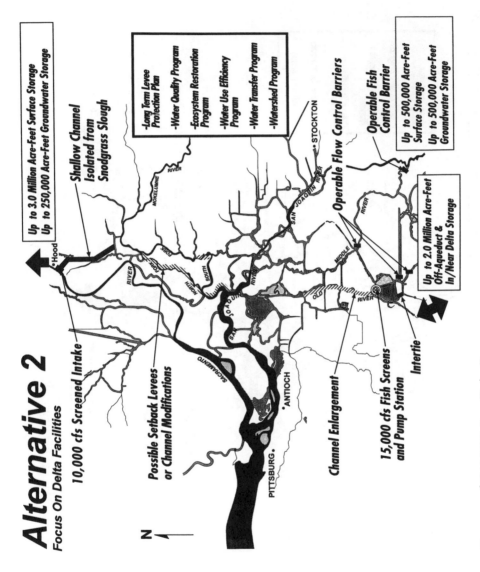

N

Up to 3.0 Million Acre-Feet Surface Storage
Up to 250,000 Acre-Feet Groundwater Storage

10,000 cfs Screened Intake

Shallow Channel
Isolated from
Snodgrass Slough

- Long Term Levee
  Protection Plan
- Water Quality Program
- Ecosystem Restoration
  Program
- Water Use Efficiency
  Program
- Water Transfer Program
- Watershed Program

Operable Flow Control Barriers

Operable Fish
Control Barrier

Up to 500,000 Acre-Feet
Surface Storage
Up to 500,000 Acre-Feet
Groundwater Storage

Up to 2.0 Million Acre-Feet
Off-Aqueduct &
In/Near Delta Storage

Possible Setback Levees
or Channel Modifications

Channel Enlargement

15,000 cfs Fish Screens
and Pump Station

Intertie

• Hood

MOKELUMNE RIVER

NORTH FORK

SOUTH FORK

RIVER

SAN JOAQUIN RIVER

• STOCKTON

MIDDLE RIVER

OLD RIVER

SACRAMENTO

PITTSBURG •

• ANTIOCH

Courtesy of CALFED Bay-Delta Program

Alternative 3
Focus on Delta Facilities

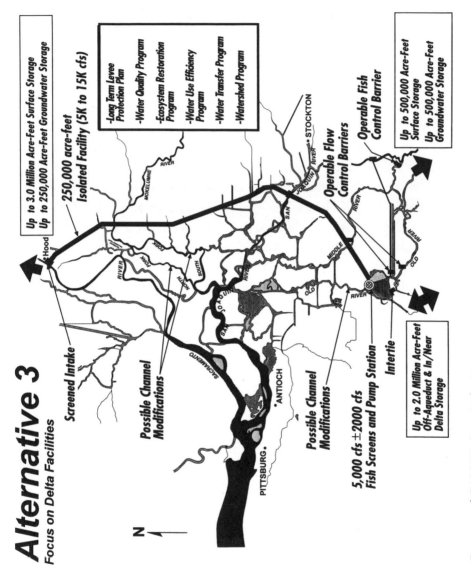

Up to 3.0 Million Acre-Feet Surface Storage
Up to 250,000 Acre-Feet Groundwater Storage

250,000 acre-feet
Isolated Facility (5K to 15K cfs)

- Long Term Levee Protection Plan
- Water Quality Program
- Ecosystem Restoration Program
- Water Use Efficiency Program
- Water Transfer Program
- Watershed Program

Up to 500,000 Acre-Feet Surface Storage
Up to 500,000 Acre-Feet Groundwater Storage

Screened Intake

Possible Channel Modifications

Possible Channel Modifications

5,000 cfs ±2000 cfs
Fish Screens and Pump Station

Intertie

Up to 2.0 Million Acre-Feet Off-Aqueduct & In/Near Delta Storage

Operable Flow Control Barriers

Operable Fish Control Barrier

N

PITTSBURG.

•ANTIOCH

•STOCKTON

MOKELUMNE RIVER

NORTH FORK

SOUTH FORK

SAN JOAQUIN RIVER

SACRAMENTO

OLD RIVER

MIDDLE RIVER

OLD RIVER

•Hood

Courtesy of CALFED Bay-Delta Program

channels. All three plans provided for more ecosystem protection than the 1982 proposal: fish and wildlife enhancement, protection for endangered species, and water quality improvement. The plans also included levee strengthening and increased water reliability through storage facilities (above and below ground) that, in combination, were equivalent to another Shasta Dam.[61]

Almost immediately, southern Californians announced support for the canal plan, while northerners and environmentalists opposed that option as well as the surface storage dams in all three plans. The rivalry intensified after CALFED, in early 1998, formally released its massive 3,500-page environmental impact statement and report (EIS/EIR) covering each plan along with an overview of how each would be implemented. In hearings scattered throughout the state, CALFED invited public comment after which the California governor and the Secretary of the Interior were expected to select one of the plans that would likely, as in 1982, go to the voters who would approve or reject the bonds needed to construct most of it. Additional funding would come from the federal government and user fees. Regardless of the option selected, the cost would be hefty (a capital expenditure of $9 billion to $10.5 billion with annual operational expenses estimated at $500 million to $600 million), though the strong California economy at the time made this less of an issue than in 1982. Implementation of the plan was expected to take thirty years.[62]

"Hide the children and the faint of heart," announced the *Los Angeles Times* in March 1998, "the Peripheral Canal debate has officially begun."[63] Quarreling mirrored the 1982 fight but there were also significant differences. Agribusiness this time supported the canal, dams, and reservoirs because all would either augment or improve the water supply and were not contingent on a hot-button issue like protection of the north-coast rivers. On the other hand, some objected strongly to CALFED's groundwater provisions out of fear that their rights to pump from the aquifers below their land would be jeopardized. Northerners and environmentalists broke ranks, with a minority coming out in favor of the canal. Prominent among them was Sunne McPeak, a former Contra Costa County supervisor and leader in the fight against the Peripheral Canal in 1982 but now cochair of the Bay-Delta Advisory Committee. She was willing to consider the new canal proposal because it would move less water than the earlier one and also included substantial provisions for conservation, environmental protection, and storage. Sharing similar views was environmentalist and northern Californian Marc Reisner, whose powerful *Cadillac Desert* (1986) had roundly indicted the West's water developers. "My idea is to give L.A. the water it needs so those people stay down there," stated Reisner. "It begins to strike you as reckless that so many people and such a humongous economy are so dependent on such a fragile water delivery system."[64]

Despite isolated northern voices of support, most environmentalists faulted all three plans and the proposals for surface dams and the canal in particular. The Natural Resources Defense Council rebuked CALFED for focusing too much on "dams and ditches" and not enough on conservation. The *San Jose Mercury News* agreed: "in our view, it is premature to talk about major new facilities until water conservation and marketing have been vigorously pursued." Emphasizing the same theme were sixteen Bay Area Democrats in Congress who, in a joint letter to the governor and Interior Secretary, "demand[ed] that water users throughout the state squeeze every drop of efficiency out of our supplies before handing taxpayers a multibillion-dollar bill for new projects." For others the problem was the inevitable population growth encouraged by more storage and additional water. "Look," stated one critic, "if you don't water it, it won't grow."[65]

The big issue, as sixteen years earlier, was *trust*. No one denied that the canal option would provide better-quality water for the Central Valley and southern California, but most northerners and environmentalists simply feared that the canal would be used, as one of them put it, "to literally suck the Sacramento River dry." Nor could they shake the fear associated with the earlier Peripheral Canal. "To us," editorialized the *Oakland Tribune*, "it looks like

CALFED indeed tried to copy the old Peripheral Canal plan and [it] . . . smells like a plain old water grab, cloaked under the palatable heading of a 'restoration' project." The executive director of the Northern California Water Association, representing northern Sacramento Valley water agencies, announced a willingness to consider a canal but only if there were assurances that the Sacramento River would not be depleted. Southland water leaders rushed to provide those assurances. "This is not a Southern California water grab," pleaded Timothy Quinn, deputy general manager of the Metropolitan Water District of Southern California. "The system will not go out of control," he promised, and he urged his colleagues "to eliminate the fear factor. That's the engine that has driven the controversy: fear of Southern California." The hope to end fear foundered in the eyes of many northerners when MWD refused to voluntarily reduce its entitlement from the State Water Project as a sign of good faith. Since earlier estimates of the water expected from the project had dropped considerably below the amount for which contracts had been issued, MWD's refusal suggested to them the agency's determination to get all the water to which it was entitled even if the expectations of others and environmental needs were not met. "Until they come up with something other than just another ploy to take more water from the north," stated an attorney for the Environmental Defense Fund, "I don't think they'll ever succeed." [66]

Alarmed at the growing bitterness and what appeared to be a replay of 1982, CALFED sought to defuse the situation in late summer 1998 by announcing a change in procedure. Instead of selecting a single proposal, the agency revealed its Preferred Program Alternative, which would phase in the bay-delta improvements, beginning with the first of the three plans and proceeding to the others only when—and if—the need for them became necessary. "The complexity of the Bay-Delta system," stated CALFED officials, "and the inability to predict future events and how the system will respond to proposed actions requires that an adaptive management philosophy and process be employed." [67]

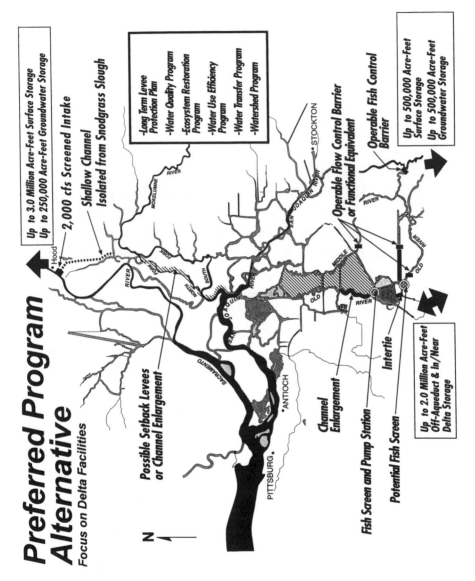

Preferred Program Alternative
Focus on Delta Facilities

N

Up to 3.0 Million Acre-Feet Surface Storage
Up to 250,000 Acre-Feet Groundwater Storage

2,000 cfs Screened Intake

Shallow Channel
Isolated from Snodgrass Slough

- Long Term Levee Protection Plan
- Water Quality Program
- Ecosystem Restoration Program
- Water Use Efficiency Program
- Water Transfer Program
- Watershed Program

Operable Fish Control Barrier

Up to 500,000 Acre-Feet Surface Storage
Up to 500,000 Acre-Feet Groundwater Storage

Operable Flow Control Barrier or Functional Equivalent

Possible Setback Levees or Channel Enlargement

Channel Enlargement

Fish Screen and Pump Station

Potential Fish Screen

Intertie

Up to 2.0 Million Acre-Feet Off-Aqueduct & In/Near Delta Storage

Hood

PITTSBURG

ANTIOCH

STOCKTON

SACRAMENTO

MOKELUMNE RIVER

SAN JOAQUIN RIVER

OLD RIVER

MIDDLE RIVER

SOUTH FORK

NORTH FORK

Courtesy of CALFED Bay-Delta Program

That olive branch produced a cry of betrayal from MWD. "Southern California's $500 billion economy, quality of life and environment will be threatened," angrily announced the agency. "That's just not right." CALFED defended itself by emphasizing that northerners were arguing the exact opposite. The need, declared the agency, was for "sufficient information" to create "general agreement . . . for future decisions and for moving beyond the first stage." At present "everyone in the process seems to believe CALFED is serving the best needs of somebody else."[68]

Two weeks later Governor Pete Wilson, though sympathetic to the canal idea, effectively quashed any hope for early construction by announcing that no such project should be attempted for at least seven years. MWD bowed to the decision as a temporary setback: "the timing isn't right." With that, the canal was put on hold and plans announced in mid-December 1998 to begin what CALFED called "Stage 1," a seven-year, $4.4 billion (of an eventual thirty-year and perhaps more than $10 billion) blending of options one and two: reenforcement of levees, improvement of water quality, reestablishment of animal and fish habitat, watershed restoration, increased water conservation, encouragement of water transfers among willing parties, and studies to determine an "appropriate mix of surface water and groundwater storage." As for the through-delta canal, these latest plans announced that it "will only be built when it is determined that . . . other CALFED actions cannot meet CALFED goals and objectives."[69]

No one was sufficiently happy with the proffered compromise for it to go forward. The south and farmers wanted a commitment to build a canal and dams, not studies and overly vague criteria. The north and environmentalists preferred no such studies but were especially upset with what they perceived as CALFED's unjustified continuing interest in surface reservoirs and dams. Taken aback but not surprised by all the wrangling, Interior Secretary Bruce Babbitt dryly noted: "In water wars, when Californians organize a firing squad, they form a circle facing inwards."[70]

Following that not inaccurate assessment, CALFED, in its search for consensus, went back once more to the drawing board and forged still another "Stage 1" plan. Released six months later, the new draft sought to give a little something to everyone. To appease the environmentalists, it reworked the words that earlier seemed to assure at least some dams: "CALFED will evaluate and determine the appropriate mix of surface water *and* groundwater storage." The new words now made dams only a possibility: "groundwater *and/or* surface water storage will be developed and constructed." In a similar gesture for greater support from the south and farmers, CALFED replaced its earlier hazy criteria for building a cross-delta canal with greater specificity: The decision for the canal would rest on three considerations: an "evaluation of how water suppliers can best provide . . . water quality of 50 ppb bromide and three ppm TOC [total organic carbon]"; an appraisal by an independent panel of experts "on CALFED's progress toward these measurable water quality goals"; and an assessment by another panel on how CALFED was progressing "toward ecosystem restoration objectives, with particular emphasis on fisheries recovery."[71]

Again, CALFED hit a brick wall. Environmentalists heatedly re-affirmed their opposition. "It's disappointing that CALFED is still considering tax-payer subsidized, damaging projects," complained a spokesman for the Audubon Society. Southlanders and farmers answered in kind: "The political pressure is overriding the engineering and the science," declared the chair of the California Avocado Commission. In an abrupt change of tactics, MWD and associated urban water agencies used CALFED's revised "Stage 1" plan as an opportunity to launch a different kind of publicity campaign on their own behalf. They backed away from their insistence on a canal and, instead, emphasized what they considered the "real" issue: "drinking-water quality . . . that meets the minimum health standards we are advocating." To MWD, CALFED's goal for reducing bromide and organic carbon was all right as a first step, but it lacked credibility because of the failure to specify dates for intermediate reductions during the seven-year phase-in period. More importantly, nothing specific was offered to decrease the salinity of delta water that now was exacerbating an already crisis situation in southern California. The salt content in water there, declared MWD's general manager, is "four to six times higher . . . than the national average," posing "critical . . . public health risks" and costing southern Californians hundreds of millions of dollars because of "additional water treatment [costs] and accelerated corrosion of not only manufacturing facilities but residential hot water heaters and home plumbing systems." Only delta water that, when mixed with local supplies, would assure a "salinity blending" of no more than 500 milligrams per liter was acceptable, stated the MWD board to CALFED in midsummer 1999. Though MWD fashioned its new campaign around water quality, it did not ignore water quantity. "Without substantially improved salinity from our Delta supply," warned an MWD spokesman, "we will require more Delta water in the future to achieve this blend." The agency demanded an annual average delivery of 1.5 million acre-feet by 2020 (its State Water Project entitlement, which it had not been receiving, was 2 million acre-feet) and a minimum of 650,000 acre-feet during severe drought years like 1977 and 1991. The catch was that to achieve these deliveries MWD would have to receive its full entitlement during wet years.[72]

Such dogged resistance all around left CALFED planners dispirited but, as reflected in the reaction to MWD's water quality and quantity demands, fully committed to staying the course. "We can't adopt specific objectives like these simply because a stakeholder requests them. We are required to look at all reasonable alternatives." Put simply, CALFED dug in its heels and refused to budge from its "study-now, decide-later approach." That approach seemed reasonable enough, but politically it was a bust. Farmers, urban water agencies, businesses, environmentalists, and fish biologists were now referring to CALFED as "Calfail" and threatening not only to desert the increasingly fragile coalition but also to turn on one another as in water wars of old.[73]

Alarmed, newly elected Governor Gray Davis decided to intervene. He settled on two courses of action. First, while sympathetic to CALFED's approach, he did not want it to stall attempts to ameliorate a host of state water woes that had received little attention if not ignored altogether: urban pollution of beaches; poor-quality drinking water; groundwater depletion; destruction of riparian habitat; flooding along the Russian, Feather, and Yuba rivers; loss of open space and farmland to unplanned development; and much more. To address the problems, he joined with legislative leaders to craft two closely related bond measures (Proposition 12 for $2.1 billion and Proposition 13 for $1.97 billion) and placed them on the state ballot for March 2000. (These were the same measures, it will be recalled, that breathed new life into the hope for a rejuvenated Los Angeles River.) To avoid the bottlenecks that had slowed the CALFED process, neither proposition called for large dams or reservoirs but, rather, stressed in their stead protection of neighborhood parks and rivers, clean air and water, conservation programs, and plans for banking water in underground aquifers that were expected to increase current supplies by a million acre-feet. Agribusiness criticized that amount as woefully inadequate and renewed its demand for dams. Few others followed its lead. Widespread support for the measures came from water agencies, environmental groups, business organizations, and residents north and south. On election day, March 7, voters gave 63 percent of their ballots to Proposition 12 and 65 percent to Proposition 13.[74]

Simultaneously with his promotion of the ballot measures, Davis teamed with Interior Secretary Babbitt to initiate a second course of action aimed at restoring CALFED's credibility and vitality. They ordered their top advisors to abandon the public meetings of so-called "stakeholders" and to devote their energies to hammering out a plan for dealing expeditiously with the state's larger water problems. All-day and late-night sessions produced, in June 2000, a carefully crafted plan: *California's Water Future: A Framework for Action.* With the plan's release, public reaction made it clear that differences among hostile camps remained, but many sharp edges were softened by the plan's downplaying or eliminating altogether of some flash-point issues and by giving the various sides something each desperately sought. Significantly, it did not blink at addressing problems—the chaotic and competitive abuse of groundwater supplies, agribusiness's increasingly agitated hostility to more water for wildlife and the environment, and increasing urban demand for water— sure to arouse opposition no matter what course of action was adopted. "The plan," explained federal and state officials, is "a delicately balanced compromise with no clear winners or losers." That compromise, observed the *Los Angeles Times,* "is a jigsaw array of individual projects to restore the environment, protect endangered fish, shore up flood control, improve the quality of water shipped to southern California, reclaim used water and conserve more water both above and below ground as a cushion against drought."[75]

The cost of the plan's seven-year first stage was $8.7 billion, nearly double the estimate for the entire 1998 plan and perhaps capable of exceeding $10 billion. Among specific provisions were: $1.3 billion for ecosystem protection in the delta, the Sacramento River corridor, and bay-delta tributaries; elimination of physical, institutional, and legal barriers to water transfers; an increase in groundwater storage of 500,000 to 1 million acre-feet; state legislation placing responsibility for groundwater management at the basinwide level and taking it away from the numerous local water districts and agencies whose environmentally destructive conflicts amounted to no management at all; additional legislation checking the waste of water in such cities as Sacramento and Modesto, which lacked water meters, by "requiring the appropriate measurement of all water uses in the State of California"; $300 million for watershed restoration and protection; $450 million for improving and maintaining the delta levee system; the purchase of 35,000 acres of inferior (due to poor drainage) San Joaquin Valley farmland, thereby freeing up better-quality Sierra Nevada runoff; regional programs in the San Francisco Bay area, Sacramento Valley, San Joaquin Valley, and southern California aimed at improving supplies to major urban areas and restoring the health of the bay-delta system; creation of a 380,000 acre-foot Environmental Water Account providing additional fish protection and preventing future water supply disruptions because of actions under the Endangered Species Act; and $1 billion for increasing groundwater storage in the Sacramento and San Joaquin valleys, for in-delta storage, and for enlarging Shasta Lake and Los Vaqueros Reservoir. The plan called for raising Shasta Dam 6 to 8 feet, thereby producing 300,000 acre-feet of additional storage to enhance fish habitat and water management generally; raising Los Vaqueros Dam 58 feet, producing 400,000 acre-feet of additional storage to improve water quality and the ability to re-spond to water emergencies; and storing surface water within the levees of the delta's islands, producing 250,000 acre-feet for fish en-hancement and management flexibility.[76]

As important as the plan's ingredients was what it did *not* con-tain. There were no provisions for major new dams or for a periph-eral canal, big or small. There was, however, authorization for *stud-ies*—not necessarily construction—of a new off-stream reservoir with a capacity of up to 1.9 million acre-feet in the Sacramento Val-ley; enlargement of Millerton Lake at Friant Dam for 250,000 to 700,000 acre-feet of additional storage; and a "screened through-delta facility" on the Sacramento River to assure cleaner water for the central and southern delta as well as for the San Joaquin Valley and southern California. This last potential project would *not* be the 44-mile trimmed-down version of the 1982 Peripheral Canal fea-tured in CALFED's Alternative 3. Rather, this conveyance, an ele-ment in Alternative 2, would be seven miles long, have a screen for protecting fish at the intake, and would be confined entirely to the north delta, where it would take water from the Sacramento River near Hood and bring it south to the Mokelumne River. The water would then move further south, via the north and south forks of the Mokelumne, to join with the San Joaquin River in the central delta and "freshen up" the water there. The State Water Project and Central Valley Project pumps near Tracy would then draw much of this good quality water into the southern delta and eventually into the SWP and CVP canals going south.[77]

Environmentalists disliked the notion of expanding reservoirs or studying the possibility of creating new ones, but they were pleased with the creation of the Environmental Water Account and the emphasis on conservation and reclamation. "There are things we don't like, but this moves the beast forward," declared an official of the Environmental Defense Fund. Many farmers, though preferring new dams and worried about the impact of the environmental provisions on farm water and land, were encouraged by the programs for increasing water supply. "In general, the benefits outweigh the detriments," stated the general manager of the Kern County Water Agency, "and we look forward to working with the governor on this package."[78]

Still, the plan provoked strong—even bitterly angry—reactions from several quarters, especially from rural residents in the northern Central Valley who, through the Regional Council of Rural Counties (a coalition of twenty-eight such counties), expressed outrage at CALFED's call for legislation mandating basinwide management of groundwater. Under the battle cry of "local management of groundwater will not be usurped," they branded the notion "an outright assault" on their local autonomy and harbinger to their water being "siphoned off . . . and more land . . . [being] taken off the tax rolls." Within weeks of the plan's release, northern opponents in the U.S. House of Representatives were vowing to fight the proposal with "every means at our disposal." In the process, critics expanded the region's enemies' list to include not only traditional foe southern California but also the environmentally beleaguered San Francisco Bay and delta area. If CALFED's "insidious" plan is approved, declared a northern congressman, "rural Northern California would become a virtual water faucet for the Bay Area and Southern California—just like the Owens Valley did." Panelists at a well-attended public meeting in Chico called by the Northern Sacramento Valley Water Forum reacted in classic NIMBY (not in my backyard) fashion: "The goal of the CALFED Program to improve water quality and quantity and to protect the environment is laudable but . . . it must not come at [our] expense."[79]

The latter concern echoed throughout much of agricultural California. "Cal-Fed proposes a massive conversion of farmland to wildlife habitat and other uses," declared a California Farm Bureau Federation press release, but it "fails to recognize the environmental benefits of keeping farmland in production and maintaining agriculture as a viable industry." In agreement was the San Joaquin Valley farmer and founder of Californians for Good Water Policy: "This 'Framework for Action' plan places a top priority on the Bay-Delta Estuary restoration and on servicing the water needs of the Metropolitan Water District of Southern California (MWD) at the expense of our own region's water supply and economies." Westlands Water District, with the lowest priority in the Central Valley, not surprisingly, made its support of CALFED's plan dependent on a quite specific condition: "a legally enforceable commitment from Cal-Fed" for Westlands's 540,000 acres.[80]

Others were unequivocal in their praise of the plan, including the MWD. The agency praised Davis and Babbitt for creating "the momentum CALFED needs to balance California's water quality and reliability demands and interests." The approval rested squarely, though not altogether directly, on the through-delta conveyance facility. MWD had earlier made it clear that water quality and how that affected quantity constituted the preeminent issue. The agency now acknowledged that the latest design for the facility, although confined to the north delta, seemed to address that issue successfully. "Metropolitan's board of directors has taken a position that it does not consider an isolated conveyance facility the definitive tool for addressing the state's water quality problems in the Bay/Delta and that any solution must be rooted in good science. We believe that the through-delta solution carefully laid out in the framework has the potential to fix the Bay-Delta and finally arrest the old regional and stakeholder disputes, which have stymied California water policy for decades." The *Ventura County Star* agreed that the plan represented a crucial turning point: "whether the state embarks on a new era of water management, or merely repeats the mistakes of the past." The Walnut Creek *Contra Costa Times* added: "There is a pressing need for CalFed to move ahead. . . . The sooner the work begins the better." Causes for optimism were the state's booming economy and the federal government's offer to contribute $2.4 billion of the total cost. Less encouraging was the resistance of some powerful farm interests, the possibility that the economy would cool, and the chance that Congress (for political, economic, or both reasons, if not others) would renege on its offer of financial help.[81]

Forging ahead, Governor Davis and Interior Secretary Babbitt formally approved the plan on August 28, 2000, but the decision to push for California legislative endorsement with only three days remaining in the 1999–2000 session proved a mistake. The rush led to two hastily drawn bills, one for initial funding and the other for a commission to oversee implementation of the plan, that generated criticism among both proponents and opponents. Bickering over the composition of the commission (virtually every interest, public and private, wanted representation), opposition among the ranks of agriculture, partisanship (Republicans saw an opportunity to embarrass Democrats Davis and Babbitt), and the chaos that invariably accompanies the closing days of a session all contributed to the narrow defeat of the bills, the commission measure by one vote in the assembly and the funding bill by two votes in the senate.[82]

No one believed that rejection of the bills meant the end of CALFED, and all agreed that new legislation, doubtless more carefully crafted, would be introduced in the next legislative session beginning in January 2001. Still, the outcome was an embarrassment to CALFED's advocates as was the bickering in the U.S. House of Representatives that prevented Congress's reauthorization of funds for CALFED by the September 30 deadline. The governor immediately vowed there would "be no delay in the implementation of the CALFED program" and to forcefully demonstrate his point released some of the funds that voters had earlier made available for CALFED's environmental work. That action and the simmering resentment of the rural north and agriculture provoked legal retaliation in the last week of September 2000—two lawsuits challenging the CALFED plan, one filed by the Regional Council of Rural Counties (fearful of losing its groundwater to the bay-delta and southern California) and the other filed by the California Farm Bureau Federation (embittered at the prospect of more agricultural water going to wildlife and the environment).[83]

The initial deliberate and rather slow CALFED process had gamely sought to paper over old enmities—north vs. south, farmers vs. cities, environmentalists vs. farmers and cities—but when that approach threatened to self-destruct and prompted state and federal leaders to accelerate the CALFED program, they unleashed what simply could not be contained. Looked at over the longer historical record, the conflicts and issues now starkly in the limelight had been begging for resolution for years. Unlike in the past, however, there now existed in CALFED a mechanism that held the hope—through determination, leadership (not always in evidence), imagination, and luck—of making a difference. Determination permeated the coalition of federal and state agencies at this critical juncture. "We have no intention of going away," declared a CALFED official, and "we expect to continue operating under the existing authorities of the [individual] CALFED agencies." Congress's failure to approve reauthorization notwithstanding, "federal agencies are still fully committed to and cooperating with the CALFED process." There was also a strong desire for "governance legislation" to strengthen CALFED's leadership and efficiency, thereby making it more than "simply a collection of federal and state agencies with their own responsibilities and authorities." As the summer of 2000 gave way to fall, the prevailing mood among supporters of CALFED was cautious optimism for what could be the largest program of environmental restoration in American history.[84]

Environmental Crisis: Central Valley

THE RECENT attempts to restore and protect the delta have overshadowed an equally intense and even longer struggle to improve water quality throughout California. Nowhere has the fight been more dramatically waged than in the Central Valley whose inhabitants had demanded first the Central Valley Project and then the State Water Project as the so-

Groundwater irrigation pump, 1978. (Courtesy of California Department of Water Resources)

lution to overdrafted aquifers and polluted drainage and groundwater. Salinity still plagues most fields and many aquifers, but another serious problem, especially in the San Joaquin Valley, is land subsidence.

Detected as early as the 1920s, land subsidence became one of the principal reasons for the Central Valley Project on the theory that an abundant new supply of water would decrease the overpumping of aquifers and their collapse, which led, in turn, to the collapse of the overlying land. As noted in chapter 5, the CVP supply that began arriving in 1951 only accelerated the mining of groundwater as farmers rushed new land into cultivation with that water while continuing to irrigate older acreage with pumps. Others also resorted to groundwater to avoid federal acreage restrictions and still others did so because CVP laterals failed to reach their property. The result was the greatest volume of land subsidence in the world due to pumping that, in turn, damaged or destroyed highways, roads, buildings, levees, and water conveyance facilities.[85]

By the 1970s some 5,200 square miles of the valley had fallen more than a foot with other areas experiencing sharper drops. Southwest of Mendota the surface had collapsed twenty-eight feet, while a sixty-eight-mile stretch of the California Aqueduct fell more than two feet between 1970 and 1994. Since 1970, imported water has lessened the rate of subsidence except during droughts, like those in 1976–1977 and 1987–1992, when cuts in supply led to increased pumping and land collapse. Similar results followed state requirements for the retention of more water in San Francisco Bay and the delta as well as the 1992 Central Valley Project Improvement Act's provisions allocating large volumes of water for environmental and wildlife enhancement.[86]

Besides collapsed aquifers and land subsidence with their attendant destruction of property, there are pollution dangers, some as adverse for wildlife and Californians elsewhere as for farmers. Again, these perils have been especially apparent in the San Joaquin Valley where agricultural runoff has created a crisis of massive proportions because of the concentration of unnaturally high levels of

Geologist Joseph Poland demonstrating land subsidence due to heavy pumping of groundwater in the San Joaquin Valley, southwest of Mendota. (Courtesy of U.S. Geological Survey)

toxic chemicals caused by irrigation flows and the residue from fertilizers and pesticides. In connection with the pollution question not only in the valley but also statewide it is important to remember that ever more sophisticated technology has allowed scientists to detect increasingly minute concentrations of toxic substances. Hence, water quality may sometimes appear to be deteriorating more rapidly than is truly the case. In the San Joaquin Valley, that is not the situation.

The western valley was brought under cultivation in the wake of the State Water Project and the introduction of federal water to the Westlands Water District. The west valley contains little natural drainage, a fact that was common knowledge to those developing the area but little publicized for fear of jeopardizing the venture. The arrival of new supplies resulted in the buildup of contaminated groundwater from agricultural runoff that had to be withdrawn to keep the threatened land—ultimately, perhaps 400,000 acres—in production. A master drain to the delta (the San Luis Drain) was proposed and construction begun in the late 1970s, but economic and environmental obstacles—how to finance it and where to dump the wastewater without adverse effects (no one in the delta wanted the drainage)—prevented completion, although the plan continues to have advocates.[87]

The lack of an outlet led to an ecological crisis in 1983 when scientists discovered that pollutants pouring from the unfinished drain, which terminated at Kesterson National Wildlife Refuge near Los Banos, were killing waterfowl and causing widespread birth deformities among the young birds that exceeded any similar outbreak ever recorded in the wild. The Reclamation Bureau's first response, in harmony with the incumbent Republican Ronald Reagan administration's desire to roll back federal restrictions on business, was to sacrifice the remaining birds by closing down Kesterson's 6,200 acres of wetlands as a refuge and announcing that surveys by Bureau regional offices throughout the West had discovered only "minor problems" and "no direct evidence of wildlife impact." This action produced such a roar of protest that the Bureau did an about-face.

Kesterson National Wildlife Refuge, site of toxic drainage water from irrigation. (Courtesy of California Department of Water Resources)

In early 1985 it invoked the Migratory Bird Treaty Act (under the U.S. Constitution, treaties, like congressionally enacted statutes, are the "supreme law of the land") and declared its intention to shut off the flow of irrigation water to those farmers who seemed primarily responsible for the toxic drainage. Some 42,000 acres would be affected. Now it was time for the farmers to protest, and in less than two weeks they got the order rescinded, with the understanding that government and agricultural interests would devise a solution.[88]

Several years and proposals later they were still trying to resolve the blight that the *Sacramento Bee,* in a series of alarming investigative reports by Tom Harris, revealed was plaguing not only Kesterson but also numerous federal water projects in the West. Despite the Bureau's earlier denials of such a widespread problem, it launched an intensive sampling and mediation effort throughout its jurisdiction. As for Kesterson, in July 1988 the state Water Resources Control Board, over the objections of skeptics, approved a Reclamation Bureau plan to cover the selenium-tainted soil with dirt trucked in from elsewhere. That $23 million project was completed the following November, but a short time later the Reclamation Bureau issued the results of a monitoring study indicating that the selenium level at Kesterson still exceeded safety limits for wildlife and that the refuge could remain dangerous for years to come. Then in late 1989 the Bureau announced a new $22 million plan to bring in 62,000 acre-feet of fresh water not only to revitalize but also to expand the existing wetlands by nearly 4,500 acres. That proposal, like the earlier ones, produced its skeptics. In the meantime, the state Department of Health Services warned residents to limit their consumption of fish and birds taken in the Kesterson area and at other wastewater ponds in the west valley.[89]

Kesterson had attracted national attention, but it was by no means an isolated problem in the valley where smaller, private holding ponds had selenium levels greater than those at the refuge. A small amount of selenium is a required nutrient for humans, but a slightly elevated level can be toxic. A U.C. Davis study of selenium in the food and livestock products produced with western San Joaquin Valley water revealed levels "high enough to justify careful monitoring" and possibly dangerous for those who are "repeat customers in direct farm-to-consumer sales." Left largely unhampered by federal prosecutors during the Republican Reagan and George Bush administrations, farmers did not begin addressing the problem until the more environmentally sensitive Bill Clinton era produced threats, like those earlier, to take action under the Migratory Bird Treaty Act. This time some farmers shut down their contaminated ponds and lakes and replaced them with clean bodies of water and wetlands. An added boost came in 1993 when the Reclamation Bureau, under the previous year's Central Valley Project Improvement Act, announced plans to buy and retire up to 7,000 acres of Westlands property with poor drainage. Bureaucratic inertia delayed the retirement program until 2000, but if it and a similar demonstration project in Kings and Tulare counties prove successful, the goal will be to retire 90,000 acres.[90]

The risks from agriculture include more than selenium and extend well beyond the valley's west side. Thirty percent of California's urban and agricultural water needs are met by groundwater, and in drought years the percentage is considerably greater. Rural populations, in particular, rely on groundwater not only for crops but also for drinking purposes. The peril lies in the vast array of insecticides, herbicides, and fungicides that are dumped on crops and then seep into groundwater supplies. (California uses more such products than any other state.) Many are safe but there is consensus among state and federal regulatory agencies that some are very dangerous and others are highly suspect. Bans on harmful substances are sometimes ignored and frequently ineffective because the poisonous pesticides have been used in such massive quantities and for so long that their presence remains in groundwater supplies for years. Though the state in 1977 and the U.S. Environmental Protection Agency two years later banned DBCP (dibromochloropropane) because of studies linking the fumigant with infertility, sterility, and cancer, scientists in 1985 found it in levels exceeding federal standards in 15 to 20 percent of all sample wells in the San Joaquin Valley. The problem also existed statewide as revealed a decade later by a U.C. Berkeley toxicology team that found this deadly chemical "responsible for contaminating more California wells than any other pesticide." The team discovered 1,700 tainted public and private wells serving 200,000 people in eighteen counties, including some in southern California. The danger remains greatest in the San Joaquin Valley, especially in the Fresno area where 50 wells, many of them in fast-developing neighborhoods, had been shut down by 1995 with another 125 still functioning despite the presence of contaminants. "DBCP is incredibly persistent," observed one of the Berkeley toxicologists. "It just won't go away."[91]

The banning of DBCP not only failed to eliminate the chemical from the environment but also did nothing to deter agribusiness from coming up with an equally deadly alternative: methyl bromide. Tests by the federal EPA determined that methyl bromide was acutely toxic to humans and depleted the Earth's protective ozone layer. These findings led to an Environmental Protection

Agency order banning the production and import of the substance by 2001. Scheduled for elimination nationwide and, through international agreement (the Montreal Protocol of 1997), worldwide by 2005, methyl bromide got a reprieve—an extension provision overriding the EPA order was slipped into a mammoth federal budget bill by a Central Valley representative just before Congress adjourned in fall 1998. Now, despite overwhelming evidence of the chemical's danger, California farmers could continue pouring it on their crops (though in increasingly smaller amounts under the law's phaseout terms) for another four years until the international ban took effect in 2005.[92]

Another incident reflecting the troubling politics of pesticide use involved aldicarb. Applied to a large portion of the state's watermelon crop in 1985, it produced what was considered the largest outbreak of illness in recent U.S. history. A thousand people reported symptoms ranging from nausea to seizures, and some women claimed to have had stillbirths following only brief illnesses. Tests in the Central Valley by the product's manufacturer revealed that the chemical went quickly through the soil to aquifers fifty feet below the surface where it persisted for as long as three years. These and other studies prompted the state Department of Health Services and the Water Resources Control Board to recommend a ban on aldicarb, but that recommendation ran afoul of Republican Governor George Deukmejian's opposition to environmental and other restrictions as unwarranted interference with economic growth. In 1989 the director of the state Department of Food and 'Agriculture, a Deukmejian political appointee, ignored the advice of the two agencies and announced that "no pollution or threat of pollution exists" with the use of aldicarb. Though he set some restrictions on the pesticide's application, critics denounced them as ineffective and his thinking as "dangerously illogical." Since he was a former president of the powerful California Farm Bureau Federation, a collection of farmers' groups, and the latest in a line of growers to head the Food and Agriculture Department, his announcement was not a complete surprise. As the *Los Angeles*

Times editorialized, however, it was an example of the Agriculture Department's "willful illogic" in failing to put the "protection of the public's health ahead of its consideration for corporate farmers' profits."[93]

To focus public attention on the pesticide problem generally, César Chávez of the United Farm Workers of America went on a fast in the summer of 1988. That fall the traditionally conservative *California Farmer,* the oldest and largest (with a circulation of 53,000) agricultural magazine in the state, noted that some grape growers were illegally using a growth-stimulating chemical. Roundly criticized by agribusiness for the disclosure, the managing editor explained that "we didn't want the industry to play into the hands of Chávez" and that "the blatant use of illegal products is a far bigger threat to the continued use of safe, properly applied chemicals than any article this magazine will ever publish." Such candor failed to sway his detractors, who forced his resignation.[94]

Not surprisingly, the volume of harmful chemicals sprayed, dumped, and dusted on California crops has continued to grow—by 129 percent between 1991 and 1995 alone. Such increases intensified environmentalists' demands for farmers to switch to "integrated pest management," a technique emphasizing changes in irrigation patterns to ward off fungus and weeds; the introduction of pest-resistant plant species; and the use of benign insects to eliminate crop pests and reduce the need for chemical agents. By the late 1990s public purchases of such organically grown fruits and vegetables were increasing nationally by 20 percent a year, despite their generally higher prices. Nonetheless, during the same period, only one-half of 1 percent of California farmland and total agricultural sales represented the organic market. Old habits, even under the closest scrutiny, die hard, a major reason for Congress's passage in 1996 of the Food Quality Protection Act.[95]

The new law directed the Environmental Protection Agency to reevaluate all pesticides over the next decade, with the EPA first targeting the OPs (organophosphates), among the deadliest and cheapest chemicals available and a source of serious concern since

Crop dusting in the Central Valley, 1992. (Courtesy of California Department of Water Resources)

at least the 1960s. OPs are efficient eradicators of the pests that attack fruits, nuts, vegetables, and cotton. Their effectiveness derives from being related to nerve gases like sarin, used in the 1995 Tokyo subway killings. A small amount on the skin can produce flulike symptoms and overexposure can blur vision, impair memory, and bring on anxiety, insomnia, headaches, chronic fatigue, and emotional instability. Evidence continues to mount of their adverse effect on farmworkers and their families, especially children. Even low exposure, like that brought home on the clothing of field laborers, can damage brain development and immune systems in young children and fetuses. Four organizations acutely concerned about pesticide poisoning (Californians for Pesticide Reform, California Rural Legal Assistance Foundation, Pesticide Action Network, and United Farm Workers of America) analyzed data collected by state and federal agencies and in 1999 released a report underscoring the need for reform. In *Fields of Poison,* they revealed that between 1991 and 1996 agricultural workers nationwide had a death rate of 20.9 per

100,000 employees as compared to a rate of 3.9 per 100,000 workers in all industries. In California there had been 3,991 instances of pesticide poisoning, an average of 665 cases a year. Field surveys turned up many incidents of exposure that had gone unreported because of fear of job loss and medical bills, the latter reflecting employee ignorance about coverage through workers' compensation. Without remedial action the future looked ever more grim, concluded the report, for "the data . . . reveal . . . increasing use of pesticides and continued high numbers of pesticide poisonings."[96]

Some observers expected the EPA evaluation process to result in the banning of OPs and many other chemicals, or at least in tougher restrictions on their use, but that hope remains largely unfulfilled. Agribusiness and the pesticide industry had not resisted the Food Quality Protection Act because it was linked to the elimination of a 1950 regulation prohibiting the sale of processed or canned foods with any detectable carcinogen levels. Once Congress passed the legislation, however, farmers and pesticide producers fought its implementation, claiming that loss of OPs and similar effective agents would increase their costs, reduce crop yields, and eliminate their profits, forcing Americans to rely on more expensive imported products. Still others predicted to the contrary that bans and tougher restrictions would cause chemical producers to drop prices on expensive, but safer, pesticides. When EPA officials indicated in 1998 that they intended to take a hard line in interpreting the legislation, farmers nationally protested. Vice President Al Gore, with hopes for a presidential run, seemed to look askance at his avowed "environmentalist" credentials by hastily creating a panel to "weigh the need to protect people against the need to protect crops" and lecturing the EPA about its responsibility to "use sound science and guarantee farmers time to make a transition to alternatives if a chemical is banned." This was scarcely an endorsement of a "hard line" approach. The EPA backed off and, instead of enforcing the law, issued brochures to grocery stores urging parents "to wash, scrub, peel, and trim" produce to eliminate pesticides.[97]

Such feeble action provoked stinging public criticism, and in

April 1999 all consumer and environmental representatives on the federal government's advisory panel on pesticides resigned in protest of EPA's dilatory performance. Distressed by the rebuke, EPA four months later finally issued its first pesticide orders under the food quality legislation (three *years* had now passed since approval of the law), banning one OP compound (methyl parathion) and limiting the quantity of another that could be used (azinphos methyl). Both had been widely applied to fruits and many vegetables common in children's diets. Predictably, farmers and pesticide companies denounced the action, claiming that EPA's review process did not meet scientific standards. Environmentalists and consumer groups, though pleased with the restrictions, believed they were "too little too late" and castigated the agency for moving so slowly and for spending so much of its time on pesticides that were either obsolete or used only minimally. Chastened once again, EPA pledged to complete its review of all OP compounds by the end of 2000, a promise that failed to deter the *Los Angeles Times* from registering its harsh opinion: "Laxity on Pesticides in Food."[98]

Even more alarming was a report issued in October 1999 by the highly respected California Public Interest Research Group (CALPIRG) revealing that pesticides were in the drinking water of 16.5 million Californians living in forty-six of the state's fifty-eight counties. Contamination was "worst" in the Central Valley, but two of the pesticides—DBCP and EDB (ethylene dibromide)—were "detected throughout the state at concentrations greater than state-established" safe levels. Moreover, many other pesticides were found for which the state had not conducted a risk assessment. CALPIRG singled out for special criticism the Department of Pesticide Regulation for its "ineffective" regulations and an upper management that had "prevented the rest of the department from doing their jobs effectively." Also harshly rebuked was the Department of Health Services for adopting "standards much weaker than an analysis of health effects alone would dictate," for "ignoring valuable data in assessing the extent of pesticide contamination," and for allowing "small water suppliers to slip through the regulatory cracks." Hope for reform came in admissions from Health Services officials that "many of the . . . guidelines are unrealistically low" and from a spokesperson for Pesticide Regulation that the "program to prevent groundwater contamination has not been preventive enough." Still, any prospect for immediate improvement was dashed when the chief of the Drinking Water Program in the Department of Health Services observed that improved "goals . . . would be good in an ideal situation, but . . . state law requires [the] . . . department to take into account feasibility, costs and benefits when devising regulations." [99]

Pesticides are not the only cause for alarm in the Central Valley. Cow manure, 80 million pounds a day and 28 billion pounds a year, fouls the landscape and poisons rivers, streams, and hundreds of square miles of underground aquifers. Toilets, sewers, and treatment plants exist for humans but not for California's more than 2,300 dairies and 1.3 million cows, each of which spews as much waste as twenty-four people. The principal pollutants in manure are nitrates and coliform bacteria, which make water unsafe for humans and kill fish and wildlife. California is the nation's number one milk producer, and Central Valley cows, especially those concentrated between Sacramento and Tulare, are a major reason for that achievement. (The largest concentration of dairy cows is in southern California's San Bernardino and Riverside counties.) In California as in the rest of the nation, crops and livestock together have outpaced factories as the major threat to water supplies. [100]

For years neither California nor the federal government responded adequately to the growing challenge created by dairies becoming "factory farms" as ever more animals were crammed into gigantic milking plants occupying increasingly less acreage and discharging ever greater amounts of feces and urine into waterways. The state and federal Clean Water acts prohibited such contamination but enforcement existed in name only. Until the late 1990s there was only one state inspector for the thousand dairy farms from Orlando, north of Sacramento, to Fresno and none for the 600 dairies between Fresno and Bakersfield. Finally, in 1998, because of increasingly flagrant violations, the state appointed four additional inspectors and began scrambling for funds to name more. During the same year, the Environmental Protection Agency, citing the federal Clean Water Act, began regulating the nation's more than 6,000 large dairies (those having in excess of 700 cows) as the factories that they had become. As a sign of its resolve, the EPA immediately fined one Central Valley dairy farmer $50,000 for allowing manure to foul a nearby highway and another dairy owner $100,000 plus ninety days in jail for ten instances of stream pollution. The EPA also targeted for inspection large hog and chicken operations (defined as those possessing more than 2,500 hogs or 100,000 chickens). This, of course, left the smaller—yet no less culpable—hog, chicken, and dairy farms virtually unchecked. Even the larger operators continued to be a major problem despite the crackdown. "Some people are trying to do the right thing, but some clearly are not," stated an EPA official in 1998. "Industry claims it's a small percentage that are the [violators], but based on what I see, I don't agree." The responsibilities of such officials are not likely to get easier. The number of large commercial dairies has been on the rise for decades, and in 1998 the J. G. Boswell Company, owner of 250,000 acres in the Central Valley and now considered the world's largest corporate farm, announced plans to create on a portion of its holdings in Kings County five dairies stocked with 55,000 cows on 7,000 acres. A couple of years later, the Kern County Board of Supervisors approved creation of two dairies southwest of Bakersfield, each housing 142,000 cows and constituting by far the county's largest dairies. And so it goes. Dairies are important to society, of course, but not unregulated ones.[101]

Past damage and that continuing as a result of livestock and pesticide pollution have contributed to the despoliation not only of San Francisco Bay and delta, but also of 10,000 square miles of aquifers and 4,000 miles of rivers and streams. In 1998 the U.S. Geological Survey released a study indicating that the nitrate concentration (residue from fertilizers) in 25 percent of the tested residential wells in the eastern San Joaquin Valley violated drinking-water standards, a finding that led to the valley's well water being ranked worse than 75 percent of the basins tested nationwide.[102] The task ahead is huge.

Environmental Crisis: Southern California

BELOW THE Tehachapis the threat from polluted water is as great as the problem in the north. Salinity has become an especially serious threat along the lower Colorado River where the concentration of salts has increased as the volume of water decreased because of evaporation losses at reservoirs and intense irrigation practices upstream. Farmers must irrigate fewer acres with the same volume of water, switch to more salt-tolerant crops, install an expensive system of tile drains, obtain more water to produce the same amount of crops, or adopt some combination of these options. The Imperial Valley has been especially hard hit, pouring millions of dollars into a struggle to control salts that, barring some unexpected technological breakthrough or infusion of new water, will inevitably be lost. If that happens, the valley will be abandoned, thus following a pattern established by many earlier civilizations stretching as far back as Sumer in the third millennium B.C.[103]

The salinity problem affects not only the Imperial Valley and other irrigated areas along the lower Colorado but also cities and agriculture elsewhere dependent on the river. While the southern California coastal plain has long experienced difficulties associated with salty imported supplies and saltwater intrusion into over-pumped aquifers near the ocean, other large areas—central Arizona and southern Nevada—are being damaged by diversions from the Colorado. The higher concentration of salts means increased costs due to corrosion of heaters and pipes, treatment of water for drinking and industrial purposes, more soap consumption, higher water-softening bills, and damage to shrubs and plants. The Metropolitan

Water District has sought to lessen the impact on southern California by blending its Colorado River supplies with less-saline northern California water (and also recharging aquifers with northern water), but this strategy has inevitably increased that agency's desire for northern water and also required greater amounts of electricity (and hence higher costs for customers) to send the water south. Much more power is required to pump water over the Tehachapis than from the Colorado.[104]

Salinity has also soured relations between the United States and Mexico. The U.S.-Mexico Treaty of 1944 guaranteed Mexico 1.5 million acre-feet from the Colorado River, but the agreement said nothing specific about water quality. The omission erupted into a bitter confrontation in 1961 when heavily saline groundwater from Wellton-Mohawk, an Arizona irrigation district, entered the river above the headgates to Mexico's Mexicali Valley, one of the richest agricultural areas in that nation. Outraged at the resulting crop losses, Mexico demanded compensation for damages and "good quality" water. The U.S. State Department, under pressure from California and the other Colorado Basin states, coldly denied that the treaty imposed any obligation "with respect to the quality of the water," but quickly took a more conciliatory position when its response generated embarrassing international publicity. Fresher water was released from American dams and a channel constructed at U.S. expense to direct the polluted drainage around the Mexican intake. Since both nations recognized that these steps would not prevent future deterioration in water quality as projects already authorized in the United States were completed, the State Department haltingly—but steadily—worked toward a longer-term solution. In 1973 the United States promised (in an agreement known as Minute 242) to maintain at an acceptable level 1.36 million acre-feet going to Mexico (plus about 100,000 acre-feet of Wellton-Mohawk drainage) and to construct just north of the border a desalination plant which, when it became operational in early 1992, was among the world's largest. Because of technical problems and delays, the plant was fourteen years late in opening, five times

Salt damage to crops, Coachella Valley. (Courtesy of U.S. Bureau of Reclamation)

more expensive (at $250 million) than the original estimate, and already obsolete in much of its technology.[105] Whether the plant will be able to maintain the promised salinity level into the more distant future remains unclear.

Salinity, however, has not been the only threat to the lower Colorado River and the millions of people in southern California, Arizona, Nevada, and northern Mexico who depend on it for drinking water and growing crops. Near Moab in southeastern Utah and only 750 feet from the river sit 10.5 million tons of radioactive uranium mill waste, accumulating since 1956 in response to the demand for processed uranium for atomic bombs and, later, for nuclear power plants. Lack of demand closed the mill in 1984 but nuclear contaminants from the waste as well as toxic chemicals and heavy metals that in high doses can cause cancer and genetic abnormalities have been steadily leaking into the Colorado River. The radioactive contamination in the river near the 130-acre, 110-foot-high pile is thirty-one times greater than allowed by Environmental Protection Agency standards. In the mid-1990s the U.S. Nuclear Regulatory Commission (NRC) concluded that moving the radioactive pile would benefit humans and wildlife but nonetheless decided that the estimated cost of at least $150 million ("and probably much more") to the firm owning the site was prohibitive. The Metropolitan Water District was among those outraged. "Costs," it lectured the NRC, "should be secondary to protecting water quality." Regardless, in April 1999 the NRC approved encasing the heap in a clay, sand, soil, and rock cap costing $19 million (plus "several million" more for groundwater clean-up) of which the federal government would contribute 56 percent.[106]

That decision sparked vigorous protests from the U.S. Interior Department, Fish and Wildlife Service, National Park Service, and others who denounced the proposal as no solution at all, since the contaminants, which rest on a floodplain above a fault line, could not be completely contained by the cap. Significantly, a cap placed on a pile of radioactive waste near Denver in the early 1990s and expected to last for at least 200 years and perhaps as long as a thousand years was crumbling by 2000, necessitating the costly removal of the pile.

Commission officials acknowledged there would be leakage at Moab but insisted that the Colorado's natural flushing action would dilute the poisons before they caused harm downstream. That rosy prediction satisfied almost no one, especially officials responsible for nearby Arches and Canyonlands national parks and for down-river Grand Canyon National Park and Glen Canyon and Lake Mead national recreation areas—all destinations for millions of visitors annually.[107]

By this time opponents to the NRC plan had grown to include cities, state agencies, and environmental groups alarmed by studies showing that nearly 30,000 gallons a day of contaminated water were leaking into the river and would continue to seep for another 270 years. The Metropolitan Water District of Southern California joined in the demands for removal of the toxic pile. Though monthly samplings indicated that the uranium concentration in MWD's Colorado River water was then about a third of the allowable federal maximum, the agency worried about the future. MWD joined with the San Diego County Water Authority and others in backing congressional legislation stripping the Nuclear Regulatory Agency of its authority over the site and transferring jurisdiction to the U.S. Department of Energy with instructions to move the pile to a safer locale, charge the federal government for the lion's share of the cost since 56 percent of the uranium went to weapons production, and bill the owner of the site for part of the expense—now estimated to total $300 million. Moving the pile would not necessarily constitute a fail-safe solution, however. To date, the Department of Energy has relocated eight uranium tailings piles on tributaries of the Colorado River without cleaning up the contaminated groundwater left behind at each site, which continues to seep into the river. The Energy Department's explanation for the inaction mirrors the one offered earlier by the NRC: "the existing contamination will be flushed or attenuated through natural process." That assumption, unsurprisingly, is not shared by everyone.[108]

In the southland, as in the Central Valley, harmful groundwater, because of agricultural pesticides, sloppy disposal of industrial and farm wastes, and overpumping, is endemic. Two hundred years ago the groundwater beneath the coastal plain existed in such abundance and so near the surface that it bubbled forth as crystal clear springs and even spouted in great artesian outpourings. These effusions also sprang from the nearby ocean floor. Local lore has it that the volume pouring up and into San Pedro Bay was so great that sailors could replenish their water stocks by dipping their buckets into the bay and never leaving their ship.

Overpumping has eliminated all but a handful of springs on the coastal plain and invited devastating saltwater intrusion (first noted as serious in the 1920s) through the same vents that earlier bubbled with fresh, clean water. Industrial and agricultural pollutants have also contaminated many of the aquifers thought safe from ocean brine. What makes the situation especially serious is that southern Californians, despite their many aqueducts, still rely on groundwater for 40 percent of their needs. For some, the reliance is much greater: the cities of San Bernardino and Riverside get nearly all their water from the ground, and Orange County relies on wells to supply 50 percent of the needs there. "These [groundwater supplies] are not replaceable in any thinkable way," stated the director of the state Department of Water Resources. "They are worth billions of dollars compared to anything you would have to do as an alternative. They are of incalculable value."[109]

They can also be incredibly dangerous as dramatized in the popular film *Erin Brockovich,* based on an actual event, which culminated in the largest penalty ever imposed in an environmental personal injury lawsuit. Three people triggered the investigation that led to the judgment: Roberta Walker, a resident of the town of Hinkley, some 130 miles northeast of Los Angeles in San Bernardino County; Edward Masry, an attorney with law offices at the time in Sherman Oaks and Rancho Mirage; and Erin Brockovich, a streetwise, tough-talking legal assistant in Masry's Sherman Oaks office. In 1992, Walker complained to Masry about the low price that Pacific Gas and Electric was offering for her home and her inability to get satisfactory results from San Bernardino County attorneys. Masry agreed to try, pro bono, to get her a better bid. "When I called a PG&E representative," recalled Masry, "he told me that he wouldn't offer any more money—that he had chased all the other attorneys from San Bernardino County away and that he wouldn't come up another dime. At the end of the conversation, we exchanged four-letter words." On returning to his office, Masry gave to Erin Brockovich for filing all the papers regarding house prices and medical tests accumulated by Walker in her dealings with PG&E. On glancing at the material to get an idea on how properly to file it, Brockovich "became curious" about the presence of medical reports on low T-cell counts and other blood problems in a file concerning a real-estate matter. As a result of that curiosity, observed Masry, "the rest is history." Four years of dogged investigation culminated

An example of land subsidence at Edwards Air Force Base in southern California. The fissure is more than a half mile long, up to fourteen feet deep, and five feet across at its widest point. (U.S. Air Force photo. Courtesy of Water Education Foundation)

in a settlement against PG&E for poisoning the groundwater of Hinkley with harmful levels of cancer-causing chromium 6 discharged from a gas-compressor plant. A landmark settlement of $333 million went to approximately 640 residents (the actual number varies constantly because, as plaintiffs die, the number of heirs and the ability to locate them varies). Masry subsequently initiated lawsuits against PG&E on behalf of other communities whose groundwater had been contaminated. News of his experiences prompted suits elsewhere as well as state inquiries into possible chromium 6 health hazards in the San Fernando Valley, Barstow, and other locales.[110]

As in the Central Valley, land subsidence due to excessive pumping has also threatened the viability of groundwater supplies. Especially hard hit have been fast-growing desert communities in Riverside, San Bernardino, and Los Angeles counties where the surface has fallen more than five feet in many areas, opening wide fissures and not only menacing groundwater but also causing millions of dollars in damage to homes, streets, utility lines, and other property. By the late 1980s and early '90s at Edwards Air Force Base, straddling the border of eastern Los Angeles and Kern counties, dozens of deep fissures had scarred the dry lake bed where the space shuttle lands, forcing the closure of one runway in January 1991 and threatening the shutdown of others. Some local officials and residents advocated conservation and slower growth as the solution, but developers opposed such "drastic decisions" and transformed the area into one of the county's largest bedroom communities.[111]

Along with continued heavy reliance on groundwater in southern California has come the pollution of aquifers. In 1986 the state Department of Health Services announced the dismaying results of a series of tests: contaminated wells were found in every southland county except one (Imperial). For some counties the news was especially distressing: of the wells tested in Los Angeles County, 40 percent were contaminated; San Bernardino County, 17 percent; Riverside County, 13 percent. In particular communities, the situation reached crisis proportions before action was taken. In El Monte, a city to the east of Los Angeles, some 750 residents in several neighborhoods served by three small water companies were told by officials in 1984 to boil their tap water before drinking it and to avoid breathing the vapors while boiling it. Two years later the residents of Glen Avon in Riverside County received notices to shift to bottled water because contamination from a toxic waste dump had polluted the aquifer from which the community was supplied. To those already suffering from what seemed to be an unusual number of illnesses, the news came as no surprise. In both El Monte and Glen Avon corrective measures were taken to restore a supply of clean water, but for other areas such action remains only a hope.[112]

Contamination was found in the aquifer underlying the densely populated San Fernando Valley, just north of downtown Los Angeles, and in the San Gabriel Valley, adjacent to Los Angeles on the northeast. The San Fernando Valley groundwater basin, the largest of four basins that constitute the aquifer and the source of 15 percent of Los Angeles's water supply, easily absorbs surface runoff, thereby helping to explain the discovery of contaminants, especially TCE (trichloroethylene) and PCE (perchloroethylene), that were first detected in 1980 in the eastern end of the aquifer near Burbank. That locale had for about a half century been a hub for Lockheed and numerous smaller aerospace firms. From there, TCE and PCE, the principal solvents for washing aircraft engines and cleaning parts, spread elsewhere in the aquifer, largely as a result of a mis-guided attempt to lessen the problem. "Because we shut off the wells [in the Burbank area] that were containing the contamina-tion," explained a Los Angeles Department of Water and Power official, "we started pulling the solvent deeper into the basin."[113]

By the mid-1980s more than half of the San Fernando basin's 112 wells exceeded the safe level for TCE and about a fourth the safe level for PCE. This was alarming for more than the extent of the pollution. More than a decade earlier TCE had been outlawed and largely replaced with PCE. The persistence and magnitude of the TCE presence years after it had been banned meant that officials were dealing with a tenacious adversary. The unsafe wells were shut down, the valley was declared a Superfund site (a designation placing it among the nation's most hazardous waste sites), and the Los Angeles Department of Water and Power was named the lead agency in cleanup efforts that included construction of four treat-ment plants by century's end with a fifth planned for completion in 2002—all paid for by the polluters. (The polluters included the federal government, which is paying half of Lockheed's assessment, since the government took control of the site during World War II and operated the facility until 1973.) These accomplishments still left more than half of the San Fernando basin's wells contaminated, but ten of them were again in service as a result of their water be-ing run through the new treatment facilities prior to distribution. Of an additional forty-eight wells in the three other basins (Sylmar, Verdugo, and Eagle Rock), twenty-seven were contaminated, with nearly all of them—some twenty-three—restored to use and their water treated. Such progress notwithstanding, great volumes of water continued unusable (130 to perhaps 200 trillion gallons) and would remain so into the foreseeable future. "If it took forty years to contaminate the basin," observed Richard Nagel, assistant watermaster for the Upper Los Angeles River Area, "it will take at least that long to clean it up."[114]

In the San Gabriel Valley, officials have spent some two decades making only minimal advances against a monumental pollution problem. In 1979 carcinogenic solvents and other deadly organic compounds released by businesses and industries were discovered in the aquifer supplying 90 percent of the water needs of the San Gabriel Valley's million residents. Twenty-five percent of the area's approximately 400 wells were shut down, and in 1984 the U.S. Environmental Protection Agency designated about 200 square miles of the valley a Superfund site.[115]

That action was unfortunately the signal for officials to haggle for years over who was responsible for the toxic mess and what kind of mechanism should be created to organize and involve local interests in the cleanup. Frustrating that task were enormous jurisdictional difficulties (three municipal water districts, forty-five private and public water companies, two watermasters, 105 water rights holders, and dozens of cities with vested interests) and the size of the aquifer (a vast subterranean lake embracing 177 square miles and extending down 4,000 to 8,000 feet). Finally, in 1990 the combatants (or at least most of them) accepted the state-created San Gabriel Basin Water Quality Authority as the agency to lead them out of chaos and toxicity. Then followed more years of finger-pointing and inaction as residents fought over the identity of the polluters who, according to EPA guidelines, had to foot the bill for the cleanup. Identification was not an easy task, for the lethal accumulations went back decades to when the San Gabriel Valley was a farming and fertilizer-using community soon joined by dairies and an influx of settlers with their household septic tanks. Then, during and following World War II, these residents were joined by millions of newcomers and nearly 50,000 businesses, many generating chemical waste.[116]

In 1997 tension escalated with the discovery of the chemical perchlorate in the aquifer supplying drinking water to three valley communities (Azusa, Irwindale, and Baldwin Park). A toxic component in rocket fuel, perchlorate can stunt growth and cause fatal anemia in adults and brain damage in fetuses. Nine wells were shut down, and because treatment methods at the time were incapable of removing the chemical, scientists rushed to develop an alternative technology before it drifted through the Whittier Narrows and into the Los Angeles River Basin. The perchlorate was traced to defense companies that used rocket fuel in the Azusa area in the 1940s, thus adding another group of polluters to those responsible for cleaning up the groundwater. EPA estimated that San Gabriel Valley cleanup costs could rise to $800 million and targeted 400 firms to pay the bill. That announcement aroused fears about the impact on the valley's economy and resistance to the technologies proposed for the cleanup. In an attempt to find a way out of the morass, the San Gabriel Basin Water Quality Authority oversaw local negotiations that in spring 1998 (*nineteen* years had now passed since pollution was first discovered) produced a plan spreading the financial burden among the public and EPA as well as the polluting businesses. As a first step in implementing that plan, especially with regards to the threat from perchlorate, local legislators in early 1999 introduced funding bills in Sacramento and Washington, D.C., on behalf of a so-called San Gabriel Basin Drinking Water Initiative. Then, later in 1999, the battle against perchlorate advanced significantly when eleven companies, under pressure of legal action by EPA, agreed to pay $200 million to remove the chemical. Such advance notwithstanding, the struggle to make safe the groundwater of the San Gabriel Valley is far from over.[117]

The subterranean basins in the western portions of nearby San Bernardino and Riverside counties have also deteriorated badly, these as a result of contaminants produced by urban sewage and cow manure from dairies. There the pollutants are salts and especially nitrates in the wastewater from some 340 dairies (home to 300,000 cows, the highest concentration of cows per acre in the world) and eight sewage treatment plants, the latter of which discharge millions of gallons of treated effluent a day into the Santa Ana River. By the 1990s half of the groundwater in the 245-square-mile Chino Basin was so contaminated with nitrates that it was undrinkable. The principal culprits were the Chino dairies, despite their allegedly being among the most regulated in the state since 1969 when a severe flood washed massive amounts of manure into residential neighborhoods. "It's too late here for prevention," declared a local water quality official in 1998, "and it's likely to get worse before it gets better."[118]

Also threatened is Orange County, which lies downstream to the southwest on the Santa Ana River and has 2 million residents who rely on groundwater supplied by the river. Besides the nitrates and other pollutants washed down from the northern counties, a serious contaminant discovered there in 1996 was MTBE (methyl tertiary butyl ether), a chemical that early tests by the U.S. Environmental Protection Agency suggested was a carcinogen. Its concentration in test wells reached as high as hundreds of thousands of parts per billion, far above the twenty to forty parts per billion considered safe by the EPA and the five parts per billion at which it can be tasted and smelled. The fear was (and is) that the chemical, detected so far only in the county's shallow groundwater supplies, will migrate into the deepest aquifers that supply drinking water to nearly half the population.[119]

Ironically, MTBE is a gasoline additive first introduced in 1979 to reduce air pollution. The principal source of the contaminant is leaking underground fuel tanks and, for reservoirs, two-stroke boat engines that can leak as much as a fourth of their fuel. Not surprisingly, its detection in Orange County was quickly followed by discoveries of the chemical in cities, towns, reservoirs, and lakes throughout the state, including Lake Tahoe where it was found as deep as ninety feet and prompted a ban on the offending engines by the local regional planning agency. Bans swiftly went into place elsewhere, with some communities following the lead of Santa Monica, which shut down affected wells and increased water rates to bring in a replacement supply. The challenge ahead is enormous, the more so because MTBE has emerged as a threat throughout the nation as a result of the federal 1990 Clean Air Act mandating its use in smoggy areas. In 1998 the Lawrence Livermore National Laboratory, confirming the worst fears, predicted that MTBE would penetrate into some of the deepest aquifers. The tab in water and dollars will likely be huge since MTBE, because of its solubility in water and long half-life, cannot now be easily removed and most treatment plants are not equipped to eliminate it. "It's a diabolical chemical. It moves up, it moves down, it moves everywhere," complained an exasperated South Lake Tahoe water official. Oil companies eventually picked up Santa Monica's $3 million annual expense for additional water, and they are currently being sued by the city to clean up the tainted supply, an action likely to be taken by similarly affected areas throughout the nation. Any cleanup costs levied against the companies will probably be passed on to consumers.[120]

Hope for eventually eliminating the problem without sacrificing air quality came in late 1998 from a team of U.C. researchers, who announced the discovery of other non-MTBE formulas that were just as effective in boosting octane and decreasing carbon monoxide emissions. The news led immediately to the introduction of legislation in California and Congress keeping the state's air pollution standards and ending the requirement for MTBE. That move, in turn, aroused fierce opposition from industrial producers of the chemical, who insisted that it was safe, and also alarm from the California Air Resources Board because of worries that deadly smog would return before a new and more effective additive could be marketed. As the debate spilled over into the next year even optimists saw no quick resolution and some predicted that a legislative ban and agreement on a new formula would still require a massive cleanup not only because of the existing damage but also because of the time needed for refineries to retool their operations and to meet market demand without creating a fuel crisis. Those speculations became a reality in March 1999 when newly elected Democratic Governor Gray Davis, responding to legislation requiring him to determine if MTBE was a hazard to humans or the environment, declared that "a significant risk to California's environment exists." He then ordered the additive eliminated from all gasoline in the state, setting as a deadline the end of 2002 and urging refiners "to step up to the plate and get this done before the deadline." A year later the Environmental Protection Agency reenforced Davis's action by invoking the Toxic Substances Control Act and issuing a nationwide ban on MTBE under a three-year phaseout plan.[121]

The pollution from businesses and industries extends to coastal waters as well as inland areas. Marinas, harbors, and storm drains regularly belch forth deadly marine-paint residues, cancer-causing PCBs (polychlorinated biphenyls), lead from the burning of leaded gasoline, toxic copper waste, raw sewage from overburdened and frequently malfunctioning city and county treatment plants, and a host of other ingredients that together make offshore water near urban areas resemble a toxic soup. Little wonder then that Santa Monica Bay, adjacent to the Los Angeles metropolitan area and once highly touted for swimming and fishing, has become one of the most polluted bodies of water in the nation.

It all began for Santa Monica Bay in 1894 with the first pipeline pouring raw sewage offshore and then worsened after 1925 when Los Angeles's newly built Hyperion sewage-treatment plant provided virtually no "treatment" before dumping raw waste a mile into the bay. The resulting sewage plume led to beach closures in the 1930s and '40s until a new plant, completed in 1950, brought a reprieve. That ended when renewed pollution sparked a fight between the city and federal health officials seeking to enforce the 1972 Clean Water Act that lasted twenty-six years until the city, only in 1998, finally began providing full secondary treatment—in other words, more enhanced treatment—of all wastewater entering the ocean. This still left Los Angeles County's Carson plant, which processes nearly as much sewage as Hyperion, free to use only primary treatment until 2002. Moreover, even with Hyperion committed to secondary treatment, problems persisted during heavy rains when the city's sewer pipes, too small to take the runoff, continued to overflow and send raw sewage into storm drains and into the bay.[122]

By the late 1990s urban runoff, especially storm-drain water during the rainy season from November to April, had become a greater source of contaminants than treated wastewater. A UCLA School of Public Health study released in 1993 and another now under way found 186 chemicals, many of them known or suspected carcinogens, entering the bay daily through storm drains releasing 60 million gallons a day of untreated runoff in dry years (like 1984 with nine inches of rainfall) and 2.3 billion gallons during wet El Niño periods (as in 1983 with thirty-four inches of precipitation).[123] For coastal waters, as with toxic substances in farming areas, banning a deadly chemical does not eliminate it from the environment. In 1998 the U.S. Environmental Protection Agency, while noting improvement in the health of waters all along the southern California coast over the preceding twenty years (largely due to the efforts of such organizations as Santa Monica Bay Restoration Project, Heal the Bay, Santa Monica BayKeeper, and the Southern California Coastal Water Research Project), nonetheless reported the presence of contaminants in 89 percent of the sand and mud offshore. DDT, outlawed in 1972, remained the most prevalent poison and, along with PCBs, was widespread in fish and considerably above safe concentrations in white croaker, a commonly caught and eaten fish in the bay. Banning DDT had diminished the chemical's presence enough to save the brown pelican and other birds but had not reduced it to a safe level in the aquatic environment. The EPA report gave Santa Monica Bay the overall lowest marks for healthy water, since the "extent and magnitude of sediment contamination was greater [there] . . . than in other [coastal] regions" studied.[124]

Hope for improvement came in January 1999 when the EPA, as a result of a lawsuit filed by environmentalists, announced plans to set pollution limits on all rivers, creeks, storm drains, and wastewater treatment facilities emptying into the ocean along the coastline of Los Angeles and Ventura counties. The ambitious plan was two decades overdue, since the federal Clean Water Act had mandated that such pollution standards be set by 1979. The goal now was to identify and regulate each polluter of the more than 130 waterways reaching the coast. The downside of the announcement was an admission that it would take thirteen years to implement the program because of inadequate EPA funding. Lessening somewhat the impact of this delay was the decision a short time later of Los Angeles city and county to divert the waters of the most polluted storm drains in their areas into existing sewage treatment systems by 2002. Good news? Not quite, for that decision still left the less offensive (yet nevertheless unhealthful) drains pouring their contents year-round onto beaches and into coastal waters. More seriously, the *most polluted* drains would continue emptying their effluent into coastal waters during the rainy winter months when the undersize and defective sewer pipes were incapable of accommodating the heavier runoff—and when surfers in great numbers inhabit the ocean in their chill-reducing (but not pollution proof) wet suits.[125]

But the reality, as affirmed by new genetic-test findings released in September 1999, was a serious threat to public health throughout the seasons. Dangerous human viruses, reported scientists at the University of Southern California's Wrigley Institute for Environmental Studies, were fouling southern California coastal waters and numerous beaches year-round. A gallon of sewage spilling onto a beach typically contained viruses for as many as 125 human diseases ranging from hepatitis and diarrhea to the common cold. Scientists remained uncertain about the concentration of viruses or bacteria required to produce illness, but an earlier study of almost 10,500 people at three Santa Monica Bay beaches with a high density of swimmers (Santa Monica, Will Rogers, and Surfrider) revealed that nearly 30 percent of those individuals swimming within 400 yards of a storm drain became sick with gastrointestinal illnesses. Of the 3,554 subjects who swam within 50 yards of a drain where viruses were known to be present, all came down with various illnesses. Heightening concern was the knowledge that viruses, unlike bacteria, do not die off quickly and many, including hepatitis, can survive for months. The new genetic-test findings reveal "a

Ballona Creek storm drain, which empties into Santa Monica Bay, with the small flow typical of dry weather visible at the bottom of the photograph. (Courtesy of Michael K. Stenstrom, University of California, Los Angeles)

different dynamic in the ocean," observed Wrigley Institute director Anthony Michaels, "and you know it's a health risk."[126]

Southern California's problems were not unique. During 1997 there were 1,141 beach closures or advisories statewide brought on by pollutants. Los Angeles County officials took 39 such actions; San Diego County, 173; Santa Barbara County, 238; and Orange County, a whopping 319; while in northern California, San Mateo County issued 223 similar orders, and San Francisco County, 101. It is important to remember that a local beach closure seldom results in great stretches of coastline being off-limits. Only about 4 percent of "beach miles" are closed on average and those areas, understandably, are near storm drains, especially during the rainy season. Still, many of California's most popular beaches are those most frequently closed, with some portions restricted throughout the year. The issue is national, though California stands among the

Ballona Creek storm drain during a heavy rain. (Courtesy of Michael K. Stenstrom, University of California, Los Angeles)

pollution leaders with 25 percent of the 1997 closures. It has since gotten worse. The seriousness of the state's difficulty received dramatic reenforcement the following year when the closures/advisories more than doubled to 3,273, forty-five percent of the national total, an increase attributed to stricter monitoring and the heavy El Niño rains of 1998. But in 1999, a near-drought La Niña year, California's closures/advisories climbed to a record 3,547, more than half the national total of 6,160. In the lead were Santa Barbara County with 1,392 postings; San Diego County, 685; Orange County, 502; and Los Angeles County, 460—all of which is a sharp reminder of the foot-dragging of local, state, and federal governments in eradicating the abysmal coastal pollution problem.[127]

That reminder helped force the completion of an embarrassingly long overdue pollution-control plan for the entire California coastline. The plan, finally released in December 1999 after four years of bickering between the state Water Resources Control Board and the state Coastal Commission over its content, happily exceeded ex-

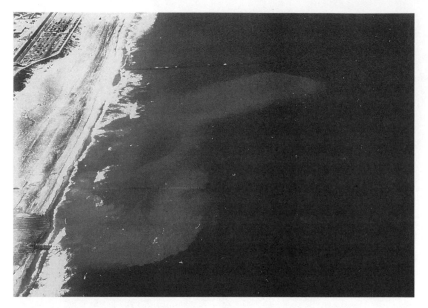

A storm-drain plume off the coast of southern California. (Courtesy of Michael K. Stenstrom, University of California, Los Angeles)

pectations in one respect: rather than dealing only with the coastal zone, as required by law, it called for standards statewide on the reasonable theory that what occurs in the mountains, foothills, and valleys can affect coastal water quality. Also boosting proponents' spirits was the federal EPA's approval of the plan in August 2000 and an award to the state of $10.5 million to get the program under way. On the other hand, the plan attracted critics for failing to set precise water-quality standards or specific deadlines for reducing pollution. Its effectiveness was further compromised by the state's failure to develop a more meaningful water monitoring system than the current one, which regularly tests only 9 percent of rivers and streams.[128] Such realities indicate that eradication of pollution along the coast—and everywhere else, for that matter—will require a more aroused public willing to press vigorously for action and, especially, to control its own unhealthful littering and dumping of toxic wastes.

Also as seriously threatened in southern California as in the Bay

Area and numerous other locales in the state are wetlands, a resource vital to flood control, water quality, and species survival by providing wildlife habitat and breeding grounds. Although, as noted earlier, more than 90 percent of the state's original wetlands have been lost, the destruction in Los Angeles County has been an even higher 94 percent. Urbanization, especially in the twentieth century, has been the principal cause of their disappearance through dikes to divert elsewhere their water supply and then construction on the dried-out soil of roads, railroads, oil wells, houses, businesses, and marinas, among the typical southern California examples. Any wetlands that survive this process are a fraction of their earlier size and frequently act as a sponge absorbing all sorts of illnesses. Ballona Wetlands on Los Angeles's west side have shrunk from their original 2,000 acres to today's less than 200 acres. The destruction of the Malibu wetlands and lagoon, more shielded from development by the rugged coastline and the immediately adjacent Santa Monica Mountains, has been less dramatic. Still, construction of the Pacific Coast Highway and upstream dams, horse ranches, and residential and retail development (and their attendant and frequently malfunctioning septic systems) have produced significant loss of wetlands. That loss diminished the wetlands' capacity to filter out pollutants, resulting in high bacteria counts at Malibu's world-famous Surfrider Beach and often illness for those who brave the area.[129]

Decades of governmental winking at the law also help explain the degraded condition of the aquifers underlying the Los Angeles, Riverside, and San Bernardino areas. So contaminated had they become by the late 1980s that the Metropolitan Water District and an old nemesis, the Environmental Defense Fund, joined forces to study ways to eliminate the toxins. Influencing MWD's decision was the realization that the traditional escape for not seriously dealing with pollution—building a massive new project—had become less likely in the wake of the Peripheral Canal defeat. Moreover, the cost of importing water from northern California and the Colorado River was by 1990 four to six times greater than obtaining an equivalent volume of groundwater. The alternative lay in cleaning up the available groundwater, acknowledged the MWD general manager, so as to meet the "demands for more surface water."[130]

Some wells have been cleaned, but the number is small and the methods remain experimental. Others have been shut down because the costs of restoration were prohibitive and the goal was decades away, and even then not assured. Expense and uncertainty prompted Beverly Hills to abandon its wells and spend up to five times more to bring in water from elsewhere. Federal officials studying the San Gabriel Valley problem acknowledged that the aquifers there may never be completely cleaned and that their best efforts may only stem the present contamination.[131]

The net result has been just a dent in pollution but there has been increased water use, some of it in the form of bottled water demanded by people who do not trust anything coming from a tap. By the late 1980s in southern California, one of three homes was using bottled water as the principal source of drinking water as compared with one in seventeen in the United States as a whole. Studies like the one released by the state Department of Health Services in 1988 suggesting an "unusually low" miscarriage rate for women drinking bottled water only intensified this trend, and a year later a survey revealed that two-thirds of Los Angeles's water customers were using filtration devices or bottled water. Department of Water and Power officials attributed the findings to unwarranted public distrust, but their explanation seemed unconvincing to many when a companion survey found that DWP employees themselves were nearly as likely to depend upon filtered or bottled water. The trend was not confined to the southland, for during the 1990s bottled water consumption nationwide increased a stunning 300 percent. Californians at that decade's end were consuming some 230 million gallons of bottled water, making them the number one U.S. imbibers, accounting for more than a fourth of such water consumed nationally.[132]

Concern over municipal water escalated with the release in early 1998 of a large-scale study sponsored by the U.S. Environmental Protection Agency, which revealed that women who drank five or more glasses daily of chlorinated tap water increased their risk of miscarriage in the first trimester. Local and state health departments found the news especially troubling because doctors frequently counseled pregnant women to drink lots of fluids. Chlorine aids water purification and kills an array of bacteria, but it also contains the contaminant THM (trihalomethane), already long suspected as a human carcinogen, which at the level found in many municipal supplies sparked the concern expressed in the study. Alarmed city officials warned pregnant women to boil water or, better yet, use an activated-charcoal filter. The Metropolitan Water District responded in 1998 with plans to substitute a more expensive ozone/carbon filtration process for chlorine treatment, with construction and retrofitting taking place over the next decade. In the meantime, EPA launched follow-up studies and many additional people joined the move to bottled water, though some did so with trepidation because such water contained insufficient amounts of tooth decay–fighting flouride and because of growing concern over the adequacy of quality standards in producing the water. That concern escalated in early 1999 when the Natural Resources Defense Council released test results of 103 brands of bottled water: a third of them contained bacteria and chemical contaminants that exceeded both government and industry standards.[133]

Subsidized Agriculture and Social Inequity

J UST AS problems of pollution have persisted, indeed, intensified, in recent years, so, too, has the resilience of agribusiness. The criticism during the fight over the Peripheral Canal of corporate agriculture's success in obtaining highly subsidized water had the ironic effect of persuading many people in high government positions that reclamation law should not be enforced but rather changed to recognize the current reality. In 1982 President Reagan's administration and corporate-farm interests nationally pressured Congress into increasing the acreage limitation from 160 acres to 960 acres—a move supported by waffling "environmentalist" Governor Jerry Brown. In addition, the residency requirement was eliminated. This represented a major victory in a decades-old battle for big agriculture whose most telling argument, especially in the hands of the highly sympathetic Reagan administration, was that the law had been effectively ignored for years. For Republicans to whom business prosperity constituted the lodestar of their political culture, the time had long passed for changing an ineffectual law—but a law which, if it remained on the statute books, might be enforced by a future administration. There were still many small farms in California (two-thirds of them were a hundred acres or less), but 80 percent of the farmland was in holdings of over a thousand acres and 10 percent of the farms accounted for 75 percent of the production and income. Under the new legislation, farms larger than 960 acres would no longer receive subsidized water but would have to pay "full cost."[134]

The concept of the family farm, long a sham, could now be declared officially dead. Nearly a half century earlier, as mentioned previously, a young anthropologist, Walter Goldschmidt, had studied the effect of farm size on the social and economic life of two San Joaquin Valley communities of about equal population (Dinuba and Arvin). Dinuba, unlike Arvin, was surrounded by small irrigated farms and had many more small businesses; a higher and more balanced distribution of income; more churches, newspapers, and community service organizations; and fewer migrant laborers.[135] In the late 1970s Dean MacCannell of the University of California at Davis canvassed conditions in five rural communities in the vicinity of the Westlands Water District (WWD), consisting of large holdings (the average farm size was 4,640 acres when water first arrived in 1968) whose owners lived elsewhere. His study, commissioned by the Reclamation Bureau and completed in 1980, reported discoveries even more dismaying than Goldschmidt's: "We have found . . . some of the worst poverty conditions (over 50 percent of the population live below the federal poverty line in some areas of the

WWD) found anywhere in the State of California. We have also found some of the lowest levels of educational attainment for both white and nonwhite populations anywhere in the State of California. . . . The median years of education completed is about 7th grade for the entire population of the study area, and about 5th grade for the Spanish surname population," which constituted "an absolute and growing majority of the population." MacCannell also noted that median family incomes were decidedly lower than those for families outside his study area: "$3,000 lower than the rest of Fresno County and $2,500 lower than the other rural areas of Fresno County." As for housing, the homes were "overcrowded and substandard when compared to the surrounding area." His only "positive" observation concerned the almost complete absence of unemployment, hardly a redeeming feature when set against a picture of crushing misery.[136]

Findings like those of MacCannell received no public notice, though they created a great stir in the Reclamation Bureau, which cut his report into so many pieces that it disappeared when incorporated into the environmental impact statement on the Reagan administration bill, noted previously, to increase the acreage limitation. Upset, MacCannell and a colleague pulled the pieces back together, added some additional material, and in 1984 published the results. By then, however, the new law was already two years old.[137]

Though agribusiness was generally pleased with the victory, those with holdings in excess of 960 acres were not satisfied and they began pressing the Reclamation Bureau to continue its old practice of circumventing the law. Neither Ronald Reagan nor his Republican successor, George Bush, found reason to object. First, Westlands Water District, not only the largest (at 650,000 acres in the late 1980s) but also among the most heavily subsidized in the nation, obtained a waiver from the Bureau on the grounds that it had a contract with the government good until the year 2007 for the old subsidized rate. For Westlands, this meant the difference between paying $17 an acre-foot and $42 an acre-foot. Then in 1987 the Reclamation Bureau delivered a gift to all corporate farmers. It concluded that holdings in excess of the 960-acre limit could continue to receive subsidized water so long as they were part of a "farm management arrangement." It was, as one critic observed, "the old leasing arrangement under a different name." Now large farms could qualify for subsidized water by dividing their holdings into trusts or partnerships of 960 acres or less. There was an outpouring of public disapproval. "Perpetuation of this program under the bureau's new regulations," observed the *Los Angeles Times,* reflecting the growing disenchantment of southern California's cities with underwriting agribusiness, "continues to subsidize a privileged group of farmers and aggravates the problem of allocating California's limited water resources in a rational fashion. It is time to stop winking at the law." [138]

The winking continued into the next year when the contracts signed forty years earlier for Central Valley Project water in the eastern San Joaquin Valley came up for renewal. The Reclamation Bureau announced that it intended to renew those with twenty-eight districts (providing 1.5 million acre-feet, about twice the amount then consumed by the city of Los Angeles) for a second forty-year period for the same amount of water. Critics blasted the decision as "crazy," a "mockery," and a violation of the national Environmental Policy Act, the Clean Water Act, and other legislation calling for a review of the expected environmental impact before granting any renewal. The Natural Resources Defense Council filed suit demanding a review, while the Environmental Protection Agency pointed to the implications of the decision for the long-standing bay-delta problem and asked the President to provide for arbitration. Urban areas also ripped the proposed action, claiming that much of the water could better serve the needs of the state's burgeoning cities. However, the Secretary of the Interior, citing a departmental legal opinion prepared by a former attorney for a Fresno agribusiness firm, replied that he was "morally and legally bound" to renew the contracts—a decision tantamount to assuring the farmers water into perpetuity—and he began renewing them.

Further protests and a challenge to the Secretary's reasoning from the White House Council on Environmental Quality led in late November 1989 to agreement by the George Bush administration to prepare an environmental impact statement but only *after* the contracts had been renewed. "That is about like holding the barn door open for the horse to escape and then studying the padlock to see if it met specifications," complained critics.[139]

Such criticisms persisted and aroused increasingly vocal demands for reform as the public became more aware of the inequities of technical compliance during the late 1980s and early 1990s. Dean MacCannell and other researchers reaffirmed the devastating effect of large-scale farm operations on nearby communities. MacCannell, in a particularly graphic 1986 study of eighty-five towns throughout the irrigated areas of the Central Valley, reported results similar to his earlier Westlands findings: "The relationships are all negative: as farm size increases the quality of community life decreases."[140]

Long-time observers also noted that as agriculture became increasingly large and industrialized, farmland, water, and crops became increasingly contaminated, not only posing a threat to the public but also harming wildlife, rivers, and fish. Equally telling, the subsidized water provided to farmers allowed them to purchase these supplies at a fraction of the cost charged urban residents. By 1990 growers were paying between $2.50 and $19.31 an acre-foot for untreated water from the federal Central Valley Project and $62 an acre-foot for untreated water from the State Water Project. The Metropolitan Water District of Southern California, on the other hand, was paying $123 for an untreated acre-foot of state water (exclusive of an additional $82 for energy to pump it down to and over the Tehachapis). The cheaper agricultural water also continued to go in enormous quantities to farmers growing some crops declared to be in surplus and yet also eligible for additional subsidies from the federal government's price-support program. The result, as in earlier years, was heavy water use by crops that produced little return. The four California crops consuming the most water (irrigated pasture, alfalfa, cotton, and rice) accounted for half of the state's water use while contributing less than 1 percent to the state's economy. All of which in 1990 prompted the director of the University of California's Water Resources Center to observe: "We've still got plenty of water. It's just misallocated." [141]

That reality, especially during the drought years of 1987–1992, was not lost on environmentalists or politically savvy government officeholders. Eliminating agriculture's excesses, they believed, was the key to meeting the demands of growing cities and to restoring and protecting wilderness areas, rivers, wildlife, and fish. To transfer at least some farm water to these other needs, however, meant grappling with formidable obstacles: the growers' traditional resistance to reform and the existence of legal institutions that tied water to the land and prohibited or made extraordinarily difficult its use elsewhere.

Water Marketing: Hope, Threat, and Challenge

TO FOSTER greater cooperation among the state's numerous water districts and other agencies and also to discourage wasteful practices, the legislature in the 1980s passed a series of laws authorizing the transfer (through sale, lease, or exchange) of water rights so long as other users and the environment were not adversely affected. The hope was that this action would eventually lead to an open market in which water would go to the highest bidders and ostensibly to "higher-value uses": specialty crops, industries, cities. Advocates realized that such a market reallocation would be difficult to achieve so long as agriculture remained heavily subsidized, and even if one should develop, its impact on wildlife, the environment, and the economies of rural communities could be devastating if the public failed to demand adequate protection. Among those most at risk in a market reallocation were the many small farm communities of the San Joaquin Valley whose residents were primarily Latino farmworkers

(230,000 people annually still labored in agriculture in the mid-1990s) and their dependents. With low incomes and little education, they were (and are) ill-equipped to deal with the challenges of water marketing and have been overlooked by the government agencies and environmental groups pushing for and involved in such change.[142]

The first significant example of water-marketing's promise (though not technically an example of marketing) occurred in the drought year of 1991 when the governor created within the Department of Water Resources a "water bank." The state purchased water for $125 an acre-foot from those farmers who had it to sell and then resold it for $175 (in order to cover administrative costs) to hard-pressed cities as well as to farmers producing high-profit crops. Initial purchases by the state proved disappointing. Some farmers were denied permission to sell by local irrigation districts, while others feared taking an action that might jeopardize their rights in the future. Still others held out because the state's water bank was not an example of true water marketing: selling water in an open market to the highest bidder. The state was the *only* bidder and it had a set price: take it or leave it. Many farmers opted out in the belief that they could force the state to double or triple its price. When heavy rains in March 1991 reduced (but did not eliminate) the demand for emergency supplies, enough farmers, now worried that the governor might cancel the program, changed their minds to allow the state to purchase some 820,000 acre-feet. Though short of the state's goal of a million acre-feet, this was still an impressive figure, more than the amount that Los Angeles was then using in a normal year. The state was sufficiently impressed to extend the water bank's life on an annual "as-needed basis."[143]

A major barrier to an open market for water in the 1980s and early 1990s lay with the federal government. Although users within a federal project could exchange water among themselves—and had done so for years—they could not engage in transfers with others. Unlike California, Washington still prohibited farmers supplied, for example, from the Central Valley Project (and those farmers used the greatest percentage of federal water in the state) from transferring their supplies outside the project's boundaries. Another obstacle to transfers lay in the scores of water districts scattered throughout the state, especially those in agricultural areas. These districts tended to have rules prohibiting the transfer of water beyond their jurisdictions. It was their way of assuring the availability of a supply adequate enough to maintain the viability of their local economies. Working through the powerful Association of California Water Agencies, they had successfully resisted even those state legislative attempts to offer economic and environmental protections in exchange for allowing individuals with more water than they needed to sell to customers outside a district. The attitude of the districts: No veto, no sale.[144]

That view conflicted directly with the desires of the state's major urban areas. In the fall of 1991, the Metropolitan Water District, in a landmark reversal of long-standing policy, publicly announced its opposition to the veto, thereby angering agricultural interests with which it had often teamed in the past to push new water projects. MWD's policy reversal was a recognition of its failure to meet its 1952 Laguna Declaration promise to supply all the needs of its member agencies. Earlier in the drought year of 1991 it had cut deliveries by a third and now, against the background of the court loss to Arizona, the setbacks in the Mono Basin and Owens Valley, and the defeat of the Peripheral Canal, MWD faced the likelihood of cutting allocations even in wet years. "We got nervous about the future," stated MWD general manager Carl Boronkay. "We didn't see any major projects coming on line."[145]

Under Boronkay's leadership the giant agency swung slowly around to seeing its salvation in transforming a decades-old ally into a target. It set its sights on a portion of the 83 percent of the state's water then going to agriculture, focusing initially on two lush prizes: the Central Valley Project with nearly 30 percent of the state's developed water and the Imperial Irrigation District, the nation's largest such district with rights to more of the Colorado River than any other agency in the basin. Boronkay made no apologies for the

Diamond Valley Lake. (Courtesy of Metropolitan Water District of Southern California)

decision. "We all like farmers, we grow up drawing crayon pictures of farmers. But there is no way . . . people are going to be denied water while farmers are spraying it on alfalfa and rice. . . . I'm laying it on the line . . . because if we don't get moving, we could be in real jeopardy."[146]

So confident was Boronkay that he ordered plans for an enormous new reservoir to hold his anticipated purchases as well as to bank whatever excess Colorado River and northern California water became available during wet years. He settled on the Domenigoni and Diamond valleys, near Hemet in southwestern Riverside County, as the site, and for about $2.25 billion, MWD transformed them into Diamond Valley Lake, which, when completed in 1999, had a capacity of 800,000 acre-feet—nearly double that of all southern California's reservoirs combined and enough to fill 1,700 Rose Bowls.[147] At the same time, Boronkay set out to change the rules of the water game so that cities could use their great resources (taxes and bonds) to seduce farmers into parting with their water. Now

The Salton Sea, Imperial Valley, and Mexicali Valley. The Imperial Valley's irrigated field patterns are visible near the center of the photograph, while the Mexicali Valley lies below the easily identified U.S.-Mexico border where the cultivated field patterns change dramatically. (Courtesy of the National Aeronautics and Space Administration)

began a case study in the hopes, complexities, and battles generated by the promise of water marketing.

The Imperial Valley, MWD, and the Market

To understand MWD's water-marketing tactics and struggles in the Imperial Valley one need only look at the valley's inefficient and wasteful water-delivery system and farming practices. The eighty-

mile-long All-American Canal and the nearly thirty-five-mile extension to the northwest (the Coachella Branch) were unlined and
lost enormous amounts of water to seepage. Even larger volumes
were lost to leaks in canal gates, inefficient laterals, and excessive
surface irrigation producing wasteful amounts of "tail water." The
preventable losses were estimated at 350,000 to 400,000 acre-feet,
enough to meet the annual needs of approximately 3 million city
dwellers. The losses along the All-American Canal moved south
into an underground aquifer straddling the U.S.-Mexico border,
while those resulting from on-farm irrigation practices flowed
north into the Salton Sea and contributed to a national environmental embarrassment.[148]

The Salton Sea, California's largest lake at thirty-five miles long
and nine to fifteen miles wide, had been a recurring phenomenon
for thousands of years as a result of Colorado River flooding. Its latest appearance came with the engineering blunder of 1905–1907
that reintroduced floodwaters into the Salton Sink, transforming
the area over the next several decades into a major stopover on the
Pacific Flyway. More than 1.5 million birds and 380 bird species (5 of
them endangered) annually visited this resting place, made increasingly crucial by the destruction of other stopovers along the flyway
by developers. By the 1960s and on into the 1980s the Salton Sea
had also become the state's most productive inland recreational
fishery. All that changed as agricultural drainage from the Imperial
Valley and raw sewage from Mexico (by way of the New and Alamo
rivers) not only polluted watercourses and the sea but also, because
evaporation is the only outlet, increased the sea's salinity and
raised the water level, damaging shoreline property.[149]

By the mid-1980s and into the 2000s the Salton Sea had become
a pitiful caricature of its earlier self. The sport fishery fell into sharp
decline while massive bird and fish die-offs, beginning as early as
the 1970s and attracting millions of flies in the spring and summer,
became ever more devastating and frequent. Over 150,000 eared
grebes died in 1992 from an undiagnosed cause; more than 15,000
birds were killed in a botulism outbreak in 1996, including 1,400 endangered California brown pelicans and more than 10 percent of all

American white pelicans in the West (the largest die-off on record of pelicans in the United States); Newcastle disease wiped out an entire colony of double-crested cormorants in 1997; and many thousands more birds died in numerous other documented events. Although scientists explained much about the avian deaths, a great deal remained a mystery into the new century. Concurrent with the bird die-offs, fish were perishing in huge numbers during epidemics and continuous episodes that left their corpses littering the shoreline. Suspected culprits in the fish die-offs were salinity and agricultural runoff, especially phosphorous and nitrogen. Studies of the sea found no evidence of bacteria harmful to humans and only minimal presence of pesticides and other toxic substances. The explanation for this better-than-expected condition—and the reason for foul conditions along portions of the waterways reaching the sea—lay in the natural cleansing of the water as it traveled up to fifty miles from farms, municipalities, and industries. On the other hand, the steady increase in phosphorous, nitrogen, and especially salts (the Salton Sea was by this time 25 percent more saline than ocean water and getting ever saltier) depleted the sea of oxygen. As a consequence, fish died by the millions and algal blooms proliferated, filling the air with the putrid smell of rotten eggs.[150]

The wildlife blight spurred public agencies such as the U.S. Fish and Wildlife Service, the Biological Resources Division of the U.S. Geological Survey, the Salton Sea Authority, and the California Department of Fish and Game to scramble for scarce funds to study and end the disaster, while, even earlier, state officials moved to stop the Imperial Valley's wasting of water. In 1984, the California Water Resources Control Board, responding to citizen complaints, found the Imperial Irrigation District, the agency that held the valley's water rights in trust, guilty of unreasonable water practices and ordered it to devise a conservation plan. Four years later the district presented a plan, but cited financial hardship in not being able to carry it out. The board promptly told the district to fund it anyway or enter into an "agreement with another entity willing to fund it."[151] This set the stage for a shotgun marriage of sorts.

Enter as suitor the Metropolitan Water District of Southern California. MWD had been trying for several years to arrange a deal like that suggested by the Water Resources Control Board. It was willing to pay for Imperial's mandated conservation measures in exchange for the water that would be saved. Talks foundered at first because of Imperial's insistence on money as well as on an overhauled delivery system. Some Imperial officials also objected to surrendering any water on the grounds that getting it back in the future would be a practical impossibility.[152] A side issue hovering over the talks emerged in protests from Mexico about the impact on that country of any improvements to the All-American Canal.

The seepage from the canal going into the aquifer straddling the border fed wells that 675 Mexican farmers used for irrigating some 33,000 acres in the Mexicali Valley, one of the most fertile and productive areas in that nation. American water interests and the State Department answered Mexico's protests with insistence that the United States had a right to conserve its own water, a response that prompted Mexico to threaten action in the World Court on the grounds that its long use of the water—twenty-five years—gave it a legal (under the principle of "abandonment") and moral right to the supply.[153]

Publicly the United States refused to budge, citing the U.S.-Mexico Water Treaty of 1944 as putting a firm cap on Mexico's share of the Colorado River. Privately, however, it entered into negotiations aimed at resolving the dispute. In talks that are still under way, the two sides are exploring such remedies as allowing Mexico to take some of its Colorado River water through the All-American Canal once its seepage problem has been eliminated. This would mean not only a better-quality supply for Mexico (because the water would be taken from a point farther upstream), but also a larger supply (since Mexico currently loses much water in its own unlined delivery canal).[154] The final outcome of the dispute is unclear, but the possibility of an international donnybrook remains, the more so because of Mexico's extraordinary population growth along the

Dead pelicans, gathered for disposal in an incinerator, following a die-off at the Salton Sea in August 1996. (Courtesy of the Salton Sea National Wildlife Refuge)

border and because some Mexican officials have long sought a pretext to force renegotiation of the 1944 treaty and increase their country's share of water from the Colorado River. These issues held (and hold) the potential for adversely affecting any transfer of Imperial Valley water.

In the meantime, MWD and the Imperial Irrigation District pushed ahead in what turned out to be a successful search for agreement. MWD offered to satisfy Imperial's demand for cash (for capital and operational expenses) so long as the price of the water did not exceed—indeed, remained below—the cost for State Water Project deliveries south of the Tehachapis (at the time $249 an acre-foot inclusive of power charges to get the water over the mountains). That flexibility—together with the mandate given Imperial by the Water Resources Control Board, a class-action suit against Imperial by Salton Sea property owners, an expensive out-of-court settlement with one such owner, and Imperial's failure to obtain a better offer from the San Diego County Water Authority—led to a

Fish die-off at the Salton Sea, August 1998. (Courtesy of Milton Friend, Executive Director, Salton Sea Science Subcommittee)

deal in late 1988 (renegotiated in some particulars and finalized in December 1989).[155]

The agreement, a landmark achievement as the first of its kind, called for a pilot project to conserve an estimated minimum of 100,000 acre-feet annually (the actual amount in 1999 was 108,500 acre-feet) that would go to MWD for thirty-five years and, if not terminated by either party, would continue. In exchange, MWD contracted to "pay the costs of a water conservation program" consisting of sixteen projects (at an estimated price of $100 million) and to compensate the valley for lost hydroelectric revenues from reduced water use. Imperial pegged the cost of water at $128 an acre-foot. Congress in 1988 registered its approval by authorizing the

A polluted irrigation canal in the Imperial Valley, 1992. (Courtesy of California Department of Water Resources)

water-conservation efforts (necessary because the government held title to the All-American Canal).[156]

One major snag delayed action on the agreement (and it would reappear to haunt later water-marketing efforts in the Imperial Valley). The Coachella Valley, located just north of the Imperial Valley, filed a lawsuit to quash the transfer. This hostile action by the Coachella Valley Water District had its origins in the 1931 allocations of Colorado River water to California cities and agriculture (popularly known as the Seven Party Agreement). Of the state's share of 4.4 million acre-feet, MWD (representing urban southern California) received 550,000 acre-feet and agriculture obtained 3.85 million acre-feet. Problems arose almost immediately among some farmers because no *specific* allocations were made to the four principal agriculture groups: Palo Verde Irrigation District, Yuma Project (California division), Imperial Irrigation District, and Coachella Valley Water District. Instead, their water was apportioned according to a less-than-satisfactory "priority" system with the first priority going to Palo Verde, the oldest water user on the river (aside from the Indians), and a second priority to the next oldest, the Yuma Project. Both were small operations, using among them about 420,000 acre-feet and leaving the bulk of the water, as a third priority, for the Imperial and Coachella valleys.[157]

Hardly any time passed before Imperial and Coachella were wrangling over their rights, with Coachella especially upset about Imperial's plans to develop new acreage outside its service area. That led to a 1934 settlement limiting Imperial's right "exclusively for [water] use in [its] . . . Service Area." Tense relations nonetheless persisted as Imperial, citing its longtime uses that predated those of the Coachella Valley, claimed prior rights to most of the water, using approximately 3.1 million acre-feet. Coachella chafed at its "last man" position that left it with only 330,000 acre-feet and worried about its increasingly heavy reliance on groundwater to meet its growing needs, overdrafting that source by as much as 200,000 acre-feet annually and threatening to exhaust its aquifer.[158]

Coachella's anger at the proposed Imperial Valley–MWD agreement was straightforward and intense: Water that it desperately needed was about to go elsewhere. To Coachella, the Imperial Valley had forfeited its right to any conserved water because the right extended only to water used in its service area, not in MWD's service area. Moreover, state and federal water law required uses to be "reasonable and beneficial." Since the state Water Resources Control Board had found the valley guilty of "wasting hundreds of thousands of acre feet of water," declared Coachella, it possessed no right to reclaimed water and hence could not sell it to MWD. Rather, such water belonged to Coachella as the next claimant in line. Everyone knew that litigation could go on for years with no one getting anything but legal bills, so an openness to compromise permeated the sharp bickering. For its efforts, Coachella in 1989 got an out-of-court settlement for half of the water expected to be conserved (that is, 50,000 acre-feet) when it could not otherwise obtain an equivalent amount from surplus flows in the Colorado River. The arrangement freed MWD to spend the next ten years implementing its conservation program, save for lining the All-American Canal, a task to which we will return later.[159]

The Imperial Valley, MWD, San Diego, and the Market

MWD left the negotiations with the Imperial Irrigation District confident that the pilot program would lead to a second agreement to reclaim the remaining water lost through inefficient farming. To MWD's chagrin, Imperial Valley landowners began experiencing "seller's remorse" and complaining that the deal had been a give-away. Their suspicion grew to a conviction after 1993 when Edward and Lee Bass, multimillionaire brothers based in Texas, began purchasing or acquiring options on thousands of acres of valley farmland (45,000 acres by the late 1990s) for which agriculture was hardly even a secondary consideration to them. The land, put in the name of the brothers' Western Farms company, came with rights to water that cost them $12.50 an acre-foot and which they planned to sell for all the market would bear—at least $400 an acre-foot. When they approached MWD with a water deal, the agency rejected it as too expensive. They then turned to Las Vegas, which sent them packing for the same reason. When they next sounded out the San Diego County Water Authority, they seemed to strike pay dirt.[160]

The Bass brothers' negotiations with San Diego took place in secret so as not to arouse opposition or troublesome complications with MWD, Imperial Valley residents, or other nearby water agencies (Coachella Valley Water District and Palo Verde Irrigation District) whose interests might not be in harmony with theirs. The brothers boasted to San Diego officials that the Imperial Irrigation District would pose no problem since they had "done a thorough job politically" in bringing its board of directors into their camp. They emphasized the need to cement a deal "as quickly as possible" so as to outmaneuver "inefficient, overstaffed, bureaucratic" MWD with a "partial fait accompli," making it difficult for the agency to thwart them. The brothers' plan was to invite as many valley farmers as were interested to join in the agreement (the hope was to generate up to 500,000 acre-feet through farmland fallowing), have San Diego pay for the water with an equity investment in their Western Farms, and then, in a series of complicated legal maneuvers, obtain title in San Diego's name to the valley's perfected rights to Colorado River water. It was a mind-boggling scheme even to those who dreamed it up.[161]

San Diego County officials decided against the proposal. They questioned the legal soundness of the plan and doubted that the Imperial Irrigation District's board of directors would ever alienate the valley's water rights. Moreover, why cut a deal with the Bass brothers when an agreement with the district would be less complicated? San Diegans now took the commonsense approach of inviting the district to the bargaining table. That move lessened but did not eliminate the Bass brothers' influence, for they remained the valley's largest landowners and had a personal contact with the irrigation district—its general manager was their former water-marketing consultant and he was widely thought to owe his current job to them.[162]

Spurring San Diego officials' drive to a water deal when earlier, it will be recalled, they had rejected an overture from the Imperial Valley subsequently accepted by MWD, were several powerful considerations: the inadequacy of its water supply and its decades-old resentment of being in the shadow of Los Angeles. San Diego had a rivalry with Los Angeles going back to the nineteenth century. Blessed by a natural harbor, San Diegans had seen themselves destined to dominate the southland as San Franciscans did northern California until Los Angeles grabbed the lead with its railroad connections, an engineered harbor at San Pedro, and water from the Owens Valley. San Diegans, strapped especially by their lack of appreciable surface and groundwater, then pinned their hopes on a pipeline of their own to bring in Colorado River water, but World War II intervened and dashed their hopes. In 1944 President Franklin Roosevelt, citing the national emergency and the need for water to supply the city's burgeoning defense industries and naval bases, issued a wartime order for San Diego to drop its plans, join MWD (which it did two years later), and take its water through the aqueduct that MWD had already completed to the coastal plain.[163]

San Diegans were bitterly disappointed at not being masters of their own house but swallowed their resentment so long as supply exceeded demand. That lasted until 1991 when the accumulated effects of drought, California's loss to Arizona in court, the 1982 defeat of the Peripheral Canal, the mandated cutbacks from Mono Basin and the Owens Valley, and Los Angeles's increased reliance on the Colorado River led to sharp reductions throughout the MWD service area. The wake-up call was especially alarming to San Diego, now the nation's sixth-largest city, because the city and county were currently using up to 25 percent of MWD's water while having preferential rights to only about 13 percent. Under severe conditions, they could expect to lose nearly 50 percent of their supply. The cut in 1991 at 31 percent was nowhere near that amount, and MWD and Los Angeles officials promised they would never approve such a drastic reduction. San Diegans, however, did not believe them; besides, the actual reduction was bad enough. "The whole nature of what we did changed . . . [with] the drought [of 1991, which] raised serious questions about our dependence," stated the chair of the San Diego County Water Authority's board of directors. In 1995, when San Diego's attempts to increase the county's preferential rights seemed to be going nowhere, the water authority reversed its view that Imperial Valley water was too expensive and, after rejecting the offer from the Bass brothers, opened talks with the Imperial Irrigation District.[164]

San Diego and Imperial bargained hard, with each side wary that the other might get an unfair advantage, and each also uneasy about dissidents at home. In the Imperial Valley, some "water ranchers," allied with the Bass brothers, wanted to sell their allocations for the highest price they could command, while other residents, including those who came together as the Coalition for a Fair Water Policy, advised against getting "too greedy" and taking actions that would destroy the area's agricultural character and economy. "Some of our farmers . . . have been mesmerized by the thought of getting rich quick for doing nothing, and are not thinking this through," cautioned Don Cox, a lone voice at the time on the board of directors of the Imperial Irrigation District (IID).[165]

Resistance on the board and in the valley increased during the summer of 1996 when the Imperial County grand jury branded as "seriously flawed" the process used to hire the IID's general manager and declared that "outside interests," a reference to the Bass brothers, "appear to have had an undue influence on the IID decision making process." Such criticism was followed a year later by the Bass brothers' sale of their holdings for $250 million (resulting in a handsome profit of $190 million) to United States Filter, the world's biggest producer of wastewater treatment equipment that now became the largest owner of farmland not only in the valley but also in southern California. The Bass brothers received payment in U.S. Filter stock, immediately making them the company's single largest shareholder, and this, instead of removing them from the scene, kept them there as part of a powerful corporation. Worried about U.S. Filter's motives, valley residents began vigorously lobbying for safeguards against any move that would destroy the area's agricultural economy and leave it a waterless wasteland. In public meetings and through organizational efforts, they demanded the outlawing of the sale of water produced through fallowing (a practice that could significantly lessen, if not eliminate, agriculture), a cap on the volume of any water transferred to San Diego, and a time limit on any agreement.[166]

San Diegans had concerns of their own, especially as news of the talks and possible agreement on sensitive issues became public. Some objected to a time limit, protesting that such a restriction would inevitably mean "leaving San Diego stranded" in the future. Others worried about taking Imperial Valley's "brackish" water rather than MWD's better-quality blend of Colorado River and northern California water. Still others resisted because, like University of San Diego economist John Christianson, a water-pricing expert, they believed that financial common sense required San Diego to work with, not against, MWD. "You get the feeling that San Diego hates Los Angeles so much," stated Christianson, "that it will take any chance to dig at L.A., even if it isn't in our best interests." For many more, the critical issue was a combination of lack of adequate information, especially about price, the reliability of the supply, and water quality. "Here we are not even close to knowing all the facts—without the facts we don't even have the luxury of making an informed bad decision," protested Gregory Quist, a member of the San Diego County Water Authority's board of directors and a resident in the northern part of the county.[167]

Despite objections and distrust on both sides, negotiators for the San Diego County Water Authority and the Imperial Irrigation District announced a tentative agreement in late 1997. The terms allowed San Diego to purchase 200,000 acre-feet (and possibly as much as 300,000) for $249 an acre-foot annually, rising to $311 in ten years. The price would be determined by a formula that could be adjusted so that San Diego always paid less than it did to MWD for an equivalent volume of water. Much of the money would go to water-conservation efforts but, even after factoring in those costs, the Imperial Valley, according to one informed observer, would earn a profit of $120 an acre-foot or $24 million annually, a gain that many San Diegans considered outrageous. The draft agreement placed the responsibility for producing most of the water (180,000 acre-feet) on the farmers but forbade them from fallowing land as a means of achieving their quota. Because of some uncertainty about how much water the farmers could produce, the terms allowed Imperial Valley to satisfy the agreement with delivery of a minimum of 130,000 acre-feet. The terms also called for a contract that would last forty-five years with an option for an additional thirty years. What would happen after that remained unclear, but those San Diegans advocating the agreement believed an even larger water market at better prices would emerge in the future.[168]

Opponents, especially water leaders in northern San Diego County, were skeptical about the promised benefits and fearful of runaway expenses. Rincon del Diablo Municipal Water District challenged the accuracy of the cost estimates, the requirement that contracted water had to be paid for even during wet years when it might not be needed, and the absence of "escape clauses" that would allow the county to take advantage of future bargains in "an open water market." Similar concerns about future profits—and an indicator of the intensity with which many on both sides sought a risk-free agreement—came from some Imperial Valley farmers: unlike the San Diego opponents, they were convinced that their water would become more valuable, rather than less, and they sought an "escape clause" of their own in the form of a much shorter contract. They also protested as too high the requirement that farmers produce 65 percent of the conserved water. Most valley residents, however, seemed to agree with Imperial Irrigation District board member William Condit's appraisal: "This partnership with San Diego . . . is the most sensible thing we can do." In late April 1998 the IID board officially approved the agreement by a four-to-one vote.[169]

San Diegans quickly followed suit. For most county water board members and many others, the promise of a large new supply of water and greater freedom from Los Angeles and MWD was irresistible. "This historic agreement heralds a new era of water supply reliability in the San Diego region," declared the water board's chair, while a state senator from the area underscored the hot-button issue: "What this is about is economic independence . . . rather than being an appendage of Los Angeles and Metropolitan [Water District]." One day after Imperial's vote, the San Diego board ratified the pact by a vote of twenty-two to six with all the dissenters coming from the northern part of the county.[170]

The Wheeling-Rate War: MWD and San Diego

Despite the agreement, the struggle was only half over. There remained the problem of moving the water from the Imperial Valley to San Diego County. Since no aqueduct existed between the two locales, the water would have to be taken ("wheeled" is the technical term) through MWD's Colorado River Aqueduct. San Diego, knowing that MWD was angry over the prospect of water it coveted going elsewhere and aware that a prohibitively high price to use the aqueduct could scuttle the deal with Imperial, looked into constructing a canal of its own. Studies suggested that such a venture would be quite expensive ($1 billion to $2 billion or more), prompting San Diego to ask Mexico to share the expenses and the canal. (Mexico was known to desire bringing some of its Colorado River water to fast-growing Tijuana on the Pacific Coast.) News of that possibility aroused opposition from the other Colorado River Basin states, which feared the impact on their rights. They vowed to fight any attempt "to put another straw in the river."[171]

Such resistance notwithstanding, San Diego persisted in its planning for a canal while recognizing that, for the short term at least, its only option lay in negotiating with MWD for space in its aqueduct. Anticipating this reality from the outset, San Diego had initiated discussions in November 1995, nearly three years before the Imperial Valley and San Diego had formalized their pact. The talks quickly turned into bitter and heated wrangling over what constituted a fair wheeling rate. San Diego sought a price based solely on the facilities and electricity needed to transport the water. MWD countered by demanding a rate based on the cost of its entire system, including the infrastructure for bringing northern California water to the southland. Such a demand was justified, reasoned MWD, because without the northern water there would be no unused capacity in the Colorado River Aqueduct available to San Diego. Moreover, the northern water enabled MWD to deliver a blended better-quality supply. Such considerations led the agency to demand a wheeling rate more than double what San Diego said it could pay.

The reasons for MWD's rate and its unhappiness with any San Diego–Imperial Valley transfer seemed patently obvious to the agency. First was San Diego's position as MWD's biggest customer, paying 24 percent of the agency's costs. The availability of Imperial Valley water would allow San Diego to reduce its purchases from MWD and hence its payments as well. At some future time or during a severe drought, it might need all the water it could get, but until then it could lessen its dependence on MWD and the funds paid to it. That possibility produced a chorus of howls from other MWD members, since they had to absorb any reduction in San Diego's portion of the agency's infrastructure and operating costs. "In essence," complained the *Ventura County Star,* San Diego is "ask-[ing] the rest of Southern California to subsidize its 'independence,' like a teenager who moves out to be free of parental rules but needs help from Mom and Dad to pay the rent." To an MWD official, the threat was far more serious: "It could be the end of the Met[ropolitan Water District] as we know it." [172]

Another reason for MWD's stance toward San Diego was the threat posed to the agency's plans for future water security, including its multibillion-dollar Diamond Valley Lake. Construction had begun in 1995, the same year in which the San Diego–Imperial Valley talks got under way. The success of the reservoir rested on getting more water from the Imperial Valley and on significant financial support from its fast-growing member communities, especially San Diego, which stood to benefit most from the facility. San Diego, of course, had plans of its own for the valley's water.

In 1996 MWD's concern about future water security broadened to include much more than a reservoir. Carl Boronkay had stepped down as general manager three years earlier but not before initiating what became a three-year appraisal of southern California's future water needs. The study's findings, released in March 1996 as the Integrated Water Resources Plan, called for an additional 1.4 million acre-feet by 2020 to meet the demands of a population expected to grow by a whopping 37 percent to 22 million. (Two years later the Southern California Association of Governments upped the increase to 43 percent and attributed the main cause to growth of the Latino community.) The plan identified sources for the needed water (increased conservation, recovery of contaminated groundwater, wastewater reclamation, and agricultural water, among others), and attached a price tag of $4.1 billion in construction projects, an annual budget increase from the current $700 million to $1.7 billion, and a doubling of household costs from $23 a month to $46.[173]

To further gird itself for shortages, especially those expected from California's loss to Arizona in the U.S. Supreme Court three decades earlier, MWD joined with other state agencies relying on the Colorado River to develop a so-called 4.4 Plan. The plan called for phasing in reductions of California's use of Colorado River water until the state was taking only its basic apportionment of 4.4 million acre-feet. Despite the court defeat, California had continued taking more than its share (sometimes nearly a million acre-feet more) because of surplus flows and the unused portions of other basin states. That excess water would one day no longer be available and, under pressure from the Secretary of the Interior, Californians began devising a strategy to cut their uses through water transfers, conservation, and storage for future use. MWD believed that the success of this plan as well as its Integrated Water Resources Plan required the full participation and cooperation of all MWD members.[174]

To MWD, these plans dramatized the recklessness of San Diego's behavior. By striking out on its own, it was not only behaving selfishly but also threatening the regional cooperation on which the welfare of millions of Californians rested. "I do not understand," complained an MWD board member, "this fixation San Diego has with moving their water through the aqueduct regardless of what it does to the rest of us."[175]

Still another reason for MWD's hard-line approach toward San Diego was its conviction that the city had greatly underpaid its share of the agency's infrastructure expenses and operating costs in comparison to other member agencies, especially Los Angeles. U.C. San Diego political scientist Steven P. Erie and former Los Angeles Department of Water and Power official Robert V. Phillips estimated that San Diego had underpaid by $2 billion (in mid-1990s dollars), while Los Angeles had overpaid by about $3 billion.[176] The wide divergence in contributions reflected nothing sinister or underhanded. It was simply a matter of timing. Los Angeles, since MWD's incorporation in 1928, had been paying for infrastructure and water rights, which it had largely not exercised because of the availability (now diminishing) of better-quality water from the Owens Valley and Mono Basin. The resulting imbalance in financial contributions, argued MWD, made San Diego morally, if not legally, obligated to cooperate with MWD in its regional approach to water development. San Diego's refusal to do so, the agency believed, was unreasonable and childish. "It's a parent-kid, haves and have-nots, big L.A.–little San Diego, sibling rivalry kind of thing," stated an MWD official. "I've been here for 25 years, and it's always been the same."[177]

Taken together, these considerations produced a demand that San Diego continue paying its full share of MWD's expenses, including those for the agency's multibillion-dollar expansion program. This meant, according to MWD's calculations in late 1996, a wheeling rate of $262 an acre-foot (plus the cost of electricity to pump the water over the mountains separating the river from the coastal plain). San Diegans denounced the figure as "outrageous" and a bald attempt to "assure MWD . . . complete control of water in Southern California." When added to what San Diego had agreed to pay for Imperial Valley water ($249 an acre-foot and rising to $311), MWD's demand eventually would drive the cost to nearly $600 an acre-foot, close to $200 more than San Diego was currently paying for MWD water ($431).[178]

Both sides modified their positions thereafter but never enough (even with state Water Resources Director David Kennedy serving as mediator) to produce an agreement. In 1997 the stalemate prompted MWD to schedule a hearing in Los Angeles County Superior Court on the validity of its wheeling formula. When San Diego and others protested use of a court in MWD's hometown, the case was transferred to San Francisco. During a preliminary hearing there, the judge seemed to question the fairness of a rate that included the cost of moving water from northern California. Since the two sides had another bargaining session scheduled in hopes of heading off a mandated settlement by the legislature, MWD used that meeting to make another offer. It fell flat.[179]

In January 1998 the San Francisco court ruled in favor of San

Diego. "MWD's inclusion of system-wide costs . . . for use of its facilities," stated the judge, "was incompatible" with state laws enacted to encourage transfers among state agencies. Not so, rejoined the Second California Court of Appeal two-and-a-half years later, in May 2000, in an opinion subsequently upheld by the state supreme court. There is nothing illegal in charging "for capital investment and system-wide costs" in order to "avoid adverse impact upon rates and charges to other [MWD] member[s]." Ironically, the decision had a greater impact on other agencies planning to wheel water through MWD's aqueduct systems than on San Diego, which arrived at a rapprochement with MWD on rates for wheeling Imperial Valley water seven months after the San Francisco court's ruling and nearly two years before the appellate court overturned it. The events preceding and following that agreement, however, precipitated other issues underscoring further the pitfalls and complexities in introducing large-scale water transfers to California.[180]

The San Francisco court's 1998 judgment served primarily to energize further those forces already thoroughly committed to water marketing. Proponents of restoring the delta complained that southern California's inability to solve its transfer problem would intensify efforts to take water from the north. Others bemoaned the possible loss of a spectacular chance to make unwitting conservationists of farmers. "This is the win-win model we've been waiting for," declared an attorney for the Environmental Defense Fund. "We gave up on idealism a long time ago. Farmers will do just as much conservation as makes sense to them economically—and no more. The way to go is with marketing, not coercion."[181]

The federal government weighed in with Secretary of the Interior Bruce Babbitt praising the concept of sending farm water to cities. "Without water markets, we can't solve the problem of meeting the future water needs of the West," he stated. While not taking sides in the MWD–San Diego imbroglio, Babbitt sternly warned Californians, as he had done more than a year earlier in 1996, to implement a plan cutting its uses to its basic 4.4 million acre-feet apportionment or face cutbacks. His threat was not an idle one, for Arizona and Nevada wanted the Secretary to award them shares of the surplus water that until now had been largely used by California. Nevada had an entitlement to 300,000 acre-feet of Colorado River water, was currently using slightly more than 200,000 acre-feet, and, because of explosive growth in the Las Vegas metropolitan area, expected to face serious shortages after 2007. Arizona was nearing its full entitlement of 2.8 million acre-feet with some of that water (and any surplus flow that could be acquired) going to replenish its groundwater basins and to support its entry into the interstate water-banking business. Its intention, through a mechanism proposed in 1997 as the "offstream storage program" and formally approved by the Interior Department two years later, was to charge Nevada and California (both in need of additional sites to store water) for "banking" supplies on their behalf—that is, storing water in its underground aquifers during wet years for future use in dry years. Nevada cheered the Arizona proposal because it would allow the state to bank that portion of its entitlement it was not now using as insurance against future shortages. MWD also endorsed the program—in fact, the agency had already begun storing water in Arizona—but MWD did not want Arizona diverting and charging the agency for surplus water that it was now taking and did not need to bank in that state.[182]

Not everyone expressed disappointment when the San Diego–MWD talks collapsed following the 1998 court decision. Those outraged by the degraded condition of the Salton Sea, for example, were fearful that a water transfer would further concentrate contaminants in that lamentable body of water. The San Diego–Imperial Valley agreement had made the valley responsible for any environmental damage to the sea resulting from the water transfer, but it also put a financial cap on the valley's liability and made any mitigation work contingent on its being able to obtain financing.[183]

With little mitigation help expected from the Imperial Valley, Congress entered the picture, further underscoring that there is nothing more complex than water politics. In 1998 as a gesture to Sonny Bono, the late entertainer and California representative in the U.S. House who had made restoring the Salton Sea his special mission, House Speaker Newt Gingrich backed a bill calling for a restoration plan and allowing California to use "surplus" Colorado River water to implement it. For an already oversubscribed river, that move aroused immediate objections from Arizona and Nevada, the other two states in the lower Colorado River Basin that would be affected by such an arrangement. Unless the bill were amended to require California to take the water from its (already overcommitted) share of 4.4 million acre-feet, they swore their opposition. Even with that, they were not ready to endorse the measure. "It seems to us," stated a Nevada representative, "that before any further federal demands for water are created, California should first implement a plan to live within the permanent supplies to which it is entitled." [184]

Just when it seemed impossible for the MWD–San Diego dispute to become any more labyrinthian, the Coachella Valley Water District in February 1998 threatened court action against the proposed transfer. The reason was similar to Coachella's lawsuit against the 1988 Imperial Valley–MWD water transfer: Coachella believed it had a prior right to any reclaimed water. That earlier fracas had ended with an out-of-court settlement, but this time Coachella dramatically increased the stakes: it wanted a right *senior* to Imperial's and an increase in its current water entitlement from 330,000 to 500,000 acre-feet. Imperial's immediate response: no deal. [185]

The Governor Intercedes

In the meantime, with the appellate court's decision upholding MWD's wheeling rates still more than a year in the future, Governor Pete Wilson increased pressure to end the MWD–San Diego impasse. He summoned both parties to his office for talks presided over by his chief of staff and state Water Resources Director David Kennedy. Even then, months elapsed with neither side surrendering enough for a deal and each seething over the other's "dirty tricks." Rumors about MWD skulduggery caused San Diego to invoke the California Public Records Act and discover a 400-page confidential report prepared by a private research firm working on behalf of MWD. The purpose had been to ferret out information—San Diego called it "digging up dirt"—on the Bass brothers' dealings with numerous San Diego and Imperial Valley officials as well as on the governor and state legislators. The investigation turned up nothing incriminating, but its discovery proved terribly embarrassing for MWD and aroused charges of "a despicable act and an abuse of public funds" from angry San Diegans.[186]

Then, not long after, MWD cried foul when it learned of documents leaked to the press describing San Diego's 1995 secret talks with the Bass brothers. Even more upset than MWD were Imperial Valley residents distressed by the apparent collusion among San Diego, the irrigation district's general manager, and the Bass brothers. Their protests led to a grand jury probe, an investigation of the San Diego County Water Authority, and the ouster (which came five months later) of the irrigation district's general manager.[187]

The revelations did nothing to improve relations between San Diego and MWD but neither did they sidetrack the talks. Instead, their own desire as well as public pressure for a resolution steeled both sides in their determination to reach a workable compromise. That meant, above all, being realistic and addressing a range of other nettlesome issues that had emerged in their interminable discussions. Those issues included Salton Sea pollution; the Imperial Valley's postponement of the lining of the All-American Canal and the question of who would do the lining and benefit from the conserved water (a similar question had come up about lining the Coachella Branch and rights to the water that would be saved there); Coachella Valley's threat to take legal action to stop the San Diego–Imperial Valley transfer; and the water rights of five bands of Mission Indians in San Diego County that Interior Department officials wished to supply with a portion of the water (16,000 acre-feet) salvaged from lining the All-American and Coachella canals. In May 1998 the magnitude and expense of dealing with these questions as well as those that had divided the two sides all along reached the governor's office. Wilson's reply: "if it was only money that separated the two agencies, the state might be willing to close the gap."[188]

The principals—MWD, San Diego, Imperial Valley, and Water Resources Director Kennedy—then secluded themselves in Palm Desert to identify the amount needed "to close the gap." They agreed that $100 million was the magic number that would subsidize what San Diego was refusing to ante up and prevent any additional financial burden on MWD members. Assuming the allocation of those funds by the state, the parties quickly arrived at the wheeling rate that San Diego should pay MWD: $90 an acre-foot (plus small annual increases) for the first twenty years and $80 (plus equally small yearly increments) thereafter. Those present then determined that for an additional $135 million they could line portions of the All-American and Coachella canals (saving nearly 100,000 acre-feet that would go toward meeting the demands of Coachella Valley and the Indians) and provide groundwater storage facilities along the Colorado River Aqueduct "for the benefit" of MWD members. These terms, in early August 1998, took the form of a memo of understanding in which MWD and San Diego formally kissed and made up, setting the stage only days later for a bill to authorize a $235-million bond issue to pay for the package.[189]

But still no brass ring. The bill aroused opposition from environmentalists and others unhappy with paying for what they believed the two agencies should finance on their own. This is "a back-room deal that sort of slipped past us," protested the Environmental Defense Fund, which joined with the Save San Francisco Bay Association in urging state legislators to defeat a "rush to judgment" bill where "the cost is so high and the details so few." When the bond proposal mushroomed to $1.7 billion for projects throughout the state, the opposing voices reached crescendo level and helped to assure its defeat. (The immediate cause of the bill's demise was the governor and agriculture's refusal to back down on the amount of storage called for in the measure.)[190]

Without losing a beat, the governor, clearly fighting on behalf of his San Diego hometown, threw his support to a recrafted bill taking the needed $235 million from the state's general fund (plus, to placate the Audubon Society, an additional $300,000 to study the legislation's impact on the Salton Sea). He then backed a tandem bill to silence the environmentalists with a plum they had sought for decades without success. The "linked" measure authorized buying and setting aside as a park (in cooperation with the federal government which would pay half the costs) Headwaters Forest, a 7,500-acre tract of ancient redwoods in northern California, the largest stand of one-thousand- to two-thousand-year-old redwoods remaining in private hands. The bill also called for the purchase of two other stands of ancient redwoods, bringing the total area targeted for preservation to about 10,000 acres.[191]

"It's illuminating—the political process at its raw core," marveled a state senator when the two bills were introduced in the final days of the legislative session. The logrolling linkage of the measures did not completely stifle the criticism by environmentalists— "extortion" shouted one protester from the senate gallery—but it took them off guard and, in late August 1998, both measures passed easily, except for the Headwaters bill in the assembly where it squeaked through with the minimum votes needed. As finally enacted, the water-transfer law, deceptively christened the Colorado River Management Program Act, formally ended (at least for the moment) the MWD–San Diego dispute.[192] Throughout the legislative struggle, MWD and San Diego representatives had suppressed years of hostility and cooperated closely in lobbying efforts. "There was MWD and the [San Diego County] Water Authority working side-by-side until all hours of the morning," recalled MWD's Annette Hubbell. "Enemies today, friends tomorrow. I wish it were that simple."[193]

One War Down, Another to Go

The legislative victory marked a major milestone, opening a new era in California policy where water is bought and sold on the open market. Though formidable obstacles had been overcome, some significant challenges remained for the San Diego–Imperial Valley transfer: obtaining a successful EIR/EIS (environmental impact report/environmental impact statement) from the state and federal governments, approvals from the state Water Resources Control Board and the Secretary of the Interior, and the willingness of Imperial Valley farmers to come up with the required water. There was also the lingering threat of a lawsuit from the Coachella Valley Water District.

Still, there were positive signs. Interior Secretary Babbitt had already gone on record as a vigorous advocate of farm-to-city transfers. Another encouraging development came two months later in November 1998 with Congress's endorsement of both the transfer and environmental restoration in the Imperial Valley. That was the purpose of the Salton Sea Reclamation Act, which directed the Interior Department to produce options for cleaning up the sea, now renamed the Sonny Bono Salton Sea National Wildlife Refuge. The task would not be easy, since Congress stipulated that the plan had to "encourage water conservation," take into consideration "transfers of water out of the Salton Sea Basin," and assume not only reduced "inflows into the . . . Basin" but also no "new or additional water from the Colorado River." This was a tall order—reclaim the Salton Sea and, at the same time, permit all transfers to go forward on less water than presently available—but Interior Secretary Babbitt boldly accepted the challenge and promised "to make ag[riculture]-to-urban transfers a reality." That goal moved a little closer in January 2000 when the Interior Department released five options ranging in cost from $300 million to $1 billion and, with several million dollars appropriated by the 1998 legislation, began cleaning up the shoreline, continuing research into the die-offs, and enhancing recreation. Significant improvement awaited agreement on a specific long-term program and securing funds to carry it out.[194]

In the meantime, the legal threat from Coachella to the San Diego–Imperial Valley transfer appeared to diminish in December 1998 when Imperial and Coachella came up with a peace plan. That lasted only until the two agencies released the terms of their pact—

technically a memo of understanding (MOU). They sought to "make nice" with each other at the expense of others, especially MWD. They called for an increase in Coachella's allocation from 330,000 acre-feet to 468,000 acre-feet and a cap on Imperial's entitlement at 3.1 million acre-feet (its current usage). The news touched off a firestorm that threatened to scuttle the Imperial Valley–San Diego transfer and to precipitate a basin-wide war over California's continued use of Colorado River water in excess of its court-mandated share. The problem was that their action was self-serving and knocked askew the delicate water-balancing dance in which southern Californians had been engaged for decades. The additional water for Coachella, when added to Imperial's share and the allocations already agreed upon for the other California users of Colorado River water (Palo Verde, the Yuma Project, and MWD), exceeded the state's 4.4 million acre-foot maximum by 138,000 acre-feet.[195]

"Where is Coachella going to get the additional supplies the MOU has promised them?" asked the chair of MWD's board of directors. He angrily answered his own question: "From Southern California [cities], that's where." Since MWD had the lowest priority among California users of Colorado River water, its customers would have to absorb that shortage or, more likely, pay premium prices to farmers to get what they needed. The agreement is "patently unfair," thundered MWD, and merely an attempt "to solve problems in the agricultural sector by taking water supplies and money away from the people of Southern California." Further galling the agency was the Imperial Valley's continued waste of water—a Reclamation Bureau study pegged the waste at about 275,000 acre-feet annually. Equity, protested MWD, demanded an end to such abuse and a fairer allocation of water: "*Conserve first, then quantify.*"[196]

Enter now Interior Secretary Babbitt and newly elected Democratic Governor Gray Davis. They sternly warned Imperial, Coachella, and MWD to resolve their differences or a settlement would be imposed on them. Davis, even with the help of hastily drafted state legislation allowing him to force a settlement, seems not to have had the authority to take such action, but Babbitt clearly did as a result of the 1963 U.S. Supreme Court decision in *Arizona* v. *California.* Congress had empowered the Interior Secretary, ruled the court on that occasion, to allocate shortages and surpluses among the lower Colorado River Basin states and also among the users *within* each state. Alarmed by Babbitt's threat, MWD, Coachella, and Imperial entered into marathon talks, mediated by an Interior Department deputy and Governor Davis's new head of the Department of Water Resources, Tom Hannigan. For eight months negotiators struggled and then, in August 1999, announced an agreement followed almost immediately by wrangling among the boards of the three agencies over the terms (not released to the public). Talks began anew, with the negotiators missing first one deadline and then another, causing great anger among the other Colorado River Basin states. They criticized Babbitt for dallying in forcing a settlement and demanded that he reduce California's water use to its legal maximum. Babbitt (and Davis) set October 15 as the final deadline, after which they would impose terms. Precisely on the designated day, following talks both heated and "going all hours," the weary negotiators announced an accord that was quickly endorsed the following week by the governing board of each agency.[197]

Three linchpin issues constituted the settlement: quantification of water use so as not to exceed California's limit of 4.4 million acre-feet; obtaining an Interior Department–approved time schedule for reducing California water use to the 4.4 million acre-feet limit; and wheeling conserved water from the Imperial Valley to San Diego County. As for quantification, the parties reaffirmed the amounts originally delineated in the 1931 Seven Party Agreement and the subsequent 1934 settlement between Imperial and Coachella: Imperial was capped at 3.1 million acre-feet, Coachella at 330,000 acre-feet, and MWD at 550,000 acre-feet, with all recognizing Palo Verde and Yuma's prior right to 420,000 acre-feet.[198]

The not-so-secret explanation for the warring parties now achieving what had earlier proved elusive was their acknowledgment, under strong outside pressure, that water was being wasted (primarily by the Imperial Valley) that could—and should—be conserved in amounts to satisfy everyone—at least for a while. This acknowledgment was embedded in the agreement's details. MWD, although officially capped at 550,000 acre-feet, was targeted for an additional 52,600 acre-feet for lining the All-American Canal and 21,500 acre-feet for lining the Coachella Canal. In addition, MWD would be credited with the 130,000 to 200,000 acre-feet destined solely for MWD-member San Diego in fulfillment of the San Diego–Imperial Valley transfer agreement. Coachella, capped at 330,000 acre-feet, could purchase an additional 100,000 acre-feet of conserved water from the Imperial Valley and also obtain a running average of 20,000 acre-feet annually from MWD (instead of the 50,000 acre-feet in nonsurplus years as originally promised for withdrawing its legal challenge to the 1988 Imperial Valley–MWD transfer agreement). As a result of such horse trading and conservation efforts, agencies ended up with water amounts that differed from their official maximum allocations but, when totaled, did not exceed 4.4 million acre-feet. Imperial (capped at 3.1 million acre-feet) would actually receive only 2.6 million acre-feet; Coachella (limited to 330,000 acre-feet) would end up with 456,000 acre-feet; and MWD (originally targeted for 550,000 acre-feet) would get approximately 850,000 acre-feet.[199]

Folded into the accord, as implied by the preceding arrangements, were other recent pacts, such as the 1989 Coachella Valley legal settlement and the 1988 MWD–Imperial Valley transfer as well as the San Luis Rey Mission Indian water claim. To resolve the last issue, the Indians obtained 11,500 acre-feet of the water conserved by lining the All-American Canal and 4,500 acre-feet of the supply resulting from lining the Coachella Canal. This produced a total of 16,000 acre-feet, the amount needed to settle the Indian claim.

Among the earlier accords, none was so critical as the proposed Imperial Valley–San Diego transfer, for only with its implementation would all the other provisions in this 1999 agreement become effective. The transfer won unanimous endorsement, with implementation anticipated for 2002 following necessary environmental reviews and federal and state approval. The total package of agreements was to last seventy-five years (and might "be extended"), though Imperial and San Diego could terminate their transfer arrangement after thirty or forty years with no effect on the other arrangements.[200]

Crucial as well to the agreement's success was the cooperation of the Interior Department and the at least implicit approval of the other Colorado River Basin states. The reason lay in the negotiators' conviction that it would take fifteen years before the water-conservation efforts and transfers would allow California to get by on 4.4 million acre-feet. Hence, they made the agreement subject to Interior's approval of a fifteen-year transition period and its willingness to manage the river's flow (through controlled releases from Lakes Mead and Powell) in a way that would allow California to gradually wean itself down to its legal maximum. This condition, they insisted, would pose no problem since their river-modeling projections indicated surpluses throughout the fifteen years as well as 60 to 70 percent of the time between 2015 and 2050.[201]

Such caveats and conditions underscored the elusive reality of what had been achieved. This was no final agreement but, at best, a framework for such an agreement—"a road map of sorts, delineating what lies ahead and what issues must be addressed," as one observer noted. Nothing would—or could—be resolved until public hearings had culminated in state and federal acquiescence, until water was flowing to San Diego, until the Interior Department had assured MWD a full aqueduct for a decade and a half, and until the agreement's terms had been reduced to legally enforceable contracts. The negotiators had signed not the usual agreement or treaty, but a preliminary document containing "Key Terms" *for* a "Settlement." Stated a witness to the pact: "In effect, it sets up the rules for the water game." But rules are important and what had been achieved was remarkable under the circumstances. The problems at hand dated back nearly forty years to when the U.S. Supreme Court had put California on notice that it would have to cut its Colorado River uses by nearly a million acre-feet—enough water for almost 8 million people. Since then, the state's population had grown by 17 million with the overwhelming portion of that increase in the south. With the day of reckoning fast approaching, the latest agreement, circumscribed as it might be, was a landmark for southern California, the state, and the entire Colorado River Basin.[202]

The most heartening sign that success was a realistic possibility came in July 2000 when, after nine months of tough and candid talks, all seven basin states and the Interior Department agreed on a plan "to wean California" over a 15-year period down to 4.4 million acre-feet. The heart of the plan was a schedule requiring California gradually to lower its river uses by specific dates over the allotted time. The success of the effort would rest heavily on implementation of the deals cut in the "Key Terms" pact of October 15, 1999. Critically important in explaining the current harmony was California's ability, after so long a time, to persuade others in the Colorado River Basin that it now took seriously its responsibility to rein in excessive water use. "For the first time," noted the general manager of the Southern Nevada Water Authority, "California is acknowledging that it has a responsibility to the larger system and that the river is not just a faucet it can turn on to get cheap water." To which an official of the Arizona Department of Water Resources added: "There's a sense of stability and certainty. You can't just cut those people off." A sentiment with which Californians heartily agreed as they collectively heaved a sigh of relief and set about trying to fulfill their promise.[203]

That commitment, as already thoroughly demonstrated by earlier events, would have to weather ever-occurring newer challenges, like the one that now came at this moment of interbasin harmony when environmentalists (led by Defenders of Wildlife and the Center for Biological Diversity) sued the federal government for additional Colorado River water to help endangered species in the Mexican delta. "Those are serious issues," responded the Interior Department, but the agency pleaded that they "be dealt with on a bilateral basis" and "kept out of the arrangements to reduce California's river use." [204] The success of that plea remained to be seen. For the moment at least a truce had emerged among users of Colorado River water in California and between California and the other basin states.

The battle over Imperial Valley's water and the host of other issues that it generated or exacerbated had loomed large in the media and government circles because the antagonists were so formidable, the prize was so great, and the regional, national, and international issues raised were so important. Less-publicized but also significant signs of the marketing era were arrangements occurring elsewhere. By 2000 more than a dozen agencies had transfer and/or "banking" (that is, storing water in underground aquifers during wet years for future use in dry years) for about 2 million acre-feet to aid such diverse locales as the Bay Area, Santa Clara Valley, the Mojave River Basin in San Bernardino County, and coastal southern California. On a short-term basis of a year or less, many districts throughout the state were transferring a considerable volume of water (as much as 500,000 acre-feet during wet years), though precise figures are unavailable because such agreements do not require state approval. [205]

MWD led the pack in the new venture of water marketing. Besides its 1988–1989 transfer arrangement with Imperial Valley for a minimum of 100,000 acre-feet, the agency had agreements with two San Joaquin Valley water storage districts. In the first, negotiated in 1994, MWD and a group of partners fashioned an arrangement with a district to bank a million acre-feet. MWD's minimum share was 350,000 acre-feet, an amount that could go higher if its banking partners failed to use their allotments. The second agreement, approved in 1997, called for MWD to purchase 40,000 to 75,000 acre-feet annually and to bank in the district's aquifer (for a fee) a minimum of 250,000 and a maximum of 350,000 acre-feet for future use. In addition, MWD had recently completed a two-year demonstration project with Palo Verde Valley farmers to bank their irrigation water (about 93,000 acre-feet a year for a total of some 186,000 acre-feet) for future MWD use and had, as well, an arrangement with an Arizona water conservation district to bank 89,000 acre-feet in that state. MWD was also well into talks with Coachella Valley Water District and Desert Water Agency for storage underground in the valley of 100,000 acre-feet annually during wet years; with Cadiz Inc. to purchase up to 2 million acre-feet of groundwater in the Cadiz and Fenner valleys (San Bernardino County) and to bank there for future use 1 million acre-feet; and with Westlands Water District for a swap: MWD would get water from Westlands in dry years in exchange for sending water to Westlands in wet years when it would be banked until needed by the farmers there. Enhancing MWD's own banking plans was the considerable property that it owned, most acquired at the time of construction of the Colorado River Aqueduct and some of the most promising of that acreage in the Hayfield and Chuckwalla valleys in Riverside County adjacent to the aqueduct. Studies indicate that 500,000 to 1 million acre-feet could be stored there. Overall, in southeastern California, MWD was currently seeking storage for 2 to 2.5 million acre-feet in three areas: Coachella Valley, Cadiz and Fenner valleys, and Hayfield and Chuckwalla valleys.[206]

Most of these and similar marketing arrangements, either under way or in the planning stage, dealt with water held by state districts or in private hands. Another enormous lode of water existed in federal projects that California's water-hungry cities, especially those belonging to the Metropolitan Water District of Southern California, had been stalking for some time. At the top of their list was the biggest prize of all: the federal government's Central Valley Project.

The Central Valley Project, "Reform," and the Market

For California's urban centers, the key to tapping water locked in the Central Valley Project lay in eliminating the federal prohibition against using it elsewhere. In 1991, while MWD's Carl Boronkay was well into his campaign for Imperial Valley water, he opened a new front in the Central Valley and found a receptive audience among environmentalists, major northern and southern California businesses, and congressional Democrats, especially Senator Bill Bradley of New Jersey and Representative George Miller of the San Francisco Bay area.

Bradley and Miller, in the face of stiff resistance from California growers, were trying to push through reforms of CVP's subsidy structure and long-term contract system and to set aside enough water to protect wildlife and fish and to restore the Sacramento–San Joaquin River Delta. At first Boronkay supported a competing but watered-down bill proposed by Republican Senator John Seymour of California, but he had second thoughts when that measure ran into strong environmental opposition. He then offered Miller and Bradley MWD's formidable backing in exchange for a provision authorizing water transfers from the CVP. Miller hesitated, since he was "very uncomfortable" with marketing. "Look, what's worse? Having subsidized agriculture wasting water, that's bad, but . . . having field after field filled with ticky-tacky subdivisions is bad as well." Despite his uneasiness, Miller believed that he and Bradley needed MWD more than the agency needed them. "The Met[ropolitan Water District] is fundamental in water politics in California," explained Miller's chief staff assistant. "You've got to have the Met on your side, and the Met was interested in the bill."[207]

A bargain was struck, yielding a bill that, with vote-producing concessions to water projects in thirteen other western states ($922 million for the Central Utah Project alone), won congressional approval in 1992 as the cumbersomely titled Reclamation Projects Authorization and Adjustment Act (the Central Valley portion of the legislation was named the Central Valley Project Improvement Act). Central Valley farmers, with the support of Governor Pete Wilson, sought in vain to persuade President George Bush to veto the measure. Bush was tempted to do so but felt compelled to sign a bill that promised funding to other states on whose electoral votes he counted in his—ultimately unsuccessful—fight for reelection.[208]

Besides allowing CVP contract holders for the first time to sell or lease their water rights for use elsewhere in California, the measure, according to its advocates and the press, had also "reformed" an old and faulty system. The law permitted renewal of existing CVP contracts, though for a shorter period (twenty-five years instead of the current forty); replaced the fixed subsidy pricing structure with a three-tier pricing system; set aside 800,000 acre-feet (600,000 acre-feet in a severe drought) of CVP water for fish and wildlife purposes; and created a $50 million annual fund to finance fish and wildlife restoration. In addition, other parts of the omnibus bill authorized federal participation in reclaiming 120,000 acre-feet in Los Angeles County (to help lessen the area's reliance on imported water and to reduce the volume of wastewater going into Santa Monica Bay) and in restoring groundwater quality in the San Gabriel Valley.

Despite the law's environmentally sensitive features, its impact as a "reform" measure is less clear, and some of what it promised was qualified in significant ways. No transfers, for instance, could be made until there had been an environmental impact study of their probable effects. Moreover, all water sales that involved transfers in excess of 20 percent of the supply in any particular district had to have the approval of the district. Since Central Valley farm interests had opposed the law, their approval of such transfers was not expected to come easily. Similarly, while contracts were reduced from forty to twenty-five years, the Secretary of the Interior was vested with *discretionary* authority to issue twenty-five-year extensions. Nor was the three-tier pricing system in lieu of the earlier fixed water subsidies a sharp departure from past practice. The three-tier system provided users with (1) 80 percent of their water at the subsidized rate; (2) 10 percent at a rate halfway between the subsidized rate and "full cost"—that is, the unsubsidized rate; and (3) 10 percent at full cost. Users could get all their water at the subsidized rate if the Interior Secretary determined they were irrigating crops that provided significant habitat value for waterfowl, a provision that proved beneficial to growers of rice, among the heaviest water-consuming crops in the state. Obviously, the law would

find its ultimate meaning, as has especially been the case with water legislation, in its *implementation,* not in its wording.

And that meaning was only dimly emerging by century's end.
Not until October 1999, seven years after the law's enactment, did
the Interior Department release an environmental impact statement clearing the way for contract renewals and programs assuring
full use of the 800,000 acre-feet for fish and wildlife. Before moving
on those fronts, however, Interior aroused the ire of farmers and urban areas south of the delta with interim actions and predictions
seen as harbingers of future peril. They included redirecting flows
in the delta to protect salmon runs and for other instream uses,
which occasionally resulted in saltier water at the pumps sending
supplies south; interim two- to three-year contracts requiring higher
costs for water and a farmer-implemented "effective water conservation program"; and predictions that future droughts could mean
a 50 percent cut in supplies for urban dwellers in the Santa Clara
Valley and, during severe drought years, no water at all for farmers
on the San Joaquin Valley's west side (the last major agricultural development in the Central Valley and hence the first to face cuts).
One by-product was the filing of multiple and continuing lawsuits
over how, when, and where the 800,000 acre-feet would be used.
Another was intense pressure on the CALFED Bay-Delta Program
and State Water Project to come up with replacement water.[209]

When the Interior Department in November 1999 finally released
its proposed long-term contracts for water, those agreements incorporated the earlier interim stipulation for "an effective water
conservation program" and set out pricing and delivery policies
that sharply increased costs, sometimes by as much as 500 percent.
The outburst from agriculture was exceeded only by the din created two months later, in January 2000, following the Reclamation
Bureau's announcement of CVP water allocations for the coming
year: deliveries to agriculture south of the delta would be cut by 55
to 60 percent (with Westlands Water District losing the most water),
while cities below the delta would experience a 25 percent reduction in supplies. "Make no mistake," angrily protested the general

manager of the Westlands Water District, "the Interior Department has drawn a line in the sand and has clearly placed the needs of fish over people."[210]

Eight months later, in August 2000, Westlands initiated what threatened to become a decades-long and multi-million-dollar civil war between farmers over the waters of the San Joaquin River. Invoking the watershed-protection and county-of-origin statutes, the district filed with the State Water Resources Control Board an application for 500,000 acre-feet, or a whopping third of the river's flow now going to farmers and some urban areas on the east side of the San Joaquin Valley. On one level, the action threatened a conflict between the behemoth industrial-size farms on the west side and the smaller farms on the east side. If successful, Westlands would have priority over the Reclamation Bureau's filings on behalf of the Central Valley Project. "It is nothing short of a direct, Pearl Harbor–type attack intended to cripple agriculture along the San Joaquin Valley's east side," declared an official of the Friant Water Users Authority in what many considered an understatement. On another level, a Westlands victory would undermine CALFED's efforts to restore San Francisco Bay and the delta and derail plans for water transfers from San Joaquin Valley farms to urban areas.[211]

Also joining the fray even before Westland's shocking announcement were environmentalists adamantly opposed to any diminution of water for wildlife and some state assembly leaders equally convinced that the Interior Department was jeopardizing the state economy and the CALFED program. The department, insisted the assembly leaders, should design an "operations plan" that "balance[s] the needs of California's environment with the realities of its economy." A month later, in February 2000, heavy rains in what had been a dry winter caused the Bureau to lessen the cut to southern agriculture to 50 percent and to propose spending $10 million in federal CALFED funds to purchase enough water to boost farm deliveries by 5 percent. The announcement did nothing to soften tensions. "The additional actions fall seriously short of providing adequate supplies," protested farmers, while environmentalists denounced the purchase plan as "using public money for private purposes." With such strongly held views being passionately argued all around, the ultimate outcome of the struggle remained cloudy.[212]

While the Central Valley Project Improvement Act caused consternation among many, MWD's Boronkay and his fellow crusaders for water marketing were delighted. "It's as if overnight a new reservoir was created," exulted Boronkay.[213] Authorizing water transfers, however, did not mean they would automatically follow. No transfers, as noted, could be made until there had been an environmental impact study of their probable effects. Moreover, all agreements were subject to a "right of first refusal" from other CVP water users willing to meet an outsider's price. Additionally, as also noted, vigorous opposition to transfers were expected from many growers. The obstacles proved formidable, for by the end of the 1990s not a single drop of CVP water had gone to anyone outside the project's service area. Moreover, the wet years after 1992 had resulted in few urban agencies going with checkbook in hand to CVP water users. The first to make the trek was MWD which, wet years notwithstanding, felt compelled to plan for the major cutbacks of Colorado River water that would inevitably come as a result of the 1963 loss to Arizona in the U.S. Supreme Court. MWD ran into significant obstacles in the Central Valley but nonetheless forged a *strategy* for obtaining water—and succeeded in getting an *agreement* for water—that hinted at monumental consequences for the future.

MWD, the San Joaquin Valley, and the Market

In the San Joaquin Valley, where many residents looked on water sales to outsiders as treasonous, there were still those who, because of misfortune, inability to pass up a financial windfall, or a host of other perfectly legitimate reasons, were willing to cut a good deal. To MWD's delight, an overture came almost immediately from a family in the heart of the valley near Los Banos. John, Jess, and Rusty Areias (the latter a Democratic state assemblyman) owned a dairy and small farm that had been in the family for seventy years. Faced with sharply dropping milk prices and cuts in water supply during drought years, they reluctantly considered selling the property. Then, with the passage of the 1992 Central Valley Project Improvement Act, they had a partial change of mind: They decided to sell their water rights and keep the property.

MWD and the Areias family began secret negotiations that in 1993 produced an agreement to sell 32,000 acre-feet to MWD over the next fifteen years. In exchange, they would receive $175 an acre-foot for water that cost them $8 an acre-foot, a $5.6 million annual transaction. That news angered the local farmers and irrigation district officials who turned out in crowds of up to 2,000 to denounce the deal as a "water grab" and the family as "traitors." Not lost on the critics was the irony of Rusty Areias agreeing to a transfer authorized by a law that he had opposed. His turnaround was attributed to the wiles of interlopers from southern California, "the region with the biggest checkbook." "MWD has swaggered in with their cash and political power and told us it's either their way or the highway," snapped one opponent. "They're going to suck this valley dry so Los Angeles can grow more suburbs and swimming pools and golf courses all the way out to Palm Springs." Since the proposed transfer did not exceed the 20 percent cap established by the 1992 law, the local irrigation district could not veto it, but that only convinced growers that they were witnessing the same "divide-and-conquer campaign . . . used 90 years ago in the Owens Valley."[214]

An unsettling disclosure by Rusty Areias that he and his family had changed their minds again about giving up farming and now intended to pump groundwater, grow crops, and operate the dairy intensified criticism and also aroused environmentalists. Pumping, they complained, would speed up the local aquifer's depletion and concentrate further the harmful salts there. To residents, the Areiases were compounding their betrayal by wanting to send good-quality water to southern California while worsening the local supply and undermining the local economy. A spokesman for the Bureau of Reclamation, the federal agency responsible for approving the required environmental impact report and the transfer, questioned the appropriateness of any agreement that might damage the Central Valley and encourage urban sprawl in southern California. "There [has been] . . . a sense of unease" about water marketing, he cautioned. "If it gets out of hand, we'll put on the brakes." With that unencouraging observation coming on top of so much criticism, MWD quietly withdrew from the area.[215]

Though rebuffed, the agency pressed on, moving further south in the San Joaquin Valley to Kern County and changing its tactics. It sought to disarm potential criticism by negotiating directly (and openly) with a *district* rather than secretly with an individual farmer or family. Such an approach would not catch residents off-guard and also held the prospect of coming away with a significantly greater volume of water. MWD at first proved only half right in its expectations. Residents were aware of the negotiations that the Arvin-Edison Water Storage District entered into with MWD, but they were upset with the agreement announced in fall 1996: 350,000 acre-feet going to MWD over twenty-five years at an annual average rate of 14,000 acre-feet. Leading the opposition were the powerful Friant Water Users Authority, which consisted of the twenty-five water districts that shared with Arvin-Edison the same delivery canal, and the Central Valley Water Coalition, an ad hoc creation of farmers and others from nearly all the same districts belonging to the Friant authority.[216]

Much of the resistance came from locals not as blessed with standby groundwater supplies as those in the Arvin-Edison district. They considered it shortsighted to send water to southern California that, if retained in the valley, could carry them through drought periods. Environmentalists also railed at the proposed transfer because it could only worsen the condition of the San Joaquin River. Agricultural diversions and polluted drainage, charged the Natural Resources Defense Council, had made the San Joaquin "one of the ten most abused rivers in America," and it would be "a terrible mistake" to divert water elsewhere "before we've done anything to address the river's environmental needs."[217]

Upset by the stinging criticism, MWD and Arvin-Edison revised their proposal in consultation with the Friant Water Authority and the Central Valley Water Coalition. The locals first insisted on establishing principles to guide all MWD attempts to secure water in the southern San Joaquin Valley. These included a prohibition against fallowing land or harming the environment and a requirement that water districts receive "permanent benefits" and suffer "no adverse water supply or cost impacts." In exchange, the growers offered MWD "access to a new water supply."[218]

Once agreed to the principles, the parties then hammered out an amended proposal, released in late 1997, that called for MWD to get 40,000 to 75,000 acre-feet annually. Unlike the earlier agreement, this water had to come from flood runoff during wet years, and its availability during dry years was contingent on the needs of Arvin-Edison growers and other surrounding landowners. The arrangement also required MWD to store a minimum of 250,000 acre-feet of its State Water Project water in Arvin-Edison's aquifer. MWD's payment for the delivered water and storage services would be based on the volume in storage: $130 per acre-foot for the initial 250,000 acre-feet and $100 per acre-foot for water in excess of that up to a maximum of 350,000 acre-feet. The arrangement was for twenty-five years (under certain conditions some components could run longer) and renewable with mutual consent. Although this plan called for more water going annually to MWD than the sharply criticized and ill-fated 1996 proposal (40,000 to 75,000 acre-feet versus 14,000 acre-feet), the water would now come from flood runoff (captured and stored underground) rather than from more reliable river flows.[219]

There now remained the need for federal and state assent to the agreement. The Reclamation Bureau as well as local, state, and congressional lawmakers promised there would be no resistance from them. The environmentalists were another matter, however, for their opposition was expected on the same grounds as before: their desire to keep water, including flood runoff, in the San Joaquin River system. This was an argument, feared MWD, that might prove persuasive to a now more environmentally sensitive State Water Resources Control Board, which had to sign off on all transfers from the Central Valley Project. Arvin-Edison farmers shared that fear, worrying that an appearance before the board would incite "environmentalists . . . [to] come out and attack their core rights." To avoid such an appearance, MWD and Arvin-Edison devised an imaginative strategy in which each got what it wanted without any CVP water leaving the project's boundaries. This was accomplished by engaging the help of a middleman agency. The plan was, first, for Arvin-Edison to transfer MWD's water to a "middleman," Kern County Water Agency. Since Kern County was in the CVP service area, the transfer would require no regulatory approval. Kern County, in turn, would supply MWD with an equal volume of water—*but this water would come from its share of State Water Project (SWP) water.* Payment for it would take the form of storage fees paid to Kern County for holding the SWP water in local aquifers until needed by MWD. As MWD official Timothy Quinn put it, "we structured something that looks like a duck, quacks like a duck, but it's not a duck. . . . It's a bona fide exchange" and "we can now implement it without having to go to the state board."[220]

The complex agreement between MWD and Arvin-Edison, which easily won the approval of both parties as well as the Friant Water Authority, reflected not only shrewd creativity but also a powerful precedent, if needed, for future acquisitions in the valley. Because of an abundance of rainfall, MWD had not implemented the plan as of late 2000, but without proposing to take a single drop of CVP water outside the service area, it had found a way to leverage that water, which promised to significantly increase its supply—and to do so without interference from environmentalists. The next step was self-evident as the agency set out on a new round of negotiations followed, in December 1999, by a statewide appeal to 500 potential sellers in both the private and public sectors. None of this was lost on other water shoppers now going to market.[221]

Among the urban interests following MWD's lead was the Los Angeles Department of Water and Power, which broadcast an appeal for supplies to replace those it was using to control dust in the

Oroville Lake, behind Oroville Dam, in February 1991, at the height of the drought of 1987–1992, showing the deeply receded water line. (Courtesy of California Department of Water Resources)

Owens Valley. Also at the head of the pack was the San Diego County Water Authority, which issued a public request for proposals from Central Valley growers. Nor were targets limited to California. MWD (soon followed by other agencies) challenged reigning policy by seeking water supplies anywhere it could get them in the Colorado River Basin.[222]

The Quest for Security and Equity

THE GOAL of water planners remains a system free and responsive enough to allow a water-short part of the state (or larger region of the nation) to obtain water quickly from areas with a surplus supply. This was the implicit outcome of the decisions to cut temporarily the flow south during the severe droughts of 1976–1977 and 1987–1992. And it was clearly embraced in the 1989 state and 1992 federal legislation making funds available to offset Los Angeles's loss of Mono Basin water and to lessen its reliance on imported water, including supplies from the Owens Valley.

Understandably, the law gives preference to cities over agriculture during droughts, and both Washington and Sacramento possess mechanisms to implement that priority. In February 1991, for example, farmers served by the State Water Project (SWP) were ordered cut off entirely while most of those supplied by the federal Central Valley Project were told to prepare for a 75 percent reduction. Those cuts angered agriculture and, in the case of state water policy, led to changes that were more symbolic than real. The Monterey Agreement of 1994 (so named after the city where the talks took place) modified the State Water Project by requiring both farm and urban users to be cut equally in future shortages of SWP water—that is, each group reduced in proportion to its annual entitlements—rather than farmers surrendering first as before. The same agreement then took the sting out of that pronouncement by stipulating that the governor could stay urban cuts by declaring a state of emergency and thereby assuring enough water for domestic consumption, fire protection, and sanitation. An order by a court or the state Water Resources Control Board could achieve the same result in times of urban peril by shifting to agriculture the responsibility for absorbing shortages.[223]

In dealing with droughts, the federal Central Valley Project essentially continues as before, adhering to a "flexible policy," according to a Reclamation Bureau official, that is sensitive to "health and safety" and by which agriculture's cuts will be "earlier and bigger" than those for urban areas and for wildlife and environmental purposes. In response to the demands of cities to know the "reliable" minimum they could expect in order to plan intelligently for droughts, the Interior Department in 1997 designed a "two-tier level of reliability": At the first level urban areas could expect "75 percent of historic use adjusted for growth and adjusted [upward] for . . . the implementation of any extraordinary water conservation action," so long as the conserved water was not misused or wasted.[224]

As for the second level, "triggered when CVP . . . supplies were severely constrained," cities would get enough water to maintain "public health and safety." Since the policy had been designed so as not "to adversely impact fulfillment of . . . environmental requirements," agriculture had to surrender the water to serve those needs and could be reduced to no water at all if necessary. To qualify for preferential treatment in times of shortage, cities had to "be implementing significant water conservation practices." Agriculture, however, as earlier, was effectively saddled with absorbing the brunt of any shortages, a burden likely to be severe in view of a CVP study revealing an overestimate of a million acre-feet in the emergency standby water available to carry users through dry years. "There's a knot tied around our water system," acknowledged a Central Valley grower, "and it will become increasingly apparent in the next drought." An ongoing attempt to untie the knot and coordinate state and federal drought policies was among the by-products of CALFED's *California's Water Future* plan released in June 2000. The plan mandated creation of the governor's Advisory Drought Planning Panel, which, two months later, began work on its charge: "[to] develop a contingency plan to reduce the impacts of critical water charges in California . . . and commit CALFED agencies to facilitate and expedite transfers within legal requirements."[225]

Even without a drought crisis, the message for the future seems clear. In confrontations between water for crops and for people (read "cities" for the latter), people will win, and they will have the law as well as the powerful weapons of the market and eminent domain to guarantee victory. The expense, bitterness, and complexity of the victory, however, will continue to be shaped by present arrangements with their heavy subsidies to agriculture (and, indirectly, to the consumers—most of them city dwellers—of California products) as well as by the future impact of such actions as the 1992 Central Valley Project Improvement Act, which permits transfers only within California, not to needy states elsewhere. The Interior Department has agreed to consider transfers among the three lower Colorado River Basin states (Arizona, California, Nevada) on a case-by-case basis and, as noted earlier, MWD and Nevada have acted on his offer to bank water in Arizona. The department has also called for marketing arrangements among all seven basin states but that proposal has yet to win the approval of the upper-basin states, some of which fear that any water sent south on even a temporary basis will be lost forever.[226]

As for California, MWD in January 1999 dropped a bombshell that reverberated throughout the agricultural industry. Precipitated by the short-lived 1998 Imperial Valley–Coachella Valley agreement that would have reduced MWD's water supply, MWD made a direct assault on agriculture's lock on the lion's share of Colorado River water. MWD asked Interior Secretary Babbitt to reappraise the allocation formula giving nearly 88 percent of the state's 4.4 million acre-foot apportionment to agriculture. Urban southern California's "need to sustain and develop its vital economy," MWD told Babbitt, "will inevitably require an assessment of whether the intra-California allocations, made by your predecessor in 1931, meet the changes that have occurred in the public's need."[227]

Farm groups throughout California, fearful that a reallocation of Colorado River water would lead to demands for similar reallocations of urban and agriculture shares elsewhere, roared their disapproval and threatened litigation. Babbitt, hoping to avert a statewide conflict, pressed MWD to back off, arguing that "these agreements and contracts . . . talk about *permanent* service" and urging sales or leases of agricultural water to urban areas as the preferred course of action. He admitted, however, that a court challenge to the 1931 allocation might be upheld, "particularly when there's a perception . . . of being unfair in the eyes of an audience of 40 million to 45 million people." MWD, after first announcing it was "standing firm," then backed off to pursue the more immediate goal of quashing the Imperial-Coachella agreement. It did not do so, however, before casting a bright spotlight on another powerful policy question: public tolerance for the sudden enormous profits going to farmers selling or leasing their water—profits made possible by taxpayer-built dams, aqueducts, and other forms of subsidization. "The [Interior] Department owes a duty to urban Southern California water users to determine . . . the public interest," MWD scolded Babbitt, and "those users hope that you will actively use [your] . . . authority for the benefit of all the citizens of California and not just those who would seek windfall profits from the re-sale of federally provided water."[228]

A demand for equity and fairness had been issued that would not go away. Even more foreboding in the thinking of many was the future of California's environment, wildlife, and quality of life as the state's engine of urbanization inevitably accelerates with massive injections of agricultural water however obtained: market transfers, large-scale government reallocations, or a combination of both.[229]

Open Spaces and Farmland: Going, Going, . . .

TO EMPHASIZE the growing power of cities and the persistence of still massive agricultural subsidies runs the risk of obscuring the threat that modern society poses to open spaces and greenbelts generally and to prime farmland in particular. Urban sprawl has gobbled up California countryside at a prodigious rate, transforming in its wake hills, mountains, and valleys that had remained virtually unchanged since the Spanish arrival. As for agricultural land, some 60,000 acres annually became housing tracts and shopping malls during the real estate boom of the 1950s, about half that amount a year by the mid-1970s, and then back again to a boom rate of about 44,000 acres by the 1990s. Whatever else might be said about farms large or small, they have contributed to a "greening" of America and serve, where they survive, as powerful and reasonably accessible antidotes to the concrete, steel, and neon of many cities. Moreover, while California produces some field crops grown in abundance elsewhere (and, hence, frequently contributes to the nation's agricultural surpluses), the state generates more income (nearly 80 percent of sales) and fame from its specialty crops, like the grapes, fruits, vegetables, and citrus products that made Los Angeles County the nation's leader in agriculture until housing tracts, concrete, and smog became the norm. Still, it bears remembering that indirect subsidies, like the tax shelters allowed corporate farmers in the 1960s and 1970s in Kern County, can lead to glutted markets even for specialty crops.[230]

It is also important to remember that in many cities and in sections of most others, where planning has been more purposeful than haphazard, water has made possible vast "urban forests" where earlier there were grasslands or few, if any, trees. Even in Los Angeles, the epitome of what many believe a city should *not* become, there are neighborhoods, once barren of shade, where trees and large plants now exceed by many times the number of people, houses, and automobiles combined. Of course, the challenge to city dwellers is to develop or import (or in some cases reintroduce) trees and plants appropriate in an environment of increasingly scarce water supplies. Some residents have accepted the challenge, though to date they have been few. During droughts, the message of selective planting is hammered into the public by the media and water officials, and a flourishing cottage industry develops almost overnight to supply books and pamphlets of the "how to do it" variety. In the past, the end of a drought has invariably meant an end to the cottage industry, with the horticulture—and water demands—of most urban neighborhoods reverting to earlier form. Tellingly, at the end of the 1990s Interior Secretary Bruce Babbitt disappointingly reported that 40 percent of the water supply of Los Angeles, Phoenix, and other western cities was used for lawns and landscaping.[231]

Also unchanged has been the steady urbanization of once productive farmland. The trend is statewide and affects not only agribusiness but also small farmers, including those avoiding pesticides and artificial fertilizers and seeking to produce crops organically. Attempts have been made, most notably in the Williamson Act of 1965, to halt the trend through special tax breaks and other incentives, with perhaps the most striking success to date occurring in Marin County. By the 1960s the remaining ranch, dairy, and farmland in the western part of the county seemed doomed by plans for freeways and suburbs until a group of alarmed conservationists, farmers committed to farming as a way of life, and political leaders came together in an uneasy but increasingly effective coalition. Despite continuing pressures for development, they had—at least as of the late 1990s—kept agriculture viable and agricultural land intact in western Marin County.[232]

The record nearly everywhere else, however, is of farmers—tax breaks and other special measures notwithstanding—succumbing to the fabulously attractive prices that developers are willing to pay. The major beneficiaries of the Williamson Act turned out to be landowners under the least pressure from developers and far from urban areas, while those on the metropolitan fringes have refused to take advantage of the law and have sold their land for great profits instead. Thus, for the majority remaining in farming, the legislation has simply provided another kind of public subsidy (the tax breaks) to a group already heavily subsidized by the public. In this sense, the law worsened the situation rather than improved it. Other unfortunate by-products have been the application of greater amounts of petrochemical fertilizers on much of the remaining acreage to increase yields and the conversion of less desirable raw land into productive acreage, thereby adding to already critical drainage and pollution problems.[233]

This does not mean there have been no attempts other than the ill-fated Williamson Act to control growth, for there has been a flurry of such activity, starting in the mid-1970s, picking up in the early

1980s, and then accelerating in the late 1980s and into the 1990s. In 1998 these efforts (sometimes misguided) included a beefed-up Williamson Act offering greater tax breaks and, even earlier, by the end of the '80s, more than 900 growth-control measures enacted throughout the state. They represented the realization of residents and community leaders that growth, long thought necessary to generate investment, jobs, and revenue for services, also meant congestion, gridlocked streets, air pollution, and general deterioration in the quality of life. Nonetheless, the outpouring of restrictions—zoning regulations, requirements to identify water sources before building new subdivisions or communities, floor-space controls, service demands, greenbelt requirements, and much more—has been invariably outpaced and effectively nullified by exploding population growth, almost all of it resulting from natural increase and international migration. The decade of the 1980s witnessed the largest population growth in California history (some 6 million people), the biggest for any state in the nation's history, and more than twice the rate of increase nationally. Except for a brief recession-induced slowdown in the early 1990s, the population surge has continued.[234]

Such growth has so far proved politically and morally impossible to change. Unlike in China, the American people have shown no desire to mandate family size or seal the borders of California and the rest of the country with tanks, mines, and Berlin-type walls, which few believe would be effective even if they were put in place. On the other hand, neither have Californians nor the American people vigorously promoted family-planning programs in the United States or abroad. Equally disappointing have been their efforts to help rebuild the economies of the countries from which many of these new residents emigrate to seek a better life in California and elsewhere in the United States. Hence, for the present, population growth continues to explode, contributing mightily to the creation of new towns, denser urban areas, and the expanding peripheries of older cities.

Southern California's coastal plain and the perimeter of San Francisco Bay have long been covered by a blanket of undifferentiated cities, but now that phenomenon is well under way in the interior agricultural valleys, including the San Joaquin Valley from Stockton southward, with Fresno among the fastest-growing cities in the state. The urbanization of 15,000 acres of Central Valley farmland each year has prompted some experts to predict the likelihood of farming no longer being the primary business of the valley. Typical of the future may be the experience of the Santa Clara Valley, the enormously fertile area south of San Jose. As late as 1965, the year when the first Williamson Act was passed, there were 52,000 acres planted in fruits, nuts, and vegetables; by 1982 there was less than half that amount of land in cultivation, and today almost nothing remains.[235] The valley is presently an area of industries, homes, smog, water pollution, and congested streets and highways. Fortunately, most of it, when viewed from the surrounding hills on a clear day, is also an urban forest masking many of the other changes. Still, the lesson seems clear. With water, like land, now subject to a market system and allowed to go blindly to the highest and most powerful bidders—invariably metropolitan areas and developers—the future holds little promise of being fundamentally different from the past.

A more painful way to check urban growth is simply to refuse to develop new water supplies or, if they are available, to refuse to accept them. Such an approach has, so far at least, proved neither popular nor successful. Santa Barbara adopted it but only after first obtaining a contract for state water and sharing in construction costs to bring the supply to the southland. Residents then forced an about-face, refusing overwhelmingly to approve bonds to finance a canal connecting the county to the state project. Their logic: no water, no unwanted development. The county's growth rate remained one of the state's lowest, but the severe drought conditions that began in 1987 produced second thoughts. At first Santa Barbara, earlier than most other California cities, adopted mandatory con-

Lake Cachuma, principal reservoir for Santa Barbara County, in the drought year of 1990. (Courtesy of California Department of Water Resources)

servation measures, some of them quite restrictive: banning lawn watering and prohibiting all but the use of hand-held buckets or drip irrigation systems to keep trees and shrubs alive; increasing water rates; stepping up groundwater pumping and exploring the possibility of temporarily transporting state water from the Central Valley through a never-used oil pipeline. By 1990, even with such measures, the city's Gibraltar Reservoir, which ordinarily supplied 30 percent of its needs, was dry. Cachuma, which provided nearly all the balance needed by the city and county and was designed to withstand a seven-year drought, had fallen to its lowest level since construction in the 1950s and was fast approaching the point where pumps would be needed to move water through the reservoir's outflow tunnel.[236]

At this point the city approved plans to build an emergency desalination facility and pondered tying the coastal area permanently into the State Water Project. Then, in June 1991, as the crisis deepened, Santa Barbara County residents voted more than two to one for state water (the hookup was completed in 1997) and voters in the city of Santa Barbara, in an advisory election, recommended turning the emergency desalination plant (completed in 1992) into a permanent facility. The $34 million plant, kept on standby during the wet years that immediately followed and then mothballed as the rainy period continued, was viewed as insurance against the closing down of the California Aqueduct in a future drought. The same rains, together with local determination not to return to predrought water-guzzling habits, made it unnecessary for Santa Barbarans to draw water from the State Water Project. Nonetheless, residents were obligated to pay roughly $4.5 million annually for their 3,000-acre-foot allotment whether or not they took the water. This prompted a founder of the Pacific Institute to conclude: "The way to deal with a water problem is no longer to seek out new supply but to look at conservation and efficiency."[237] Reasonable enough, but a final judgment for Santa Barbara must await future severe and prolonged droughts.

A more promising approach to containing urban sprawl and preserving farmland emerged in the Napa Valley in 1990 when vineyardists and environmentalists, worried about the disappearance of the area's famed wines, successfully promoted a county initiative requiring a popular vote on all major decisions to transform farmland into housing tracts, malls, business parks, or anything else. Opponents appealed the new law but state supreme court approval of it five years later inspired its replication or transformation into new guises in Santa Rosa, Healdsburg, Ventura, Pleasanton, Sebastopol, Rohnert Park, and elsewhere. Activists have also designed tandem measures. One, recently adopted by five Ventura County cities, seeks to lock in growth boundaries by taking the power to approve developments from city and county officials and putting it in the hands of the electorate, while another tries to prevent runaway commercial development by mandating voter approval for any attempt to rezone residential areas for nonresidential uses.[238]

Such measures seem to be a piecemeal approach toward what residents in and around Portland, Oregon, did in a more direct and larger way to control urban sprawl two decades ago. In 1979, in response to state legislation requiring every city and county to devise a plan for controlling municipal expansion, they created a "growth boundary" (modified once since then) that encircled the city and twenty-three nearby towns. Some residents feared that limiting urban expansion would lead to escalating housing costs and smaller homes. Those concerned were technically correct: prices did go up and typical lot sizes decreased—but not out of line with what has occurred in many parts of California. Portland residents still overwhelmingly support their "great wall" and remain in easy distance of vast stretches of greenery.[239]

The decision in Portland—and now increasingly in many California communities—to place control over urban growth in the electorate's hands reflects popular distrust and disgust with elected officials and bureaucrats. Powerful justification for that distrust is evident in the experience of southern California's Santa Monica Mountains, a rugged expanse of 160 square miles in western Los Angeles County. Thanks to federal and state expenditures of more than $400 million, about 44 percent of the area was made a preserve two decades ago, while the remainder was targeted for limited development in a growth-control plan adopted by the county board of supervisors that allowed for about a thousand homes. By 1998, some 2,200 homes had been built, and there were plans for an additional 2,400. This was accomplished all quite legally and through such otherwise reasonable devices as variances and waivers. Over the years, developers obtained scores of them: one allowed 204 homes on land approved for 37; another 1,272 homes where 620 had been designated. Most individual variances and waivers were modest in their impact and not attention-getters— for example, 28 houses where 24 were supposed to be built and 41 where 12 had been planned—but, taken together, they amounted to a building boom. Investigative reporters for the *Los Angeles Times* attributed the boom primarily to campaign donations, especially those going to the county supervisor representing the area. Variances and waivers also came in exchange for developers' promises to construct affordable housing (not always built) and as a result of county officials allowing builders to count roads and other public rights of way as part of their property and to take advantage of still other complex formulas interpreted so as to produce more houses rather than fewer.[240]

Another example of abuse in the county that unfolded thirty miles north of Los Angeles is the massive Newhall Ranch housing project, the largest proposed in Los Angeles County history and nearly ten times bigger than what was allowed under the county's general plan. It is also an undertaking for which opponents say an adequate water supply has not been identified and is destined for a floodplain zoned for agriculture alongside an almost wild river—that is, an unchannelized river, the last in Los Angeles County—doomed to be straitjacketed in concrete for the project. The venture seeks to produce an entire city of 60,000 people; 21,615 homes; a 200-acre business park and golf course; and a high school, a middle school, and five elementary schools. Despite strong public opposition, the project garnered the support of the Los Angeles County Board of Supervisors after the builder reduced the original number of houses by 11 percent, agreed to add homes for low- and moderate-income families, and donated 246 acres for neighborhood parks and 6,138 acres for open space. Not unimportant were the hefty contributions received by all five supervisors from the developer, the powerful Newhall Land and Farming Company.[241]

The decision led to a lawsuit by nearby Ventura County plus the cities of Oxnard, Ventura, and Santa Paula—all convinced that the development would decrease their groundwater supplies, harm fish and bird species, and adversely affect agriculture in the Santa Clarita Valley. Joining the suit, now transferred to Kern County to avoid conflict-of-interest charges, were the Sierra Club and other environmental groups alarmed about the impact of the development on endangered species, as well as the state attorney general's office, concerned that the project would have "serious adverse environmental consequences, which will affect the public and natural resources of the state." In June 2000 the Kern County judge agreed with the critics, ruling that the developers had neither demonstrated the existence of an adequate water supply nor produced an acceptable assessment of the venture's impact on fish, wildlife, and the environment. "Shrinking the project is a very real possibility," a Ventura County attorney observed elatedly, while a county supervisor thought the shrinkage in houses could be dramatic: "Now they could be stuck with none." Not so, countered a Newhall official: "At first blush we see these as fairly minor issues." The Los Angeles Board of Supervisors thought otherwise, for three months later it withdrew its approval of the project's environmental impact report. Whatever the outcome, the undertaking has the weight of tradition on its side. "There's a history in California for 150 years that if you create the demand, the water will follow," observed a lobbyist. "It's the dirty little secret of the development industry."[242]

In 1995 the state legislature had sought to eliminate that "dirty little secret" by requiring local governments to assess an area's existing and projected water supply before approving new developments. This Costa Act (named for its sponsor) ostensibly sought to reverse the age-old practice of first approving large subdivisions and industrial expansion and finding the water later. The law turned out to be more symbolic than real. First off, it applied only to projects consisting of 500 or more units. Little imagination is required to realize that it will not take too many projects of 499 or fewer houses to devour landscape just as effectively as bigger projects. Second, the law did *not* apply to the large number of proposals submitted to local agencies before the legislation's passage and still undergoing review. Third, the law was unenforceable because it did not require local governments to deny building permits even if their assessments determined there was not enough water. Finally, the Costa Act could not contain urban expansion so long as there were farmers willing to sell or lease water and buyers willing to pay the going rate. Legislation addressing some of these flaws, though not the critical last one, was being considered in 2000.[243]

In the same year that the act gained approval, more than a hundred new towns and subdivisions were on drawing boards in the Central Valley alone for an expected 2 million people, 30,000 acres of commercial development, and 44 golf courses. In October 1995 a team of University of California and private researchers released the first detailed study, two years in the making, of the projected urbanization of California farmland. On the basis of current trends, they predicted that over the next forty-five years the state would lose more than a million acres of cropland at an annual cost of $5.3 billion and witness a tripling of Central Valley population from 4 million to 12 million and a loss of $1 billion annually in public services. Put simply: a mass of people accompanied by a sharp decline in the quality of life. Highway 99, which bisects the valley lengthwise, would become an almost unbroken chain of cities sitting under a blanket of smog and stretching 300 miles from Sacramento to Bakersfield. "There is a choice," stated an official of the American Farmland Trust, which had funded the study. If so, the choice to date has been to fulfill the researchers' prediction.[244]

An "institutional mirage" encouraging the notion that Californians can somehow find all the water necessary for development into the distant future is the Monterey Agreement of 1994, mentioned earlier in connection with state drought policy for agriculture and urban areas. Prior to the agreement, entered into by the state Department of Water Resources and nearly all the SWP water users, every contract stipulated that if shortages became permanent, allotments would be reduced to match actual supplies. The agreement eliminated that requirement, immediately provoking strong criticism from environmentalists and many other concerned Californians. In *Planning and Conservation League* v. *Department of Water Resources,* they challenged the action on the grounds that it encouraged unplanned development by ignoring the reality of an oversubscribed State Water Project: contracts for 4.2 million acre-feet a year but only about 2.5 million acre-feet available for delivery. They lost at the superior court level but obtained a unanimous favorable ruling from the Third District Court of Appeal. "The entitlements represent nothing more than hopes, expectations, water futures or, as the parties refer to them, 'paper water,'" declared the court in September 2000, and "contractors surely cannot be entitled to water nature refuses to provide." Still, lectured the court, "there is certainly the possibility that local decision-makers are seduced by contractual entitlements and approve projects dependent on water worth little more than a wish and a prayer."[245]

Still hopeful that open space can be preserved and boasting a plan of his own in the late 1990s for aiding agriculture was environmentalist Marc Reisner. He believed that farmland could be protected by assuring growers a reliable water supply at low cost in exchange for their agreeing to keep land in production for twenty to forty years. This is an interesting notion, but it seems to resemble another form of agricultural subsidy (of which there have been too many). Yet, as author David Carle has observed: "Increasing such benefits even further . . . recognizes that farmers must have incentives to stand up to multimillion-dollar development offers."[246]

Certainly, Reisner himself did not underestimate the power of soaring population growth and the urban market for agricultural water. After giving some thought in 1998 to joining U.S. Filter (the firm discussed earlier in connection with Imperial Valley water and the Bass brothers, who became U.S. Filter's largest single stockholder), Reisner instead took a part-time job with Vidler Water Company, a business involved in water transfer and storage projects in the San Joaquin Valley and three other western states. Much of the balance of his time was spent as a sort of real estate agent with his first major client being the owner of 13,000-acre Madera Ranch whose property he marketed as a vast underground storage reservoir. He thought that he had it sold when the Reclamation Bureau offered him about $50 million (his commission would be as high as 5 percent), but the deal fell through as a result of neighbors complaining that poor-quality water might be put into the aquifer or that their own groundwater might be stolen. Also opposed were environmentalists who objected to CALFED offering to help the Reclamation Bureau to purchase the property. Reisner did not let this initial disappointment undermine his faith in water marketing's eventual success and his own along with it. "I'm too old not to be making money anymore," he observed in April 1999, a conviction reenforced by a recent bout with cancer that left him determined to provide for his family's security. Sadly, a little more than a year later, in July 2000, Reisner died of cancer at the age of fifty-one.[247]

A Confusion of Laws

USHROOMING POPULATION, developers' zeal, agricultural subsidies, pesticides, and other forms of pollution only partially explain the persistence of environmentally destructive water practices. The entire body of water law itself has been—and remains—a major culprit because of flawed statutes and legal principles out of step with the times. Also behind the confusion is the badly fragmented water management system that, along with the patchwork of laws, has emerged from the cauldron of legislative and court battles over a century and a half.

Typical is the status of groundwater which, as already noted, is of crucial importance to the ecological and economic health of California (and the West generally). The state's groundwater reserves are enormous, some 850 million acre-feet, although the usable capacity is less than half that amount because of quality considerations and the cost of extraction. Underground supplies presently account for about 30 percent of the water used in the state and much more than that amount during drought periods. Despite the immensity of groundwater reserves, the volume extracted greatly exceeds the rate of natural replenishment during dry years and even in normal years exceeds that rate (currently by 1.6 million acre-feet) with a considerably greater overdraft for aquifers in highly developed urban and agricultural areas.[248] Careful management to control overdrafts is a self-evident need, but the reality is that groundwater has seldom been subject to meaningful management and remains at the whim of contradictory laws.

A fundamental problem is that the law has traditionally distinguished groundwater from surface water by holding that the paramount right to subterranean supplies belongs to owners of overlying land. This is a principle, as will be recalled, found in Hispanic practice, though in American jurisprudence it is traceable to the common law and the lingering power of the Blackstonian notion that land ownership carries with it dominion over a wedge extending from the earth's center into space. The principle remained adequate so long as settlers focused their energies on the more easily acquired surface water. By the turn of the twentieth century, however, with the spread of powerful electricity- and gasoline-driven pumps and increased—frequently fierce—competition among landowners claiming rights to the same aquifer, the need for new guidelines became obvious.

The state supreme court responded in 1903 with the "correlative" rights doctrine. That rule, as announced in *Katz* v. *Walkinshaw,* held that if there were multiple owners above an aquifer, each possessed a "correlative" or reciprocal right to a reasonable volume of water.[249] Groundwater not needed by overlying landowners, and hence considered surplus, could be acquired by others through the doctrine of prior appropriation: first in time, first in right. It also could be acquired by "prescription"—that is, by individuals who went unchallenged in taking more than their correlative share or in appropriating nonsurplus subterranean water. Thus, groundwater became subject to correlative, appropriative, and prescriptive rights, a circumstance that led to a legal free-for-all resulting in unchecked pumping and overdrafted aquifers.

Nearly a half century later, the state supreme court in 1949 sought to inject order into a patently destructive situation by creating the doctrine of "mutual prescription." This principle, set out in *Pasadena* v. *Alhambra,* awarded prescriptive rights to the users of an overdrafted aquifer and established a formula for determining the quantity of each party's right.[250] That formula called for determining each user's highest five years of pumping and then reducing proportionately the uses until the total did not exceed the safe yield of the aquifer.

The 1949 decision, rather than bringing improvement, sparked a rush to the pumphouse as people sought to set their uses at as high an average as possible. Waste, environmental degradation, and legal conflict accelerated, especially in densely populated and rapidly growing southern California, where communities overdrew the resource to the injury of everyone. In 1951 state lawmakers sought to lessen the pressure for uncontrolled pumping by permitting southern Californians to rely on alternative surface supplies without losing their unused groundwater rights. Two years later the legislature offered additional relief to the southland by vesting the state Water Rights Board with authority to obtain injunctions against southern California pumpers whose actions threatened to destroy aquifers through intrusion of ocean water. More recently, in August 2000, the California Supreme Court hinted that the judiciary has the authority to impose order on the chaotic groundwater situation. Since that issue was not directly before the court in *Barstow* v. *Mojave Water Agency,* the remarks (in a footnote) carried no legal weight, but they suggested a course of action of considerable significance: "If Californians expect to harmonize water shortages with a fair allocation of future use, courts should have some discretion to limit the future of groundwater use of an overlying owner . . . and reduce to a reasonable level the amount the overlying user takes from an overdrafted basin."[251]

Despite significant progress in water management in the Santa Clara Valley and in parts of southern California the issue remains grave virtually everywhere (Arizona and New Mexico are the only western states that have made especially impressive advances) and at the crisis stage in the San Joaquin Valley. There planning is in a shambles, water is allocated on the basis of location rather than need, and overdrawn basins in many locales frequently result in land subsidence so serious that aquifers collapse and cannot be re-filled. A ballot initiative in 1982 was the last major attempt to bring order to this sad chaos, but it failed primarily because of farmer op-position. The problem remains essentially as described more than two decades ago by the Governor's Commission to Review Cali-fornia Water Rights Law: "California's groundwater is usually avail-able to any pumper, public or private, who wants to extract it, re-gardless of the impact of extraction on neighboring groundwater pumpers or on the general community." Those extractions, short of reform or a major influx of new water, will inevitably drop water levels to a point where pumping is economically impossible or will exhaust the aquifers altogether. But reform, as noted earlier in this chapter, is what CALFED seeks in the plan that it released in mid-2000, calling for basinwide management of groundwater and elimination of the current chaotic and environmentally destructive practice of management by numerous local water districts and agencies—a practice that has meant no management at all. Many farmers have called for all-out war against the state legislation re-quired to bring about this change.[252]

Other flaws derive from such legal uncertainties as the exact scope of the rights claimed by appropriators and riparians. In 1914 the state for the first time required all new appropriators on a stream to obtain a permit for a specific volume of water. Before that, many rights went unrecorded and a significant number—perhaps a quar-ter of the state's annual water demand—remain that way. Similarly troublesome is the indeterminate quantity of most riparian rights. Such uncertainties encourage costly litigation, frustrate planning, and undermine attempts at efficient and wise water use. Another unfortunate legacy of riparianism is the rigid requirement that water be used only on lands along streams and lakes, thus preventing its reassignment to nonriparian areas where the need may be greater.[253]

The state constitutional amendment of 1928 checked riparians (and appropriators as well) by mandating that all uses be "reasonable," but not surprisingly that action introduced another element of legal uncertainty by prompting debate over the meaning of *reasonable*. The courts have eliminated many of the grosser abuses, and the legislature took some important steps toward reform. In 1979, it qualified the "use it or lose it" principle of appropriation law by stipulating that rights to water unused *because of conservation* would not be lost. In other words, if a person achieved the same goal using less water—for example, by installing drip irrigation technology—the right to the saved water was not diminished. The following year lawmakers again encouraged conservation efforts by granting rights to reclaimed wastewater to the person salvaging the water.[254] While impressive, such advances have been few, slow in coming, and deceptive, especially where the availability of cheap subsidized water has discouraged conservation efforts. Overall, legal reform has been fitful, piecemeal, and frequently inconclusive.

Another legal uncertainty lies in the politically sensitive "area of origin" statutes that protect counties and other locales from exportation of their water. The uncertainty derives largely from the laws never having been exercised to recover a single drop of water.[255] Still, the statutes possess great political significance, and two of them, as noted earlier, were invoked in August 2000 by Westlands Water District against the Central Valley Project.

There are four such state laws, the earliest coming in 1931 in response to the state's filings on unappropriated water for its anticipated statewide water project. Alarm from those fearing an Owens Valley–like raid caused the legislature to prohibit depriving a "county in which the water . . . originates of any such water necessary for [its] . . . development." [256] This is one of the laws that West-lands has invoked, but there is widespread misapprehension that it is all encompassing; it actually has narrow applicability. It cannot be used against earlier transfers, like those affecting Hetch Hetchy, Mono Basin, and the Owens Valley, and it can be invoked only against water appropriations for the 1931 State Water Plan, some of which were assigned two years later to the Reclamation Bureau for the Central Valley Project and the remainder going to the eventual State Water Project. Even then, its protection is not absolute. It is applicable to the CVP but only to the extent permitted by federal law, and that law can always be changed to deny its applicability. As for the State Water Project, the 1959 Burns-Porter Act stipulated that the state's water contracts could not be abrogated while the bonds remained outstanding. The bonds will not terminate until 2035 or when they are paid off, now projected to be around 2029. Another limitation on the county-of-origin statute is the state's power of eminent domain. "If public necessity requires water for southern counties," note legal scholars Harold E. Rogers and Alan H. Nichols, "the state as a last resort can always override private north-ern water rights by condemnation." Among the reasons that the county-of-origin statute has not been tested is that so far there has been little or no need to do so. When the Department of Water Re-sources built Oroville Dam and initiated the State Water Project, it signed contracts for 800,000 acre-feet with the prior appropriators on the Feather River in order to protect their rights. Moreover, the department has established the policy of selling water to area-of-origin residents who desire it. [257]

A second law similar to the county-of-origin statute and also be-ing invoked by Westlands is the "watershed protection" provision in the 1933 Central Valley Project Act. That provision, which ap-plies only to appropriations for the CVP, states that a "watershed or area . . . immediately adjacent thereto [possesses] . . . the prior right to all of the water reasonably required to adequately supply the beneficial needs of the watershed . . . or any of the inhabitants." [258] Besides being subject to veto by federal legislation, the law offers the potential for disputes over such vague language as the "area immediately adjacent" to the watershed of origin.

As the search for water intensified in later decades, pressure for protection focused increasingly on specific rivers and river systems. The earliest and, arguably, the least effective of these efforts targeted the Sacramento–San Joaquin River delta. The state Delta Protection Act of 1959 grandly stipulated that "no person, corporation or public or private agency or the State or the United States should divert water from the channels of the Sacramento–San Joaquin Delta to which the users within said Delta are entitled." [259] By protecting only the water to which delta users are "entitled," the act seems merely to assure them of rights that they already possess.

More far-reaching were 1984 state laws aimed at so-called protected areas—a vast collection of locales that included Mono Basin; all the lands drained by the Sacramento, San Joaquin, Truckee, Carson, Walker, Calaveras, and Mokelumne rivers; and all the north-coast rivers from the Russian to the Oregon border. The legislation authorized residents of these places to purchase water from developers "intending to export water for use outside the protected area." [260] Though wide in scope, these laws, like earlier statutes, did not apply to any previous diversions. Moreover, they did not provide the stronger protection against dams accorded to those rivers (or portions of them) in the federal wild and scenic system. Nonetheless, close observers are convinced that this legislation and the other untested statutes will be at the center of future donnybrooks as the competition for water intensifies.

Also uncertain and a source of great anxiety among California water managers is the extent of federal water rights. They result from the government's ownership of national forests, parks, monuments, other public lands, and especially Indian reservations. The U.S. Supreme Court, in a series of cases, has held that the government possesses rights to enough water to fulfill the primary purposes for which these lands were set aside. The issue of Indian rights is particularly important to Californians not only because of the large number of reservations in the state (all are small but most are in arid areas where water is crucial), but also because many of the reservations (including the nation's largest, the Navajo) are in the Colorado River Basin where California has a vital stake. Nearly a century ago the U.S. Supreme Court held, in *Winters* v. *United States* (1908), that Indian reservations possessed a special water right not lost through nonuse. In 1963, in the same *Arizona* v. *California* decision in which Arizona emerged the victor, the court pegged the extent of the Indian right as the water needed to develop "all the practicably irrigable acreage" on a reservation.[261] Since agriculture is the heaviest consumer of water, the decision sent shock waves throughout the state and the West. The ultimate meaning of the decision for water users—Indian and non-Indian—is as yet uncertain because of lawsuits under way, planned, and possible, but it is patently clear that Indians can no longer be ignored in water planning.

Chaotic Management

THE LEGAL uncertainties are matched by a water management system that is fragmented and egregiously localized. In a sense, it exhibits the centrifugal, fractional tendencies of the American federal system carried to some kind of logical extreme. The basic idea, as James Madison conceived it, was to divide and balance powers, horizontally and vertically, so as to prevent government from becoming too powerful. The question now, in California (and western) water matters, is whether government is so hobbled and confused that, as a total complex of institutions, it cannot provide reasonable supervision and guidance at all.

In California, water management responsibilities are divided among at least nine major federal agencies (Interior Department, Reclamation Bureau, Fish and Wildlife Service, Environmental Protection Agency, Commerce Department, National Marine Fisheries

Service, Army Corps of Engineers, Agriculture Department, Natural Resources Conservation Service), eight major state organizations (Resources Agency, Department of Water Resources, Department of Fish and Game, state Environmental Protection Agency, Water Resources Control Board, Department of Health Services, Department of Food and Agriculture, Department of Pesticide Regulation), and nearly a thousand public and private entities at the regional and local levels—and many of these agencies overlap each other. Even at the highest levels there are numerous other entities exercising some control—the Federal Power Commission and California Public Utilities Commission, to name two of the more important.[262] State and federal governments frequently consult with one another and each has occasionally authorized another agency to oversee a pet task, but only once in the state's history have they sought meaningfully to coordinate their efforts on a single project—the CALFED Bay-Delta Program—and the verdict is still out on that one. Statewide there is no coordinating authority or management program; there is no one "in charge." The result is that cooperation in critical matters such as pollution control, dam releases, and environmental protection has often been mandated by the courts.

A case in point was the foot-dragging created by the Interior Department's refusal to acknowledge that it was bound by the 1986 state supreme court decision giving California's Water Resources Control Board authority to regulate water supplied by both the federal Central Valley Project and the State Water Project. And in 1990 the U.S. Supreme Court added to California concerns when it held (in *California* v. *Federal Energy Regulatory Commission*) that state officials had no authority over water flowing from streams into hydroelectric plants, whether the plants were public or private. That authority, declared the court, belonged solely to federal officials because all hydroelectric plants operate under licenses granted by the Federal Energy Regulatory Commission.[263] The decision especially alarmed environmentalists, who viewed the commission as more interested in promoting increased power production than in protecting fish, the environment, or recreation. Happily, there are signs, as noted earlier, that the commission is adopting a more environmentally sensitive stance. Still, the major point remains clear: the federal government has been, and will remain, a key player in decisions involving water in California—and Washington has frequently been an uncooperative player.

Cooperative water management among agencies within California itself is even further from an optimum norm. The fragmentation among regional and local public agencies is staggering and now epitomized by the approximately thousand so-called special districts involved in some aspect of water supply—irrigation, generation of hydroelectricity, recreation, flood control, sewage treatment, and much more. According to careful studies, these districts (most of fairly recent creation, between 1950 and 1970) are ordinarily managed by boards of directors made up of a homogeneous, single-interest body of people representing the larger water users and guided by a rigid set of goals: maximization of water use at minimum cost with little or no regard for the environment or for the welfare of the people of California. In these districts, directors are more often appointed than elected and, when elected, obtain office with ballots distributed according to acreage held (or value of acreage held) rather than according to the principle of one person, one vote. Not surprisingly, voter turnout for these elections is egregiously low under such circumstances. Moreover, directors are served by engineering staffs who share their views and help reenforce the insularity of decision-making. A study of nearly 1,400 elections over a four-year period concluded that "there is relatively little participation in water districts, either in competition among candidates seeking office or in voters turning out at the polls to exercise their franchise."[264]

The need for cooperative water management extends well beyond California to the entire West and, so far as California is concerned, especially to the states of the Colorado River Basin. Decades of conflict have produced significant advances in what is popularly called the "Law of the River"—the Colorado River Compact (1922), the Boulder Canyon Act (1928), the U.S.-Mexico Water Treaty (1944), *Arizona* v. *California* (1963), the Upper Basin Compact (1948), the Central Arizona Project (1968), and more. Such achievements notwithstanding, there is still monumental bickering, misunderstanding, and failure to deal effectively with pollution, salinity, environmental protection and restoration, Indian water rights, water for Mexico, water marketing, and so much else. Frustration has prompted some water leaders to demand an overhaul or even complete rejection and redrafting of the 1922 compact and a lot of what followed it. Others are amazed at how well that agreement has withstood the test of time and made so much possible while increasingly accommodating too long ignored environmental values and Indian water claims.

But there is no denying that much remains to be done, and it could clearly be facilitated by more openness, communication, and cooperation among those for whom water is a common and fundamental concern. Part of the problem is structural. River basins possess no permanent mechanisms for bringing together on a regular basis the stakeholders empowered to take action—state, federal, environmental, and tribal leaders. The states along the headwaters of the Colorado have an Upper Colorado River Commission empowered "to do all things necessary, proper or convenient in the performance of its duties."[265] Its members, however, are limited to representatives of upper-basin state governments and a presidential appointee representing the federal government. Still, a *basin-wide* commission, even if it consisted only of federal and state delegates, would represent a major advance today when the lower-basin states have no mechanisms for addressing common problems among themselves, much less with the upper basin. The lower basin is essentially a creature of the Secretary of the Interior whom the 1963 *Arizona* v. *California* decision installed as its watermaster.[266] Scores of conferences, symposia, special task forces, and government advisory committees have studied the problems facing the Colorado and other river basins, but until there is in place a meaningful mechanism for taking action, the reports will continue to flow with little or nothing significant being done on a timely basis. And time is of the essence.[267]

Calls for Reform, Fanciful and Otherwise

MODERN CALIFORNIA has attracted numerous critics, many with plans for setting aright all that they perceive is askew. The state's environmental problems seem peculiarly capable of stimulating an extraordinary reawakening of the utopian, deeply romantic thinking about society and nature that flourished in such earlier eras as those of the Transcendentalists and communal-utopian theorists of the Age of Jackson in the 1830s and 1840s, or the advocates of the communal movements of the 1960s and 1970s. Donald Worster, in a fascinating and provocative account of water-resource development, sees contemporary California and the West as the creation and creature of "a coercive, monolithic, and hierarchical system ruled by a power elite based on the ownership of capital and expertise." His "elite" are the water brokers—agribusiness and government agencies, especially the Reclamation Bureau—whose minions "impose their outlook and their demands on nature, as they do on the individual and the small human community." Change, he believes, is possible only through "redesigning the West as a network of more or less discrete, self-contained watershed settlements"— hundreds of small communities "not participating to any great extent in the national or world marketplace, concentrating instead on producing food and fiber for local use." These communities, he predicts, would somehow result in "a more open, free, and democratic" people who would see a river as "a reflection of their own liberated minds, running free and easy."[268]

The message seems to be that people can free themselves from their bureaucratic masters by dismantling elaborate hydraulic systems, retreating to small communities not needing such systems, and in the process of liberating rivers and nature generally also liberate themselves. This is a message that others have advocated, including Peter Berg and Raymond Dasmann who more than two decades ago called for "reinhabiting" California through the "massive redistribution of land to create smaller farms" and then joining "a biotic community and ceasing to be its exploiter." Success, they concluded, also required the establishment of a new and "separate state" consisting of "watershed governments appropriate to maintaining local life-places."[269]

This vision has a certain appeal, but it seems out of touch with modern urban society and a world (increasing by some 250,000 persons daily or 90 million annually) where production only for local needs—even if limited to California and the West—appears a practical impossibility if not undesirable. It shares much (albeit with an important caveat or two) with the Jeffersonian dream of the yeoman farmer, with the hoped-for edens of the nineteenth-century irrigation crusaders, and with the aspirations of those who fought for the Reclamation Act. It forgets that many people's vision of hell is life on a farm or in a small town. Worster implicitly acknowledges the utopian character of his own vision by admitting that its implementation would result in profit losses, the tearing down of much (how much is unclear) of the present infrastructure for moving and storing water, and the redistribution of people to other regions—a requirement that would surely necessitate coercive, not to say totalitarian, measures incongruent with a more "open" and "free" society.

Left unanswered is how numerous watershed communities can be created and stabilized without so controlling nature as virtually to eliminate wilderness, especially those rivers "running free and easy." Nearly all rivers, including the Colorado, Sacramento–San Joaquin, and their myriad tributaries, are far from placid in their natural state. English naval captain Edward Belcher in an 1837 visit to the Sacramento Valley observed "unequivocal proofs of the power of the flood-streams" and noted that the "annual rains . . . in severe seasons" transform the valley into "one immense sea, leaving only the few scattered eminences which art or nature have produced, as so many islets or spots of refuge."[270]

Even southern California's many sluggish and "upside down" streams regularly became raging torrents, devouring banks and flooding adjacent countryside. The first California flood on record took place in 1770 on the Los Angeles River. "We . . . saw the Porciúncula River . . . and forded it," noted Fray Juan Crespi on January 17, "observing on its sands rubbish, fallen trees, and pools on either side, for a few days previously there had been a great flood which had caused it to leave its bed."[271] As noted earlier, dams offer no foolproof protection, but floodplain farming along uncontrolled rivers (and the entire Central Valley is a flood plain) seems incongruous with the dream of those like Worster for communities that "would want little, enjoy much" and "find abundance." Worster, Berg, Dasmann, and others who share their views are nonetheless completely on target in arguing for the need for a substantial rethinking of the way society has dealt with the West's precious water resources.

As committed as these critics to a more democratic society and unpolluted environment, but perhaps less utopian, are reform advocates like René Dubos, Martin Krieger, and Eric Jubler. They acknowledge the reality of population pressures which, they believe, are incompatible with the survival of uncontrolled nature. Their concern is not with the subjugation of nature—"humanization of Earth" is their deceptive euphemism—but with how it is done. In *The Wooing of Earth* (1980), Dubos, a Frenchman, calls for establishing around the world "new environments that are ecologically sound, aesthetically satisfying, economically rewarding, and favorable to the continued growth of civilization." Though acknowledging that preservation of some wilderness is commendable, he believes that the "environmental crisis has been discussed to death" and "human beings can improve on nature."[272] He covets a future with relatively few large cities, people dispersed on small farms in the countryside, and greater democracy, but the clear and sparkling rivers that he envisages are, like nature generally, carefully managed.

Wendell Berry, in *The Unsettling of America* (1977), goes even further by advocating not only the dismantling of cities nationally but their replacement with small homesteads, thereby pushing the wish for decentralization and agricultural self-sufficiency to its logical extreme.[273] Roderick Nash, an eloquent spokesman for wilderness preservation, finds such a prospect illogical and dismaying. "If a family of four endeavored to supply itself with food and fuel on a forty-acre farm," he writes, "the present population of the United States would require 2,200,000,000 acres which is more land than exists in the forty-eight [contiguous] states." Most troubling to Nash and other preservationists about the views of Berry, Dubos, and others like them with their dreams of Edens on earth is that "wilderness is just as dead in the garden as it is in the concrete wasteland." Nash's hope for wilderness is straightforward. Humanity, he pleads, should "keep the options of the future open with regard to something [wilderness] that, by definition, mankind can never create."[274]

Nash could have also added, as Dubos does, that the relentless growth in population ranks among the most serious—some insist *the* most serious—threat to nature, free or controlled, and to humankind generally. It took 1,700 years from the time of Christ for the world's population to double. Since then population has doubled three times, now standing at 5 billion, and is expected to double again and reach 10 billion within eighty years. The growth is greatest in the Third World, but it is also significant in industrialized nations where lifestyles more severely tax ecosystems and resources. "While overpopulation in poor nations tends to keep them poverty-stricken," notes Stanford University population expert Paul Ehrlich, "overpopulation in rich nations tends to undermine the life-support capacity of the entire planet."[275] Such an observation helps underscore the ultimate futility of designing a water policy—or virtually any policy, for that matter—without acknowledging and also addressing this reality.

The fate of all bodies of water is intertwined with human values about the quality of life and the number of people any part of the world can properly support. Closer to home, the message to Californians is the folly of continuing to encourage the influx of people, whether new residents, developers, or farmers, into areas where the environment is already overburdened and despoiled. The message is also about the tragedy of California's rapidly disappearing open spaces and world-renowned farmland through unchecked urbanization and an accelerating market in agricultural water.

8 Reflections

*M*odern California, with
its booming economy (eighth
among the nations of the world
if measured separately) and its
number one ranking nationally
in population, agriculture, and
industry, dominates the Amer-

ican West and much of the nation like a colossus and exercises great influence not only in Washington (perhaps best measured by its ability to attract more federal dollars—38 percent more—than any other state) but also in foreign capitals.[1] An engine contributing mightily to these achievements has been the passion of Californians to capture the water of other regions as reflected in the thousands of miles of aqueducts crisscrossing the state and extending to the eastern border where they tap into the scarce supplies of much of the American West. To outsiders, California is the feared water hustler *nonpareil,* while to those within the state, there have been (and remain) a host of water seekers of varying strength and influence struggling with one another over increasingly limited supplies. Some of these internecine conflicts are better known than others. The "north" against the "south" stands deceptively at the grossest level of generalization. The variations on the theme, however, can be multiplied many times: Los Angeles versus Owens Valley/Mono Basin, San Francisco versus Hetch Hetchy and the preservationists, Army Corps of Engineers against the Reclamation Bureau, Metropolitan Water District of Southern California versus San Diego and the Imperial Valley, Pacific Gas and Electric against the Interior Department, Los Angeles versus the San Fernando Valley cities, the state Water Resources Control Board against the Reclamation Bureau, the California Farm Bureau Federation versus the state Department of Water Resources, and so on in increasing number and complexity, as this account has demonstrated.

Note that the battles have sometimes been between and among those groups traditionally identified as providing "water leaders" or as being part of a "water establishment," "water industry," and "water lobby"—that is, those whose collective actions have straitjacketed the state's rivers and given California its reputation as a water imperialist. This "establishment," however, has never been a monolith driven by a single purpose or vision, save the idea that water (and nature generally) exists to serve humankind. Rather, as this account has suggested, it has consisted of many discrete groups,

both in and outside the state, each with its own (frequently chang-
ing) agenda that has sometimes led to conflict (for example, the
California Farm Bureau Federation's opposition to the Peripheral
Canal), at other times to foot-dragging (the Metropolitan Water
District's last minute and reluctant support of the State Water Project), and on still other occasions to compromises and alliances resulting in a major undertaking (the joining of the Imperial Valley,
Reclamation Bureau, and Los Angeles on behalf of the Boulder
Canyon Project). The alliances have often been fleeting but their
frequency and composition have been such as to create in California the world's largest and most complex hydraulic system. The
success of that system in promoting growth has ironically intensified internal competition for water, especially between urban
and agricultural interests, and made less likely those city-farm alliances that produced the monumental projects of the past.

As Californians built their water system, they left along the way
significant institutions and other signposts: new systems of water
law that spread throughout the American West; the introduction
for the first time of engineering principles in such ventures as hydraulicking and, later, other flood-control and reclamation projects
that served as the basis for subsequent large-scale public and private undertakings; innovations such as the irrigation district and
mutual water company, which, although not living fully up to expectations in California, nonetheless encouraged settlement, especially in other parts of the West which borrowed and improved
upon the original designs; invention of a pueblo water right that set
Los Angeles upon its course of becoming the preeminent city of the
West and a pacesetter for the nation and, in many ways, the world;
the first great urban aqueducts—one to the Owens Valley that profoundly accelerated Los Angeles's growth and the other to Hetch
Hetchy Valley, which had a similar impact on much of the San Francisco Bay area and also precipitated the first major clash between
preservationists and conservationists; the Boulder Canyon Project,
the first of the federal government's massive multipurpose under-

MAJOR WATER PROJECTS
OF CALIFORNIA

Goose Lake

Shasta Lake

Clear Lake

Lake Berryessa

Lake Oroville

Feather River

AMERICAN RIVER

TEHAMA-COLUSA CANAL

SACRAMENTO RIVER

Sacramento

Lake Tahoe

San Francisco

CONTRA COSTA CANAL

MOKELUMNE AQUEDUCT

HETCH HETCHY

Hetch Hetchy Res.

SAN JOAQUIN AQUEDUCT

Mono Lake

OWENS R.

San Luis Reservoir

DELTA MENDOTA CANAL

MADERA CANAL

SAN JOAQUIN RIVER

Millerton Lake

Tinemaha Reservoir

LOS ANGELES AQUEDUCT

TURLOCK CANAL

FRIANT-KERN CANAL

KERN RIVER

Bakersfield

CALIFORNIA AQUEDUCT

Santa Barbara

Castaic Lake

Van Norman Res.

Los Angeles

Lake Mathews

Lake Perris

COLORADO RIVER AQUEDUCT

ARIZONA

SAN DIEGO AQUEDUCTS

Salton Sea

COACHELLA BRANCH

ALL AMERICAN CANAL

San Diego

NEVADA

N

0 20 40 60 80 100 MILES
0   50   100   150   200 KILOMETERS

——— RIVERS
- - - - CANALS/AQUEDUCTS

takings and the one responsible for putting the Reclamation Bureau on the path to becoming the most powerful federal agency in the West; and the California Water Project, the largest hydraulic enterprise ever launched by a state. Other examples could be cited, but these are indicative of the historical significance of the state's experience.

That experience has not been uniformly positive, as attested by the overabundance of evidence, both historical and more recent, of environmental despoliation, wretched working conditions for those harvesting California's bountiful crops, and increased threats to the health of all life. Some critics have attributed California's (and the West's) land, water, labor, and environmental problems generally to "immense centralized institutions" ruled by oppressive bureaucratic elites who have manipulated water resources in their own self-interest. There is some truth in this observation, but, as noted earlier, to see California's water leaders as part of a "centralized" group or ruling through "a coercive, monolithic, and hierarchical system" runs directly contrary to the reality of a war of fragmented authorities. More compelling explanations are found in a compound of interest-group pressures, local and regional considerations, political trade-offs, and the larger context of American political culture in which the national culture and its reverberations within California help explain actions that may otherwise be incorrectly attributed to a conspiratorial power elite. Then, too, there is the need to appreciate more fully the historical record's longer reach. Bureaucracies have been important, but individual Americans with their digging sticks, axes, firearms, shovels, and votes (where available, whether exercised or not) have always played a critical role in shaping the environment—a role reflecting attitudes toward nature.

At the outset, American Indians, Spaniards, and Mexicans, as the California experience attests, left relatively few marks on the land. For the Indians, a desire to live in symbiosis with nature guided their actions, including those of groups like the Owens Valley Paiute, who practiced irrigation in precontact California and operated within a communal system in which labor was freely given and leaders were selected by the people. Spaniards and Mexicans belonged to societies convinced that the New World's resources were divine gifts to be exploited as higher authority directed, but it was an authority that, in matters involving water, emphasized the preeminence of community rights, the inequity of monopoly, and the need to measure all actions by the extent to which they promoted *bien procumunal*—the common good. In Spanish and Mexican California, the notorious exception in practice, if not in theory, involved the treatment of the Indians.

In contrast to the Hispanic emphasis on community, the Americans pouring into California after the mid-nineteenth century were single-minded and aggressively self-seeking in their pursuit of wealth, not at all surprising for a profoundly individualistic people possessing a tenaciously exploitive tradition extending back nearly four centuries. There seemed no need to conserve timber or soil or minerals or water or any other natural resource when the supply appeared limitless and richer frontiers were just beyond the horizon. Such conviction catapulted settlement across the Appalachians, into the Old Northwest and Old Southwest, and onto the eastern prairies. When the waves of pioneers reached the Mississippi River Valley, their vision blurred momentarily as they considered the vast semiarid and arid expanse before them, but their confidence returned with the discovery of precious metals in California and elsewhere.

Despite California's sparse water supply, the newcomers, drawing upon eastern practices and reacting to environmental realities, devised institutions to compensate for the scarcity and to promote their economic self-interest. In doing so, they warred constantly among themselves—no civil disputes of a public nature so preoccupied the courts as controversies over water—while also managing to persuade local, state, and federal governments to endorse their conflicting legal positions. In such an expensive, conflictive, pell-mell rush for wealth, the winners were those with capital, wit, and luck who—whether mining magnates, railroad nabobs, or land and water barons—managed to bribe officials, otherwise skirt the law, or offer enough concessions to the less fortunate (often in the form of such palliatives as William Chapman's small irrigated tracts) to quash or sidetrack effective reform.

When a special interest, like the hydraulic miners who overreached themselves in the late nineteenth century, threatened the lives, livelihoods, and sensibilities of too many Californians, the courts put them out of business. In subsequent years, the discontent aroused by monopolies of land and water resources, violations of reclamation law, heavily subsidized agribusiness, scandalous working conditions for agricultural labor, and environmental abuse was largely siphoned off or otherwise neutralized by a booming economy. The California population doubled nearly every generation following the gold rush, with the overwhelming majority of newcomers gravitating to the mushrooming metropolitan centers in search of health, pleasure, homes, and jobs in the rapidly expanding commercial, transportation, oil, motion picture, service, defense, and myriad other industries. Except for an occasional and modest reform of water institutions, most Californians felt no compelling reason to change the system. Rather, the opposite became true as they took great pride—as measured in newspaper pronouncements, popular magazines, chamber of commerce brochures, and (especially) ballot-box returns—in the state's hydraulic, industrial, and agricultural achievements.

Powerful bureaucracies and special corporate interests have also played a monumental role in shaping modern California. The fundamental explanation for the contemporary waterscape, however, is to be found in the fact that the public has historically tolerated and, until recently, vigorously supported great water projects. Individual citizens cast votes for the Owens River aqueduct, the extension to Mono Basin, the Hetch Hetchy project, the Colorado River Aqueduct, the original Central Valley Project, and the State Water Project. They also elected the representatives who fought in Congress for the Boulder Canyon Project and for appropriations for all

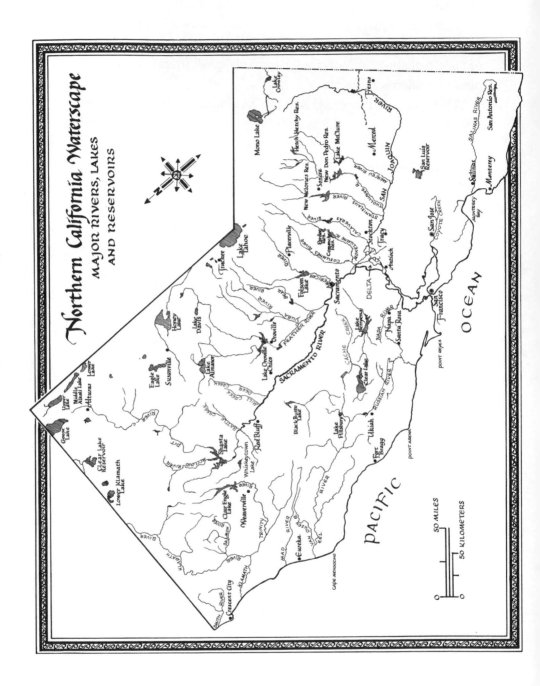

Northern California Waterscape

MAJOR RIVERS, LAKES AND RESERVOIRS

PACIFIC OCEAN

50 MILES

50 KILOMETERS

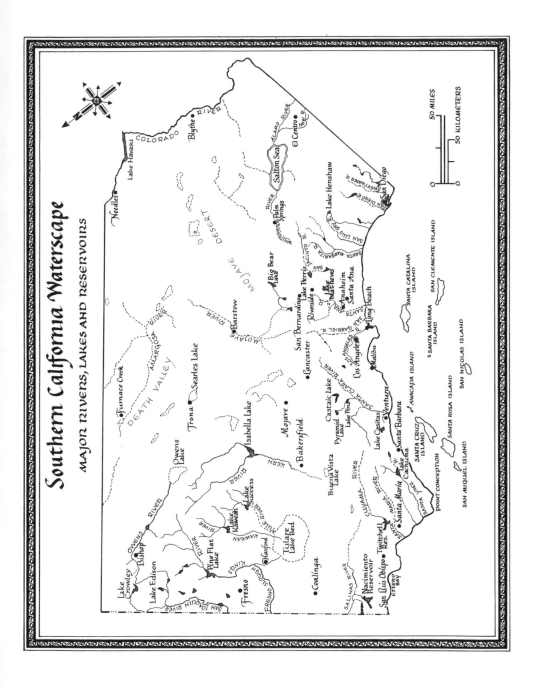

Southern California Waterscape

MAJOR RIVERS, LAKES AND RESERVOIRS

the federal ventures in California and who winked at the "technical compliance" loopholes in reclamation law. More recently, they have begun to challenge the wisdom of earlier actions and have used their ballots to defeat the Peripheral Canal package, to pressure their representatives in Washington and Sacramento to derail major new water projects, and to enact a host of environmental and preservation bills.

The record, as unfolded here, reveals past and continuing abuses by government agencies and agribusiness as well as attempts to manipulate the people's will, but just as clear is the ultimate authority of the electorate. Where powerful bureaucracies have come into existence—the Los Angeles Department of Water and Power, the Metropolitan Water District of Southern California, the Reclamation Bureau, and others—voters directly or through their elected representatives created them and can eliminate or change them. They can also change the rules governing the hundreds of local districts that tend to resist change and operate undemocratically. This is not to say that such adjustments will come quickly or easily. Moreover, ballot issues involving water are complex, often confusing, and may, as seems to have occurred in the struggle over the Stanislaus, lead to an unintended result at the polls. This merely underscores realities faced by all democracies in today's complex technological age. No one has ever argued that democracy is a perfect form of government.

Imperfect as it is, the democratic process has accommodated advances in water management and environmental protection during the last several decades, and it continues to foster struggles in courts and legislative halls to hold onto and increase those gains— in the Owens Valley, at Mono Lake, and through such devices as the public trust doctrine and other measures. These advances have occurred, as might be expected in a representative system, *where the public has been informed, vigilant, and active.* On balance, however, the gains have been largely piecemeal, often undermined by lack of enforcement, and frequently more symbolic than real, especially when the appointees to regulatory agencies lack the commitment or resources to carry out their duties effectively. There has not yet emerged at the highest levels leadership capable of designing and winning public support for an intelligent and practical overall water policy that accounts for the complex—and often clashing—entanglements among federal, state, and local governments and private interests.

Failure of that leadership to emerge among elected officials has created a vacuum into which the public frequently steps with initiatives, many of them hastily drafted and, out of frustration, designed to attempt massive reform all at once. A telling example was Proposition 128 (or "Big Green") which appeared on California's November 1990 ballot and would have forced numerous environmental reforms and also created a new elective Office of Environmental Advocate. There were many reasons for its nearly two-to-one rejection at the polls, but certainly among them was the measure's extraordinary complexity and length (nearly eleven pages of small print in the state's ballot pamphlet) that all but denied the average voter the opportunity to make an intelligent decision.

It could be contended that the first task of a responsible electorate would be to demand an end to the confusion in government. That confusion, arguably the result of an excess of Madisonian democracy with its focus on localism, has contributed mightily to the internecine conflict so characteristic of California's water management experience. However, this *is* the American system, for Americans do profoundly believe in widely shared and dispersed power among the people at large, and it is a system that has immense potential for liberating ideas and energies.

Still, the seriousness of the problems and the complexity of the issues, involving as they do government at all levels as well as the private sector, clamor for reform. They deserve the attention of the nation's best minds in and out of government: a task force approach. Ultimately what seems clearly warranted is a coordinating agency authorized to *take charge*. The challenge lies in the design of the appropriate mechanism and the nature of its accountability to the people—for it *must be accountable* in a region where water is so critical to the life of every community. The issue has thus far proven beyond the capability of legislatures, is not suited to resolution by the courts, and is too complex (and important) to be left to the vicissitudes of the initiative process.

Certainly among the highest priorities of any leadership should be a thorough overhaul of the system of agricultural subsidies that encourages the production of low-value, water-intensive surplus crops. The growers of such crops are actually subsidized twice by taxpayers, once in the form of cheap water and again in the form of federal price supports and supply controls, which in effect pay farmers to take some of their land out of production. Reform of the subsidy structure would go a long way toward correcting other deleterious by-products—such as waste, pollution, and land subsidence—of an industry that accounts for the overwhelming lion's share (now 77 percent) of California water use. While agriculture is important to the California economy and helps to stabilize it in downturns,[2] it is also an industry that has demonstrated an ability to get along on less water. According to a 1984 study by Henry Vaux, Jr., and Richard Howitt, two University of California resource economists, a cutback of 10 percent in farm water use (at that time approximately 83 percent of the state's developed supply) would have met California's urban needs for the next twenty years and "wouldn't do any serious harm to the agricultural community." By the late 1990s their prediction seemed to be squarely on target. As a result of water transfers and conservation on farms (and in cities), urban areas were still growing and agricultural water use had fallen 6 percent (and will fall further as water marketing comes increasingly into play). In the meantime, observed Vaux and Howitt in 1998, none of this had hurt California agriculture's position in the national or global economy.[3]

Also significantly enhancing California's ability to meet its future needs would be more efficient use of aquifers as storage receptacles. Aquifers are ready-made, have a usable capacity estimated presently at 140 million acre-feet or about four times the capacity of surface reservoirs (the state's total annual rain- and snowfall is approximately 200 million acre-feet), and avoid the characteristically heavy water losses attributable to evaporation at surface reservoirs. Hoover Dam's Lake Mead and Glen Canyon Dam's Lake Powell together lose 2 million acre-feet a year to evaporation, more than 10 percent of the Colorado River's average flow and enough to supply a city the size of Los Angeles.[4]

Some use of aquifers for storage is being made, but it is minimal, with groundwater pollution and overdraft, rather than cleanup and replenishment, being the norm. Significant progress will require far more effective pollution controls than those now in place, meaningful groundwater management, and a major reform of groundwater law. The lack of clear vested rights to groundwater encourages pumpers to take it without paying for it, thereby eliminating any incentive to protect its quality, invest in reclaiming it, or pay for developing groundwater storage facilities. Exacerbating the problem are the weaker self-cleansing properties of groundwater than those for surface supplies, resulting in much longer time intervals for any improvement.[5] Some headway has been made, but policymakers do not yet seem to fully understand that it is invariably less expensive to avoid contamination than to eliminate it. Moreover, the law must cease making a false distinction between groundwater and surface supplies, recognize that they are interconnected and part of the same hydrologic cycle, and prevent the unrestrained extractions that now encourage exhaustion of aquifers, seawater intrusion in coastal areas, and land subsidence.

California's urban areas, though utilizing far less water than agriculture, nonetheless contain the preponderance of voters and are capable of effecting major institutional change in the state and exerting enormous pressure for reforms in Washington. First, however, city dwellers need to change their own attitudes and practices. Incredible as it may seem as we enter a new millennium, many cities, including Sacramento and Fresno, have yet to install water meters, thereby conveying the nonsensical notion that water exists in unlimited abundance and at virtually no cost.[6] Experience suggests that urban dwellers change their practices only grudgingly and incrementally, and even then only in response to penalties and economic incentives, while their attitudes change little if at all. In the severe droughts of 1976–1977 and 1987–1992 requests for voluntary cutbacks from local governments and water agencies in hard-hit areas failed to produce the required savings, thus leading to mandated conservation measures, including such penalties as fines, increased water rates, and restricted service for offenders. Significant water savings were achieved only when nearly every community in the state adopted some kind of required conservation code.

Even so, many residents and officials responsible for enforcing the codes winked at the restrictions, with the extent of noncompliance tending to vary according to a community's perception of the drought threat. For example, in 1977 Los Angeles residents, in response to mandated cutbacks of 10 percent per household, reduced the city's overall water consumption by 13 percent. What appeared at first to be a commendable achievement, however, dims on discovery that some 100,000 of the city's households failed to reduce their consumption by the required amount or to stop such practices as watering lawns during the hottest daylight hours, between 10:00 a.m. and 4:00 p.m., and hosing, rather than sweeping, sidewalks and driveways. The drought of 1987–1992 witnessed a repeat performance, with Los Angeles issuing more than 22,000 citations. Despite numerous violations during both droughts, no one, not even flagrant repeat lawbreakers, had their water supply restricted or turned off. The violations and lack of enforcement in 1976–1977 reflected Los Angeles's (and southern California's) secure position at the time because of a surplus supply in the Colorado River Basin. In northern California, however, especially in Marin and Monterey counties where the 1976–1977 drought was particularly severe and there was no standby surplus, mandatory water conservation, strict enforcement, and heightened public awareness resulted in dramatically reduced water consumption—53 percent less than normal in the area served by the Marin Municipal Water District, 38 percent less in the North Marin Water District, and 47 percent less in the Monterey Bay area. Once the drought crisis passed, however, people even in these areas tended to revert to their usual wasteful practices as rapidly as the residents of southern California.[7]

The drought of 1987–1992 prompted some water leaders to conclude that there had to be a better way. First to react were northerners, especially water managers in Marin County where memories of the earlier devastating drought remained fresh and where at one point during that crisis restaurants had been required to serve food on paper plates in order to meet water-conservation requirements. Rather than waiting until the new dry cycle reached a crisis stage that would require mandated cutbacks, the North Marin Water District announced its strategy: "Go after programs that use less water automatically."[8]

Those programs included a combination of water-pricing formulas and financial incentives to encourage conservation: upping the price for each cubic foot of water each time a customer's uses escalated beyond a certain point, thus making it increasingly expensive to use water; offering financial incentives to replace lawns (identified as the single heaviest water user) with Xeriscapes, dry landscapes capable of existing on little rainfall; providing subsidies and rebates to residents willing to install low-flow toilets (water for toilets represented the single biggest usage indoors) and low-flow showerheads (the next largest indoor usage was for showers and baths). Other communities followed, and sometimes preceded, Marin residents in adopting these strategies—Goleta in Santa Barbara County was the first city in California to require low-flow toilets in new construction, and Monterey Peninsula Water Management District went a step further by compelling the installation of low-flow toilets in older properties when they were sold or when

remodeled with the addition of a new bathroom or with a significant increase (25 percent or more) in a home's overall square footage.
The communities adopting such practices, however, remained a
small minority.[9]

By 1988 with the state in what the Department of Water Resources designated a "critically dry" stage (the department's term for
the most severe period), the contrast in water-consumption patterns between the handful of conservation-conscious communities
and most California cities was dramatic. While Goleta during the
previous year had reduced daily water consumption to 150 gallons
per person, the figure for nearby Santa Barbara was 12 percent higher
at 169 gallons, for Los Angeles 179 gallons, and for Beverly Hills a
staggering 332 gallons, the latter figure suggesting that more affluent
areas, whose residents were able and willing to pay higher rates to
keep landscaping lush, tended to be more flagrant water users.[10]
During the increasingly dry months that followed, water consumption in most California communities began to decline, but that was
primarily the result of mandated cutbacks like those adopted during the drought of 1976–1977 (or threats to mandate cutbacks if a
community's collective usage did not fall by a specified percentage)
and because of rapidly declining or exhausted reservoirs.[11]

All of which suggests that, as each drought ends, most Californians will lapse into their wasteful ways just as they did when earlier emergencies passed. A recent ten-year study of the monthly
water bills of Los Angeles Department of Water and Power customers concludes that, "after a drought, 50-75 percent of the gains
that were made in water-use reduction are lost." Those not lost appear to be the result of water-saving technology such as low-flow
toilets and showerheads. "Behaviorally, people tend to backslide,"
states UCLA sociologist Richard Berk, who conducted the research,
"almost completely reverting to their original water-use patterns."[12]
Also indicative of such behavior was the demand of many Californians for the elimination of water restrictions when the cooler than
usual summer of 1991 and heavier precipitation in the winter of
1992 resulted in higher reservoir levels. The key issue, as suggested

by Berk's research, becomes how to persuade people to adopt water-saving technology that can outlast their fickle behavior. In a subsequent study of Los Angeles, San Francisco, and East Bay homeowners, Berk and Daniel Schulman found that a crucial incentive was a rebate. "Even for the smallest rebates tested," they observed, "large fractions of respondents seemed ready to accept the rebate offer," and "increasing the rebates increased the adoption rate" until it reached "a little over half the respondents."[13] The implications of these findings for government and the private sector are self-evident.

Prominent water managers question whether California will ever be entirely free from "drought" conditions. The combination of the water lost by court decision to Arizona, the still uncertain demands created by environmental legislation and court decisions, the continued rapid population growth, the economic and political obstacles to a major new water project, and the determination of farmers—so far at least—to sell or lease only reclaimed or surplus water suggests a future of permanent shortage even if there are (and perhaps in spite of) careful management strategies. "Californians face water shortages now, and will face increasing shortages in the future," declared the state Department of Water Resources in 1998, following one of the wettest winters on record.[14]

Such observations underscore both the need for changes in attitude and the possibilities of what might be achieved through well-crafted reforms, especially when combined with efforts to reclaim wastewater. The drought of 1987–1992 renewed interest in desalting seawater (Santa Barbara, Morro Bay, Marina, and Avalon on Santa Catalina Island have desalination plants—some only on standby for severe droughts—while other communities are considering them), but the process remains very expensive ($1,000 to $2,000 an acre-foot), much more so than wastewater reclamation ($500 to $1,200 an acre-foot). California now produces some 323,000 acre-feet of recycled water that would otherwise be lost to the state's hydrologic system, but the state Department of Water Resources estimates that almost 1.1 million acre-feet could be acquired by 2020 through reclaiming wastewater alone. Such a goal depends on securing funds for projects still in the planning stage.[15]

Among the most impressive recent advances in conservation and wastewater reclamation have taken place in what some thought would have been the least likely locale—southern California. Despite the area's nationwide reputation as a water ogre and its tendency to backslide into wasteful habits following droughts, the southland is working to recast its image and practices. Leadership has come primarily from the usually maligned water agencies now worried that severe shortages may occur before adequate agricultural water or other supplies can be secured.

Spurred by the 1987–1992 drought and the examples set by Marin County, Goleta, and Monterey, the Los Angeles Department of Water and Power in 1995 released a detailed Urban Water Management Plan aimed at making more "efficient use of water resources . . . in an environmentally responsible manner." The department actually initiated major parts of the plan as early as 1990 when it began giving away or offering rebates on ultra-low-flush toilets. By the end of the decade it had distributed more than 850,000 toilets and inspired MWD and other southern California water agencies to disperse another 675,000 for a total of 1.5 million. The city also gave away showerheads and offered cash incentives to those who purchased high-efficiency washing machines while, at the same time, mandating low-flow showerheads and low-flush toilets in every home sold. The Los Angeles program led to savings of 9 billion gallons annually. As a result of such savings and increased water-recycling efforts (the latter producing nearly 27,500 acre-feet) Los Angeles at the end of the '90s was using about the same volume of water as it did in 1970 despite a population increase of nearly a million. The accomplishment did not go unnoticed by the environmental community. "The Department of Water and Power is one of the great iconic villains of the environmental movement," stated an attorney for the Natural Resources Defense Council, but it is "at risk now of destroying its symbolic value to the movement."[16]

MWD by the end of the '90s was acquiring a similar reputation. Its conservation and reclamation efforts constituted a critical part of its 1996 Integrated Water Resources Plan designed to meet the needs of a fast-growing population while also helping to wean southern California off Colorado River water until it was taking no more than its basic allocation of 4.4 million acre-feet. Those efforts paid off handsomely, producing by 1999 some 700,000 acre-feet a year, an achievement that allowed the agency that year to support its customers with the same volume of water as it did in 1986 even though the population of its service area had grown by 3 million. Such advances notwithstanding, even the water agencies recognized that more could be done, as a Los Angeles example illustrates: 60 percent of the city's homes by the end of the 1990s still used older water-guzzling toilets (3.6 to 7 gallons per flush versus 1.6 gallons), lawns and landscaping accounted for 40 percent of water use, and millions of gallons continued to pour into the ocean from sewage plants and storm drains.[17]

That Californians—and all Americans, for that matter—have abused the land and waterscape and failed to develop a coherent water policy hardly seems surprising for a people with a centuries-old tradition of exploitation and with a (perhaps illogical) desire to accommodate simultaneously growth, environmental restoration, and at least some wilderness preservation. Still, there are hopeful signs: the environmental legislation and the occasional attempts to focus some of the best minds on the issues, most notably in the 1978 report of the Governor's Commission to Review California Water Rights Law which, despite then-Governor Jerry Brown's failure to follow through vigorously on the commission's recommendations after asking for them, sparked the most effective of recent reforms. Nonetheless, the record of abuse, the growing multitudes of people, and humanity's peculiar tolerance for fouling its nest by increments once thought intolerable are dismaying and underscore the immensity of the task faced by those seeking to inform and arouse the public.

So, too, does the irony of environmentalists joining with cities in a powerful coalition for water marketing that, without appropriate constraints, could accelerate the urbanization of open spaces and farmland and, withal, the despoliation of a once Golden State. The irony is all the more disconcerting because the environmentalists place the responsibility for designing and implementing the needed constraints solely on the fast-growing urban areas that have historically proved incapable of controlling their runaway expansion. "The environmental community feels very strongly that growth management is something that California desperately needs," stated the executive director of the Save San Francisco Bay Association in 1993. "We hope that southern California, at some point, figures out that growth control is in the interest of the survival of southern California. There's going to be . . . terrifying consequences in southern California. Not just environmental, but quality of life and for the future of the southern California economy."[18] So true, not only of southern California, but also of the East Bay, San Jose, Sacramento, Fresno, Modesto, Bakersfield, and numerous other locales. Environmentalists, especially at the local level, have not ignored the issue, but the environmental leadership has yet to acknowledge the magnitude of its responsibility to marshal its considerable followers and resources and to participate meaningfully in resolving the problem.

And that problem derives from the powerful reality that Californians are not so much facing a water problem as a *land-use* problem. California's (and the nation's) exploding population notwithstanding, leaders at all levels of government have thus far been unwilling or unable to invest the resources needed to make *current* cities more livable, appealing, healthful, and safe—in a word, more *attractive* to people so they do not feel compelled to flee an undesirable urban environment only to replicate it endlessly across the map and into the future. Nor have leaders devised effective land- and water-use constraints aimed at preserving the remaining open spaces while also respecting property rights in a way that does not unfairly enrich at public expense those agricultural interests holding rights to 77 percent of the state's developed water supply—a supply made possible by taxpayer-funded subsidies. Without such changes, there seems little hope of containing the urbanization of the countryside or assuring future generations an opportunity to enjoy whatever is left of those qualities that once made California one of the most desirable places on earth.

Because California possesses a greater array of spectacular natural wonders in proximity to great population centers than any other state (or nation), it has attracted an especially eloquent group of champions who have focused extensively or entirely on the Golden State: Raymond Dasmann in *The Destruction of California* (1965) and *California's Changing Environment* (1981); Richard Lillard in *Eden in Jeopardy* (1966); Roderick Nash in *Wilderness and the American Mind* (3d ed., 1982); Donald Worster in *Rivers of Empire* (1985); Marc Reisner in *Cadillac Desert* (1986); Tim Palmer in *The Stanislaus* (1982) and *Endangered Rivers and the Conservation Movement* (1986); Robert Gottlieb in *A Life of Its Own* (1988); John Walton in *Western Times and Water Wars* (1992); John Hart in *Storm over Mono* (1996); David Carle in *Drowning the Dream* (2000); David Brower in his many books for the Sierra Club; William Kahrl, Tom Harris, Nancy Vogel, and Tom Knudson in their insightful reporting and observations in the *Sacramento Bee;* Rita Schmidt-Sudman, Sue McClurg, and Josh Newcom in their publications through the Water Education Foundation; the Pacific Institute's studies of California water; and the photographers Edward Weston and Ansel Adams, among many others. These individuals have attracted their challengers—most notably, Charles Zurhorst in *The Conservation Fraud* (1970), Bernard J. Frieden in *The Environmental Protection Hustle* (1979), Joseph Gughemetti and Eugene D. Wheeler in *The Taking* (1980)—but the critics notwithstanding, the advocates of change have contributed powerfully to the public's increasing awareness of the fragility of the land and the waterscape.

For the long and short term, the overriding message of those concerned with California's (and the nation's) water supplies is for society to adopt attitudes and institutions that meaningfully address today's enormous population pressures and wasteful and environmentally damaging practices. Fundamentally, this means continuing those efforts at informing and encouraging the electorate to abandon those attitudes and institutions that were born of an earlier era when abundance encouraged abuse.

Notes

Preface

1. Karl Wittfogel, *Oriental Despotism: A Comparative Study of Total Power* (New Haven: Yale University Press, 1957). For other views, most of them challenging Wittfogel, see René Millon, "Variations in Response to the Practice of Irrigation Agriculture," in Richard B. Woodbury, ed., *Civilizations in Desert Lands* (Salt Lake City: University of Utah Anthropological Paper No. 62, Dec. 1962), 56–88; Theodore Downing and McGuire Gibson, eds., *Irrigation's Impact on Society* (Tucson: University of Arizona Press, 1974); and William Mitchell, "The Hydraulic Hypothesis," *Current Anthropology* 14 (1973): 532–534. A work in American history influenced by Karl Wittfogel is Donald Worster's *Rivers of Empire: Water, Aridity, and the Growth of the American West* (New York: Pantheon, 1985), which draws upon Wittfogel's assumptions about centralized water control and despotism to describe the emergence in the American West of what he calls "the greatest hydraulic society ever built in history," a society characterized by "a coercive, monolithic, and hierarchical system, ruled by a power elite based on the ownership of capital and expertise" (pp. 7, 276). Other scholars of western water have produced findings more in harmony with my own than Worster's. See, for example, Donald Pisani, *To Reclaim a Divided West: Water, Law, and Public Policy* (Albuquerque: University of New Mexico Press, 1992); James E. Sherow, *Watering the Valley: Development along the High Plains Arkansas River, 1870–1950* (Lawrence: University Press of Kansas, 1990); Daniel Tyler, *The Last Water Hole in the West: A History of the Northern Colorado Water Conservancy District and the Colorado–Big Thompson Project* (Niwot, Colo.: University Press of Colorado, 1992); Susan M. Stacy, *When the River Rises: Flood Control*

on the Boise River, 1943–1985 (Boulder: Institute of Behavioral Science, University of Colorado; College of Social Sciences and Public Affairs, Boise State University, 1993); Richard Sadler and Richard Roberts, *The Weber River Basin: Grass Roots Democracy and Water Development* (Logan: Utah State University Press, 1994); John Walton, *Western Times and Water Wars: State, Culture, and Rebellion in California* (Berkeley and Los Angeles: University of California Press, 1992); Robert Gottlieb and Margaret FitzSimmons, *Thirst for Growth: Water Agencies as Hidden Government in California* (Tucson: University of Arizona Press, 1991).

2. Robert Kelley, *Battling the Inland Sea: American Political Culture, Public Policy, and the Sacramento Valley, 1850–1986* (Berkeley and Los Angeles: University of California Press, 1989), xv.

Chapter 1: The Aboriginal Waterscape

1. Sherburne F. Cook, *The Population of the California Indians, 1769–1970* (Berkeley and Los Angeles: University of California Press, 1976), 43; Cook, "Historical Demography," in Robert Heizer, ed., *California,* vol. 3 of *Handbook of North American Indians* (Washington, D.C.: Smithsonian Institution, 1978), 91; Russell Thornton, *American Indian Holocaust and Survival: A Population History Since 1492* (Norman: University of Oklahoma Press, 1987), 28–29.

2. California Department of Water Resources, "California Water Plan Update," *Bulletin 160–98* (Sacramento: California Department of Water Resources, Nov. 1998), chap. 1, p. 2, chap. 3, pp. 48–51; *Bulletin 160–98: Executive Summary,* chap. ES4, p. 4.

3. Robert F. Heizer and Albert B. Elsasser, *The Natural World of the California Indians* (Berkeley and Los Angeles: University of California Press, 1980), 210–211.

4. For a sampling of the conflicting views of the Indian as ecologist in prehistoric America, see Paul S. Martin and Richard B. Klein, eds., *Quaternary Extinctions: A Prehistoric Revolution* (Tucson: University of Arizona Press, 1984), 357–370, 451–465; passim; Paul S. Martin, "Prehistoric Overkill," in P. S. Martin and H. E. Wright, Jr., eds., *Pleistocene Extinctions: The Search for a Cause* (New Haven: Yale University Press, 1967), 75–120; Calvin Martin, *Keepers of the Game* (Berkeley and Los Angeles: University of California Press, 1978), 167–171; Jared M. Diamond, "The Environmentalist Myth," *Nature* 324 (Nov. 26, 1986): 19–20.

5. D. Demetracopoulou Lee, "Linguistic Reflection of Wintu Thought," *International Journal of American Linguistics* 10 (1944): 186–187; S. A. Barrett, "Pomo Myths," *Bulletin of the Public Museum of the City of Milwaukee* 14 (Nov. 6, 1933): 51, 53, 68, 77–78, 82–83, 456, passim; Edward W. Gifford and Gwendoline H. Block, *California Indian Nights Entertainments* (Glendale, Calif.: Arthur H. Clark Co., 1930), 186–187, passim; Alfred L. Kroeber, *Yurok Myths* (Berkeley and Los Angeles: University of California Press, 1976), passim; Dorothy Demetracopoulou and Cora DuBois, "A Study of Wintu Mythology," *Journal of American Folklore* 45 (1932): 404–495; Cora DuBois and Dorothy Demetracopoulou, "Wintu Myths," *University of California Publications in American Archaeology and Ethnology* vol. 28, no. 5 (Berkeley: University of California Press, 1931): passim.

6. Emil W. Haury, *The Hohokam* (Tucson: University of Arizona Press, 1976); George J. Gumerman, ed., *Exploring the Hohokam: Prehistoric Desert Peoples of the American Southwest* (Albuquerque: University of New Mexico Press, 1991); Michael C. Meyer, *Water in the Hispanic Southwest: A Social and Legal History, 1550–1850* (Tucson: University of Arizona Press, 1984), 17; Eric Wolf, *Sons of the Shaking Earth* (Chicago: University of Chicago Press, 1962), 74–76.

7. Elna Bakker, *An Island Called California* (Berkeley and Los Angeles: University of California Press, 1971), 123–133, passim; A. Starker Leopold, *Wild California: Vanishing Lands, Vanishing Wildlife* (Berkeley and Los Angeles: University of California Press, 1985), 55–70; Kenneth Thompson, "Historic Flooding in the Sacramento Valley," *Pacific Historical Review* 29 (Nov. 1960): 349–360; S. T. Harding, *Water in California* (Palo Alto, Calif.: N-P Publications, 1960), 4–5.

8. William Preston, *Vanishing Landscapes: Land and Life in the Tulare Lake Basin* (Berkeley and Los Angeles: University of California Press, 1981); Bakker, *An Island Called California,* 223–227; passim; Leopold, *Wild California,* 24, 26; Community and Organization Research Institute, University of California, Santa Barbara, *The Future of Mono Lake* (Riverside: University of California Water Resources Center Report no. 68, Feb. 1988), 6.

9. *The World Encompassed by Sir Francis Drake* (1628; n.p.: Readex Micropoint, 1966), 79–80; Otto von Kotzebue, *A New Voyage Round the World, in the Years 1823, 24, 25, and 26,* 2 vols. (London: Henry Colburn and Richard Bentley, 1830), 2: 144.

10. William L. Kahrl, ed., *The California Water Atlas* (Sacramento:

Governor's Office of Planning and Research, 1979), 4, 10, 12, 14, 17; Leopold, *Wild California,* 56, 68; Raymond F. Dasmann, *California's Changing Environment* (San Francisco: Boyd & Fraser Publishing Co., 1981), 5–8; Bakker, *An Island Called California,* 147–157, passim.

11. The California Department of Water Resources indicates that agricultural water use is 33.8 million acre-feet and that of urban areas is 8.8 million acre-feet, but these figures are too high. The agricultural estimate refers to water *applied* to crops and does not account for return flow to a stream that is available for use by others downriver, while the urban figure does not take into consideration water that is reclaimed and then recycled for further use. Such adjustments result in 28 million acre-feet of agricultural water use and 8.5 million acre-feet for cities. The figure for agriculture comes from studies conducted by Henry Vaux, Jr., a University of California resource economist (Vaux to the author, March 12, 1999). On "new recycled water" (323,000 acre-feet or approximately 0.3 million acre-feet), see California Department of Water Resources, "California Water Plan Update," *Bulletin 160–98: Executive Summary* (Sacramento: California Department of Water Resources, Nov. 1998), chap. 3, p. ES3-9; and interview with Susan Tatayon, manager, water recycling, California Department of Water Resources, April 14, 1999. See also California Department of Water Resources, *Bulletin 160–98,* chap. 1, p. 2, chap. 3, pp. 1–2, 12–13, 25; California Department of Water Resources, "California Water Plan Update," *Bulletin 160–93,* 2 vols. (Sacramento: California Department of Water Resources, Oct. 1994), 1: 5–7; California Department of Water Resources, "California Water: Looking to the Future," *Bulletin 160–87* (Sacramento: San Diego Department of Water Resources, Nov. 1987), 22, 31; California Department of Water Resources and California Water Resources Control Board, "Policies and Goals for California Water Management: The Next 20 Years—Public Review Draft," *DWR/SWRCB Bulletin 4* (Sacramento: California Department of Water Resources, June 1981), 38; interview with Karl Hauge, supervising engineering geologist, California Department of Water Resources, June 12, 1991; California Department of Water Resources, "Ground Water Basins in California," *Bulletin 118–80* (Sacramento: California Department of Water Resources, Jan. 1980); Kahrl, ed., *California Water Atlas,* 3–4, 6, 9.

12. Henry F. Díaz and Vera Markgraf, eds., *El Niño: Historical and Paleoclimatic Aspects of the Southern Oscillation* (New York: Cambridge

University Press, 1992); S. G. Philander, "El Niño," *Oceanus* 35 (1992): 56–65; Jeffrey F. Mount, *California Rivers and Streams: The Conflict between Fluvial Process and Land Use* (Berkeley and Los Angeles: University of California Press, 1995), 152–157; David W. Stahle et al., "Tree-Ring Data Document 16th Century Megadrought over North America," *EOS: Transactions of the American Geophysical Union* 81 (Mar. 21, 2000): 124–125; Metropolitan Water District of Southern California, *News Release,* May 23, 2000; *Los Angeles Times,* May 24, 2000.

13. California Department of Water Resources, "California Water Plan Update," *Bulletin 160–93,* 2 vols. (Sacramento: California Department of Water Resources, Oct. 1994): 1: 50.

14. These figures, taken from National Weather Service data, are based on a rainfall year of January 1 through December 31.

15. Scott Stine, "Extreme and Persistent Drought in California and Patagonia during Mediaeval Time," *Nature* 369 (June 16, 1994): 546–549; Stahle et al., "Tree-Ring Data Document 16th Century Megadrought over North America," 124–125.

16. California Department of Water Resources, "Annual Precipitation for California since 1600 Reconstructed from Western North American Tree Rings," by Harold C. Fritts and Geoffrey A. Gordon (July 1980): 38–40, copy in S-9, item 3981, California Department of Water Resources Archives, Sacramento; Fritts and Gordon, "Reconstructed Annual Precipitation for California," in M. K. Hughes et al., eds., *Climate from Tree Rings* (Cambridge, Eng.: Cambridge University Press, 1982), 190–191; Edmund Schulman, "Tree-Ring Hydrology in Southern California," *University of Arizona Bulletin* 18 (July 1947): 33. See also Harold C. Fritts, G. Robert Lofgren, and Geoffrey A. Gordon, "Variations in Climate since 1602 as Reconstructed from Tree Rings," *Quaternary Research* 12 (1979): 18–46; Edmund Schulman, "Precipitation Records in California Tree Rings," in *Proceedings of the Sixth Pacific Science Congress, 1939,* 6 vols. (Berkeley and Los Angeles: University of California Press, 1940–1943), 3: 707–717; Schulman, "Runoff Histories in Tree Rings of the Pacific Slope," *Geographical Review* 35 (Jan. 1945): 59–73; H. B. Lynch, *Rainfall and Stream Run-off in Southern California since 1769* (Los Angeles: Metropolitan Water District of Southern California, 1931); U.S. Department of Agriculture, Weather Bureau, *Climatic Summary of the United States: Section 18—Southern California and Owens Valley* (Washington, D.C.: Government Printing Office, 1932), p. 18-4;

S. T. Harding, "Recent Variations in the Water Supply of the Western Great Basin," *Archive Series Report No. 16* (Berkeley: University of California Water Resources Center Archives, 1965); Arthur Douglas, "Past Air-Sea Interaction over the Eastern North Pacific Ocean as Revealed by Tree Ring Data" (Ph.D. dissertation, University of Arizona, 1976); J. M. Guinn, "A History of California Floods and Drought," *Publications of the Historical Society of Southern California* 1 (1890): 33–39; Kahrl, ed., *California Water Atlas,* 6.

17. Ralph L. Beals and Joseph A. Hester, Jr., "A New Ecological Typology of the California Indians," in Robert F. Heizer and M. A. Whipple, eds., *The California Indians: A Source Book,* 2d ed. (Berkeley and Los Angeles: University of California Press, 1971), 73–83; Heizer and Elsasser, *Natural World,* 10–22, 42, 56, 57–58; Cook, *Population of the California Indians,* 40–43.

18. A. L. Kroeber, "The Nature of Land-Holding Groups in Aboriginal California," in Robert F. Heizer, ed., *Aboriginal California: Three Studies in Culture History* (Berkeley: University of California Archaeological Research Facility, 1963), 111; Beals and Hester, "New Ecological Typology," 74–82; Heizer and Elsasser, *Natural World,* 7, 9–10, 57–113.

19. Heizer and Elsasser, *Natural World,* 73–75; Beals and Hester, "New Ecological Typology," 81; William Strong, *Aboriginal Society in Southern California* (1929; Banning, Calif.: Malki Museum Press, 1972), 38; Julian H. Steward, "Ecological Aspects of Southwestern Society," *Anthropos* 32 (1937): 89; Sidney W. Mintz, "The Role of Water in Steward's Cultural Ecology," *Journal of the Steward Anthropological Society* 11 (Fall 1979): 25.

20. Quoted in Lee, "Linguistic Reflection of Wintu Thought," 187; see also B. W. Aginsky, "Population Control in the Shanel (Pomo) Tribe," *American Sociological Review* 4 (1939): 209–216; Heizer and Elsasser, *Natural World,* 23, 26, 33–34, 211, passim.

21. Henry T. Lewis, *Patterns of Indian Burning in California: Ecology and Ethnohistory* (Ramona, Calif.: Ballena Press, 1973); Lowell J. Bean and Harry W. Lawton, "Some Explanations for the Rise of Cultural Complexity in Native California with Comments on Proto-Agriculture and Agriculture," in ibid., v–xlvii; Walter Ebeling, *Handbook of Indian Foods and Fiber of Arid America* (Berkeley and Los Angeles: University of California Press, 1986), 183; Heizer and Whipple, *California Indians,* 22; David W. Peri and Scott M. Patterson, "The Basket Is in the Roots, That's Where It Begins," in Thomas C.

Blackburn and Kat Anderson, eds., *Before the Wilderness: Environmental Management by Native Californians* (Menlo Park. Calif.: Ballena Press, 1993), 175–194; Florence C. Shipek, "An Example of Intensive Plant Husbandry: The Kumeyaay of Southern California," in David R. Harris and Gordon C. Hillman, eds., *Foraging and Farming: The Evolution of Plant Exploitation* (London: Unwin Hyman, 1989), 159–170; James Cornett, "Indians and the Desert Fan Palm," *Masterkey* (1987): 12–17; M. Kat Anderson, Michael G. Barbour, and Valerie Whitworth, "A World of Balance and Plenty: Land, Plants, Animals, and Humans in a Pre-European California," in Ramón A. Gutiérrez and Richard J. Orsi, eds., *Contested Eden: California Before the Gold Rush* (Berkeley: University of California Press, 1997), 12–47.

22. Robert F. Heizer, "Prehistoric Central California: A Problem in Historical-Development Classification," *University of California Archaeological Survey Report No. 41* (Berkeley: Department of Anthropology, University of California, 1958), 19–26; Herbert J. Spinden, "The Origin and Distribution of Agriculture in America," *Proceedings of the 19th International Congress of Americanists, 1915* (Washington, D.C., 1915), 269–276; Carl O. Sauer, "American Agricultural Origins: A Consideration of Nature and Culture," in Robert H. Lowie, ed., *Essays in Anthropology Presented to A. L. Kroeber in Celebration of His Sixtieth Birthday, June 11, 1936* (Berkeley: University of California Press, 1936), 294–295; S. J. Jones, "Some Regional Aspects of Native California," in Heizer and Whipple, eds., *California Indians,* 88–89; Ebeling, *Handbook of Indians Foods,* 167–168 (quote p. 168).

23. Julian H. Steward, "Irrigation without Agriculture," *Papers of the Michigan Academy of Science, Arts and Letters* 12 (1930): 149–156; Mintz, "Role of Water in Steward's Cultural Ecology," 17–32.

24. Harry W. Lawton, Philip J. Wilke, Mary DeBecker, and William M. Mason, "Agriculture among the Paiute of Owens Valley," *Journal of California Anthropology* 3 (Summer 1976): 13–50; Ebeling, *Handbook of Indian Foods,* 136–137, 151.

25. Lawton et al., "Agriculture among the Paiute," 33, 39–41.

26. Mark N. Cohen, *The Food Crisis in Prehistory* (New Haven: Yale University Press, 1977).

27. Paul D. Bouey, in "Population Pressure and Agriculture in Owens Valley," *Journal of California and Great Basin Anthropology* 1 (Summer 1979): 162–170, directly addresses Cohen's thesis in *Food Crisis.* See also Lawton et al., "Agriculture among the Paiute," 15.

28. Lawton et al., "Agriculture among the Paiute," 41–43.

29. Edward F. Castetter and Willis H. Bell, *Yuman Indian Agriculture* (Albuquerque: University of New Mexico Press, 1951), 1–65, 97–130.

30. Ibid., 74, 131–166, 238; Cook, *Population of the California Indians,* 43, 46.

31. Karl A. Wittfogel, *Oriental Despotism: A Comparative Study of Total Power* (New Haven: Yale University Press, 1957). More flexible than Wittfogel is Donald Worster in *Rivers of Empire* (New York: Pantheon, 1985), 32, but he seems not to take adequately into account the points raised in Lawton et al., "Agriculture among the Paiute," 18, 37, 41, 44–45. See also Ebeling, *Handbook of Indian Foods,* 153–154, but cf. 799, where he seems to contradict himself and is less persuasive. For a summary of anthropological studies of different irrigation societies, see René Millon, "Variations in Response to the Practice of Irrigation Agriculture," in Richard B. Woodbury, ed., *Civilizations in Desert Lands* (Salt Lake City: University of Utah Anthropological Paper No. 62, Dec. 1962), 56–88. See also Theodore Downing and McGuire Gibson, eds., *Irrigation's Impact on Society* (Tucson: University of Arizona Press, 1974); and William Mitchell, "The Hydraulic Hypothesis," *Current Anthropology* 14 (Dec. 1973): 532–534.

32. Frederic Hicks, "The Influence of Agriculture on Aboriginal Socio-Political Organization in the Lower Colorado River Valley," *Journal of California Anthropology* 1 (Winter 1974): 133–144.

33. Castetter and Bell, *Yuman Indian Agriculture,* 72–73; Hicks, "Influence of Agriculture," 137–141, passim.

34. Lawton et al., "Agriculture among the Paiute," 18.

35. Quoted in Heizer and Elsasser, *Natural World,* 210.

Chapter 2: Hispanic Patterns

1. *Las siete partidas del sabio rey don Alfonso* (1265; 4 vols.; Madrid, 1789), pt. 3, title 28, law 1.

2. Genesis 9:7.

3. Roderick Nash, *Wilderness and the American Mind,* 3d ed. (New Haven: Yale University Press, 1982), 9.

4. Thomas F. Glick, *Irrigation and Society in Medieval Valencia* (Cambridge, Mass.: Harvard University Press, 1970), 4, 5, 207.

5. Quoted in William H. Hall, *Irrigation Development* (Sacramento: Superintendent of State Printing, 1886), 386. See also Robert I.

Burns, "Irrigation Taxes in Early Mudejar Valencia: The Problems of Alfarda," *Speculum* 44 (1969): 560–567.

6. Donald E. Smith and Frederick J. Teggart, eds., *Diary of Gaspar de Portolá during the California Expedition of 1769–1770* (Berkeley: University of California Press, 1909), 39; Francisco Palóu, *Historical Memoirs of New California,* ed. Herbert E. Bolton, 4 vols. (Berkeley: University of California Press, 1926), 2: 82; Ray Brandes, trans., *The Costansó Narrative of the Portolá Expedition* (Newhall, Calif.: Hogarth Press, 1970), 83, 90.

7. Palóu, *Historical Memoirs,* 2: 82.

8. Ibid., 100, 101, 316, 323, 324, 359, 361.

9. Antonio María Bucareli y Ursúa, Instructions, Aug. 17, 1773, articles 12 and 13, California Archives, vol. 52: 327–328, Bancroft Library, University of California, Berkeley.

10. Felipe de Neve, Instructions for the Founding of the Pueblo of Los Angeles, Aug. 26, 1781, in "Los Angeles vs. United States," Land Grant Case 386, Southern District, pp. 38–40, Bancroft Library; Oscar O. Winther, "The Story of San Jose, 1777–1869: California's First Pueblo," *California Historical Society Quarterly* 14 (Mar.–June, 1935): 5; Diego de Borica to presidio commandants, Jan. 9, 1795, California Archives, 23: 402–403.

11. Zephyrin Engelhardt, *San Diego Mission* (San Francisco: James H. Barry Co., 1920), 54–56; Engelhardt, *The Missions and Missionaries of California,* 4 vols. (San Francisco: James H. Barry Co., 1908–1915), 4: 535; R. Louis Gentilcore, "Missions and Mission Lands of Alta California," *Annals of the Association of American Geographers* 51 (Mar. 1961): passim; Palóu, *Historical Memoirs,* 2: 319, 320.

12. Winther, "Story of San Jose," 7.

13. Robert F. Heizer and Albert B. Elsasser, *The Natural World of the California Indians* (Berkeley and Los Angeles: University of California Press, 1980), 56.

14. Palóu, *Historical Memoirs,* 3: 301.

15. Conde del Valle de Orizaba, Dec. 20, 1805, California Archives, 12: 14–16; Engelhardt, *Missions and Missionaries,* 2: 517; Florian Guest, "The Establishment of the Villa de Branciforte," *California Historical Quarterly* 41 (Mar. 1962): 29–50; Daniel Garr, "Villa de Branciforte: Innovation and Adaptation on the Frontier," *The Americas* 35 (July 1978): 95–109.

16. *Recopilación de leyes de los reynos de las Indias* (1681; 4 vols., Madrid: Ediciones Cultura Hispánica, [1681] 1973), bk. 4, title 17, law 5.

17. Antonio María Bucareli y Ursúa, Instructions, Aug. 17, 1773, articles 5 to 12, California Archives, 52: 325–327.

18. Felipe de Neve, Regulations, June 1, 1779, in *Reglamento para el gobierno de la provincia de Californias* (1784; San Francisco: Grabhorn Press, 1929), title 14.

19. Plan of Pitic, California Archives, 52: 340–357. An English translation can be found in John W. Dwinelle, *The Colonial History: City of San Francisco,* 4th ed. (San Francisco: Towne & Bacon, 1867), addenda 7. For the dating of the Plan, see Michael Meyer, *Water in the Hispanic Southwest: A Social and Legal History, 1550–1850* (Tucson: University of Arizona Press, 1984), 30–35.

20. Plan of Pitic, article 6; *Recopilación,* bk. 4, title 17, law 7; Pedro Fages to José Argüello, Aug. 14, 1786, in "Los Angeles vs. United States," 126–127.

21. Plan of Pitic, article 20.

22. Plan of Pitic, articles 20 and 24; Records of the Los Angeles Ayuntamiento, May 27, 1836, 2 Span. 211–212, 2 Eng. 153, Los Angeles City Archives.

23. Felipe de Neve, Regulations, June 1, 1779, in *Reglamento,* title 14.

24. Records of the Los Angeles Ayuntamiento, Mar. 23, 1839, 2 Span. 633, 2 Eng. 483; Jan. 29, 1844, 2 Span. 757, 2 Eng. 550; June 16, 1838, 2 Span. 569–571, 2 Eng. 438–439.

25. Felipe de Neve to Teodoro Croix, Oct. 29, 1781, California Archives, 22: 306–307; Diego de Borica to Alberto de Córdoba, May 15, 1797, California Archives, 14: 259; Guest, "Establishment of the Villa de Branciforte," 35–36, 39.

26. Felipe de Neve, Regulations, June 1, 1779, in *Reglamento,* title 14, section 18; Plan of Pitic, articles 21 and 24.

27. John Q. Ressler, "Indian and Spanish Water Control on New Spain's Northwest Frontier," *Journal of the West* 7 (Jan. 1968): 15–16; see also Ressler, "Spanish Mission Water Systems: Northwest Frontier of New Spain" (M.A. thesis, University of Arizona, 1965).

28. See, for example, Records of the Los Angeles Ayuntamiento, Jan. 21, 1836, 2 Span. 143, 2 Eng. 101; June 9, 1836, 2 Span. 215, 2 Eng. 156–157; June 30, 1836, 2 Span. 219–220, 2 Eng. 161; Feb. 11, 1837, 2 Span. 352–353, 2 Eng. 272; Aug. 3, 1839, 2 Span. 692, 2 Eng. 516.

29. Plan of Pitic, article 7.

30. Meyer, *Water,* 120; Meyer, "The Living Legacy of Hispanic Groundwater Law in the Contemporary Southwest," *Journal of the Southwest* 31 (Autumn 1989): 296–297.

31. Meyer, *Water,* 148.

32. W. W. Robinson, *Land in California* (Berkeley and Los Angeles: University of California Press, 1948), 47–48, 69, passim; Robert G. Cleland, *The Cattle on a Thousand Hills: Southern California, 1850–1880,* 2d ed. (San Marino, Calif.: Huntington Library, 1951), 8, passim.

33. Meyer, *Water,* 122–123, 129–130, 138; *Los Angeles vs. Baldwin: Supreme Court of the State of California: Respondent's Points and Authorities* (n.p., n.d.), 29, copy in California Supreme Court Records, vol. 465, California State Library.

34. Marginal note dated Oct. 20, 1784, by Pedro Fages on petition submitted by José María Verdugo in "Julio Berdugo [Verdugo] vs. United States," San Rafael Grant, Land Grant Case 381, Southern District, pp. 26–27, Bancroft Library; Verdugo to Diego de Borica, Dec. 4, 1797, ibid., 27–30; marginal note dated Oct. 21, 1784, on petition submitted by Manuel Pérez Nieto, in George Tays, "Transcriptions and Translations of Original Documents Relating to Ranchos in Los Angeles County," 3 vols. (typescript in Bancroft Library, 1939), vol. 3, "La Zanja."

35. Meyer, *Water,* 156.

36. Plan of Pitic, articles 2 and 19.

37. Robinson, *Land in California,* 56; Cleland, *Cattle on a Thousand Hills,* passim.

38. *San Diego* v. *Cuyamaca Water Co.,* 209 Cal. 122 (1930); *Cartwright* v. *Public Service Co. of New Mexico,* 66 N. Mex. 64 (1958). For a recent analysis of the Hispanic documents of New Mexico, which concludes that "the pueblo rights doctrine can only be seen as unhistorical and fictitious," see Daniel Tyler, *The Mythical Pueblo Rights Doctrine: Water Administration in Hispanic New Mexico* (El Paso: Texas Western Press, 1990), 45.

39. Zephyrin Engelhardt, *San Fernando Rey: The Mission of the Valley* (Chicago: Franciscan Herald Press, 1927), 5, 6; Palóu, *Historical Memoirs,* 2: 137.

40. Engelhardt, *San Fernando Rey,* 92, 97, 99, 102.

41. José Argüello to Governor of California, Mar. 26, 1810, California Archives, 12: 303–304; *Los Angeles vs. Baldwin: Transcript on Appeal from Seventeenth District Court, Los Angeles County* (March 16, 1878), 44–47. The transcripts and briefs cited in this section are in the California Supreme Court Records, California State Library, Sacramento, and in the Los Angeles County Law Library, Los Angeles.

42. *Vernon Irrigation Co. vs. Los Angeles: Supreme Court of the State of California—Closing Brief for Appellant* (1894), 35–39.

43. The errors and omissions in the documents that Los Angeles filed in the *Vernon* case helped fuel a major assault on the pueblo right theory in the 1960s. *Los Angeles vs. San Fernando et al.: California Court of Appeal, Second Appellate District—Appendix to Respondents' Brief* (Mar. 14, 1968), vol. 1, app. A, p. 58.

44. Edith B. Webb, *Indian Life at the Old Missions* (Los Angeles: W. F. Lewis, 1952), 77; Engelhardt, *San Fernando Rey,* passim.

45. *Los Angeles vs. San Fernando et al.: California Court of Appeal, Second Appellate District—Appendix to Respondents' Brief,* vol. 1, app. A, pp. 48–49.

46. Hubert Howe Bancroft, *History of California,* 7 vols. (San Francisco: The History Co., 1886–1890), 2: 111; H. B. Lynch, *Rainfall and Stream Run-Off in Southern California since 1769* (Los Angeles: Metropolitan Water District of Southern California, 1931),1–3. See also Lester Rowntree and Robert Raburn, "Rainfall Variability and California Mission Agriculture: An Analysis from Harvest and Tree Ring Data," in James W. Scott, ed., *Yearbook of the Association of Pacific Coast Geographers, 1980* (Corvallis: Oregon State University Press, 1980), 42: 31–44.

47. Engelhardt, *San Fernando Rey,* 97; Lynch, *Rainfall and Stream Run-Off,* 2–4; David Hornbeck, "Economic Growth and Change at the Missions of Alta California, 1769–1846," in David H. Thomas, ed., *Columbian Consequences,* vol. 2, *Archaeological and Historical Perspectives on the Spanish Borderlands West* (Washington, D.C.: Smithsonian Institution Press, 1989), 428–429; Robert Archibald, *The Economic Aspects of the California Missions* (Washington, D.C.: Academy of American Franciscan History, 1978), xii, 74–186.

48. Quoted in Archibald, *Economic Aspects,* 113.

49. Testimony of José Polanco, June 23, 1829, in "Julio Berdugo [Verdugo] vs. United States," San Rafael Grant, Land Grant Case 381, Southern District, 100–103, Bancroft Library; Guillermo Cota to Comandante General, June 26, 1829, in ibid., 95–98; Lynch, *Rainfall and Stream Run-Off,* 1, 4.

50. Records of the Los Angeles Ayuntamiento, Apr. 7, 1836, 2 Span. 181–182, 2 Eng. 133; Apr. 14, 1836, 2 Span. 199–200, 2 Eng. 143–144; Lynch, *Rainfall and Stream Run-Off,* 1, 4.

51. *Los Angeles vs. Baldwin: Transcript on Appeal,* 70, 71.

52. Robert G. Cowan, *Ranchos of California* (Fresno, Calif.: Academy Library Guild, 1956), 21, 34, 76, 105; W. W. Robinson, *San Fer-*

nando Valley (Los Angeles: Title Insurance and Trust Co., 1951), 18–19; "Diseños" (MS, n.d.), 378, call no. 170/508, Dept. of Special Collections, University Research Library, University of California, Los Angeles; Robert H. Becker, *Diseños of California Ranchos: Maps of Thirty-Seven Land Grants, 1822–1846* (San Francisco: Book Club of California, 1964), chap. 32; Lynch, *Rainfall and Stream Run-Off*, 5; Cleland, *Cattle on a Thousand Hills*, passim.

53. Junípero Serra to Francisco Pangua, Dec. 8, 1782, in Antonine Tibesar, ed., *Writings of Junípero Serra*, 4 vols. (Washington, D.C.: Academy of American Franciscan History, 1954–1966), 4: 171, 167–175; *Los Angeles vs. San Fernando et al.: Appendix to Respondents' Brief*, 1: app. C, I-98.

54. Miguel José de Azanza to Diego de Borica, Aug. 7, 1798, California Archives, 52: 44–45; Borica to Azanza, Dec. 3, 1798, ibid., 24: 434; Raymundo Carrillo to José Joaquín de Arrillaga, Aug. 1, 1801, ibid., 52: 45.

55. Marques de Casafuerte, decrees of Dec. 20, 1731, and May 12, 1733, both in *Brief of Everett Bell et al.: Texas et al. vs. Valmont Plantations et al.* (n.p., n.d.), app. A; William Corner, comp. and ed., *San Antonio de Béxar: A Guide and History* (San Antonio: Bainbridge & Corner, 1890), 47; Betty E. Dobkins, *The Spanish Element in Texas Water Law* (Austin: University of Texas Press, 1959), 114–118; Thomas F. Glick, *The Old World Background of the Irrigation System of San Antonio, Texas* (El Paso: Texas Western Press, 1972), 33–36. For the New Mexico situation, see Tyler, *Mythical Pueblo Rights Doctrine*, quote on 45.

56. Meyer, *Water*, 146–164; David J. Langum, *Law and Community on the Mexican California Frontier* (Norman: University of Oklahoma Press, 1987), 271.

57. See, for example, Tyler, *Mythical Pueblo Rights Doctrine*, 27, 35–36, 39–41.

58. Frank Adams, "The Historical Background of California Agriculture," in Claude B. Hutchison, ed., *California Agriculture* (Berkeley and Los Angeles: University of California Press, 1946), 10.

59. Sherburne F. Cook, *The Conflict between the California Indian and White Civilization: The Indian versus the Spanish Mission* (Berkeley: University of California Press, 1943), 23: 96n.

60. Quoted in Archibald, *Economic Aspects*, 94–95; George Phillips, "Indians in Los Angeles, 1781–1875: Economic Integration, Social Disintegration," *Pacific Historical Review* 49 (Aug. 1980): 431–435.

61. Pedro Fages, Instructions, Jan. 13, 1787, California Archives, 3: 145–149; William Mason, "Fages' Code of Conduct toward Indians, 1787," *Journal of California Anthropology* 2 (Summer 1975): 96–98.

62. Phillips, "Indians in Los Angeles," 435–444, passim; Hubert Howe Bancroft, *California Pastoral* (San Francisco: The History Co., 1888), 438.

Chapter 3: The American Takeover

1. Sherburne F. Cook, *The Population of the California Indians, 1769–1970* (Berkeley and Los Angeles: University of California Press, 1976), 44; Cook, "Historical Demography," in Robert F. Heizer, ed., *California,* vol. 8 of *Handbook of North American Indians* (Washington, D.C.: Smithsonian Institution, 1978), 91, 93; U.S. Department of Commerce, Bureau of the Census, *Historical Statistics of the United States* (Washington, D.C.: Government Printing Office, 1975), pt. 1, 25.

2. See, for example, Records of the Los Angeles Ayuntamiento, Mar. 23, 1839, 2 Span. 633, 2 Eng. 483; Jan. 29, 1844, 2 Span. 757, 2 Eng. 550, Los Angeles City Archives; Morton Horwitz, *The Transformation of American Law, 1780 to 1860* (Cambridge, Mass.: Harvard University Press, 1977), 32–42, passim.

3. Robert Kelley, *Battling the Inland Sea: American Political Culture, Public Policy, and the Sacramento Valley, 1850–1986* (Berkeley and Los Angeles: University of California Press, 1989), 14.

4. The following discussion of American political culture relies heavily on Robert Kelley's brilliant insights and analyses in "The Interplay of American Political Culture and Public Policy: The Sacramento River as a Case Study," *Journal of Policy History* 1, no. 1 (1989): 1–23; "Ideology and Political Culture from Jefferson to Nixon," *American Historical Review* 82 (June 1977): 531–562; and *The Cultural Pattern in American Politics: The First Century* (New York: Alfred A. Knopf, 1979). See also Lee Benson, *The Concept of Jacksonian Democracy: New York as a Test Case* (Princeton: Princeton University Press, 1961); Daniel Walker Howe, *The Political Culture of the American Whigs* (Chicago: University of Chicago Press, 1979); and Paul Kleppner, *The Third Electoral System, 1853–1892* (Chapel Hill: University of North Carolina Press, 1979).

5. Kelley, "The Interplay of American Political Culture and Public Policy," 5–16; Royce D. Delmatier, Clarence F. McIntosh, and Earl G.

Waters, eds., *The Rumble of California Politics, 1848–1970* (New York: Wiley, 1970), 15, 33–35, 40–124, 449–455; William Henry Ellison, *A Self-Governing Dominion: California, 1848–1860* (Berkeley and Los Angeles: University of California Press, 1950), passim.

6. For mining techniques in gold-rush California, see John W. Caughey, *Gold Is the Cornerstone* (Berkeley and Los Angeles: University of California Press, 1948); Rodman Paul, *California Gold* (Cambridge, Mass.: Harvard University Press, 1947); and Paul, *Mining Frontiers of the Far West, 1848–1880* (New York: Holt, Rinehart and Winston, 1963).

7. Paul W. Gates, *History of Public Land Law Development* (Washington, D.C.: Public Land Law Review Commission, 1968), 152–163, 236–240, 705–706; Roy M. Robbins, *Our Landed Heritage: The Public Domain, 1776–1970,* 2d ed. (Lincoln: University of Nebraska Press, 1976), 67–68; Benjamin F. Shambaugh, "Frontier Land Clubs or Claims Associations," *American Historical Association Annual Report* (1900): 67–85; *U.S. Statutes at Large* 5 (1841): 453.

8. Quoted in Samuel C. Wiel, *Water Rights in the Western States,* 3d ed., 2 vols. (San Francisco: Bancroft-Whitney Co., 1911), 1: 72.

9. Wiel, *Water Rights,* 1: pts. 1 and 2; Charles H. Shinn, *Mining Camps: A Study in American Frontier Government* (1884; New York: Harper and Row, 1965), 105–258.

10. *Cal. Stats.,* chap. 5, sec. 621 (1851); *U.S. Statutes at Large,* 14 (1866): 251, 253; see also *U.S. Statutes at Large,* 16 (1870): 217; and 17 (1872): 91. The principle of priority in water appropriation did not originate in the California mines—it has been traced to the Middle Ages in Europe and to the 1840s in New England (where it was discarded by mid-century)—but the doctrine, following its emergence in California, spread rapidly to other areas, covered a greater variety of uses, and otherwise had greater significance than the earlier examples. For some of those earlier examples, see William E. Colby, "The Freedom of the Miner and Its Influence on Water Law," in Max Radin, ed., *Legal Essays in Tribute to Orrin Kip McMurray* (Berkeley: University of California Press, 1935), 67–84; Horwitz, *Transformation of American Law,* 41–42.

11. Clesson S. Kinney, *A Treatise in the Law of Irrigation and Water Rights,* 2d ed., 4 vols. (San Francisco: Bender-Moss, 1912), 2: 1098–1124; Robert G. Dunbar, *Forging New Rights in Western Waters* (Lincoln: University of Nebraska Press, 1983), 78–85.

12. This is not to deny that the appropriation doctrine prohibited

waste and allowed owners to possess only what they could use, but, as this account demonstrates, such requirements did not prevent vast quantities of California water and prime agricultural land from falling into the hands of large corporations. For the evolution of the appropriation doctrine in California, see Wells A. Hutchins, *The California Law of Water Rights* (Sacramento: California State Printing Division, 1956), 67–178; see also Kinney, *Treatise in the Law of Irrigation and Water Rights,* passim; and Wiel, *Water Rights,* passim.

13. Douglas R. Littlefield, "Water Rights during the California Gold Rush: Conflicts over Economic Points of View," *Western Historical Quarterly* 14 (Oct. 1983): 420–421, 431.

14. L. P. Brockett, *Our Western Empire: Or the New West Beyond the Mississippi* (Philadelphia: Bradley, Garretson & Co., 1881), 106–107 (quote); see also Philip Ross May, *Origins of Hydraulic Mining in California* (Oakland: Holmes Book Co., 1970), 40–47; Randall E. Rohe, "Hydraulicking in the American West: The Development and Diffusion of a Mining Technique," *Montana, the Magazine of Western History* 35 (Spring 1985): 20–24; Robert L. Kelley, *Gold vs. Grain: The Hydraulic Mining Controversy in California's Sacramento Valley—A Chapter in the Decline of Laissez-Faire* (Glendale, Calif.: Arthur H. Clark Co., 1959), passim.

15. *Second Report of the State Mineralogist of California* (Sacramento: State Printing Office, 1882), app. 159; Frank T. Gilbert, Harry L. Wells, and W. L. Chambers, *History of Butte County, California* (San Francisco: Harry L. Wells, 1882), 212–213; Taliesin Evans, "Hydraulic Mining in California," *Century Magazine* 25 (Jan. 1883): 331, 334; Rohe, "Hydraulicking in the American West," 24–25; Sacramento *Record-Union,* Feb. 5, 1877.

16. Kelley, *Gold vs. Grain,* passim; Kelley, "The Mining Debris Controversy in the Sacramento Valley," *Pacific Historical Review* 25 (Nov. 1956): 331–346.

17. *Woodruff* v. *North Bloomfield,* 9 Sawyer 441; 18 F. 753 (9th Cir. 1884).

18. This section leans substantially on Robert Kelley's outstanding *Battling the Inland Sea,* passim, as well as his "Interplay of American Political Culture and Public Policy," 1–23; and his "Taming the Sacramento: Hamiltonianism in Action," *Pacific Historical Review* 34 (Feb. 1965): 21–49. See also Kenneth Thompson, "Historic Flooding in the Sacramento Valley," *Pacific Historical Review* 29 (Nov. 1960): 349–360.

19. Kelley, *Battling the Inland Sea,* chap. 2; Gates, *History of Public*

Land Law Development, 323; Joseph Ellison, *California and the Nation, 1850–1869* (Berkeley: University of California Press, 1927), 38.

20. *Cal. Stats.,* chap. 352 (1861), 355–361.

21. Ibid., chap. 415 (1868), 514–521; Kelley, *Battling the Inland Sea,* 47–57; Delmatier et al., eds., *Rumble of California Politics,* 31–33, 54–59; Richard H. Peterson, "The Failure to Reclaim: California State Swamp Land Policy and the Sacramento Valley, 1850–1866," *Southern California Quarterly* 56 (Spring 1974): 45–60.

22. Kelley, *Battling the Inland Sea,* 58–61; S. T. Harding, *Water in California* (Palo Alto, Calif.: N-P Publications, 1960), 142–143.

23. Paul W. Gates, "Public Land Disposal in California," in James H. Shideler, ed., *Agriculture in the Development of the Far West* (Washington, D.C.: Agricultural History Society, 1975), 166; Harding, *Water in California,* 143; Kelley, *Battling the Inland Sea,* 61–63.

24. Kelley, *Battling the Inland Sea,* 63, 177–219.

25. James Kent, *Commentaries on American Law,* ed. Charles M. Barnes, 13th ed., 4 vols. (Boston: Little, Brown, & Co., 1884), 3: 439.

26. *Cal. Stats.* (April 13, 1850), 219.

27. *Cal. Stats.,* chap. 5, sec. 621 (1851); *Cal. Civil Code,* title 7, secs. 1410–1422 (1872); *Irwin* v. *Phillips,* 5 Cal. 140 (1855); *Crandall* v. *Woods,* 8 Cal. 136 (1857).

28. Wiel, *Water Rights,* 1: 133.

29. *Ferrea* v. *Knipe,* 28 Cal. 340, 341–345 (1865); Horwitz, *Transformation of American Law,* 32–42, passim.

30. Gilbert Fite, *The Farmers' Frontier, 1865–1900* (New York: Holt, Rinehart and Winston, 1966), 158.

31. Paul W. Gates, "California Land Policy and Its Historical Context: The Henry George Era," in Paul Gates et al., *Four Persistent Issues* (Berkeley: University of California Institute of Governmental Studies, 1978), 7, 14; Central Pacific Railroad Co., Board of Directors, *Annual Report, 1882* (San Francisco: H. S. Crocker & Co., 1883), 58.

32. Gates, "Public Land Disposal," 160, 175; Gates, "California Land Policy," 19; Fite, *Farmers' Frontier,* 165.

33. Gates, "Public Land Disposal," 159, 172; Gates, "California Land Policy," 7–10; Albert Camarillo, *Chicanos in a Changing Society* (Cambridge, Mass.: Harvard University Press, 1979); Leonard Pitt, *The Decline of the Californios* (Berkeley and Los Angeles: University of California Press, 1966); Robert G. Cleland, *The Cattle on a Thousand Hills,* 2d ed. (San Marino, Calif.: Huntington Library, 1951).

34. Rodman Paul, "The Wheat Trade between California and the United Kingdom," *Mississippi Valley Historical Review* 45 (Dec. 1958):

391–412; Paul, *The Far West and the Great Plains in Transition, 1859–1900* (New York: Harper & Row, 1988), 227–228, passim.

35. Paul, *Far West,* 227; Fite, *Farmers' Frontier,* 166.

36. Steven Stoll, *The Fruits of Natural Advantage: Making the Industrial Countryside in California* (Berkeley and Los Angeles: University of California Press, 1998); John H. White, *The Great Yellow Fleet: A History of American Railroad Refrigerator Cars* (San Marino, Calif.: Golden West Books, 1986), 86, passim; Fite, *Farmers' Frontier,* 167–168, 170–171.

37. Donald Pisani, *From the Family Farm to Agribusiness* (Berkeley and Los Angeles: University of California Press, 1984), 440; Donald Worster, *Rivers of Empire* (New York: Pantheon, 1985), 100.

38. Fite, *Farmers' Frontier,* 168–169.

39. Legislative Irrigation Committee of the State Irrigation Convention, *Address to the Legislature of the State of California, Twenty-sixth Session* (n.p., [1885]), 3, 4–5, 15.

40. Alonzo Phelps, *Contemporary Biography of California's Representative Men* (San Francisco: A. L. Bancroft and Co., 1881), 325–328; Pisani, *From the Family Farm,* 193–203.

41. Quoted in Pisani, *From the Family Farm,* 194.

42. Margaret Aseman Cooper, "Land, Water, and Settlement in Kern County, California" (M.A. thesis, University of California, Berkeley, 1954), chaps. 3, 4, and 6.

43. James B. Haggin, *The Desert Lands of Kern County, Cal.* (San Francisco, 1877), vii.

44. Henry Miller, "Autobiographical Statement" (1891), 9, Bancroft Library, University of California, Berkeley.

45. Gates, "Public Land Disposal," 172; William D. Lawrence, "Henry Miller and the San Joaquin Valley" (M.A. thesis, University of California, Berkeley, 1933), 23, 60, passim; M. Catherine Miller, *Flooding the Courtrooms: Law and Water in the Far West* (Lincoln: University of Nebraska Press, 1993); David Igler, "When Is a River Not a River: Reclaiming Nature's Disorder in *Lux* v. *Haggin,*" *Environmental History* 1 (Apr. 1996): 52–69; Igler, *Industrial Cowboys: Miller & Lux and the Transformation of the Far West* (Berkeley and Los Angeles: University of California Press, forthcoming).

46. John Clay, *My Life on the Range* (Chicago: The Author, 1924), 27 ("selfish, grasping . . ."); *Kern County Californian* (Bakersfield), Apr. 23, 1881. The *Kern County Californian* frequently reprinted articles on the suit appearing in other newspapers.

47. *Lux* v. *Haggin,* 69 Cal. 255 (1886).

48. Wells A. Hutchins, *Water Rights Laws in the Nineteen Western States,* 3 vols. (Washington, D.C.: U.S. Department of Agriculture, 1971–1977), 3: 286–300, 333–358, 408–418, 423–435, 441–467, 478–498, 505–527, 571–601.

49. In the final agreement, both sides contributed to the cost of the dam, the riparians received a right to the river during the months of lowest flow, and the water impounded by the dam was divided with a third going to the riparians and two-thirds to the appropriators. Edward F. Treadwell, *The Cattle King,* rev. ed. (Boston: Christopher Publishing House, 1950), 93; Pisani, *From the Family Farm,* 243.

50. Lucien Shaw, "The Development of the Law of Waters in the West," *California Law Review* 10 (1922): 444; Lawrence, "Henry Miller and the San Joaquin Valley," 64.

51. *Stockton Daily Independent,* July 28, 1886; Pisani, *From the Family Farm,* 236.

52. Quoted in Fite, *Farmers' Frontier,* 169. See also Thomas E. Malone, "The California Irrigation Crisis of 1886: Origins of the Wright Act" (Ph.D. dissertation, Stanford University, 1965), 197–204, passim; Pisani, *From the Family Farm,* chap. 9; California Department of Engineering, "Irrigation Districts in California, 1887–1915," by Frank Adams, *Bulletin No. 2* (Sacramento: State Printing Office, 1917), 8; California Department of Public Works, Division of Engineering and Irrigation, "Irrigation Districts in California," by Frank Adams, *Bulletin No. 21* (Sacramento: California Department of Public Works, 1929), 13–17.

53. Malone, "California Irrigation Crisis," 189–196; Pisani, *From the Family Farm,* 132–133.

54. *Crandall* v. *Woods,* 8 Cal. 136 (1857); Shaw, "Development of the Law of Waters," passim; Fite, *Farmers' Frontier,* 169–171; Harding, *Water in California,* 80.

55. California Department of Engineering, *Bulletin No. 2,* 8–9, 34–47, 105–118; California Department of Public Works, *Bulletin No. 21,* passim; Gates, "Public Land Disposal," 160; Gates, "California Land Policy," 4; Lawrence J. Jelinek, *Harvest Empire: A History of California Agriculture,* 2d ed. (San Francisco: Boyd and Fraser, 1982), 53; Pisani, *From the Family Farm,* 264.

56. Malone, "California Irrigation Crisis," 208–217; Pisani, *From the Family Farm,* 259–279.

57. George and Helen Beattie, *Heritage of the Valley: San*

Bernardino's First Century (Pasadena, Calif.: San Pasqual Press, 1939), 170–310; Flora B. Houston, "The Mormons in California, 1846–1857" (M.A. thesis, University of California, Berkeley, 1929).

58. William H. Hall, *Irrigation in [Southern] California* (Sacramento: State Printing Office, 1888), 616–621; Richard D. Bateman, "Anaheim Was an Oasis in a Wilderness," *Journal of the West* 4 (Jan. 1965): 1–20; Dorothea Paule, "The German Settlement at Anaheim" (M.A. thesis, University of Southern California, 1952); Vincent P. Carosso, *The California Wine Industry: A Study of the Formative Years* (Berkeley: University of California Press, 1951), 60–73; Mildred Yorba MacArthur, *Anaheim: "The Mother Colony"* (Los Angeles: Ward Ritchie Press, 1959), 3–26, passim.

59. Hall, *Irrigation in [Southern] California,* 222–244; Merlin Stonehouse, "The Michigan Excursion for the Founding of Riverside, California," *Michigan History* 45 (Sept. 1961): 193–209; Tom Patterson, *A Colony for California: Riverside's First Hundred Years* (Riverside, Calif.: Press-Enterprise Co., 1971), 31–61, 85–102; William E. Smythe, *The Conquest of Arid America,* rev. ed. (New York: Macmillan Co., 1905), 97–105.

60. J. A. Alexander, *The Life of George Chaffey* (Melbourne: Macmillan & Co., 1928), 32–58, passim; Hall, *Irrigation in [Southern] California,* 336–338, 359–363; Beatrice Lee, "The History and Development of the Ontario Colony" (M.A. thesis, University of Southern California, 1929); R. Louis Gentilcore, "Ontario, California, and the Agricultural Boom of the 1880s," *Agricultural History* 34 (Apr. 1960): 77–87.

61. Clark C. Spence, *The Rainmakers: American "Pulviculture" to World War II* (Lincoln: University of Nebraska Press, 1980), 65–66.

62. Ibid., 71, 76, 159n.

63. Thomas W. Patterson, "Hatfield the Rainmaker," *Journal of San Diego History* 16 (Winter 1970): 2–27; Paul A. Hatfield, "The Hatfield Brothers, Rainmakers" (University of California, Los Angeles, Oral History Program, 1972); Spence, *Rainmakers,* 80–81.

64. *Los Angeles Herald,* Dec. 2, 3, 8, and 11, 1904; *Los Angeles Times,* Dec. 3, 6, and 7, 1904; U.S. Dept. of Agriculture, Weather Bureau, *Climatic Summary of the United States: Section 18 — Southern California and Owens Valley* (Washington, D.C.: Government Printing Office, 1932), p. 18-4; June Oxford, "Rain at the Drop of a Hatfield," *Californians* 6 (May–June 1988): 38–43.

65. Quoted in Spence, *Rainmakers,* 84.

66. Quoted in Shelley J. Higgins, *This Fantastic City San Diego*

(San Diego: City of San Diego, 1956), 182; see also Oxford, "Rain at the Drop of a Hatfield," 40; Patterson, "Hatfield," 13–27.

67. International Irrigation Congress, *Official Report of the International Irrigation Congress Held at Los Angeles, California, October, 1893* (Los Angeles: Los Angeles Chamber of Commerce, 1893), 109.

68. Panics, or depressions in financial values, were fairly frequent in the volatile U.S. economy of the nineteenth century and occurred in 1837, 1857, 1873, and 1893. Gates, *History of Public Land Law Development,* 638–643, 648, 650–651; Robbins, *Our Landed Heritage,* 328–329.

69. Kelley, "Ideology and Political Culture from Jefferson to Nixon," 548, passim; Kelley, *Battling the Inland Sea,* 249–251; Robert Wiebe, *The Search for Order, 1877–1920* (New York: Hill and Wang, 1967), passim; Ballard C. Campbell, Jr., *Representative Democracy: Public Policy and Midwestern Legislatures in the Later Nineteenth Century* (Cambridge, Mass.: Harvard University Press, 1980); Stephen Skowronek, *Building a New American State: The Expansion of National Administrative Capacities, 1877–1920* (Cambridge, Eng.: Cambridge University Press, 1982); Morton Keller, *Affairs of State: Public Life in Late Nineteenth Century America* (Cambridge, Mass.: Harvard University Press, 1977).

70. J. Leonard Bates, "Fulfilling American Democracy: The Conservation Movement, 1907–1921," *Mississippi Valley Historical Review* 44 (June 1957): 31; Samuel P. Hays, *Conservation and the Gospel of Efficiency: The Progressive Conservation Movement, 1890–1920* (Cambridge, Mass.: Harvard University Press, 1959), 265. See also Samuel Haber, *Efficiency and Uplift: Scientific Management in the Progressive Era, 1890–1920* (Chicago: University of Chicago Press, 1964), passim; Kelley, *Battling the Inland Sea,* 251–255.

71. Smythe, *Conquest of Arid America,* 266–267. For a splendid discussion of Smythe, see the introduction by Lawrence B. Lee in the 1969 reissue of Smythe's *Conquest of Arid America* (Seattle: University of Washington Press, 1969).

72. U.S. House, *H. Doc. 141,* 55 Cong., 2 sess. (1897), 58; Smythe, *Conquest of Arid America,* xxvii, 271; Martin E. Carlson, "William E. Smythe: Irrigation Crusader," *Journal of the West* 7 (Jan. 1968): 41–47.

73. Andrew Hudanick, Jr., "George Hebard Maxwell: Reclamation's Militant Evangelist," *Journal of the West* 14 (July 1975): 108–121; Hays, *Conservation and the Gospel of Efficiency,* 9–12, passim; Donald J. Pisani, *To Reclaim a Divided West: Water, Law, and Public Policy, 1848–1902* (Albuquerque: University of New Mexico Press,

1992); William D. Rowley, *Reclaiming the Arid West: The Career of Francis G. Newlands* (Bloomington: Indiana University Press, 1996).

74. *U.S. Statutes at Large* 22 (1902): 390.

75. *Cong. Rec.,* 35 Cong., 1 sess. (1902), 6758.

76. "Irrigation of Arid Lands," *S. Doc. 446,* 57 Cong., 1 sess. (1902), 21.

Chapter 4: Urban Imperialism

1. U.S. Department of Commerce, Bureau of the Census, *Thirteenth Census of the United States, 1910,* vol. 2, *Population* (Washington, D.C.: Government Printing Office, 1913), 140; *Fifteenth Census of the United States, 1930,* vol. 3, *Population* (Washington, D.C.: Government Printing Office, 1931), pt. 1, 6.

2. U.S. Department of Commerce, Bureau of the Census, *Fifteenth Census of the United States, 1930,* vol. 1: 18–19.

3. *Cal. Stats.,* chap. 60 (1850), chap. 78 (1851), chap. 65 (1854); M. C. Desnoyers, *The Ordinances and Resolutions of the City of Los Angeles* (Los Angeles: Herald Publishing Co., 1875), 64; Report to the Committee on Water Supply, July 27, 1877, Los Angeles City Archives, 12: 863–925.

4. U.S. Bureau of the Census, *Fifteenth Census: Population,* vol. 1: 18–19; Glenn S. Dumke, *The Boom of the Eighties in Southern California* (San Marino, Calif.: Huntington Library, 1944), passim.

5. Los Angeles City Archives, 34: 406.

6. Harris Newmark, *Sixty Years in Southern California, 1853– 1913,* 4th ed. (Los Angeles: Zeitlin & Ver Brugge, 1970), 322; J. M. Guinn, *A History of California and an Extended History of Los Angeles and Environs,* 3 vols. (Los Angeles: Historic Record Co., 1915), 1: 391.

7. Los Angeles, Common Council Records (July 20, 1868), 6: 251–252, Los Angeles City Archives; Vincent Ostrom, *Water & Politics: A Study of Water Policies and Administration in the Development of Los Angeles* (Los Angeles: Haynes Foundation, 1953), 40–44.

8. Lawrence M. Friedman, *A History of American Law,* 2d ed. (New York: Simon & Schuster, 1985), 358–363, 556; Harold M. Hyman and William M. Wiecek, *Equal Justice Under Law: Constitutional Development, 1835–1875* (New York: Harper & Row, 1982), 343, 344, 347–349.

9. *Crandall* v. *Woods,* 8 Cal. 136 (1857); *Union Water Co.* v. *Crary,* 25 Cal. 504 (1864); *Davis* v. *Gale,* 32 Cal. 26 (1867).

10. Leon T. Davis, *Law and Lawyers: One Hundred Twenty-Eight*

Years in the History of Los Angeles (Los Angeles: The Author, 1950?), 23 (quote); W. W. Robinson, *Lawyers of Los Angeles* (Los Angeles: Los Angeles Bar Association, 1959), 50.

11. *Los Angeles vs. Baldwin: Transcript on Appeal from Seventeenth District Court, Los Angeles County* (Mar. 16, 1878), 88–89. The transcripts and briefs for the cases cited in this section are in the California Supreme Court Records, California State Library, Sacramento, and in the Los Angeles County Law Library, Los Angeles.

12. *Eddy v. Simpson,* 3 Cal. 249, 252 (1853); Samuel C. Wiel, *Water Rights in the Western States,* 3d ed., 2 vols. (San Francisco: Bancroft-Whitney Co., 1911), 2: 1–21.

13. *Cal. Stats.,* chap. 447, art. 2, sec. 1 (1874).

14. *Los Angeles vs. Baldwin: Transcript on Appeal,* 8–13, 19–21, 94–96.

15. *Los Angeles v. Baldwin,* 53 Cal. 469 (1879); *Los Angeles vs. San Fernando et al.: California Court of Appeal, Second Appellate District—Appendix to Respondents' Brief* (Mar. 14, 1968), vol. 1, app. A, 58.

16. *Feliz vs. Los Angeles: Transcript on Appeal from Seventeenth District Court, Los Angeles County* (Nov. 9, 1880), 3–10, 72 (quote).

17. Ibid., 68, 71, 75.

18. *Feliz vs. Los Angeles: Supreme Court of the State of California—Respondents' Points and Authorities* (Apr. 22, 1881), 3, 4, 6–9; see also *Elms vs. Los Angeles: Supreme Court of the State of California—Respondents' Points and Authorities* (Apr. 19, 1881), a brief submitted by plaintiffs in a related case decided at the same time.

19. *Feliz v. Los Angeles,* 58 Cal. 73, 79 (1881); for a similar decision in the related case, see *Elms v. Los Angeles,* 58 Cal. 80 (1881).

20. *Feliz v. Los Angeles,* 58 Cal. 79–80.

21. *Lux v. Haggin,* 69 Cal. 255, 329, 331 (1886).

22. *Vernon Irrigation Co. v. Los Angeles,* 106 Cal. 237, 250, 251 (1895); *Vernon Irrigation Co. vs. Los Angeles: Transcript on Appeal from the Superior Court of Los Angeles* (Nov. 8, 1893), 66; *Los Angeles Times,* Mar. 10, 1895.

23. *Vernon Irrigation Co. vs. Los Angeles: Supreme Court of the State of California—Closing Brief for Appellant* (July 12, 1894), 35 (quote); *Vernon Irrigation Co. vs. Los Angeles: Transcript on Appeal,* 53–55, 91; *Vernon Irrigation Co. vs. Los Angeles: Supreme Court of the State of California—Appellant's Brief* (Dec. 8, 1893), 4, passim.

24. Peter L. Reich, "Mission Revival Jurisprudence: State Courts and Hispanic Water Law since 1850," *Washington Law Review* 69 (Oct. 1994): 869–906.

25. *Los Angeles* v. *Pomeroy,* 124 Cal. 597 (1899); *Los Angeles* v. *Hunter* and *Los Angeles* v. *Buffington,* 156 Cal. 603 (1909); California Department of Public Works, Division of Water Resources, "South Coastal Basin Investigation: Geology and Ground Water Storage Capacity of Valley Fill," *Bulletin No. 45* (Sacramento: State Printing Office, 1934), 21.

26. *Los Angeles* v. *Pomeroy,* 124 Cal. 597, 649–650 (1899); W. W. Robinson, *Land in California* (Berkeley and Los Angeles: University of California Press, 1948), 244; J. B. Lippincott, "William Mulholland — Engineer, Pioneer, Raconteur," *Civil Engineering* 2 (Feb.–Mar. 1941): 162 (quote).

27. *Los Angeles Times,* Dec. 4, 1898, Aug. 18, 1899; Ostrom, *Water & Politics,* 46.

28. Ostrom, *Water & Politics,* 45.

29. Los Angeles, *Charter of the City of Los Angeles as Adopted January, 1889 and Amended January, 1903* (Los Angeles: Southern California Printing Co., 1903), 57.

30. Ibid., 57–62; Ostrom, *Water & Politics,* 51–115, passim; J. Gregg Layne, *Water and Power for a Great City: A History of the Department of Water and Power of the City of Los Angeles to December 1950* (Los Angeles: Los Angeles Department of Water and Power, 1952), 74–110, 177–231, passim. See also Samuel P. Hays, *Conservation and the Gospel of Efficiency* (Cambridge, Mass.: Harvard University Press, 1959).

31. Los Angeles Board of Water Commissioners, *Third Annual Report* (Los Angeles: Geo. Rice & Sons), 23; Los Angeles Aqueduct Investigation Board, *Report of the Aqueduct Investigation Board to the City Council of Los Angeles* (Los Angeles: Los Angeles City Council, Aug. 31, 1912), 42 (copy in the library of the Los Angeles Department of Water and Power); Ostrom, *Water & Politics,* 144, 146.

32. For an informative biography of Mulholland from the perspective of an admiring granddaughter, see Catherine Mulholland, *William Mulholland and the Rise of Los Angeles* (Berkeley and Los Angeles: University of California Press, 2000); see also H. A. Van Norman, "William Mulholland," *American Society of Civil Engineers Transactions* 101 (1936): 1605; Lippincott, "Mulholland," 106; Robert W. Matson, *William Mulholland: A Forgotten Forefather* (Stockton, Calif.: Pacific Center for Western Studies, University of the Pacific, 1976), 8–9; Arthur L. Littleworth and Eric L. Garner, *California Water* (Point Arena, Calif.: Solano Press Books, 1995), 3.

33. Lippincott, "Mulholland," 161; Matson, *Mulholland,* 10–11.

34. Charles A. Moody, "Los Angeles and the Owens River," *Out West* 23 (Oct. 1905): 424–425; Matson, *Mulholland,* 12, 35–36.

35. *Los Angeles Times,* July 29, 1905; Los Angeles Department of Public Works, *First Annual Report of the Chief Engineer of the Los Angeles Aqueduct to the Board of Public Works* (Los Angeles: Los Angeles Department of Public Works, Mar. 15, 1907), 17.

36. *Los Angeles Times,* July 29, 1905; *Los Angeles Examiner,* July 30, 1905; Los Angeles Department of Public Works, *First Annual Report of the Chief Engineer,* 8–17.

37. Los Angeles Department of Public Works, *First Annual Report of the Chief Engineer,* 18; see also Los Angeles Aqueduct Investigation Board, *Report,* 42, 53; *Los Angeles Examiner,* Aug. 25, 1905; Abraham Hoffman, *Vision or Villainy: Origins of the Owens Valley–Los Angeles Water Controversy* (College Station, Tex.: Texas A&M Press, 1981), 64–66; William L. Kahrl, *Water and Power: The Conflict over Los Angeles' Water Supply in the Owens Valley* (Berkeley and Los Angeles: University of California Press, 1982), 48–49, 54.

38. Hoffman, *Vision or Villany,* 79; Kahrl, *Water and Power,* 108–126; Los Angeles Aqueduct Investigation Board, *Report,* 53–54.

39. Los Angeles Aqueduct Investigation Board, *Report,* 35; see also ibid., 10, 36–37, 41–42; Los Angeles Department of Public Works, *First Annual Report of the Chief Engineer,* 23, 46, 84; *Los Angeles Times,* Aug. 5, 1905; *Los Angeles Examiner,* Aug. 5, 1905; Los Angeles Department of Public Service, *Complete Report on Construction of the Los Angeles Aqueduct* (Los Angeles: Los Angeles Department of Public Service, 1916), 13.

40. *Los Angeles Times,* Sept. 8, 1905; *Los Angeles Examiner,* June 13, 1907; *Los Angeles Herald,* June 13, 1907.

41. *Los Angeles Herald,* Aug. 30, Sept. 3, 1905; *Los Angeles Examiner,* July 30, 1905.

42. *Los Angeles Herald,* Sept. 2, 1905; *Los Angeles Examiner,* July 31, 1905; U.S. Department of Agriculture, Weather Bureau, *Climatic Summary of the United States: Section 18—Southern California and Owens Valley* (Washington, D.C.: Government Printing Office, 1932), p. 18-4. For differing views about the existence of a drought, see Hoffman, *Vision or Villainy,* 97n, 242; Kahrl, *Water and Power,* 84–87; Gordon R. Miller, "Los Angeles and the Owens River Aqueduct" (Ph.D. dissertation, Claremont Graduate School, 1977), 255–259.

43. *Los Angeles Herald,* Aug. 31, 1905.

44. Kahrl, *Water and Power,* 89; U.S. Department of Agriculture, *Climatic Summary,* pp. 18-4 to 18-5; Hoffman, *Vision or Villainy,* 141–144; Ostrom, *Water & Politics,* 55.

45. Newmark, *Sixty Years in Southern California,* 535, 546; Los Angeles Department of Water and Power, *Water and Power Facts* (Los Angeles: Los Angeles Department of Water and Power, 1971), 10, 13; Nelson S. Van Valen, "Power Politics: The Struggle for Municipal Ownership of Electric Utilities in Los Angeles, 1905–1937" (Ph.D. dissertation, Claremont Graduate School, 1964), passim.

46. Elting E. Morison, ed., *The Letters of Theodore Roosevelt,* 5 vols. (Cambridge, Mass.: Harvard University Press, 1952), 5: 315; *U.S. Statutes at Large,* 34 (1906): 801.

47. Boyle Workman, *The City That Grew* (Los Angeles: Southland Publishing Co., 1936), 316; Los Angeles Dept. of Public Service, *Complete Report,* 26.

48. *Los Angeles Times,* Apr. 15, 1913.

49. Ostrom, *Water & Politics,* 155, 156–157.

50. Los Angeles City Council, *Report on the Los Angeles Aqueduct: After an Investigation Authorized by the City Council of Los Angeles,* by Edward Johnson and Edward S. Cobb (Los Angeles: Los Angeles City Council, July 15, 1912), 17; Catherine Mulholland, *The Owensmouth Baby: The Making of a San Fernando Valley Town* (Northridge, Calif.: Santa Susana Press, 1987), 74.

51. *Los Angeles Examiner,* Aug. 24, 25, and 28, 1905; Los Angeles Aqueduct Investigation Board, *Report,* 42.

52. Los Angeles Aqueduct Investigation Board, *Report,* 38. See also Robert Gottlieb and Irene Wolt, *Thinking Big: The Story of the Los Angeles Times* (New York: G. P. Putnam's Sons, 1977), 146–147, passim.

53. Los Angeles Aqueduct Investigation Board, *Report,* 3.

54. Quoted in Kahrl, *Water and Power,* 119.

55. Ibid., 126–127, 143, 202; Kenneth Q. Volk and Edgar A. Rowe, "Joseph Barlow Lippincott," *American Society of Civil Engineers Transactions* 108 (1943): 1546.

56. Cope Rand Means Company, "Recent Purchases of Water in Owens Valley by City of Los Angeles" (Nov. 1923), file 12, Thomas H. Means Papers, University of California Water Resources Center Archives, Berkeley; "Additional Water Supply for City of Los Angeles in Owens Valley and Mono Basin" (Jan. 1924), file 13, ibid.; "Purchasing of Water in Owens Valley by City of Los Ange-

les" (Aug. 1925), file 14, ibid.; Ostrom, *Water & Politics,* 127. For a close study of the conflicts of the 1920s and more, see John Walton, *Western Times and Water Wars: State, Culture, and Rebellion in California* (Berkeley and Los Angeles: University of California Press, 1992). More pessimistic in his appraisal than Walton is Robert A. Sauder in *The Lost Frontier: Water Diversion in the Growth and Destruction of Owens Valley Agriculture* (Tucson: University of Arizona Press, 1994).

57. Kahrl, *Water and Power,* 353–354, 358; U.S. Department of the Interior, Bureau of Indian Affairs, Sacramento Land Operations Office, *Multiple Purpose Water Resources Investigations: Owens Valley Region Indian Reservations, California* (Sacramento: Government Printing Office, June 1976).

58. Layne, *Water and Power,* passim; Kahrl, *Water and Power,* 330–340.

59. Kahrl, *Water and Power,* 335–340, 405.

60. Los Angeles Department of Public Works, Bureau of the Los Angeles Aqueduct, *Sixth Annual Report of the Bureau of the Los Angeles Aqueduct to the Board of Public Works* (Los Angeles: Department of Public Works, 1911), 42 (first quote); Charles F. Outland, *Man-Made Disaster: The Story of St. Francis Dam,* rev. ed. (Glendale, Calif.: Arthur H. Clark Co., 1977), 193–259, passim; Matson, *Mulholland,* 64 (second quote); J. David Rogers, "Reassessment of the St. Francis Dam Failure," in Bernard W. Pipkin and Richard J. Proctor, eds., *Engineering Geology Practice in Southern California* (Belmont, Calif.: Southern California Section, Association of Engineering Geologists, 1992), 639–666; Rogers, "A Man, a Dam, and a Disaster," *Southern California Quarterly* 77 (Spring/Summer 1995): 1–109; Catherine Mulholland, "William Mulholland and the St. Francis Dam," ibid., 111–137.

61. Quoted in Matson, *Mulholland,* 64.

62. Los Angeles City Council, *Report on the Los Angeles Aqueduct,* 8–9; F. C. Finkle, "Los Angeles Aqueduct Mistakes," *Journal of Electricity, Power and Gas* 34 (Jan. 9, 1915): 25–28; Finkle, "Los Angeles' $40,000,000 White Elephant," *Irrigation Age* 30 (May 1915): 200–202, 216; Kahrl, *Water and Power,* 164, 314–315, 490 n. 37.

63. *Engineering News-Record* 115 (July 25, 1935): 136; *Western Construction News* 10 (Aug. 1935): 35, 239; see also *Transactions of the American Society of Civil Engineers* 101 (1936): 1604–1608.

64. Clifford M. Zierer, ed., *California and the Southwest* (New York: John Wiley & Sons, Inc., 1956), 336, passim; William L. Kahrl, ed.,

The California Water Atlas (Sacramento: California Governor's Office of Planning and Research, 1979), 35.

65. *Cal. Stats.,* chap. 720 (1931); "Report of Senate Special Investigating Committee on Water Situation in Inyo and Mono Counties" (May 6, 1931), in *Journal of the Senate: Forty-Ninth Session of the California Legislature, 1931* (Sacramento: State Printing Office, 1941), 2447–2452.

66. San Francisco Board of Supervisors, *Reports on the Water Supply of San Francisco, California, 1900 to 1908* (San Francisco: Britton & Ray, 1908), 3; San Francisco City and County, *San Francisco Water & Power: A History of the Municipal Water Department and Hetch Hetchy System* (San Francisco: City and County of San Francisco, 1985), 8; Ray W. Taylor, *Hetch Hetchy* (San Francisco: Ricardo J. Orozco, 1926), 15–16.

67. Quoted in Taylor, *Hetch Hetchy,* 18.

68. San Francisco City and County Board of Supervisors, *Proceedings Had in Board of Supervisors and Reports of Engineer in the Matter of Furnishing Water Supplies for the City and County of San Francisco* (San Francisco: Spaulding & Barto, 1875), 5–13; San Francisco Board of Supervisors, *Reports on the Water Supply,* 7; Marsden Manson, "Early History of San Francisco Water Supply, 1871–1906" (1906), file 1, Max J. Bartell Papers, University of California Water Resources Center Archives; Taylor, *Hetch Hetchy,* 20–21, 40.

69. San Francisco Board of Supervisors, *Reports on the Water Supply,* 38.

70. Ibid., 113–115, 129–130.

71. Ibid., 129.

72. Taylor, *Hetch Hetchy,* 60; see also Walton Bean, *Boss Ruef's San Francisco* (Berkeley and Los Angeles: University of California Press, 1952), 141–144.

73. *San Francisco Bulletin,* Sept. 29, 1906.

74. San Francisco Board of Supervisors, *Reports on the Water Supply,* 219.

75. Michael L. Smith, *Pacific Visions: California Scientists and the Environment, 1850–1915* (New Haven: Yale University Press, 1987), 172.

76. John Muir, "The Hetch Hetchy Valley," *Sierra Club Bulletin* 6 (Jan. 1908): 219; Muir, "The Endangered Valley," *Century* 77 (Jan. 1909): 469; Holway R. Jones, *John Muir and the Sierra Club: The Battle for Yosemite* (San Francisco: Sierra Club, 1965), 173; Michael P.

Cohen, *The History of the Sierra Club, 1892–1970* (San Francisco: Sierra Club, 1988), 1–10.

77. Muir, "Hetch Hetchy Valley," 211, 220; Muir, *The Yosemite* (New York: The Century Co., 1912), 261–262; Muir, *My First Summer in the Sierra* (Boston: Houghton Mifflin Co., 1911), 205, 354.

78. Lyman Abbott, "Saving the Yosemite Park," *Outlook* 91 (Jan. 30, 1909): 235–236; Robert Underwood Johnson, "A High Price to Pay for Water," *Century* 76 (Aug. 1908): 632–634; Johnson, "Dismembering Your National Park," *Outlook* 91 (Jan.–Apr. 1909): 252–253; Roderick Nash, *Wilderness and the American Mind,* 3d ed. (New Haven: Yale University Press, 1982), chap. 10.

79. Marsden Manson to G. W. Woodruff, Apr. 6, 1910, carton 1, Marsden Manson Papers, Bancroft Library, University of California, Berkeley; Marsden Manson, "San Francisco's Side of the Hetch Hetchy Reservoir Matter," *Twentieth Century* 2 (June 1910): 271; San Francisco Board of Supervisors, *Reports on the Water Supply,* 116.

80. Jones, *Muir and the Sierra Club,* 97–98, 127–131; Kendrick Clements, "Politics and the Park: San Francisco's Fight for Hetch Hetchy, 1908–1913," *Pacific Historical Review* 48 (May 1979): 190–191, 194, 201, 208; Hays, *Conservation and the Gospel of Efficiency,* 193–195, passim.

81. Clements, "Politics and the Park," 195–200, 203–206.

82. "Hetch Hetchy Valley: Report of Advisory Board of Army Engineers to the Secretary of the Interior on Investigations Relative to Sources of Water Supply for San Francisco and Bay Communities," *H. Doc. 54,* 63 Cong., 1 sess. (Feb. 19, 1913), 51.

83. Hays, *Conservation and the Gospel of Efficiency,* 148–149; Clements, "Politics and the Park," 206.

84. Clements, "Politics and the Park," 209–210, 211–212.

85. House Committee on Public Lands, *Hearings on Hetch Hetchy Dam Site, H.R. 6281,* 63 Cong., 1 sess. (1913), 278–363; Clements, "Politics and the Park," 209–211.

86. *Cong. Rec.,* 63 Cong., 2 sess. (Dec. 19, 1913), 1189; Richard Lowitt, "The Hetch Hetchy Controversy, Phase II: The 1913 Senate Debate," *California History* 74 (Summer 1995): 190–203, 220.

87. Quoted in Jones, *Muir and the Sierra Club,* 168.

88. William Issel and Robert W. Cherny, *San Francisco, 1865–1932: Politics, Power, and Urban Development* (Berkeley and Los Angeles: University of California Press, 1986), 176, 184; Lawrence Kinnaird, *History of the Greater San Francisco Bay Region,* 3 vols. (New

York: Lewis Historical Publishing Co., 1966), 2: 301–302; San Francisco Public Utilities Commission, *San Francisco Water: Report of the City and County of San Francisco to the State Water Resources Control Board* (San Francisco: Public Utilities Commission of the City and County of San Francisco, 1987), 46, passim.

89. San Francisco City and County, *San Francisco Water & Power,* 33, passim; Kinnaird, *San Francisco,* 2: 305.

90. Issel and Cherny, *San Francisco,* 183–184; Kinnaird, *San Francisco,* 2: 305–306; Kahrl, ed., *California Water Atlas,* 31; Roger Lotchin, "John Francis Neylan: San Francisco Irish Progressive," in James P. Walsh, ed., *San Francisco Irish: 1850–1876* (San Francisco: Irish Literary & Historical Society, 1978), 99–104.

91. Kinnaird, *San Francisco,* 2: 305–306; Issel and Cherny, *San Francisco,* 182–184; Kahrl, ed., *California Water Atlas,* 31.

92. "Hetch Hetchy Valley: Report of the Advisory Board of Army Engineers," 50; Ted Wurm, *Hetch Hetchy and Its Dam Railroad* (Berkeley: Howell-North, 1973), 191–193, 222; Kahrl, ed., *California Water Atlas,* 31; S. T. Harding, *Water in California* (Palo Alto, Calif.: N-P Publications, 1960), 120.

93. Kinnaird, *San Francisco,* 2: 296–297; Erwin Cooper, *Aqueduct Empire* (Glendale Calif.: Arthur H. Clarke Co., 1968), 55; Kahrl, ed., *California Water Atlas,* 31; Walter R. McLean, "From Pardee to Buckhorn: Water Resources Engineering and Water Policy in the East Bay Municipal Utility District, 1927–1991" (Regional Oral History Office, Bancroft Library, University of California, Berkeley, 1995), chaps. 6–9, 11; Harold Raines, "Water Rights on the Mokelumne River and Legal Issues at the East Bay Municipal Utility District, 1927–1966" (Regional Oral History Office, Bancroft Library, University of California, Berkeley, 1995); John B. Reilly, "Water Rights and Legal Issues at the East Bay Municipal Utility District, 1951–1983" (Regional Oral History Office, Bancroft Library, University of California, Berkeley, 1995–1996).

94. *Los Angeles Times,* Aug. 7 and 23, 1987.

95. George E. Mowry, *The California Progressives* (Berkeley and Los Angeles: University of California Press, 1951), 7–9, 23–85, 133, passim.

96. Taylor, *Hetch Hetchy,* 20; Frank J. Taylor, *Land of Homes* (Los Angeles: Powell, 1929); Robert M. Fogelson, *The Fragmented Metropolis: Los Angeles, 1850–1930* (Cambridge, Mass.: Harvard University

Press, 1967), chap. 7, passim; T. H. Watkins and R. R. Olmsted, *Mirror of the Dream: An Illustrated History of San Francisco* (San Francisco: Scrimshaw Press, 1976); Paul C. Johnson and Richard Reinhardt, *San Francisco: As It Is, As It Was* (Garden City, N.Y.: Doubleday, 1979); David Clark, *Los Angeles: A City Apart—An Illustrated History* (Woodland Hills, Calif.: Windsor Publications, 1981).

97. The Hines quotation is in *Los Angeles Times,* Feb. 24, 1991. See also Hines, *Richard Neutra and the Search for Modern Architecture* (New York: Oxford University Press, 1982); Kevin Starr, *Material Dreams: Southern California through the 1920s* (New York: Oxford University Press, 1990), 184–196, passim; Terence G. Young, "Constructing an Urban Forest: A Cultural Biogeography in Middle-Class Los Angeles, 1930–1980" (M.A. thesis, University of California, Los Angeles, 1987); Esther McCoy, *Five California Architects* (New York: Reinhold, 1960); David Gebhard et al., *A Guide to Architecture in San Francisco & Northern California,* 2d ed. (Santa Barbara: Peregrine Smith, 1976); David Gebhard and Robert Winter, *A Guide to Architecture in Los Angeles & Southern California* (Santa Barbara: Peregrine Smith, 1977); Reyner Banham, *Los Angeles: The Architecture of Four Ecologies* (New York: Harper & Row, 1971), 31, 95–109, 161–198, passim.

Chapter 5: Hydraulic Society Triumphant

1. Wallace Stegner, *Beyond the Hundredth Meridian: John Wesley Powell and the Second Opening of the West* (Boston: Houghton Mifflin Co., 1954).

2. Arthur P. Davis, *The Single Tax from the Farmer's Standpoint* (Minneapolis: 1897); *Pacific Builder and Engineer,* July 11, 1914; Gene Gressley, "Arthur Powell Davis, Reclamation, and the West," *Agricultural History* 42 (July 1968): 241–257.

3. League of the Southwest, "Minutes" (Denver, Aug. 25–27, 1920), 34, box 477, Imperial Irrigation District Papers, Imperial, Calif.; Arthur Powell Davis to J. B. Lippincott, Oct. 10, 1902, file 187, Colorado River Project, 1902–1919, Bureau of Reclamation Papers, Record Group 115, National Archives.

4. For a splendid study of the Salt River Project, see Karen L. Smith, *The Magnificent Experiment: Building the Salt River Reclamation Project* (Tucson: University of Arizona Press, 1986). See also

Michael C. Robinson, *Water for the West: The Bureau of Reclamation, 1902–1977* (Chicago: Public Works Historical Society, 1979), 20–23.

5. J. A. Alexander, *The Life of George Chaffey* (Melbourne: Macmillan & Co., 1928), 292; "Irrigation in Imperial Valley, California," *S. Doc. 246,* 60 Cong., 1 sess. (1908), 14–15; Otis B. Tout, *The First Thirty Years, 1901–1931* (San Diego: O. B. Tout, 1931), 29–40, 45–50, 162, 190.

6. H. T. Cory, *The Imperial Valley and the Salton Sink* (San Francisco: J. J. Newbegin, 1915), 1271–1291; Tout, *First Thirty Years,* 97–105; Alexander, *Chaffey,* 303; William deBuys, *Salt Dreams: Land & Water in Low-Down California* (Albuquerque: University of New Mexico Press, 1999), chaps. 6–8.

7. House Committee on Irrigation of Arid Lands, *Hearings on All-American Canal in Imperial County, Calif., H.R. 6044,* 66 Cong., 1 sess. (1919), 116; Norris Hundley, jr., "The Politics of Reclamation: California, the Federal Government, and the Origins of the Boulder Canyon Act—A Second Look," *California Historical Quarterly* 52 (Winter 1973): 300–304.

8. "Report on H.R. 6044 for Relief of Imperial Valley, California," Aug. 21, 1919, p. 13, file 711.1216M/494, Records of the Department of State, Record Group 59, National Archives; House Committee on Irrigation of Arid Lands, *Hearings on All-American Canal in Imperial and Coachella Valleys, Calif., H.R. 6044 and H.R. 11553,* 66 Cong. (1920), 94, 142, 261, 290.

9. U.S. Dept. of Commerce, *Statistical Abstract of the United States, 1921* (Washington, D.C.: Government Printing Office, 1922), 7: 46; "Federal Reclamation by Irrigation," *S. Doc. 92,* 68 Cong., 1 sess. (1924), xi–xvi, passim; Donald J. Pisani, *To Reclaim a Divided West: Water, Law, and Public Policy, 1848–1902* (Albuquerque: University of New Mexico Press, 1992), 329–335, passim; Donald C. Jackson, "Engineering in the Progressive Era: A New Look at Frederick Haynes Newell and the U.S. Reclamation Service," *Technology and Culture* 34 (July 1993): 539–574; Michael C. Robinson, *Water for the West: The Bureau of Reclamation, 1902–1977* (Chicago: Public Works Historical Society, 1979), 43–44; Norris Hundley, jr., "The Great American Desert Transformed: Aridity, Exploitation, and Imperialism in the Making of the Modern American West," in M. T. El-Ashry and Diana C. Gibbons, eds., *Water and Arid Lands of the Western United States* (New York: Cambridge University Press, 1988), 38–39.

10. Arthur Maass, *Muddy Waters: The Army Engineers and the Nation's Rivers* (Cambridge, Mass.: Harvard University Press, 1951), 21, 61–259; Arthur E. Morgan, *Dams and Other Disasters: A Century of the Army Corps of Engineers in Civil Works* (Boston: Porter Sargent, 1971), chap. 9, passim; Robinson, *Water for the West,* 26–27; Alfred R. Golzé, *Reclamation in the United States* (Caldwell, Idaho: Caxton Printers, 1961), 190, 197, 207–217, 297–298, passim; Albert N. Williams, *The Water and the Power* (New York: Duell, Sloan and Pearce, 1951), 214–264, 330–333, passim.

11. William E. Warne, "Administration of the Department of Water Resources, 1961–1966" (Regional Oral History Office, Bancroft Library, University of California, Berkeley, 1981), 120; *Cong. Rec.,* 67 Cong., 2 sess. (1922), 5929, 5985; "Problems of Imperial Valley and Vicinity," *S. Doc. 142,* 67 Cong., 2 sess. (1922); Beverly Moeller, *Phil Swing and Boulder Dam* (Berkeley and Los Angeles: University of California Press, 1971).

12. James R. Kluger, *Turning on Water with a Shovel: The Career of Elwood Mead* (Albuquerque: University of New Mexico Press, 1992); Robinson, *Water for the West,* 45–48; Paul W. Gates, *History of Public Land Law Development* (Washington, D.C.: Public Land Law Review Commission, 1968), 678–691.

13. W. S. Norviel to Carl Hayden, May 6, 1922, copy in file 1-M/311, Herbert Hoover Papers, Hoover Presidential Library, West Branch, Iowa; Colorado River Commission, "Hearings" (Denver, Mar. 31, 1922), 70, file 032, Colorado River Project, Bureau of Reclamation Papers.

14. *Wyoming* v. *Colorado,* 259 U.S. 419 (1922).

15. Norris Hundley, jr., *Water and the West: The Colorado River Compact and the Politics of Water in the American West* (Berkeley and Los Angeles: University of California Press, 1975), 187–214, passim; Frederick L. Zimmermann and Mitchell Wendell, *The Interstate Compact since 1925* (Chicago: Council of State Governments, 1951), 5, 13–16; Vincent Thursby, *Interstate Cooperation: A Study of the Interstate Compact* (Washington, D.C.: Government Printing Office, 1953); National Water Commission, *Interstate Water Compacts,* by Jerome C. Muys (Washington, D.C.: Government Printing Office, 1971).

16. W. S. Norviel, "Report of W. S. Norviel, Colorado River Commissioner, State of Arizona" (n.d.), 6, file 1-M/315, Herbert Hoover Papers, Hoover Presidential Library, West Branch, Iowa; Richard E.

Sloan, "Pact Criticism Is Largely on What It Does Not Say," *Arizona Mining Journal* 6 (Jan. 15, 1923): 58. Sloan was Norviel's advisor.

17. *Journal of the Senate: Sixth State Legislature of Arizona, 1923* (Phoenix: Arizona Senate, 1923), 131; *Arizona Republican* (Phoenix), Jan. 24, 1923.

18. House Committee on Irrigation and Reclamation, *Hearings on Protection and Development of Lower Colorado River Basin, H.R. 2903,* 68 Cong., 1 sess. (1924), 97.

19. Samuel B. Nelson, "Water for Los Angeles" (Oral History Program, University of California, Los Angeles, 1988), 65; see also *Cal. Stats.,* chap. 429 (1927); Metropolitan Water District of Southern California, *History and First Annual Report* (Los Angeles: Metropolitan Water District of Southern California, 1939), 37–51, 310–313; Jerome W. Milliman, "The History, Organization and Economic Problems of the Metropolitan Water District of Southern California" (Ph.D. dissertation, University of California, Los Angeles, 1956), 83–90, 102–105; William L. Kahrl, *Water and Power: The Conflict over Los Angeles' Water Supply in the Owens Valley* (Los Angeles and Berkeley: University of California Press, 1982), 268, 301.

20. It was in 1953 that Los Angeles's votes on the MWD board of directors first dropped below 50 percent (to 48.74 percent). Metropolitan Water District of Southern California, *Sixteenth Annual Report, 1953–1954* (Los Angeles: Metropolitan Water District of Southern California, 1954), xvi; *Cal. Stats.,* chap. 429, sec. 6 (1927); Milliman, "Metropolitan Water District," 102, 112–115; Vincent Ostrom, *Water & Politics: A Study of Water Policies and Administration in the Development of Los Angeles* (Los Angeles: Haynes Foundation, 1953), 193–194.

21. Milliman, "Metropolitan Water District," 114–115; Ostrom, *Water & Politics,* 169, 193–195; Kazuto Oshio, "Who Pays and Who Benefits? Metropolitan Water Politics in Twentieth-Century Southern California," *Japanese Journal of American Studies* no. 8 (1997): 63–89.

22. *Cal. Stats.,* chap. 429, sec. 6 (1927).

23. *Cong. Rec.,* 70 Cong., 2 sess. (1928), 389.

24. Moeller, *Phil Swing,* 87, 119; "Hoover Dam Documents," *H. Doc. 717,* 80 Cong., 2 sess. (2d ed., 1948), 47–48.

25. *Cong. Rec.,* 70 Cong., 2 sess. (1928), 603, 837–838; *U.S. Statutes at Large* 45 (1928): 1057–1066; 46 (1929): 3000; *Cal. Stats.* (Mar. 4, 1929), chaps. 15–16, 37–39; Norris Hundley, jr., "Clio Nods:

Arizona v. *California* and the Boulder Canyon Act: A Reassessment," *Western Historical Quarterly* 3 (Jan. 1972): 17–51.

26. "Hoover Dam Documents," *H. Doc. 717,* app. 601.

27. California Department of Public Works, Division of Engineering and Irrigation, "Irrigation Districts in California," by Frank Adams, *Bulletin 21* (Sacramento: State Printing Office, 1929), 339; Paul S. Taylor, "Water, Land, and Environment in Imperial Valley: Law Caught in the Winds of Politics," *Natural Resources Journal* 13 (Jan. 1973): 4; Paul S. Taylor, *Mexican Labor in the United States: Imperial Valley, California,* vol. 6, no. 1 (Berkeley: University of California Publications in Economics, 1928), 33, 94, passim; Paul G. Barnett, *Imperial Valley: The Land of Sun and Subsidies* (Davis: California Institute for Urban Studies, 1978).

28. *Decisions of the Secretary of the Interior,* 71 (1964): 528; Taylor, "Water, Land, and Environment," 4, 8; Paul W. Gates, *History of Public Land Law Development* (Washington, D.C.: Government Printing Office, 1968), 696; Robinson, *Water for the West,* 102; Ernest Leonard, "The Imperial Irrigation District" (Ph.D. dissertation, Claremont Graduate School, 1972); Ann Foley Scheuring, ed., *A Guidebook to California Agriculture* (Berkeley and Los Angeles: University of California Press, 1983), 27; Paul S. Taylor, "Mexican Migration and the 160-Acre Water Limitation," *California Law Review* 63, no. 3 (1975): 740–741; T. Lynn Smith, "A Study of Social Stratification in the Agricultural Sections of the U.S.: Nature, Data, Procedures, and Preliminary Results," *Rural Sociology* 34 (Dec. 1969): 509.

29. "Hoover Dam Documents," *H. Doc. 717,* 65–80, 84–85, 131–132; Metropolitan Water District of Southern California, *History and First Annual Report,* 1938 (Los Angeles: Metropolitan Water District of Southern California, 1939).

30. Remi Nadeau, *The Water Seekers* (Garden City, N.Y.: Doubleday & Co., 1950), 233–237; "Hoover Dam Documents," *H. Doc. 717,* 131–132; *United States* v. *Arizona,* 295 U.S. 174 (1935); *U.S. Statutes at Large* 49 (1935): 1039.

31. Keith Nobriga, planning and resources division, MWD, to the author, Aug. 26, 1998; Kahrl, *Water and Power,* 348–349; *Los Angeles Times,* Apr. 4, 1990.

32. The figures on urban southern California's contribution to the construction and operation of Hoover Dam were supplied by John L. Scott, engineer, planning and resources division, Metropolitan Water District of Southern California, May 7, 1999. See also

Warren W. Butler, chair, MWD Board of Directors, to Board of Directors, Dec. 16, 1952 (quote), copy in possession of the author; U.S. Department of Commerce, Bureau of the Census, *Sixteenth Census of the United States: 1940—Population,* vol. 2, *Characteristics of the Population* (Washington, D.C.: Government Printing Office, 1943), 629; U.S. Department of Commerce, Bureau of the Census, *U.S. Census of the Population: 1970,* vol. 1, *Characteristics of the Population,* pt. 6, sec. 1, *California* (Washington, D.C.: Government Printing Office, 1973), 6-6; U.S. Department of Commerce, Bureau of the Census, *County Data Book* (Washington, D.C.: Government Printing Office, 1947), 78; U.S. Department of Commerce, Bureau of the Census, *County and City Data Book, 1972* (Washington, D.C.: Government Printing Office, 1973), 55, 66; Hundley, "Great American Desert Transformed," 52–53; Gerald D. Nash, *The American West in the Twentieth Century: A Short History of an Urban Oasis* (Englewood Cliffs, N.J.: Prentice-Hall, 1973), 201–202; Nash, *The Federal Landscape: An Economic History of the Twentieth-Century West* (Tucson: University of Arizona Press, 1999).

33. *Cal. Stats.,* 822 (1911), 586 (1913); Frank Adams to W. F. McClure, Feb. 11 and 19, 1913, folder 13, Frank Adams Papers, University of California Water Resources Center Archives, Berkeley. For a more detailed discussion of Progressive actions, see Donald Pisani, *From the Family Farm to Agribusiness: The Irrigation Crusade in California and the West, 1850–1931* (Berkeley and Los Angeles: University of California Press, 1984), chap. 11.

34. Pisani, *From the Family Farm,* 355–356; California Department of Engineering, "Irrigation Districts in California, 1887–1915," by Frank Adams, *Bulletin No. 2* (Sacramento: State Printing Office, 1917), 47–59; California Department of Public Works, *Bulletin No. 21,* 40–41.

35. Robert Kelley, *Battling the Inland Sea: American Political Culture, Public Policy, and the Sacramento Valley, 1850–1986* (Berkeley and Los Angeles: University of California Press, 1989), 286–293, 297–307.

36. Paul S. Taylor, "Central Valley Project: Water and Land," *Western Political Quarterly* 2 (June 1949): 228; William L. Kahrl, ed., *The California Water Atlas* (Sacramento: California Governor's Office of Planning and Research, 1979), 47.

37. Pisani, *From the Family Farm,* 303–308, 320–334, 388.

38. Frank Adams, "Frank Adams, University of California, on Ir-

rigation, Reclamation, and Water Administration" (Regional Oral History Office, Bancroft Library, University of California, Berkeley, 1959), 249. Adams had earlier anticipated many of the flaws in the Progressive Era reforms, but his advice was sought too late in the legislative process to be acted upon. Adams to W. F. McClure, Feb. 11 and 19, 1913, file 13, Frank Adams Papers, University of California Water Resources Center Archives, Berkeley. See also California Department of Public Works, *Bulletin No. 21,* 40–43, 403; Pisani, *From the Family Farm,* 356, 368–377; Lawrence Jelinek, *Harvest Empire: A History of California Agriculture,* 2d ed. (San Francisco: Boyd & Fraser Publishing Co., 1982), 53, 63.

39. Jelinek, *Harvest Empire,* 63.

40. *Cal. Stats.,* chap. 1727 (1921); Pisani, *From the Family Farm,* 390–391.

41. Merrill R. Goodall and John D. Sullivan, "Water District Organization: Political Decision Systems," in Ernest A. Engelbert, ed., *California Water Planning and Policy: Selected Issues* (Davis: University of California Water Resources Center, Davis, 1979), 207–227; James Jamieson, Sidney Sonenblum, Werner Z. Hirsch, Merrill R. Goodall, and Harold Jaffee, *Some Political and Economic Aspects of Managing California Water Districts* (Los Angeles: UCLA Institute of Government and Public Affairs, 1974), 9–48, 97–183; David L. Martin, "California Water Politics: The Search for Local Control" (Ph.D. dissertation, Claremont Graduate School, 1973); California Department of Water Resources, "General Comparison of Water District Acts," *Bulletin 155–94* (Sacramento: California Department of Water Resources, March 1994); Jelinek, *Harvest Empire,* 63.

42. Sucheng Chan, *This Bittersweet Soil: The Chinese in California Agriculture, 1860–1910* (Berkeley and Los Angeles: University of California Press, 1987); Chan, *Asian Californians* (San Francisco: Boyd & Fraser Publishing Co., 1990); Linda and Theo Majka, *Farm Workers, Agribusiness, and the State* (Philadelphia: Temple University Press, 1982), chaps. 2–4; Cletus Daniel, *Bitter Harvest: A History of California Farm Workers, 1870–1941* (Ithaca, N.Y.: Cornell University Press, 1981); Mark Reisler, *By the Sweat of Their Brow: Mexican Immigrant Labor in the United States, 1900–1945* (Westport, Conn.: Greenwood Press, 1976); Jelinek, *Harvest Empire,* 70.

43. "Annual Report of the Surveyor-General for 1856," in *Appendix to Assembly Journals for the Eighth Session of the Legislature of the State of California* (Sacramento: James Allen, 1857), 26.

44. U.S. Department of Agriculture, Bureau of Agricultural Economics, *History of Legislation and Policy Formation of the Central Valley Project,* by Mary Montgomery and Marion Clawson (Berkeley: U.S. Bureau of Agricultural Economics, 1946), 9–10, 21, passim; Kelley, *Battling the Inland Sea,* 202–207; Pisani, *From the Family Farm,* 154–190, 393, 396–398; Robert Bradford Marshall, *Irrigation of Twelve Million Acres in the Valley of California* (Sacramento: California State Irrigation Association, Mar. 16, 1919); *Sacramento Union,* Sept. 29, 1919. Marshall's activities can best be followed in his papers in the Bancroft Library at the University of California, Berkeley.

45. *Journal of the Senate: Forty-Fourth Session of the California Legislature, 1921* (Sacramento: State Printing Office, 1921), 1269; *Journal of the Assembly: Forty-Fourth Session of the California Legislature, 1921* (Sacramento: State Printing Office, 1921), 2326; H. H. Wadsworth to Harold Wadsworth, Feb. 7, 1921, file 376, Adams Papers; "Marshall Plan—Data and Reports," file 615.021, California Department of Water Resources Archives, Sacramento; Arthur D. Angel, "Political and Administrative Aspects of the Central Valley Project of California" (Ph.D. dissertation, University of California, Los Angeles, 1944), 41, 60–62, passim; Pisani, *From the Family Farm,* 400–415. For evidence of the persistence of California Progressivism into the 1920s, save for some waning of influence between 1923 and 1925, see Jackson K. Putnam, "The Persistence of Progressivism in the 1920's: The Case of California," *Pacific Historical Review* 35 (Aug. 1966): 395–411; Putnam, *Modern California Politics,* 3d ed. (San Francisco: Boyd & Fraser Publishing Co., 1990), chap. 1.

46. *Herminghaus* v. *Southern California Edison,* 200 Cal. 81 (1926); M. Catherine Miller, "Water Rights and the Bankruptcy of Judicial Action: The Case of *Herminghaus* v. *Southern California Edison,*" *Pacific Historical Review* 58 (Feb. 1989): 83–107.

47. Governor's Commission to Review California Water Rights Law, *Final Report* (Sacramento: State of California, Dec. 1978), 9.

48. *California Water Code,* sec. 10505 (1931); *Cal. Stats.,* chap. 720 (1931). As an added concession to the north, the Central Valley Project Act of 1933 contained a so-called watershed protection provision stating that a watershed possessed a "prior right to all of the water reasonably required . . . to adequately supply the beneficial needs of the watershed . . . or any of the inhabitants." *California Water Code,* sec. 11460 (1933); *Cal. Stats.,* chap. 1042 (1933); California Department of Water Resources, "California State Water Project,"

vol. 1: "History, Planning, and Early Progress," *Bulletin No. 200* (Sacramento: California Resources Agency, Nov. 1974), 11–12; *California Attorney General's Opinions*, 25 (1955): 8; ibid., 29 (1957): 136.

49. California Department of Public Works, Division of Water Resources, "Report to Legislature of 1931 on State Water Plan," *Bulletin No. 25* (Sacramento: State Printing Office, 1930), 33–57. Hyatt had been working on the plan for years. See, for example, Hyatt, "A State Water Policy for California" (paper presented to the American Water Works Association, June 12, 1928), file 1, Edward Hyatt Papers, University of California Water Resources Center Archives. See also *Pacific Purchasor* 12 (July 1931): 7, 25, copy in file 2, ibid.

50. Robert Kelley, "Ideology and Political Culture from Jefferson to Nixon," *American Historical Review* 82 (June 1977): 531–562; Kelley, *The Cultural Pattern in American Politics: The First Century* (New York: Knopf, 1979); Kelley, *The Shaping of the American Past* (Englewood Cliffs, N.J.: Prentice-Hall, 1986); Otis L. Graham, Jr., *An Encore for Reform: The Old Progressives and the New Deal* (New York: Oxford University Press, 1967); Graham, *Toward a Planned Society: From Roosevelt to Nixon* (New York: Oxford University Press, 1976).

51. Kelley, "Ideology and Political Culture," 551–553; Kelley, *Battling the Inland Sea,* 331–332; Harris G. Warren, *Herbert Hoover and the Great Depression* (New York: Oxford University Press, 1959); Albert U. Romasco, *Poverty of Abundance: Hoover, the Nation, and the Great Depression* (New York: Oxford University Press, 1965).

52. Kelley, "Ideology and Political Culture," 551–553; David Burner, *The Politics of Provincialism: The Democratic Party in Transition, 1918–1932* (New York: Knopf, 1968); Louis L. Gerson, *The Hyphenate in Recent American Politics and Diplomacy* (Lawrence: University of Kansas Press, 1964); Robert S. McElvaine, *The Great Depression* (New York: New York Times Books, 1984); Frank Freidel, *Franklin Roosevelt: Launching the New Deal* (Boston: Little, Brown & Co., 1973); William E. Leuchtenburg, *Franklin D. Roosevelt and the New Deal, 1932–1940* (New York: Harper & Row, 1963), chaps. 3–8, passim.

53. Kelley, *Battling the Inland Sea,* 332.

54. Michael P. Rogin and John L. Shover, *Political Change in California: Critical Elections and Social Movements, 1890–1966* (Westport, Conn.: Greenwood, 1970), chap. 5; Putnam, *Modern California Politics,* chaps. 2–3.

55. *Journal of the Senate: Fiftieth Session of the California Legislature, 1933* (Sacramento: State Printing Office, 1933), 3428; *Journal of the As-*

sembly: Fiftieth Session of the California Legislature, 1933 (Sacramento: State Printing Office, 1933), 4506–4507.

56. Lawrence B. Lee, "California Water Politics: Depression Genesis of the Central Valley Project, 1933–1944," *Journal of the West* 24 (Oct. 1985): 65–66; Charles E. Coate, "Water, Power, and Politics in the Central Valley Project, 1933–1967" (Ph.D. dissertation, University of California, Berkeley, 1969), 11, passim; Angel, "Political and Administrative Aspects," 42–56.

57. Quoted in Coate, "Water, Power, and Politics," 20; see also Angel, "Political and Administrative Aspects," 67–78.

58. *Journal of the California Senate, 1933,* 3428; *Journal of the California Assembly, 1933,* 4506–4507. In this book, as noted elsewhere, southern California is defined as generally the area below the Tehachapis and encompassing eight counties: San Diego, Imperial, Orange, Riverside, San Bernardino, Los Angeles, Ventura, and Santa Barbara.

59. Quoted in U.S. Department of Agriculture, Bureau of Agricultural Economics, *History of Legislation,* 51.

60. Coate, "Water, Power, and Politics," 26, 28; Angel, "Political and Administrative Aspects," 78–84; U.S. Department of Agriculture, Bureau of Agricultural Economics, *History of Legislation,* 51–61; Jack T. Casey, "Legislative History of the Central Valley Project, 1933–1949" (Ph.D. dissertation, University of California, Berkeley, 1949), 34–37.

61. California Secretary of State, *Statement of the Vote of California at the Special Election Held December 19, 1933, on Referendum Measure* (Sacramento: State Printing Office, 1934).

62. U.S. Department of Agriculture, Bureau of Agricultural Economics, *History of Legislation,* 81, 84–87; *U.S. Statutes at Large* 50 (1937): 844, 850. For a thoughtful appraisal of the relationship among the federal government, water, and the Central Valley both before and after Congress authorized the Reclamation Bureau to take over the Central Valley Project, see Steven Hirsch, "Zealous Intruder or Reluctant Leader? The Federal Government's Increasing Presence in Managing Water in California's Central Valley" (master's thesis, California State University, Fullerton, 1995).

63. "Central Valley Project Documents, Part One," *H. Doc. 416,* 84 Cong., 2 sess. (1956); "Central Valley Documents, Part Two," *H. Doc. 246,* 85 Cong., 1 sess. (1957); S. T. Harding, "Background of California Water and Power Problems," *California Law Review* 38

(Oct. 1950): 547–571; Erwin Cooper, *Aqueduct Empire* (Glendale, Calif: Arthur H. Clark Co., 1968), 149–153. For a splendid analysis of how the Central Valley Project affected one community (Fresno), see Todd A. Shallat, *Water and the Rise of Public Ownership on the Fresno Plain, 1850 to 1978* (Fresno: Fresno Public Works Department, 1978), chaps. 5–6. For the activities of a California congressman deeply involved in the politics of the Central Valley Project in the 1950s, see Stephen P. Sayles, "Clair Engle and the Politics of California Reclamation, 1943–1960" (Ph.D. dissertation, University of New Mexico, 1978); U.S. Department of the Interior, Bureau of Reclamation, *The Central Valley Project: "It's about Water"* (Sacramento: U.S. Bureau of Reclamation, 2000).

64. Lee, "California Water Politics," 68, 71.

65. U.S. Department of Agriculture, Bureau of Agricultural Economics, *Agricultural Land Ownership and Operation in the Southern San Joaquin Valley,* by Edwin E. Wilson and Marion Clawson (Berkeley, mimeo., June 1945), 28. For the 1926 amendment stipulating the terms for disposing of excess lands, see *U.S. Statutes at Large* 44 (1926): 636.

66. *U.S. Statutes at Large* 34 (1906): 117; Goizé, *Reclamation in the United States,* 70–75; Lee, "California Water Politics," 76, passim.

67. U.S. Department of the Interior, Bureau of Reclamation, *The Story of the Columbia Basin Project* (Washington, D.C.: Government Printing Office, 1964); Richard K. Pelz, ed., *Federal Reclamation and Related Laws Annotated,* 3 vols. (Washington, D.C.: Government Printing Office, 1972), 1: 596; 2: 728–735; Robinson, *Water for the West,* 63–64; Golzé, *Reclamation in the United States,* 176–187; Charles McKinley, *Uncle Sam in the Pacific Northwest* (Berkeley: University of California Press, 1952); George Sundborg, *Hail Columbia: The Thirty Year Struggle for Grand Coulee Dam* (New York: Macmillan, 1954); Donald Swain, "The Bureau of Reclamation and the New Deal, 1933–1940," *Pacific Northwest Quarterly* 61 (July 1970): 145–146.

68. John Steinbeck, *Grapes of Wrath* (New York: Viking Press, 1939); Carey McWilliams, *Factories in the Field* (1939; Santa Barbara and Salt Lake City: Peregrine Smith, Inc., 1971); Majka, *Farm Workers,* chaps. 5–7, passim; Daniel, *Bitter Harvest,* passim; Jelinek, *Harvest Empire,* 67; Leuchtenberg, *Roosevelt and the New Deal,* 138–139, 141–142.

69. Clayton Koppes, "Public Water, Private Land: Origins of the Acreage Limitation Controversy, 1933–1953," *Pacific Historical Re-*

view 47 (Nov. 1978): 617; David Seckler, ed., *California Water: A Study in Resource Management* (Berkeley and Los Angeles: University of California Press, 1971), 260.

70. Pelz, ed., *Federal Reclamation and Related Laws,* 1: 612–613, 712; Koppes, "Public Water, Private Land," 612–613, 616; National Reclamation Association, *Proceedings: Irrigation War Food Conference and 12th Annual Meeting, National Reclamation Association, Denver, Colorado, October 27–28–29, 1943* (Washington, D.C.: National Reclamation Association, [1944]), 202.

71. Koppes, "Public Water, Private Land," 617; Sidney T. Harding, "A Life in Western Water Development" (Regional Oral History Office, Bancroft Library, University of California, Berkeley, 1967), 237–241, 307–309.

72. Maass, *Muddy Waters,* 228–238; Harry S. Truman to Earl Warren, Apr. 10, 1946, file F3640:3555, Earl Warren Papers, California State Archives, Sacramento; Lee, "California Water Politics," 79–80; Richard P. Simpson, "The Campaign for State Purchase of the Central Valley Project, 1945–1955" (M.A. thesis, Stanford University, 1956), 77–78, passim. The contention of Arthur Maass and Raymond Anderson that small farmers along the Kings River joined with large farmers to oppose acreage limitation because of a shared commitment to "local control" has been challenged by Patricia Ballard. Maass and Anderson, . . . *And the Desert Shall Rejoice: Conflict, Growth, and Justice in Arid Environments* (Cambridge, Mass.: MIT Press, 1978), 271–273; Patricia L. Ballard, ". . . And Conflict Shall Prevail: Reclamation Law, Water Districts, and Politics in the Kings River Service Area of California—An Alternative Framework for Analysis" (M.A. thesis, University of California, Los Angeles, 1980), 35–52.

73. Senate Special Committee to Study Problems of American Small Business, "Small Business and the Community: A Study in Central Valley of California on Effects of Scale of Farm Operations," *Committee Print 13,* 79 Cong., 2 sess. (1946), 6; Walter Goldschmidt, *As You Sow* (New York: Harcourt, Brace & Co., 1947); Richard Kirkendall, "Social Science in the Central Valley of California: An Episode," *California Historical Society Quarterly* 43 (Sept. 1964): 195–218; Koppes, "Public Water, Private Land," 618.

74. Ernesto Galarza, *Merchants of Labor: The Mexican Bracero Story* (Santa Barbara: McNally & Loftin, 1964); Paul S. Taylor, "Walter Goldschmidt's Baptism by Fire: Central Valley Water Politics," in

James P. Loucky and Jeffrey R. Jones, eds., *Paths to the Symbolic Self: Essays in Honor of Walter Goldschmidt* (Los Angeles: Department of Anthropology, University of California, Los Angeles, 1976), 129–140; Jelinek, *Harvest Empire,* 74, 83–84; Kirkendall, "Social Science in the Central Valley," 200–209; Richard Kirkendall, *Social Scientists and Farm Politics in the Age of Roosevelt* (Columbia: University of Missouri Press, 1965), 224.

75. Koppes, "Public Water, Private Land," 621. The delightful description of Straus's eyebrows comes from Donald Worster, *Rivers of Empire* (New York: Pantheon, 1985), 247.

76. Koppes, "Public Water, Private Land," 621.

77. Ibid; David A. Kathka, "The Bureau of Reclamation in the Truman Administration: Personnel, Politics, and Policy" (Ph.D. dissertation, University of Missouri, 1976), 27–28, 61–62, passim.

78. Senate Committee on Public Lands, *Hearings on Exemption of Certain Projects from Land-Limitation Provisions of Federal Reclamation Laws, S. 912,* 80 Cong., 1 sess. (1947), passim; Sheridan Downey, *They Would Rule the Valley* (San Francisco: Sheridan Downey, 1947), 3.

79. For an admirable analysis of "technical compliance," see Koppes, "Public Water, Private Land," 624–635; see also Straus's testimony in Senate Committee on Public Lands, *Hearings on Exemption of Certain Projects,* passim; and the typescript record of a meeting between Reclamation Bureau officials and Central Valley landowners in "Minutes of Meeting, July 29, 1947," file 5.2, Ralph M. Brody Papers, University of California Water Resources Center Archives, Berkeley.

80. Koppes, "Public Water, Private Land," 635; Lawrence B. Lee, "Reclamation and Irrigation," in Howard R. Lamar, ed., *The Reader's Encyclopedia of the American West* (New York: Crowell, 1977), 1003.

81. Joseph L. Sax, "Selling Reclamation Water Rights: A Case Study in Federal Subsidy Policy," *Michigan Law Review* 64 (Nov. 1965): 13–46.

82. Elmo Richardson, *Dams, Parks & Politics: Resource Development and Preservation in the Truman-Eisenhower Era* (Lexington: University Press of Kentucky, 1973), 114.

83. Ibid., 158–163.

84. Ibid., 94; see also 36, 73, passim.

85. *San Francisco Chronicle,* Nov. 28, 1939; *Sacramento Bee,* Nov. 28, 1939; J. B. Black to John C. Page, Aug. 1, 1941, file 614.24,

California Department of Water Resources Archives; "Statement on Behalf of the Pacific Gas and Electric Company" (Mar. 4, 1942), file 614.2521, ibid.; J. B. Black, "Statement before the [U.S.] Senate Committee on Appropriations on the Central Valley Project in California" (June 9, 1943), ibid.; Coate, "Water, Power, and Politics," 129–137, 168–169; Robert E. Burke, *Olson's New Deal for California* (Berkeley: University of California Press, 1953), 100–106.

86. Coate, "Water, Power, and Politics," 139–142; Lee, "California Water Politics," 76–77; Paul Goyne, "Developing the Empire of Tomorrow: The California Farm Bureau Federation, the California State Grange, and the Central Valley Project, 1933–1952" (paper in possession of the author, 1989), 15.

87. Earl Warren to California's U.S. Senators and Congressmen, May 14, 1946, file F3640:3555, Warren Papers; Warren to William F. Knowland and Sheridan Downey, June 13, 1946, ibid.; Warren, "Statement . . . to the United States Senate" (June 4, 1948), file F3640:3564, ibid.; Putnam, *Modern California Politics,* 33–35; Leo Katcher, *Earl Warren: A Political Biography* (New York: McGraw-Hill, 1967), 213, passim; Richard B. Harvey, *Earl Warren, Governor of California* (Jericho, N.Y.: Exposition Press, 1969), passim.

88. For the contracts that constituted the agreement, see "Central Valley Documents, Part Two," 286–298, 305–323. See also Coate, "Water, Power and Politics," 152, 162–163, 170–173.

89. Quoted in Coate, "Water, Power, and Politics," 176.

90. Ibid., 175, 206, 225, passim.

91. Comptroller General of the United States, *Congress Should Reevaluate the 160-Acre Limitation on Land Eligible to Receive Water from Federal Water Resources Projects* (Washington, D.C.: Comptroller General of the United States, 1972), 10.

92. S. T. Harding, "The Hassle over the Central Valley Project" (May 22, 1953), file 116-2, S. T. Harding Papers, University of California Water Resources Center Archives; *Commonwealth* 29 (June 1, 1953): 120–121; Alten B. Davis, "The Excess Land Law in the Central Valley of California" (Ph.D. dissertation, University of California, Berkeley, 1962), 34–47.

93. "Landownerships in Excess of 10,000 Acres, State Service Area, San Joaquin Valley Portion, Kern County, California" (1959), file 1.3, Brody Papers. After the State Water Project was approved, there were changes in owners and sizes of landholdings, but many of the same corporations remained in the area and the sizes of the

holdings continued to be among the largest in the nation. See, for example, Don Villarejo, *New Lands for Agriculture: The California State Water Project* (Davis, Calif.: California Institute for Rural Studies, 1981), 3, 6–7; Leslie W. Senger, "Irrigated Agricultural Developments on the Southern 'West Side' of the San Joaquin Valley with Special Reference to Major Oil Company Holdings" (Ph.D. dissertation, University of California, Los Angeles, 1972), chap. 4. See also Harvey O. Banks, "California Water Project, 1955–1961" (Regional Oral History Office, Bancroft Library, University of California, Berkeley, 1967), 15, 34; McWilliams, *California,* 332–333; Ellen Liebman, *California Farmland: A History of Large Agricultural Landholdings* (Totowa, N.J.: Rowman & Allanheld, 1983), 145, app. B; Sidney Kossen, "California's $2 Billion Thirst," *Harper's Magazine* 222 (Mar. 1961): 100.

94. U.S. Geological Survey, "Ground-Water Conditions in the Mendota-Huron Area, Fresno and Kings Counties, California," *Water-Supply Paper 1360-G* (Washington, D.C.: Government Printing Office, 1957), 409, 412, 440, passim; U.S. Department of Agriculture, "Replenishment of Ground Water Supplies by Artificial Means," by Dean C. Muckel, *Technical Bulletin No. 1195* (Washington, D.C.: U.S. Department of Agriculture, 1959), 31, passim.

95. Ibid.; Cooper, *Aqueduct Empire,* 164–166.

96. California Water Resources Board, "Water Resources of California," *Bulletin No. 1* (Sacramento: State Printing Office, 1951), 17, 22, 70; California Water Resources Board, "Water Utilization and Requirements of California," *Bulletin No. 2,* 2 vols. (Sacramento: California Water Resources Board, June 1955), 2: 236; California Economic Development Agency, *California Statistical Abstract, 1961* (Sacramento: State Printing Office, 1961), 49.

97. California Water Resources Board, *Report on Feasibility of Feather River Project and Sacramento–San Joaquin Delta Diversion Projects Proposed as Features of the California Water Plan* (Sacramento: California Department of Public Works, May 1951), chaps. 2–3; Kahrl, ed., *California Water Atlas,* 51; Cooper, *Aqueduct Empire,* 246.

98. California Department of Water Resources, *Bulletin No. 200,* 121; see also ibid., 7–9.

99. *Ivanhoe v. McCracken,* 357 U.S. 275 (1958).

100. Putnam, *Modern California Politics,* 41–43.

101. Harvey P. Grody, "From North to South: The Feather River Project and Other Legislative Water Struggles in the 1950s," *South-*

ern *California Quarterly* 60 (Fall 1978): 289–293; Cooper, *Aqueduct Empire,* 193. See also Harvey P. Grody, "The California Legislature and Comprehensive Water Resources Development: 1941–1959" (Ph.D. dissertation, University of California, Los Angeles, 1971), chap. 8.

102. William H. Jennings, "William H. Jennings, Water Lawyer" (Oral History Program, University of California, Los Angeles, 1967), 101–111; William R. Gianelli, "The California State Department of Water Resources, 1967–1973" (Regional Oral History Office, Bancroft Library, University of California, Berkeley, 1986), 74–75; C. W. Bradbury to Harvey Banks, Nov. 23, 1956, file 601.20, California Department of Water Resources Archives; *San Francisco Chronicle,* Nov. 21, 1956; *Oroville Mercury,* Nov. 23, 1956.

103. Quoted in Royce D. Delmatier, Clarence F. McIntosh, and Earl G. Waters, eds., *The Rumble of California Politics, 1848–1970* (New York: John Wiley & Sons, 1970), 341.

104. The emphasis is Brown's. Edmund G. Brown, Sr., "The California Water Project: Personal Interest and Involvement in the Legislation, Public Support, and Construction, 1950–1966" (Regional Oral History Office, Bancroft Library, University of California, Berkeley, 1981), 29; Ralph Brody, "Revising Legislation and Building Public Support for the California Water Project, 1959–1960; Brief History of the Westlands Water District" (Regional Oral History Office, Bancroft Library, University of California, Berkeley, 1981), 10. Brown's role can be followed in additional detail in his papers in the Bancroft Library.

105. Brown, "California Water Project," 29.

106. Delmatier et al., eds., *Rumble of California Politics,* 341; Grody, "From North to South," 300.

107. *Cal. Stats.,* chap. 1762 (1959); Ralph M. Brody, "Essential Provisions of the Bond Act," *Western Water News* 11 (Sept. 1959): A and D; California Department of Water Resources, *Bulletin No. 200,* 12–13; Brody, "Revising Legislation," 29–30; Gianelli, "California State Department of Water Resources," 74–75; Jennings, "William H. Jennings: Water Lawyer," 101–111; Cooper, *Aqueduct Empire,* 224–225; Grody, "From North to South," 308; George L. Baker, "Family Farming vs. Land Monopoly; Westlands' Ralph Brody," *California Journal* 7 (Sept. 1976): 293; David Sandino, senior staff counsel, Office of the Chief Counsel, California Department of Water Resources, to the author, Sept. 4, 1998.

108. Brown, "California Water Project," 16–17, 62; Banks, "California Water Project," 34, 36; Gianelli, "California State Department of Water Resources," 20; Brody, "Revising Legislation," 9; Robert A. Skinner, "Progress of the Metropolitan Water District: Recollections" (Oral History Program, University of California, Los Angeles, 1970), 52.

109. *Cal. Stats.,* chap. 1762 (1959), 4240; Brown, "California Water Project," 16–17; Brody, "Revising Legislation," 13 ff.

110. Brown, "California Water Project," 8; Grody, "From North to South," 299; Banks, "California Water Project," 68.

111. *Journal of the Senate: 1959 Session of the California Legislature* (Sacramento: State Printing Office, 1959), 2943; *Journal of the Assembly: 1959 Session of the California Legislature* (Sacramento: State Printing Office, 1959), 5660–5661; *Cal. Stats.,* chap. 1762 (1959).

112. Quoted in Grody, "From North to South," 300; see also Brown, "California Water Project," 21; Brody, "Revising Legislation," 25 ff.

113. *Los Angeles Times,* Oct. 27, 1960; *San Francisco Chronicle,* Oct. 27, 1960; California Department of Water Resources, *Bulletin No. 200,* 9; Cooper, *Aqueduct Empire,* 235–236; Robert H. Boyle, John Graves, and T. H. Watkins, *The Water Hustlers* (San Francisco: Sierra Club, 1971), 165, 166.

114. Quoted in Cooper, *Aqueduct Empire,* 234; see also Banks, "California Water Project," 61–62; *Imperial Valley Press* (El Centro), July 16, 1959; *Los Angeles Examiner,* Aug. 28, 1960; *Los Angeles Times,* Oct. 13, 1960; *Santa Ana Register* Mar. 17, 1960; *San Diego Union,* Sept. 22, 1960.

115. Cooper, *Aqueduct Empire,* 205–207, 225, 237–238.

116. Kahrl, *Water and Power,* 403.

117. Preston Hotchkis, Sr., "One Man's Dynamic Role in California Politics and Water Development, and World Affairs" (Regional Oral History Office, Bancroft Library, University of California, Berkeley, 1980), 102.

118. Skinner, "Progress of the Metropolitan Water District," 60–66; Joseph Jensen, "Developing California's Natural Resources" (Oral History Program, University of California, Los Angeles, 1970), 155–158; Brown, "California Water Project," 37–39; Jennings, "William H. Jennings: Water Lawyer," 116–126; Warne, "Administration of the Department of Water Resources," 94–97.

119. Ibid.

120. California Secretary of State, *Statement of Vote, General Election, 1960* (Sacramento: State Printing Office, 1960), 23; William E. Warne, "California Comes of Age" (Speech Delivered on Jan. 13, 1961), file 1961-1, William E. Warne Papers, University of California Water Resources Center Archives.

121. California Department of Water Resources, "Management of the California State Water Project," *Bulletin No. 132–87* (Sacramento: California Department of Water Resources, Sept. 1987), 4, 7; California Department of Water Resources, "The California State Water Project in 1974," *Bulletin No. 132–74* (Sacramento: California Department of Water Resources, June 1974), iii, 11–15; Cooper, *Aqueduct Empire,* 244; California Department of Water Resources, *State Water Project Atlas* (Sacramento: California Department of Water Resources, 2000).

122. California Department of Water Resources, *Bulletin No. 200,* 25–29; Warne, "Administration of the Department of Water Resources," 60–66; Gianelli, "California State Department of Water Resources," 12–34, 41–43; interview with Viju Patel, power manager, Division of Operations and Maintenance, California Department of Water Resources, Dec. 13, 1990.

123. Brown, "California Water Project," 43. See also California Department of Water Resources, "Contract between the State of California Department of Water Resources and the Metropolitan Water District of Southern California for a Water Supply, November 4, 1960," pp. 30/1–30/2, copy in folder 1.12, Brody Papers; Brody, "Revising Legislation," 22–23; Warne, "Administration of the Department of Water Resources," 87–92; Banks, "California Water Project," 46–47, 70; Gianelli, "California State Department of Water Resources," 26–27.

124. Banks, "California Water Project," 29–30; California Department of Water Resources, "Contract between the State of California Department of Water Resources and the Metropolitan Water District of Southern California for a Water Supply, November 4, 1960," sec. C, folder 1.12, Brody Papers.

125. Warne, "Administration of the Department of Water Resources," 88–90; Brown, "California Water Project," 30–31; California Department of Water Resources, "Contract between the State of California Department of Water Resources and the Metropolitan Water District of Southern California for a Water Supply, November 4, 1960," pp. 21/1–21/2, file 1.12, Brody Papers; Gianelli,

"California State Department of Water Resources," 26–27; California Department of Water Resources, *Bulletin No. 200,* 25; Michael Storper and Richard Walker, *The Price of Water: Surplus and Subsidy in the California State Water Project* (Berkeley: University of California Institute of Governmental Studies, 1984), 3, 10; Richard Walker and Michael Storper, "The California Water System: Another Round of Expansion?" *Public Affairs Report: Bulletin of the Institute of Governmental Studies* 20 (Apr. 1979): 5; George L. Baker and Tom DeVries, "Water," *New West* (June 16, 1980): 36–37.

126. Villarejo, *New Lands for Agriculture,* 3, 15; Storper and Walker, *Price of Water,* 1, passim.

127. Warne, "Administration of the Department of Water Resources," 90; cf. Jensen, "Developing California's Natural Resources"; Skinner, "Progress of the Metropolitan Water District"; Banks, "California Water Project"; and Brody, "Revising Legislation," among others. MWD later argued unpersuasively that there was no subsidy. See Warren J. Abbott, "'Myth vs. Reality': Agricultural Subsidies and the State Water Project" (Los Angeles: Metropolitan Water District of Southern California, photocopy, Jan. 21, 1986); and Michael Storper, "Subsidies in the State Water Project: A Reply to the MWD" (Los Angeles: The Author, photocopy, n.d.). Copies of both papers in possession of the author.

128. Brown, "California Water Project," 31; interview with Kevin Donhoff, associate engineer, State Water Project Branch, Metropolitan Water District of Southern California, Dec. 5, 1990; interview with Walt Blanksvard, senior engineer, State Water Project Branch, Metropolitan Water District of Southern California, Dec. 13, 1990; California Department of Water Resources, "Management of the California State Water Project," *Bulletin 132–89* (Sacramento: California Department of Water Resources, Sept. 1989), 282.

129. Villarejo, *New Lands for Agriculture,* 1, 9–12.

130. Walker and Storper, "California Water System," 6; E. Phillip LeVeen, "Reclamation Policy at a Crossroads," *Public Affairs Report: Bulletin of the Institute of Governmental Studies* 19 (Oct. 1978): 4; Don Villarejo, *How Much Is Enough? Federal Water Subsidies and Agriculture in California's Central Valley* (Davis: California Institute for Rural Studies, 1986).

131. Galarza, *Merchants of Labor,* passim; Majka, *Farm Workers,* chaps. 8–12; Richard B. Craig, *The Bracero Program: Interest Groups and Foreign Policy* (Austin: University of Texas Press, 1971), 47,

54–55, 84–86, 157–197, passim; Miriam J. Wells, *Regulation of the Farm Labor Market: An Assessment of Farm Labor Protection under California's Agricultural Labor Relations Act* (Davis: California Institute for Rural Studies, 1989); *Los Angeles Times,* May 4, 1987, July 11, 1989, May 27 and 28, 1999; Harold O. Carter and George Goldman, *The Measure of California Agriculture: Its Impact on the State Economy,* rev. ed. (Oakland: University of California Division of Agriculture and Natural Resources, 1998), 42.

132. Cooper, *Aqueduct Empire,* 262.

Chapter 6: Hydraulic Society on the Defensive

1. Senate Committee on Irrigation and Reclamation, *Hearings on Arizona Water Resources, S. Res. 304,* 78 Cong., 2 Sess. (1945), 1, 42, passim.

2. House Committee on Interior and Insular Affairs, *Hearings on the Central Arizona Project, H.R. 1500 and H.R. 1501,* 82 Cong., 1 sess. (1951), 739–756, passim; Rich Johnson, *The Central Arizona Project, 1918–1968* (Tucson: University of Arizona Press, 1977), chaps, 2–4.

3. "Hoover Dam Documents," *H. Doc. 717,* 80 Cong., 2 sess. (1948), 108; Norris Hundley, jr., *Dividing the Waters: A Century of Controversy between the United States and Mexico* (Berkeley and Los Angeles: University of California Press, 1966), chap. 5.

4. *Arizona* v. *California et al.,* 373 U.S. 564, 565 (1963); Norris Hundley, jr., "Clio Nods: *Arizona* v. *California* and the Boulder Canyon Act—A Reassessment," *Western Historical Quarterly* 3 (Jan. 1972): 17–51; *U.S. Statutes at Large* 82 (1968): 885. For an earlier but quickly forgotten precedent for the 1963 decision, see Douglas R. Littlefield, "Interstate Water Conflicts, Compromises, and Compacts: The Rio Grande, 1880–1938" (Ph.D. dissertation, University of California, Los Angeles, 1987).

5. Robert A. Skinner to William E. Warne, Feb. 13, 1964, file 1.24, Ralph M. Brody Papers, University of California Water Resources Center Archives, Berkeley; Skinner to Ralph M. Brody, Feb. 14, 1964, ibid.; California Department of Water Resources, "California State Water Project," vol. 1, "History, Planning, and Early Progress," *Bulletin No. 200* (Sacramento: California Resources Agency, Nov. 1974), 16, 22; Robert A. Skinner, "Progress of the Metropolitan Water District: Recollections" (Oral History Program, University of California, Los Angeles, 1966), 67–70.

6. Aldo Leopold, "The Conservation Ethic," *Journal of Forestry* 31 (Oct. 1933): 634–643; Leopold, *A Sand County Almanac and Sketches Here and There* (New York: Oxford University Press, 1949), 224–225. See also Stephen Fox, *The American Conservation Movement: John Muir and His Legacy* (Madison: University of Wisconsin Press, 1985); Curt Meine, *Aldo Leopold: His Life and Work* (Madison: University of Wisconsin Press, 1988); Roderick Nash, *The Rights of Nature: A History of Environmental Ethics* (Madison: University of Wisconsin Press, 1989); Donald Worster, *Nature's Economy: A History of Ecological Ideas,* 2d ed. (New York: Cambridge University Press, 1994); Donald Fleming, "Roots of the New Conservation Movement," *Perspectives in American History* 6 (1972): 7–91.

7. Samuel P. Hays, *Beauty, Health, and Permanence: Environmental Politics in the United States, 1955–1985* (New York: Cambridge University Press, 1987), 34.

8. Rachel Carson, *Silent Spring* (Boston: Houghton Mifflin, 1962); Linda Lear, *Rachel Carson: Witness for Nature* (New York: Henry Holt, 1997); Rice Odell, *Environmental Awakening: The New Revolution to Protect the Earth* (Cambridge, Mass.: Ballinger Publishing Co., 1980), 1–6; Craig R. Humphrey and Frederick R. Buttel, *Environment, Energy and Society* (Belmont, Calif.: Wadsworth Publishing Co., 1982), 120, 132, passim; Victor B. Scheffer, *The Shaping of Environmentalism in America* (Seattle: University of Washington Press, 1991); Hays, *Beauty, Health, and Permanence,* 52–60.

9. Hays, *Beauty, Health, and Permanence,* 40–54, 530–531.

10. Two of these laws required environmental investigations whose nearly similar official names have sometimes led to confusion. The National Environmental Policy Act, passed by Congress in 1969, mandated a "detailed statement" on any federal action that could reasonably be expected to have a major effect on the environment. The resulting statement, not surprisingly, came to be known as "Environmental Impact *Statement*" (EIS). In 1970 the California legislature enacted a similar law, the California Environmental Quality Act, which obligated state and local agencies to prepare an "Environmental Impact *Report*" (EIR), the contents of which, for all practical purposes, mirror those produced by the federal requirement. In those instances when both state and federal agencies are involved in the same project, each must prepare its respective EIS and EIR or cooperate on a single EIS/EIR. *U.S. Code,* vol. 42, secs. 4321 et seq. (1969); *California Public Resources Code,* secs. 21000 et seq. (1970); Michael Remy, *Guide to the Environmental Quality Act*

(*CEQA*), 7th ed. (Point Arena, Calif.: Solano Press Books, 1993); Hays, *Beauty, Health, and Permanence,* 40–54; Arthur L. Littleworth and Eric L. Garner, *California Water* (Point Arena, Calif.: Solano Press Books, 1995), 71–72, 113–114, 123–124, 142–143, 211–222.

11. Susan R. Neel, "Irreconcilable Differences: Reclamation, Preservation, and the Origins of the Echo Park Dam Controversy" (Ph.D. dissertation, University of California, Los Angeles, 1990), traces the beginnings of the dispute to changing values about reclamation and preservation in the 1930s and 1940s, and Mark W. T. Harvey has provided a splendid overview of the dispute and its larger significance in *A Symbol of Wilderness: Echo Park and the American Conservation Movement* (Albuquerque: University of New Mexico Press, 1994). See also Elmo Richardson, *Dams, Parks, & Politics: Resource Development & Preservation in the Truman-Eisenhower Era* (Lexington: University Press of Kentucky, 1973), 56–70, 129–152; Susan R. Neel, "Newton Drury and the Echo Park Dam Controversy," *Forest & Conservation History* 38 (Apr. 1994): 55–56; Byron Pearson, "Newton Drury of the National Park Service: A Reappraisal," *Pacific Historical Review* 68 (Aug. 1999): 397–424; Eliot Porter, *The Place No One Knew: Glen Canyon on the Colorado* (San Francisco: Sierra Club, 1963); Russell Martin, *Glen Canyon and the Struggle for the Soul of the West* (New York: Henry Holt, 1989); Mark W. T. Harvey, "Echo Park, Glen Canyon, and the Postwar Wilderness Movement," *Pacific Historical Review* 60 (Feb. 1991): 43–67; Owen Stratton and Phillip Sirotkin, *The Echo Park Controversy* (University, Ala.: University of Alabama Press, 1959); Dean E. Mann, Gary D. Weatherford, and Phillip Nichols, "Legal-Political History of Water Resource Development in the Upper Colorado River Basin," *Lake Powell Research Project Bulletin No. 4* (Los Angeles: National Science Foundation, Sept. 1974); "Echo Park Controversy Resolved," *Living Wilderness* 20 (Winter-Spring 1955–1956): 23–43; David Perlman, "Our Winning Fight for Dinosaur," *Sierra Club Bulletin* 41 (Jan. 1956): 5–8; Jared Farmer, *Glen Canyon Dammed: Inventing Lake Powell and the Canyon Country* (Tucson: University of Arizona Press, 1999).

12. U.S. Congress, *Congressional Quarterly Fact Sheet* (Nov. 1, 1969): 3019–3031; Roderick Nash, *Wilderness and the American Mind,* 3d ed. (New Haven: Yale University Press, 1982), 227–235; U.S. Department of the Interior, "News Release" (Oct. 1, 1993).

13. Lou Cannon, "The Reagan Years," *California Journal* 5 (Nov.

1974): 362–363; *Cal. Stats.,* chap. 1259 (1972); Frank Stead and Walt Anderson, "The California Water Plan: Onward and Upward," *Cry California* 11 (Summer 1976): 12–13; Tim Palmer, *Endangered Rivers and the Conservation Movement* (Berkeley and Los Angeles: University of California Press, 1986), 77, 155.

14. William E. Warne, "Administration of the Department of Water Resources, 1961–1966" (Regional Oral History Office, Bancroft Library, University of California, Berkeley, 1979), 67; Ralph M. Brody, "Revising Legislation and Building Public Support for the California Water Project, 1959–1960; Brief History of the Westlands Water District" (Regional Oral History Office, Bancroft Library, University of California, Berkeley, 1981), 43; William R. Gianelli, "The California State Department of Water Resources, 1967–1973" (Regional Oral History Office, Bancroft Library, University of California, Berkeley, 1986), 48.

15. California Department of Water Resources, *Bulletin No. 200,* 40–44; Richard Walker and Michael Storper, "The California Water System: Another Round of Expansion?" *Public Affairs Report: Bulletin of the Institute of Governmental Studies* 20 (Apr. 1979): 2; W. Turrentine Jackson and Alan M. Paterson, *The Sacramento–San Joaquin Delta: The Evolution and Implementation of Water Policy* (Davis: University of California Water Resources Center, June 1977), 15–100, passim.

16. Interagency Delta Committee, *Plan of Development: Sacramento–San Joaquin Delta* (Sacramento: Interagency Delta Committee, Jan. 1965); California Department of Water Resources, *Bulletin No. 200,* 41–42; Jackson and Paterson, *Sacramento–San Joaquin Delta,* 96–98.

17. California Department of Water Resources, *The Peripheral Canal of the Sacramento–San Joaquin Delta* (Sacramento: California Resources Agency, Dec. 1966), 3, 8–9.

18. "Statement of W. C. Bryant, Engineer-Manager, on Behalf of the Kern County Water Agency before the Joint Senate and Assembly Water Committees Hearing on the Bureau of Reclamation Report on the Peripheral Canal Unit" (Sept. 17, 1969), file 071.41: Peripheral Canal, California Department of Water Resources Archives, Sacramento.

19. "Statement of the Metropolitan Water District of Southern California in Support of Peripheral Canal Unit" (Sept. 17, 1969), ibid.; John Hart, "The Delta: The Living (or Dying?) Heart of California,"

Cry California 12 (Summer 1977): 49; Walker and Storper, "California Water System," 5; Don Villarejo, *New Lands for Agriculture: The California State Water Project* (Davis: California Institute for Rural Studies, 1981), 15.

20. Walker and Storper, "California Water System," 5 (quote); see also John Hart, "One System, Many Masters: Happenstance Water Development," *Cry California* 12 (Fall 1977): 9–10; Hart, "The Delta," 45–50; Elizabeth Johnson, "The Delta Canal, Anything But a Peripheral Issue: Get Ready for the Water War of the 80s," *California Journal* 11 (Oct. 1980): 376–378; Harry Dennis, *Water and Power: The Peripheral Canal and Its Alternatives* (San Francisco: Friends of the Earth, 1981); and the extensive coverage in the San Francisco, Sacramento, and Los Angeles newspapers.

21. California Department of Water Resources, "Water Conservation in California," *Bulletin No. 198* (Sacramento: California Resources Agency, May 1976), 42–46, 87–89, passim; Walker and Storper, "California Water System," 6.

22. See, for example, E. Phillip LeVeen, "Reclamation Policy at a Crossroads," *Public Affairs Report: Bulletin of the Institute of Governmental Studies* 19 (Oct. 1978): 9; John Raphael, "Quality or Quantity? The Uncertain Fate of Delta Water," *Cry California* 14 (Spring 1979): 22–25; Nicholas Arguimbau, "Water Conservation: L.A. Is Not the Villain, New Developments Are Not the Answer," ibid. (Summer 1979), 27–32; Jonathan Kirsch, "The Politics of Water," *New West* 4 (Sept. 10, 1979): 48–50, 63–70; Villarejo, *New Lands for Agriculture,* 12–15.

23. LeVeen, "Reclamation Policy at a Crossroads," 5. See also George L. Baker, "Family Farming vs. Land Monopoly: Westlands' Ralph Brody—The $81,500 Public Servant," *California Journal* 7 (Sept. 1976): 293–296.

24. Baker, "Family Farming vs. Land Monopoly," 294.

25. Brody vehemently denied Baker's charges at the time. Four years later, in an interview, he offered a defense of his and Westlands' actions grounded essentially on the Reclamation Bureau's technical-compliance policy. See "Westlands' Brody Replies," *California Journal* 7 (Nov. 1976): 362 and 392; Brody, "Revising Legislation," 80–85.

26. Quoted in Kirsch, "The Politics of Water," 65. See also John A. Nejedly, "Contra Costa and the Peripheral Canal" (July 10, 1986), file 071.41: Peripheral Canal, California Department of Wa-

ter Resources Archives; Delta Water Users Association to California Senate Committee on Water Resources and Assembly Committee on Water, Sept. 11, 1969, ibid.; Arthur Miller, "Delta Water Controversy Stalls Construction of the Peripheral Canal, Last Major Link in the State Water Project," *California Journal* 4 (Jan. 1973): 11–14.

27. Francis C. Lindsay to California Assembly Committee on Water, Sept. 12, 1969, file 071.41: Peripheral Canal, California Department of Water Resources Archives; Trout Unlimited to Joint California Senate-Assembly Interim Committees on Water and Water Resources, Sept. 15, 1969, ibid.; *Los Angeles Times,* Sept. 5, 1974, Jan. 6, 1975.

28. California Department of Water Resources, *Bulletin 132–72* (Sacramento: California Resources Agency, 1972), 17; Miller, "Delta Water Controversy," 11–14; *California* v. *United States,* 438 U.S. 645 (1978); California Department of Water Resources, "The California State Water Project—1978 Activities and Future Management Plans," *Bulletin 132–79* (Sacramento: California Resources Agency, Nov. 1979), 17, 60; California Department of Water Resources, "The California State Water Project—Current Activities and Future Management Plans," *Bulletin 132–80* (Sacramento: California Resources Agency, Oct. 1980), 1–14, 20; *United States* v. *State Water Resources Control Board,* 182 Cal.App.3d 82 (1986).

29. Gianelli, "California State Department of Water Resources," 44; Miller, "Delta Water Controversy," 14.

30. James M. Dourgarian, "The Peripheral Canal: Environmental Concerns Catch up with Southern Thirst," *California Journal* 6 (July 1975): 249; Jackson and Paterson, *Sacramento–San Joaquin Delta,* 173.

31. Quoted in Stephanie S. Pincetl, "The Environmental Policies and Politics of the Brown Administration" (Ph.D. dissertation, University of California, Los Angeles, 1985), 176. See also *Los Angeles Times,* June 21, 1982.

32. Quoted in Ronald B. Robie, "The State Department of Water Resources, 1975–1983" (Regional Oral History Office, Bancroft Library, University of California, Berkeley, 1989), 71.

33. By this time the dispute over water quality standards had become enmeshed in other federal-state jurisdictional battles, the most notorious involving the filling of the reservoir behind New Melones Dam on the Stanislaus River. *California* v. *United States,* 438

U.S. 645 (1978); Timothy J. Beaton, "Breathing New Life into Section 8 of the 1902 Reclamation Act: *California v. United States," University of Colorado Law Review* 50 (Winter 1979): 207–229; Robie, "State Department of Water Resources," 71–75; California Department of Water Resources, "Delta Water Facilities," *Bulletin 76* (Sacramento: California Resources Agency, July 1978), 6–7, 30–32; California Department of Water Resources, *Bulletin 132–79,* 1–3, 16–20; *Bulletin 132–80,* 1–14, 20; Tony Quinn, "The Impact of the Drought on California's Political Climate," *California Journal* 8 (July 1977): 245; Hal Rubin, "California's Canal Conflict (Peripheral, Not Panama)," ibid. 9 (Jan. 1978): 17–18; Ed Salzman, "The Brown Record," ibid. (June 1978), 175.

34. California Department of Water Resources, *Bulletin 132–79,* 1–8; *Bulletin 132–80,* iii, 1–14; *Journal of the Senate: 1979–1980 Session of the California Legislature* (Sacramento: State Printing Office, 1980), 8246; *Journal of the Assembly: 1979–1980 Session of the California Legislature* (Sacramento: State Printing Office, 1980), 17743; Robie, "State Department of Water Resources," 76–77.

35. *Journal of the Senate: 1979–1980 Session of the California Legislature,* 12594; *Journal of the Assembly: 1979–1980 Session of the California Legislature,* 17105; California Department of Water Resources, "The California State Water Project—Current Activities and Future Management Plans," *Bulletin 132–81* (Sacramento: California Resources Agency, Nov. 1981), iii, 4–11; California Secretary of State, *Statement of Vote: General Election, November 4, 1980* (Sacramento: State Printing Office, 1980), 32; *Los Angeles Times,* June 8, 9, and July 11, 1980.

36. Robie, "State Department of Water Resources," 77.

37. California Department of Water Resources, *Bulletin 132–80,* 33–36; *San Francisco Chronicle,* July 19, 1980; *Los Angeles Times,* July 19, 1980.

38. *Los Angeles Times,* Feb. 1, 1981; Daniel J. Blackburn, "The Farm Bureau's Big Switch on the Big Ditch," *California Journal* 12 (March 1981): 91; Sari Sommarstrom, "How Safe the North Coast Streams?" *California Tomorrow* 17 (Spring 1982): 25, 28; *County of Del Norte v. United States,* cert. denied, 469 U.S. 1189 (1985).

39. *Sacramento Bee,* July 19, 1980; Johnson, "The Delta Canal," 378.

40. *Healdsburg Tribune,* Dec. 17, 1980; Blackburn, "Farm Bureau's Big Switch," 90–91.

41. Blackburn, "Farm Bureau's Big Switch," 90–91; *Bakersfield*

Californian, Mar. 6, 1981; *Sacramento Bee,* Mar. 26, 1981; *Los Angeles Times,* Feb. 8, 1982.

42. Dennis, *Water and Power,* 52; *Los Angeles Times,* Feb. 8, 1982.

43. Johnson, "The Delta Canal," 377, 378; Don Villarejo, *New Lands for Agriculture: The California State Water Project* (Davis: California Institute for Rural Studies, 1981); George L. Baker and Tom DeVries, "Water," *New West* 5 (June 16, 1980): 35–40, 42, 44, 46. Letters of opposition poured in to Director of Water Resources Ronald Robie and Governor Brown, who usually referred them to Robie for response. See Peripheral Canal Correspondence Books, Ronald B. Robie Papers, University of California Water Resources Center, Berkeley; Robie, "State Department of Water Resources," 68–76.

44. California Department of Water Resources, *Peripheral Canal,* 8–9; William R. Gianelli, "Phase Two" (June 8, 1973), 4, file 1973-8, William R. Gianelli Papers, University of California Water Resources Center Archives; California Department of Water Resources, *Department of Water Resources Position on Proposition 9 (SB 200)—Delta Projection, Peripheral Canal and Other Facilities* (Sacramento: California Resources Agency, Apr. 1982), 12, copy in file S9, item 4143, California Department of Water Resources Archives; Ronald Robie to Helen Freed, June 24, 1980, Peripheral Canal Correspondence, Robie Papers; Gerald Meral to Roger Hedgecock, July 23, 1980, ibid.; *San Francisco Chronicle,* Apr. 17, 1982; Blackburn, "Farm Bureau's Big Switch," 89; Dennis, *Water and Power,* 53–54, passim.

45. *Sacramento Bee,* Mar. 26, 1981, May 20, 1982.

46. Ibid., Mar. 19, 1981, Apr. 14, 1982; *Sacramento Union,* Mar. 26, 1981; *Alameda Times-Star,* Mar. 30, 1982; *Journal Commerce Review* (Los Angeles), Mar. 29, 1982; *San Francisco Chronicle,* Apr. 29, 1982; *Los Angeles Times,* Feb. 8, Apr. 17, 1982; California Department of Water Resources, "The California State Water Project—Current Activities and Future Management Plans," *Bulletin 132–82* (Sacramento: California Resources Agency, Nov. 1982), 4.

47. California Secretary of State, *Statement of Vote: Primary Elections, June 8, 1982* (Sacramento: State Printing Office, 1982), 45; California Department of Water Resources, *Bulletin 132–82,* 4–6.

48. *Los Angeles Times,* Jan. 22 and 24, 1985, Aug. 7, 8, and 9, 1984, Jan. 20, 1986, Apr. 15, 1988, May 10, 1989, May 4, Sept. 2, and Oct. 9, 1990, Mar. 25 and Apr. 9, 1991; John Hart, "The Bay and the Delta: Still in Trouble," *California Tomorrow* 17 (Spring 1982): 14–15.

49. Antonio Rossman, "Water: Where Do We Go from Here?"

California Journal 13 (Sept. 1982): 349–350; Dan Carson, "Water Wars '87: New Bills Revive North-South Struggle," ibid. 17 (Aug. 1987): 378–382; Cheryl Clark, "Breaking the Faith—Southern California Dissidents: We Don't Need Northern Water Now," ibid. 16 (May 1985): 197; Dan Meyers, "Searching for a Solution to the Delta's Costly Problems," ibid. 14 (July 1983): 268–269; Ed Mendel, "Policy, Plumbing and Peace," *Golden State Report* 2 (Dec. 1986): 29–32; *County of Del Norte v. United States,* 732 F.2d 1462 (9th Cir. 1984); cert. denied, 469 U.S. 1189 (1985).

50. *Los Angeles vs. San Fernando et al.: Appendix to Respondents' Brief* (n.p., n.d.), vol. 1, app. A, 57; *Los Angeles v. San Fernando et al.,* 14 Cal.3d 199, 217 (1975); *Glendale News-Press,* Mar. 18, 1968.

51. *Los Angeles v. San Fernando et al.,* 14 Cal.3d 246.

52. *Los Angeles vs. San Fernando et al.: California Court of Appeal, Second Appellate District—Appendix to Respondents' Brief* (March 14, 1968), vol. 1, app. A, 64.

53. David B. Chatfield and Bruce M. Bertram, "Water Rights of the City of Los Angeles: Power-Politics and the Courts," *San Fernando Valley Law Review* 6 (Spring 1978): 173; *Glendale News-Press,* May 16, 1975; *Los Angeles Times,* May 13, 1975.

54. Mark Twain, *Roughing It* (Hartford, Conn.: American Publishing Co., 1872), 265.

55. Ron Bass, "The Troubled Waters of Mono Lake," *California Journal* 9 (Oct. 1979): 349–350; Daniel Chasan, "Mono Lake vs. Los Angeles: A Tug-of-War for Precious Water," *Smithsonian* 11 (Feb. 1981): 42–50; David Graber, "Mono Lake Is Dying: Who Cares?" *Cry California* 14 (Summer 1979): 33–36; National Research Council, *The Mono Basin Ecosystem: Effects of Changing Lake Level* (Washington, D.C.: National Academy Press, 1987), 1–3, 92–110, passim; Community and Organization Research Institute, University of California, Santa Barbara, *The Future of Mono Lake* (Riverside: University of California Water Resources Center Report No. 68, Feb. 1988), ix, 1–6.

56. William L. Kahrl, *Water and Power: The Conflict over Los Angeles' Water Supply in the Owens Valley* (Berkeley and Los Angeles: University of California Press, 1982), 405–406, 430, passim.

57. *Cal. Stats.,* chap. 368, sec. 1460 (1943), chap. 1344, sec. 1 (1945); *California Water Code,* secs. 1460 (1943), 106.5 (1945).

58. Community and Organization Research Institute, *Future of Mono Lake,* ix, 1–6, 18, app. B, passim; National Research Council,

Mono Basin Ecosystem, 107–109, 196–198; California Department of Water Resources, "California Water Plan Update," *Bulletin 160–98* (Sacramento: California Department of Water Resources, Nov. 1998), chap. 9, p. 20.

59. California Department of Water Resources, *Report of Interagency Task Force on Mono Lake* (Sacramento: California Department of Water Resources, Dec. 1979), 7, 45–52, 55, app. H and I; see also files 089.21, 626.1, and S-9, item 3935, California Department of Water Resources Archives; Bass, "Trouble Waters of Mono Lake," 350; Chasan, "Mono Lake vs. Los Angeles," 47.

60. Harrison C. Dunning, "A New Front in the Water Wars: Introducing the 'Public Trust' Factor," *California Journal* 14 (May 1983): 189–190; Dunning, "The Significance of California's Public Trust Easement for California's Water Rights Law," *U.C. Davis Law Review* 14 (Winter 1980): 357–398.

61. *National Audubon Society v. Superior Court of Alpine County,* 33 Cal.3d 419 (1983); cert. denied, 464 U.S. 977 (1983).

62. Dunning, "A New Front in the Water Wars," 189.

63. Harrison C. Dunning, "The Public Right to Use Water in Place," in Robert E. Beck, ed., *Water and Water Rights,* 7 vols. (Charlottesville, Va.: Michie, 1996), 4: pt. VI, 103–113; *National Audubon Society v. Superior Court of Alpine County,* 33 Cal.3d 452.

64. *National Audubon Society v. Superior Court of Alpine County,* 33 Cal.3d 419 (1983); cert. denied, 464 U.S. 977 (1983); *Los Angeles Times,* Nov. 8, 1983.

65. *Los Angeles Times,* Aug. 28, 1986, Sept. 21, 1988; National Research Council, *Mono Basin Ecosystem,* passim; Community and Organization Research Institute, *Future of Mono Lake,* passim.

66. National Research Council, *Mono Basin Ecosystem,* 2, 4–5, 16, 206–211; Community and Organization Research Institute, *Future of Mono Lake,* ix, xi; *Los Angeles Times,* May 3, Sept. 21 and 26, 1988.

67. *In the Matter of Mono Lake Water Rights Cases, Coordinated Proceeding, Nos. 2284 and 2288,* El Dorado County Superior Court, Aug. 22, 1989; *California Trout, Inc. v. State Water Resources Control Board,* 207 Cal.App.3d 584 (1989); *Los Angeles Times,* Apr. 28, 1988, Apr. 27 and 29, Sept. 24, Dec. 7, 1989, Mar. 2 and 29, 1990; interview with Glenn Singley, manager of Mono Basin studies, Aqueduct Division, Los Angeles Department of Water and Power, Sept. 28, 1989; Community and Organization Research Institute, *Future of Mono Lake,* 2.

68. *Los Angeles Times,* June 17, Sept. 24 and 27, 1989; Casey Skinner, "Mono Lake," *California Journal* 20 (May 1989): 220 (quote). See also *Smithsonian* 11 (Feb. 1981): 42–50; *Harper's* 262 (Mar. 1981): 61–70; *National Geographic* 160 (Oct. 1981): 504–525; *Audubon* 82 (Spring 1980): 98–125; *Sports Illustrated* 58 (May 30, 1983): 76–90; *Time* 133 (Apr. 3, 1989): 8–10.

69. *In the Matter of Mono Lake Water Rights Cases, Coordinated Proceeding, Nos. 2284 and 2288,* El Dorado County Superior Court, April 17, 1991.

70. *Los Angeles Times,* Oct. 5, 1993; John Hart, *Storm over Mono: The Mono Lake Battle and the California Water Future* (Berkeley and Los Angeles: University of California Press, 1996), 106, 132, 164–165, 168–169.

71. Hart, *Storm over Mono,* 57–58, 123–178; Los Angeles Department of Water and Power, Water Resources and Planning Business Unit, *Urban Water Management Plan: Fiscal Year 1997–1998 Update* (Los Angeles: Los Angeles Department of Water and Power, 1998), 4–5; *Los Angeles Times,* Dec. 14 and 19, 1993, Sept. 18, 21, 29, 1994.

72. Hart, *Storm over Mono,* 179; David Carle, *Drowning the Dream: California's Water Choices at the Millennium* (Westport, Conn.: Praeger, 2000), 185.

73. Quoted in Judith and Neil Morgan, "California's Parched Oasis," *National Geographic* 149 (Jan. 1976): 123.

74. *County of Inyo* v. *Yorty,* 32 Cal.App.3d 795 (1973); *County of Inyo* v. *City of Los Angeles,* 61 Cal.App.3d 91 (1976); 71 Cal.App.3d 185 (1977); 78 Cal.App.3d 82 (1978); 124 Cal.App.3d 1 (1981); *Los Angeles Times,* Aug. 30, Sept. 16 and 17, 1976, Oct. 18, 1987.

75. *County of Inyo* v. *City of Los Angeles,* 71 Cal.App.3d 185 (1977); 124 Cal.App.3d. 1, 9, 11 (1981).

76. *Los Angeles Times,* July 14, 1983.

77. Ibid., Apr. 18, 1984, Feb. 5, 1985, Oct. 18, 1987.

78. Ibid., June 6, 1986.

79. Ibid., Apr. 1 and 2, May 11, Aug. 2, Sept. 21, 1989, June 10 and Oct. 1, 1990; "Agreement between the County of Inyo and the City of Los Angeles . . ." (Aug. 1, 1989), copy in possession of the author.

80. *Los Angeles Times,* Apr. 1 and Sept. 29, 1990; *Inyo Register* (Bishop), Nov. 7, 9 and Dec. 7 and 14, 1990; interview with Dale Plumb, editor, *Inyo Register,* Dec. 12 and 14, 1990.

81. Inyo County Board of Supervisors, "Resolution No. 91–66"

(Oct. 15, 1991), 6–7 passim, copy in possession of the author; Los Angeles Board of Water and Power Commissioners, "Resolution No. 92–099" (Oct. 15, 1991), copy in possession of the author; *Los Angeles Times,* Oct. 16, 1991; *Inyo Register* (Bishop), Oct. 20, 1991.

82. Inyo County Board of Supervisors, "Resolution No. 91–66" (Oct. 15, 1991), 6–7, passim, copy in possession of the author; Los Angeles Board of Water and Power Commissioners, "Resolution No. 92–099" (Oct. 15, 1991), copy in possession of the author; *Los Angeles v. County of Inyo: Superior Court of Inyo County, Case No. 12098 — Stipulation and Order for Judgment* (Oct. 18, 1991); *Los Angeles Times,* Oct. 16, 1991; *Inyo Register* (Bishop), Oct. 20, 1991; Inyo County Water Department, *Owens Valley Water Reporter,* Nov. 1, 1991, Dec. 1993.

83. *County of Inyo v. City of Los Angeles: California Third District Court of Appeal—Notification of Settlement [from the Owens Valley Indian Water Commission]* (Feb. 13, 1992), 1 ("a settlement"); interview with Terry Cawelti, executive director, Owens Valley Indian Water Commission; *County of Inyo v. City of Los Angeles: California Third District Court of Appeal— Opening Brief Submitted by Amicus [sic] Curiae California Department of Fish and Game and the California State Lands Commission Regarding the Inadequacy of the Environmental Impact Report* (June 24, 1993), 2 ("applaud these efforts . . ."), 3 ("water management practices"; "Instead of analyzing . . ."; "Details of the mitigation . . ."); *County of Inyo v. City of Los Angeles: California Third District Court of Appeal—Amicus Brief of Sierra Club* (July 21, 1993); *County of Inyo v. City of Los Angeles: California Third District Court of Appeal—Brief of Amici Curiae Owens Valley Committee and Carla Scheidlinger in Opposition to Application for Discharge of Peremptory Writ* (July 23, 1993); *County of Inyo v. City of Los Angeles: California Third District Court of Appeal— Opening Brief Submitted by Amicus Curia [sic] Stan Matlick Regarding the Inadequacy of the Environmental Impact Statement* (July 22, 1993); Inyo County Water Department, *Owens Valley Water Reporter,* Dec. 22, 1991, Feb. 1997.

84. "Memo of Understanding between the City of Los Angeles Department of Water and Power, the County of Inyo, the California Department of Fish and Game, the California State Lands Commission, the Sierra Club, the Owens Valley Committee, and Carla Scheidlinger" (March 24, 1997), 6 ("multiple resource values"), 8 ("healthy, functioning . . ."), 33 ("based upon holistic . . ."), copy in possession of the author; *Los Angeles Times,* Jan. 29, 1997; *County*

of *Inyo v. City of Los Angeles: California Third District Court of Appeal—Order Granting Motion for Discharge of Peremptory Writ of Mandate* (May 29, 1997); Inyo County Water Department, *Owens Valley Water Reporter,* Feb. and July 1997.

85. "Memo of Understanding between the City of Los Angeles Department of Water and Power, the County of Inyo, the California Department of Fish and Game, the California State Lands Commission, the Sierra Club, the Owens Valley Committee, and Carla Scheidlinger" (March 24, 1997), 10 ("continuous flow"); Great Basin Unified Air Pollution Control District, *Owens Valley PM-10 Planning Area Demonstration of Attainment State Implementation Plan* (Bishop, Calif.: Great Basin Unified Air Pollution Control District, July 1997), pp. 1-1, 2-8, 2-9, 3-1, passim; *Los Angeles Times,* Dec. 17, 1996 ("When we see the white cloud . . ." and the quotes that follow).

86. Interview with Theodore Schade, project manager, Great Basin Unified Air Pollution Control District, July 31, 1998; *Los Angeles Times,* Dec. 17, 1996.

87. *Los Angeles Times,* Dec. 17 (quote) and 18, 1996.

88. Great Basin Unified Air Pollution Control District, *Owens Valley PM-10 Planning Area,* pp. ES-1 to ES-13, 5-1 to 5-22, passim; interview with Theodore Schade, July 31, 1998; *Los Angeles Times,* July 3, 1997.

89. *Los Angeles Times,* July 3, 1997 (quote), Aug. 21, Dec. 11 and 18, 1997, Apr. 29, May 23, June 26, 1998.

90. Interview with Theodore Schade, April 29, 1998.

91. For the *Los Angeles Times* quotes, see the issues for Dec. 18, 1996, Jan. 29, June 20, Nov. 12, 1997, Apr. 30, 1998; see also ibid., May 28, July 2, 1997, July 17, 1998.

92. Ibid., Oct. 29, 1997; Howard J. Nelson, *The Los Angeles Metropolis* (Dubuque, Iowa: Kendall/Hunt, 1983), 112.

93. A measure of Freeman's success was that, during the subsequent scorching summer of 2000 when much of California was facing blackouts and soaring electricity bills (for example, San Diego had doubled its rates), DWP, after dramatically reducing its debt, was planning a rate reduction and had a surplus of electricity that it was selling for immense profits elsewhere in the state. The downside of this achievement was that it was also due to MWD "running its power plants full-bore," including several that were "among the dirtiest the city-run facility operates." The result in August 2000 was a $14 million fine, the largest ever levied by the South Coast Air Quality Management District, and a district order requiring that the

polluting plants be rebuilt or fitted with newer technology between 2001 and 2008 at an estimated $40 million. Nonetheless, MWD's profits selling excess electricity had reached some $45 million that summer. *Los Angeles Times,* Oct. 29, Nov. 16, 19, 23, Dec. 12, 13, 18, 1997, Jan. 30, Feb. 11, 12, 26, Mar. 1, 14, 19, 21, 26, May 18 ("transform . . ."), July 16, 1998, Aug. 3, 30, 2000 ("running . . .").

94. "Memorandum of Agreement between the City of Los Angeles and the Great Basin Unified Air Pollution Control District" (July 15, 1998), copy in possession of the author.

95. *Los Angeles Times,* July 16, 1998 (quotes), Aug. 18, 1999.

96. Ibid., July 31 ("Our people . . ."; "There's no free lunch . . ."; "If our wells go . . ."); Aug. 9, 2000 ("We continue . . .").

97. *Fullerton* v. *State Water Resources Control Board,* 90 Cal.App.3d 590 (1979); *California Trout, Inc.* v. *State Water Resources Control Board,* 90 Cal.App.3d 816 (1979).

98. *National Audubon Society* v. *Superior Court of Alpine County,* 33 Cal.3d 419 (1983), cert. denied, 464 U.S. 977 (1983); Dunning, "Public Right to Use Water in Place," 103–113; *California Trout, Inc.* v. *State Water Resources Control Board,* 207 Cal.App. 584 (1989).

99. The "recent state and federal legislation" was the federal Central Valley Project Improvement Act of 1992 and state Proposition 204 approved by the voters in 1996. Interview with Andrew Sawyer, assistant chief counsel, State Water Resources Control Board, Feb. 22, 1999; *Cal. Stats.,* chap. 663, sec. 2 (1991); *Cal. Water Code,* sec. 1707 (1991).

100. Keith Nobriga, planning and resources division, MWD, to the author, Aug. 5 and 28, 1998; Metropolitan Water District of Southern California, *Southern California's Integrated Water Resources Plan: Executive Summary—Report No. 1107* (Los Angeles: Metropolitan Water District of Southern California, March 1996), p. E-5.

101. Jerome W. Milliman, "The History, Organization and Economic Problems of the Metropolitan Water District of Southern California" (Ph.D. dissertation, University of California, Los Angeles, 112–114; Keith Nobriega, MWD, to the author, Aug. 5, 1998; *Los Angeles Times,* Apr. 10, 1991.

Chapter 7: Water Policy at a Crossroads

1. W. Turrentine Jackson and Stephen D. Mikesell, *The Stanislaus River Drainage Basin and the New Melones Dam* (Davis: University of California Water Resources Center, June 1979), 42–95; Tim

Palmer, *Stanislaus: The Struggle for a River* (Berkeley and Los Angeles: University of California Press, 1982), 46–60.

2. Jackson and Mikesell, *Stanislaus River Drainage Basin,* 101–102; Tim Palmer, *Endangered Rivers and the Conservation Movement* (Berkeley and Los Angeles: University of California Press, 1986), 125.

3. William R. Gianelli, "Wild Rivers—Who Needs 'Em" (Speech to the Eel River Water Council, July 28, 1972), file 1972–12, William R. Gianelli Papers, University of California Water Resources Center Archives, Berkeley; Palmer, *Stanislaus,* 66–77; Jackson and Mikesell, *Stanislaus River Drainage Basin,* 145–154.

4. Palmer, *Stanislaus,* 77–112 (the Brown quote is on p. 103); Jackson and Mikesell, *Stanislaus River Drainage Basin,* 154–157.

5. California Secretary of State, *Statement of the Vote: General Election, November 5, 1974* (Sacramento: State Printing Office, 1974); Palmer, *Stanislaus,* 111.

6. California Water Resources Control Board, *Decision 1422* (Sacramento: California Water Resources Control Board, Apr. 4, 1973), 18.

7. *California* v. *United States,* 438 U.S. 645 (1978); *United States* v. *California State Water Resources Control Board,* 694 F.2d 1171 (1982); California Department of Water Resources, "Management of the California State Water Project," *Bulletin 132–83* (Sacramento: California Resources Agency, Nov. 1983), 155–156.

8. Palmer, *Stanislaus,* 163, 168.

9. *Los Angeles Times,* July 6, 1980; House Committee on Interior and Insular Affairs, *Hearings on Amendment to the Wild and Scenic Rivers Act by Designating Certain Segments of the Stanislaus River in California as a Component of the National Wild and Scenic River System, H.R. 4223,* 96 Cong., 1 sess. (1979), passim; Samuel P. Hays, *Beauty, Health, and Permanence: Environmental Politics in the United States, 1955–1985* (New York: Cambridge University Press, 1987), 58, 509.

10. Palmer, *Stanislaus,* 236–272; Palmer, *Endangered Rivers,* 127; California Department of Water Resources, *Bulletin 132–83,* 155–156.

11. Palmer, *Endangered Rivers,* 128.

12. Ibid.

13. *Wild and Scenic Rivers Act* (federal), *U.S. Code,* vol. 16, sec. 1271 (1968); *Wild and Scenic Rivers Act* (California), *Public Resources Code,* sec. 5093.50 (1972).

14. Although Governor Gray Davis, in October 1999, signed

legislation placing thirty-nine miles of the south fork of the Yuba River in the state system, he announced that official recognition of the new status would be delayed until January 1, 2001, so that flood protection could be provided for downstream communities. *Cal. Stats.,* chap. 1016 (Oct. 10, 1999); *Sacramento Bee,* Oct. 12, 1999. See also California Department of Water Resources, "California Water Plan Update," *Bulletin 160–93,* 2 vols. (Sacramento: California Department of Water Resources, Oct. 1994), 1: 28–30; California Department of Water Resources, "California Water Plan Update," *Bulletin 160–98* (Sacramento: California Department of Water Resources, Nov. 1998), chap. 4, p. 34, app. 2A, p. 6; *Los Angeles Times,* Dec. 9 and 27, 1988, Aug. 5, 1989; Palmer, *Endangered Rivers,* 258, 284–88; Constance Elizabeth Hunt and Verne Huser, *Down by the River: The Impact of Federal Water Projects and Policies on Biological Diversity* (Washington, D.C.: Island Press, 1988), 11.

15. Metropolitan Water District of Southern California, *News Release* (Jan. 11, 2000); U.S. Department of the Interior, Bureau of Reclamation, *Shasta Dam and Reservoir Enlargement: Appraisal Assessment of the Potential for Enlarging Shasta Dam and Reservoir—Draft* (Denver: U.S. Bureau of Reclamation, May 1998); CALFED Bay-Delta Program, Storage and Refinement Team, *Facility Descriptions and Updated Cost Estimates for Shasta Lake Enlargement* (Sacramento: CALFED Bay-Delta Program, Oct. 1997); CALFED Bay-Delta Program, Storage and Refinement Team, *Facility Descriptions and Updated Cost Estimates for Millerton Lake Enlargement* (Sacramento: CALFED Bay-Delta Program, Oct. 1997); CALFED Bay-Delta Program, Storage and Refinement Team, *Facility Descriptions and Updated Cost Estimates for Los Vaqueros Reservoir Enlargement* (Sacramento: CALFED Bay-Delta Program, Oct. 1997); *Sacramento Bee,* July 13, 1998.

16. Los Angeles Department of Water and Power, "Report on the History of Chatsworth Reservoir and the Status of the Reservoir Property," in Duane L. Georgeson to Ric Villasenor, Aug. 28, 1989, copy in possession of the author; *Los Angeles Times,* Apr. 7, July 16, Oct. 3 and 16, 1999.

17. *Los Angeles Times,* Oct. 20, 1999.

18. Palmer, *Endangered Rivers,* 229; Friends of the River, *Rivers Reborn: Removing Dams and Restoring Rivers in California* (Sacramento: Friends of the River, 1999), 14 ("the mother of all . . ."); *San Francisco Chronicle,* July 15 and 16, 1998; *San Jose Mercury News,* July 17, 1998; *New York Times,* July 15, 1998; *Los Angeles Times,* Jan. 12, 1999.

19. U.S. Army Corps of Engineers, Northwestern Division, *Co-*

lumbia River Fish Mitigation: Lower Snake River Reservoir Drawdown Studies (Portland, Ore.: U.S. Army Corps of Engineers, Aug. 1998); U.S. Army Corps of Engineers, Walla Walla District, *Lower Snake River Juvenile Salmon Migration Feasibility Study: Natural River Drawdown* (Walla Walla, Wash.: U.S. Army Corps of Engineers, Oct. 1998); *USA Today,* May 6, 1998; *San Francisco Chronicle,* July 15, 1998; *Los Angeles Times,* June 21, 1998 (quote), July 2, 1999; Patrick Joseph, "The Battle of the Dams," *Smithsonian* 29 (Nov. 1998): 48–61.

20. Joseph E. Stevens, *Hoover Dam: An American Adventure* (Norman: University of Oklahoma Press, 1988), 245 (Ickes quote); *New York Times,* July 15, 1998 (Babbitt quote); *San Jose Mercury News,* July 17, 1998. For an elaboration of Babbitt's views, see his "Western Water Policy—From Reclamation to Restoration" (Address at the Natural Resource Center's Program on Western Water Law and Policy, Boulder, Colo., June 8, 1999), copy in possession of the author.

21. William L. Kahrl, *The California Water Atlas* (Sacramento: California Governor's Office of Planning and Research, 1979), 75; Edward Goldsmith and Nicholas Hildyard, *The Social and Environmental Effects of Large Dams* (San Francisco: Sierra Club, 1984), 1–15, 331–332, passim; Marc Reisner, *Cadillac Desert: The American West and Its Disappearing Water* (New York: Viking, 1986), 490–494.

22. California Department of Water Resources, *Bulletin 160–98,* chap. 3, p. 24, chap. 8, p. 10; National Research Council, *Improving American River Flood Frequency Analyses* (Washington, D.C.: National Academy Press, 1999); *Sacramento Bee,* Nov. 23 and 25, 1997, Jan. 10, Feb. 10 and 28, 1999.

23. California Department of Water Resources, *Bulletin 160–98,* chap. 8, p. 10, chap. 10, p. 6; *Los Angeles Times,* June 11, 1997; Robert Kelley, *Battling the Inland Sea: American Political Culture, Public Policy, and the Sacramento Valley, 1850–1986* (Berkeley and Los Angeles: University of California Press, 1989), 314 (quote).

24. Lisa L. Ely et al., "A 5000-Year Record of Extreme Floods and Climate Change in the Southwestern United States," *Science* 262 (Oct. 15, 1993): 410–412; *Sacramento Bee,* Nov. 23 and 24 (quote), 1997.

25. *Los Angeles Times,* Jan. 25, 1997; *Sacramento Bee,* Nov. 23, 1997.

26. *Sacramento Bee,* Nov. 23 and 25, 1997.

27. Ibid., Nov. 25, 1997 (both quotes).

28. Goldsmith and Hildyard, *Social and Environmental Effects of Large Dams,* 111–112; Kahrl, ed., *California Water Atlas,* 74–75.

29. Hal Rubin, "The Political Aftershocks of Carter's Auburn Dam Decision," *California Journal* 8 (May 1977): 159–161; Luther J. Carter, "Auburn Dam: Earthquake Hazards Imperil $1-Billion Project," *Science* 197 (Aug. 12, 1977): 643–644, 646–649; Palmer, *Endangered Rivers,* 2, 44, 115–118; California Department of Water Resources, *Bulletin 160–98,* chap. 3, p. 24, chap. 7, p. 19; *Los Angeles Times,* June 28, 1996; *Sacramento Bee,* Oct. 16, 1998, Jan. 10, Feb. 10 and 28, 1999; U.S. Department of the Interior, Bureau of Reclamation, *Folsom Dam Modification Report: New Outlets Plan* (Sacramento: Bureau of Reclamation, Central California Area Office, Feb. 1998).

30. California Department of Water Resources, *Bulletin 160–93,* I, 54.

31. Goldsmith and Hildyard, *Social and Environmental Effects of Large Dams,* 219–224; *Sacramento Bee,* Nov. 26, 1997 (quote).

32. *Sacramento Bee,* Nov. 23–27, 1997.

33. "A Unified National Program for Managing Flood Losses," *H. Doc. 465,* 89 Cong., 2 sess. (Aug. 10, 1966); Howard C. Kunreuther and Gilbert F. White, "The Role of the National Insurance Program in Reducing Losses and Promoting Wise Use of Floodplains," *Water Resources Update* no. 95 (Spring 1994): 31–35; Gilbert F. White, *Choice of Adjustment to Floods* (Chicago: University of Chicago, Department of Geography Research Paper No. 93, 1964); White, *The Control and Development of Floodplain Areas* (Albany, N.Y.: Matthew Bender & Co., 1961); White et al., *Flood Hazard in the United States: A Research Assessment* (Boulder: University of Colorado, Institute of Behavioral Science, 1975); *Sacramento Bee,* Nov. 24, 1997.

34. *Los Angeles Times,* Jan. 13, 1997.

35. Luna B. Leopold, "Flood Hydrology and Floodplain," *Water Resources Update* no. 95 (Spring 1994): 11–14; Andrew Brookes, *Channelized Rivers: Perspectives for Environmental Management* (Chichester, U.K.: John Wiley & Sons, 1988); Jeffrey F. Mount, *California Rivers and Streams: The Conflict between Fluvial Process and Land Use* (Berkeley and Los Angeles: University of California Press, 1995), 268–286, 309–310, passim; *Sacramento Bee,* Nov. 27, 1997.

36. Kunreuther and White, "Role of the National Flood Insurance Program," 32, passim; *Sacramento Bee,* Nov. 27, 1997; Mike Davis, *Ecology of Fear: Los Angeles and the Imagination of Disaster* (New York: Metropolitan Books, 1998), 48–50, 129, 135. For a thoughtful analysis of the interaction between land-use practices and the dynamics of rivers, see Mount, *California Rivers and Streams.*

37. *Sacramento Bee,* Nov. 27, 1997 (quote). Leopold has offered

many thoughtful suggestions for improving floodplain management. See, for example, his "Flood Hydrology and the Floodplain," 11–14; and Luna B. Leopold and Thomas Maddock, Jr., *The Flood Control Controversy: Big Dams, Little Dams, and Land Management* (New York: Ronald Press, 1954). For more on Leopold, see his oral history: "Hydrology, Geomorphology, and Environmental Policy: U.S. Geological Survey, 1950–1972, and U.C. Berkeley, 1972–1987" (Regional Oral History Office, Bancroft Library, University of California, Berkeley, 1990–1991).

38. Los Angeles County Board of Engineers, Flood Control, *Reports of the Board of Engineers, Flood Control, to the Board of Supervisors, Los Angeles County, California* (Los Angeles: Los Angeles County Board of Engineers, 1915); U.S. Geological Survey, "Floods of March 1938 in Southern California," by Harold C. Troxell et al., *Water-Supply Paper 844* (Washington, D.C.: U.S. Geological Survey, 1942), 381–384; U.S. Department of War, Engineer Office, *Flood Control in the Los Angeles County Drainage Area* (Los Angeles: U.S. Engineer Office, 1938); U.S. Department of War, Engineer Office, *Report on Engineering Aspects: Flood of March 1938* (Los Angeles: U.S. Engineer Office, May 1939); U.S. Department of War, Engineer Office, *Los Angeles County Drainage Area Flood Control,* by Edwin C. Kolton (Los Angeles: U.S. Engineer Office, Sept. 1939); Lawrence H. Daingerfield, "Southern California Rain and Flood, February 27 to March 4, 1938," *Monthly Weather Review* 66 (May 1938): 139–143; Los Angeles County Flood Control District, *Flood of March 2, 1938,* by M. F. Burke (Los Angeles: Los Angeles County Flood Control District, May 20, 1938); Los Angeles County Board of Engineers, Flood Control, *A Report on Floods, River Phenomena and Rainfall in the Los Angeles Region, California,* by J. W. Reagan (Los Angeles: Los Angeles County Board of Engineers, 1939); U.S. Army Corps of Engineers, Los Angeles District, *Los Angeles County Drainage Area Review: Final Feasibility Study, Interim Report, and Environmental Impact Statement* (Los Angeles: U.S. Army Corps of Engineers, Los Angeles District, Dec. 1991), 20–21, 40–41; Richard Bigger, *Flood Control in Metropolitan Los Angeles* (Berkeley: University of California Press, 1959), 1–3, passim; U.S. Geological Survey, "Urban Sprawl and Flooding in Southern California," by S. E. Rantz, *Geological Survey Circular 601-B* (Washington, D.C.: U.S. Geological Survey, 1970); U.S. Geological Survey, "California: Floods and Droughts," by R. A. Hunrichs, *Water-Supply Paper W2375* (Washington, D.C.: U.S. Geological Survey,

1991), 197–206; Anthony F. Turhollow, *A History of the Los Angeles District, U.S. Army Corps of Engineers, 1898–1965* (Los Angeles: U.S. Army Corps of Engineers, Los Angeles District, 1975), 144–146, 158, passim; Howard J. Nelson, *The Los Angeles Metropolis* (Dubuque, Iowa: Kendall/Hunt, 1983), 88–94; *Los Angeles Times,* Dec. 26, 1994, Oct. 25, 1997, June 29 and Sept. 13, 1998. For the fullest overall treatments of the Los Angeles River, see Blake Gumprecht, *The Los Angeles River: Its Life, Death, and Possible Rebirth* (Baltimore: Johns Hopkins University Press, 1999); and Jared Orsi, "Hazardous Metropolis: Flooding and Urban Ecology in Los Angeles" (Ph.D. dissertation, University of Wisconsin, Madison, 1999).

39. U.S. Army Corps of Engineers, *Los Angeles County Drainage Area Review,* i–ii, 180–183; Mount, *California Rivers and Streams,* 290–291; *Los Angeles Times,* Oct. 25, 1997, June 29, 1998.

40. U.S. Army Corps of Engineers, *Los Angeles County Drainage Area Review,* i–ii, 140–183; *Los Angeles Times,* July 26, 1995, Aug. 11, 1996, June 29 and July 3, 1998, Mar. 18, 1999. A similar movement to reclaim and preserve the nearby twenty-nine-mile-long San Gabriel River is under way. *Los Angeles Times,* Apr. 4, 1999.

41. *Los Angeles Times,* July 26, 1995, Aug. 11, 1996, June 29 and July 3, 1998, Oct. 16, 1999; *Long Beach Press-Telegram,* June 29, July 22, 2000.

42. *Cal. Stats.,* chap. 789 (Oct. 10, 1999), sec. 32602(a) (quote).

43. *Official Sample Ballot and Voter Information: Primary Election, March 7, 2000,* p. 5; *Cal. Stats.,* chap. 52 (June 30, 2000); Patrick Wright, deputy secretary for policy development, California Resources Agency, to the author, Aug. 7, 2000; interview with Steven Treanor, division chief, Southern Division, California Department of Parks and Recreation, Sept. 5, 2000; *San Diego Union-Tribune,* June 25, 2000 (quotes).

44. CALFED Bay-Delta Program, *Draft Programmatic Environmental Impact Statement/Environmental Impact Report: Long-Term Levee Protection Plan* (Sacramento: CALFED Bay-Delta Program, Mar. 1998), 2, 6, app. A, p. A2; California Department of Water Resources, "Delta Levees Investigation," *Bulletin 192–82* (Sacramento: California Department of Water Resources, Dec. 1982), 36–38, passim; Ed Winkler, principal engineer, MWD, to the author, June 20, 2000; Susan Davis, "When the Levees Break," *California Waterfront Age* 5 (Fall 1989): 31–33; Davis, "That Sinking Feeling," *California* 14 (Dec. 1989): 98, 148–149; California Department of Water Resources, *Dis-*

covering and Rediscovering the Fragility of Levees and Land in the Sacramento–San Joaquin Delta, 1870–1879 and Today, by John Thompson (Sacramento: California Resources Agency, Mar. 1982); Hal Rubin, "Dilemma in the Delta—Balancing Competing Interests," *California Journal* 7 (Aug. 1976): 278, 279.

45. California Department of Water Resources, *Bulletin 192–82,* 35–58; Davis, "When the Levees Break," 33; Mount, *California Rivers and Streams,* 304–308; California Energy Commission, *The Impacts of Global Warming on California* (Sacramento: California Energy Commission, June 1989); David Rind, "The Greenhouse Effect: Reality and Potential Consequences," in *Proceedings, Seventeenth Biennial Conference on Ground Water, San Diego, California, September 25– 26, 1989* (Davis: University of California Water Resources Center, Davis; California Department of Water Resources and California Water Resources Control Board, 1990), 69–72; Robert E. Trenberth, "Climate Change and Climate Variability: The Climate Record," in Committee on Climate Uncertainty and Water Resources Management, Water Science and Technology Board, Commission on Geosciences, Environment, and Resources, comp., *Managing Water Resources in the West under Conditions of Climate Uncertainty* (Washington, D.C.: National Academy Press, 1991), 47–70; John Dracup and Donald R. Kendall, "Climate Uncertainty: Implications for Operation of Water Control Systems," in ibid., 177–216; California Department of Water Resources, *Bulletin 160–93,* 1: 252; California Department of Water Resources, *Bulletin 160–98,* chap. 8, pp. 27–28.

46. CALFED Bay-Delta Program, *Draft Programmatic Environmental Impact Statement/Environmental Impact Report* (Sacramento: CALFED Bay-Delta Program, Mar. 1998); Davis, "When the Levees Break," 32–33; California Department of Water Resources, "California Water: Looking to the Future," *Bulletin 160–87* (Sacramento: California Department of Water Resources, Nov. 1987), 14, 24–25.

47. California Department of Water Resources, *Bulletin 160–93,* 1: 256–257; *Cal. Stats.,* chap. 1302 (1976); Davis, "When the Levees Break," 35 (Buddemier quote); *Los Angeles Times,* Jan. 13, 2000 (National Research Council quote); Daniel B. Botkin, "Global Warming: What It Is, What Is Controversial about It, and What We Might Do in Response to It," *UCLA Journal of Environmental Law and Policy* 9, no. 2 (1991): 119–142; Gil Davis, "Greenhouse California," *Golden State Report* 3 (Mar. 1987): 24–31; James R. Fleming, *Histori-*

cal Perspectives on Climate Change (New York: Oxford University Press, 1998); Konstantin Y. Vinnikov et al., "Global Warming and Northern Hemisphere Sea Ice Extent," *Science* 286 (Dec. 3, 1999): 1934–1937.

48. CALFED Bay-Delta Program, *Revised Phase II Report: Draft Programmatic EIS/EIR Technical Appendix* (Sacramento: CALFED Bay-Delta Program, June 1999), 43–47, 131, passim; California Department of Water Resources, *Bulletin 160–98,* chap. 4, pp. 46–51; California Department of Water Resources, "Management of the California State Water Project," *Bulletin 132–87* (Sacramento: California Department of Water Resources, Sept. 1987), 55–56; California Department of Water Resources and Department of Fish and Game, "Selenium Behavior in the Sacramento–San Joaquin Estuary, California," by Gregory A. Cutter, *Technical Report 18* (Sacramento: California Department of Water Resources, Sept. 1988); California Department of Water Resources, *Bulletin 160–93,* 1: 120–126, 188–207; *Los Angeles Times,* Sept. 19, 1986, Oct. 7 and 31, 1999; Joseph E. Bodovitz, Melvin B. Lane, and E. Clement Shute, Jr., "The San Francisco Bay Conservation and Development Commission, 1964–1973" (Regional Oral History Office, Bancroft Library, University of California, Berkeley, 1984); Barry Bunshoft, Esther Gulick, Catherine Kerr, and Sylvia McLaughlin, "Save San Francisco Bay Association, 1961–1986" (Regional Oral History Office, Bancroft Library, University of California, Berkeley, 1985–1986); Joel W. Hedgpeth, "Marine Biologist and Environmentalist: Pycnogonids, Progress, and Preserving Bays, Salmon, and Other Living Things" (Regional Oral History Office, Bancroft Library, University of California, Berkeley, 1992), 244–265.

49. U.S. Geological Survey, "California Wetland Resources," by G. L. Bertoldi and Walter C. Swain, *Water-Supply Paper 2425* (Washington, D.C.: U.S. Geological Survey, 1996), 127–134; U.S. Fish and Wildlife Service, *Wetlands—Losses in the United States, 1780's to 1980's,* by Thomas E. Dahl (Washington, D.C.: U.S. Fish and Wildlife Service, 1990), 6; California Department of Parks and Recreation, *California Wetlands: An Element of the California Outdoor Recreation Planning Program* (Sacramento: California Resources Agency, Sept. 1988), 19–20, passim; California Department of Water Resources, *Bulletin 160–98,* chap. 4, pp. 39–51; Richard F. Ambrose and Johannes Feddema, "Wetlands," in Richard Berk and Arthur M. Winer, eds., *Southern California Environmental Report Card [1998]* (Los

Angeles: UCLA Institute of the Environment, 1998), 32–34; Ann Vileisis, *Discovering the Unknown Landscape: A History of America's Wetlands* (Washington, D.C.: Island Press, 1997), chaps. 13–17; National Wetlands Policy Forum, *Protecting America's Wetlands: An Action Agenda* (Washington, D.C.: Conservation Foundation, 1988); Paul D. Cylinder et al., *Wetlands Regulation: A Complete Guide to Federal and California Programs* (Point Arena, Calif.: Solano Press Books, 1995); Samuel P. Hays, *Beauty, Health, and Permanence: Environmental Politics in the United States, 1955–1985* (New York: Cambridge University Press, 1987), 150–151; California Department of Water Resources, *Bulletin 160–93,* 1: 219–221.

50. *Cal. Stats.,* chap. 284 (1967); California Water Quality Control Board, "Useful Waters for California," *Publication No. 37* (Sacramento: California Water Quality Control Board, 1967), 71; Paul R. Bonderson, "Executive Officer, Regional and State Water Pollution and Water Quality Control Boards, 1950–1966" (Regional Oral History Office, Bancroft Library, University of California, Berkeley, 1980), chap. 2; California Water Resources Control Board, *Toward Clean Water: A Progress Report for 1974 and 1975* (Sacramento: California Water Resources Control Board, n.d.), i; Mary Ellen Leary, "The Water Resources Control Board," *California Journal* 16 (Mar. 1985): 110; Jerome B. Gilbert, "Problem Drinkers," *Golden State Report* 2 (Dec. 1986): 34–35.

51. Leary, "Water Resources Control Board," 110–112; Paul R. Bonderson, "Executive Officer, Regional and State Water Pollution and Water Quality Control Boards, 1950–1966" (Regional Oral History Office, Bancroft Library, University of California, Berkeley, 1980), 70–71.

52. *United States* v. *State Water Resources Control Board,* 182 Cal.App.3d 82 (1986); *United States* v. *California State Water Resources Control Board,* 694 F.2d 1171 (1982); California Department of Water Resources, *Bulletin 132–87,* 55–56, *Bulletin 160–87,* 14, 24–25, passim; *Los Angeles Times,* May 29, June 8, Sept. 19, 1986.

53. *Los Angeles Times,* Nov. 4, 13, 14, Dec. 3, 1988; Richard Zeiger, "Water, Water," *California Journal* 19 (Mar. 1988): 105–106.

54. *Los Angeles Times,* Nov. 4, 14, Dec. 3, 21, 1988, Jan. 28, 1989.

55. California Department of Water Resources, *Bulletin 160–98,* app. 2A, pp. 8–9; *Los Angeles Times,* Jan. 20, 1989, Sept. 10, 1998.

56. *Cong. Rec.,* 102 Cong., 2 sess. (Oct. 5, 1992), 138, pt. 3:

H11572–H11625; "Reclamation Projects Authorization and Adjustment Act of 1992," *H. Doc. 102-1016,* 102 Cong., 2 sess. (Oct. 5, 1992).

57. California Department of Water Resources, *Bulletin 160–98,* app. 2A, p. 9.

58. Mark Cowin, DWR/CALFED, to the author, Oct. 6, 2000 (quote). For several years it was impossible to determine from CALFED's publications the precise state and federal agencies that constituted the organization. Its public documents indicated that there were fifteen such agencies, but the lists accompanying those statements (as well as the lists printed on its correspondence, announcements of meetings, news releases, and the like) identified twenty agencies—six state and fourteen federal. Inquiries failed to elicit a clear explanation, but CALFED eventually came up with a list that dovetailed with the number claimed: state (Resources Agency, Department of Water Resources, Department of Fish and Game, Environmental Protection Agency, State Water Resources Control Board, Department of Food and Agriculture) and federal (Department of the Interior, Bureau of Reclamation, Fish and Wildlife Service, Environmental Protection Agency, Department of Commerce, National Marine Fisheries Service, U.S. Army Corps of Engineers, Department of Agriculture, Natural Resources Conservation Service). See CALFED's website: www.calfed.water.ca.gov/.

59. CALFED Bay-Delta Program, *Executive Summary: Draft Programmatic Environmental Impact Statement/Environmental Impact Report* (Sacramento: CALFED Bay-Delta Program, Mar. 1998), 1–2, passim; California Department of Water Resources, *Bulletin 160–98,* chap. 2, pp. 14–16.

60. CALFED Bay-Delta Program, *Revised Phase II Report [June 1999],* 43; CALFED Bay-Delta Program, *Executive Summary;* CALFED Bay-Delta Program, *Program Goals and Objectives: Draft Programmatic EIS/EIR* (Sacramento: CALFED Bay-Delta Program, Mar. 1998); California Department of Water Resources, *Bulletin 160–98,* chap. 6, p. 27; *Sacramento Bee,* June 26, 1996; *Los Angeles Times,* July 11, 12, Oct. 17, Dec. 18, 1997; Feb. 15, 2000.

61. Ibid.

62. CALFED Bay-Delta Program, *Executive Summary,* passim; CALFED Bay-Delta Program, *Program Goals and Objectives;* CALFED Bay-Delta Program, *Commonly Asked Questions about the*

CALFED Bay-Delta Program (Sacramento: CALFED Bay-Delta Program, 1998); *San Jose Mercury News,* Apr. 19, 1998; *San Diego Union-Tribune,* Apr. 19, 1998; *Los Angeles Times,* Oct. 7, 1996, Dec. 18, 1997, Mar. 17, 1998.

63. *Los Angeles Times,* Mar. 17, 1998.

64. *Sacramento Bee,* Apr. 14, 1998 (Reisner quote); Reisner, *Cadillac Desert; Fresno Bee,* July 24, 1998; *Los Angeles Times,* Mar. 17, 1998; *Contra Costa Times* (Walnut Creek), Dec. 19, 1998.

65. *Los Angeles Times,* Mar. 17 (NRDC quote), 19 ("don't water it" quote), 1998; *San Jose Mercury News,* Apr. 19, 1998; *San Francisco Chronicle,* June 25, 1998 (sixteen Democrats' quote).

66. *Los Angeles Times,* Mar. 17 ("suck the Sacramento River dry" and second Quinn quote), May 3 and 12, Sept. 18 (EDF quote), 1998; *Oakland Tribune,* June 23, 1998; *San Francisco Chronicle,* July 16, 1998 (first Quinn quote); *San Diego Union-Tribune,* Nov. 10, 1998.

67. CALFED Bay-Delta Program, *Developing a Draft Preferred Program Alternative* (Sacramento: CALFED Bay-Delta Program, Aug. 5, 1998); CALFED Bay-Delta Program, *Draft Preferred Program Alternative: 30-Year Policy Framework* (Sacramento: CALFED Bay-Delta Program, Aug. 14, 1998), 1 (quote).

68. *Los Angeles Times,* Sept. 15, 1998 (MWD and CALFED quotes).

69. CALFED Bay-Delta Program, *Revised Phase II Report* (Sacramento: CALFED Bay-Delta Program, Dec. 18, 1998), chaps. 4 and 5 ("appropriate mix . . . ," p. 108; "will only be built . . . ," p. 111); *Los Angeles Times,* Sept. 26, 1998 ("timing isn't right").

70. *San Jose Mercury News,* Dec. 19, 1998 (Babbitt quote).

71. CALFED Bay-Delta Program, *Revised Phase II Report [Dec. 1998],* 108 (emphasis added); CALFED Bay-Delta Program, *Revised Phase II Report [June 1999],* 126 (emphasis added), 131; *Contra Costa Times* (Walnut Creek), Dec. 19, 1998; *Bakersfield Californian,* Dec. 18, 1998; *Fresno Bee,* Dec. 18, 1998; *San Francisco Examiner,* Dec. 17, 1998; *San Francisco Chronicle,* Dec. 19, 1998; *Sacramento Bee,* Dec. 18, 26, 1998; *Wall Street Journal,* Dec. 21, 1998; Steve Evans, "CALFED Pursuing 14 Dam Projects," *Headwaters* (Winter 1999): 10–12; Sue McClurg, "CALFED and the Delta Fix," *Western Water* (Jan.–Feb. 1999): 4–13.

72. *Los Angeles Times,* Sept. 16 ("It's disappointing . . ."; "The political pressure . . ."), and Sept. 23, 1999 ("real," "drinking-water

quality . . ."; "four to six . . ."; "critical . . ."; "additional water treatment . . ."); Metropolitan Water District of Southern California,
"Statement of Needs for the CALFED Bay-Delta Program" (July 23,
1999), 2 ("salinity blending"); Metropolitan Water District of Southern California, "Metropolitan Water District of Southern California:
Policy Direction Regarding CALFED Bay-Delta Program" (July 23,
1999), copies of the preceding two items in possession of the author; *Political Pulse Newsletter,* Aug 27, 1999; CALFED Bay-Delta Program *News,* Aug. 1999; *San Diego Union-Tribune,* Sept. 8, 1999.

73. Mark Cowin, CALFED, to the author, Oct. 19, 1999 ("We
can't adopt . . ."); *Sacramento Bee,* Sept. 5, 1999 ("study-now . . .");
Los Angeles Times, June 12, 2000 ("Calfail").

74. *Official Sample Ballot and Voter Information: [California] Primary
Election, March 7, 2000,* p. 5; *Los Angeles Times,* Mar. 9, 2000; *Cal.
Stats.,* chap. 2000 (2000).

75. CALFED Bay-Delta Program, *California's Water Future: A
Framework for Action* (Sacramento: CALFED Bay-Delta Program,
June 9, 2000); *San Francisco Chronicle,* June 10, 2000 ("stakeholders");
Sacramento Bee, June 10 and 11, Aug. 29 ("The plan . . ."), 2000; *Los
Angeles Times,* June 8, 12, 2000 ("is a jigsaw . . ."); *San Diego Union-
Tribune,* June 8, 2000; *Contra Costa Times* (Walnut Creek), June 10,
2000.

76. CALFED Bay-Delta Program, *California's Water Future,* 10–21,
30, passim ("requiring the appropriate . . ." p. 27); Ed Winkler, principal engineer, MWD, to the author, July 7 and 18, 2000; Office of
the California Governor, *News Release,* June 9, 2000.

77. CALFED Bay-Delta Program, *California's Water Future,* 13–
14, 19–20 ("screened through-Delta facility," p. 19), Appendix G;
Ed Winkler, MWD, to the author, June 13, 20, and 21 ("freshen
up"), 2000.

78. *San Jose Mercury News,* June 7, 2000 ("There are things . . .");
Bakersfield Californian, June 7, 2000 ("In general . . .").

79. *Chico Enterprise-Record,* June 21 ("outright assault"; "siphoned
off . . ."), Aug. 20, 2000 ("local management . . ."; "the goal . . .");
Grass Valley Union, Aug. 19 ("insidious"; "rural Northern California . . ."); *San Diego Union-Tribune,* June 29, 2000 ("every means . . .");
Redding Record Searchlight, June 21, 2000; *Sacramento Bee,* June 30,
2000.

80. California Farm Bureau Federation, *News Release,* Aug. 24,

2000 ("Cal-Fed proposes . . ."); *Fresno Bee,* Aug. 30, 2000 ("This 'Framework for Action' . . ."); *San Francisco Examiner,* Aug. 29, 2000 ("a legally enforceable . . .").

81. Metropolitan Water District of Southern California, *News Release,* June 9, 2000 ("have created . . ."; "Metropolitan's board . . ."); *Sacramento Bee,* June 14, 2000; *Ventura County Star,* Aug. 31, 2000 ("whether the state . . ."); *Contra Costa Times* (Walnut Creek), Aug. 30, 2000 ("There is a pressing . . .").

82. *Sacramento Bee,* Aug. 29, 2000; *San Jose Mercury News,* Aug. 29, Sept. 2, 2000; *Contra Costa Times* (Walnut Creek), Aug. 22, 27, 28, and 29, 2000; *Modesto Bee,* Aug. 22, 2000; *Redding Record Searchlight,* Aug. 23, 26, and 27, Sept. 2, 2000; *Los Angeles Times,* Aug. 29, 2000; Regional Council of Rural Counties, *News Release,* Sept. 1, 2000; Capitol Bureau Chief, "Fallout from CALFED Defeat," Sept. 2, 2000.

83. Joining the Regional Council of Rural Counties in the lawsuit were the Central Delta Water Agency and the South Delta Water Agency. *Contra Costa Times* (Walnut Creek), Sept. 14, 2000 ("be no delay . . ."); *Sacramento Bee,* Sept. 14 and 28, 2000; *Los Angeles Times,* Sept. 27, Oct. 1, 2000; California Farm Bureau Federation, *News Release,* Sept. 28, 2000. A related lawsuit was filed by the Municipal Water District of Orange County against the California Resources Agency for actions that could increase costs of restoring the quality of northern California water. *Orange County Register* (Santa Ana), Sept. 29, 2000.

84. Mark Cowin, DWR/CALFED, to the author, Aug. 30, 1999, Oct. 6, 2000 (quotes).

85. A. K. Williamson and D. E. Prudie, "Simulation of Flow and Compaction in the Regional Aquifer System of the Central Valley of California, U.S.A.," in A. I. Johnson, Laura Carbogin, and L. Ubertini, eds., *Land Subsidence: Proceedings of the Third International Symposium on Land Subsidence, 1984* (Wallingford, Oxfordshire: International Association of Hydrological Sciences, 1986), 271–280; Nikola P. Prokopovich, "Origin and Treatment of Hydrocompaction in the San Joaquin Valley, CA, USA," ibid., 537–546; Prokopovich and M. J. Marriott, "Cost of Subsidence to the Central Valley Project, CA," *Bulletin of the Association of Engineering Geologists* 20 no. 3 (1983): 325–332; U.S. Geological Survey, "Ground-Water Conditions in the Mendota-Huron Area, Fresno and Kings Counties, California," *Water-Supply Paper 1360-G* (Washington, D.C.: Gov-

ernment Printing Office, 1957), 409, 412, 440, passim; U.S. Department of Agriculture, "Replenishment of Ground Water Supplies by Artificial Means," by Dean C. Muckel, *Technical Bulletin No. 1195* (Washington, D.C.: U.S. Department of Agriculture, 1959), 31, passim; Erwin Cooper, *Aqueduct Empire: A Guide to Water in California—Its Turbulent History and Its Management Today* (Glendale, Calif.: Arthur H. Clark Co., 1968), 164–166; Inter-Agency Committee on Land Subsidence in the San Joaquin Valley, *Proposed Program for Investigating Land Subsidence in the San Joaquin Valley, California* (Sacramento: Inter-Agency Committee on Land Subsidence in the San Joaquin Valley, Feb. 1955); Inter-Agency Committee on Land Subsidence in the San Joaquin Valley, *Progress Report on Land-Subsidence Investigations in the San Joaquin Valley, California, through 1957* (Sacramento: Inter-Agency Committee on Land Subsidence in the San Joaquin Valley, 1958); Alfred R. Golzé, *Land Subsidence: Why the State Is Concerned* (Sacramento: California Department of Water Resources, 1965); Blair-Westfall Associates, *Land Subsidence in the Firebaugh Soil Conservation District* (Fresno, Calif.: Blair-Westfall Associates, 1966); Joseph F. Poland, *Land Subsidence in the Santa Clara Valley, Alameda, San Mateo, and Santa Clara Counties, California* (Washington, D.C.: U.S. Geological Survey, 1971).

86. California Department of Water Resources, *Bulletin 160–98,* chap. 3, pp. 51–52; Joseph F. Poland et al., *Land Subsidence in the San Joaquin Valley, California, as of 1972* (Sacramento: U.S. Geological Survey, 1973); William B. Bull and Raymond E. Miller, *Land Subsidence Due to Ground-Water Withdrawal in the Los Banos–Kettleman City Area, California* (Washington, D.C.: U.S. Geological Survey, 1975); Joseph F. Poland, "The Occurrence and Control of Land Subsidence Due to Ground-Water Withdrawal with Special Reference to the San Joaquin and Santa Clara Valleys" (Ph.D. dissertation, Stanford University, 1981); Richard L. Ireland, Joseph F. Poland, and Francis F. Riley, *Land Subsidence in the San Joaquin Valley, California, as of 1980* (Sacramento: U.S. Geological Survey, 1982); Joseph F. Poland and Richard L. Ireland, *Land Subsidence in the Santa Clara Valley, California, as of 1982* (Denver: U.S. Geological Survey, 1988).

87. California Water Resources Control Board, Environmental Protection Agency, *1996 California Water Quality Assessment Report* (Sacramento: California Water Resources Control Board, Jan. 1997), section on Region 5; U.S. Bureau of Reclamation, California Department of Water Resources, and California Water Resources Con-

trol Board, *San Joaquin Valley Interagency Drainage Program: Agricultural Drainage and Salt Management in the San Joaquin Valley* (Fresno, Calif.: San Joaquin Valley Interagency Drainage Program, June 1979); U.S. Department of the Interior, Bureau of Reclamation, Mid-Pacific Region, *San Luis Drain, Central Valley Project, California* (Sacramento: U.S. Bureau of Reclamation, 1983); *San Francisco Chronicle,* Nov. 25, 1983; *Los Angeles Times,* Apr. 22, 1984; *San Jose Mercury News,* July 7, 2000.

88. John A. Izbicki, *Chemical Quality of Agricultural Drainage Water Tributary to Kesterson Reservoir, Fresno and Merced Counties, California, January and August 1984* (Sacramento: U.S. Geological Survey, 1989); California Water Resources Control Board, *Kesterson Reservoir Closure and Cleanup Plan* (Sacramento: California Water Resources Control Board, 1985); California Department of Water Resources, *Bulletin 160–93,* 1: 44–46; *Migratory Bird Treaty Act, U.S. Code,* vol. 16, secs. 661 et seq.; Don Villarejo, *Agricultural Land Ownership and Operations in the 49,000 Acre Drainage Study Area of the Westlands Water District: A Report to the Assembly Office of Research* (Sacramento: Assembly Office of Research, 1985); *Los Angeles Times,* Mar. 16, 18, and 29, May 21, Dec. 12, 1985; *Sacramento Bee,* Sept. 8, 1985 (quote).

89. *Sacramento Bee,* Sept. 8, 9, 10, 1985; see also Tom Harris, *Death in the Marsh* (Washington, D.C.: Island Press, 1991). See as well *Los Angeles Times,* July 6, Oct. 12, 19, 28, Nov. 20, 1988, Jan. 15, Nov. 26, 1989, Mar. 13, 1990.

90. John A. Izbicki, *Chemical Quality of Water at 14 Sites near Kesterson National Wildlife Refuge, Fresno and Merced Counties, California* (Sacramento: U.S. Geological Survey, 1984); Ray Coppock, *Resources at Risk in the San Joaquin Valley: Selenium, Human Health, and Irrigated Agriculture* (Davis: University of California Agricultural Issues Center, Cooperative Extension, Salinity/Drainage Task Force, and Water Resources Center [1988]), 8 (quote); Neil M. Dubrovsky et al., *Influence of Redox Potential on Selenium Distribution in Ground Water, Mendota, Western San Joaquin Valley, California* (Sacramento: U.S. Geological Survey, 1990); California Department of Water Resources, *Bulletin 160–93,* 1: 45–46; *Los Angeles Times,* Mar. 30, 1993; Water Education Foundation, *Press Release,* Nov. 30, 1993; *San Diego Union-Tribune,* Dec. 14, 1999.

91. California Department of Water Resources, *Bulletin 160–98,* chap. 3, pp. 48–51, passim; William S. Pease et al., *Pesticide Contamination of Groundwater in California* (Berkeley: California Policy

Seminar, University of California, Berkeley, 1995), xiv ("responsible for contaminating . . ."), 3, 11, 17, 29, passim; U.S. Department of the Interior, Geological Survey, "Water Quality in the San Joaquin–Tulare Basins, California, 1992–95," by Neil M. Dubrovsky et al. *Circular 1159* (Denver: U.S. Geological Survey, 1998), 3, 19, passim; *Los Angeles Times,* June 12, 1995 (quote); California Department of Health Services, *DBCP in Drinking Water: What Does It Mean?* (Berkeley: California Department of Health Services, Dec. 1989); Luhdorff and Scalmanini, Consulting Engineers, *State Water Resources Control Board Groundwater "Hot Spots" Project: Well Testing and Site Characterization—Fresno Area* (Sacramento: California Water Resources Control Board, Feb. 1986); U.S. Department of the Interior, Geological Survey, *Nitrate and Pesticides in Groundwater in the Eastern San Joaquin Valley, California,* by Karen R. Burow, Sylvia V. Stork, and Neil M. Dubrovsky (Sacramento: U.S. Geological Survey, 1998); California Water Resources Control Board, Toxic Substances Control Program, *Water Quality and Pesticides: A California Risk Assessment Program,* by David B. Cohen and Gerald W. Bowes (Sacramento: California Water Resources Control Board, Dec. 1984); California Auditor General, *Report by the Office of the Auditor General to the Joint Legislative Audit Committee: The State Lacks Data Necessary to Determine the Safety of Pesticides* (Sacramento: California Auditor General, Aug. 1984); Ramlit Associates, Inc., *Groundwater Contamination by Pesticides: A California Assessment—Submitted to State Water Resources Control Board* (Berkeley: Ramlit Associates, Inc., June 1983); California Water Resources Control Board, Toxic Substances Control Program, *1, 2-Dichloropropane (1, 2-D) 1, 3-Dichloropropene (1, 3-D),* by David B. Cohen et al. (Sacramento: California Water Resources Control Board, Aug. 1983); Harold G. Alford and Mary P. Ferguson, eds., *Pesticides in Soil and Groundwater* (Berkeley: Agricultural Sciences Publications, 1982); California Water Resources Control Board, *Significance of Pesticides from Irrigated Agriculture in California* (Sacramento: California Water Resources Control Board, Sept. 1979); California Department of Water Resources, "Investigation of Ground Water Contamination by Dibromochloropropane in the Dinuba Area" (Aug. 1980), file S-9, item 3986, California Department of Water Resources Archives, Sacramento; Hal Rubin, "The Toxic Chemical Storm over California," *California Journal* 10 (Dec. 1979): 413–416; Douglas Foster, "The Growing Battle over Pesticides in Drinking Water," ibid. 14 (May 1983): 178; Stephen Green,

"Glitches, Gremlins, and Swoap: Staggering Along the Road to Toxic Waste Reform in California," ibid. 16 (Sept. 1985): 345–348; Rick Rodriguez, "Regulating Pesticides," ibid. 16 (Oct. 1985): 401–404; Ray Sotero, "Food Safety: Carrots, Cucumbers, and Cancer," ibid. 21 (Mar. 1990): 157–158, 161; James Nelson, "The Pesticide Problem: Working Can Be Hazardous to Your Health," *Cry California* 12 (Summer 1977): 59–62. See also William B. Deichmann, *Pesticides and the Environment: A Continuing Controversy* (New York: Intercontinental Medical Book Corporation, 1973), 215–231, passim; *Los Angeles Times,* Feb. 23, Mar. 13, 23, May 2, Sept. 5, 1986, Feb. 21, July 6, 1988.

92. U.S. Environmental Protection Agency, *U.S. Methyl Bromide Phase Out* (Washington, D.C.: U.S. Environmental Protection Agency, 2000); California Department of Pesticide Regulation, *Notice of Proposed Changes in the Regulations of the Department of Pesticide Regulation: Methyl Bromide Field Fumigations* (Sacramento: California Department of Pesticide Regulation, 2000); *Los Angeles Times,* Jan. 19, 2000 ("We're very disappointed . . ."); *Sacramento Bee,* Jan. 19, 2000; California Department of Food and Agriculture, Office of Pesticide Consultation and Analysis, *Methyl Bromide: An Impact Assessment* (Sacramento: California Department of Food and Agriculture, 1996); California Environmental Protection Agency, Department of Pesticide Regulation, *Review of Restrictions on the Use of Methyl Bromide: A Report to the Legislature* (Sacramento: California Environmental Protection Agency, 1996); U.S. Environmental Protection Agency, *Review of Control Options for Methyl Bromide in Commodity Treatment,* by Glenn DeWolf (Washington, D.C.: U.S. Environmental Protection Agency, 1996); House Committee on Agriculture, Subcommittee on Forestry, Resource Conservation, and Research, *Hearings on Review of the Phaseout of Methyl Bromide,* 105 Cong., 2 sess. (1998); California Hazard Evaluation and Information Service, *Methyl Bromide* (Berkeley: Hazard Evaluation and Information Service, 1990); U.S. General Accounting Office, *Pesticides: The Phaseout of Methyl Bromide in the United States* (Washington, D.C.: General Accounting Office, 1995); California Department of Health Services, *Methyl Bromide (Chemical Name Bromomethane)* (Berkeley: California Department of Health Services, 1981); U.S. Department of Health and Human Services, *Teratologic Assessment of Butylene Oxide, Styrene Oxide and Methyl Bromide,* by Melvin R. Sikov et al. (Cincinnati: U.S. Department of Health and Human Services, 1981); California Department of Public Health, Bureau of Occupational

Health, "Methyl Bromide Poisoning," *Occupational Health Bulletin* G (March 1956); California Department of Public Health, Bureau of Occupational Health, "Methyl Bromide," *Occupational Health Bulletin No. 5* (1945); *Los Angeles Times,* June 29, 1993, Jan. 17 and Mar. 13, 1996; *Sacramento Bee,* Oct. 16, 1998; *Wall Street Journal* (California), Dec. 8, 1999.

93. *Los Angeles Times,* Oct. 31 ("no pollution . . ."), Nov. 1 ("dangerously illogical"; "willful illogic . . ."), 1989, Sept. 17, 1990. See also Rodriguez, "Regulating Pesticides," 403–404; Vic Pollard, "Seed of the Tainted Watermelons," *Golden State Report* 1 (Fall 1985): 30–32.

94. *San Francisco Chronicle,* Aug. 14, 1988; *Los Angeles Times,* May 31, Aug. 5, Sept. 16 ("we didn't want . . ."), 28, Oct. 21, 1988; Richard Steven Street, "The Big Fix: How Some Growers Fixed Their Grapes Illegally to Get an Edge on the Market," *California Farmer* 269 (Sept. 3, 1988): 8–9, 13–15.

95. Harold O. Carter and George Goldman, *The Measure of California Agriculture: Its Impact on the State Economy,* rev. ed. (Oakland: University of California Division of Agriculture and Natural Resources, 1998), 19; *Food Quality Protection Act of 1996, U.S. Statutes at Large* 110 (1996): 1489; *Los Angeles Times,* Sept. 19, 1997. For an optimistic view of the future for organic farming in California, see Elizabeth Schilling, "From Fad to Fortune: Organic Agriculture Grows Up," *California Journal* 26 (May 1995): 23–25.

96. Robert Gordan, "Poisons in the Fields: The United Farm Workers, Pesticides, and Environmental Politics," *Pacific Historical Review* 68 (Feb. 1999): 51–77; Paul G. Barnett, *Survey of the Research on the Impacts of Pesticides on Agricultural Workers and the Rural Environment* (Davis: California Institute for Rural Studies, Feb. 1989); Margaret Reeves et al., *Fields of Poison: California Farmworkers and Pesticides* (San Francisco: Californians for Pesticide Reform, 1999), 6–9, passim (quote, pp. 6–7); *Los Angeles Times,* July 12, 1998.

97. *Los Angeles Times,* July 12, 1998 (Gore quotes), Feb. 21, 1999 ("to wash . . .").

98. Ibid., Aug. 4, 1999 ("too little too late" and "Laxity on . . ." [editorial page]); see also news article in ibid. on the same date.

99. California Public Interest Research Group, *Toxics on Tap: Pesticides in California Drinking Water Sources,* by Brad Heavner (San Francisco: Californians for Pesticide Reform, Oct. 27, 1999), 6–9 (quotes); *Los Angeles Times,* Oct. 27, 1999 ("many of the . . ."; "goals . . .").

100. California Water Resources Control Board, Environmental Protection Agency, *1996 California Water Quality Assessment Report,* section on Region 5; California Water Resources Control Board, *Nitrate in Drinking Water: Report to the Legislature* (Sacramento: California Water Resources Control Board, 1988); H. H. Davis, "Monitoring and Evaluation of Water Quality under Central Valley Dairy Sites," in *Proceedings of the California Plant and Soil Conference, January 1995* (Visalia, Calif.: American Society of Agronomy and California Fertilizer Association, 1995), 158–164; *Los Angeles Times,* Apr. 28, 1998, Feb. 14, 1999; *San Francisco Chronicle,* Dec. 4, 1998.

101. California Water Resources Control Board, *1996 California Water Quality Assessment Report,* passim; Davis, "Monitoring and Evaluation of Water Quality under Central Valley Dairy Sites," passim; *Los Angeles Times,* Apr. 28, 1998 (quote), Feb. 14, 1999; *Bakersfield Californian,* Jan. 16 and 21, July 26, 2000.

102. *Los Angeles Times,* Apr. 28, 1998; U.S. Department of the Interior, Geological Survey, *Circular 1159.* This study should be read in conjunction with an interview given to a reporter for the *Fresno Bee* and published on May 1, 1998.

103. California Department of Water Resources, *Bulletin 160–98,* chap. 3, pp. 68, 70–71; California Department of Water Resources, *Bulletin 160–93,* 1: 127–128, 2: 261–262; Vernon E. Valantine, "Impacts of Colorado River Salinity," *Journal of the Irrigation and Drainage Division, American Society of Civil Engineers* 100 (Dec. 1974): 500–501; B. Delworth Gardner and Clyde E. Stewart, "Agriculture and Salinity," in Dean F. Peterson and A. Berry Crawford, eds., *Values and Choices in the Development of the Colorado River Basin* (Tucson: University of Arizona Press, 1978), 121–143; Myron Holburt, *California's Stake in the Colorado River,* rev. ed. (Los Angeles: Colorado River Board of California, 1979), 20–22; Thorkild Jacobsen and Robert M. Adams, "Salt and Silt in Ancient Mesopotamian Agriculture," *Science* 128 (Nov. 21, 1958): 1252.

104. California Department of Water Resources, *Bulletin 160–98,* chap. 7, pp. 59–60; Valantine, "Impacts of Colorado River Salinity," 503–504; Josh Newcom, "Getting Serious about Salt: Urban Water Purveyors Seek Solution to Mounting Problem," *Western Water* (Sept.–Oct. 1999): 4–13.

105. Norris Hundley, jr., *Dividing the Waters: A Century of Controversy between the United States and Mexico* (Berkeley and Los Angeles: University of California Press, 1966), 153–180; "Minute 242," *Inter-*

national Legal Materials 12 (1973): 1105; U.S. Department of State *Bulletin* 69 (1973): 395; California Department of Water Resources, *Bulletin 160–98,* chap. 3, pp. 70–71; *El Universal* (México, D.F.), Aug. 30, 1973; House Committee on Interior and Insular Affairs, *Hearings on Colorado River Basin Salinity Control, H.R. 12165,* 93 Cong. 2 sess. (1974), passim; U.S. Section, International Boundary and Water Commission, *Joint Projects of the United States and Mexico through the International Boundary and Water Commission* (n.p., [1982]); Myron Holburt, "International Problems," in Peterson and Crawford, eds., *Values and Choices,* 220–237; Norris Hundley, jr., "The West against Itself: The Colorado River—An Institutional History," in Gary D. Weatherford and F. Lee Brown, eds., *New Courses for the Colorado River: Major Issues for the Next Century* (Albuquerque: University of New Mexico Press, 1986), 37–39; *Los Angeles Times,* Mar. 8, 1992; California Department of Water Resources, *Bulletin 160–98,* chap. 3, pp. 70–71.

106. The years when the plant was operational and the cost estimates for the mitigation plans were obtained in interviews with Myron ("Mike") Fliegel, Division of Waste Management, U.S. Nuclear Regulatory Commission, June 29, 1999; and Richard Blubaugh, executive vice president, Atlas Corporation, June 29, 1999. *San Diego Union-Tribune,* Oct. 9, 1998 (MWD quote); U.S. Nuclear Regulatory Commission, Office of Nuclear Material Safety and Safeguards, *Final Technical Evaluation Report for the Proposed Revised Reclamation Plan for the Atlas Corporation Moab Mill* (Washington, D.C.: U.S. Nuclear Regulatory Commission, March 1997); U.S. Nuclear Regulatory Commission, Office of Nuclear Material Safety and Safeguards, *Final Technical Evaluation Report for the Proposed Revised Reclamation Plan for the Atlas Corporation Moab Mill,* 2 vols. and Supplement (Washington, D.C.: U.S. Nuclear Regulatory Commission, Apr. 1999); *Los Angeles Times,* Apr. 20, 1997; *Sacramento Bee,* Jan. 23, 1999; Josh Newcom, "Hot Debate over Hot Tailings," *River Report* (Spring 1999): 10–11; *San Diego Union-Tribune,* Jan. 10, 2000.

107. *Los Angeles Times,* Apr. 20, 1997; *Sacramento Bee,* Jan. 23, 1999; *San Diego Union-Tribune,* Jan. 10, 2000.

108. David Mathes, remediation project engineer, U.S. Department of Energy, to the author, July 23, 1999 (Energy Department quote); *San Diego Union-Tribune,* Oct. 9, 1998; *San Bernardino Sun,* Oct. 10, 1998; *Sacramento Bee,* Jan. 23, 1999; *North County Times* (Escondido), Feb. 12, 1999, Jan. 14 and 15, 2000; *San Diego Union-*

Tribune, Jan. 10 and 14, 2000; Metropolitan Water District of Southern California, *News Release,* Feb. 8, 2000; Associated Press, Feb. 12, 2000.

109. Joseph F. Poland, *Summary Statement of Ground-Water Conditions and Saline Contamination along the Coast of Orange County, California* (Santa Ana: Orange County Water District, 1947); Orange County Water District, *Statement Regarding the Present Condition of the Underground Water Basin of Orange County* (Santa Ana, Calif.: Orange County Water District, 1945); Joe A. Moreland and John A. Singer, *A Study of Deep Aquifers Underlying Coastal Orange County, California* (Menlo Park, Calif.: U.S. Geological Survey, 1969); California Department of Water Resources, *Bulletin 160–98,* chap. 3, pp. 52–53; Brian Thomas, MWD, to the author, Dec. 22, 1998; *Los Angeles Times,* Dec. 10, 1989 (quote); *Orange County Register* (Santa Ana), Mar. 15, 1960; William Blomquist, *Dividing the Waters: Governing Groundwater in Southern California* (San Francisco: Institute for Contemporary Studies, 1992), 249; John A. Izbicki et al., "Seawater Intrusion in Aquifers Underlying the Oxnard Plain, Ventura County, California," in Johannes DeVries and Jeff Woled, eds., *Ground Water and Future Supply: Proceedings of the Twenty-First Biennial Conference on Ground Water, September 15–16, 1997* (Davis: University of California Water Resources Center, Nov. 1998), 65–67.

110. Edward L. Masry to the author, Apr. 24 and May 3, 2000; *Los Angeles Times* (Ventura County Edition), Mar. 19, 2000; *San Diego Union-Tribune,* Mar. 27, 2000; *San Bernadino County Sun,* Apr. 12, 2000; *Riverside Press-Enterprise,* Aug. 20, 2000; *Los Angeles Times,* Aug. 20, 22, 23, 24, and 31, 2000.

111. C. J. Londquist et al., *Hydrogeology and Land Subsidence, Edwards Air Force Base, Antelope Valley, California, January 1989–December 1991* (Sacramento: U.S. Geological Survey, 1993); James C. Blodgett and J. S. Williams, *Land Subsidence and Problems Affecting Land Use at Edwards Air Force Base and Vicinity, California* (Sacramento: U.S. Geological Survey, 1992); *Los Angeles Times,* Mar. 17, 1991.

112. *Los Angeles Times,* Dec. 10, 1989, Mar. 17, 1991.

113. Duane Georgeson, "Case Study of Ground Water Contamination in the San Fernando Basin," in *Proceedings: Seventeenth Biennial Conference on Ground Water, September 25–26, 1989, San Diego, California* (Riverside: University of California Water Resources Center, Riverside; California Department of Water Resources, and State Water Resources Control Board, May 1990): 126 (quote); Melvin L.

Blevins and John F. Mann, Jr., "Management of Upper Los Angeles River Area (ULARA) Ground Water Contamination," in *Proceedings of the Nineteenth Biennial Conference on Ground Water, September 13– 14, 1993, Sacramento, California* (Davis: University of California Centers for Water and Wildlife Resources, Dec. 1994): 116–132; California Department of Water Resources, *Bulletin 160–98,* chap. 7, p. 60.

114. Interview with Richard Nagel, assistant watermaster for the Upper Los Angeles River Area, Los Angeles Department of Water and Power, June 1, 1999 (quote); Georgeson, "Case Study of Ground Water Contamination," 125–128; Upper Los Angeles River Area Watermaster, *Watermaster Service in the Upper Los Angeles River Area, Los Angeles County, 1994–95 Water Year* (Los Angeles: Upper Los Angeles River Area Watermaster, May 1996); Tom Harmon, "Groundwater Quality," in Richard Berk and Arthur M. Winer, eds., *Southern California Environmental Report Card, 1999* (Los Angeles: UCLA Institute of the Environment, 1999), 23–31; *Los Angeles Daily News,* Jan. 21, 1999; *Los Angeles Times,* Jan. 20 and 21, 2000. See also U.S. Geological Survey, "A Conceptional Ground-Water-Quality Monitoring Network for San Fernando Valley, California," by James G. Setmire, *Water-Resources Investigations Report 84-4128* (Sacramento: U.S. Geological Survey, 1985).

115. California Department of Water Resources, *Bulletin 160–98,* chap. 7, p. 60; *Los Angeles Times,* Dec. 10, 1989, May 13 and June 11, 1990; Luhdorff and Scalmanini, Consulting Engineers, *State Water Resources Control Board Groundwater "Hot Spots" Project: Well Testing and Site Characterization—Los Angeles Area* (Woodland, Calif.: Luhdorff and Scalmanini, 1986).

116. *Los Angeles Times,* Mar. 19, 1994; *San Gabriel Valley Daily Tribune,* Apr. 20, 1998.

117. *San Gabriel Valley Daily Tribune,* Apr. 20, 1998, Jan. 14, 1999; *Los Angeles Times,* Mar. 19, 1994, Jan. 1, 1996, Mar. 2, Sept. 16, 1999; *Pasadena Star News,* Mar. 2 and 4, 1999.

118. California Water Resources Control Board, Environmental Protection Agency, *1996 California Water Quality Assessment Report,* section on Region 8; California Water Resources Control Board, *Nitrate in Drinking Water,* 13–21; Camp Dresser & McKee Inc., *Nitrate Impact Study Report: Prepared for Santa Ana Watershed Project Authority* (Ontario, Calif.: Camp Dresser & McKee Inc., 1989); Lanny J. Lund, *Sources and Sinks of Nitrogen and Other Inorganic Constituents in the*

Santa Ana River above Prado Dam (Riverside: Department of Soil and Environmental Sciences, University of California, Riverside, 1992); Carmen A. Burton, John A. Izbicki, and Katherine S. Paybins, *Water-Quality Trends in the Santa Ana River at MWD Crossing and Below Prado Dam, Riverside County, California* (Sacramento: U.S. Geological Survey, 1998); Sue McClurg, "Watershed Management," *Western Water* (Nov.–Dec. 1995): 12; *Los Angeles Times,* September 29, 1989, June 11, 1990, Apr. 28, 1998 (quote), Feb. 14, 1999.

119. Lawrence Livermore National Laboratory, *An Evaluation of MTBE Impacts to California Groundwater Resources* (Livermore, Calif.: Lawrence Livermore National Laboratory, 1998); National Governors Association, *The National Debate about the Gasoline Additive MTBE,* by Martha Bohm (Washington, D.C.: National Governors Association, 1999); Steven A. Book, "MTBE and Perchlorate in California Drinking Water," in DeVries and Woled, eds., *Ground Water and Future Supply,* 241–244; California Department of Water Resources, *Bulletin 160–98,* chap. 3, p. 65; Monica Schwarze, "The Knock against MTBE," *Metropolitan Water District of Southern California Aqueduct* 65, no. 1 (1999): 2–3; *Orange County Register* (Santa Ana), June 28, 1998; *San Diego Union-Tribune,* Oct. 3, 1998; *Los Angeles Times,* Jan. 6, 1999.

120. Ibid.; *Sacramento Bee,* Dec. 11, 1998; Reuters News Service, Jan. 13, 2000; Associated Press Release, Jan. 22, 2000 ("It's a diabolical chemical . . ."); *San Diego Union-Tribune,* Mar. 20, 2000; *Los Angeles Times,* June 20, 22, July 6, 7, and 9, 2000; *ENN News,* Aug. 15, 2000.

121. *Los Angeles Times,* Nov. 17, 1998, Mar. 24, 26 (Davis quotes), Dec. 6, 1999, Mar. 21, 2000; *Orange County Register* (Santa Ana), June 28, 1998; *San Francisco Chronicle,* Dec. 15, 1998, Jan. 20, 1999; *San Diego Union-Tribune,* Mar. 20, 2000.

122. Los Angeles Department of Public Works, Bureau of Sanitation, *City San: Hyperion Treatment Plant* (Los Angeles: Los Angeles Department of Public Works, 1998); Michael K. Stenstrom, "Wastewater Treatment," in Berk and Winer, eds., *Southern California Environmental Report Card [1998],* 16–25; *Los Angeles Times,* Dec. 8, 1998.

123. The volume of runoff into the bay produced by different amounts of rainfall is based on a formula developed by Michael K. Stenstrom, professor in the Civil and Environmental Engineering Department, University of California, Los Angeles. For a preliminary study, see Kenneth M. Wong, Eric W. Strecker, and Michael K. Stenstrom, "GIS to Estimate Storm-Water Pollutant Mass Load-

ings," *Journal of Environmental Engineering* 123 (Aug. 1997): 737–745; see also Michael K. Stenstrom, "Stormwater Impact," in Berk and Winer, eds., *Southern California Environmental Report Card, 1999,* 12–21. For the study on the chemicals detected in the bay, see I. H. Suffet et al., *Chemical Contaminant Release into the Santa Monica Bay: A Pilot Study* (Los Angeles: Environmental Health Sciences, School of Public Health, University of California, Los Angeles, 1993).

124. Santa Monica Bay Restoration Project, *Taking the Pulse of the Bay: The State of the Bay, 1998* (Monterey Park, Calif.: Santa Monica Bay Restoration Project, 1998); Heal the Bay and the Los Angeles & San Gabriel Rivers Watershed Council, *Visions for the River: A Conference, May 4, 1996* (Santa Monica, Calif.: Heal the Bay, 1996); Heal the Bay, *Proceedings of the Southern California Watershed Conference: "Making Watersheds Work"* (Santa Monica: Heal the Bay, 1995); Santa Monica Bay Restoration Project, *Priority Actions for Bay Restoration* (Monterey Park, Calif.: Santa Monica Bay Restoration Project, 1992); Southern California Coastal Water Research Project, *Annual Report, 1992–93* (Westminster, Calif.: Southern California Coastal Water Research Project, 1994); Deidre J. McDermott, *Polychlorinated Biphenyls in Marine Organisms off Southern California* (El Segundo, Calif.: Southern California Coastal Water Research Project, 1975); David R. Young, *Trace Elements in Seafood Organisms Around Southern California Municipal Wastewater Outfalls* (Sacramento: California Water Resources Control Board, 1978); Southern California Coastal Water Research Project, *Coastal Water Research* (El Segundo, Calif.: Southern California Coastal Water Research Project, 1974); Southern California Coastal Water Research Project, *The Effects of the Ocean Disposal of Municipal Wastes* (El Segundo, Calif.: Southern California Coastal Water Research Project, 1978); *Los Angeles Times,* Aug. 29, 1993, Feb. 12, 1998 (quote).

125. *Los Angeles Times,* Jan. 20, Mar. 30, May 13, 1999.

126. Ibid., Sept. 5 (quote) and 6, 1999; Robert W. Haile et al., "The Health Effects of Swimming in Ocean Water Contaminated by Storm Drain Runoff," *Epidemiology* 10 (July 1999): 355–363.

127. *Los Angeles Times,* Aug. 3, 1998, Aug. 4, 2000; Stenstrom, "Stormwater Impact," in Berk and Winer, eds., *Southern California Environmental Report Card, 1999,* 16. For a detailed and alarming investigation of how humans have harmed species and polluted the waters along California's 1,100-mile coastline, see the five-part series "Pacific Blues" by reporters Tom Knudson and Nancy Vogel in the *Sacramento Bee,* Dec. 22–26, 29, 1996.

128. California Water Resources Control Board and California Coastal Commission, *California's Nonpoint Source Management Plan,* 2 vols. (Sacramento: California Water Resources Control Board, 1999); *Los Angeles Times,* Dec. 15 and 22, 1999; *San Diego Union-Tribune,* Dec. 15, 1999, Jan. 12, 2000; *Escondido North County Times,* Aug. 1, 2000.

129. Ambrose and Feddema, "Wetlands," in Berk and Winer, eds., *Southern California Environmental Report Card [1998],* 26–34; *Malibu Surfside News,* Mar. 25, 1999; *Malibu Times,* Aug. 5, 1999; *Los Angeles Times,* Apr. 30, 1999.

130. *Los Angeles Times,* Sept. 29, 1987, June 11, 1990 (quote).

131. Ibid., Dec. 10, 1989.

132. Lisa Dunlap, "It's Good to Know What You're Gulping: Bottled Water Is Not Necessarily Better Than Tap, Says a UCR Microbiologist [Marilyn Yates]," *Fiat Lux* (Apr. 2000): 16–17; *Los Angeles Times,* Jan 16, May 15, 1986, May 24, 1988, Sept. 20, Nov. 18, 1989.

133. Kirsten Waller et al., "Trihalomethanes in Drinking Water and Spontaneous Abortion," *Epidemiology* 9 (March 1998): 134–140; Dunlap, "It's Good to Know What You're Drinking," 16–17; Brian Thomas, assistant chief, planning and resources division, Metropolitan Water District of Southern California, to the author, Dec. 22, 1998; California Department of Water Resources, *Bulletin 160–98,* chap. 3, pp. 66–67; *Philadelphia Inquirer,* Dec. 14, 1998; *New York Times,* Nov. 3, 1998; *Orange County Register* (Santa Ana), Nov. 9, 1998; *Los Angeles Times,* Feb. 10, 11, 12, 19, 1998, Mar. 31, 1999.

134. *U.S. Statutes at Large* 96 (1982): 1263; Lawrence J. Jelinek, *Harvest Empire: A History of California Agriculture,* 2d ed. (San Francisco: Boyd & Fraser Publishing Co., 1982), 89; Don Villarejo, *Getting Bigger: Large Scale Farming in California* (Davis: California Institute for Rural Studies, 1980); Don Villarejo, *Agricultural Land Ownership and Operations; Los Angeles Times,* Dec. 8, 1981, Sept. 30, 1982.

135. Walter Goldschmidt, *Small Business and the Community: A Study in the Central Valley of California on Effects of Scale of Farm Operations,* in U.S. Senate Special Committee to Study Problems of American Small Business, 79 Cong., 2 sess. (1946), Committee Print 13.

136. Dean MacCannell, *Draft Report on Current Social Conditions in the Communities in and near the Westlands Water District* (Davis: University of California, [1980]), 3–4, copy in possession of the author; Trudy Wischemann (an associate of Dean MacCannell) to the author, Jan. 12, 1990. See also Merrill D. Goodall, John D. Sullivan,

and Timothy de Young, *California Water: A New Political Economy* (Montclair, N.J.: Allanheld, Osmun, 1978), 100, passim; Charles Wollenberg, "The Small Farmer Deserves a Chance," *Cry California* 14 (Winter 1978–79): 18–24.

137. Trudy Wischemann to the author, Jan. 12, 1990; Dean Mac-Cannell and Jerry White, "The Social Costs of Large-Scale Agriculture: The Prospects of Land Reform in California," in Charles C. Geisler and Frank J. Popper, eds., *Land Reform, American Style* (Totowa, N.J.: Rowman & Allanheld, 1984), 35–55. See also Joseph R. Rocha, "A Study of Four San Joaquin Valley Communities: Firebaugh, Mendota, Kerman, and Orange Cove" (Ph.D. dissertation, Claremont Graduate School, 1974), which concluded that "the physical and social amenities of moderate sized farm communities were superior to those of large agribusiness oriented communities" (p. 100).

138. *Los Angeles Times,* July 25, 28, Aug. 4, 1986, Apr. 15, 1987, Nov. 20, 1989. See also Don Villarejo, *How Much Is Enough? Federal Water Subsidies and Agriculture in California's Central Valley* (Davis: California Institute for Rural Studies, 1986); E. Phillip LeVeen and Laura B. King, *Turning Off the Tap on Federal Water Subsidies,* vol. 1: *The Central Valley Project* (San Francisco: Natural Resources Defense Council, 1985).

139. *Los Angeles Times,* Nov. 30, Dec. 12, 1988, Jan. 2, Feb. 26, July 1 and 10, Nov. 3 and 30, and Dec. 1, 1989 (quote), Jan. 7 and Mar. 15, 1990.

140. Dean MacCannell, "The Effect of Agricultural Scale on Communities," in *Proceedings: Sustainability of California Agriculture— A Symposium* (Davis: University of California, Davis, 1986), 236. See also Louis E. Swanson, ed., *Agriculture and Community Change in the U.S.: The Congressional Research Reports* (Boulder: Westview Press, 1988); Barbara Grondin, "Does Big Agribusiness Spell Community Doom?" *California Farmer* (May 3, 1986): 8, 12, 22.

141. The higher price of $19.31 an acre-foot of CVP water for growers was for an uninterruptible supply, while the $62 an acre-foot for SWP water does not include $10 for pumping charges within the valley. Patricia Watters, resource specialist, Metropolitan Water District of Southern California, to the author, April 1, 1999; interview with Watters, April 6, 1999; Marc Reisner and Sarah Bates, *Overtapped Oasis: Reform or Revolution for Western Water* (Washington, D.C.: Island Press, 1990), 32–33, passim; *Los Angeles Times,* Oct. 16, 1990 (quote), Apr. 7, 1991.

142. *Cal. Stats.,* chap. 933 (1980), chap. 1655 (1984), chaps. 364, 918, 970, 1241, 1384 (1986); Tom Stallard, "Local Concern vs. Statewide Desires," in DeVries and Woled, eds., *Ground Water and Future Supply,* 207–208; Harold O. Carter and George Goldman, *The Measure of California Agriculture: Its Impact on the State Economy,* rev. ed. (Oakland: University of California Division of Agriculture and Natural Resources, 1998), 42; Don Villarejo, *93640 at Risk: Farmers, Workers and Townspeople in an Era of Water Uncertainty* (Davis: California Institute for Rural Studies, 1996). See also California Department of Water Resources, *Bulletin 160–87,* 110; Richard W. Wahl, *Water Marketing in California: Past Experiences, Future Prospects* (Los Angeles: Reason Foundation, Policy Study 162, July 1993); Kenneth D. Frederick, ed., *Scarce Water and Institutional Change* (Washington, D.C.: Resources for the Future, Inc., 1986); Henry J. Vaux, Jr., "Growth and Water in the South Coast Basin of California," in M. T. El-Ashry and Diana C. Gibbons, eds., *Water and Arid Lands of the Western United States* (New York: Cambridge University Press, 1988), 233–279; Charles V. More and Richard E. Howitt, "The Central Valley of California," ibid., 85–126; Phelps, Moore, and Graubard, *Efficient Water Uses in California,* passim; Myron B. Holburt, Richard W. Atwater, and Timothy H. Quinn, "Water Marketing in Southern California," *American Water Works Association Journal* 80 (March 1988): 38–45; Brent M. Haddad, *Rivers of Gold: Designing Markets to Allocate Water in California* (Washington, D.C.: Island Press, 2000).

143. California Department of Water Resources, *Bulletin 160–98,* chap. 3, pp. 53, 55–59 (quote on p. 56), chap. 6, pp. 25–30; Lloyd S. Dixon, Nancy Y. Moore, and Susan W. Schechter, *California's 1991 Drought Water Bank: Economic Impacts in the Selling Regions* (Santa Monica, Calif.: Rand, 1993); Roger G. Potter and Susan Tatayon, "State Interest in Water Banking/Conjunctive Use," in DeVries and Woled, eds., *Ground Water and Future Supply,* 27–34; *Los Angeles Times,* Mar. 8, 11, 13, and 18, Apr. 6 and 18, May 9, June 5 and 22, Nov. 19, 1991.

144. *Los Angeles Times,* Oct. 16, 1990, Mar. 14, June 5, July 17, Aug. 21 and 26, Nov. 20, 1991, Feb. 20, 1992.

145. William Fulton, *The Reluctant Metropolis: The Politics of Urban Growth in Los Angeles* (Point Arena, Calif.: Solano Press Books, 1997), 118 (quote); *Los Angeles Times,* Aug. 12, Sept. 25, 1991.

146. Carl Boronkay and Timothy H. Quinn, "Passage of the Cen-

tral Valley Project Improvement Act, 1991–1992: The Metropolitan Water District Perspective" (Regional Oral History Office, Bancroft Library, University of California, Berkeley, 1997), 31–33, 61–62; *Los Angeles Times,* Aug. 11, 12 (quote), 1991.

147. California Department of Water Resources, *Bulletin 160–98,* chap. 7, p. 54; Metropolitan Water District of Southern California, *News Release* (Jan. 11, 2000). Metropolitan Water District of Southern California, *Wheeling: Gearing for the Future of Water Marketing* (Los Angeles: Metropolitan Water District of Southern California, Feb. 1997), 19, 21; Joe Pomento, "The Last Water Hole in the West," *Metropolitan Water District of Southern California Aqueduct* 64, no. 3 (1998): 2–3; *Bond Buyer,* Dec. 4, 1998; *Los Angeles Times,* Apr. 12, 1993, Aug. 3, 1997; *Hemet Press-Enterprise,* May 11 and 12, 1999.

148. Colorado River Board of California, *Annual Report, 1982* (Sacramento: State Printing Office, 1983), 5; *Imperial Irrigation District v. State Water Resources Control Board,* 186 Cal.App.3d 1160 (1986); California Department of Water Resources, *Bulletin 160–87,* 106; John L. Scott, MWD, to the author, May 7 and 20, 1999.

149. U.S. Department of the Interior, Fish and Wildlife Service, *Saving the Salton Sea: A Research Needs Assessment* (Washington, D.C.: U.S. Fish and Wildlife Service, Oct. 1997), 1–2, passim; California Department of Water Resources, *Bulletin 160–87,* 106–107; California Department of Water Resources, *Bulletin 160–98,* chap. 9, pp. 35–38; Michael J. Cohen, Jason I. Morrison, and Edward P. Glenn, *Haven or Hazard: The Ecology and Future of the Salton Sea* (Oakland: Pacific Institute for Studies in Development, Environment, and Security, Feb. 1999); William deBuys, *Salt Dreams: Land & Water in Low-Down California* (Albuquerque: University of New Mexico Press, 1999); chap. 15; Wayne W. Carmichael, "The Toxins of Cyanobacteria," *Scientific American* 270 (Jan. 1994): 78–86; Joe Pomento, "The Salton Sea: Can It Be Saved?" *Metropolitan Water District of Southern California Aqueduct* 64, no. 2 (1998): 2–3; *Los Angeles Times,* Sept. 4, 1996, June 8, Oct. 6, 1997, Feb. 8, Mar. 6, 1998; *Riverside Press-Enterprise,* May 5, 1998; *Sacramento Bee,* May 10, 1998; *Desert Sun* (Palm Springs), July 21, 2000.

150. The massive fish die-offs caused many to believe that the fish population was declining, but later studies found that it was booming and exacerbating the problem. Part of subsequent planning to restore the sea called for harvesting the fish to decrease the overpopulation. U.S. Department of the Interior, Bureau of Recla-

mation, *Guide to the Salton Sea Restoration Project and EIS/EIR* (Washington, D.C.: Bureau of Reclamation, 2000); U.S. Department of the Interior, Bureau of Reclamation, and Salton Sea Authority, *Draft Salton Sea Restoration Project Environmental Impact Statement/ Environmental Impact Report* (Boulder City, Nev.: U.S. Bureau of Reclamation, Jan. 2000), pp. 3-1 to 3-33, 3-74 to 3-95, 3-141 to 3-155 passim; U.S. Department of the Interior, Fish and Wildlife Service, *Saving the Salton Sea,* 1–3, 5–6, 33–35, 45, 47, 49; Milton Friend, executive director, Salton Sea Science Subcommittee, to the author, Nov. 29, 1999; Salton Sea Authority, *Proceedings of the Salton Sea Symposium, January 13, 1994* (Indian Wells, Calif.: Salton Sea Authority, 1994); U.S. Department of the Interior, Bureau of Reclamation, *The Salton Sea Restoration Project: Opportunities and Challenges* (Washington, D.C.: U.S. Bureau of Reclamation, 1999); *Los Angeles Times,* May 23, 1999, Jan. 14, 2000; *San Diego Union-Tribune,* Jan. 21, 2000; *San Jose Mercury News,* Jan. 23, 2000.

151. *Imperial Irrigation District* v. *State Water Resources Control Board,* 186 Cal.App.3d 1160 (1986); California Department of Water Resources, *Bulletin 160–87,* 106; Colorado River Board of California, *Executive Director's Monthly Report* (Los Angeles: Colorado River Board of California, photocopy, Sept. 13, 1988), 3.

152. *Los Angeles Times,* Nov. 10, Dec. 22, 1987, March 1, Nov. 10 and 13, 1988.

153. Thomas Waller, "Southern California Water Politics and U.S.-Mexican Relations: Lining the All-American Canal," *Journal of Borderlands Studies* 7 (Fall 1992): 7, 17–26; *New York Times,* Oct. 1, 1989.

154. Interview with Manuel R. Ybarra, secretary, United States Section, International Boundary and Water Commission, April 20, 1998; *San Diego Union-Tribune,* Feb. 28, 1999.

155. Imperial Irrigation District and Metropolitan Water District of Southern California, "Agreement for the Implementation of a Water Conservation Program and Use of Conserved Water" (Dec. 22, 1988); "Water Conservation Agreement between the Metropolitan Water District of Southern California and Imperial Irrigation District" (Dec. 19, 1989), copies of both documents in possession of the author; Colorado River Board of California, *Executive Director's Monthly Report* (Los Angeles: Colorado River Board of California, photocopy, Dec. 13, 1988), 3; Patricia Watters, MWD, to the author, June 8, 1999; *Los Angeles Times,* Dec. 14 and 29, 1988,

Oct. 16, 1990; *Imperial Valley Press* (El Centro), Dec. 18, 1988, Dec. 13, 1989, Jan. 11, 1990.

156. Based on cost and other considerations, present plans call for building a lined canal alongside the older canal. "Water Conservation Agreement between the Metropolitan Water District of Southern California and Imperial Irrigation District" (Dec. 19, 1989). Prior to implementation of the sixteen projects (subsequently regrouped as "conservation" and "augmentation" projects), they were modified in certain particulars. Jan Matusak, principal engineer, planning and resources division, Metropolitan Water District, to the author, Feb. 11 and 16, 1999, June 16, 2000. See also *U.S. Statutes at Large* 102 (1988): 4005; John Scott, MWD, to the author, May 7, 1999; *Los Angeles Times,* July 13, 1998.

157. "Agreement: Requesting the Division of Water Resources of the State of California to Apportion California's Share of the Waters of the Colorado River among the Various Applicants and Water Users Therefrom in the State, Consenting to Such Apportionments, and Requesting Similar Apportionments by the Secretary of the Interior of the United States" (Aug. 18, 1931) in "Hoover Dam Documents," *H. Doc. 717,* 80 Cong., 2 sess. (1948), app. 1003; Phillip J. Pace, "Water-Use Efficiency: The Key to California's Future" (March 11, 1999), in Metropolitan Water District of Southern California, *Direct Line: Colorado River Update* (March 1999).

158. "Agreement of Compromise" (Feb. 14, 1934), in "Hoover Dam Documents," app. 1107, p. A64 ("exclusively for . . ."); *Riverside Press-Enterprise,* Oct. 19, 1999; *Imperial Valley Press* (El Centro), Oct. 20, 1999; *North County Times* (Escondido), Oct. 19, 1999.

159. Thomas E. Levy, Coachella Valley Water District, to Carl Boronkay, MWD, Feb. 1, 1989 ("wasting hundreds . . ."); *Coachella Valley Water District vs. Imperial Irrigation District, Metropolitan Water District of Southern California, and Acting Secretary of the Interior: Complaint for Declarative and Injunctive Relief,* United States District Court, Southern District of California, February 1, 1989; "Water Conservation Agreement between the Metropolitan Water District of Southern California and Imperial Irrigation District" (Dec. 19, 1989); Brian Thomas, MWD, to the author, Sept. 18, 1998, copies of all the preceding documents in the possession of the author.

160. There are four Bass brothers (Sid, Robert, Edward, and Lee), but Edward and Lee were the major players in the Imperial Valley through their ownership of Western Farms. Koenig & Dorsey, "Re-

search Report on the Bass Brothers: Confidential" (1997), copy in possession of the author; *Imperial Valley Press* (El Centro), June 13, 1994, May 18, June 9 and 23, 1995, June 3, Oct. 14, 1996, Aug. 5, 1997; *Los Angeles Times,* Oct. 2, 1995, Aug. 25, 1996, May 19, 1997; *Wall Street Journal,* July 1, 1998.

161. The information and quotations in this paragraph come from documents in the files of the San Diego County Water Authority that were leaked to the press. See *Wall Street Journal,* July 1, 1998 (quotes); *Imperial Valley Press* (El Centro), July 6 and 26, 1998; *San Diego Union-Tribune,* July 3, 1998.

162. *Imperial Valley Press* (El Centro), June 1, 1995, Dec. 8, 1998; *Los Angeles Times,* Oct. 2, 1995, Aug. 25, May 19, 1996; Robert Campbell, "Presentation to the Southern California Water Committee: The SDCWA/IID Water Conservation and Transfer Agreement— Water Resource Management for 21st Century" (Jan. 29, 1998), copy in possession of the author.

163. Robert M. Fogelson, *The Fragmented Metropolis: Los Angeles, 1850–1930* (Cambridge, Mass.: Harvard University Press, 1967), 43–62, passim; "Hoover Dam Documents," *H. Doc. 717,* 80 Cong., 2 sess. (1948), 136, apps. 1010, 1011, 1012, 1014; *Los Angeles Times,* Apr. 29, 1996.

164. Len Novarro, "Water War," *San Diego Homes/Gardens* (Mar. 1998): 13–14 (quote); *Los Angeles Times,* Apr. 29, 1996, Aug. 3, 1997.

165. Coalition for a Fair Water Policy, "Conditions for a Water Transfer Agreement" (Oct. 14, 1996); Coalition for a Fair Water Policy to Imperial Irrigation District, Mar. 25, 1997, copies of the preceding items in possession of the author; *Los Angeles Times,* May 19, 1997 ("water ranchers"); *Imperial Valley Press* (El Centro), June 1, 9 ("too greedy"), 23 (Cox quote), 28, 1995.

166. *Imperial County Grand Jury Report* (July 1996), copy in possession of the author; *Money Magazine* (Oct. 1, 1997), 117; *Wall Street Journal,* Aug. 4, 1997; *New York Times,* Apr. 23, 1998; *Imperial Valley Press* (El Centro), June 13, July 26, Aug. 7, Oct. 17, 1996, Aug. 5, 8, 11 and 15, Sept. 23, 1997.

167. *Los Angeles Times,* Oct. 2, 1995 ("brackish"), Mar. 3, 1996 ("leaving San Diego stranded"), Apr. 29, 1996 (Christianson quote), Aug. 25, 1996, May 19 and Aug. 3, 1997; Gregory Quist to Mark Watton, Aug. 7, 1996, copy in possession of the author.

168. "Agreement for Transfer of Conserved Water by and between Imperial Irrigation District and San Diego County Water Authority" (Dec. 15, 1997). The draft agreement established a formula

for determining the price rather than giving specific dollar figures. The costs per acre-foot given here were supplied by Rodney T. Smith, economic consultant and participant in the negotiations on behalf of the Imperial Irrigation District. Smith to the author, Apr. 2, 1998; see also Smith, "Summary of Pricing Provisions, IID–San Diego Water Conservation and Transfer Agreement" (Mar. 9, 1998); Imperial Irrigation District, "Quantity Provisions of IID/SDCWA Water Conservation and Transfer Agreement Prepared for IID Public Workshop" (Mar. 23, 1998); San Diego County Water Authority, "Summary of Basic Terms: IID–San Diego Water Conservation Transfer Agreement: Summary of Basic Terms" (Dec. 11, 1997), copies of all the preceding items in possession of the author. See, in addition, Campbell, "The SDCWA/IID Water Transfer Agreement"; *Imperial Valley Press* (El Centro), Dec. 11, 1997; *San Diego Daily Transcript,* Dec. 12, 1997; *San Diego Union-Tribune,* Dec. 12, 1997; *North County Times* (Escondido), Dec. 12, 1997; *Los Angeles Times,* May 19, Dec. 12, 1997.

169. Rincon del Diablo Municipal Water District to Christine Frahm, chair, San Diego County Water Authority, Apr. 2, 1998 (quotes); Frahm to Rincon del Diablo Municipal Water District, Apr. 6, 1998, copies of the preceding items in possession of the author; *North County Times* (Escondido), Apr. 5, 1998; *Imperial Valley Press* (El Centro), Dec. 11, 12, 14, and 17, 1997, Jan. 23, Feb. 13, Apr. 29, 1998 (Condit quote).

170. SDCWA, "News Release," Apr. 29, 1998 (quote of chair of San Diego water board), copy in possession of the author; *San Diego Union-Tribune,* Apr. 30, 1998; *Los Angeles Times,* Dec. 12, 1997 (state senator's quote). For the agreement as approved, see "Agreement for Transfer of Conserved Water by and between Imperial Irrigation District and San Diego County Water Authority" (April 29, 1998), copy in possession of the author.

171. Interview with Brian Thomas, MWD, May, 12, 1998 ("to put another straw in the river"); Ken Weinberg, director of water resources, SDCWA, to SDCWA Board of Directors, May 7, 1998 (there are two memos with this date from Weinberg to the board, each dealing with different aspects of possible "joint cooperation [with Mexico on a] . . . conveyance of Colorado River water to the San Diego/Tijuana region," copies in possession of the author); *Los Angeles Times,* Mar. 3, Apr. 29, and Aug. 25, 1996; *San Diego Union-Tribune,* Sept. 7 and 8, 1999.

172. Heightening the stakes in the dispute were approaches

made to MWD by several other authorities wanting to wheel water (for example, Santa Margarita Water District, San Bernardino Valley Water District, Western Water). "These requests were for significantly smaller amounts and had less impact," recalled an MWD official, "but the policy concern was real." One result was MWD's adoption in November 1996 of a wheeling rate policy that guided the agency's dealings with San Diego and the price it set. Brian Thomas, MWD, to the author, Oct. 9, 1998; "Metropolitan's Policy Principles for Wheeling" (November 19, 1996), in Metropolitan Water District of Southern California, *Wheeling,* 4; *Ventura County Star,* Dec. 28, 1997 ("ask[ing] the rest . . ."); *Wall Street Journal,* July 11, 1997 (quote of MWD official); *Los Angeles Times,* Mar. 3, 1996, May 28, Aug. 3, Oct. 14, 1997.

173. Metropolitan Water District of Southern California, *Southern California's Integrated Water Resources Plan—Report Number 1107: Executive Summary* (Los Angeles: Metropolitan Water District of Southern California, March 1996), 5, 10–19.

174. Colorado River Board of California, "Colorado River Board 4.4 Plan: California's Use of Its Colorado River Allocation" (Draft: Dec. 17, 1997); Bruce Babbitt, Address to the Colorado River Water Users Association (Dec. 19, 1996), 3, 6–7; Babbitt, Address to the Colorado River Water Users Association (Dec. 18, 1997), 4–6; Babbitt, Address to the Colorado River Water Users Association (Dec. 17, 1998), 1–4; MWD Negotiating Team to MWD Board of Directors, Jan. 6, 1999, copies of the previous items in possession of the author; California Department of Water Resources, *Bulletin 160–98,* chap. 7, pp. 56–57; Sue McClurg, "Cutting Colorado River Use: The California Plan," *Western Water* (Nov.–Dec. 1998): 4–13.

175. *Los Angeles Times,* Dec. 26, 1997; see also ibid., March 3 and May 19, 1996.

176. Ibid., Mar. 3, 1996.

177. Ibid., Apr. 29, 1996.

178. General Manager, MWD, to MWD Board of Directors, Nov. 5, 1996, copy in possession of the author; *Los Angeles Times,* May 19, 1997. The $431 an acre-foot paid by San Diego to MWD was for treated water. MWD, *Wheeling,* 11.

179. Interview with Brian Thomas, MWD, May 12, 1998; MWD, *Wheeling,* 13, 17; *Los Angeles Times,* Dec. 12, 1997.

180. Though San Diego's agreement with MWD for wheeling Imperial Valley water was not affected by the appellate and supreme court rulings, plans to wheel water from other sources—

and San Diego had such plans—would be affected. *Metropolitan Water District of Southern California* v. *All Persons Interested in the Matter of . . . Certain Wheeling Rates: Los Angeles County Superior Court [Assigned to San Francisco County Superior Court]* (San Francisco, Jan. 12, 1998), 5 ("MWD's inclusion . . ."); Metropolitan Water District of Southern California, *News Release,* May 30, 2000 ("to charge . . ."); Metropolitan Water District of Southern California, *News Release,* Sept. 14, 2000.

181. *San Diego Daily Transcript,* Dec. 29, 1997; *New York Times,* Apr. 23, 1998 (part of EDF quote); *Los Angeles Times,* May 19, 1997 (part of EDF quote).

182. Bruce Babbitt, Address to the Colorado River Water Users Association (Dec. 19, 1996), 5–7; Babbitt, Address to the Colorado River Water Users Association (Dec. 18, 1997), 3; Babbitt, Address to the Colorado River Water Users Association (Dec. 17, 1998), 4; Phillip J. Pace, chair, MWD Board of Directors, to Bruce Babbitt, Jan. 25, 1999; Jan Matusak, principal engineer, planning and resources division, MWD, to the author, Jan. 15, 1999; John R. Wodraska, MWD general manager, to Dale Ensminger, Boulder Canyon Operations Office, Bureau of Reclamation, Apr. 3 and Oct. 21, 1998; Wodraska to James Green, Lower Colorado Regional Office, Bureau of Reclamation, Apr. 3, 1998; Rita Pearson, Arizona Department of Water Resources, to Lower Colorado Regional Office, Bureau of Reclamation, Apr. 1, 1998, copies of the preceding items in possession of the author; *Federal Register,* vol. 62, no. 250 (Dec. 31, 1997): 68492–68500, vol. 63, no. 32 (Feb. 18, 1998): 8160, vol. 63, no. 182 (Sept. 21, 1998): 50183, vol. 64, no. 210 (Nov. 1, 1999): 58986–59009; Josh Newcom, "Saving for a Dry Day: Innovative Storage Plan Could Stretch Colorado River Supply," in *River Report* (Winter 1998): 1, 4–9; *Wall Street Journal,* July 11, 1997; *San Diego Daily Transcript,* Dec. 29, 1997; *Los Angeles Times,* May 19, 1996, Dec. 12, 19, and 26, 1997; *Las Vegas Sun,* Dec. 18, 1998; *San Diego Union-Tribune,* Dec. 13, 1999.

183. California Department of Water Resources, *Bulletin 160–98,* chap. 9, pp. 57–58; "Agreement for Transfer of Conserved Water by and between Imperial Irrigation District and San Diego County Water Authority," article 8.1, sec. d, pp. 41–42; *Los Angeles Times,* Oct. 26 and 31, 1989; *San Diego Union-Tribune,* Dec. 20, 1997.

184. *Las Vegas Review Journal,* Mar. 13, 1998 (quote); *Los Angeles Times,* Feb. 8 and 26, Mar. 6, 1998.

185. Thomas Levy, CVWD, to Maureen Stapleton, SDCWA,

Feb. 16, 1998; David N. Kennedy to Christine Frahm, SDCWA, and Jack Foley, MWD, Jan. 5, 1998; Imperial Irrigation District, "The IID Proposal to Resolve Dispute with CVWD" (Mar. 5, 1997); Imperial Irrigation District, "News Release: IID Will Not Bow to Coachella's Unreasonable Demands" (Mar. 25, 1997); Imperial Irrigation District, "IID Proposal to Resolve Outstanding Dispute with CVWD" (Jan. 27, 1998), copies of all the preceding items in possession of the author; *Imperial Valley Press* (El Centro), Oct. 17, 1996, Dec. 11 and 12, 1997; *Los Angeles Times,* Nov. 29, 1996.

186. Koenig & Dorsey, "Research Report on the Bass Brothers: Confidential" (1997); *San Diego Union-Tribune,* Jan. 9, 1998 ("dirty tricks"); *North County Times* (Escondido), Jan. 7 ("despicable . . .") and 9 ("digging up dirt"), 1998.

187. *Wall Street Journal,* July 1, 1998; *Imperial Valley Press* (El Centro), June 30, July 5, 8, 13, 15, and 26, 1998. For the firing of the general manager, see *Los Angeles Times,* Jan. 7, 1999.

188. Brian Thomas, MWD, to the author, Oct. 5, 1998 (Wilson quote); California Department of Water Resources, *Bulletin 160–98,* chap. 9, pp. 54–55; Bruce Babbitt, Address to the Colorado River Water Users Association (Dec. 18, 1997), 5; Babbitt, Address to the Colorado River Water Users Association (Dec. 17, 1998), 1–2.

189. "Memorandum of Understanding of Essential Terms of a Contract between MWD and SDCWA" (Aug. 10, 1998), copy in possession of the author; Brian Thomas, MWD, to the author, Aug. 26, Oct. 5 and 6, 1998.

190. Save San Francisco Bay Association and Environmental Defense Fund to James Costa and Michael Machado, Aug. 12, 1998, copy in possession of the author; *Los Angeles Times,* Aug. 11 ("a back-room . . .") and 17, 1998; *San Diego Union-Tribune,* Aug. 7, 1998; *San Diego Daily Transcript,* Aug. 11, 1998; *Imperial Valley Press* (El Centro), Aug. 7 and 11, 1998; Brian Thomas, MWD, to the author, Oct. 5, 1998.

191. *Los Angeles Times,* Aug. 29 and 31, 1998; Brian Thomas, MWD, to the author, Oct. 5, 1998.

192. *Cal. Stats.,* chap. 7, sec. 12560 (1998); *Los Angeles Times,* Aug. 31 (state senator's quote), Sept. 1 ("extortion"), 1998; *Imperial Valley Press* (El Centro), Aug. 11, 1998. The redwoods were purchased in an agreement reached in March 1999. *Los Angeles Times,* Mar. 3, 1999.

193. Annette Hubbell, MWD, to the author, Sept. 3, 1998.

194. "Salton Sea Reclamation Act of 1998," *U.S. Statutes at Large*, 112 (Nov. 12, 1998): 3377; Bruce Babbitt, Address to Colorado River Water Users Association (Dec. 17, 1998), 5 (quote); U.S. Department of the Interior, Bureau of Reclamation, *Guide to the Salton Sea Restoration Project and EIS/EIR;* U.S. Department of the Interior, Bureau of Reclamation, and Salton Sea Authority, *Draft Salton Sea Restoration Project Environmental Impact Statement/Environmental Impact Report;* U.S. Department of the Interior, Bureau of Reclamation, Salton Sea Authority, *Draft Figures to Accompany Salton Sea Restoration Project Environmental Impact Statement/Environmental Impact Report* (Boulder City, Nev.: U.S. Bureau of Reclamation, Jan. 2000); U.S. Department of the Interior, *News Release,* Jan. 13, Aug. 1, 2000; Michelle Nijhuis, "Accidental Refuge," *High Country News* 32 (June 19, 2000): 1, 8–13; *San Diego Union-Tribune,* Jan. 12, 2000; *Riverside Press-Enterprise,* Jan. 13 and 14, 2000; *Los Angeles Times,* Jan. 14, Aug. 2, 2000.

195. "IID/CVWD/DOI Memorandum of Understanding Regarding Quantification of Colorado River Rights" (Dec. 16, 1998), copy in possession of the author.

196. Phillip J. Pace, chair, MWD Board of Directors, "Water-Use Efficiency: The Key to California's Future," in *Metropolitan Water District of Southern California Direct Line: Colorado River Update* (Mar. 1999), quotes, emphasis is in the original; see also "Summary Remarks by Timothy H. Quinn, Acting General Manager, Metropolitan Water District of Southern California, for Joint Hearing of [California] Assembly Water, Parks and Wildlife Committee and Senate Agriculture and Water Resources Committee" (March 17, 1999), copies of the preceding two items in possession of the author; Marvin E. Jensen and Ivan A. Walter, *Assessment of 1987–1996 Water Use by the Imperial Irrigation District Using Water Balance and Cropping Data: Special Report Prepared for the U.S. Bureau of Reclamation, Boulder City, Nevada* (Boulder City, Nev.: U.S. Bureau of Reclamation, June 1997), 6, 35, 37, 41, 42; *Imperial Valley Press* (El Centro), Jan. 22, Mar. 14, 1999; *Sacramento Bee,* Feb. 28, 1999; *San Diego Union-Tribune,* Mar. 8, 11, and 18, 1999; *Los Angeles Times,* Mar. 12, 1999.

197. *Arizona* v. *California et al.,* 373 U.S. 564, 565 (1963); Norris Hundley, jr., *Water and the West: The Colorado River Compact and the Politics of Water in the American West* (Berkeley and Los Angeles: University of California Press, 1975), 304–305; Jeffrey Kightlinger, senior deputy counsel, MWD, to the author, Oct. 14, 1999 ("going all

hours"); *Los Angeles Times,* Aug. 5, Oct. 16, 1999; *North County Times* (Escondido), Oct. 16 and 20, 1999; *San Diego Union-Tribune,* Oct. 16, 1999; *San Diego Business Journal,* Oct. 25, 1999.

198. "Key Terms for Quantification Settlement among the State of California, IID, CVWD and MWD" (October 15, 1999); "Synopsis of Quantification Settlement among California, IID, CVWD and MWD" (October 18, 1999), copies of both documents in possession of the author. The San Diego County Water Authority participated in the talks but, as a member of MWD, it was MWD, not San Diego, that signed the agreement.

199. "Key Terms for Quantification Settlement," sec. 3: Water Budget during the Quantification Period; sec. 3C: Summary of Water Budgets during Quantification Period; Jeffrey Kightlinger, senior deputy counsel, MWD, to the author, Nov. 1 and 4, 1999; Dennis B. Underwood, executive assistant to the general manager, MWD, to the author, Nov. 5, 1999.

200. Ibid. For the quote, see "Key Terms for Quantification Settlement," sec. 5: Quantification Period, pt. B, Extension.

201. "Key Terms for Quantification Settlement," exhibit A: Surplus Criteria for Management of the Colorado River; *San Diego Union-Tribune,* Dec. 13, 1999.

202. "Key Terms for Quantification Settlement"; *North County Times* (Escondido), Oct. 20, 1999 ("a road map . . ."; "In effect . . .").

203. U.S. Department of the Interior, *News Release* (July 27, 2000); U.S. Bureau of Reclamation, *News Release* Aug. 4, 2000; *Federal Register,* 65 (Aug. 8, 2000): 48531–48538, (Sept. 22, 2000): 57371; Jan Matusak, MWD, to the author, July 31, Aug. 9, 2000; *Los Angeles Times,* Dec. 18, 1999 ("For the first time . . ."); *San Diego Union-Tribune,* July 26, 27, 2000 ("There's a sense . . ."); *Las Vegas Sun,* July 26, 2000; *New York Times,* July 28, 2000; *Ventura County Star,* Aug. 3, 2000.

204. *Las Vegas Review-Journal,* June 28, July 26, 2000 ("Those are serious issues . . ."); Michelle Nijhuis, "A River Resurrected: The Colorado River Delta Gets a Second Chance," *High Country News* 32 (July 3, 2000): 1, 10–13; *Los Angeles Times,* June 29, 2000; *San Bernardino County Sun,* June 29, 2000; *Riverside Press-Enterprise,* June 29, 2000.

205. Interview with Jeanine Jones, principal engineer, California Department of Water Resources, Jan. 21, 1999; California Department of Water Resources, *Bulletin 160–98,* chap. 3, pp. 57–59.

206. It should be noted that the volume of MWD water con-

served and transferred under the arrangement with Imperial Irrigation District varies and can exceed the minimum of 100,000 acrefeet. In 2000, for example, it amounted to 109,460 acre-feet. The agreements mentioned in this paragraph between MWD and the two San Joaquin Valley water districts were with Semitropic Water Storage District (1994) and Arvin-Edison Water Storage District (1997). "Agreement Between the Metropolitan Water District of Southern California and Semitropic Water Storage District and Its Improvement Districts for a Metropolitan-Semitropic Water Banking and Exchange Program" (Dec. 12, 1994); "Agreement between Arvin-Edison Water Storage District and the Metropolitan Water District of Southern California for a Water Management Program" (Dec. 19, 1997); George Little, project manager, resources procurement branch, MWD, to the author, Feb. 9 and 11, 1999; Jan Matusak, principal engineer, planning and resources division, MWD, to the author, June 16 and 20, 2000; Dirk Marks, principal engineer, State Water Project branch, MWD, to the author, June 21, 2000; Imperial Irrigation District and Metropolitan Water District of Southern California, "Agreement for the Implementation of a Water Conservation Program and Use of Conserved Water" (Dec. 22, 1988); Metropolitan Water District of Southern California and Imperial Irrigation District, "Water Conservation Agreement Between the Metropolitan Water District of Southern California and Imperial Irrigation District" (Dec. 19, 1989), copies of the above agreements and correspondence in possession of the author; California Department of Water Resources, *Bulletin 160–98,* chap. 3, pp. 57–59; U.S. Department of the Interior, Palo Verde Irrigation District, Metropolitan Water District of Southern California, Imperial Irrigation District, and Coachella Valley Water District, "Agreement for the Implementation of a Test Land Fallowing Program and Use of Saved Water" (May 22, 1992), copy in the possession of the author; Metropolitan Water District of Southern California and U.S. Bureau of Land Management, *Draft Environmental Impact Report/Environmental Impact Statement: Cadiz Groundwater Storage and Dry-Year Supply Program, San Bernardino County, California* (Los Angeles: Metropolitan Water District of Southern California, Nov. 1999); Metropolitan Water District of Southern California, *The Metropolitan Water District of Southern California Water Revenue Bonds, 1999 Authorization, Series A* (Los Angeles: Metropolitan Water District of Southern California, Nov. 2, 1999; *Fresno Bee,* June 26, 2000.

207. There were more bills dealing with the Central Valley Proj-

ect than those of Seymour and Miller-Bradley. Some preceded and accompanied these two, and on occasion, Bradley and Miller each had their own individual bills. Boronkay and Quinn, "Passage of the Central Valley Project Improvement Act, 1991–1992: The Metropolitan Water District Perspective," 33–38, 62–111; Daniel P. Beard, "Passage of the Central Valley Project Improvement Act, 1991–1992: The Role of George Miller" (Regional Oral History Office, Bancroft Library, University of California, Berkeley, 1995), 21 (first two quotes), 29 (third quote). Seymour's bill also authorized water transfers, but Boronkay believed that the support for the Miller-Bradley measure coming from businesses and environmentalists (for example, Bank of America, Transamerica, Share the Water, Save San Francisco Bay Association, Environmental Defense Fund, Natural Resources Defense Council) gave it a better chance of passage. Richard K. Golb, "Passage of the Central Valley Project Improvement Act, 1991–1992: The Role of John Seymour" (Regional Oral History Office, Bancroft Library, University of California, Berkeley, 1996), 25–27, 43–44; Beard, "Passage of the Central Valley Project Improvement Act, 1991–1992: The Role of George Miller," 21–23, 29; Carl Boronkay and Warren J. Abbott, "Water Conflicts in the Western United States," *Studies in Conflict and Terrorism* 20 (1997): 144; Thomas J. Graff and David R. Yardas, "Passage of the Central Valley Project Improvement Act, 1991–1992: Environmental Defense Fund Perspective" (Regional Oral History Office, Bancroft Library, University of California, Berkeley, 1994), 65, passim; Barry Nelson, "Passage of the Central Valley Project Improvement Act, 1991–1992: Executive Director, Save San Francisco Bay Association" (Regional Oral History Office, Bancroft Library, University of California, Berkeley, 1993), 9–13, 69–70. For an inside view of agriculture's attempt to defeat the Miller-Bradley Bill, see Jason Peltier, "Passage of the Central Valley Project Improvement Act, 1991–1992: Manager, Central Valley Project Water Association" (Regional Oral History Office, Bancroft Library, University of California, Berkeley, 1993); and Stuart Somach, "Passage of the Central Valley Project Improvement Act, 1991–1992: The Central Valley Project Water Association Perspective" (Regional Oral History Office, Bancroft Library, University of California, Berkeley, 1998).

208. *Reclamation Projects Authorization and Adjustment Act of 1992,* U.S. Statutes at Large 106 (Oct. 10, 1992): 4706; *Central Valley Project Improvement Act,* ibid., 4706, secs. 3401–3412; *Cong. Rec.,* 102 Cong.,

2 sess. (Oct. 5, 1992), 138, pt. 3: H11572–H11625; "Reclamation Projects Authorization and Adjustment Act of 1992," *H. Doc. 102-1016,* 102 Cong., 2 sess. (Oct. 5, 1992): U.S. Department of the Interior, Bureau of Reclamation, *Central Valley Project Improvement Act: Draft Programmatic Environmental Impact Statement,* 9 vols. (Sacramento: U.S. Government Printing Office, Sept. 1997); U.S. Department of the Interior, Bureau of Reclamation, *Central Valley Project Improvement Act: Supplement to the Draft Programmatic Environmental Impact Statement* (Sacramento: U.S. Government Printing Office, June 1999); *Los Angeles Times,* Oct. 9 and Nov. 3, 1992; *Washington Post,* Nov. 3, 1992; *New York Times,* Oct. 13, 1992.

209. U.S. Department of the Interior, Bureau of Reclamation, *Central Valley Project Improvement Act: Final Programmatic Environmental Impact Statement* (Sacramento: U.S. Government Printing Office, Oct. 1999); U.S. Department of the Interior, Bureau of Reclamation, *Central Valley Project, California: Interim Renewal Contract* (Sacramento: U.S. Bureau of Reclamation, June 21, 1994, to Nov. 3, 1999), 32 ("effective water conservation . . ."); California Department of Water Resources, *Bulletin 160–98,* chap. 2, pp. 8–11; Sue McClurg, "Central Valley Project Improvement Act Update," *Western Water* (Jan.–Feb. 2000): pp. 4–13.

210. U.S. Department of the Interior, Bureau of Reclamation, *Central Valley Project, California: Draft of Long-Term Renewal Contract* (Sacramento: U.S. Bureau of Reclamation, Nov. 2, 1992), 32 ("an effective water . . ."); interview with Sam Cervantes, public involvement specialist, U.S. Bureau of Reclamation, Feb. 15, 2000; U.S. Bureau of Reclamation, *News Release: Preliminary Water Allocation,* Jan. 21, 2000; *San Diego Union-Tribune,* Jan. 21, 2000 ("Make no mistake . . .").

211. James Snow, assistant to the general manager, Westlands Water District, to Harry Schueller, chief, Division of Water Rights, State Water Resources Control Board, Aug. 4, 2000; Westlands Water District, "Application to Appropriate Water" (Aug. 4, 2000), copies of the preceding items in possession of the author; California Water Code, sections 10505 and 11460; *Bakersfield Californian,* Aug. 8, 2000 ("It is nothing short . . .").

212. McClurg, "Central Valley Project Improvement Act Update," 4 ("operations plan . . ."), 14; U.S. Bureau of Reclamation, *News Release: Bureau of Reclamation Announces Initial Water Allocations for Water Year 2000,* Feb. 17, 2000; Westlands Water District, *News*

Release, Feb. 17, 2000 ("The additional actions . . ."); *San Francisco Examiner,* Feb. 18, 2000 ("using public money . . ."); *Sacramento Bee,* Feb. 18, 2000.

213. *Los Angeles Times,* Oct. 31, 1992.

214. MWD General Manager to MWD Board of Directors, Oct. 20, 1993, copy in Water Resources Center Archives, University of California, Berkeley; Boronkay and Quinn, "Passage of the Central Valley Project Improvement Act, 1991–1992: The Metropolitan Water District Perspective," 123–125; *Los Angeles Times,* July 3, 1994 (quotes); U.S. Bureau of Reclamation, "Summary: Transfer of Central Valley Project Water Pursuant to Section 3405(a) of the Central Valley Project Improvement Act" (April 29, 1998), copy in possession of the author; interview with S. Gale Heffler-Scott, water transfer manager, U.S. Bureau of Reclamation, Sacramento Office, April 28, 1998.

215. Bureau of Reclamation, "Summary: Transfer of Central Valley Project Water"; *Los Angeles Times,* July 3, 1994 (quote).

216. Bureau of Reclamation, "Summary: Transfer of Central Valley Project Water"; MWD General Manager to MWD Board of Directors, Sept. 30, 1997; Brian Thomas, MWD, to the author, Aug. 26, 1998; Boronkay and Quinn, "Passage of the Central Valley Project Improvement Act, 1991–1992: The Metropolitan Water District Perspective," 125–126, 132–133; *Los Angeles Times,* July 29, 1997.

217. *Los Angeles Times,* July 29, 1997.

218. MWD General Manager to MWD Board of Directors, Nov. 21, 1997 (quotes), copy in possession of the author; *Los Angeles Times,* Dec. 13, 1997.

219. MWD General Manager to MWD Board of Directors, Nov. 21, 1997; Gordon E. Little, project manager, resources procurement branch, MWD, to the author, Dec. 9 and 10, 1998; Dirk Reed, principal engineer and manager, resources procurement, planning and resources division, MWD, to the author, Nov. 12 and Dec. 10, 1998.

220. It should be noted that the agreements called for an additional cost to MWD of about $25 an acre-foot to transport its SWP water to the Arvin-Edison area. "Agreement between Arvin-Edison Water Storage District and the Metropolitan Water District of Southern California for a Water Management Program" (Dec. 19, 1997). Dirk Reed, MWD, to the author, Nov. 12, 1998; Gordon E. Little, MWD, to the author, Dec. 10 and 14, 1998; Jeffrey Kightlinger,

MWD, to the author, Oct. 11, 1999; interview with S. Gale Heffler-Scott, Bureau of Reclamation, Jan. 20, 1999; Boronkay and Quinn, "Passage of the Central Valley Project Improvement Act, 1991–1992: The Metropolitan Water District Perspective," 134–137 (Arvin-Edison quote, 134; Quinn quote, 135).

221. Metropolitan Water District of Southern California, *Direct Line,* Dec. 16, 1999.

222. Brian Thomas, MWD, to the author, Aug. 26, 1998.

223. The Monterey Agreement also aided urban areas by requiring agricultural contractors to permanently transfer "on a willing buyer–willing seller basis" 130,000 acre-feet of their water to urban areas and it benefited all contractors by restructuring the SWP debt so as to significantly reduce charges to users. The Monterey Agreement was followed in 1995 by a Monterey Amendment, a revision of the contracts for SWP water. "The Monterey Agreement—Statement of Principles" (Dec. 1, 1994), copy in possession of the author; David Sandino, senior staff counsel, Office of the Chief Counsel, California Department of Water Resources, to the author, Feb. 14, 1999; *Los Angeles Times,* Sept. 24, 1989, Feb. 24, Mar. 5, 8, and 11, 1991.

224. Interview with Donna Tegelman, specialist for water rights, contracts, and acreage limitation, Central Valley Project, Bureau of Reclamation, Feb. 17, 1999 ("flexible policy," "health and safety," "earlier and bigger"). The Central Valley Project Improvement Act stipulated that "nothing" in the legislation "shall require the [Interior] Secretary to operate the project in a way that jeopardizes "human health or safety." *U.S. Statutes at Large* 106 (Oct. 10, 1992): 4706, sec. 3406(b). The "two-tier" policy was issued as an interim measure pending completion of CVP water-yield studies and an environmental impact statement. See U.S. Fish and Wildlife Service and U.S. Bureau of Reclamation to "Interested Party" regarding "Central Valley Project Improvement Act Administrative Proposal on Urban Water Supply Reliability," June 9, 1997 (quotes on "two-level" policy), copy in possession of the author. For assistance in correctly understanding the "two-tier" policy, I thank Melvin D. Wallace, water contracts specialist, U.S. Bureau of Reclamation.

225. U.S. Fish and Wildlife Service and U.S. Bureau of Reclamation to "Interested Party," June 9, 1997 (quotes on "second level"); *Sacramento Bee,* Oct. 31, 1999 (There's a knot . . ."); California Department of Water Resources, *News Release,* Aug. 28, 2000 ("develop a . . .").

226. At the present time, Babbitt will not consider proposals for permanent transfers. His explanation: "In recognition of the permanent nature of State allocations established under the Boulder Canyon Project Act, and prudential considerations as well, I will not approve permanent transfers. I will look favorably on transfers of sufficient duration to permit efficiency and stability in arrangements for the use of Colorado River water." Bruce Babbitt, Address to the Colorado River Water Users Association (Dec. 8, 1995), 19, 21 (quote); Babbitt, Address to the Colorado River Water Users Association (Dec. 19, 1996), 7–8.

227. Phillip J. Pace to Bruce Babbitt, Jan. 18, 1999, copy in possession of the author. The 1931 intra-California allocations are popularly known as the Seven Party Agreement. See "Hoover Dam Documents," *H. Doc. 717,* 80 Cong., 2 sess. (2d ed., 1948), app. 1003, pp. A479–A483.

228. Phillip J. Pace to Babbitt, Jan. 25, 1999 (". . . owes a duty . . ."), copy in possession of the author; *Los Angeles Times,* Jan. 22, 1999 (Babbitt's quotes and MWD quote: "standing firm"); Metropolitan Water District of Southern California, "Approaches to Implementing Metropolitan's Policy Regarding Required Volume of Colorado River Water Supplies" (statement drafted on January 6, 1999, and approved by the board on January 12, 1999), copy in possession of the author; *Imperial Valley Press* (El Centro), Jan. 12 and 14, 1999. For MWD backing off from its request for a reallocation of the 1931 apportionments, see Phillip J. Pace, "Water-Use Efficiency: The Key to California's Future."

229. For thoughtful discussions of possible safeguards, see Santos V. Gomez and Anna Steding, *California Water Transfers: An Evaluation of the Economic Framework and a Spatial Analysis of the Potential Impacts* (Oakland: Pacific Institute for Studies in Development, Environment, and Security, Apr. 1998); Pen Loh and Santos V. Gomez, *Water Transfers in California: A Framework for Sustainability and Justice* (Oakland: Pacific Institute for Studies in Development, Environment, and Security, 1996).

230. Valerie C. Kircher, "The Legislative Battle over Preserving Agricultural Land," *California Journal* 7 (May 1976): 155–157; Jerome B. Siebert, "Agriculture: Will the Cornucopia Run Dry?" ibid. 21 (Jan. 1990): 42; American Farmland Trust, *Risks, Challenges and Opportunities: Agriculture, Resources and Growth in a Changing Central Valley* (San Francisco: American Farmland Trust, 1989), 14, passim; Dan Walters, "Punching Holes in the Williamson Act," ibid. 14

(Dec. 1983): 459–461; Robert Lawrence, "Agriculture: Seeds of Change," *Cry California* 11 (Summer 1976): 55–58; John H. Dresslar, "Agricultural Land Preservation in California: Time for a New View," *Ecology Law Quarterly* 8, no. 2 (1979): 303–338; California Department of Food and Agriculture, *California Agriculture: Statistical Review, 1987* (Sacramento: California Department of Food and Agriculture, 1988), 1–3, 9–10; Don Villarejo, *New Lands for Agriculture: The California State Water Project* (Davis: California Institute for Rural Studies, 1981), 9–12.

231. Bruce Babbitt, "Western Water Policy—From Reclamation to Restoration" (Address to Natural Resource Law Center's Program on Western Water Law and Policy, June 8, 1999), 2, copy in possession of the author.

232. John Hart, *Farming on the Edge: Saving Family Farms in Marin County, California* (Berkeley and Los Angeles: University of California Press, 1991).

233. Walters, "Punching Holes in the Williamson Act," 459–461; California Land-Use Task Force, *The California Land: Planning for a People* (Sacramento: Planning and Conservation Foundation, 1975), 47–53; Steven Witt, "The Struggle to Legislate Protection for Agricultural Lands," *California Tomorrow* 18 (Winter 1983): 18–23.

234. Stephen Levy, *California Population Characteristics: What the 1990 Census Will Show, What the Next Decade Will Bring* (Palo Alto, Calif.: Center for Continuing Study of the California Economy, 1990), 2–7; Center for Continuing Study of the California Economy, *California Population Characteristics, 1992 Edition* (Palo Alto, Calif.: Center for Continuing Study of the California Economy, 1992), viii–ix, passim; Center for Continuing Study of the California Economy, *California Economic Growth: 1999 Edition* (Palo Alto, Calif.: Center for Continuing Study of the California Economy, 1999), 1–2 to 4–13; *Cal. Stats.,* chap. 353 (1998); Madelyn Glickfeld and Ned Levine, *Regional Growth . . . Local Reaction: The Enactment and Effects of Local Growth Control and Management Measures in California* (Cambridge, Mass.: Lincoln Institute of Land Policy, 1992), x–xi, 1–9, passim; California Department of Water Resources, *Bulletin 160–98,* chap. 4, pp. 4–7. See also Leon F. Bouvier and Lindsey Grant, *How Many Americans? Population, Immigration, and the Environment* (San Francisco: Sierra Club Books, 1994); Steve H. Murdock, *An America Challenged: Population Change and the Future of the United States* (Boulder, Colo.: Westview Press, 1995).

235. American Farmland Trust, *Alternatives for Future Urban*

Growth in California's Central Valley: The Bottom Line for Agriculture and Taxpayers (Washington, D.C.: American Farmland Trust, Oct. 1995); Yvonne Jacobson, *Passing Farms, Enduring Values* (Los Gatos, Calif.: William Kaufman, Inc., 1984), 233, 236; *Los Angeles Times,* May 29, 1990, Nov. 25, 1991. For the transformation in the Antelope Valley near Los Angeles, see *Los Angeles Times,* July 6, 1990.

236. *Los Angeles Times,* Mar. 1 and 11, Apr. 1 and 11, May 7, 1990; James Kimo Campbell, "The No-Growth Politics of Cutting off Water," *California Journal* 6 (July 1975): 251–252; Jerry Rankin, "Why Santa Barbara Voted No on State Water," ibid., 10 (Oct. 1979): 362–364.

237. City of Santa Barbara, *Newsletter* (Fall 1990); *Los Angeles Times,* Apr. 11, Aug. 13 and 18, 1990, June 6, 1991, Mar. 2, 2000 (quote); *Santa Barbara News-Press,* June 5, 1991, Aug. 27, 2000; City of Santa Barbara, *The City of Santa Barbara Charles Meyer Desalination Facility* (Santa Barbara: Santa Barbara Public Works Department, April 8, 1997); City of Santa Barbara, *The State Water Project as a Component of the City of Santa Barbara Water Supply* (Santa Barbara: Santa Barbara Public Works Department, Jan. 1998).

238. *DeVita v. County of Napa,* 9 Cal.4thSer., 763 (1995); *Los Angeles Times,* Nov. 11, 1995, Nov. 29, 1996, Feb. 7, 1999.

239. Carl Abbott, Deborah Howe, and Sy Adler, *Planning the Oregon Way: A Twenty-Year Evaluation* (Corvallis: Oregon State University Press, 1994); Carl Abbott, "Planning the Oregon Way: A Quarter Century of Growth Management," *Renewable Resources Journal* 16 (Autumn 1998): 14–19; C. Robert Steringer and Kurt Wanless, "Symposium on Oregon Land Use: The Twenty-Fifth Anniversary of SB 100—Introduction," *University of Oregon Law Review* 77 (Fall 1998): 807–844; Gerrit Knaap and Arthur C. Nelson, *The Regulated Landscape: Lessons on State Land Use Planning from Oregon* (Cambridge, Mass.: Lincoln Institute of Land Policy, 1992); Carl Abbott, *Portland: Planning, Politics, and Growth in a Twentieth-Century City* (Lincoln: University of Nebraska Press, 1983), 257–258, passim; Richard Lacayo, "The Brawl over Sprawl," *Time* 153 (Mar. 22, 1999): 45–48; Andres Duany, Elizabeth Plater-Zyberk, and Jeff Speck, *Suburban Nation: The Rise and Sprawl and the Decline of the American Dream* (San Francisco: North Point Press, 2000).

240. *Los Angeles Times,* Dec. 27, 1998.

241. Lynne Plambeck, "Los Angeles County's Last Unchannel-

ized River—The Santa Clara," *Headwaters* (Winter 1999); 8–9; *Los Angeles Times,* Nov. 23, 1998; ibid. (Ventura County Edition), Feb. 16, 25, 27, Mar. 3, 4, and 29, 2000; *San Francisco Examiner,* Jan. 3, 1999.

242. *Los Angeles Times,* Nov. 23, 1998 ("There's a history . . ."), Mar. 29, 1999; ibid. (Ventura County Edition), Feb. 16, 25, 27, Mar. 3 ("serious adverse . . .") and 4; ibid. (Los Angeles County Edition) June 2 ("Shrinking the project . . ."; "At first blush . . ."), June 3 ("Now they could . . ."), Aug. 30, 2000; *San Francisco Examiner,* Jan. 3, 1999; Newhall Land and Farming Company, *Company Press Release: Newhall Ranch Ruling Received,* June 1, 2000.

243. *Cal. Stats.,* chap. 881, sec. 65302 (1995); *California Assembly Bill 1219* (as amended May 16, 2000); *Los Angeles Times,* June 6, Aug. 14, Sept. 19, 1995, Jan. 6, June 18 and 19, 2000; *San Diego Union-Tribune,* Jan. 13, 2000; *Inland Valley Daily Bulletin* (Ontario), June 28, 2000; *Wall Street Journal,* July 20, 2000.

244. American Farmland Trust, *Alternatives for Future Urban Growth in California's Central Valley,* passim; *Los Angeles Times,* Oct. 29, 1995 (quote); Steven C. Blank, a U.C. Davis economist, predicts that "the production of food and other agricultural products will disappear from the United States because it will become unprofitable to tie up resources into farming and ranching." Blank, *The End of Agriculture in the American Portfolio* (Westport, Conn.: Quorum Books, 1998). More hopeful but worried are American Farmland Trust, *The Central Valley's New Towns: Destiny or Disaster* (Davis, Calif.: American Farmland Trust, Jan. 1995); Council for Agricultural Science and Technology, *Future of Irrigated Agriculture* (Ames, Iowa: Council for Agricultural Science and Technology, 1996); National Research Council, *A New Era for Irrigation* (Washington, D.C.: National Academy Press, 1996); Alvin D. Sokolow, *Farmland Policy in California's Central Valley: State, County, and City Roles* (Berkeley: California Policy Seminar, 1997); *Report of the Agricultural Task Force for Resource Conservation and Economic Growth in the Central Valley* (Sacramento: California Farm Bureau Federation, 1998).

245. *Planning and Conservation League* v. *Department of Water Resources* (Sept. 15, 2000, SO [Slip Opinion] CO24576, Cal. App. 3d [typed opinion]); *Sacramento Bee,* Sept. 19, 2000 ("institutional mirage").

246. Marc Reisner, *Water Policy and Farmland Protection: A New Approach to Saving California's Best Agricultural Lands* (Washington,

D.C.: American Farmland Trust, 1997); David Carle, *Drowning the Dream: California's Water Choices at the Millennium* (Westport, Conn.: Praeger, 2000), 179–180.

247. *Santa Barbara News-Press,* Apr. 11, 1999 (Reisner quote); *Sacramento Bee,* Apr. 11, 1999, July 28, 2000; *Los Angeles Times,* July 25, 2000; *San Francisco Chronicle,* Aug. 6, 2000.

248. California Department of Water Resources, *Bulletin 160–98,* chap. 1, p. 2, chap. 3, pp. 7, 48–51; *Bulletin 160–93,* 1: 5–7; *Bulletin 160–87,* 31–34.

249. *Katz* v. *Walkinshaw,* 141 Cal. 116 (1903).

250. *Pasadena* v. *Alhambra,* 33 Cal.2d 905 (1949).

251. *Cal. Stats.,* chap. 1361 (1951); chap. 1690 (1953); *Barstow* v. *Mojave Water Agency* (Aug. 21, 2000, SO [Slip Opinion] 71728, Cal. 4th [typed opinion, p. 25, note 13 {quote}]).

252. Governor's Commission to Review California Water Rights Law, *Final Report* (Sacramento: Governor's Commission to Review California Water Rights Law, Dec. 1978), 136; Harrison C. Dunning, a U.C. Davis law professor and member of the commission, to the author, May 27, 1998; California Department of Water Resources, *Bulletin 160–98,* chap. 3, pp. 70–72; California Water Resources Control Board and California Department of Water Resources, "Policies and Goals for California Water Management," 38, 48–49; Samuel E. Wood, "Putting It All in One Bucket," *Cry California* 12 (Fall 1977): 17–20; Gary Weatherford, Kim Malcolm, and Barbara Andrews, "California Groundwater Management: The Sacred and the Profane," *Natural Resources Journal* 22 (Oct. 1982): 1031–1043; Blomquist, *Dividing the Waters;* David J. Guy and Jennifer Cordua, "Conjunctive Use from the Ground Up: The Need to Protect Landowners' Rights to Ground Water," in DeVries and Woled, eds., *Ground Water and Future Supply,* 139–147; Carl Hague, "Ground Water Management in California," ibid., 179–185; William Blomquist, "Political or Hydrologic Management," ibid., 187–193; CALFED Bay-Delta Program, *California's Water Future,* 14–16; *Chico Enterprise-Record,* June 21, 2000; *Redding Record Searchlight,* June 21, 2000.

253. Gerald D. Bowden, Stahrl W. Edmunds, and Norris C. Hundley, jr., "Institutions: Customs, Laws and Organizations," in Ernest A. Engelbert and Ann Foley Scheuring, eds., *Competition for California Water: Alternative Resolutions* (Berkeley and Los Angeles: University of California Press, 1982), 170–171; Donald Pisani, "Wa-

ter Law Reform in California, 1900–1913," *Agricultural History* 54 (Apr. 1980): 295–317.

254. *Cal. Stats.,* chap. 1112, sec. 2 (1979) and chap. 933 (1980); *California Water Code,* sec. 1011(a) (1979) and sec. 1010 (1980).

255. David Sandino, California Department of Water Resources, to the author, Sept. 4, 1998.

256. *California Water Code,* sec. 10505 (1931).

257. *Cal. Stats.,* chap. 1762, sec. 12937 (1959); David Sandino, DWR, to the author, Sept. 14, 1998, Oct. 6, 2000; Harrison C. Dunning, U.C. Davis School of Law, to the author, Sept. 5 and 9, 2000; Harold E. Rogers and Alan H. Nichols, *Water for California: Planning, Law and Practice, Finance,* 2 vols. (San Francisco: Bancroft-Whitney, 1967) 1: 115–117 (quote, p. 116). See also Andrew H. Sawyer, "Area of Origin: Protection for Local Needs in Ground Water Management," in DeVries and Woled, eds., *Ground Water and Future Supply,* 173–177.

258. *California Water Code,* sec. 11460 (1933); *Cal. Stats.,* chap. 1042 (1933); Rogers and Nichols, *Water for California,* 116–117. For a careful analysis of the watershed-protection and county-of-origin provisions, see *California Attorney General's Opinions,* 25 (1955): 8; ibid., 29 (1957): 136.

259. *California Water Code,* sec. 12201 (1959).

260. Ibid., secs. 1215–1222 (1984).

261. *Arizona* v. *California et al.,* 373 U.S. 596, 598–601 (1963); *Winters* v. *United States,* 207 U.S. 564 (1908); Norris Hundley, jr., "The Dark and Bloody Ground of Indian Water Rights: Confusion Elevated to Principle," *Western Historical Quarterly* 9 (Oct. 1978): 455–482; Hundley, "The 'Winters' Decision and Indian Water Rights: A Mystery Reexamined," ibid. 13 (Jan. 1982): 17–42. For the meaning of the federal reserved rights doctrine as it applies to the national forests, see *United States* v. *New Mexico,* 438 U.S. 696 (1978).

262. John Hart, "One System, Many Masters," *Cry California* 12 (Fall 1977): 2–10; Charles E. Phelps, Nancy Y. Moore, and Morlie H. Graubard, *Efficient Water Use in California: Water Rights, Water Districts, and Water Transfers* (Santa Monica: Rand, 1978); Goodall, Sullivan, and De Young, *California Water,* 4–16; James Jamieson, Sidney Sonenblum, Werner Z. Hirsch, Merrill R. Goodall, and Harold Jaffee, *Some Political and Economic Aspects of Managing California Water Dis-*

tricts (Los Angeles: UCLA Institute of Government and Public Affairs, 1974), 9–25.

263. *United States* v. *State Water Resources Control Board,* 182 Cal.App.3d 82 (1986); *California* v. *Federal Energy Regulatory Commission,* 110 S.Ct. 2024 (1990); *Los Angeles Times,* Sept. 19, 1986, June 7, 1989, May 2, 1990. See also Doris O. Dawdy, *Congress in Its Wisdom: The Bureau of Reclamation and the Public Interest* (Boulder, Colo.: Westview Press, 1989); and Ronald B. Robie, "The Delta Decisions—The Quiet Revolution in California Water Rights," *Pacific Law Journal* 19 (1988): 1111–1142.

264. Jamieson et al., *Some Political and Economic Aspects,* 14–15, 41–42, 97–183 (the quotation is on p. 183); California Department of Water Resources, "Interim Statewide Alpha Listing of Water Service Agencies" (Mar. 1989), copy in California Department of Water Resources Archives. See also Robert Gottlieb and Margaret Fitz-Simmons, *Thirst for Growth: Water Agencies as Hidden Government in California* (Tucson: University of Arizona Press, 1991); Blomquist, "Political or Hydrologic Management," in DeVries and Woled, eds., *Ground Water and Future Supply,* 187–193; Hague, "Ground Water Management in California," ibid., 179–185; David L. Martin, "California Water Politics: The Search for Local Control" (Ph.D. dissertation, Claremont Graduate School, 1973); Patricia L. Ballard, ". . . And Conflict Shall Prevail: Reclamation Law, Water Districts, and Politics in the Kings River Service Area of California—An Alternative Framework for Analysis" (M.A. thesis, University of California, Los Angeles, 1980), 53–83.

265. Upper Colorado River Basin Compact (Oct. 11, 1948), in "Hoover Dam Documents," *H. Doc. 717,* app. 231, p. A174 (quote); Jean S. Breitenstein, "The Upper Colorado River Basin Compact," *State Government* 22 (1949): 214–216, 225.

266. *Arizona* v. *California,* 373 U.S. 564, 565 (1963).

267. For a sampling of the paper trail, see Western Water Policy Review Advisory Commission, *Water in the West: Challenge for the Next Century* (Springfield, Va.: National Technical Information Service, June 1998); Western Water Policy Review Advisory Commission, *Indian Water—1997, Trends and Directions in Federal Water Policy: A Summary of the Conference Proceedings, March 1997,* by Todd Olinger (Springfield, Va.: National Technical Information Service, 1997); Water Education Foundation, *75th Anniversary: Colorado River Compact—Symposium Proceedings* (Sacramento: Water Education Foun-

dation, May 1997); Grand Canyon Trust, *Proceedings Report: The Colorado River Workshop, February 26–28, 1996—Issues, Ideas, and Directions* (Phoenix, Ariz.: Grand Canyon Trust, 1996); D. D. Fort, V. L. Gabin, and E. Pinnes, *Managing Groundwater Quality and Quantity in the Western States—A Report to the Environmental Protection Agency* (San Francisco: Natural Heritage Institute, 1993); Interagency Floodplain Management Committee, *Sharing the Challenge: Floodplain Management into the 21st Century* (Washington, D.C.: Government Printing Office, 1994); Committee to Review the Glen Canyon Environmental Studies, *Colorado River Ecology and Dam Management: Proceedings of a Symposium, May 24–25, 1990, Santa Fe, New Mexico* (Washington, D.C.: National Academy Press, 1991); Committee on Restoration of Aquatic Ecosystems, *Restoration of Aquatic Ecosystems: Science, Technology, and Public Policy* (Washington, D.C.: National Academy Press, 1992); Committee on Groundwater Recharge, *Groundwater Recharge Using Waters of Impaired Quality* (Washington, D.C.: National Academy Press, 1994); Western Governors' Association, *White Paper on Federal Water Policy Coordination* (Denver: Western Governors' Association, 1989); Western Governors' Association, *Resolution 96-012: Open Space* (Denver: Western Governors' Association, 1996); Western States Water Council, *Settlement of Indian Reserved Water Rights Claims: Proceedings of a Symposium, Portland, Oregon, September 6–8, 1995* (Midvale, Utah: Western States Water Council, 1995); Western States Water Council, *Water Policy and Growth Management* (Denver: Western Governors' Association, 1995).

268. Donald Worster, *Rivers of Empire: Water, Aridity, and the Growth of the American West* (New York: Pantheon, 1985), 7, 331–335.

269. Peter Berg and Raymond Dasmann, "Reinhabiting California," *Not Man Apart* 7 (Mid-Sept., 1977): 6–7.

270. Edward Belcher, *Narrative of a Voyage Round the World, Performed in Her Majesty's Ship Sulphur during the Years 1836–1842,* 2 vols. (London: Henry Colburn, 1843), 2: 123, 124.

271. Francisco Palóu, *Historical Memoirs of New California,* ed. Herbert E. Bolton, 4 vols. (Berkeley: University of California Press, 1926), 2: 256–257.

272. René Dubos, *The Wooing of Earth* (New York: Charles Scribner's Sons, 1980), xiv, 159; see also Dubos, *A God Within* (New York: Charles Scribner's Sons, 1972); Dubos, *The Resilience of Ecosystems* (Boulder: Colorado Associated University Press, 1978); Martin Krieger, "What's Wrong with Plastic Trees," *Science* 179 (Feb. 2,

1973): 446–454; Eric Jubler, "Let's Open Up Our Wilderness Areas," *Reader's Digest* 100 (May 1972): 125–128; Jubler, "The Wilderness: Just How Wild Should It Be?" *Trends* 9 (1972): 15–18.

273. Wendell Berry, *The Unsettling of America: Culture & Agriculture* (San Francisco: Sierra Club, 1977), 30–38, 218–223, passim.

274. Roderick Nash, *Wilderness and the American Mind,* 3d ed. (New Haven: Yale University Press, 1982), 380, 381, 388; see also Nash, *The Rights of Nature: A History of Environmental Ethics* (Madison: University of Wisconsin Press, 1989).

275. Paul R. Ehrlich and Anne H. Ehrlich, "Population, Plenty, and Poverty," *National Geographic* 174 (Dec. 1988): 916; *Los Angeles Times,* July 27, 1999. See also Bouvier and Grant, *How Many Americans.*

Chapter 8: Reflections

1. U.S. Department of Commerce, Bureau of the Census, *Statistical Abstract of the United States, 1999* (Washington, D.C.: Government Printing Office, 1999), 28, 355, 682, 841. The nations with economies larger than that of California as of 1997, the year for which the latest data were available at the time of publication, were the United States ($7.783 trillion), Japan ($4.182 trillion), Germany ($2.321 trillion), France ($1.542 trillion), the United Kingdom ($1.231 trillion), Italy ($1.160 trillion), and China ($1.055 trillion). California's gross state product in 1997 was $1.033 trillion. Ibid., 841; California Department of Finance, *California Statistical Abstract, 1999* (Sacramento: California Department of Finance, Dec. 1999), 211.

2. Frequently, the practice has been to denigrate agriculture's economic importance by contrasting its enormous appetite for water with its small contribution to the state's gross product—about 2 percent of a nearly $1 trillion economy. Forgotten in such a comparison is that agriculture is among the state's biggest industries and, if you include linked industries (processing and so forth), accounts for $76 billion annually (increasing its share of the state's economy to 7.9 percent) and for more than a half million jobs. Harold O. Carter and George Goldman, *The Measure of California Agriculture: Its Impact on the State Economy,* rev. ed. (Oakland: University of California Division of Agriculture and Natural Resources, 1998), 44–45, 54–55, passim.

Note that the percentage given in the text for current agricultural water use (77) is derived from figures different from those employed by the California Department of Water Resources (DWR). DWR states that agricultural water use is 33.8 million acre-feet and that of urban areas is 8.8 million acre-feet. These figures are too high. The agricultural estimate refers to water *applied* to crops and does not account for return flow to a stream that is available for use by others downriver, while the urban figure does not take into consideration water that is reclaimed and then recycled for further use. Such adjustments result in 28 million acre-feet of agricultural water use and 8.5 million acre-feet for cities. The figure for agriculture comes from studies conducted by Henry Vaux, Jr., a University of California resource economist (Vaux to the author, March 12, 1999). On "new recycled water" (323,000 acre-feet or approximately 0.3 million acre-feet), see California Department of Water Resources, "California Water Plan Update," *Bulletin 160–98: Executive Summary* (Sacramento: California Department of Water Resources, Nov. 1998), chap. 3, p. ES3-9; and interview with Susan Tatayon, manager, water recycling, California Department of Water Resources, April 14, 1999.

3. California Department of Water Resources, "California Water: Looking to the Future," *Bulletin 160–87* (Sacramento: California Department of Water Resources, Nov. 1987), 16; Henry Vaux, Jr., and Richard Howitt, "Managing Water Scarcity: An Evaluation of Interregional Transfers," *Water Resources Research* 20 (1984): 785–792; *Los Angeles Times,* Oct. 16, 1990 (quotation), Jan. 16, 1999; Henry Vaux, Jr., to the author, March 26, 1998. As agricultural water use (and acreage) declined during the 1980s and early 1990s, the value of farm productivity increased by 34 percent "as growers abandoned marginal land, employed the most modern irrigation technologies, and switched to higher-valued crops." Council for Agricultural Science and Technology, *Future of Irrigated Agriculture* (Ames, Iowa: Council for Agriculture and Technology, 1996), 37. See also Richard E. Howitt, "Effects of Water Marketing on the Farm Economy," in Harold O. Carter, Henry J. Vaux, Jr., and Ann F. Scheuring, eds., *Sharing Scarcity: Gainers & Losers in Water Marketing* (Davis: University of California Agricultural Issues Center, 1994), 97–132; Richard E. Howitt and Henry J. Vaux, Jr., "Competing Demands for California's Scarce Water," in A. Dinar and E. T. Loehman, eds., *Water Quantity/Quality Management and Conflict Resolution* (Westport, Conn.: Praeger Publishers, 1995), 271–287.

4. California Department of Water Resources, *Bulletin 160–98,*

chap. 1, pp. 2–5, chap. 3, pp. 1–2, 12–13, 48–51; University of California Water Resources Center, *California Water,* no. 4 (Fall 1990); William L. Kahrl, ed., *The California Water Atlas* (Sacramento: California Governor's Office of Planning and Research, 1979), v; Bruce Babbitt, "Western Water Policy—From Reclamation to Restoration" (Address at the Natural Resources Center's Program on Western Water Law and Policy, June 3, 1999), 3, copy in possession of the author.

5. Henry Vaux, Jr., to the author, March 8, 1999.

6. Babbitt, "Western Water Policy," 2.

7. Kahrl, ed., *California Water Atlas,* 77; Rasa Gustaitis, "Water Conservation: The Untapped Well," *Cry California* 16 (Summer 1981): 85–89; *Los Angeles Times,* Apr. 1 and 30, 1990; Barry Tuller, Los Angeles Department of Water and Power, to the author, Oct. 21, 1993.

8. *Los Angeles Times,* Feb. 2, 1988 (quote), Dec. 24, 1989, Apr. 1, 1990.

9. *San Francisco Examiner,* Mar. 11, 1990; *Los Angeles Times,* Feb. 2, 1988, Apr. 1, 1990.

10. California Department of Water Resources, "Urban Water Use in California," *Bulletin 166–44* (Sacramento: California Department of Water Resources, Aug. 1994), pp. A-100, A-102, A-113, A-125; William Ferguson, water supply planner, Santa Barbara Public Works Department, to the author, Feb. 18, 1988. A 1991 study conducted by the Metropolitan Water District of more than 2,900 people scattered across southern California concluded: "Household income is the best single indicator of household water use. People earning higher incomes use more water." Metropolitan Water District of Southern California, *Focus,* no. 1 (1991): 5.

11. California Department of Water Resources, *Bulletin 166–44,* pp. A-100, A-113, A-125; Ferguson to the author, Feb. 18, 1998; *Los Angeles Times,* June 13, July 10, 14, and 25, Aug. 17 and 22, Sept. 4 and 5, 1990.

12. Quoted in Dan Gordan, "Low Water Marks," *Challenge: Research at UCLA, 1996* (Los Angeles: Office of the UCLA Vice Chancellor for Research, 1966), 9.

13. Based on their past research, Berk and Schulman believe that the rate of adoption they found was "too high by perhaps 15 percent," thus suggesting a more reliable and conservative rate of 42.5 percent which is still remarkable. Richard Berk and Daniel Schulman, "Managing the Demand for Water by Subsidizing the Purchase of Water-Efficient Technology" (Feb. 1998), 31, 32, copy in posses-

sion of the author; see also Berk, "Water Conservation," in Richard Berk and Arthur M. Winer, eds., *Southern California Environmental Report Card [1998]* (Los Angeles: UCLA Institute of the Environment, 1998), 10–15.

14. California Department of Water Resources, *Bulletin 160–98,* chap. 10, p. 4.

15. California Department of Water Resources, *Bulletin 160–98: Executive Summary,* chap. 3, p. ES3-9; *Bulletin 160–98,* chap. 6, p. 34; interview with Lynn Johnson, chief, Office of Water Recycling, California Water Resources Control Board, July 22, 1998; interview with Susan Tatayon, California Department of Water Resources, April 15, 1999.

16. Los Angeles Department of Water and Power, *Urban Water Management Plan for the City of Los Angeles* (Los Angeles: Los Angeles Department of Water and Power, Nov. 1995), chap. 1, p. 1 ("efficient use . . ."); Los Angeles Department of Water and Power, Water Resources and Planning Business Unit, *Urban Water Management Plan: Fiscal Year 1997–1998 Annual Update* (Los Angeles: Los Angeles Department of Water and Power, 1998); Los Angeles Department of Water and Power, "Water Conservation Programs" (July 1, 1999), copy in possession of the author; Stephen A. Ott, waterworks engineer, water recycling group, Los Angeles Department of Water and Power, to the author, Sept. 29, 1999; *Los Angeles Times,* June 15 ("The Department of Water and Power . . ."), Dec. 24, 1999.

17. Phillip J. Pace, "Dividing the Water: A Colorado Plan That Ensures California's Future," *Metropolitan Water District of Southern California Aqueduct* 65, no. 2 (1999): 5; Ott to the author, Oct. 4, 1999; Metropolitan Water District of Southern California, *Southern California's Integrated Water Resources Plan—Report 1107* (Los Angeles: Metropolitan Water District of Southern California, March 1996); *Los Angeles Times,* June 15, 1999; *Imperial Valley Press* (El Centro), Sept. 6, 1999.

18. Barry Nelson, "The Passage of the Central Valley Project Improvement Act, 1991–1992: Executive Director, Save San Francisco Bay Association" (Regional Oral History Office, Bancroft Library, University of California, Berkeley, 1993), 72–73.

Bibliography

The items found in the bibliography proved especially valuable in preparing this book but they do not represent all the sources consulted (interviews, solicited opinions, and legal briefs, for example, appear only in the relevant notes) and are just an approximation of the vast array of materials available on the complex and controversial topics touched on in this account. The scores of manuscript and other source materials obtained from individuals, public agencies, and private groups and identified in the notes as "in possession of the author" will be deposited in the Manuscripts Division, Department of Special Collections, Young Research Library, University of California, Los Angeles.

Archival Materials and Selected Unpublished Papers

Abbott, Warren J. "'Myth vs. Reality': Agricultural Subsidies and the State Water Project." Los Angeles: Metropolitan Water District of Southern California, photocopy, Jan. 21, 1986. (Copy in possession of the author.)

Adams, Frank. Adams Papers. University of California Water Resources Center Archives, Berkeley.

Bartell, Max J. Bartell Papers. University of California Water Resources Center Archives, Berkeley.

Berk, Richard, and Daniel Schulman. "Managing the Demand for Water by Subsidizing the Purchase of Water-Efficient Technology." Feb. 1998. (Copy in possession of the author.)

Brody, Ralph M. Brody Papers. University of California Water Resources Center Archives, Berkeley.

Brown, Edmund G., Sr. Brown Papers. Bancroft Library, University of California, Berkeley.

California Archives. Bancroft Library, University of California, Berkeley.

California Department of Water Resources. "Annual Precipitation for California since 1600 Reconstructed from Western North American Tree Rings," by Harold C. Fritts and Geoffrey A. Gordon. July 1980. (Copy in S-9, item 3981, California Department of Water Resources Archives, Sacramento.)

California Department of Water Resources Archives, Sacramento.

California Governors and California State Agencies. Papers. California State Archives, Sacramento.

California Land Grant Papers. Bancroft Library, University of California, Berkeley.

Gianelli, William R. Gianelli Papers. University of California Water Resources Center Archives, Berkeley.

Goyne, Paul. "Developing the Empire of Tomorrow: The California Farm Bureau Federation, the California State Grange, and the Central Valley Project, 1933–1952." 1998. (Copy in possession of the author.)

Harding, S. T. Harding Papers. University of California Water Resources Center Archives, Berkeley.

Hoover, Herbert. Hoover Papers. Hoover Presidential Library, West Branch, Iowa.

Hyatt, Edward. Hyatt Papers. University of California Water Resources Center Archives, Berkeley.

Imperial Irrigation District Papers. Imperial, California.

Koenig & Dorsey. "Research Report on the Bass Brothers: Confidential." 1997. (Copy in possession of the author.)

Los Angeles Ayuntamiento Records. Los Angeles City Archives.

Los Angeles Common Council Records. Los Angeles City Archives.

Manson, Marsden. Manson Papers. Bancroft Library, University of California, Berkeley.

Means, Thomas H. Means Papers. University of California Water Resources Center Archives, Berkeley.

Miller, Henry. "Autobiographical Statement." 1891. Bancroft Library, University of California, Berkeley.

Robie, Ronald R. Robie Papers. University of California Water Resources Center Archives, Berkeley.

Storper, Michael. "Subsidies in the State Water Project: A Reply to the MWD." Los Angeles: photocopy, 1986. (Copy in possession of the author.)

Tays, George. "Transcriptions and Translations of Original Documents Relating to Ranchos in Los Angeles County." 3 vols., 1939. (Typescript in Bancroft Library, University of California, Berkeley.)

United States Bureau of Reclamation Papers. Record Group 115. National Archives.

United States Department of State Papers. Record Group 59. National Archives.

Warne, William E. Warne Papers. University of California Water Resources Center Archives, Berkeley.

Warren, Earl. Warren Papers. California State Archives, Sacramento.

Oral Histories

Adams, Frank. "Frank Adams, University of California, on Irrigation, Reclamation, and Water Administration." Regional Oral History Office, Bancroft Library, University of California, Berkeley, 1959.

Banks, Harvey O. "California Water Project, 1955–1961." Regional Oral History Office, Bancroft Library, University of California, Berkeley, 1967.

Beard, Daniel P. "Passage of the Central Valley Project Improvement Act, 1991–1992: The Role of George Miller." Regional Oral History Office, Bancroft Library, University of California, Berkeley, 1995.

Bodovitz, Joseph E., Melvin B. Lane, and E. Clement Shute, Jr. "The San Francisco Bay Conservation and Development Commission, 1964–1973." Regional Oral History Office, Bancroft Library, University of California, Berkeley, 1984.

Bonderson, Paul R. "Executive Officer, Regional and State Water Pollution and Water Quality Control Boards, 1950–1966." Regional Oral History Office, Bancroft Library, University of California, Berkeley, 1980.

Boronkay, Carl, and Timothy H. Quinn. "The Passage of the Central Valley Project Improvement Act, 1991–1992: The Metropolitan Water District Perspective." Regional Oral History Office, Bancroft Library, University of California, Berkeley, 1997.

Brody, Ralph M. "Revising Legislation and Building Public Support for the California Water Project, 1959–1960; Brief History of the Westlands Water District." Regional Oral History Office, Bancroft Library, University of California, Berkeley, 1981.

Brown, Edmund G., Sr. "The California Water Project: Personal Interest and Involvement in the Legislation, Public Support, and Construction, 1950–1966." Regional Oral History Office, Bancroft Library, University of California, Berkeley, 1981.

Bunshoft, Barry, Esther Gulick, Catherine Kerr, and Sylvia McLaughlin. "Save San Francisco Bay Association, 1961–1986." Regional Oral History Office, Bancroft Library, University of California, Berkeley, 1985–1986.

Gianelli, William R. "The California State Department of Water Resources, 1967–1973." Regional Oral History Office, Bancroft Library, University of California, Berkeley, 1986.

Golb, Richard K. "Passage of the Central Valley Project Improvement Act, 1991–1992: The Role of John Seymour." Regional Oral History Office, Bancroft Library, University of California, Berkeley, 1996.

Graff, Thomas J., and David R. Yardas. "Passage of the Central Valley Project Improvement Act, 1991–1992: Environmental Defense Fund Perspective." Regional Oral History Office, Bancroft Library, University of California, Berkeley, 1994.

Harding, Sidney T. "A Life in Western Water Development." Regional Oral History Office, Bancroft Library, University of California, Berkeley, 1967.

Hatfield, Paul A. "The Hatfield Brothers, Rainmakers." Oral History Program, University of California, Los Angeles, 1972.

Hedgpeth, Joel W. "Marine Biologist and Environmentalist: Pycnogonids, Progress, and Preserving Bays, Salmon, and Other Living Things." Regional Oral History Office, Bancroft Library, University of California, Berkeley, 1992.

Hotchkis, Preston, Sr. "One Man's Dynamic Role in California Politics and Water Development, and World Affairs." Regional Oral History Office, Bancroft Library, University of California, Berkeley, 1980.

Jennings, William H. "William H. Jennings, Water Lawyer." Oral History Program, University of California, Los Angeles, 1967.

Jensen, Joseph. "Developing California's Natural Resources." Oral History Program, University of California, Los Angeles, 1970.

Leopold, Luna B. "Hydrology, Geomorphology, and Environmental Policy: U.S. Geological Survey, 1950–1972, and U.C. Berkeley, 1972–1987." Regional Oral History Office, Bancroft Library, University of California, Berkeley, 1990–1991.

McLean, Walter R. "From Pardee to Buckhorn: Water Resources Engineering and Water Policy in the East Bay Municipal Utility District, 1927–1991." Regional Oral History Office, Bancroft Library, University of California, Berkeley, 1995.

Nelson, Barry. "Passage of the Central Valley Project Improvement Act, 1991–1992: Executive Director, Save San Francisco Bay Association." Regional Oral History Office, Bancroft Library, University of California, Berkeley, 1993.

Nelson, Samuel B. "Water for Los Angeles." Oral History Program, University of California, Los Angeles, 1988.

Peltier, Jason. "Passage of the Central Valley Project Improvement Act, 1991–1992: Manager, Central Valley Project Water Association." Regional Oral History Office, Bancroft Library, University of California, Berkeley, 1993.

Raines, Harold. "Water Rights on the Mokelumne River and Legal Issues at the East Bay Municipal Utility District, 1927–1966." Regional Oral History Office, Bancroft Library, University of California, Berkeley, 1995.

Reilly, John B. "Water Rights and Legal Issues at the East Bay Municipal Utility District, 1951–1983." Regional Oral History Office, Bancroft Library, University of California, Berkeley, 1995–1996.

Robie, Ronald B. "The State Department of Water Resources,

1975–1983." Regional Oral History Office, Bancroft Library, University of California, Berkeley, 1988.

Skinner, Robert A. "Progress of the Metropolitan Water District: Recollections." Oral History Program, University of California, Los Angeles, 1970.

Somach, Stuart. "Passage of the Central Valley Project Improvement Act, 1991–1992: The Central Valley Project Water Association Perspective." Regional Oral History Office, Bancroft Library, University of California, Berkeley, 1998.

Warne, William E. "Administration of the Department of Water Resources, 1961–1966." Regional Oral History Office, Bancroft Library, University of California, Berkeley, 1981.

Newspapers and Periodicals

Alameda Times-Star

American Society of Civil Engineers Transactions

Arizona Republican (Phoenix); after 1930, *Arizona Republic*

Audubon

Bakersfield Californian

Bond Buyer

California Water (University of California Water Resources Center)

Chico Enterprise-Record

Commonwealth

Contra Costa Times (Walnut Creek)

Desert Sun (Palm Springs)

El Universal (México, D.F.)

Engineering News-Record

Fresno Bee

Glendale News-Press

Harper's

Healdsburg Tribune

Hemet Press-Enterprise

Imperial Valley Press (El Centro)

Inland Valley Daily Bulletin (Ontario)

Inyo Register (Bishop)

Journal Commerce Review (Los Angeles)

Kern County Californian

Las Vegas Review-Journal

Las Vegas Sun

Long Beach Press-Telegram

Los Angeles Daily News

Los Angeles Examiner

Los Angeles Herald

Los Angeles Times

Malibu Surfside News

Malibu Times

Modesto Bee

Money Magazine

National Geographic

New York Times

Newsletter (City of Santa Barbara)

North County Times (Escondido)

Oakland Tribune

Orange County Register (Santa Ana)

Oroville Mercury

Owens Valley Water Reporter (Inyo County Water Department)

Pacific Builder and Engineer

Pasadena Star News

Philadelphia Inquirer

Political Pulse Newsletter

Redding Record Searchlight

Riverside Press-Enterprise

Sacramento Bee

Sacramento Record-Union

Sacramento Union

Salt Lake Tribune

San Bernardino Sun

San Diego Business Journal

San Diego Daily Transcript

San Diego Union

San Diego Union-Tribune

San Francisco Bulletin

San Francisco Chronicle

San Francisco Examiner

San Gabriel Valley Daily Tribune

San Jose Mercury News

Santa Ana Register

Santa Barbara News-Press

Smithsonian

Sports Illustrated

Stockton Daily Independent

Time

Ventura County Star

Wall Street Journal

Washington Post

Western Construction News

Western Water

Court Cases

Arizona v. *California et al.,* 373 U.S. 564 (1963).

Barstow v. *Mojave Water Agency* (Aug. 21, 2000, SO [Slip Opinion] 71728, Cal. 4th [typed opinion])

California v. *Federal Energy Regulatory Commission,* 110 S.Ct. 2024 (1990).

California v. *United States,* 438 U.S. 645 (1978).

California Trout, Inc. v. *State Water Resources Control Board,* 90 Cal.App.3d 816 (1979).

California Trout, Inc. v. *State Water Resources Control Board,* 207 Cal.App.3d 584 (1989).

Cartwright v. *Public Service Co. of New Mexico,* 66 N. Mex. 64 (1958).

County of Del Norte v. *United States,* 732 F.2d 1462 (9th Cir. 1984); cert. denied, 469 U.S. 1189 (1985).

County of Del Norte v. *United States,* 469 U.S. 1189 (1985).

County of Inyo v. *City of Los Angeles,* 61 Cal.App.3d 91 (1976); 71 Cal.App.3d 185 (1977); 78 Cal.App.3d 82 (1978); 124 Cal.App.3d 1 (1981).

County of Inyo v. *Yorty,* 32 Cal.App.3d 795 (1973).

Crandall v. *Woods,* 8 Cal. 136 (1857).

Davis v. *Gale,* 32 Cal. 26 (1867).

DeVita v. *County of Napa,* 9 Cal.4thSer., 763 (1995).

Eddy v. *Simpson,* 3 Cal. 249 (1853).

Elms v. *Los Angeles,* 58 Cal. 80 (1881).

Feliz v. *Los Angeles,* 58 Cal. 73 (1881).

Ferrea v. *Knipe,* 28 Cal. 340 (1865).

Fullerton v. *State Water Resources Control Board,* 90 Cal.App.3d 590 (1979).

Herminghaus v. *Southern California Edison,* 200 Cal. 81 (1926).

Imperial Irrigation District v. *State Water Resources Control Board,* 186 Cal.App.3d 1160 (1986).

Irwin v. *Phillips,* 5 Cal. 140 (1855).

Ivanhoe v. *McCracken,* 357 U.S. 275 (1958).

Katz v. *Walkinshaw,* 141 Cal. 116 (1903).

Kidd v. *Laird,* 15 Cal. 161 (1860).

Los Angeles v. *Baldwin,* 53 Cal. 469 (1879).

Los Angeles v. *Buffington,* 156 Cal. 603 (1909).

Los Angeles v. *Hunter,* 156 Cal. 603 (1909).

Los Angeles v. *Pomeroy,* 124 Cal. 597 (1899).

Los Angeles v. *San Fernando et al.,* 14 Cal.3d 199 (1975).

Lux v. *Haggin,* 69 Cal. 255 (1886).

National Audubon Society v. *Superior Court of Alpine County,* 33 Cal.3d 419 (1983); cert. denied, 464 U.S. 977 (1983).

Nevada County & Sacramento Canal Co. v. *Kidd,* 37 Cal. 282 (1869).

Pasadena v. *Alhambra,* 33 Cal.2d 905 (1949).

Planning and Conservation League v. *Department of Water Resources* (Sept. 15, 2000, SO [Slip Opinion] CO 24576, Cal. App. 3d [typed opinion])

San Diego v. *Cuyamaca Water Co.,* 209 Cal. 122 (1930).

Union Water Co. v. *Crary,* 25 Cal. 504 (1864).

United States v. *Arizona,* 295 U.S. 174 (1935).

United States v. *New Mexico,* 438 U.S. 696 (1978).

United States v. *California State Water Resources Control Board,* 694 F.2d 1171 (1982).

United States v. *State Water Resources Control Board,* 182 Cal.App.3d 82 (1986).

Vernon Irrigation Co. v. *Los Angeles,* 106 Cal. 237 (1895).

Winters v. *United States,* 207 U.S. 564 (1908).

Woodruff v. *North Bloomfield,* 9 Sawyer 441; 18 F. 753 (1884).

Wyoming v. *Colorado,* 259 U.S. 419 (1922).

Government Publications

ARIZONA

Journal of the House.
Journal of the Senate.

CALIFORNIA

Auditor General. *Report by the Office of the Auditor General to the Joint Legislative Audit Committee: The State Lacks Data Necessary to Determine the Safety of Pesticides.* Sacramento: California Auditor General, Aug. 1984.

Colorado River Board of California. *Annual Reports..*

———. *California's Stake in the Colorado River.* Los Angeles: Colorado River Board of California, various editions.

———. *Executive Director's Monthly Reports.*

Department of Engineering. "Irrigation Districts in California, 1887–1915," by Frank Adams. *Bulletin No. 2.* Sacramento: State Printing Office, 1917.

Department of Finance. *California Statistical Abstracts, 1999.* Sacramento: California Department of Finance, Dec. 1999.

Department of Food and Agriculture. *California Agriculture: Statistical Review, 1987.* Sacramento: California Department of Food and Agriculture, 1988.

———. Office of Pesticide Consultation and Analysis. *Methyl Bromide: An Impact Assessment.* Sacramento: California Department of Food and Agriculture, 1996.

Department of Health Services. *DBCP in Drinking Water: What Does It Mean?* Berkeley: California Department of Health Services, Dec. 1989.

———. *Methyl Bromide (Chemical Name Bromomethane).* Berkeley: California Department of Health Services, 1981.

Department of Justice. *Opinions of the Attorney General of California.*

Department of Parks and Recreation. *California Wetlands: An Element of the California Outdoor Recreation Planning Program.* Sacramento: California Resources Agency, Sept. 1988.

Department of Pesticide Regulation. *Notice of Proposed Changes in the Regulations of the Department of Pesticide Regulation: Methyl Bromide Field Fumigations.* Sacramento: California Department of Pesticide Regulation, 2000.

Department of Public Health. Bureau of Occupational Health. "Methyl Bromide." *Occupational Health Bulletin No. 5* (1945).

———. Bureau of Occupational Health. "Methyl Bromide Poisoning." *Occupational Health Bulletin G* (March 1956).

Department of Public Works. Division of Engineering and Irrigation. "Irrigation Districts in California," by Frank Adams. *Bulletin No. 21.* Sacramento: California Department of Public Works, 1929.

————. Division of Water Resources. "Report to Legislature of 1931 on State Water Plan." *Bulletin No. 25.* Sacramento: State Printing Office, 1930.

————. Division of Water Resources. "South Coastal Basin Investigation: Geology and Ground Water Storage Capacity of Valley Fill." *Bulletin No. 45.* Sacramento: State Printing Office, 1934.

Department of Water Resources. "California State Water Project." Vol. 1: "History, Planning, and Early Progress." *Bulletin 200.* Sacramento: California Resources Agency, Nov. 1974.

————. "The California State Water Project—Current Activities and Future Management Plans." *Bulletin 132–80.* Sacramento: California Resources Agency, Oct. 1980.

————. "The California State Water Project—Current Activities and Future Management Plans." *Bulletin 132–81.* Sacramento: California Resources Agency, Nov. 1981.

————. "The California State Water Project—Current Activities and Future Management Plans." *Bulletin 132–82.* Sacramento: California Resources Agency, Nov. 1982.

————. "The California State Water Project in 1974." *Bulletin No. 132–74.* Sacramento: California Department of Water Resources, June 1974.

————. "The California State Water Project—1978 Activities and Future Management Plans." *Bulletin 132–79.* Sacramento: California Resources Agency, Nov. 1979.

————. "California Water: Looking to the Future." *Bulletin 160–87.* Sacramento: California Department of Water Resources, Nov. 1987.

————. "California Water Plan Update." *Bulletin 160–93.* 2 vols. Sacramento: California Department of Water Resources, Oct. 1994.

————. "California Water Plan Update." *Bulletin 160–98.* Sacramento: California Department of Water Resources, Nov. 1998.

————. "California Water Plan Update." *Bulletin 160–98: Executive Summary.* Sacramento: California Department of Water Resources, Nov. 1998.

————. "Delta Levees Investigation." *Bulletin 192–82*. Sacramento: California Department of Water Resources, Dec. 1982.

————. "Delta Water Facilities." *Bulletin 76*. Sacramento: California Resources Agency, July 1978.

————. *Department of Water Resources Position on Proposition 9 (SB 200)—Delta Protection, Peripheral Canal and Other Facilities.* Sacramento: California Resources Agency, Apr. 1982.

————. *Discovering and Rediscovering the Fragility of Levees and Land in the Sacramento–San Joaquin Delta, 1870–1879 and Today,* by John Thompson. Sacramento: California Resources Agency, Mar. 1982.

————. "General Comparison of Water District Acts." *Bulletin 155–94*. Sacramento: California Department of Water Resources, Mar. 1994.

————. "Ground Water Basins in California." *Bulletin 118–80*. Sacramento: California Department of Water Resources, Jan. 1980.

————. "Management of the California State Water Project, 1972." *Bulletin 132–72*. Sacramento: California Resources Agency, 1972.

————. "Management of the California State Water Project." *Bulletin 132–83*. Sacramento: California Resources Agency, Nov. 1983.

————. "Management of the California State Water Project." *Bulletin 132–87*. Sacramento: California Department of Water Resources, Sept. 1987.

————. "Management of the California State Water Project." *Bulletin 132–89*. Sacramento: California Department of Water Resources, Sept. 1989.

————. *The Peripheral Canal of the Sacramento–San Joaquin Delta.* Sacramento: California Resources Agency, Dec. 1966.

————. *Report of Interagency Task Force on Mono Lake.* Sacramento: California Department of Water Resources, Dec. 1979.

————. "Urban Water Use in California." *Bulletin 166–4*. Sacramento: California Department of Water Resources, Aug. 1994.

————. "Water Conservation in California." *Bulletin 198.* Sacramento: California Resources Agency, May 1976.

Department of Water Resources and Department of Fish and Game. "Selenium Behavior in the Sacramento–San Joaquin Estuary, California," by Gregory A. Cutter. *Technical Report 18.* Sacramento: California Department of Water Resources, Sept. 1988.

Department of Water Resources and Water Resources Control Board. "Policies and Goals for California Water Management: The Next 20 Years—Public Review Draft." *DWR/ SWRCB Bulletin 4.* Sacramento: California Department of Water Resources, June 1981.

Economic Development Agency. *California Statistical Abstract, 1961.* Sacramento: State Printing Office, 1961.

Energy Commission. *The Impacts of Global Warming on California.* Sacramento: California Energy Commission, June 1989.

Environmental Protection Agency. Department of Pesticide Regulation. *Review of Restrictions on the Use of Methyl Bromide: A Report to the Legislature.* Sacramento: California Environmental Protection Agency, 1996.

Governor's Commission to Review California Water Rights Law. *Final Report.* Sacramento: Governor's Commission to Review California Water Rights Law, Dec. 1978.

Hazard Evaluation and Information Service. *Methyl Bromide.* Berkeley: California Hazard Evaluation and Information Service, 1990.

Interagency Delta Committee. *Plan of Development: Sacramento– San Joaquin Delta.* Sacramento: Interagency Delta Committee, Jan. 1965.

Journal of the Assembly.

Journal of the Senate.

Public Resources Code.

Secretary of State. *Statement of the Vote of California at the Special Election Held December 19, 1933, on Referendum Measure.* Sacramento: State Printing Office, 1934.

———. *Statement of Vote: General Election, 1960.* Sacramento: State Printing Office, 1960.

———. *Statement of Vote: General Election, November 5, 1974.* Sacramento: State Printing Office, 1974.

———. *Statement of Vote: General Election, November 4, 1980.* Sacramento: State Printing Office, 1980.

———. *Statement of Vote: Primary Election, June 8, 1982.* Sacramento: State Printing Office, 1982.

State Mineralogist. *Second Report of the State Mineralogist of California.* Sacramento: State Printing Office, 1882.

Statutes.

Water Code.

Water Quality Control Board. "Useful Waters for California." *Publication No. 37.* Sacramento: California Water Quality Control Board, 1967.

Water Resources Board. *Report on Feasibility of Feather River Project and Sacramento–San Joaquin Delta Diversion Projects Proposed as Features of the California Water Plan.* Sacramento: California Department of Public Works, May 1951.

———. "Water Resources of California." *Bulletin No. 1.* Sacramento: State Printing Office, 1951.

———. "Water Utilization and Requirements of California." *Bulletin No. 2.* 2 vols. Sacramento: California Water Resources Board, June 1955.

———. Water Resources Control Board. *Decision 1422.* Sacramento: California Water Resources Control Board, Apr. 4, 1973.

———. *Kesterson Reservoir Closure and Cleanup Plan.* Sacramento: California Water Resources Control Board, 1985.

———. *Nitrate in Drinking Water: Report to the Legislature.* Sacramento: California Water Resources Control Board, 1988.

———. *Significance of Pesticides from Irrigated Agriculture in California.* Sacramento: California Water Resources Control Board, Sept. 1979.

———. *Toward Clean Water: A Progress Report for 1974 and 1975.* Sacramento: California Water Resources Control Board, n.d.

———. Environmental Protection Agency. *1996 California Water Quality Assessment Report.* Sacramento: California Water Resources Control Board, Jan. 1997.

———. Toxic Substances Control Program. *1, 2-Dichloropropane (1, 2-D) 1, 3-Dichloropropene (1, 3-D),* by David B. Cohen et al. Sacramento: California Water Resources Control Board, Aug. 1983.

———. Toxic Substances Control Program. *Water Quality and Pesticides: A California Risk Assessment Program,* by David B. Cohen and Gerald W. Bowes. Sacramento: California Water Resources Control Board, Dec. 1984.

——— and California Coastal Commission. *California's Nonpoint Source Management Plan.* 2 vols. Sacramento: California Water Resources Control Board, 1999.

CALIFORNIA AND THE UNITED STATES

CALFED Bay-Delta Program. *Commonly Asked Questions about the CALFED Bay-Delta Program.* Sacramento: CALFED Bay-Delta Program, 1998.

———. *Developing a Draft Preferred Program Alternative.* Sacramento: CALFED Bay-Delta Program, Aug. 5, 1998.

———. *Draft Preferred Program Alternative: 30-Year Policy Framework.* Sacramento: CALFED Bay-Delta Program, Aug. 14, 1998.

———. *Draft Programmatic Environmental Impact Statement/ Environmental Impact Report.* Sacramento: CALFED Bay-Delta Program, Mar. 1998.

———. *Draft Programmatic Environmental Impact Statement/ Environmental Impact Report: Long-Term Levee Protection Plan.* Sacramento: CALFED Bay-Delta Program, Mar. 1998.

———. *Executive Summary: Draft Programmatic Environmental Impact Statement/Environmental Impact Report.* Sacramento: CALFED Bay-Delta Program, Mar. 1998.

———. *Facility Descriptions and Updated Cost Estimates for Millerton Lake Enlargement.* Sacramento: CALFED Bay-Delta Program, Oct. 1997.

————. *Facility Descriptions and Updated Cost Estimates for Shasta Lake Enlargement.* Sacramento: CALFED Bay-Delta Program, Oct. 1997.

————. *News* (various issues).

————. *Program Goals and Objectives: Draft Programmatic EIS/EIR.* Sacramento: CALFED Bay-Delta Program, Mar. 1998.

————. *Revised Phase II Report.* Sacramento: CALFED Bay-Delta Program, Dec. 18, 1998.

————. *Revised Phase II Report: Draft Programmatic EIS/EIR Technical Appendix.* Sacramento: CALFED Bay-Delta Program, June 1999.

————. Storage and Refinement Team. *Facility Descriptions and Updated Cost Estimates for Los Vaqueros Reservoir Enlargement.* Sacramento: CALFED Bay-Delta Program, Oct. 1997.

LOS ANGELES

Aqueduct Investigation Board. *Report of the Aqueduct Investigation Board to the City Council of Los Angeles.* Los Angeles: Los Angeles City Council, Aug. 31, 1912. (Copy in the library of the Los Angeles Department of Water and Power.)

Board of Water Commissioners. *Third Annual Report.* Los Angeles: Geo. Rice & Sons, n.d.

Charter of the City of Los Angeles as Adopted January, 1889 and Amended January, 1903. Los Angeles: Southern California Printing Co., 1903.

City Council. *Report on the Los Angeles Aqueduct: After an Investigation Authorized by the City Council of Los Angeles,* by Edward Johnson and Edward S. Cobb. Los Angeles: Los Angeles City Council, July 15, 1912.

Department of Public Service. *Complete Report on Construction of the Los Angeles Aqueduct.* Los Angeles: Los Angeles Department of Public Service, 1916.

Department of Public Works. *First Annual Report of the Chief Engineer of the Los Angeles Aqueduct to the Board of Public Works.* Los Angeles: Los Angeles Department of Public Works, Mar. 15, 1907.

———. Bureau of the Los Angeles Aqueduct. *Sixth Annual Report of the Bureau of the Los Angeles Aqueduct to the Board of Public Works.* Los Angeles: Department of Public Works, 1911.

———. Bureau of Sanitation. *City San: Hyperion Treatment Plant.* Los Angeles: Los Angeles Department of Public Works, 1998.

Department of Water and Power. *Urban Water Management Plan for the City of Los Angeles.* Los Angeles: Los Angeles Department of Water and Power, Nov. 1995.

———. *Water and Power Facts.* Los Angeles: Los Angeles Department of Water and Power, 1971.

———. *Water and Power for a Great City: A History of the Department of Water and Power of the City of Los Angeles to December 1950.* By J. Gregg Layne. Los Angeles: Los Angeles Department of Water and Power, 1952.

———. Water Resources and Planning Business Unit. *Urban Water Management Plan: Annual Updates.*

LOS ANGELES COUNTY

Board of Engineers. Flood Control. *A Report on Floods, River Phenomena and Rainfall in the Los Angeles Region, California,* by J. W. Reagan. Los Angeles: Los Angeles County Board of Engineers, 1939.

———. Flood Control. *Reports of the Board of Engineers, Flood Control, to the Board of Supervisors, Los Angeles County, California.* Los Angeles: Los Angeles County Board of Engineers, 1915.

Flood Control District. *Flood of March 2, 1938,* by M. F. Burke. Los Angeles: Los Angeles County Flood Control District, May 20, 1938.

METROPOLITAN WATER DISTRICT OF SOUTHERN CALIFORNIA

Metropolitan Water District of Southern California. *Annual Reports.*

———. *Aqueduct* (various issues).

———. *Direct Line* (various issues).

———. *Focus* (various issues).

———. *History and First Annual Report.* Los Angeles: Metropolitan Water District of Southern California, 1939.

―――. *The Metropolitan Water District of Southern California Water Revenue Bonds, 1999 Authorization, Series A.* Los Angeles: Metropolitan Water District of Southern California, Nov. 2, 1999.

―――. *Southern California's Integrated Water Resources Plan—Report No. 1107.* Los Angeles: Metropolitan Water District of Southern California, Mar. 1996.

―――. *Wheeling: Gearing for the Future of Water Marketing.* Los Angeles: Metropolitan Water District of Southern California, Feb. 1997.

―――― and U.S. Bureau of Land Management. *Draft Environmental Impact Report/Environmental Impact Statement: Cadiz Groundwater Storage and Dry-Year Supply Program, San Bernardino County, California.* Los Angeles: Metropolitan Water District of Southern California, Nov. 1999.

SAN FRANCISCO

City and County. *San Francisco Water & Power: A History of the Municipal Water Department and Hetch Hetchy System.* San Francisco: City and County of San Francisco, 1985.

City and County Board of Supervisors. *Proceedings Had in Board of Supervisors and Reports of Engineer in the Matter of Furnishing Water Supplies for the City and County of San Francisco.* San Francisco: Spaulding & Barto, 1875.

―――. *Reports on the Water Supply of San Francisco, California, 1900 to 1908.* San Francisco: Britton & Ray, 1908.

Public Utilities Commission. *San Francisco Water: Report of the City and County of San Francisco to the State Water Resources Control Board.* San Francisco: Public Utilities Commission of the City and County of San Francisco, 1987.

UNITED STATES

Army Corps of Engineers. Los Angeles District. *Los Angeles County Drainage Area Review: Final Feasibility Study, Interim Report, and Environmental Impact Statement.* Los Angeles: U.S. Army Corps of Engineers, Los Angeles District, Dec. 1991.

―――. Northwestern Division. *Columbia River Fish Mitigation:*

Lower Snake River Reservoir Drawdown Studies. Portland, Ore.: U.S. Army Corps of Engineers, Aug. 1998.

———. Walla Walla District. *Lower Snake River Juvenile Salmon Migration Feasibility Study: Natural River Drawdown.* Walla Walla, Wash.: U.S. Army Corps of Engineers, Oct. 1998.

Comptroller General. *Congress Should Reevaluate the 160-Acre Limitation on Land Eligible to Receive Water from Federal Water Resources Projects.* Washington, D.C.: Comptroller General of the United States, 1972.

Congress. *Congressional Quarterly Fact Sheet.*

———. *Congressional Record.*

———. House of Representatives. Documents and Reports:

55 Cong., 2 sess. *H. Doc. 141.* 1897.

63 Cong., 1 sess. "Hetch Hetchy Valley: Report of Advisory Board of Army Engineers to the Secretary of the Interior on Investigations Relative to Sources of Water Supply for San Francisco and Bay Communities." *H. Doc. 54.* Feb. 19, 1913.

80 Cong., 2 sess. "Hoover Dam Documents." *H. Doc. 717.* 1948.

84 Cong., 2 sess. "Central Valley Project Documents, Part One." *H. Doc. 416.* 1956.

85 Cong., 1 sess. "Central Valley Project Documents, Part Two." *H. Doc. 246.* 1957.

89 Cong., 2 sess. "A Unified National Program for Managing Flood Losses." *H. Doc. 465.* Aug. 10, 1966.

102 Cong., 2 sess. "Reclamation Projects Authorization and Adjustment Act of 1992." *H. Doc. 102–1016.* Oct. 5, 1992.

———. House of Representatives. Hearings:

Committee on Agriculture. Subcommittee on Forestry, Resource Conservation, and Research. *Hearings on Review of the Phaseout of Methyl Bromide.* 105 Cong., 2 sess., 1998.

Committee on Interior and Insular Affairs. *Hearings on Amendment to the Wild and Scenic Rivers Act by Designating Certain Segments of the Stanislaus River in California as a*

Component of the National Wild and Scenic River System.
H.R. 4223. 96 Cong., 1 sess., 1979.

———. *Hearings on the Central Arizona Project. H.R. 1500 and
H.R. 1501.* 82 Cong., 1 sess., 1951.

———. *Hearings on Colorado River Basin Salinity Control. HR.
12165.* 93 Cong., 2 sess., 1974.

Committee on Irrigation of Arid Lands. *Hearings on All-
American Canal in Imperial and Coachella Valleys, Calif.,
H.R. 6044 and H.R. 11553.* 66 Cong., 1919.

———. *Hearings on All-American Canal in Imperial County,
Calif., H.R. 6044.* 66 Cong., 1 sess., 1919.

Committee on Irrigation and Reclamation. *Hearings on Protection and Development of Lower Colorado River Basin, H.R.
2903.* 68 Cong., 1 sess., 1924.

Committee on Public Lands. *Hearings on Hetch Hetchy Dam
Site, H.R. 6281.* 63 Cong., 1 sess., 1913.

Congress. Senate. Documents and Reports:

57 Cong., 1 sess. *Doc. 446.* 1902.

60 Cong., 1 sess. "Irrigation in Imperial Valley, California,"
S. Doc. 246. 1908.

67 Cong., 2 sess. "Problems of Imperial Valley and Vicinity,"
S. Doc. 142. 1922.

68 Cong., 1 sess. "Federal Reclamation by Irrigation," *S. Doc.
92.* 1924.

79 Cong., 2 sess. Special Committee to Study Problems of
American Small Business. *Small Business and the Community: A Study in the Central Valley of California on Effects
of Scale of Farm Operations,* by Walter Goldschmidt.
Committee Print 13. 1946.

———. Senate. Hearings:

Committee on Irrigation and Reclamation. *Hearings on Arizona Water Resources, S. Res. 304.* 78 Cong., 2 sess.,
1945.

Committee on Public Lands. *Hearings on Exemption of Certain
Projects from Land-Limitation Provisions of Federal Reclamation Laws, S. Res. 912.* 80 Cong., 1 sess., 1947.

Department of Agriculture. "Replenishment of Ground Water
    Supplies by Artificial Means," by Dean C. Muckel. *Technical
    Bulletin No. 1195.* Washington, D.C.: U.S. Department of
    Agriculture, 1959.

———. *Water Rights Laws in the Nineteen Western States,* by Wells A.
    Hutchins. 3 vols. Washington, D.C.: U.S. Department of
    Agriculture, 1971–1977.

———. Bureau of Agricultural Economics. *Agricultural Land Own-
    ership and Operation in the Southern San Joaquin Valley,* by
    Edwin E. Wilson and Marion Clawson. Berkeley: mimeo.,
    June 1945.

———. Bureau of Agricultural Economics. *History of Legislation and
    Policy Formation of the Central Valley Project,* by Mary Mont-
    gomery and Marion Clawson. Berkeley: U.S. Bureau of Agri-
    cultural Economics, 1946.

———. Weather Bureau. *Climatic Summary of the United States: Sec-
    tion 18—Southern California and Owens Valley.* Washington,
    D.C.: Government Printing Office, 1932.

Department of Commerce. Bureau of the Census. *County and City
    Data Book, 1972.* Washington, D.C.: Government Printing
    Office, 1973.

———. Bureau of the Census. *County Data Book.* Washington,
    D.C.: Government Printing Office, 1947.

———. Bureau of the Census. *Sixteenth Census of the United States:
    1940—Population, vol. 2, Characteristics of the Population.* Wash-
    ington, D.C.: Government Printing Office, 1943.

———. Bureau of the Census. *Statistical Abstract of the United
    States, 1999.* Washington, D.C.: Government Printing Office,
    1999.

———. Bureau of the Census. *U.S. Census of the Population: 1970.*
    Vol. 1, *Characteristics of the Population,* pt. 6, sec. 1, *California.*
    Washington, D.C.: Government Printing Office, 1973.

Department of Health and Human Services. *Teratologic Assessment
    of Butylene Oxide, Styrene Oxide and Methyl Bromide,* by
    Melvin R. Sikov et al. Cincinnati: U.S. Department of Health
    and Human Services, 1981.

Department of the Interior. *Decisions of the Secretary of the Interior.*

————. Bureau of Indian Affairs. Sacramento Land Operations Office. *Multiple Purpose Water Resources Investigation: Owens Valley Region Indian Reservations, California.* Sacramento: U.S. Government Printing Office, June 1976.

————. Bureau of Reclamation. *The Central Valley Project: "It's about Water."* Sacramento: U.S. Bureau of Reclamation, 2000.

————. Bureau of Reclamation. *Central Valley Project, California: Draft of Long-Term Renewal Contract.* Sacramento: U.S. Bureau of Reclamation, Nov. 2, 1999.

————. Bureau of Reclamation. *Central Valley Project, California: Interim Renewal Contract.* Sacramento: U.S. Bureau of Reclamation, June 21, 1994–Nov. 3, 1999.

————. Bureau of Reclamation. *Central Valley Project Improvement Act: Draft Programmatic Environmental Impact Statement.* Sacramento: U.S. Government Printing Office, Sept. 1997.

————. Bureau of Reclamation. *Central Valley Project Improvement Act: Final Programmatic Environmental Impact Statement.* Sacramento: U.S. Government Printing Office, Oct. 1999.

————. Bureau of Reclamation. *Central Valley Project Improvement Act: Supplement to the Draft Programmatic Environmental Impact Statement.* Sacramento: U.S. Government Printing Office, June 1999.

————. Bureau of Reclamation. *Folsom Dam Modification Report: New Outlets Plan.* Sacramento: Bureau of Reclamation, Central California Area Office, Feb. 1998.

————. Bureau of Reclamation. *Guide to the Salton Sea Restoration Project and EIS/EIR.* Washington, D.C.: U.S. Bureau of Reclamation, 2000.

————. Bureau of Reclamation. *The Salton Sea Restoration Project: Opportunities and Challenges.* Washington, D.C.: U.S. Bureau of Reclamation, 1999.

————. Bureau of Reclamation. *Shasta Dam and Reservoir Enlargement: Appraisal Assessment of the Potential for Enlarging Shasta Dam and Reservoir—Draft.* Denver: U.S. Bureau of Reclamation, May 1998.

————. Bureau of Reclamation. *The Story of the Columbia Basin Project.* Washington, D.C. Government Printing Office, 1964.

————. Bureau of Reclamation. California Department of Water Resources. California Water Resources Control Board. *San Joaquin Valley Interagency Drainage Program: Agricultural Drainage and Salt Management in the San Joaquin Valley.* Fresno, Calif.: San Joaquin Valley Interagency Drainage Program, June 1979.

————. Bureau of Reclamation. Mid-Pacific Region. *San Luis Drain, Central Valley Project, California.* Sacramento: U.S. Bureau of Reclamation, 1983.

————. Bureau of Reclamation and Salton Sea Authority. *Draft Figures to Accompany Salton Sea Restoration Project Environmental Impact Statement/Environmental Impact Report.* Boulder City, Nev.: U.S. Bureau of Reclamation, Jan. 2000.

————. Bureau of Reclamation and Salton Sea Authority. *Draft Salton Sea Restoration Project Environmental Impact Statement/ Environmental Impact Report.* Boulder City, Nev.: U.S. Bureau of Reclamation, Jan. 2000.

————. Fish and Wildlife Service. *Saving the Salton Sea: A Research Needs Assessment.* Washington, D.C.: U.S. Fish and Wildlife Service, Oct. 1997.

————. Fish and Wildlife Service. *Wetlands—Losses in the United States, 1780's to 1980's,* by Thomas E. Dahl. Washington, D.C.: U.S. Fish and Wildlife Service, 1990.

————. Geological Survey. "California: Floods and Droughts," by R. A. Hunrichs. *Water-Supply Paper W2375.* Washington, D.C.: U.S. Geological Survey, 1991.

————. Geological Survey. "California Wetland Resources," by G. L. Bertoldi and Walter C. Swain, 127–134. *Water-Supply Paper 2425.* Washington, D.C.: U.S. Geological Survey, 1996.

————. Geological Survey. "A Conceptual Ground-Water-Quality Monitoring Network for San Fernando Valley, California," by James G. Setmire. *Water-Resources Investigations Report 84-4128.* Sacramento: U.S. Geological Survey, 1985.

————. Geological Survey. "Floods of March 1938 in Southern California," by Harold C. Troxell et al. *Water-Supply Paper 844.* Washington, D.C.: U.S. Geological Survey, 1942.

————. Geological Survey. "Ground-Water Conditions in the

Mendota-Huron Area, Fresno and Kings Counties, California." *Water-Supply Paper 1360-G.* Washington, D.C.: Government Printing Office, 1957.

———. Geological Survey. *Nitrate and Pesticides in Groundwater in the Eastern San Joaquin Valley, California,* by Karen R. Burow, Sylvia V. Stork, and Neil M. Dubrovsky. Sacramento: U.S. Geological Survey, 1998.

———. Geological Survey. "Overview of Water Resources in Owens Valley, California." *Water-Resources Investigations Report 86-4357.* Sacramento: U.S. Geological Survey, 1987.

———. Geological Survey. "Urban Sprawl and Flooding in Southern California," by S. E. Rantz. *Geological Survey Circular 601-B.* Washington, D.C.: U.S. Geological Survey, 1970.

———. Geological Survey. "Water Quality in the San Joaquin–Tulare Basins, California, 1992–95," by Neil M. Dubrovsky et al. *Circular 1159.* Denver: U.S. Geological Survey, 1998.

———. Geological Survey. "Water Resources Data: Arizona, Water Year 1981." *Water-Data Report AZ-81-1.* Tucson: U.S. Geological Survey, 1983.

Department of War. Engineer Office. *Flood Control in the Los Angeles County Drainage Area.* Los Angeles: U.S. Engineer Office, 1938.

———. Engineer Office. *Los Angeles County Drainage Area Flood Control,* by Edwin C. Kolton. Los Angeles: U.S. Engineer Office, Sept. 1939.

———. Engineer Office. *Report on Engineering Aspects: Flood of March 1938.* Los Angeles: U.S. Engineer Office, May 1939.

Environmental Protection Agency. *Review of Control Options for Methyl Bromide in Commodity Treatment,* by Glenn DeWolf. Washington, D.C.: U.S. Environmental Protection Agency, 1996.

———. *U.S. Methyl Bromide Phase Out.* Washington, D.C.: U.S. Environmental Protection Agency, 2000.

Federal Register (various issues).

General Accounting Office. *Pesticides: The Phaseout of Methyl Bromide in the United States.* Washington, D.C.: General Accounting Office, 1995.

National Water Commission. *Interstate Water Compacts,* by Jerome C. Muys. Washington, D.C.: Government Printing Office, 1971.

Nuclear Regulatory Commission. Office of Nuclear Material Safety and Safeguards. *Final Technical Evaluation Report for the Proposed Revised Reclamation Plan for the Atlas Corporation Moab Mill.* Washington, D.C.: U.S. Nuclear Regulatory Commission, Mar. 1997.

———. Office of Nuclear Material Safety and Safeguards. *Final Technical Evaluation Report for the Proposed Revised Reclamation Plan for the Atlas Corporation Moab Mill.* 2 vols. and supplement. Washington, D.C.: U.S. Nuclear Regulatory Commission, Apr. 1999.

United States and Mexico, International Boundary and Water Commission. "Flow of the Colorado River and Other Western Boundary Streams and Related Data." *Western Water Bulletin, 1981.* Washington, D.C.: U.S. Department of State, 1991.

United States Section, International Boundary and Water Commission. *Joint Projects of the United States and Mexico through the International Boundary and Water Commission.* N.p., 1982.

Statutes at Large.

Articles, Essays, and Chapters

Abbott, Carl. "Planning the Oregon Way: A Quarter Century of Growth Management." *Renewable Resources Journal* 16 (Autumn 1998): 14–19.

Abbott, Lyman. "Saving the Yosemite Park." *Outlook* 91 (Jan. 30, 1909): 234–236.

Adams, Frank. "The Historical Background of California Agriculture." In *California Agriculture,* ed. Claude B. Hutchison, 1–50. Berkeley and Los Angeles: University of California Press, 1946.

Adams, Robert M., and Thorkild Jacobsen. "Salt and Silt in Ancient Mesopotamian Agriculture." *Science* 128 (Nov. 21, 1958): 1251–1258.

Aginsky, B. W. "Population Control in the Shanel (Pomo) Tribe." *American Sociological Review* 4 (1939): 209–216.

Ambrose, Richard F., and Johannes Feddema. "Wetlands." In *Southern California Environmental Report Card [1998],* eds. Richard Berk and Arthur M. Winer, 26–34. Los Angeles: UCLA Institute of the Environment, 1998.

Anderson, M. Kat, Michael G. Barbour, and Valerie Whitworth. "A World of Balance and Plenty: Land, Plants, Animals, and Humans in a Pre-European California." In *Contested Eden: California Before the Gold Rush,* ed. Ramón A. Gutiérrez and Richard J. Orsi, 12–47. Berkeley: University of California Press, 1997.

Anderson, Walt, and Frank Stead. "The California Water Plan: Onward and Upward." *Cry California* 11 (Summer 1976): 8–13.

Arguimbau, Nicholas. "Water Conservation: L.A. Is Not the Villain, New Developments Are Not the Answer." *Cry California* 14 (Summer 1979): 27–32.

Baker, George L. "Family Farming vs. Land Monopoly: Westlands' Ralph Brody—The $81,500 Public Servant." *California Journal* 7 (Sept. 1976): 293–296.

Baker, George L., and Tom DeVries. "Water." *New West* (June 16, 1980): 35–46.

Barrett, S. A. "Pomo Myths." *Bulletin of the Public Museum of the City of Milwaukee* 14 (Nov. 6, 1933).

Bass, Ron. "The Troubled Waters of Mono Lake." *California Journal* 9 (Oct. 1979): 349–350.

Bateman, Richard D. "Anaheim Was an Oasis in a Wilderness." *Journal of the West* 4 (Jan. 1965): 1–20.

Bates, J. Leonard. "Fulfilling American Democracy: The Conservation Movement, 1907–1921." *Mississippi Valley Historical Review* 44 (June 1957): 29–57.

Beals, Ralph L., and Joseph A. Hester, Jr. "A New Ecological Typology of the California Indians." In *The California Indians: A Source Book,* ed. Robert F. Heizer and M. A. Whipple, 73–83. 2d ed. Berkeley and Los Angeles: University of California Press, 1971.

Bean, Lowell J., and Harry W. Lawton. "Some Explanations for the Rise of Cultural Complexity in Native California with Comments on Proto-Agriculture and Agriculture." In *Patterns* of *Indian Burning in California: Ecology and Ethnohistory,* ed. Henry T. Lewis, v–xlvii. Ramona, Calif.: Ballena Press, 1973.

Beaton, Timothy J. "Breathing New Life into Section 8 of the 1902 Reclamation Act: *California v. United States.*" *University of Colorado Law Review* 50 (Winter 1979): 207–229.

Berg, Peter, and Raymond Dasmann. "Reinhabiting California." *Not Man Apart* 7 (Mid-Sept., 1977): 6–7.

Berk, Richard. "Water Conservation." In *Southern California Environmental Report Card [1998],* ed. Richard Berk and Arthur M. Wincr, 10–15. Los Angeles: UCLA Institute of the Environment, 1998.

Bertram, Bruce M., and David B. Chatfield. "Water Rights of the City of Los Angeles: Power-Politics and the Courts." *San Fernando Valley Law Review* 6 (Spring 1978): 151–194.

Blackburn, Daniel J. "The Farm Bureau's Big Switch on the Big Ditch." *California Journal* 12 (Mar. 1981): 88–92.

Blevins, Melvin L., and John F. Mann, Jr. "Management of Upper Los Angeles River Area (ULARA) Ground Water Contamination." In *Proceedings of the Nineteenth Biennial Conference on Ground Water, September 13–14, 1993, Sacramento, California,* 113–132. Davis: University of California Centers for Water and Wildlife Resources, Dec. 1994.

Blomquist, William. "Political or Hydrologic Management." In *Ground Water and Future Supply: Proceedings of the Twenty-First Biennial Conference on Ground Water, November 15–16, 1997,* 187–193. Davis: University of California Water Resources Center, Nov. 1998.

Book, Steven A. "MTBE and Perchlorate in California Drinking Water." In *Ground Water and Future Supply: Proceedings of the Twenty-First Biennial Conference on Ground Water, September 15–16, 1997,* ed. Johannes DeVries and Jeff Woled, 241–244. Davis: University of California Water Resources Center, Nov. 1998.

Boronkay, Carl, and Warren J. Abbott. "Water Conflicts in the Western United States." *Studies in Conflict and Terrorism* 20 (1997): 137–166.

Botkin, Daniel B. "Global Warming: What It Is, What Is Controversial about It, and What We Might Do in Response to It."

UCLA *Journal of Environmental Law and Policy* 9, no. 2 (1991): 119–142.

Bouey, Paul D. "Population Pressure and Agriculture in Owens Valley." *Journal of California and Great Basin Anthropology* 1 (Summer 1979): 162–170.

Bowden, Gerald D., Stahrl W. Edmunds, and Norris C. Hundley. "Institutions: Customs, Laws and Organizations." In *Competition for California Water: Alternative Resolutions,* ed. Ernest A. Engelbert and Ann Foley Scheuring, 163–182. Berkeley and Los Angeles: University of California Press, 1982.

Breitenstein, Jean S. "The Upper Colorado River Basin Compact." *State Government* 22 (1949): 214–216, 225.

Brody, Ralph M. "Essential Provisions of the Bond Act." *Western Water News* 11 (Sept. 1959): pp. A and D.

———. "Westlands' Brody Replies." *California Journal* 7 (Nov. 1976): 362–392.

Burns, Robert I. "Irrigation Taxes in Early Mudejar Valencia: The Problems of Alfarda." *Speculum* 44 (1969): 560–567.

Campbell, James Kimo. "The No-Growth Politics of Cutting off Water." *California Journal* 6 (July 1975): 251–252.

Cannon, Lou. "The Reagan Years." *California Journal* 5 (Nov. 1974): 360–366.

Carlson, Martin E. "William E. Smythe: Irrigation Crusader." *Journal of the West* 7 (Jan. 1968): 41–47.

Carmichael, Wayne W. "The Toxins of Cyanobacteria." *Scientific American* 270 (Jan. 1994): 78–86.

Carson, Dan. "Water Wars '87: New Bills Revive North-South Struggle." *California Journal* 17 (Aug. 1987): 378–382.

Carter, Luther J. "Auburn Dam: Earthquake Hazards Imperil $1-Billion Project." *Science* 197 (Aug. 12, 1977): 643–644, 646–649.

Chasan, Daniel Jack. "A Matter of Blind Opposition." *Audubon* 82 (Jan. 1980): 98–125.

———. "Mono Lake vs. Los Angeles: A Tug-of-War for Precious Water." *Smithsonian* 11 (Feb. 1981): 42–50.

Clark, Cheryl. "Breaking the Faith—Southern California Dissidents: We Don't Need Northern Water Now." *California Journal* 16 (May 1985): 194–198.

Clements, Kendrick. "Politics and the Park: San Francisco's Fight for Hetch Hetchy, 1908–1913." *Pacific Historical Review* 48 (May 1979): 1185–1215.

Colby, William E. "The Freedom of the Miner and Its Influence on Water Law." In *Legal Essays in Tribute to Orrin Kip McMurray,* ed. Max Radin, 67–84. Berkeley: University of California Press, 1935.

Conniff, Richard. "A Deal That Might Save a Sierra Gem." *Time* 133 (Apr. 3, 1989): 8–11.

Cook, Sherburne F. "Historical Demography." In *California,* vol. 3 of *Handbook of North American Indians,* ed. Robert F. Heizer, 91–98. Washington, D.C.: Smithsonian Institution, 1978.

Cornett, James. "Indians and the Desert Fan Palm." *Masterkey* (1987): 12–17.

Daingerfield, Lawrence H. "Southern California Rain and Flood, February 27 to March 4, 1938." *Monthly Weather Review* 66 (May 1938): 139–143.

Davis, Gil. "Greenhouse California." *Golden State Report* 3 (Mar. 1987): 24–31.

Davis, H. H. "Monitoring and Evaluation of Water Quality under Central Valley Dairy Sites." In *Proceedings of the California Plant and Soil Conference, January 1995,* 158–164. Visalia, Calif.: American Society of Agronomy and California Fertilizer Association, 1995.

Davis, Susan. "That Sinking Feeling." *California* 14 (Dec. 1989): 98, 148–149.

———. "When the Levees Break." *California Waterfront Age* 5 (Fall 1989): 30–39.

Demetracopoulou, Dorothy, and Cora DuBois. "A Study of Wintu Mythology." *Journal of American Folklore* 45 (1932): 375–500.

———. "Wintu Myths." *University of California Publications in American Archaeology and Ethnology* Vol. 28, no. 5. Berkeley: University of California Press, 1931.

Diamond, Jared M. "Archeology: The Environmentalist Myth." *Nature* 324 (Nov. 6, 1986): 19–20.

Dourgarian, James M. "The Peripheral Canal: Environmental Concerns Catch Up with Southern Thirst." *California Journal* 6 (July 1975): 249–250.

Dracup, John, and Donald R. Kendall. "Climate Uncertainty: Implications for Operation of Water Control Systems." In *Managing Water Resources in the West under Conditions of Climate Uncertainty,* comp. Committee on Climate Uncertainty and Water Resources Management, Water Science and Technology Board, Commission on Geosciences, Environment, and Resources, 177–216. Washington, D.C.: National Academy Press, 1991.

Dresslar, John H. "Agricultural Land Preservation in California: Time for a New View." *Ecology Law Quarterly* 8, no. 2 (1979): 303–338.

Dunlap, Lisa. "It's Good to Know What You're Gulping: Bottled Water Is Not Necessarily Better Than Tap, Says a UCR Microbiologist [Marylynn Yates]." *Fiat Lux* (Apr. 2000): 16–17.

Dunning, Harrison C. "A New Front in the Water Wars: Introducing the 'Public Trust' Factor." *California Journal* 14 (May 1983): 189–190.

———. "The Public Right to Use Water in Place." In *Water and Water Rights,* ed. Robert E. Beck. 7 vols. (Charlottesville, Va.: Michie, 1996) 4: pt. VI, 103–113.

———. "The Significance of California's Public Trust Easement for California's Water Rights Law." *U.C. Davis Law Review* 14 (Winter 1980): 357–398.

"Echo Park Controversy Resolved." *Living Wilderness* 20 (Winter-Spring 1955–1956): 23–43.

Ehrlich, Paul R., and Anne H. Ehrlich. "Population, Plenty, and Poverty." *National Geographic* 174 (Dec. 1988): 914–945.

Ely, Lisa L., et al. "A 5000-Year Record of Extreme Floods and Climate Change in the Southwestern United States." *Science* 262 (Oct. 15, 1993): 410–412.

Evans, Steve. "CALFED Pursuing 14 Dam Projects." *Headwaters* (Winter 1999): 10–12.

Evans, Taliesin. "Hydraulic Mining in California." *Century Magazine* 25 (Jan. 1883): 323–338.

Finkle, F. C. "Los Angeles Aqueduct Mistakes." *Journal of Electricity, Power and Gas* 34 (Jan. 9, 1915): 27–28.

———. "Los Angeles' $40,000,000 White Elephant." *Irrigation Age* 30 (May 1915): 201, 202, 216.

Fleming, Donald. "Roots of the New Conservation Movement." *Perspectives in American History* 6 (1972): 7–91.

Foster, Douglas. "The Growing Battle over Pesticides in Drinking Water." *California Journal* 14 (May 1983): 177–179.

Fritts, Harold C., and Geoffrey A. Gordon. "Reconstructed Annual Precipitation for California." In *Climate from Tree Rings,* ed. M. K. Hughes et al., 185–191. Cambridge, Eng.: Cambridge University Press, 1982.

Fritts, Harold C., G. Robert Lofgren, and Geoffrey A. Gordon. "Variations in Climate since 1602 as Reconstructed from Tree Rings." *Quaternary Research* 12 (1979): 18–46.

Gardner, B. Delworth, and Clyde E. Stewart. "Agriculture and Salinity." In *Values and Choices in the Development of the Colorado River Basin,* ed. Dean F. Peterson and A. Berry Crawford, 121–143. Tucson: University of Arizona Press, 1978.

Garr, Daniel. "Villa de Branciforte: Innovation and Adaptation on the Frontier." *The Americas* 35 (July 1978): 95–109.

Gates, Paul W. "California Land Policy and Its Historical Context: The Henry George Era." In *Four Persistent Issues,* ed. Paul Gates et al., 1–24. Berkeley: University of California Institute of Governmental Studies, 1978.

———. "Public Land Disposal in California." In *Agriculture in the Development of the Far West,* ed. James H. Shideler, 158–178. Washington, D.C.: Agricultural History Society, 1975.

Gentilcore, R. Louis. "Missions and Mission Lands of Alta California." *Annals of the Association of American Geographers* 51 (Mar. 1961): 46–72.

———. "Ontario, California, and the Agricultural Boom of the 1880s." *Agricultural History* 34 (Apr. 1960): 77–87.

Georgeson, Duane. "Case Study of Ground Water Contamination in the San Fernando Basin." In *Proceedings: Seventeenth Biennial Conference on Ground Water, September 25–26, 1989, San Diego, California,* 125–128. Riverside: University of California Water Resources Center, Riverside; California Department of Water Resources; and State Water Resources Control Board, May 1990.

Gilbert, Bil. "Is This a Holy Place?" *Sports Illustrated* 58 (May 30, 1983): 76–90.

Gilbert, Jerome B. "Problem Drinkers." *Golden State Report* 2 (Dec. 1986): 34–35.

Goodall, Merrill R., and John D. Sullivan. "Water District Organization: Political Decision Systems." In *California Water Planning and Policy: Selected Issues,* ed. Ernest A. Engelbert, 207–227. Davis: University of California Water Resources Center, Davis, 1979.

Gordan, Dan. "Low Water Marks." In *Challenge: Research at UCLA, 1996,* 9. Los Angeles: Office of the UCLA Vice Chancellor for Research, 1996.

Gordan, Robert. "Poisons in the Fields: The United Farm Workers, Pesticides, and Environmental Politics." *Pacific Historical Review* 68 (Feb. 1999): 51–77.

Graber, David. "Mono Lake Is Dying: Who Cares?" *Cry California* 14 (Summer 1979): 33–36.

Green, Stephen. "Glitches, Gremlins, & Swoap: Staggering Along the Road to Toxic Waste Reform in California." *California Journal* 16 (Sept. 1985): 344–348.

Gressley, Gene. "Arthur Powell Davis, Reclamation, and the West." *Agricultural History* 42 (July 1968): 241–257.

Grody, Harvey P. "From North to South: The Feather River Project and Other Legislative Water Struggles in the 1950s." *Southern California Quarterly* 60 (Fall 1978): 287–326.

Grondin, Barbara. "Does Big Agribusiness Spell Community Doom?" *California Farmer* (May 3, 1986): 8, 12, 22.

Guest, Florian. "The Establishment of the Villa de Branciforte." *California Historical Quarterly* 41 (Mar. 1962): 29–50.

Guinn, J. M. "A History of California Floods and Drought." *Publications of the Historical Society of Southern California* 1 (1890): 33–39.

Gustaitis, Rasa. "Water Conservation: The Untapped Well." *Cry California* 16 (Summer 1981): 85–89.

Guy, David J., and Jennifer Cordua. "Conjunctive Use from the Ground Up: The Need to Protect Landowners' Rights to Ground Water." In *Ground Water and Future Supply: Proceedings from the Twenty-First Biennial Conference on Groundwater, September 15–16, 1997,* ed. Johannes DeVries and Jeff Woled, 139–147. Davis: University of California Water Resources Center, Nov. 1998.

Hague, Carl. "Ground Water Management in California." In *Ground Water and Future Supply: Proceedings of the Twenty-First Biennial Conference on Ground Water, September 15–16, 1997,* ed. Johannes DeVries and Jeff Woled, 179–185. Davis: University of California Water Resources Center, Nov. 1998.

Haile, Robert W., et al. "The Health Effects of Swimming in Ocean Water Contaminated by Storm Drain Runoff." *Epidemiology* 10 (July 1999): 355–363.

Harding, Sidney T. "Background of California Water and Power Problems." *California Law Review* 38 (Oct. 1950): 547–571.

———. "Recent Variations in the Water Supply of the Western Great Basin." *Archive Series Report No. 16.* Berkeley: University of California Water Resources Center Archives, 1965.

Harmon, Tom. "Groundwater Quality." In *Southern California Environmental Report Card, 1999,* ed. Richard Berk and Arthur M. Winer, 22–31. Los Angeles: UCLA Institute of the Environment, 1999.

Hart, John. "The Bay and the Delta: Still in Trouble." *California Tomorrow* 17 (Spring 1982): 14–15.

———. "The Delta: The Living (or Dying?) Heart of California." *Cry California* 12 (Summer 1977): 45–50.

———. "One System, Many Masters: Happenstance Water Development." *Cry California* 12 (Fall 1977): 2–10.

Harvey, Mark. "Echo Park, Glen Canyon, and the Postwar Wilderness Movement." *Pacific Historical Review* 60 (Feb. 1991): 43–67.

Heizer, Robert F. "Prehistoric Central California: A Problem in Historical-Development Classification." *University of California Archaeological Survey Report No. 41.* Berkeley: Department of Anthropology, University of California, 1958.

Hicks, Frederic. "The Influence of Agriculture on Aboriginal Socio-Political Organization in the Lower Colorado River Valley." *Journal of California Anthropology* 1 (Winter 1974): 133–144.

Holburt, Myron B. "International Problems." In *Values and Choices in the Development of the Colorado River Basin,* ed. Dean F. Peterson and A. Berry Crawford, 220–237. Tucson: University of Arizona Press, 1978.

Holburt, Myron B., Richard W. Atwater, and Timothy H. Quinn. "Water Marketing in Southern California." *American Water Works Association Journal* 80 (Mar. 1988): 38–45.

Hornbeck, David. "Economic Growth and Change at the Missions of Alta California, 1769–1846." In *Columbian Consequences.* Vol. 2, *Archaeological and Historical Perspectives on the Spanish Borderlands West,* ed. David H. Thomas, 423–433. Washington, D.C.: Smithsonian Institution Press, 1989.

Howitt, Richard E. "Effects of Water Marketing on the Farm Economy." In *Sharing Scarcity: Gainers & Losers in Water Marketing,* ed. Harold E. Carter, Henry J. Vaux, Jr., and Ann F. Scheuring, 97–132. Davis: University of California Agricultural Issues Center, 1994.

Howitt, Richard E., and Henry J. Vaux, Jr. "Competing Demands for California's Scarce Water." In *Water Quantity/Quality Management and Conflict Resolution,* ed. A. Dinar and E. T. Loehman, 271–287. Westport, Conn.: Praeger Publishers, 1995.

Hudanick, Andrew, Jr. "George Hebard Maxwell: Reclamation's Militant Evangelist." *Journal of the West* 14 (July 1975): 108–121.

Hundley, Norris, jr. "Clio Nods: *Arizona* v. *California* and the Boulder Canyon Act—A Reassessment." *Western Historical Quarterly* 3 (Jan. 1972): 17–51.

———. "The Dark and Bloody Ground of Indian Water Rights: Confusion Elevated to Principle." *Western Historical Quarterly* 9 (Oct. 1978): 455–482.

———. "The Great American Desert Transformed: Aridity, Exploitation, and Imperialism in the Making of the Modern American West." In *Water and Arid Lands of the Western United States,* ed. M. T. El-Ashry and Diana C. Gibbons, 21–83. New York: Cambridge University Press, 1988.

————. "The Politics of Reclamation: California, the Federal Government, and the Origins of the Boulder Canyon Act—A Second Look." *California Historical Quarterly* 52 (Winter 1973): 292–325.

————. "Water and the West in Historical Imagination." *Western Historical Quarterly* 27 (Spring 1996): 5–31.

————. "The West against Itself: The Colorado River—An Institutional History." In *New Courses for the Colorado River: Major Issues for the Next Century,* ed. Gary D. Weatherford and F. Lee Brown, 9–49. Albuquerque: University of New Mexico Press, 1986.

————. "Whither Californians and Their Water: Environmental Preservation or Environmental Destruction?" *Southern California Quarterly* 82 (2000): 75–100.

————. "The 'Winters' Decision and Indian Water Rights: A Mystery Reexamined." *Western Historical Quarterly* 13 (Jan. 1982): 17–42.

Igler, David. "When Is a River Not a River: Reclaiming Nature's Disorder in *Lux* v. *Haggin.*" *Environmental History* 1 (Apr. 1996): 52–69.

Izbicki, John, et al. "Seawater Intrusion in Aquifers Underlying the Oxnard Plain, Ventura County, California." In *Ground Water and Future Supply: Proceedings of the Twenty-First Biennial Conference on Ground Water, September 15–16, 1997,* ed. Johannes DeVries and Jeff Woled, 65–67. Davis: University of California Water Resources Center, Nov. 1998.

Jackson, Donald C. "Engineering in the Progressive Era: A New Look at Frederick Haynes Newell and the U.S. Reclamation Service." *Technology and Culture* 34 (July 1993): 539–574.

Jacobsen, Thorkild, and Robert M. Adams. "Salt and Silt in Ancient Mesopotamian Agriculture." *Science* 128 (Nov. 21, 1958): 1252.

Jarvis, Michaela. "Toxic Cover-Up?" *California Journal* 21 (June 1990): 277–280.

Johnson, Elizabeth. "The Delta Canal, Anything But a Peripheral Issue: Get Ready for the Water War of the 80's." *California Journal* 11 (Oct. 1980): 376–378.

Johnson, Robert Underwood. "Dismembering Your National Park." *Outlook* 91 (Jan.–Apr. 1909): 252–253.

———. "A High Price to Pay for Water." *Century* 76 (Aug. 1908): 632–634.

Jones, S. J. "Some Regional Aspects of Native California." In *The California Indians: A Source Book,* ed. Robert F. Heizer and M. A. Whipple, 84–96. 2d ed. Berkeley and Los Angeles: University of California Press, 1971.

Joseph, Patrick. "The Battle of the Dams." *Smithsonian* 29 (Nov. 1998): 48–61.

Jubler, Eric. "Let's Open up Our Wilderness Areas." *Reader's Digest* 100 (May 1972): 125–128.

———. "The Wilderness: Just How Wild Should It Be?" *Trends* 9, no. 1 (1972): 15–18.

Kaufman, Richard F. "The Anatomy of the Great California Water Debate." *Journal of the West* 34 (Oct. 1995): 77–87.

Kelley, Robert. "Ideology and Political Culture from Jefferson to Nixon." *American Historical Review* 82 (June 1977): 531–562.

———. "The Interplay of American Political Culture and Public Policy: The Sacramento River as a Case Study." *Journal of Policy History* 1, no. 1 (1989): 1–23.

———. "The Mining Debris Controversy in the Sacramento Valley." *Pacific Historical Review* 25 (Nov. 1956): 331–346.

———. "Taming the Sacramento: Hamiltonianism in Action." *Pacific Historical Review* 34 (Feb. 1965): 21–49.

Kircher, Valerie C. "The Legislative Battle over Preserving Agricultural Land." *California Journal* 7 (May 1976): 155–157.

Kirkendall, Richard. "Social Science in the Central Valley of California: An Episode." *California Historical Society Quarterly* 43 (Sept. 1964): 195–218.

Kirsch, Jonathan. "The Politics of Water." *New West* 14 (Sept. 10, 1979): 48–70.

Koppes, Clayton. "Public Water, Private Land: Origins of the Acreage Limitation Controversy, 1933–1953." *Pacific Historical Review* 47 (Nov. 1978): 607–636.

Kossen, Sidney. "California's $2 Billion Thirst." *Harper's* 222 (Mar. 1961): 94–95, 100–102.

Krieger, Martin. "What's Wrong with Plastic Trees." *Science* 179 (Feb. 2, 1973): 446–455.

Kroeber, A. L. "The Nature of Land-Holding Groups in Aboriginal California." In *Aboriginal California: Three Studies in Culture History,* ed. Robert F. Heizer, 81–120. Berkeley: University of California Archaeological Research Facility, 1963.

Kunreuther, Howard C., and Gilbert F. White. "The Role of the National Insurance Program in Reducing Losses and Promoting Wise Use of Floodplains." *Water Resources Update,* no. 95 (Spring 1994): 31–35.

Lacayo, Richard. "The Brawl over Sprawl." *Time* 153 (Mar. 22, 1999): 45–48.

Lawrence, Robert. "Agriculture: Seeds of Change." *Cry California* 11 (Summer 1976): 55–58.

Lawton, Harry W., Philip J. Wilke, Mary DeBecker, and William M. Mason. "Agriculture among the Paiute of Owens Valley." *Journal of California Anthropology* 3 (Summer 1976): 13–50.

Leary, Mary Ellen. "The Water Resources Control Board." *California Journal* 16 (Mar. 1985): 110–112.

Lee, D. Demetracopoulou. "Linguistic Reflection of Wintu Thought." *International Journal of American Linguistics* 10 (1944): 181–187.

Lee, Lawrence B. "California Water Politics: Depression Genesis of the Central Valley Project, 1933–1944." *Journal of the West* 24 (Oct. 1985): 63–81.

———. "Reclamation and Irrigation." In *The Reader's Encyclopedia of the American West,* ed. Howard R. Lamar, 1000–1005. New York: Crowell, 1977.

Leopold, Aldo. "The Conservation Ethic." *Journal of Forestry* 31 (Oct. 1933): 634–643.

Leopold, Luna B. "Flood Hydrology and Floodplain." *Water Resources Update,* no. 95 (Spring 1994): 11–14.

LeVeen, E. Phillip. "Reclamation Policy at a Crossroads." *Public Affairs Report: Bulletin of the Institute of Governmental Studies* 19 (Oct. 1978).

Lippincott, J. B. "William Mulholland—Engineer, Pioneer, Raconteur." *Civil Engineering* 2 (Feb.–Mar. 1941): 105–107, 161–164.

Littlefield, Douglas R. "Water Rights during the California Gold Rush: Conflicts over Economic Points of View." *Western Historical Quarterly* 14 (Oct. 1983): 415–434.

Lotchin, Roger. "John Francis Neylan: San Francisco Irish Progressive." In *The San Francisco Irish: 1850–1876,* ed. James P. Walsh, 86–110. San Francisco: Irish Literary and Historical Society, 1978.

Lowitt, Richard. "The Hetch Hetchy Controversy, Phase II: The 1913 Senate Debate." *California History* 74 (Summer 1995): 190–203, 220.

MacCannell, Dean. "The Effect of Agricultural Scale on Communities." In *Proceedings: Sustainability of California Agriculture— A Symposium,* 233–240. Davis: University of California, Davis, 1986.

MacCannell, Dean, and Jerry White. "The Social Costs of Large-Scale Agriculture: The Prospects of Land Reform in California." In *Land Reform, American Style,* ed. Charles C. Geisler and Frank J. Popper, 35–55. Totowa, N.J.: Rowman & Allanheld, 1984.

McClurg, Sue. "CALFED and the Delta Fix." *Western Water* (Jan.–Feb. 1999): 4–13.

———. "Central Valley Project Improvement Act Update." *Western Water* (Jan.–Feb. 2000): 4–13.

———. "Cutting Colorado River Use: The California Plan." *Western Water* (Nov.–Dec. 1998): 4–13.

———. "Watershed Management." *Western Water* (Nov.–Dec. 1995): 12.

Mann, Dean E., Gary D. Weatherford, and Phillip Nichols. "Legal-Political History of Water Resource Development in the Upper Colorado River Basin." *Lake Powell Research Project Bulletin No. 4.* Los Angeles: National Science Foundation, Sept. 1974.

Manson, Marsden. "San Francisco's Side of the Hetch Hetchy Reservoir Matter." *Twentieth Century* 2 (June 1910): 270–274.

Martin, Paul S. "Prehistoric Overkill." In *Pleistocene Extinctions:*

The Search for a Cause, ed. P. S. Martin and H. E. Wright, Jr.,
75–120. New Haven: Yale University Press, 1967.

Mason, William. "Fages' Code of Conduct toward Indians, 1787."
Journal of California Anthropology 2 (Summer 1975): 90–100.

Mendel, Ed. "Policy, Plumbing and Peace." *Golden State Report* 2
(Dec. 1986): 29–32.

Meyer, Michael. "The Living Legacy of Hispanic Groundwater
Law in the Contemporary Southwest." *Journal of the Southwest* 31 (Autumn 1989): 287–299.

Meyers, Dan. "Searching for a Solution to the Delta's Costly
Problems." *California Journal* 14 (July 1983): 268–269.

Miller, Arthur. "Delta Water Controversy Stalls Construction of
the Peripheral Canal, Last Major Link in the State Water Project." *California Journal* 4 (Jan. 1973): 11–14.

Miller, M. Catherine. "Water Rights and the Bankruptcy of Judicial
Action: The Case of *Herminghaus* v. *Southern California
Edison.*" *Pacific Historical Review* 58 (Feb. 1989): 83–107.

Millon, René. "Variations in Response to the Practice of Irrigation
Agriculture." In *Civilizations in Desert Lands,* ed. Richard B.
Woodbury, 56–88. Salt Lake City: University of Utah An-
thropological Paper No. 62, Dec. 1962.

Mintz, Sidney W. "The Role of Water in Steward's Cultural Ecology." *Journal of the Steward Anthropological Society* 11 (Fall
1979): 17–32.

"Minute 242." *International Legal Materials* 12 (1973): 1105.

Mitchell, William. "The Hydraulic Hypothesis." *Current Anthropology* 14 (Dec. 1973): 532–534.

Moody, Charles A. "Los Angeles and the Owens River." *Out West*
23 (Oct. 1905): 417–442.

Moore, Charles V., and Richard E. Howitt. "The Central Valley
of California." In *Water and Arid Lands of the Western United
States,* ed. M. T. El-Ashry and Diana C. Gibbons, 85–126.
New York: Cambridge University Press, 1988.

Morgan, Judith, and Neil Morgan. "California's Parched Oasis."
National Geographic 149 (Jan. 1976): 98–127.

Muir, John. "The Endangered Valley." *Century* 77 (Jan. 1909):
464–469.

———. "The Hetch Hetchy Valley." *Sierra Club Bulletin* 6 (Jan. 1908): 95–109.

Mulholland, Catherine. "William A. Mulholland and the St. Francis Dam." *Southern California Quarterly* 77 (Spring/Summer 1995): 111–137.

Neel, Susan R. "Newton Drury and the Echo Park Dam Controversy." *Forest & Conservation History* 38 (Apr. 1994): 56–66.

Nelson, James. "The Pesticide Problem: Working Can Be Hazardous to Your Health." *Cry California* 12 (Summer 1977): 59–62.

Newcom, Josh. "Getting Serious about Salt: Urban Water Purveyors Seek Solution to Mounting Problem." *Western Water* (Sept.–Oct. 1999): 4–13.

———. "Hot Debate over Hot Tailings." *River Report* (Spring 1999): 10–11.

———. "Saving for a Dry Day: Innovative Storage Plan Could Stretch Colorado River Supply." *River Report* (Winter 1998): 1, 4–9.

Nijhuis, Michelle. "Accidental Refuge." *High Country News* 32 (June 19, 2000): 1, 8–13.

———. "A River Resurrected: The Colorado River Delta Gets a Second Chance." *High Country News* 32 (July 3, 2000): 1, 10–13.

Norman, H. A. "William Mulholland." *American Society of Civil Engineers Transactions* 101 (1936): 1604–1608.

Novarro, Len. "Water War." *San Diego Homes/Gardens* (Mar. 1998): 1–16.

Oshio, Kazuto. "Who Pays and Who Benefits? Metropolitan Water Politics in Twentieth-Century Southern California." *Japanese Journal of American Studies,* no. 8 (1997): 63–89.

Oxford, June. "Rain at the Drop of a Hatfield." *Californians* 6 (May–June 1988): 38–41.

Pace, Phillip J. "Dividing the Water: A Colorado Plan That Ensures California's Future." *Metropolitan Water District of Southern California Aqueduct* 65, no. 2 (1999): 4–5.

———. "Water-Use Efficiency: The Key to California's Future." In *Metropolitan Water District of Southern California Direct Line: Colorado River Update* (March 1999).

Patterson, Thomas W. "Hatfield the Rainmaker." *Journal of San Diego History* 16 (Winter 1970): 3–27.

Paul, Rodman. "The Wheat Trade between California and the United Kingdom." *Mississippi Valley Historical Review* 45 (Dec. 1958): 391–412.

Pearson, Byron. "Newton Drury of the National Park Service." *Pacific Historical Review* 68 (Aug. 1999): 397–424.

Peri, David W., and Scott M. Patterson. "The Basket Is in the Roots, That's Where It Begins." In *Before the Wilderness: Environmental Management by Native Californians,* ed. Thomas C. Blackburn and Kat Anderson, 175–194. Menlo Park, Calif.: Ballena Press, 1993.

Perlman, David. "Our Winning Fight for Dinosaur." *Sierra Club Bulletin* 41 (Jan. 1956): 5–8.

Peterson, Richard H. "The Failure to Reclaim: California State Swamp Land Policy and the Sacramento Valley, 1850–1866." *Southern California Quarterly* 56 (Spring 1974): 45–60.

Philander, S. G. "El Niño." *Oceanus* 35 (1992): 56–65.

Phillips, George. "Indians in Los Angeles, 1781–1875: Economic Integration, Social Disintegration." *Pacific Historical Review* 49 (Aug. 1980): 427–451.

Pisani, Donald. "Water Law Reform in California, 1900–1913." *Agricultural History* 54 (Apr. 1980): 295–317.

Plambeck, Lynne. "Los Angeles County's Last Unchannelized River—The Santa Clara." *Headwaters* (Winter 1999): 8–9.

Pollard, Vic. "Seed of the Tainted Watermelons." *Golden State Report* 1 (Fall 1985): 30–32.

Pomento, Joe. "The Last Water Hole in the West." *Metropolitan Water District of Southern California Aqueduct* 64, no. 3 (1998): 2–3.

———. "The Salton Sea: Can It Be Saved?" *Metropolitan Water District of Southern California Aqueduct* 64, no. 2 (1998): 2–3.

Potter, Roger G., and Susan Tatayon. "State Interest in Water Banking/Conjunctive Use." In *Ground Water and Future Supply: Proceedings of the Twenty-First Biennial Conference on Ground Water, September 15–16, 1997,* ed. Johannes DeVries and Jeff

Woled, 27–34. Davis: University of California Water Resources Center, Nov. 1998.

Prokopovich, Nikola P. "Origin and Treatment of Hydrocompaction in the San Joaquin Valley, CA, USA." In *Land Subsidence: Proceedings of the Third International Symposium on Land Subsidence,* ed. A. I. Johnson, Laura Carbogin, and L. Ubertini, 537–546. Wallingford, Oxfordshire: International Association of Hydrological Sciences, 1986.

Prokopovich, Nikola P., and M. J. Marriott. "Cost of Subsidence to the Central Valley Project, CA." *Bulletin of the Association of Engineering Geologists* 20, no. 3 (1983): 325–332.

Putnam, Jackson K. "The Persistence of Progressivism in the 1920's: The Case of California." *Pacific Historical Review* 35 (Aug. 1966): 395–411.

Quinn, Tony. "The Impact of the Drought on California's Political Climate." *California Journal* 8 (July 1977): 244–245.

Rankin, Jerry. "Why Santa Barbara Voted No on State Water." *California Journal* 10 (Oct. 1979): 362–364.

Raphael, John. "Quality or Quantity? The Uncertain Fate of Delta Water." *Cry California* 14 (Spring 1979): 22–25.

Reich, Peter L. "Mission Revival Jurisprudence: State Courts and Hispanic Water Law since 1850." *Washington Law Review* 69 (Oct. 1994): 869–925.

Ressler, John Q. "Indian and Spanish Water Control on New Spain's Northwest Frontier." *Journal of the West* 7 (Jan. 1968): 10–17.

Rind, David. "The Greenhouse Effect: Reality and Potential Consequences." In *Proceedings of the Seventeenth Biennial Conference on Ground Water, San Diego, California, September 25–26, 1989.* Davis: University of California Water Resources Center, Davis; California Department of Water Resources and California Water Resources Control Board, 1990.

Robie, Ronald B. "The Delta Decisions—The Quiet Revolution in California Water Rights." *Pacific Law Journal* 19 (1988): 1111–1142.

Rodriguez, Rick. "Regulating Pesticides." *California Journal* 16 (Oct. 1985): 401–404.

Rogers, J. David. "A Man, a Dam, and a Disaster." *Southern California Quarterly* 77 (Spring/Summer 1995): 1–109.

———. "Reassessment of the St. Francis Dam Failure." In *Engineering Geology Practice in Southern California,* ed. Bernard W. Pipkin and Richard J. Proctor, 639–666. Belmont, Calif.: Southern California Section, Association of Engineering Geologists, 1992.

Rohe, Randall E. "Hydraulicking in the American West: The Development and Diffusion of a Mining Technique." *Montana, the Magazine of Western History* 35 (Spring 1985): 18–35.

Rossman, Antonio. "Water: Where Do We Go from Here?" *California Journal* 13 (Sept. 1982): 349–350.

Rowe, Edgar A., and Kenneth Q. Volk. "Joseph Barlow Lippincott." *American Society of Civil Engineers Transactions* 108 (1943): 1543–1550.

Rowntree, Lester, and Robert Raburn. "Rainfall Variability and California Mission Agriculture: An Analysis from Harvest and Tree Ring Data." In *Yearbook of the Association of Pacific Coast Geographers, 1980,* ed. James W. Scott, 31–44. Corvallis: Oregon State University Press, 1980.

Rubin, Hal. "California's Canal Conflict (Peripheral, Not Panama)." *California Journal* 9 (Jan. 1978): 17–18.

———. "Dilemma in the Delta—Balancing Competing Interests." *California Journal* 7 (Aug. 1976): 277–279.

———. "The Political Aftershocks of Carter's Auburn Dam Decision." *California Journal* 8 (May 1977): 159–161.

———. "The Toxic Chemical Storm over California." *California Journal* 10 (Dec. 1979): 413–416.

Salzman, Ed. "The Brown Record." *California Journal* 9 (June 1978): 173–176.

Sauer, Carl O. "American Agricultural Origins: A Consideration of Nature and Culture." In *Essays in Anthropology Presented to A. L. Kroeber in Celebration of his Sixtieth Birthday, June 11, 1936,* ed. Robert H. Lowie, 294–295. Berkeley: University of California Press, 1936.

Sawyer, Andrew H. "Area of Origin: Protection for Local Needs in Ground Water Management." In *Ground Water and Future*

Supply: Proceedings of the Twenty-First Conference on Ground Water, November 15–16, 1997, ed. Johannes DeVries and Jeff Woled, 173–177. Davis: University of California Water Resources Center, Nov. 1998.

Sax, Joseph L. "Selling Reclamation Water Rights: A Case Study in Federal Subsidy Policy." *Michigan Law Review* 64 (Nov. 1965): 13–46.

Schilling, Elizabeth. "From Fad to Fortune: Organic Agriculture Grows Up." *California Journal* 26 (May 1995): 23–25.

Schulman, Edmund. "Precipitation Records in California Tree Rings." In *Proceedings of the Sixth Pacific Science Congress, 1939.* Vol. 3: 707–717. Berkeley and Los Angeles: University of California Press, 1940–1943.

———. "Runoff Histories in Tree Rings of the Pacific Slope." *Geographical Review* 35 (Jan. 1945): 59–73.

———. "Tree-Ring Hydrology in Southern California." *University of Arizona Bulletin* 18 (July 1947), 5–36.

Schwarze, Monica. "The Knock against MTBE." *Metropolitan Water District of Southern California Aqueduct* 65, no. 1 (1999): 2–3.

Shambaugh, Benjamin F. "Frontier Land Clubs or Claims Associations." *American Historical Association Annual Report* (1900): 67–85.

Shaw, Lucien. "The Development of the Law of Waters in the West." *California Law Review* 10 (1922): 443–460.

Shipek, Florence C. "An Example of Intensive Plant Husbandry: The Kumeyaay of Southern California." In *Foraging and Farming: The Evolution of Plant Exploitation,* ed. David R. Harris and Gordon C. Hillman, 159–170. London: Unwin Hyman, 1989.

Siebert, Jerome B. "Agriculture: Will the Cornucopia Run Dry?" *California Journal* 21 (Jan. 1990): 41–43.

Skinner, Casey. "Mono Lake." *California Journal* 20 (May 1989): 217–220.

Sloan, Richard E. "Pact Criticism Is Largely on What It Does Not Say." *Arizona Mining Journal* 6 (Jan. 15, 1923): 58.

Smith, T. Lynn. "A Study of Social Stratification in the Agricultural Sections of the U.S.: Nature, Data, Procedures, and Preliminary Results." *Rural Sociology* 34 (Dec. 1969): 496–509.

Sommarstrom, Sari. "How Safe the North Coast Streams?" *California Tomorrow* 17 (Spring 1982): 25, 28.

Sotero, Ray. "Food Safety: Carrots, Cucumbers, and Cancer." *California Journal* 21 (Mar. 1990): 157–161.

Spinden, Herbert J. "The Origin and Distribution of Agriculture in America." *Proceedings of the 19th International Congress of Americanists, 1915* (Washington, D.C., 1915): 269–276.

Stahle, David W., et al. "Tree-Ring Data Document 16th Century Megadrought over North America." *EOS: Transactions of the American Geophysical Union* 81 (Mar. 21, 2000): 124–125.

Stallard, Tom. "Local Concerns vs. Statewide Desires." In *Ground Water and Future Supply: Proceedings of the Twenty-First Biennial Conference on Ground Water, September 15–16, 1997,* ed. Johannes DeVries and Jeff Woled, 207–208. Davis: University of California Water Resources Center, Nov. 1998.

Stead, Frank M. "California's Natural Reservoirs." *Cry California* 12 (Fall 1977): 14–16.

Stegner, Page. "Water and Power: The Owens Valley Water War." *Harper's* 262 (Mar. 1981): 1570.

Stenstrom, Michael K. "Stormwater Impact." In *Southern California Environmental Report Card, 1999,* ed. Richard Berk and Arthur M. Winer, 12–21. Los Angeles: UCLA Institute of the Environment, 1999.

———. "Wastewater Treatment." In *Southern California Environmental Report Card [1998],* ed. Richard Berk and Arthur M. Winer, 16–25. Los Angeles: UCLA Institute of the Environment, 1998.

Steringer, C. Robert, and Kurt Wanless. "Symposium on Oregon Land Use: The Twenty-Fifth Anniversary of SB 100—Introduction." *University of Oregon Law Review* 77 (Fall 1998): 807–844.

Steward, Julian H. "Ecological Aspects of Southwestern Society." *Anthropos* 32 (1937): 87–104.

———. "Irrigation without Agriculture." *Papers of the Michigan Academy of Science, Arts and Letters* 12 (1930): 149–156.

Stine, Scott. "Extreme and Persistent Drought in California and

Patagonia during Mediaeval Time." *Nature* 369 (June 16, 1994): 546–549.

Stonehouse, Merlin. "The Michigan Excursion for the Founding of Riverside, California." *Michigan History* 45 (Sept. 1961): 193–209.

Street, Richard Steven. "The Big Fix: How Some Growers Fixed Their Grapes Illegally to Get an Edge on the Market." *California Farmer* 269 (Sept. 3, 1988): 8–9, 13–15.

Swain, Donald. "The Bureau of Reclamation and the New Deal, 1933–1940." *Pacific Northwest Quarterly* 61 (July 1970): 137–146.

Taylor, Paul S. "Central Valley Project: Water and Land." *Western Political Quarterly* 2 (June 1949): 228–253.

———. "Mexican Migration and the 160-Acre Water Limitation." *California Law Review* 63, no. 3. (1975): 732–750.

———. "Walter Goldschmidt's Baptism by Fire: Central Valley Water Politics." In *Paths to the Symbolic Self: Essays in Honor of Walter Goldschmidt,* ed. James P. Loucky and Jeffrey R. Jones, 129–140. Los Angeles: Department of Anthropology, University of California, Los Angeles, 1976.

———. "Water, Land, and Environment in Imperial Valley: Law Caught in the Winds of Politics." *Natural Resources Journal* 13 (Jan. 1973): 1–35.

Thompson, Kenneth. "Historic Flooding in the Sacramento Valley." *Pacific Historical Review* 29 (Nov. 1960): 349–360.

Trenberth, Robert E. "Climate Change and Climate Variability: The Climate Record." In *Managing Water Resources in the West under Conditions of Climate Uncertainty,* comp. Committee on Climate Uncertainty and Water Resources Management, Water Science and Technology Board, Commission on Geosciences, Environment, and Resources, 47–70. Washington, D.C.: National Academy Press, 1991.

Valantine, Vernon E. "Impacts of Colorado River Salinity." *Journal of the Irrigation and Drainage Division, American Society of Civil Engineers* 100 (Dec. 1974): 495–510.

Vaux, Henry J., Jr. "Growth and Water in the South Coast Basin of California." In *Water and Arid Lands of the Western United*

States, ed. M. T. El-Ashry and Diana C. Gibbons, 233–279. New York: Cambridge University Press, 1988.

Vaux, Henry J., Jr., and Richard Howitt. "Managing Water Scarcity: An Evaluation of Interregional Transfers." *Water Resources Research* 20 (1984): 785–792.

Vinnikov, Konstantin Y., et al. "Global Warming and Northern Hemisphere Sea Ice Extent." *Science* 286 (Dec. 3, 1999): 1934–1937.

Walker, Richard, and Michael Storper. "The California Water System: Another Round of Expansion?" *Public Affairs Report: Bulletin of the Institute of Governmental Studies* 20 (Apr. 1979).

Waller, Kirsten, et al. "Trihalomethanes in Drinking Water and Spontaneous Abortion." *Epidemiology* 9 (Mar. 1998): 134–140.

Waller, Thomas. "Southern California Water Politics and U.S.-Mexican Relations: Lining the All-American Canal." *Journal of Borderlands Studies* 7 (Fall 1992): 1–32.

Walters, Dan. "Punching Holes in the Williamson Act." *California Journal* 14 (Dec. 1983): 459–461.

Weatherford, Gary, Kim Malcolm, and Barbara Andrews. "California Groundwater Management: The Sacred and the Profane." *Natural Resources Journal* 22 (Oct. 1982): 1031–1043.

Williamson, A. K., and D. E. Prudie. "Simulation of Flow and Compaction in the Regional Aquifer System of the Central Valley of California, U.S.A." In *Land Subsidence: Proceedings of the Third International Symposium on Land Subsidence, 1984,* ed. A. I. Johnson, Laura Carbogin, and L. Ubertini, 271–280. Wallingford, Oxfordshire: International Association of Hydrological Sciences, 1986.

Winther, Oscar O. "The Story of San Jose, 1777–1869: California's First Pueblo." California Historical Society Quarterly 14 (Mar.–June 1935): 3–27, 147–174.

Witt, Steven. "The Struggle to Legislate Protection for Agricultural Lands." *California Tomorrow* 18 (Winter 1983): 18–23.

Wollenberg, Charles. "The Small Farmer Deserves a Chance." *Cry California* 14 (Winter 1978–79): 18–24.

Wong, Kenneth M., Eric W. Strecker, and Michael K. Stenstrom. "GIS to Estimate Storm-Water Pollutant Mass Loadings." *Journal of Environmental Engineering* 123 (Aug. 1997): 737–745.

Wood, Samuel E. "Putting It All in One Bucket." *Cry California* 12 (Fall 1977): 17–20.

Young, Gordon. "The Troubled Waters of Mono Lake." *National Geographic* 160 (Mar. 1981): 504–519.

Zeiger, Richard. "Water, Water." *California Journal* 19 (Mar. 1988): 104–109.

Books, Monographs, and Pamphlets

Abbott, Carl. *Portland: Planning, Politics, and Growth in a Twentieth-Century City.* Lincoln: University of Nebraska Press, 1983.

Abbott, Carl, Deborah Howe, and Sy Adler. *Planning the Oregon Way: A Twenty-Year Evaluation.* Corvallis: Oregon State University Press, 1994.

Abrahamson, Dean E., ed. *The Challenge of Global Warming.* Covelo, Calif.: Island Press, 1989.

Alexander, J. A. *The Life of George Chaffey.* Melbourne: Macmillan & Co., 1928.

Alford, Harold G., and Mary P. Ferguson, eds. *Pesticides in Soil and Groundwater.* Berkeley: Agricultural Sciences Publications, 1982.

American Farmland Trust. *Alternatives for Future Urban Growth in California's Central Valley: The Bottom Line for Agriculture and Taxpayers.* Washington, D.C.: American Farmland Trust, Oct. 1995.

———. *The Central Valley's New Towns: Destiny or Disaster.* Davis, Calif.: American Farmland Trust, Jan. 1995.

———. *Risks, Challenges and Opportunities: Agriculture, Resources and Growth in a Changing Central Valley.* San Francisco: American Farmland Trust, 1989.

Anderson, Raymond, and Arthur Maass. *. . . And the Desert Shall Rejoice: Conflict, Growth, and Justice in Arid Environments.* Cambridge, Mass.: MIT Press, 1978.

Archibald, Robert. *The Economic Aspects of the California Missions.* Washington, D.C.: Academy of American Franciscan History, 1978.

Bakker, Elna. *An Island Called California.* Berkeley and Los Angeles: University of California Press, 1971.

Bancroft, Hubert Howe. *California Pastoral.* San Francisco: The History Co., 1888.

———. *History of California.* 7 vols. San Francisco: The History Co., 1886–1890.

Banham, Reyner. *Los Angeles: The Architecture of Four Ecologies.* New York: Harper & Row, 1971.

Barnett, Paul G. *Imperial Valley: The Land of Sun and Subsidies.* Davis: California Institute for Urban Studies, 1978.

———. *Survey of the Research on the Impacts of Pesticides on Agricultural Workers and the Rural Environment.* Davis: California Institute for Rural Studies, Feb. 1989.

Bean, Walton. *Boss Ruef's San Francisco.* Berkeley and Los Angeles: University of California Press, 1952.

Beattie, George, and Helen Beattie. *Heritage of the Valley: San Bernardino's First Century.* Pasadena, Calif.: San Pasqual Press, 1939.

Becker, Robert H. *Diseños of California Ranchos: Maps of Thirty-Seven Land Grants, 1822–1846.* San Francisco: Book Club of California, 1964.

Belcher, Edward. *Narrative of a Voyage Round the World, Performed in Her Majesty's Ship Sulphur during the Years 1836–1842.* 2 vols. London: Henry Colburn, 1843.

Benson, Lee. *The Concept of Jacksonian Democracy: New York as a Test Case.* Princeton: Princeton University Press, 1961.

Berry, Wendell. *The Unsettling of America: Culture & Agriculture.* San Francisco: Sierra Club, 1977.

Bigger, Richard. *Flood Control in Metropolitan Los Angeles.* Berkeley: University of California Press, 1959.

Blackburn, Thomas C., and Kat Anderson, eds. *Before the Wilderness: Environmental Management by Native Californians.* Menlo Park, Calif.: Ballena Press, 1993.

Blair-Westfall Associates. *Land Subsidence in the Firebaugh Soil Conservation District.* Fresno, Calif.: Blair-Westfall Associates, 1966.

Blank, Steven C. *The End of Agriculture in the American Portfolio.* Westport, Conn.: Quorum Books, 1998.

Blodgett, James C., and J. S. Williams. *Land Subsidence and Problems Affecting Land Use at Edwards Air Force Base and Vicinity, California.* Sacramento: U.S. Geological Survey, 1992.

Blomquist, William. *Dividing the Waters: Governing Groundwater in Southern California.* San Francisco: Institute for Contemporary Studies, 1992.

Bouvier, Leon, and Lindsey Grant. *How Many Americans? Population, Immigration, and the Environment.* San Francisco: Sierra Club Books, 1994.

Boyle, Robert H., John Graves, and T. H. Watkins. *The Water Hustlers.* San Francisco: Sierra Club, 1971.

Brandes, Ray, trans. *The Costansó Narrative of the Portolá Expedition.* Newhall, Calif.: Hogarth Press, 1970.

Brigham, Jay L. *Empowering the West: Electrical Politics Before FDR.* Lawrence: University of Kansas Press, 1998.

Brockett, L. P. *Our Western Empire: Or the New West Beyond the Mississippi.* Philadelphia: Bradley, Garretson & Co., 1881.

Brookes, Andrew. *Channelized Rivers: Perspectives for Environmental Management.* Chichester, U.K.: John Wiley & Sons, 1988.

Brower, David. *Not Man Apart: Lines from Robinson Jeffers.* San Francisco: Sierra Club, [1962].

———. *Wilderness: America's Living Heritage.* San Francisco: Sierra Club, [1962].

———, ed. *Wildlands in Our Civilization.* San Francisco: Sierra Club, [1964].

Bull, William B., and Raymond E. Miller. *Land Subsidence Due to Ground-Water Withdrawal in the Los Banos–Kettleman City Area, California.* Washington, D.C.: U.S. Geological Survey, 1975.

Burke, Robert E. *Olson's New Deal for California.* Berkeley: University of California Press, 1953.

Burner, David. *The Politics of Provincialism: The Democratic Party in Transition, 1918–1932.* New York: Knopf, 1968.

Burton, Carmen A., John A. Izbicki, and Katherine S. Paybins. *Water-Quality Trends in the Santa Ana River at MWD Crossing and below Prado Dam, Riverside County, California.* Sacramento: U.S. Geological Survey, 1998.

Buttel, Frederick R., and Craig R. Humphrey. *Environment, Energy and Society.* Belmont, Calif.: Wadsworth Publishing Co., 1982.

California Jurisprudence: A Complete and Modern Statement of the Law and Practice of the State of California. 2d ed. Vols. 51 and 52. San Francisco: Bancroft-Whitney Co., 1959.

California Land-Use Task Force. *The California Land: Planning for a People.* Sacramento: Planning and Conservation Foundation, 1975.

California Public Interest Research Group. *Toxic on Tap: Pesticides in California Drinking Water Sources,* by Brad Heavner. San Francisco: Californians for Pesticide Reform, Oct. 27, 1999.

Camarillo, Albert. *Chicanos in a Changing Society.* Cambridge, Mass.: Harvard University Press, 1979.

Campbell, Ballard C., Jr. *Representative Democracy: Public Policy and Midwestern Legislatures in the Later Nineteenth Century.* Cambridge, Mass.: Harvard University Press, 1980.

Camp Dresser & McKee Inc. *Nitrate Impact Study Report: Prepared for Santa Ana Watershed Project Authority.* Ontario, Calif.: Camp Dresser & McKee Inc., 1989.

Carle, David. *Drowning the Dream: California's Water Choices at the Millennium.* Westport, Conn.: Praeger, 2000.

Carosso, Vincent P. *The California Wine Industry: A Study of the Formative Years.* Berkeley: University of California Press, 1951.

Carson, Rachel. *Silent Spring.* Boston: Houghton Mifflin, 1962.

Carter, Harold O., and George Goldman. *The Measure of California Agriculture: Its Impact on the State Economy.* Rev. ed. Oakland: University of California Division of Agriculture and Natural Resources, 1998.

Castetter, Edward F., and Willis H. Bell. *Yuman Indian Agriculture.* Albuquerque: University of New Mexico Press, 1951.

Caughey, John W. *Gold Is the Cornerstone.* Berkeley and Los Angeles: University of California Press, 1948.

Center for Continuing Study of the California Economy. *California Economic Growth: 1999 Edition.* Palo Alto, Calif.: Center for Continuing Study of the California Economy, 1999.

———. *California Population Characteristics, 1992 Edition.* Palo Alto, Calif.: Center for Continuing Study of the California Economy, 1992.

Central Pacific Railroad Co., Board of Directors. *Annual Report, 1882.* San Francisco: H. S. Crocker & Co., 1883.

Chan, Sucheng. *Asian Californians.* San Francisco: Boyd & Fraser Publishing Co., 1990.

———. *This Bittersweet Soil: The Chinese in California Agriculture, 1860–1910.* Berkeley and Los Angeles: University of California Press, 1987.

Cherney, Robert W., and William Issel. *San Francisco, 1865–1932: Politics, Power, and Urban Development.* Berkeley and Los Angeles: University of California Press, 1986.

Clark, David. *Los Angeles: A City Apart—An Illustrated History.* Woodland Hills, Calif.: Windsor Publications, 1981.

Clay, John. *My Life on the Range.* Chicago: The Author, 1924.

Cleland, Robert G. *The Cattle on a Thousand Hills: Southern California, 1850–1880.* 2d ed. San Marino, Calif.: Huntington Library, 1951.

Cohen, Mark N. *The Food Crisis in Prehistory.* New Haven: Yale University Press, 1977.

Cohen, Michael J., Jason I. Morrison, and Edward P. Glenn. *Haven or Hazard—The Ecology and Future of the Salton Sea.* Oakland: Pacific Institute for Studies in Development, Environment, and Security, 1999.

Cohen, Michael P. *The History of the Sierra Club, 1892–1970.* San Francisco: Sierra Club, 1988.

Committee on Groundwater Recharge. *Groundwater Recharge Using Waters of Impaired Quality.* Washington, D.C.: National Academy Press, 1994.

Committee on Restoration of Aquatic Ecosystems. *Restoration of*

Aquatic Ecosystems: Science, Technology, and Public Policy. Washington, D.C.: National Academy Press, 1992.

Committee to Review the Glen Canyon Environmental Studies. *Colorado River Ecology and Dam Management: Proceedings of a Symposium, May 24–25, 1990, Santa Fe, New Mexico.* Washington, D.C.: National Academy Press, 1991.

Community and Organization Research Institute, University of California, Santa Barbara. *The Future of Mono Lake.* Riverside: University of California Water Resources Center Report No. 68, Feb. 1988.

Cook, Sherburne F. *The Conflict between the California Indian and White Civilization: The Indian versus the Spanish Mission.* Berkeley: University of California Press, 1943.

———. *The Population of the California Indians, 1769–1970.* Berkeley and Los Angeles: University of California Press, 1976.

Cooper, Erwin. *Aqueduct Empire: A Guide to Water in California—Its Turbulent History and Its Management Today.* Glendale, Calif.: Arthur H. Clark Co., 1968.

Coppock, Ray. *Resources at Risk in the San Joaquin Valley: Selenium, Human Health, and Irrigated Agriculture.* Davis: University of California Agricultural Issues Center, Cooperative Extension, Salinity/Drainage Task Force, and Water Resources Center, [1988].

Corner, William, comp. and ed. *San Antonio de Béxar: A Guide and History.* San Antonio: Bainbridge & Corner, 1890.

Cory, H. T. *The Imperial Valley and the Salton Sink.* San Francisco: J. J. Newbegin, 1915.

Council for Agricultural Science and Technology. *Future of Irrigated Agriculture.* Ames, Iowa: Council for Agricultural Science and Technology, 1996.

Cowan, Robert G. *Ranchos of California.* Fresno, Calif.: Academy Library Guilds, 1956.

Craig, Richard B. *The Bracero Program: Interest Groups and Foreign Policy.* Austin: University of Texas Press, 1971.

Cylinder, Paul D., et al. *Wetlands Regulation: A Complete Guide to Federal and California Programs.* Point Arena, Calif.: Solano Press Books, 1995.

Daniel, Cletus. *Bitter Harvest: A History of California Farm Workers, 1870–1941.* Ithaca, N.Y.: Cornell University Press, 1981.

Dasmann, Raymond F. *California's Changing Environment.* San Francisco: Boyd & Fraser Publishing Co., 1981.

————. *The Destruction of California.* New York: Macmillan, 1965.

Davis, Arthur P. *The Single Tax from the Farmer's Standpoint.* Minneapolis: n.p., 1897.

Davis, Leon T. *Law and Lawyers: One Hundred Twenty-Eight Years in the History of Los Angeles.* Los Angeles: The Author, [1950?].

Davis, Margaret Leslie. *Rivers in the Desert: William Mulholland and the Inventing of Los Angeles.* New York: HarperCollins, 1993.

Davis, Mike. *Ecology of Fear: Los Angeles and the Imagination of Disaster.* New York: Metropolitan Books, 1998.

Dawdy, Doris O. *Congress in Its Wisdom: The Bureau of Reclamation and the Public Interest.* Boulder, Colo.: Westview Press, 1989.

deBuys, William. *Salt Dreams: Land & Water in Low-Down California.* Albuquerque: University of New Mexico Press, 1999.

Deichmann, William B. *Pesticides and the Environment: A Continuing Controversy.* New York: Intercontinental Medical Book Corporation, 1973.

Delmatier, Royce D., Clarence F. McIntosh, and Earl G. Waters, eds. *The Rumble of California Politics, 1848–1970.* New York: John Wiley & Sons, 1970.

Dennis, Harry. *Water and Power: The Peripheral Canal and Its Alternatives.* San Francisco: Friends of the Earth, 1981.

Desnoyers, M. C. *The Ordinances and Resolutions of the City of Los Angeles.* Los Angeles: Herald Publishing Co., 1875.

Díaz, Henry F., and Vera Markgraf, eds. *El Niño: Historical and Paleoclimatic Aspects of the Southern Oscillation.* New York: Cambridge University Press, 1992.

Dixon, Lloyd, Nancy Y. Moore, and Susan W. Schechter. *California's 1991 Drought Water Bank: Economic Impacts in the Selling Regions.* Santa Monica, Calif.: Rand, 1993.

Dobkins, Betty E. *The Spanish Element in Texas Water Law.* Austin: University of Texas Press, 1959.

Downey, Sheridan. *They Would Rule the Valley.* San Francisco: Sheridan Downey, 1947.

Downing, Theodore, and McGuire Gibson, eds. *Irrigation's Impact on Society.* Tucson: University of Arizona Press, 1974.

Duany, Andres, Elizabeth Plater-Zyberk, and Jeff Speck. *Suburban Nation: The Rise and Sprawl and the Decline of the American Dream.* San Francisco: North Point Press, 2000.

Dubos, René. *A God Within.* New York: Charles Scribner's Sons, 1972.

———. *The Resilience of Ecosystems.* Boulder: Colorado Associated University Press, 1978.

———. *The Wooing of Earth.* New York: Charles Scribner's Sons, 1980.

Dubrovsky, Neil M., et al. *Influence of Redox Potential on Selenium Distribution in Ground Water, Mendota, Western San Joaquin Valley, California.* Sacramento: U.S. Geological Survey, 1990.

Dumke, Glenn S. *The Boom of the Eighties in Southern California.* San Marino, Calif.: Huntington Library, 1944.

Dunbar, Robert G. *Forging New Rights in Western Waters.* Lincoln: University of Nebraska Press, 1983.

Dwinelle, John W. *The Colonial History: City of San Francisco.* 4th ed. San Francisco: Towne & Bacon, 1867.

Ebeling, Walter. *Handbook of Indian Foods and Fiber of Arid America.* Berkeley and Los Angeles: University of California Press, 1986.

El-Ashry, M. T., and Diana C. Gibbons, eds. *Water and Arid Lands of the Western United States.* New York: Cambridge University Press, 1988.

Elkind, Sarah S. *Bay Cities and Water Politics: The Battle for Resources in Boston and Oakland.* Lawrence: University Press of Kansas, 1998.

Ellison, Joseph. *California and the Nation, 1850–1869.* Berkeley: University of California Press, 1927.

Ellison, William Henry. *A Self-Governing Dominion: California, 1848–1860.* Berkeley and Los Angeles: University of California Press, 1950.

Engelhardt, Zephyrin. *The Missions and Missionaries of California.* 4 vols. San Francisco: James H. Barry Co., 1908–1915.

———. *San Diego Mission.* San Francisco: James H. Barry Co., 1920.

———. *San Fernando Rey: The Mission of the Valley.* Chicago: Franciscan Herald Press, 1927.

Farmer, Jared. *Glen Canyon Dammed: Inventing Lake Powell and the Canyon Country.* Tucson: University of Arizona Press.

Fite, Gilbert. *The Farmers' Frontier, 1865–1900.* New York: Holt, Rinehart and Winston, 1966.

Fleming, James R. *Historical Perspectives on Climate Change.* New York: Oxford University Press, 1998.

Fogelson, Robert M. *The Fragmented Metropolis: Los Angeles, 1850–1930.* Cambridge, Mass.: Harvard University Press, 1967.

Fort, D. D., V. L. Gabin, and E. Pinnes. *Managing Groundwater Quality and Quantity in the Western States—A Report to the Environmental Protection Agency.* San Francisco: Natural Heritage Institute, 1993.

Fox, Stephen. *The American Conservation Movement: John Muir and His Legacy.* Madison: University of Wisconsin Press, 1985.

Frederick, Kenneth D., ed. *Scarce Water and Institutional Change.* Washington, D.C.: Resources for the Future, Inc., 1986.

Freidel, Frank. *Franklin Roosevelt: Launching the New Deal.* Boston: Little, Brown & Co., 1973.

Freiden, Bernard J. *The Environmental Protection Hustle.* Cambridge, Mass.: MIT Press, 1979.

Freidman, Lawrence M. *A History of American Law.* 2d ed. New York: Simon & Schuster, 1985.

Friends of the River. *Rivers Reborn: Removing Dams and Restoring Rivers in California.* Sacramento: Friends of the River, 1999.

Fulton, William. *The Reluctant Metropolis: The Politics of Urban Growth in Los Angeles.* Point Arena, Calif.: Solano Press Books, 1997.

Galarza, Ernesto. *Merchants of Labor: The Mexican Bracero Story.* Santa Barbara, Calif.: McNally & Loftin, 1964.

Gates, Paul W. *History of Public Land Law Development.* Washington, D.C.: Public Land Law Review Commission, 1968.

Gebhard, David, and Robert Winter. *A Guide to Architecture in Los Angeles & Southern California.* Santa Barbara: Peregrine Smith, 1977.

Gebhard, David, et al. *A Guide to Architecture in San Francisco & Northern California.* 2d ed. Santa Barbara: Peregrine Smith, 1976.

Gerson, Louis L. *The Hyphenate in Recent American Politics and Diplomacy.* Lawrence: University of Kansas Press, 1964.

Gifford, Edward W., and Gwendoline H. Block. *California Indian Nights Entertainments.* Glendale, Calif.: Arthur H. Clark Co., 1930.

Gilbert, Frank T., Harry L. Wells, and W. L. Chambers. *History of Butte County, California.* San Francisco: Harry L. Wells, 1882.

Glick, Thomas F. *Irrigation and Society in Medieval Valencia.* Cambridge, Mass.: Harvard University Press, 1970.

———. *The Old World Background of the Irrigation System of San Antonio, Texas.* El Paso: Texas Western Press, 1972.

Glickfeld, Madelyn, and Ned Levine. *Regional Growth . . . Local Reaction: The Enactment and Effects of Local Growth Control and Management Measures in California.* Cambridge, Mass.: Lincoln Institute of Land Policy, 1992.

Goldschmidt, Walter. *As You Sow.* New York: Harcourt, Brace & Co., 1947.

Goldsmith, Edward, and Nicholas Hildyard. *The Social and Environmental Effects of Large Dams.* San Francisco: Sierra Club, 1984.

Golzé, Alfred R. *Land Subsidence: Why the State Is Concerned.* Sacramento: California Department of Water Resources, 1965.

———. *Reclamation in the United States.* Caldwell, Idaho: Caxton Printers, 1961.

Gómez, Santos V., and Anna Steding. *California Water Transfers: An Evaluation of the Economic Framework and a Spatial Analysis of the Potential Impacts.* Oakland: Pacific Institute for Studies in Development, Environment, and Security, 1998.

Goodall, Merrill D., John D. Sullivan, and Timothy de Young. *California Water: A New Political Economy.* Montclair, N.J.: Allanheld, Osmun, 1978.

Gottlieb, Robert. *A Life of Its Own: The Politics and Power of Water.* San Diego: Harcourt Brace Jovanovich, 1988.

Gottlieb, Robert, and Irene Wolt. *Thinking Big: The Story of the Los Angeles Times.* New York: G. P. Putnam's Sons, 1977.

Gottlieb, Robert, and Margaret FitzSimmons. *Thirst for Growth: Water Agencies as Hidden Government in California.* Tucson: University of Arizona Press, 1991.

Graham, Otis L., Jr. *An Encore for Reform: The Old Progressives and the New Deal.* New York: Oxford University Press, 1967.

———. *Toward a Planned Society: From Roosevelt to Nixon.* New York: Oxford University Press, 1976.

Grand Canyon Trust. *Proceedings Report: The Colorado River Workshop, February 26–28, 1996—Issues, Ideas, and Directions.* Phoenix, Ariz.: Grand Canyon Trust, 1996.

Great Basin Unified Air Pollution Control District. *Owens Valley PM-10 Planning Area Demonstration of Attainment State Implementation Plan.* Bishop, Calif.: Great Basin Unified Air Pollution Control District, July 1997.

Gughemetti, Joseph, and Eugene D. Wheeler. *The Taking.* Palo Alto, Calif.: Hidden House Publications, 1981.

Guinn, J. M. *A History of California and an Extended History of Los Angeles and Environs.* 3 vols. Los Angeles: Historic Record Co., 1915.

Gumerman, George J., ed. *Exploring the Hohokam: Prehistoric Desert Peoples of the American Southwest.* Albuquerque: University of New Mexico Press, 1991.

Gumprecht, Blake. *The Los Angeles River: Its Life, Death, and Possible Rebirth.* Baltimore: Johns Hopkins University Press, 1999.

Guthrie, Frank E., and Jerome J. Perry, eds. *Introduction to Environmental Toxicology.* New York: Elsevier, 1980.

Haber, Samuel. *Efficiency and Uplift: Scientific Management in the Progressive Era, 1890–1920.* Chicago: University of Chicago Press, 1964.

Haddad, Brent M. *Rivers of Gold: Designing Markets to Allocate Water in California.* Washington, D.C.: Island Press, 2000.

Haggin, James B. *The Desert Lands of Kern County, Cal.* San Francisco: n. p., 1877.

Hall, William H. *Irrigation Development.* Sacramento: Superintendent of State Printing, 1886.

———. *Irrigation in [Southern] California.* Sacramento: State Printing Office, 1888.

Harding, Sidney T. *Water in California.* Palo Alto, Calif.: N-P Publications, 1960.

Harris, Tom. *Death in the Marsh.* Washington, D.C.: Island Press, 1991.

Hart, John. *Farming on the Edge: Saving Family Farms in Marin County, California.* Berkeley and Los Angeles: University of California Press, 1991.

———. *Storm over Mono: The Mono Lake Battle and the California Water Future.* Berkeley and Los Angeles: University of California Press, 1996.

Harvey, Mark W. T. *A Symbol of Wilderness: Echo Park and the American Conservation Movement.* Albuquerque: University of New Mexico Press, 1994.

Harvey, Richard B. *Earl Warren, Governor of California.* Jericho, N.Y.: Exposition Press, 1969.

Haury, Emil W. *The Hohokam.* Tucson: University of Arizona Press, 1976.

Hays, Samuel P. *Beauty, Health, and Permanence: Environmental Politics in the United States, 1955–1985.* New York: Cambridge University Press, 1987.

———. *Conservation and the Gospel of Efficiency: The Progressive Conservation Movement, 1890–1920.* Cambridge, Mass.: Harvard University Press, 1959.

Heal the Bay. *Proceedings of the Southern California Watershed Conference: "Making Watersheds Work."* Santa Monica, Calif.: Heal the Bay, 1995.

Heal the Bay and the Los Angeles & San Gabriel Rivers Watershed Council. *Visions for the River: A Conference, May 4, 1996.* Santa Monica, Calif.: Heal the Bay, 1996.

Heizer, Robert F., and Albert B. Elsasser. *The Natural World of the*

Johnson, Rich. *The Central Arizona Project, 1918–1968.* Tucson: University of Arizona Press, 1977.

Jones, Holway R. *John Muir and the Sierra Club: The Battle for Yosemite.* San Francisco: Sierra Club, 1965.

Kahrl, William L. *Water and Power: The Conflict over Los Angeles' Water Supply in the Owens Valley.* Berkeley and Los Angeles: University of California Press, 1982.

Kahrl, William L., ed. *The California Water Atlas.* Sacramento: Governor's Office of Planning and Research, 1979.

Katcher, Leo. *Earl Warren: A Political Biography.* New York: McGraw-Hill, 1967.

Keller, Morton. *Affairs of State: Public Life in Late Nineteenth Century America.* Cambridge, Mass.: Harvard University Press, 1977.

Kelley, Robert. *Battling the Inland Sea: American Political Culture, Public Policy, and the Sacramento Valley, 1850–1986.* Berkeley and Los Angeles: University of California Press, 1989.

———. *The Cultural Pattern in American Politics: The First Century.* New York: Knopf, 1979.

———. *Gold vs. Grain: The Hydraulic Mining Controversy in California's Sacramento Valley—A Chapter in the Decline of Laissez-Faire.* Glendale, Calif.: Arthur H. Clark Co., 1959.

———. *The Shaping of the American Past.* Englewood Cliffs, N.J.: Prentice-Hall, 1986.

Kent, James. *Commentaries on American Law,* ed. Charles M. Barnes. 13th ed. 4 vols. Boston: Little, Brown, & Co., 1884.

Kinnaird, Lawrence. *History of the Greater San Francisco Bay Region.* 3 vols. New York: Lewis Historical Publishing Co., 1966.

Kinney, Clesson S. *A Treatise in the Law of Irrigation and Water Rights.* 2d ed. 4 vols. San Francisco: Bender-Moss, 1912.

Kirkendall, Richard. *Social Scientists and Farm Politics in the Age of Roosevelt.* Columbia, Mo.: University of Missouri Press, 1965.

Kleppner, Paul. *The Third Electoral System, 1853–1892.* Chapel Hill: University of North Carolina Press, 1979.

Kluger, James R. *Turning on Water with a Shovel: The Career of Elwood Mead.* Albuquerque: University of New Mexico Press, 1992.

Knaap, Gerrit, and Arthur C. Nelson. *The Regulated Landscape: Les-*

sons on *State Land Use Planning from Oregon.* Cambridge, Mass.: Lincoln Institute of Land Policy, 1992.

Kroeber, Alfred L. *Yurok Myths.* Berkeley and Los Angeles: University of California Press, 1976.

Langum, David J. *Law and Community on the Mexican California Frontier.* Norman: University of Oklahoma Press, 1987.

Las siete partidas del sabio rey don Alfonso. [1265] 4 vols. Madrid, 1789.

Lawrence Livermore National Laboratory. *An Evaluation of MTBE Impacts to California Groundwater Resources.* Livermore, Calif.: Lawrence Livermore National Laboratory, 1998.

Layne, J. Gregg. *Water and Power for a Great City: A History of the Department of Water and Power of the City of Los Angeles to December 1950.* Los Angeles: Los Angeles Department of Water and Power, 1952.

Lear, Linda. *Rachel Carson: Witness for Nature.* New York: Henry Holt, 1997.

Legislative Irrigation Committee of the State Irrigation Convention. *Address to the Legislature of the State of California, Twenty-Sixth Session.* N.p. [1885].

Leopold, Aldo. *A Sand County Almanac and Sketches Here and There.* New York: Oxford University Press, 1949.

Leopold, A. Starker. *Wild California: Vanishing Lands, Vanishing Wildlife.* Berkeley and Los Angeles: University of California Press, 1985.

Leopold, Luna B., and Thomas Maddock, Jr. *The Flood Control Controversy: Big Dams, Little Dams, and Land Management.* New York: Ronald Press, 1954.

Leuchtenburg, William E. *Franklin D. Roosevelt and the New Deal, 1932–1940.* New York: Harper & Row, 1963.

LeVeen, E. Phillip, and Laura B. King. *Turning Off the Tap on Federal Water Subsidies.* Vol. 1: *The Central Valley Project.* San Francisco: Natural Resources Defense Council, 1985.

Levy, Stephen. *California Population Characteristics: What the 1990 Census Will Show, What the Next Decade Will Bring.* Palo Alto, Calif.: Center for Continuing Study of the California Economy, 1990.

Lewis, Henry T. *Patterns of Indian Burning in California: Ecology and Ethnohistory.* Ramona, Calif.: Ballena Press, 1973.

Liebman, Ellen. *California Farmland: A History of Large Agricultural Landholdings.* Totowa, N.J.: Rowman & Allanheld, 1983.

Lillard, Richard. *Eden in Jeopardy.* New York: Knopf, 1966.

Littleworth, Arthur L., and Eric L. Garner. *California Water.* Point Arena, Calif.: Solano Press Books, 1995.

Loh, Penn, and Santos V. Gómez. *Water Transfers in California: A Framework for Sustainability and Justice.* Oakland: Pacific Institute for Studies in Development, Environment, and Security, 1996.

Londquist, C. J., et al. *Hydrogeology and Land Subsidence, Edwards Air Force Base, Antelope Valley, California, January 1989–December 1991.* Sacramento: U.S. Geological Survey, 1993.

Luhdorff and Scalmanini, Consulting Engineers. *State Water Resources Control Board Groundwater "Hot Spots" Project: Well Testing and Site Characterization—Fresno Area.* Sacramento: California Water Resources Control Board, Feb. 1986.

———. *State Water Resources Control Board Groundwater "Hot Spots" Project: Well Testing and Site Characterization—Los Angeles Area.* Woodland, Calif.: Luhdorff and Scalmanini, 1986.

Lund, Lanny J. *Sources and Sinks of Nitrogen and Other Inorganic Constituents in the Santa Ana River above Prado Dam.* Riverside: Department of Soil and Environmental Sciences, University of California, Riverside, 1992.

Lynch, H. B. *Rainfall and Stream Run-Off in Southern California since 1769.* Los Angeles: Metropolitan Water District of Southern California, 1931.

Maass, Arthur. *Muddy Waters: The Army Engineers and the Nation's Rivers.* Cambridge, Mass.: Harvard University Press, 1951.

MacArthur, Mildred Yorba. *Anaheim: "The Mother Colony."* Los Angeles: Ward Ritchie Press, 1959.

MacCannell, Dean. *Draft Report on Current Social Conditions in the Communities in and near the Westlands Water District.* Davis: University of California, [1980].

McClurg, Sue. *Water and the Shaping of California.* Sacramento: Heyday Books and Water Education Foundation, 2000.

McCoy, Esther. *Five California Architects.* New York: Reinhold, 1960.

McDermott, Deidre. *Polychlorinated Biphenyls in Marine Organisms off Southern California.* El Segundo, Calif.: Southern California Coastal Water Research Project, 1975.

McElvaine, Robert S. *The Great Depression.* New York: New York Times Books, 1984.

McKinley, Charles. *Uncle Sam in the Pacific Northwest.* Berkeley: University of California Press, 1952.

McWilliams, Carey. *Factories in the Field.* [1939] Santa Barbara and Salt Lake City: Peregrine Smith, Inc., 1971.

Majka, Linda, and Theo Majka. *Farm Workers, Agribusiness, and the State.* Philadelphia: Temple University Press, 1982.

Malone, Michael P., and Richard W. Etulain. *The American West: A Twentieth-Century History.* Lincoln: University of Nebraska Press, 1989.

Marshall, Robert Bradford. *Irrigation of Twelve Million Acres in the Valley of California.* Sacramento: California State Irrigation Association, Mar. 16, 1919.

Martin, Calvin. *Keepers of the Game.* Berkeley and Los Angeles: University of California Press, 1978.

Martin, Paul S., and Richard B. Klein, eds. *Quaternary Extinctions: A Prehistoric Revolution.* Tucson: University of Arizona Press, 1984.

Martin, Russell. *Glen Canyon and the Struggle for the Soul of the West.* New York: Henry Holt, 1989.

Matson, Robert W. *William Mulholland: A Forgotten Forefather.* Stockton, Calif.: Pacific Center for Western Studies, University of the Pacific, 1976.

May, Philip Ross. *Origins of Hydraulic Mining in California.* Oakland: Holmes Book Co., 1970.

Meine, Curt. *Aldo Leopold: His Life and Work.* Madison: University of Wisconsin Press, 1988.

Meyer, Michael C. *Water in the Hispanic Southwest: A Social and Legal History, 1550–1850.* Tucson: University of Arizona Press, 1984.

Miller, M. Catherine. *Flooding the Courtrooms: Law and Water in the Far West.* Lincoln: University of Nebraska Press, 1993.

Moeller, Beverly. *Phil Swing and Boulder Dam.* Berkeley and Los Angeles: University of California Press, 1971.

Moreland, Joe A., and John A. Singer. *A Study of Deep Aquifers Underlying Coastal Orange County, California.* Menlo Park, Calif.: U.S. Geological Survey, 1969.

Morgan, Arthur E. *Dams and Other Disasters: A Century of the Army Corps of Engineers in Civil Works.* Boston: Porter Sargent, 1971.

Morison, Elting E., ed. *The Letters of Theodore Roosevelt.* 5 vols. Cambridge, Mass.: Harvard University Press, 1952.

Mount, Jeffrey F. *California Rivers and Streams: The Conflict between Fluvial Process and Land Use.* Berkeley and Los Angeles: University of California Press, 1995.

Mowry, George E. *The California Progressives.* Berkeley and Los Angeles: University of California Press, 1951.

Muir, John. *My First Summer in the Sierra.* Boston: Houghton Mifflin Co., 1911.

———. *The Yosemite.* New York: The Century Co., 1912.

Mulholland, Catherine. *The Owensmouth Baby: The Making of a San Fernando Valley Town.* Northridge, Calif.: Santa Susana Press, 1987.

———. *William Mulholland and the Rise of Los Angeles.* Berkeley and Los Angeles: University of California Press, 2000.

Murdock, Steve H. *An America Challenged: Population Change and the Future of the United States.* Boulder, Colo.: Westview Press, 1995.

Nadeau, Remi. *The Water Seekers.* Garden City, N.Y.: Doubleday & Co., 1950.

Nash, Gerald D. *The American West in the Twentieth Century: A Short History of an Urban Oasis.* Englewood Cliffs, N.J.: Prentice-Hall, 1973.

———. *The Federal Landscape: An Economic History of the Twentieth-Century West.* Tucson: University of Arizona Press, 1999.

Nash, Roderick. *The Rights of Nature: A History of Environmental Ethics.* Madison: University of Wisconsin Press, 1989.

———. *Wilderness and the American Mind.* 3d ed. New Haven: Yale University Press, 1982.

National Governors Association. *The National Debate about the Gasoline Additive MTBE,* by Martha Bohm. Washington, D.C.: National Governors Association, 1999.

National Reclamation Association. *Proceedings: Irrigation War Food Conference and 12th Annual Meeting, National Reclamation Association, Denver, Colorado, October 27–28–29, 1943.* Washington, D.C.: National Reclamation Association, [1944].

National Research Council. *Improving American River Flood Frequency Analyses.* Washington, D.C.: National Academy Press, 1999.

———. *The Mono Basin Ecosystem: Effects of Changing Lake Level.* Washington, D.C.: National Academy Press, 1987.

———. *A New Era for Irrigation.* Washington, D.C.: National Academy Press, 1997.

National Wetlands Policy Forum. *Protecting America's Wetlands: An Action Agenda.* Washington, D.C.: Conservation Foundation, 1988.

Nelson, Howard J. *The Los Angeles Metropolis.* Dubuque, Iowa: Kendall/Hunt, 1983.

Newmark, Harris. *Sixty Years in Southern California, 1853–1913.* 4th ed. Los Angeles: Zeitlin & Ver Brugge, 1970.

Odell, Rice. *Environmental Awakening: The New Revolution to Protect the Earth.* Cambridge, Mass.: Ballinger Publishing Co., 1980.

Official Sample Ballot and Voter Information: [California] Primary Election, March 7, 2000.

Olmstead, R. R., and T. H. Watkins. *Mirror of the Dream: An Illustrated History of San Francisco.* San Francisco: Scrimshaw Press, 1976.

Orange County Water District. *Statement Regarding the Present Condition of the Underground Water Basin of Orange County.* Santa Ana: Orange County Water District, 1945.

Ostrom, Vincent. *Water & Politics: A Study of Water Policies and Administration in the Development of Los Angeles.* Los Angeles: Haynes Foundation, 1953.

Outland, Charles F. *Man-Made Disaster: The Story of St. Francis Dam.* Rev. ed. Glendale, Calif.: Arthur H. Clark Co., 1977.

Palmer, Tim. *America by Rivers.* Washington, D.C.: Island Press, 1996.

———. *Endangered Rivers and the Conservation Movement.* Berkeley and Los Angeles: University of California Press, 1986.

———. *Stanislaus: The Struggle for a River.* Berkeley and Los Angeles: University of California Press, 1982.

Palóu, Francisco. *Historical Memoirs of New California.* Ed. Herbert E. Bolton. 4 vols. Berkeley: University of California Press, 1926.

Patterson, Tom. *A Colony for California: Riverside's First Hundred Years.* Riverside, Calif.: Press-Enterprise Co., 1971.

Paul, Rodman. *California Gold.* Cambridge, Mass.: Harvard University Press, 1947.

———. *The Far West and the Great Plains in Transition, 1859–1900.* New York: Harper & Row, 1988.

———. *Mining Frontiers of the Far West, 1848–1880.* New York: Holt, Rinehart and Winston, 1963.

Pease, William S., et al. *Pesticide Contamination of Groundwater in California.* Berkeley: California Policy Seminar, University of California, Berkeley, 1995.

Pelz, Richard K., ed. *Federal Reclamation and Related Laws Annotated.* 3 vols. Washington, D.C.: Government Printing Office, 1972.

Phelps, Alonzo: *Contemporary Biography of California's Representative Men.* San Francisco: A. L. Bancroft and Co., 1881.

Phelps, Charles E., Nancy Y. Moore, and Morlie H. Graubard. *Efficient Water Use in California: Water Rights, Water Districts, and Water Transfers.* Santa Monica: Rand, 1978.

Pisani, Donald J. *From the Family Farm to Agribusiness: The Irrigation Crusade in California and the West, 1850–1931.* Berkeley and Los Angeles: University of California Press, 1984.

———. *To Reclaim a Divided West: Water, Law, and Public Policy, 1848–1902.* Albuquerque: University of New Mexico Press, 1992.

Pitt, Leonard. *The Decline of the Californios.* Berkeley and Los Angeles: University of California Press, 1966.

Poland, Joseph F. *Land Subsidence in the Santa Clara Valley, Alameda, San Mateo, and Santa Clara Counties, California.* Washington, D.C.: U.S. Geological Survey, 1971.

————. *Summary Statement of Ground-Water Conditions and Saline Contamination along the Coast of Orange County, California.* Santa Ana: Orange County Water District, 1947.

Poland, Joseph F., and Richard L. Ireland. *Land Subsidence in the Santa Clara Valley, California, as of 1982.* Denver: U.S. Geological Survey, 1988.

Poland, Joseph F., et al. *Land Subsidence in the San Joaquin Valley, California, as of 1972.* Sacramento: U.S. Geological Survey, 1973.

Porter, Eliot. *The Place No One Knew: Glen Canyon on the Colorado.* San Francisco: Sierra Club, 1963.

Preston, William. *Vanishing Landscapes: Land and Life in the Tulare Lake Basin.* Berkeley and Los Angeles: University of California Press, 1981.

Putnam, Jackson K. *Modern California Politics, 1917–1980.* 3d ed. San Francisco: Boyd & Fraser Publishing Co., 1990.

Ramlit Associates, Inc. *Groundwater Contamination by Pesticides: A California Assessment—Submitted to State Water Resources Control Board.* Berkeley: Ramlit Associates, Inc., June 1983.

Recopilacíon de leyes de los reynos de las Indias. [1681] 4 vols. Madrid: Ediciones Cultura Hispánica, 1973.

Reeves, Margaret, et al. *Fields of Poison: California Farmworkers and Pesticides.* San Francisco: Californians for Pesticide Reform, 1999.

Reglamento para el gobierno de la provincia de Californias. [1784] San Francisco: Grabhorn Press, 1929.

Reisler, Mark. *By the Sweat of Their Brow: Mexican Immigrant Labor in the United States, 1900–1945.* Westport, Conn.: Greenwood Press, 1976.

Reisner, Marc. *Cadillac Desert: The American West and Its Disappearing Water.* New York: Viking, 1986.

————. *Water Policy and Farmland Protection: A New Approach to Saving California's Best Agricultural Lands.* Washington, D.C.: American Farmland Trust, 1997.

Reisner, Marc, and Sarah Bates. *Overtapped Oasis: Reform or Revolution for Western Water.* Washington, D.C.: Island Press, 1990.

Remy, Michael. *Guide to the Environmental Quality Act (CEQA).* 7th ed. Point Arena, Calif.: Solano Press Books, 1993.

Report of the Agricultural Task Force for Resource Conservation and Economic Growth in the Central Valley. Sacramento: California Farm Bureau Federation, 1998.

Richardson, Elmo. *Dams, Parks & Politics: Resource Development and Preservation in the Truman-Eisenhower Era.* Lexington: University Press of Kentucky, 1973.

Robbins, Roy M. *Our Landed Heritage: The Public Domain, 1776–1970.* 2d ed. Lincoln: University of Nebraska Press, 1976.

Robinson, Michael C. *Water for the West: The Bureau of Reclamation, 1902–1977.* Chicago: Public Works Historical Society, 1979.

Robinson, W. W. *Land in California.* Berkeley and Los Angeles: University of California Press, 1948.

———. *Lawyers of Los Angeles.* Los Angeles: Los Angeles Bar Association, 1959.

———. *San Fernando Valley.* Los Angeles: Title Insurance and Trust Co., 1951.

Rogers, Harold D., and Alan H. Nichols. *Water for California: Planning, Law & Practice, Finance.* San Francisco: Bancroft-Whitney, 1967.

Rogin, Michael P., and John L. Shover. *Political Change in California: Critical Elections and Social Movements, 1890–1966.* Westport, Conn.: Greenwood, 1970.

Romasco, Albert U. *Poverty of Abundance: Hoover, the Nation, and the Great Depression.* New York: Oxford University Press, 1965.

Rowley, William D. *Reclaiming the Arid West: The Career of Francis G. Newlands.* Bloomington: Indiana University Press, 1996.

Sadler, Richard, and Richard Roberts. *The Weber River Basin: Grass Roots Democracy and Water Development.* Logan: Utah State University Press, 1994.

Salton Sea Authority. *Proceedings of the Salton Sea Symposium, January 13, 1994.* Indian Wells, Calif.: Salton Sea Authority, 1994.

San Francisco City and County. *San Francisco Water & Power: A His-*

tory of the Municipal Water Department and Hetch Hetchy System. San Francisco: City and County of San Francisco, 1985.

Santa Barbara. *The City of Santa Barbara Charles Meyer Desalination Facility*. Santa Barbara: Santa Barbara Public Works Department, Jan. 1998.

Santa Monica Bay Restoration Project. *Priority Actions for Bay Restoration*. Monterey Park, Calif.: Santa Monica Bay Restoration Project, 1992.

————. *Taking the Pulse of the Bay: The State of the Bay, 1998*. Monterey Park, Calif.: Santa Monica Bay Restoration Project, 1998.

Sauder, Robert A. *The Lost Frontier: Water Diversion in the Growth and Destruction of Owens Valley Agriculture*. Tucson: University of Arizona Press, 1994.

Scheffer, Victor B. *The Shaping of Environmentalism in America*. Seattle: University of Washington Press, 1991.

Scheuring, Ann Foley, ed. *A Guidebook to California Agriculture*. Berkeley and Los Angeles: University of California Press, 1983.

Schneider, Stephen H. *Global Warming*. San Francisco: Sierra Club Books, 1989.

Seckler, David, ed. *California Water: A Study in Resource Management*. Berkeley and Los Angeles: University of California Press, 1971.

Shallat, Todd A. *Water and the Rise of Public Ownership on the Fresno Plain, 1850–1978*. Fresno: Fresno Public Works Department, 1978.

Sherow, James E. *Watering the Valley: Development along the High Plains Arkansas River, 1870–1950*. Lawrence: University Press of Kansas, 1990.

Shinn, Charles H. *Mining Camps: A Study in American Frontier Government*. [1884] New York: Harper and Row, 1965.

Sirotkin, Phillip, and Owen Stratton. *The Echo Park Controversy*. University, Ala.: University of Alabama Press, 1959.

Skowronek, Stephen. *Building a New American State: The Expansion of National Administrative Capacities, 1877–1920*. Cambridge, Eng.: Cambridge University Press, 1982.

Smith, Donald E., and Frederick J. Teggart, eds. *Diary of Gaspar de*

Portolá during the California Expedition of 1769–1770. Berkeley: University of California Press, 1909.

Smith, Karen L. *The Magnificent Experiment: Building the Salt River Reclamation Project.* Tucson: University of Arizona Press, 1986.

Smith, Michael L. *Pacific Visions: California Scientists and the Environment, 1850–1915.* New Haven: Yale University Press, 1987.

Smythe, William E. *The Conquest of Arid America.* Rev. ed. New York: Macmillan Co., 1905.

———. *The Conquest of Arid America,* ed. Lawrence B. Lee. Seattle: University of Washington Press, 1969.

Sokolow, Alvin. *Farmland Policy in California's Central Valley: State, County, and City Roles.* Berkeley: California Policy Seminar, 1997.

Southern California Coastal Water Research Project. *Annual Report, 1992–93.* Westminster, Calif.: Southern California Coastal Water Research Project, 1994.

———. *Coastal Water Research.* El Segundo, Calif.: Southern California Coastal Water Research Project, 1974.

———. *The Effects of the Ocean Disposal of Municipal Wastes.* El Segundo, Calif.: Southern California Coastal Water Research Project, 1978.

Spence, Clark C. *The Rainmakers: American "Pulviculture" to World War II.* Lincoln: University of Nebraska Press, 1980.

Stacy, Susan M. *When the River Rises: Flood Control on the Boise River, 1943–1985.* Boulder: Institute of Behavioral Science, University of Colorado, and College of Social Sciences and Public Affairs, Boise State University, 1993.

Starr, Kevin. *Material Dreams: Southern California through the 1920s.* New York: Oxford University Press, 1990.

Stegner, Wallace. *Beyond the Hundredth Meridian: John Wesley Powell and the Second Opening of the West.* Boston: Houghton Mifflin Co., 1954.

Steinbeck, John. *Grapes of Wrath.* New York: Viking Press, 1939.

Stevens, Joseph E. *Hoover Dam: An American Adventure.* Norman: University of Oklahoma Press, 1988.

Stoll, Steven. *The Fruits of Natural Advantage: Making the Industrial*

Countryside in California. Berkeley and Los Angeles: University of California Press, 1998.

Storper, Michael, and Richard Walker. *The Price of Water: Surplus and Subsidy in the California State Water Project.* Berkeley: University of California Institute of Governmental Studies, 1984.

Strong, William. *Aboriginal Society in Southern California.* [1929] Banning, Calif.: Malki Museum Press, 1972.

Suffet, I. H., et al. *Chemical Contaminant Release into the Santa Monica Bay: A Pilot Study.* Los Angeles: Environmental Health Sciences, School of Public Health, University of California, Los Angeles, 1993.

Sundborg, George. *Hail Columbia: The Thirty Year Struggle for Grand Coulee Dam.* New York: Macmillan, 1954.

Swanson, Louis E., ed. *Agriculture and Community Change in the U.S.: The Congressional Research Reports.* Boulder: Westview Press, 1988.

Taylor, Frank J. *Land of Homes.* Los Angeles: Powell, 1929.

Taylor, Paul S. *Mexican Labor in the United States: Imperial Valley, California.* Vol. 6, no. 1. Berkeley: University of California Publications in Economics, 1928.

Taylor, Ray W. *Hetch Hetchy.* San Francisco: Ricardo J. Orozco, 1926.

Thornton, Russell. *American Indian Holocaust and Survival: A Population History since 1492.* Norman: University of Oklahoma Press, 1987.

Thrusby, Vincent. *Interstate Cooperation: A Study of the Interstate Compact.* Washington, D.C.: Government Printing Office, 1953.

Tibesar, Antonine, ed. *Writings of Junípero Serra.* 4 vols. Washington, D.C.: Academy of American Franciscan History, 1954–1966.

Tout, Otis B. *The First Thirty Years, 1901–1931.* San Diego: O. B. Tout, 1931.

Treadwell, Edward F. *The Cattle King.* Rev. ed. Boston: Christopher Publishing House, 1950.

Turhollow, Anthony F. *A History of the Los Angeles District, U.S. Army Corps of Engineers, 1898–1965.* Los Angeles: U.S. Army Corps of Engineers, Los Angeles District, 1975.

Twain, Mark. *Roughing It.* Hartford, Conn.: American Publishing Co., 1872.

Tyler, Daniel. *The Last Water Hole in the West: A History of the Northern Colorado Water Conservancy District and the Colorado–Big Thompson Project.* Niwot, Colo.: University Press of Colorado, 1992.

———. *The Mythical Pueblo Rights Doctrine: Water Administration in Hispanic New Mexico.* El Paso: Texas Western Press, 1990.

Upper Los Angeles River Area Watermaster. *Watermaster Service in the Upper Los Angeles River Area, Los Angeles County, 1994–95 Water Year.* Los Angeles: Upper Los Angeles River Area Watermaster, May 1996.

Vileisis, Ann. *Discovering the Unknown Landscape: A History of America's Wetlands.* Washington, D.C.: Island Press, 1997.

Villarejo, Don. *Agricultural Land Ownership and Operations in the 49,000 Acre Drainage Study Area of the Westlands Water District: A Report to the Assembly Office of Research.* Sacramento: Assembly Office of Research, 1985.

———. *Getting Bigger: Large Scale Farming in California.* Davis: California Institute for Rural Studies, 1980.

———. *How Much Is Enough? Federal Water Subsidies and Agriculture in California's Central Valley.* Davis: California Institute for Rural Studies, 1986.

———. *New Lands for Agriculture: The California State Water Project.* Davis: California Institute for Rural Studies, 1981.

———. *93640 at Risk: Farmers, Workers and Townspeople in an Era of Water Uncertainty.* Davis: California Institute for Rural Studies, 1996.

Von Kotzebue, Otto. *A New Voyage Round the World, in the Years 1823, 24, 25, and 26.* 2 vols. London: Henry Colburn and Richard Bentley, 1830.

Wahl, Richard W. *Water Marketing in California: Past Experiences, Future Prospects.* Los Angeles: Reason Foundation, Policy Study 162, July 1993.

Walton, John. *Western Times and Water Wars: State, Culture, and Rebellion in California.* Berkeley and Los Angeles: University of California Press, 1992.

Warren, Harris G. *Herbert Hoover and the Great Depression.* New York: Oxford University Press, 1959.

Water Education Foundation. *75th Anniversary: Colorado River Compact—Symposium Proceedings.* Sacramento: Water Education Foundation, May 1997.

Webb, Edith B. *Indian Life at the Old Missions.* Los Angeles: W. F. Lewis, 1952.

Wells, Miriam J. *Regulation of the Farm Labor Market: An Assessment of Farm Labor Protection under California's Agricultural Labor Relations Act.* Davis: California Institute for Rural Studies, 1989.

Wendell, Mitchell, and Frederick L. Zimmermann. *The Interstate Compact since 1925.* Chicago: Council of State Governments, 1951.

Western Governors' Association. *Resolution 96-012: Open Space.* Denver: Western Governors' Association, 1996.

———. *White Paper on Federal Water Policy.* Denver: Western Governors' Association, 1989.

Western States Water Council. *Settlement of Indian Reserved Water Rights Claims: Proceedings of a Symposium, Portland, Oregon, September 6–8, 1995.* Midvale, Utah: Western States Water Council, 1995.

———. *Water Policy and Growth Management.* Denver: Western Governors' Association, 1995.

Western Water Policy Review Advisory Commission. *Indian Water—1997, Trends and Directions in Federal Water Policy: A Summary of the Conference Proceedings, March 1997,* by Todd Olinger. Springfield, Va.: National Technical Information Service, 1997.

———. *Water in the West: Challenge for the Next Century.* Springfield, Va.: National Technical Information Service, June 1998.

White, Gilbert F. *Choice of Adjustment to Floods.* Chicago: University of Chicago, Department of Geography Research Paper No. 93, 1964.

———. *The Control and Development of Floodplain Areas.* Albany, N.Y.: Matthew Bender & Co., 1961.

——— et al. *Flood Hazard in the United States: A Research Assessment.* Boulder: University of Colorado, Institute of Behavioral Science, 1975.

White, John H. *The Great Yellow Fleet: A History of American Railroad*

Refrigerator Cars. San Marino, Calif.: Golden West Books, 1986.

Wiebe, Robert. *The Search for Order, 1877–1920.* New York: Hill and Wang, 1967.

Wiel, Samuel C. *Water Rights in the Western States.* 3d ed. 2 vols. San Francisco: Bancroft-Whitney Co., 1911.

Williams, Albert N. *The Water and the Power.* New York: Duell, Sloan and Pearce, 1951.

Wittfogel, Karl A. *Oriental Despotism: A Comparative Study of Total Power.* New Haven: Yale University Press, 1957.

Wolf, Eric. *Sons of the Shaking Earth.* Chicago: University of Chicago Press, 1962.

Workman, Boyle. *The City That Grew.* Los Angeles: Southland Publishing Co., 1936.

The World Encompassed by Sir Francis Drake. [1628] n.p.: Readex Micropoint, 1966.

Worster, Donald. *Nature's Economy: A History of Ecological Ideas.* 2d ed. New York: Cambridge University Press, 1994.

———. *Rivers of Empire: Water, Aridity, and the Growth of the American West.* New York: Pantheon, 1985.

Wurm, Ted. *Hetch Hetchy and Its Dam Railroad.* Berkeley: Howell-North, 1973.

Young, David R. *Trace Elements in Seafood Organisms around Southern California Municipal Wastewater Outfalls.* Sacramento: California Water Resources Control Board, 1978.

Zierer, Clifford M., ed. *California and the Southwest.* New York: John Wiley & Sons, Inc., 1956.

Zurhorst, Charles. *The Conservation Fraud.* New York: Cowles Book Co., 1970.

Dissertations and Theses

Angel, Arthur D. "Political and Administrative Aspects of the Central Valley Project of California." Ph.D. dissertation, University of California, Los Angeles, 1944.

Ballard, Patricia L. ". . . And Conflict Shall Prevail: Reclamation Law, Water Districts, and Politics in the Kings River Service

Area of California—An Alternative Framework for Analysis." M.A. thesis, University of California, Los Angeles, 1980.

Casey, Jack T. "Legislative History of the Central Valley Project, 1933–1949." Ph.D. dissertation, University of California, Berkeley, 1949.

Coate, Charles E. "Water, Power, and Politics in the Central Valley Project, 1933–1967." Ph.D. dissertation, University of California, Berkeley, 1969.

Cooper, Margaret Aseman. "Land, Water, and Settlement in Kern County, California." M.A. thesis, University of California, Berkeley, 1954.

Davis, Alten B. "The Excess Land Law in the Central Valley of California." Ph.D. dissertation, University of California, Berkeley, 1962.

Douglas, Arthur. "Past Air-Sea Interaction over the Eastern North Pacific Ocean as Revealed by Tree Ring Data." Ph.D. dissertation, University of Arizona, 1976.

Grody, Harvey P. "The California Legislature and Comprehensive Water Resources Development: 1941–1959." Ph.D. dissertation, University of California, Los Angeles, 1971.

Hirsch, Steven. "Zealous Intruder or Reluctant Leader? The Federal Government's Increasing Presence in Managing Water in California's Central Valley." M.A. thesis, California State University, Fullerton, 1995.

Houston, Flora B. "The Mormons in California, 1846–1857." M.A. thesis, University of California, Berkeley, 1929.

Kathka, David A. "The Bureau of Reclamation in the Truman Administration: Personnel, Politics, and Policy." Ph.D. dissertation, University of Missouri, 1976.

Lawrence, William D. "Henry Miller and the San Joaquin Valley." M.A. thesis, University of California, Berkeley, 1933.

Lee, Beatrice. "The History and Development of the Ontario Colony." M.A. thesis, University of Southern California, 1929.

Leonard, Ernest. "The Imperial Irrigation District." Ph.D. dissertation, Claremont Graduate School, 1972.

Littlefield, Douglas R. "Interstate Water Conflicts, Compromises, and Compacts: The Rio Grande, 1880–1938." Ph.D. dissertation, University of California, Los Angeles, 1987.

Malone, Thomas E. "The California Irrigation Crisis of 1886: Origins of the Wright Act." Ph.D. dissertation, Stanford University, 1965.

Martin, David L. "California Water Politics: The Search for Local Control." Ph.D. dissertation, Claremont Graduate School, 1973.

Miller, Gordon R. "Los Angeles and the Owens River Aqueduct." Ph.D. dissertation, Claremont Graduate School, 1977.

Milliman, Jerome W. "The History, Organization and Economic Problems of the Metropolitan Water District of Southern California." Ph.D. dissertation, University of California, Los Angeles, 1956.

Neel, Susan R. "Irreconcilable Differences: Reclamation, Preservation, and the Origins of the Echo Park Dam Controversy." Ph.D. dissertation, University of California, Los Angeles, 1990.

Orsi, Jared. "Hazardous Metropolis: Flooding and Urban Ecology in Los Angeles." Ph.D. dissertation, University of Wisconsin, Madison, 1999.

Paterson, Alan. "Rivers and Tides: The Story of Water Policy Management in California's Sacramento–San Joaquin Delta." Ph.D. dissertation, University of California, Davis, 1978.

Paule, Dorothea. "The German Settlement at Anaheim." M.A. thesis, University of Southern California, 1952.

Pincetl, Stephanie S. "The Environmental Policies and Politics of the Brown Administration." Ph.D. dissertation, University of California, Los Angeles, 1985.

Poland, Joseph F. "The Occurrence and Control of Land Subsidence Due to Ground-Water Withdrawal with Special Reference to the San Joaquin and Santa Clara Valleys." Ph.D. dissertation, Stanford University, 1981.

Ressler, John Q. "Spanish Mission Water Systems: Northwest Frontier of New Spain." M.A. thesis, University of Arizona, 1965.

Rocha, Joseph R. "A Study of Four San Joaquin Valley Communities: Firebaugh, Mendota, Kerman and Orange Cove." Ph.D. dissertation, Claremont Graduate School, 1974.

Sayles, Stephen P. "Clair Engle and the Politics of California Reclamation, 1943–1960." Ph.D. dissertation, University of New Mexico, 1978.

Simpson, Richard P. "The Campaign for State Purchase of the Central Valley Project, 1945–1955." M.A. thesis, Stanford University, 1956.

Van Valen, Nelson S. "Power Politics: The Struggle for Municipal Ownership of Electric Utilities in Los Angeles, 1905–1937." Ph.D. dissertation, Claremont Graduate School, 1964.

Waller, Thomas S. "The Politics of Agricultural Water Conservation in the Border Region of the Californias." Ph.D. dissertation, University of California, San Diego, 1993.

Young, Terence G. "Constructing an Urban Forest: A Cultural Bio-Geography in Middle-Class Los Angeles, 1930–1980." M.A. thesis, University of California, Los Angeles, 1987.

Index

and water quality, 321. *See also* flood control; hydroelectricity; irrigation; reservoirs

Dasmann, Raymond, 539, 540, 563

Davis, Arthur Powell: and Boulder Canyon Project, 205–6, 209–11, 214; and Owens Valley aqueducts, 163, 166

Davis, Gray: and CALFED, 418–19, 423, 424; and MTBE, 452–53; and MWD-Coachella-Imperial water transfers, 495–96; and Yuba River status, 628–29n14

Davis, Martha, 346

Davis, Pauline, 283

Davis-Grunsky Act, 283

DBCP (dibromochloropropane), 432, 437

DDT (dichlorodiphenyltrichloroethane), 309, 454

debris flows, 385–86

Dedrick, Claire, 322

Defenders of Wildlife, 499

deficit: water, 2. *See also* water shortages

delta. *See* Sacramento–San Joaquin Delta

Delta Cross Channel, 257, 259*fig*

Delta-Mendota Canal, 257, 258, 259*fig*

Delta Protection Act (1959), 533

delta smelt, 407

Democratic party: and acreage limitation, 271, 272; Areias, 506–7; and Boulder Canyon Project, 215–16, 222; and CALFED, 413; and cross-filing, 251; and CVP, 253–55, 265, 502; and depressions, 114, 247–48, 249–51, 309; early history, 67–69, 70, 71; and environmental movement, 309–10, 311; and flood control, 80, 81, 83, 84; and MTBE, 452–53; and New Melones

Dam, 369, 371–73; and North-South debates, 68, 83; and Peripheral Canal, 321, 322, 324, 333; political culture, 67–69, 71, 83, 113, 114, 115, 120, 248–51, 366; Progressive, 113, 114, 115, 120; and SWP, 281–86

Denver, radioactive waste management, 443

depressions, 585n68; Great (1930s), 189, 247–48, 249–52, 253, 255, 263, 267, 309; panic (1890s), 113, 114, 117, 120, 247, 585n68; after World War I, 241–42, 267

desalination, 284, 440–41, 520–21, 559–60

Desert Land Act (1877), 113

deserts, 200; aboriginal California, 16, 18; Imperial Valley, 230*fig*

Desert Water Agency, 501

Destruction of California (Dasmann), 563

Detention Dam, proposed, 385

Deukmejian, George, 333, 342, 345, 403–4, 433

development ethic, 374; and floodplain management, 386–88; and groundwater depletion, 447; water for growth rather than need, 154, 166, 171, 231, 288–89, 304; water supply following demand, 524–26. *See also* speculators; urbanization

Diamond Valley, 375

Diamond Valley Lake, 375, 469–70, 469*fig*, 485

Diazinon, 398

Dinosaur National Monument, 311

Dinuba, 266, 462

Disabled American Veterans, 269

dispute resolution, Hispanic, 59–60

ditches: inefficient irrigation with, 318; *zanja madre* (main irrigation ditch), 43–45, 50, 124–25, 126*fig*. *See also* canals

diversion. *See* water diversion

Domenigoni Valley, 375, 469

Dominy, Floyd, 272

Dos Rios Dam proposal, 312–13

Douglas, Helen Gahagan, 271

Downey, Sheridan, 268–70

Drake, Francis, 8

"dream power," Indian, 24

drinking water: bottled, 447, 460–61; desalination, 440–41; groundwater used for, 432, 445; Hispanic era, 44–45; pesticides in, 437–38; polluted, 447–51; quality standards, 393, 408, 417. *See also* water use

drought: American period, 90, 96, 107, 112, 117; annual water deficit during, 2; California Aqueduct shut down during, 322, 521; Central Valley, 241–42, 291*map*, 427; conservation during, 363–64, 516, 519–20, 556–58; cutbacks in water deliveries during, 418, 468, 480, 504, 511–513; and CVP endorsement, 252; driest on record (1976–1977), 9, 291*map*, 322, 511, 556–57, 558; dry farming and, 90; El Niño/La Niña and, 9, 457; Great Plains, 108; groundwater use, 528; Hispanic era, 36–37, 55, 57; landscaping compatible with, 516, 557; land subsidence during, 427; Los Angeles, 153, 216, 345, 355, 362, 556; and Mono Lake, 338; and

Proposition 8 (1980), 325, 327, 328, 329, 332
Proposition 12 (2000), 391–92, 419
Proposition 13 (2000), 391–92, 419
Proposition 17 (1974), 368–69, 371
Proposition 128 "Big Green" (1990), 553
Providencia, Rancho, 58
Provincias Internas, 41
Public Affairs Reports, 318
public power. *See* municipal power system; public vs. private power
public trust doctrine, 340–47, 361, 404
public vs. private power: CVP and, 249, 253, 254, 259, 262, 272–76; DWP and, 357; Los Angeles, 155; and Marshall Plan, 244; San Francisco, 189–90
public water. *See* municipal water system
Pueblo Indians, Southwest, 4, 19, 47, 60
pueblos (villages or towns), 33, 34, 35; Indian labor, 60, 61–62; land grants, 39–40, 48–49; water rights, 47, 49–60; water systems, 35, 36–38, 42–45, 48–49, 61
pueblo water rights, 51–60, 545; Los Angeles claims, 51–58, 127–40, 154, 156, 170, 197, 334–35, 545
pumping, water: Areias groundwater, 507–8; Arizona groundwater, 304; CALFED and, 412, 417, 420, 421, 422, 424, 527, 530; California Aqueduct, 298 fig, 302; CAP, 311–12; Central Valley groundwater, 427; charges, 653n141; gasoline- or electricity-powered, 239, 528; and groundwater management, 528–30; and groundwater rights (unclear), 555; Owens Valley groundwater, 347–53, 359, 362; San Fer-

nando Valley groundwater, 54, 55, 135, 137, 334, 335, 447–49; San Gabriel Valley groundwater, 447–50, 460, 503; San Joaquin Valley groundwater, 239, 277–78, 297, 317, 530; Santa Barbara conservation measures, 520; southern California groundwater, 444–45, 529; Tracy Pumping Plant, 259 fig, 315; Whitsett Pumping Plant, 236 fig. *See also* hydraulic systems

Quechan (Yuma) Indians, 21
Quinn, J. D., 287
Quinn, Timothy, 414, 510
Quist, Gregory, 482

Racanelli decision, 404
race: discrimination based on, 308. *See also* ethnic composition
Radical Reconstruction, 69, 82–83
radioactive waste, 442–44
railroads: competition for transcontinental passengers, 124; land for, 88; Los Angeles connections, 105, 390 fig, 479; Owens Valley, 164; owners, 160; refrigerated cars, 90–91, 103, 240
rainfall. *See* precipitation
rainmaking, 15, 36–37, 107–12, 110–11 figs
Raker, John E., 184
Raker Act (1913), 184–93
rancherías (Indian villages), 33
Rancho Cahuenga, 58
Rancho El Encino, 58
Rancho Ex-Mission de San Fernando, 58
Rancho Los Feliz, 129, 132
Rancho Los Nietos, 48
Rancho Providencia, 58
ranchos, 31; American takeover, 88–89, 94, 96; Indian labor, 61, 63; San Fernando Valley, 51–52, 58; water

rights, 47–50, 58, 129, 131; water systems, 61
Rancho San Rafael, 48
Rand Corporation, Santa Monica, 232
rationing, water, 322, 363–64
Reagan, Ronald: and Dos Rios Dam proposal, 312–13; environmental movement and, 310, 312–13; and Hetch Hetchy, 194; and Kesterson pollution, 429, 431; New Melones Dam supported by, 367–68, 373; and Peripheral Canal, 321–22; subsidies to agribusiness/increased acreage limitation supported by, 295, 461–62, 463
rebates, for water conservation, 559
reclamation: of wastewater, 346, 531, 559–60. *See also* reclamation law
Reclamation Act (1902), 115–20, 240, 262–72, 539; and Boulder Canyon Project, 206, 209, 210, 223–26; CVP and, 260–72, 275, 276; and subsidies to agribusiness, 270, 275, 319, 461–64; "technical compliance," 269–76, 319, 465. *See also* acreage limitation
Reclamation and Swampland Act (1861), 81–82
Reclamation Bureau. *See* U.S. Bureau of Reclamation
reclamation district, 82, 396. *See also* swampland district
reclamation law, 115–20, 549; Reclamation and Swampland Act (1861), 81–82; Reclamation Projects Authorization and Adjustment Act (1992), 502–4. *See also* Central Valley Project Improvement Act (1992); Reclamation Act (1902)

MWD created (1928), 216; and north-coast river protection, 327; and Peripheral Canal, 313–15, 317–18, 320–21, 322, 323, 324–25, 329, 330, 332–33; pollution of coastal waters, 453–59, 503; pollution of groundwater, 440–53, 460, 503; population growth (1980s–1990s), 362, 485; precipitation patterns, 10; radioactive waste, 442–44; rainmaking, 108–9; salinity problems, 418, 440–42; and State Water Plan, 246–47; and SWP, 279–302, 307–8, 314, 317–18, 337; urbanization, 231–34, 302, 508, 519; water conservation, 560–61; waterscape, 551 *map;* wetlands, 459. *See also* Coachella Valley Water District; Imperial Irrigation District; Imperial Valley; Los Angeles County; Los Angeles Department of Water and Power; Metropolitan Water District of Southern California; Orange County; Riverside County; San Bernardino County; San Diego County; San Diego County Water Authority; San Fernando Valley; Santa Barbara County; Ventura County
Southern California Association of Governments, 485
Southern California Coastal Water Research Project, 454
Southern California Country (McWilliams), 162
Southern Nevada Water Authority, 499
Southern Oscillation, 9
Southern Pacific Company, 277
Southern Pacific Land Company, 277

Southern Pacific Railroad, 88, 105, 390 *fig*
Southwest: flood history, 381; Old, 548; Pueblo Indians, 4, 19, 47, 60. *See also* Arizona; New Mexico
Spain: attitude toward water, 28, 29–31; "Garden of," 30; law, 28, 30–31, 38–43, 47, 48, 53, 54, 101, 131, 134, 136, 137, 335; overseas empire, 27–64; political culture, 28, 29–31, 38–43. *See also* Spanish era
Spanish era (1769–1821), 28, 30, 43, 51, 53. *See also* Hispanic era
special districts (water districts), 536
speculators: American period, 87–89, 91, 103; Central Valley, 87–89, 91; Imperial Valley, 223–24
Sports Illustrated, 344
Spreckels, Rudolph, 182, 244
Spring Valley Water Works, 172–83 passim, 189, 197, 198, 199
Standard Oil, 277
Stanford University: Ehrlich on population, 541; and Mono ecosystem, 339–40; National Performance of Dams Program, 386
Stanislaus, The (Palmer), 563
Stanislaus Canyon, 369–73
Stanislaus River, 366–73, 372 *fig,* 374, 386. *See also* New Melones Dam
stare decisis (respect for precedent), 134, 335
State Department, U.S., 441
state water commission, 237, 240
State Water Plan (1931), Hyatt's, 246–47, 252, 532
State Water Project (SWP), 204, 246, 276–302, 292 *map,* 425–27;

agribusiness and, 281, 287, 295–301, 317, 319–20, 465, 608–9 n93; bond issues, 280, 284–87, 290, 294, 314, 532; Brown (Pat) and, 281–90, 293 *fig,* 295, 299, 320, 325–26; CALFED and, 414, 418, 421; cost of acre-foot, 474–76, 653 n141; costs of project, 280, 284, 286–87, 289, 294–97; county-of-origin law and, 281, 284, 286, 287–88, 307–8, 532; deliveries during drought, 418, 512; delta and, 279, 280, 284, 397; hydroelectricity, 294–95; Los Angeles and, 288–90, 337; Monterey Agreement (1994), 512, 525–26, 669 n223; Monterey Amendment (1995), 669 n223; MWD and, 283–84, 287–90, 296, 297–99, 340, 405, 414, 418, 509; Peripheral Canal and, 314–17; phases, 307–8, 313–14; plans, 278–80; and saltwater intrusion, 281, 291 *map;* San Joaquin Valley and, 277–79, 281, 286, 291, 293, 317, 337, 340, 429, 510; and Santa Barbara County, 520–21; subsidies to agriculture, 287, 295–301, 319–20, 465; volume in acre-feet, 293–94; and water marketing, 296–99, 504, 509, 510; water quality standards, 321, 404; Wild and Scenic Rivers Act and, 313. *See also* California Aqueduct
State Water Resources Act (1945), 278–79
statutory law, 86, 129
Steinbeck, John, 263, 264
Stephens, William, 244
Steward, Julian, 18
Still (E. M. and E. C.) Company, 277
Stockton, 101, 519

Text and display: Stempel Schneidler
Composition: G & S Typesetters
Maps: Madge Kelley
Index: Barbara Roos